HUMAN INFORMATION PROCESSING

An Introduction to Psychology

Second Edition

HUMAN
INFORMATION
PROCESSING

An Introduction to Psychology

Second Edition

PETER H. LINDSAY

University of Toronto

DONALD A. NORMAN

University of California, San Diego

ACADEMIC PRESS   *New York   San Francisco   London*

A Subsidiary of Harcourt Brace Jovanovich, Publishers

ACADEMIC PRESS, INC.
111 Fifth Avenue, New York, New York 10003

United Kingdom Edition published by
ACADEMIC PRESS, INC. (LONDON) LTD.
24/28 Oval Road, London NW1

Library of Congress Cataloging in Publication Data

Lindsay, Peter H
  Human information processing.

  Bibliography: p.
  1. Human information processing. I. Norman,
Donald A., joint author. II. Title. [DNLM:
1. Perception. 2. Communication. 3. Psycholinguistics. BF455 L749h]
BF455.L494 1977   153   76-27448
ISBN 0–12–450960–6

Illustrations for cover and text by Leanne Hinton

Preface

The field flourishes: the study of human information processing continues to produce important insights into our understanding of human mental processes. New phenomena challenge the old ideas. New ideas have advanced our understanding of old phenomena. Each year, new developments enrich our knowledge and widen the scope of behaviors that we can begin to comprehend.

This second edition of *Human Information Processing* was written to reflect recent developments, as well as anticipate new directions, in this flourishing field. We believe that the ideas of human information processing are relevant to all human activities, most especially those of human interactions. We discuss all the traditional areas, of course, but we go on: consciousness, states of awareness, multiple levels of processing (and of awareness), interpersonal communication, emotion, and stress. In doing this, we tried to keep on the scientific side of the narrow division between scientifically based speculation and fantasy.

We believe our extensions of the area of information processing research show how the scientific analyses of this book can help illuminate many if not all human phenomena. Even if substantive experimental research has not yet been performed in many fields, this is no reason to deny that these fields exist. Adding these topics enhances the generality of this course. (Still, note the things we have left out, including most of the phenomena of abnormal psychology: a good area for your students to try their own extensions of the basic principles of this book.)

In this revision, we have tried to remedy the shortcomings of the earlier edition. We, too, teach from this book, and thus we, too, have encountered some problems in the first edition. A few chapters were obscure (or just plain difficult—such as Chapter 2). Others were difficult in parts, while some chapters worked very well. Furthermore, the first edition had an unwanted and accidental emphasis on masculine activity. We have therefore "desexed" the book. This may seem to be a subtle issue, but to some people (including us) it is important.

This edition is a thorough, extensive revision. We have reordered the chapters, reordered and reworded the material. We have deleted a lot and added a lot. Each chapter contains two new features: a preview and a review of terms and concepts. We have revised and updated the "Suggested Readings" section at the end of each chapter. Throughout the book, our aim was to maintain the more exciting and intriguing parts of the old edition while including current research findings, adding greater breadth of coverage, and explaining ideas better.

New to this edition is a comprehensive study guide, written by Ross Bott and Allen Munro expressly to accompany this text. The study guide is not the usual fill-in-the-blanks workbook. It is much more than that: it is actually a miniature text in its own right, explaining new concepts, amplifying and extending this text. The study guide reflects our experience in using the book in a self-paced course, and we recommend its use, either in a PSI course or as a valuable supplement in a lecture course.

Our goal remains the same as it was with the first edition—to try to convey the excitement of modern psychology to the beginning student. We want to explain what we, as researchers, are doing. We want to get the student actively involved in working with the concepts of psychology, rather than simply committing to memory long lists of facts and experiments. We want to communicate how we think and how we approach the study of the human mind. We hope that the second edition has brought this book closer to this ideal.

Acknowledgments

As the material in the book was rewritten, we were guided by a number of professional reviewers. Lynn Cooper (of Cornell) advised us on the perception chapters. Donald I. A. MacLeod (of the University of California, San Diego) and Fred Wightman (of Northwestern) advised us on the visual and auditory material, respectively. Steve Hillyard and Larry Squire (both at the University of California, San Diego) read the material on neural information processing and the neural basis of memory and offered numerous good suggestions. Allen Munro (of the University of California, San Diego) and Pamela Munro (of the University of California, Los Angeles) gave voluminous comments on our material on language, saving us from the errors of the first edition. And Elissa Newport (of the University of California, San Diego) and Dedre Gentner (of the University of Washington) commented on the developmental material and on language. These people have aided the technical content of the book immensely.

The contents of the book owe much to those who helped with the first edition. We thank the LNR Research Group, and in particular, David Rumelhart, for their continuing inspiration.

Joyce Farrell helped to compile all the material, editing our rough manuscripts, commenting upon the material, and putting together readable pages from our scribbles. Kris Stewart typed the final manuscript.

Julie Lustig, as usual, supervised the whole operation, from cajoling the authors to correcting the spelling, from suggesting topics to rewriting sections. Leanne Hinton came back again from her academic duties (at the University of Texas, Dallas) to add more demons, to redo drawings, and to add new illustrations. Her drawings have played an important role in the book, and we are pleased that she was able to help illustrate this edition.

FIGURE, TABLE, AND QUOTATION CREDITS

| Figures 1-9 and 7-18 | From J. Thurston and R. G. Carraher, *Optical illusions and the visual arts.* © 1966 Litton Educational Publishing, Inc. Reprinted by permission of Van Nostrand Reinhold Company. |
| Figure 1-28 | From James J. Gibson, *Perception of the visual* |

	world (Boston: Houghton Mifflin Company, 1950). Used by permission of the publisher.
Figure 2-7	From S. Polyak, *The vertebrate visual system.* Copyright © 1957 by the University of Chicago Press, and used by permission.
Figure 3-3	From Stevens (1961b). Copyright 1961 by the American Association for the Advancement of Science.
Figure 3-17	From D. B. Judd, Basic correlates of the visual stimulus. In S. S. Stevens (Ed.), *Handbook of experimental psychology.* New York: Wiley, 1951. By permission of John Wiley & Sons, Inc.
Figure 3-22	From Wald (1964). Copyright 1964 by the American Association for the Advancement of Science.
Figures 4-4 and 4-5	From Denes and Pinson (1963). Courtesy of Bell Telephone Laboratories, Incorporated.
Figure 4-13	Photograph from Bredberg *et al.* (1970). Copyright 1970 by the American Association for the Advancement of Science.
Figure 5-2	From Robinson and Dadson (1956). By permission of the Institute of Physics and the Physical Society.
Figure 5-3	Illustration courtesy of C. G. Conn, Ltd., Oak Brook, Illinois.
Figures 5-7 and 5-9	From E. Zwicker and B. Scharf, Model of loudness summation. *Psychology Review,* 1965, 72, 3-26. Copyright 1965 by the American Psychological Association. Reprinted by permission.
Figure 5-11	Excerpted by permission from *Consumer Reports,* July 1975. Copyright 1975 by Consumers Union of United States, Inc., Mount Vernon, New York.
Figures 5-13 and 5-14	From J. Zwislocki, Analysis of some auditory characteristics. In D. R. Luce, R. R. Bush, and E. Galanter (Eds.), *Handbook of mathematical psychology,* Vol. III. New York: Wiley, 1965. By permission of John Wiley & Sons, Inc.
Figure 5-20	From R. R. Fay, Auditory frequency stimulation in the goldfish (*Carassius, Auratus*). *Journal of Comparative Physiological Psychology,* 1970, 73(2), 175–180. Copyright 1970 by the

	American Psychological Association. Reprinted by permission.
Figure 6-1	From Pomeranz and Chung (1970). Copyright 1970 by the American Association for the Advancement of Science.
Figure 6-24	From Hurvich and Jameson (1974). Copyright 1974 by the American Psychological Association. Reprinted by permission.
Table 7-3	Table adapted from pp. 176–177 and 303 of *The sound pattern of English* by Noam Chomsky and Morris Halle. Copyright © 1968 by Noam Chomsky and Morris Halle. By permission of Harper & Row, Publishers, Inc.
Figure 8-9	From B. B. Murdock, Jr., The retention of individual items. *Journal of Experimental Psychology*, 1961, *62*, 618–625. Copyright 1961 by the American Psychological Association. Reprinted by permission.
Figures 9-1, 9-3, and 9-4	From B. B. Murdock, Jr., The serial effect of free recall. *Journal of Experimental Psychology*, 1962, *64*, 482–488. Copyright 1962 by the American Psychological Association. Reprinted by permission.
Figure 11-5	Adapted from Kandel (1974) in *The neurosciences, third study program*, F. O. Schmitt (Ed.) by permission of The M.I.T. Press, Cambridge, Massachusetts. Copyright © 1974 by The M.I.T. Press.
Figure 11-9	From Squire *et al.* (1975). Copyright 1975 by the American Association for the Advancement of Science.
Figure 11-13	Graph from E. H. Lenneberg, *Biological foundations of language*. New York: Wiley, 1967. By permission of John Wiley & Sons, Inc.
Table 13-3	From R. Brown and C. Hanlon, Derivational complexity and order of acquisition in child speech. In J. R. Hayes (Ed.), *Cognition and the development of language*. New York: Wiley, 1970. By permission of John Wiley & Sons, Inc.
Figure 14-7	From Herbert A. Simon and Allen Newell, *Human problem solving* © 1971. By permis-

	sion of Prentice-Hall, Inc., Englewood Cliffs, New Jersey.
Figure 15-4	From N. Kleitman, Sleep and wakefulness (2nd ed.). Copyright © 1963 by the University of Chicago Press, and used by permission.
Quotation, Pp. 648ff.	From S. Milgram, Behavioral study of obedience, *Journal of Abnormal and Social Psychology*, 1963, 67, 371–378. Copyright 1963 by the American Psychological Association. Reprinted by permission.
Figures 16-7 and 16-8	From S. Siegal and L. E. Fouraker, *Bargaining and group decision making: Experiments in bilateral monopoly.* Copyright 1960 by McGraw-Hill, Inc. Used with permission of McGraw-Hill Book Company.
Figure 17-1	Reprinted from D. B. Lindsay, Psychophysiology and motivation. In M. R. Jones (Ed.), *Nebraska symposium on motivation*, by permission of University of Nebraska Press. Copyright © 1957 by the University of Nebraska Press.
Figures A-3 and A-4	From Stevens (1966a). Copyright 1966 by the American Association for the Advancement of Science.
Table A-2	From Stevens (1961a). In W. A. Rosenblith (Ed.), *Sensory communication*, by permission of The M.I.T. Press, Cambridge, Massachusetts. Copyright © 1961 by The M.I.T. Press.

Contents

4. THE AUDITORY SYSTEM

5. THE DIMENSIONS OF SOUND

7. PATTERN RECOGNITION AND ATTENTION

8. THE MEMORY SYSTEMS

9. USING MEMORY

13. LEARNING AND COGNITIVE DEVELOPMENT

14. PROBLEM SOLVING AND DECISION MAKING

17. STRESS AND EMOTION

APPENDIX A. MEASURING PSYCHOLOGICAL VARIABLES

HUMAN INFORMATION PROCESSING

An Introduction to Psychology

Second Edition

1 Human perception

PREVIEW

The senses—seeing, hearing, touching, tasting, feeling—are the windows to the world. These sensory organs feed the brain information about the environment, and the brain interprets this information, matching what is happening with what previously happened. The operations of the sensory system and how they transform the sensory data into perceptual experience are clearly of central importance to human functioning. This chapter begins that study—human perception—the mechanisms that operate upon sensory information, interpreting, classifying, and organizing arriving information.

We start by examining the nature of the problem: What does it take to recognize the sensory information about an object? Start with a simple problem: recognizing the letters of the alphabet. We look at a letter and immediately recognize it. But how is this done? What are the mental mechanisms that perform this task? It turns out that the task is much harder than might appear. Indeed, scientists still do not know how it is done. Examination of the simple task of recognizing letters introduces the complexities of perception.

This chapter provides an introduction to some of the more interesting phenomena of perception and poses some of the puzzles faced by those who would attempt to unravel the structures. Actually, we study perception all the way through Chapter 7. The four chapters that follow this one (Chapters 2 through 5) go into quite a bit of detail about the systems of most interest for human communication: the visual system and the auditory system. Then, in Chapter 6, we examine the structure of the nervous system, learning how the signals are processed by the brain. Finally, in Chapter 7, we return to the problems originally posed in this chapter, this time with sufficient knowledge that we can suggest some answers.

But no one yet knows the final answers; despite intensive effort on the part of many scientists from a number of different fields, the mysteries of the perceptual system remain hidden. We are making progress, but we still have a long way to go. Moreover, as the descriptions in Chapters 1 through 6 suggest and as Chapter 7 makes explicit, one cannot really study one mental process in isolation from the others. Human perception is intimately related to the process of human attention and memory. We will probably not understand one of these until we understand the others. But attention and memory are also related to other systems, to language, to development, to human activity. The study of human perception ultimately becomes the study of the human.

An important part of this chapter is the study of psychological mechanisms. We start by describing a mechanism that we know is wrong. We do this to show how one studies psychological processes: thinking deeply about an issue, analyzing the phenomena, and then testing your ideas against data, against real observations. It seems easiest to do this with the template mechanism, because it is easy to understand, even though we know it is quite incorrect. This way, we can also point out how we discard what might seem to be a useful idea.

In fact, the major thing to learn from this chapter is an appreciation of the importance and the difficulty of the topic. How we see and hear is clearly important, yet a full understanding of how it happens still eludes us. This chapter is designed to illustrate the basic phenomena and the basic tools used to study them.

INTERPRETING SENSORY MESSAGES

The goal is to understand the mechanisms of perception. The task before us is to discover the psychological processes that are operating and as much as possible of the wiring diagram of the neural networks that are involved. The problems are numerous. When we read the printed letters on a page of text, the conversion from the visual symbols on the page to meaningful phrases in the mind is performed rapidly and without effort. Similarly, speech is heard as meaningful words, not as a jumble of sounds that must somehow then be translated to make sense. When we walk about in the environment, we recognize the objects before us immediately and without effort. If there is a sound on the left, we hear it on the left. When we come to a curb, we step up or down at the right time, and when we pick up a pencil, no conscious thought processes are involved, either in the recognition of that object as a pencil, in the control of the arms and hands to grasp the object, or in the way by which the pencil gets put to use.

We start the story of perception with the study of pattern recognition: how the external signals arriving at the sense organs are converted into meaningful perceptual experiences. Ordinarily, the objects and events around us are recognized with such apparent ease and immediacy that it is easy to assume that the operations involved are simple and direct. But the experience of engineers has proven the illusiveness of the task. There exists no machine that is capable of recognizing sounds and symbols normally encountered in the environment. The numerous attempts to build pattern recognition systems have failed to achieve the flexibility and power of the perceptual systems of even primitive animals. Let us start by seeing why the task is so difficult.

Matching templates

Template matching is the simplest of all the possible schemes for classifying and recognizing patterns. For template matching, there must be some representation—a template—for each of the patterns to be recognized. Recognition is accomplished by matching the external signal against the internal template. The one that matches best identifies the pattern present.

Consider how a template scheme might work in detecting signals that are presented visually. Suppose the task is to recognize letters of the alphabet. For the present discussion, assume that when a letter is presented, its image falls upon the rear surface of the eye, the area called the *retina*. The retina is composed of many hundreds of thousands of light-sensitive nerve cells, called *receptors*. Details of how these receptors operate will be discussed in later chapters; for the moment, let us see how they might be interconnected to recognize the letters of the alphabet.

FIGURE 1-1

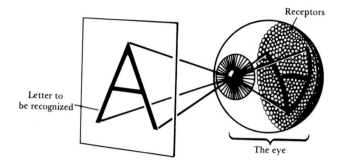

If the letter **A** is presented to the eye, it excites a pattern of receptors on the retina. If we were to interconnect these receptors together to a single detector cell, we would have a template of receptor cells specifically designed to detect the occurrence of the letter **A**. Thus, a possible template for **A** is shown in Figure 1-2.¹ When the light pattern

FIGURE 1-2

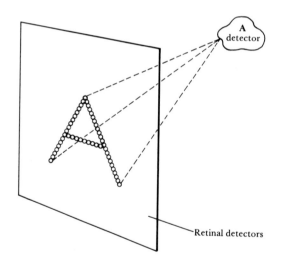

stimulates just the right set of receptors, the "**A** detector" begins responding vigorously.

---

¹ In the diagrams that follow, the fact that the lens of the eye inverts the image is conveniently ignored. This makes it easier to draw the diagrams and talk about the various pattern recognition schemes. Obviously, the principles of connecting together the receptors are unchanged whether the retinal image be upside down or rightside up.

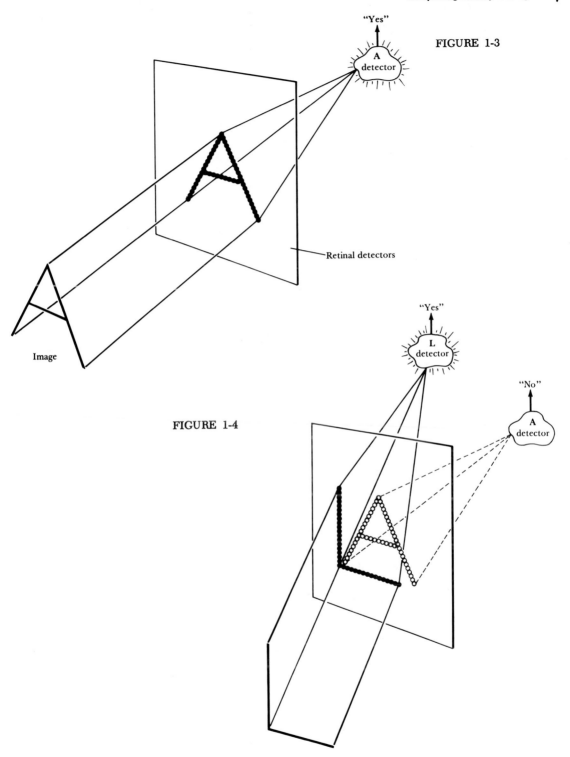

FIGURE 1-3

FIGURE 1-4

Figure 1-4

A different selection of receptors makes a template for **L**. Still another arrangement produces a template for **N**. By continuing in this fashion, it is possible to make templates for each pattern to be recognized.

Template matching is a straightforward scheme for recognizing patterns. Note that it does have one interesting feature: It matches the incoming pattern against all of the possible templates simultaneously. That is, it doesn't have to go through the cumbersome procedure of trying out a succession of templates one at a time to find the one that fits best. It looks for all of the letters at the same time: The template that provides the closest match to the incoming pattern is the one that is most strongly activated.

This simple version, however, is easy to dismiss as a model of human pattern recognition. Look what happens if the letter is printed slightly crooked, too big, or too small, respectively:

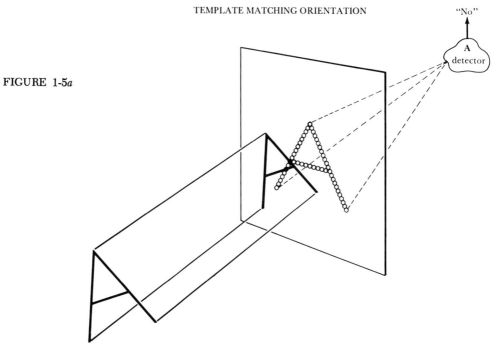

TEMPLATE MATCHING ORIENTATION

FIGURE 1-5a

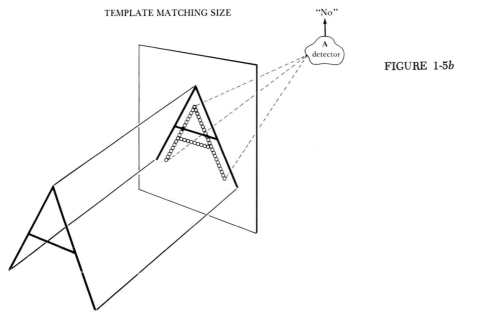

TEMPLATE MATCHING SIZE

"No"

FIGURE 1-5b

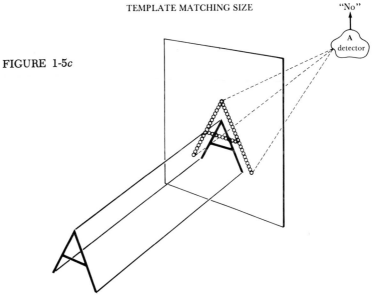

TEMPLATE MATCHING SIZE

"No"

FIGURE 1-5c

Thus, the system fails unless it has an exact template for the incoming pattern.

There is a choice of strategies for modifying the template scheme to handle these problems. More templates can be added—one for each possible size and orientation of the letter to be recognized:

TEMPLATE MATCHING DIFFERENT SIZES

FIGURE 1-6

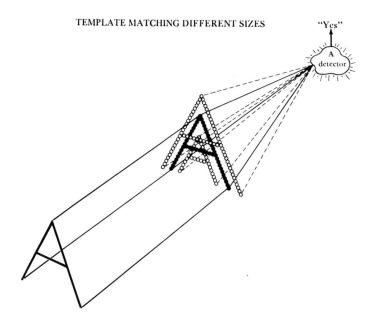

Alternatively, the symbols can be preprocessed to put them into a standard format before attempting a template match.

Many computer programs and machines that use a template system for recognizing patterns perform preprocessing. Before attempting to recognize the pattern, the letter is rotated so that its long axis is vertically oriented. It is then scaled in size to a preset height and width. Finally, the preprocessed signal is matched against a standard set of templates.

FIGURE 1-7

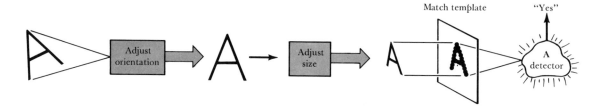

The best known working example of a template-matching scheme illustrates some of its limitations as a method for pattern recognition. On the bottom of bank checks, the bank identification number and checking account number are printed in special characters that can be read both by humans and by the check-sorting machines connected to the computers of the bank's clearing house. The characters are read off the check by a scanning device and are identified by an electronic template-matching system. Note the characters.

FIGURE 1-8

A great deal of effort went into designing them to be as distinct as possible from one another. They must be printed on the checks with a special machine to ensure the exact size and positioning of the letters. When the checks are read by the scanning device, misalignment can lead to errors. Template matching is the simplest scheme to build; it is also the easiest to go wrong.

It seems unlikely that templates could account for human pattern recognition. The variety in the patterns that must be dealt with poses considerable problems for a template scheme. They can be handled, but each must be treated as a special case, and the system soon becomes very complex and unwieldy. Moreover, a template scheme cannot recognize novel versions of patterns for which it has no template. Humans can succeed. Clearly then, a more powerful and flexible system is needed to account for the capabilities of human pattern recognition.

There are several different aspects of the simple template scheme that cause difficulties. Primarily, templates lack flexibility. That is, either there is an exact template for the particular pattern that is to be recognized or the system fails. We have seen that preprocessing helps minimize this rigidity. It is possible to compensate for size changes of preprocessing. But in general, preprocessing is very likely not able to compensate.

The template scheme can be called data-driven. Look at Figure 1-7; the operations are set into operation by arriving data. They proceed from left to right, from the presentation of the data to the next box, to the next, and so on. The processing is initiated by the arrival of data and proceeds in smooth, logical progression to the recognition of the item. Each stage of analysis does its thing, getting inputs (data) and doing something with them. The outputs of each stage are the input data that drive the next

DATA-DRIVEN AND CONCEPTUALLY DRIVEN PROCESSING

stage. With a data-driven system, nothing happens until we put in the data at one end. Then it all gets neatly processed and out pops the answer. Unfortunately, perception is not this simple. Look at Figure 1-9. Here we cannot recognize the object until we know what it is. A data-driven system will not work for this figure.

FIGURE 1-9   *R. C. James (photographer).*

Here we see some of the organizational processes that are operating during the interpretation of a visual image. To see that it is a picture of a dalmation dog (facing to the left), information not present in the picture must be added. Once the dog can be seen, it is difficult not to see it. The knowledge that the picture is of a dog seems to speed up the whole interpretive process: When you know what to look for, it is easier to see it.

Whenever knowledge of the possible interpretation or *conceptualization* of something helps in perceiving that thing, we say the processing is conceptually driven. That is, the processing starts with conceptualization of what might be present and then looks for confirming evidence, biasing the processing mechanisms to give the expected result. In the diagram of the template mechanism shown in Figure 1-7, conceptually driven processing would proceed from the right part of the figure toward the left, as is shown in Figure 1-10. In some ways a conceptually driven system is just the opposite of a data-driven system. A data-driven system works from what is actually present, and so it goes from left-to-right in Figure 1-10. A conceptually driven system works from what is expected, and so it goes from right-to-left in Figure 1-10.

As Figure 1-10 shows, conceptually driven processing and data-driven processing almost always occur together, with each direction of processing contributing something to the total analysis. Certainly, Figure 1-9 could not be interpreted without the incoming data. Moreover, because it is quite possible to look at Figure 1-9 for the first time, with no pre-

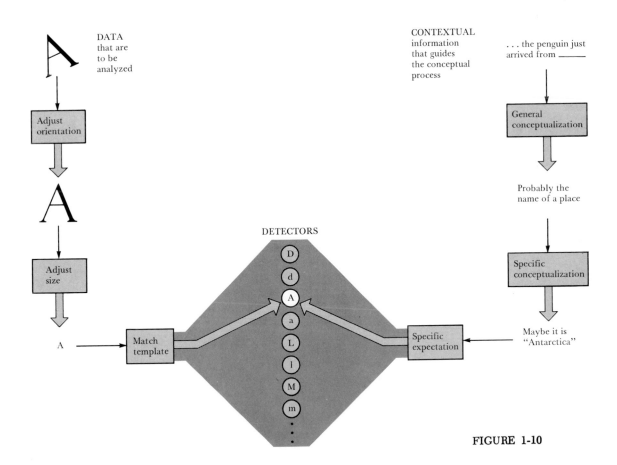

FIGURE 1-10

vious knowledge of what it might be, and see the dalmation dog, even the conceptualizations about the possible interpretations that operate the conceptually driven analysis come from data-driven processing. We will have a lot more to say about this complex situation in later chapters.

SOME PERCEPTUAL PHENOMENA

Before continuing our analysis of the possible mechanisms of pattern recognition, we need to know more. First, we need to know more about the nature of perception, about the types of difficulties humans have in perceiving things. Second, we need to know more about the machinery of the mind, about the operation of the human sensory systems, and about the mechanisms by which nerve cells operate and communicate with each other. Finally, after analysis of the phenomena and the mechanisms, we can begin to piece together what is happening. In the remainder of this chapter we concentrate upon a discussion of the phenomena of perception, with heavy emphasis on visual perception. The next four chapters discuss the operations of the human sensory system: Chapters 2 and 3 discuss the visual system and Chapters 4 and 5 cover the auditory system. Then, Chapter 6 presents a description of the operations of the basic cells that comprise the human nervous system: the neurons. Chapter 6 discusses how neurons can communicate with one another and how they might be interconnected to form specialized detectors. Finally, in Chapter 7, we return to the problem of pattern recognition and attempt to piece together the information that is known today about both perception and the nervous system into a general picture of how perceptual processes operate.

Things do not always appear as they actually are. What we see or hear is not always what is. Often, the perceptual system makes errors: Sometimes we see illusions, sometimes the perceptual system requires time to recover from prolonged stimulation, and sometimes it requires time to interpret the image presented to it. All these phenomena are valuable to us because the mechanics of a system are frequently revealed primarily through its errors and distortions. When all works smoothly and properly, it is difficult to know where to begin the search. But when failures occur, the analysis of those failures can be very revealing. So now let us examine some perceptual phenomena for the basic principles that can be extracted from them.

Let us start by examining how sensory information gets interpreted. We bring the interpretation process into awareness through tricks. First, we *degrade the image*, making interpretation difficult (if not impossible). Second, we provide *competing organizations*, making possible several conflicting interpretations of the same image. Third, we provide *organization without meaning* to see how past experience affects the process.

Ordinarily, the interpretation of sensory messages proceeds so rapidly and automatically that we are seldom aware of the complexity of the task. The processes must be slowed up a bit so that the mechanisms involved become apparent. One way of doing this is by reducing the amount of visual information available, as illustrated by the picture of the dalmation dog (Figure 1-9).

An image may be ambiguous because of a lack of relevant information or a surplus of irrelevant data. It can also be ambiguous because of the existence of several different ways of constructing a meaningful interpretation. Under these conditions, we have difficulty in interpreting the image in two distinct ways at the same time. A work by the artist Salvador Dali illustrates the point.

Competing organizations

Salvador Dali, "The Slave Market with Disappearing Bust of Voltaire." **FIGURE 1-11** *Collection: Mr. and Mrs. A. Reynolds Morse. Photograph courtesy of Salvador Dali Museum, Cleveland, Ohio.*

The title gives the clue to the alternative interpretations of Dali's work: *Slave Market with Disappearing Bust of Voltaire*. In the very center of the picture are two undersized nuns standing shoulder to shoulder. But with a different perceptual organization, the faces of the nuns become the eyes of Voltaire, the joining of their shoulders becomes a nose, the slash of white across their waists becomes a chin. One way of putting the information together produces a perception of miniature figures, the alternative way produces an oversized sculpture of a head. The two perceptions are, to some extent, incompatible ways of organizing the visual information: It is difficult to perceive both views simultaneously.

ORGANIZING AUDITORY PERCEPTIONS

The tendency to attend to and organize selectively the data provided by sensory systems is a very general characteristic of all perceptual experiences. When one conversation is extracted from out of the many around us, that conversation becomes *figure*. All other sounds in the environment become *ground*. The effect is most noticeable in a crowded party, where it is possible to switch attention from one conversation to another. Each time, the new conversation stands out clearly and sharply in consciousness while the others recede fuzzily into the background. (This phenomenon is treated in Chapter 7 in the discussion of attention.)

In music, the organization of our perceptions into figure and ground is well known. Composers often present different melodic lines simultaneously, knowing that the listener will attend primarily to one. In fact, it is possible to make one solo instrument sound as if it were playing two melodic lines at the same time. The player alternates between a high series and a low series of notes. The listener finds that he can listen to the high notes and find one line of the music or to the low notes and find the other line. He perceives the alternating notes as two distinct themes.

Look at this example of the technique in a segment of music from a piece for a solo flute. We have separated the two themes for you by screening the lower line. Note that the composer (Telemann) maintains a clear separation between the themes by separating the notes and forcing the flute player to alternate between one theme and the other. The listener can choose to follow

FIGURE 1-12

either the high or the low theme. Whichever line is attended to becomes the figure. The intervening notes are heard as background accompaniment.

In many ways the richness of music depends upon perceptual organizations. We pick out a theme and follow it. We hear the bass, pick it up for a while, then pass on to another instrument. We learn to follow the pattern from instrument to instrument. As the same piece of music is listened to over and over again, new themes can be discovered. The theme attended to at the moment is the figure. Everything else is the ground. Go back and listen to some music, something complex like Bach or Stravinsky or some good jazz or rock. Try out different ways of listening to the music. The variety of possible organizations is not obvious until you begin to notice them. It may take dozens of listenings to a piece before a particular pattern stands out clearly and distinctly. Like visual perceptions, knowing what to listen for seems to help, but once a particular way of organizing the music has been found, it is difficult to avoid from then on.

Does the ability to organize and separate out particular components of the visual image rely entirely on being able to construct familiar perceptions? Not at all. During the interpretation of a visual message,   *Organization without meaning*

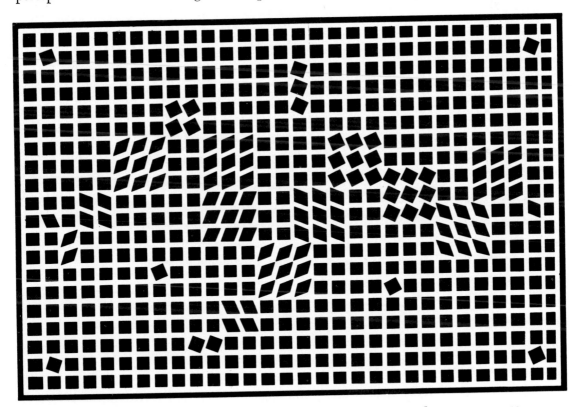

Victor Vasarely, "Tlinko." 1956. From Vasarely 1, p. 120, Editions du Griffon, Neuchâtel-Suisse.   FIGURE 1-13

FIGURE 1-14　*François Morellet, "Screen Painting: 0°, 22°5, 45°, 67°5." Collection: Museum of Modern Art, Paris. Courtesy of the artist.*

we seem to segregate and treat as a unit any grouping which has some distinguishing characteristic. Clusters of similar shapes or breaks in a repetitive pattern stand out as figures. A classic maxim for composing an interesting graphic pattern is to make sure to provide a focal point of interest by including some type of break in any repetitive pattern. Many contemporary artists are masters at discovering the variety of compositions that can be used to provide interesting groupings of figure

Figures 1-13 & 1-14　　and ground. We have just seen some samples of their works.

How do you break up these images? What do you look at? Why do the organizations keep changing in some of the pictures? These paintings have illustrated several different points. First, the objects need be neither meaningful nor familiar for the organizational principles to work. Second, it is difficult, if not impossible, to prevent the organization of information. Look at these figures carefully. The organization fluctuates, sometimes taking one form, sometimes another. But there is usually some structure to the pictures, even if the artist has deliberately tried

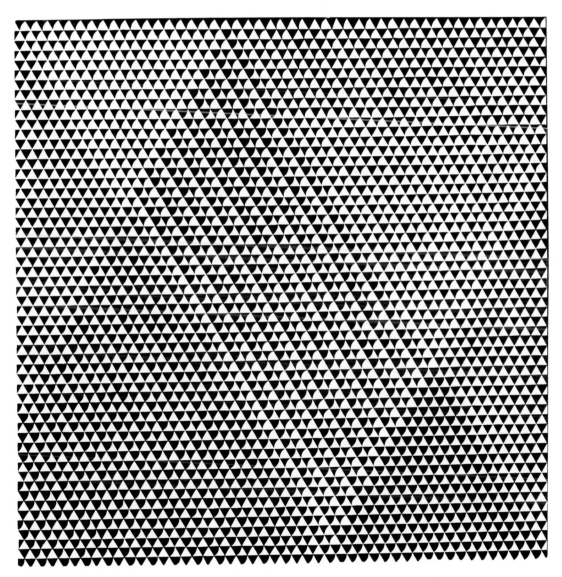

Bridget Riley, "Tremor." 1962. 48 × 48 inches. Courtesy of Mr. David M. Winton. FIGURE 1-15

to avoid standard forms of organization. The viewer puts it in. Figure 1-15 is especially interesting, since it can be perceived as a set of long, horizontal, rectangular tubes, or vertical ones, or simply as patterns of large, shifting triangles. But whatever the pattern, one is almost always present. Whether the figure be meaningful or not, familiar or novel, the data-driven and conceptually driven processes interact to impose organization upon it.

Making the data fit the conceptualization

Other important aspects of the organization of visual information can be demonstrated by illusions. The point of an illusion is to design an ambiguous set of sensory inputs in order to tease out some characteristics of the perceptual system through an analysis of the kinds of errors made. In this way, it is often possible to examine in more detail operations of the system that normally are not observable. Consider Figure 1-16 It could represent either an object lying down (Figure 1-17) or standing up (Figure 1-18).

To make the object,[2] take a piece of fairly heavy paper, fold it and set it up as shown in Figure 1-19. When you have set it up, view it with one eye closed from a point directly in line and slightly above the fold: The point labeled O. At first, the paper looks like the one in Figure 1-17. If you continue to stare at it intently, the paper will suddenly stand up and look like the one in Figure 1-18 It takes a little concentration and practice, but do it. The illusion is worth it. When you see it as in Figure 1-18, gently move your head slowly back and forth (remember to use only one eye). Note what happens to the object.

There are two distinct ways of organizing the image of the figure. When the object is perceived as lying down, all of the depth information fits together. When it is standing up, the shadows and contours are not quite what they should be (which makes the object appear somewhat luminous). When you move your head, the object seems to be made of a rubbery substance that twists and turns. This comes about because when the head is moved, the image of the near point of the fold moves across the retina faster than the image of the far point. This is the normal pattern of stimulation for parts of the scene at different depths—a phenomenon known as *motion parallax*. When the object is seen in its true orientation, this motion parallax cue coincides with the motion. When the object is seen as standing up, however, all the points along the fold appear to be equally distant. The only way the motion cues can be consistent with the vertical organization is if the object itself twists

[2] It is instructive to try out all of these illusions yourself: Little can be learned simply by reading about them.

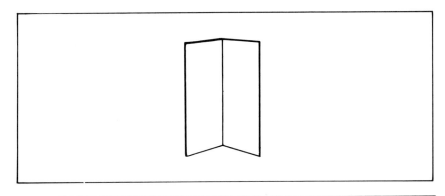

FIGURE 1-16

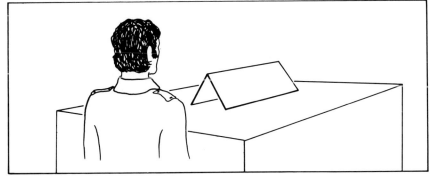

FIGURE 1-17

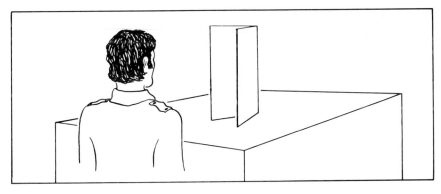

FIGURE 1-18

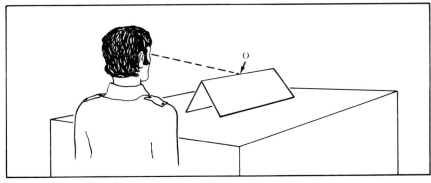

FIGURE 1-19

and turns. Even though you know very well that the object cannot be behaving in that way, the sensory data force you to perceive it as though it were. All of the sensory data are used to construct a consistent interpretation of the visual world.

Before you put away the paper, try it once more. This time, place the paper so that it is strongly lit from the side. When it switches from a horizontal to a vertical orientation, pay particular attention to the changes in the apparent brightness of the side of the object that is in the shadow. Can you explain these brightness differences?

THE IMPORTANCE
OF RULES

The last few examples have all illustrated a common theory: Sensory evidence must be interpreted. But what are the rules that govern the interpretation?

Look at Figure 1-20 The immediate perception is of a group of three-dimensional blocks, some overlapping others. The question is, what information is used to determine how the different areas in the block combine to form figures? How is it known that areas 20 and 18 come from the same figure, or, to pick a more difficult example, areas 3 and 29? To

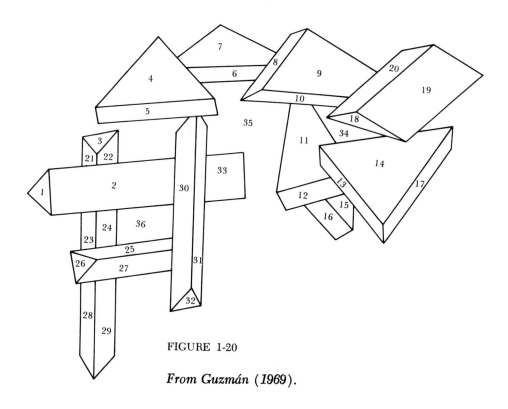

FIGURE 1-20

From Guzmán (1969).

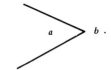

L – Vertex where two
lines meet

Fork – Three lines forming angles
smaller than 180°

FIGURE 1-21

*From Guzmán
(1969).*

Arrow – Three lines meeting at a
point, with one of the angles
bigger than 180°

T – Three concurrent lines, two
of them collinear

K – Two of the vertices are collinear
with the center, and the other
two fall in the same side of such
a line

X – Two of the vertices are collinear
with the center, and the other
two fall in opposite sides of
such a line

Peak – Formed by four or more lines,
when the central vertex is the
tallest part of the intersection.

Multi – Vertices formed by four or more
lines, and not falling in any
of the preceding types

do this task requires consideration of the lines and angles extracted
from the image. It turns out that there are several methods by which
this figure can be disentangled. This particular diagram comes from
the work of Guzmán (1969), a computer scientist interested in determining rules by which computers might do the task.

Guzmán analyzed a number of scenes of this type and concluded that
the most important information about overlap came from a consideration
of intersections, the spot where several contours intersect each other (see
Figure 1-21 . If the intersection forms an **L**, for example, it is likely that
the surface to the left (*a*) belongs to a different body than the surface

to the right (*b*). With a **fork,** however, all three surfaces can belong to the same body: *d, e,* and *f.* An **arrow** usually signifies two bodies, one that contains surfaces *h* and *i,* the other containing *j.*

It is the intersection labeled **T** that often contains the most important clues for the construction of the final picture. A **T** often signifies that one object is in front of another, so that surfaces *k* and *l* belong to one body that passes behind body *m.* Hence, when one **T** is found, it is important to see if others are around, other **T**'s that will line up properly with the first.

In Figure 1-22 the two **T**'s that are marked are sufficient to identify that surfaces *o* and *p* belong together, surfaces *r* and *s* belong together, and that *o* and *r* are the same surface, as are *p* and *s.* With the additional information provided by the **fork** that *r, s,* and *z* are part of the same body, the entire figure is unambiguously interpreted: *q* is one body: *o, p, r, s,* and *z* are another; *u* is the background.

FIGURE 1-22

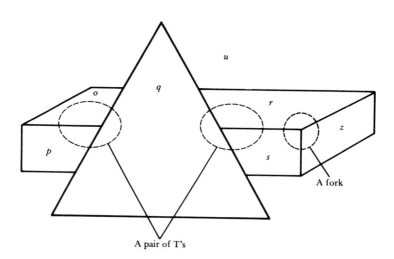

This analysis has only illustrated some simple principles operating in the interpretation of simple line drawings. To understand more complex scenes we need more information. Thus, shadows can play an important role in putting together the components of a picture, as shown in Figure 1-23.

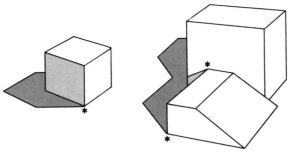

FIGURE 1-23

From Waltz (1975).

(*a*) In these scenes the starred junctions provide evidence the two objects or the object and table *touch*.

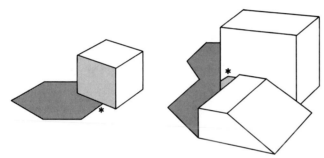

(*b*) In these scenes the starred junctions provide evidence the two objects or the object and table *do not touch*.

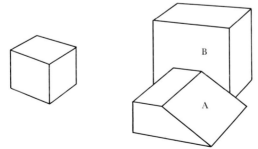

(*c*) In these scenes there is no evidence to use to relate the objects to each other or to the table; it is not possible to decide whether they touch or not.

Even shadows will not suffice for a complete understanding of an image: we need to know what objects are being represented. Look at Figure 1-24. Here the two cone shapes are seen to be different objects: one is a street, the other is the top part of a building. These cones are drawn almost identically, yet they represent quite different objects. The cone on the left is obviously oriented vertically. The sides do not appear to be parallel. The same size cone on the right is a street receding away to the distance. The sides appear parallel. The same visual information can be interpreted quite differently. Here, as with most visual perception, the interpretation of a part of the scene cannot be performed until there is a conceptualization of the entire scene.

These examples show the use of two different sources of information: first, the specific information about the picture gathered by analysis of the intersecting lines; second, an interpretation of the meaning conveyed by those intersections. There is a combination of the information conveyed by the local features of the picture with a consideration of the global interpretation. This dual process—of feature extraction and interpretation—is closely related to the distinction already encountered between data-driven and conceptually driven processing. These processes will come up repeatedly as we examine the perceptual experience. Moreover, the implications of this dual process of perception make themselves felt not only in the analysis of things like blocks, but also in situations where there is conflict between the implications of the local features and the global interpretation. When these contradictions arise, the resulting perception shows the conflict in rather obvious ways.

Perception of space   We normally perceive space to be three-dimensional. Distant objects take up a smaller angle than they do when close up. Textures change with distance and with viewing angle. Lines converge in the distance. Assuming that humans normally live and move about in a three-dimensional world, it makes sense that the visual apparatus has evolved to piece together a three-dimensional representation of the images that it sees. Let us try out some rules that it might have adopted to see how they work in explaining some phenomena.

Whenever a visual pattern is encountered in which lines or edges are converging, there are two options in interpreting it. It could be a two-dimensional object viewed straight on, in which case the lines are truly converging, or, it could be a three-dimensional object viewed at an angle, in which case the lines may really be parallel and the apparent convergence is a result of distance.

Rene Magritte, "Les Promenades d'Euclide." Courtesy of The Minneapo-lis Institute of Arts.   FIGURE 1-24

FIGURE 1-25   *Jeffrey Steele, "Baroque Experiment: Fred Maddox." Collection: Hon.*
Anthony Samuel. Courtesy of the artist.

The ability to see things in depth does not depend on familiarity with the objects. In Figure 1-25 a painting by Jeffrey Steele, a compelling illusion of depth is created by a very precise use of perspective in an endlessly repeated pattern.

Horizontal contours that are equally spaced in the environment are projected onto the retina with smaller and smaller separations. Look at the design shown in Figure 1-26.

FIGURE 1-26

From Carraher and Thurston (1968).

If we start at the middle of the pattern and follow up to the right, it appears to recede in the distance because the line spacing is systematically reduced. In fact, if you examine the geometry of the figure with care, you see that the gradient of line spacings gives rather precise angle and distance information. This is illustrated in Figure 1-27 where the different line gradients seen by an observer are shown as a plane surface that has a series of equally spaced horizontal lines tilted away from him. The spacing of the lines tells unambiguously the angle of the surface. Distance is not known, however, since in this diagram, the same gradient of line spacings can be the result of any distance from the eye (assuming that there is no way of knowing the actual spacing of the horizontal lines). Note, however, that if the information about the sides of the surface is available, as it is in the figure, then further constraints are put upon the situation.

Figure 1-27 shows that as a plane surface is tilted, equally spaced horizontal lines become more tightly packed in the furthest parts of the retinal image, and the projected lengths of the lines also decrease. This phenomenon, the well-known distance gradient, is responsible for many optical illusions.

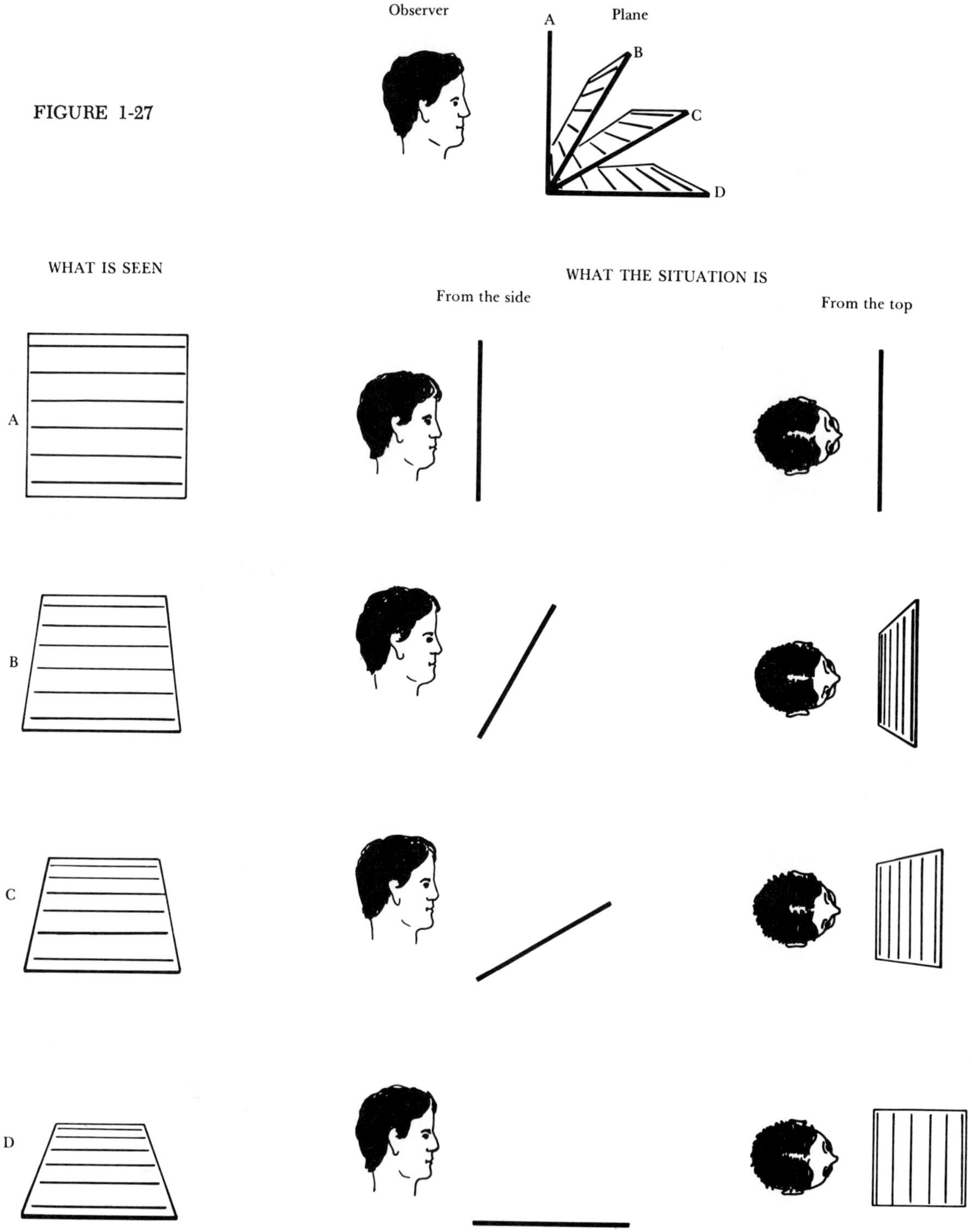

Observer   A   Plane

B

C

D

FIGURE 1-27

WHAT IS SEEN   WHAT THE SITUATION IS

From the side   From the top

A

B

C

D

The first illusion can be seen in Figure 1-26, where the end of the object that is perceived to be more distant is also perceived to be larger, even though (actually, because) the vertical lines of the drawing are all the same length. This diagram presents conflicting information to the observer, so it is no surprise that the resolution of the interpretation is also a conflict.

It does not take much to present depth information. Many different types of surface gradients will do the trick, as shown in Figure 1-28. When a rectilinear object is viewed straight on, the intersecting lines formed by its contours form right angles. As the object is tilted and rotated in space, the angles in the retinal image diverge from right angles. The degree of divergence depends on the orientation of the object in space. By interpreting that divergence from right angles as a result of depth, distance information can be extracted.

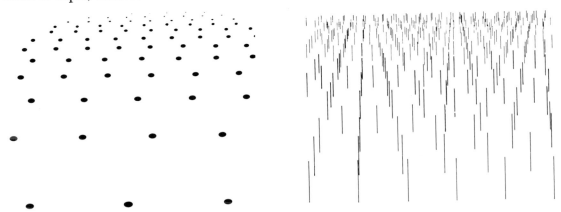

From Gibson (1950).   FIGURE 1-28

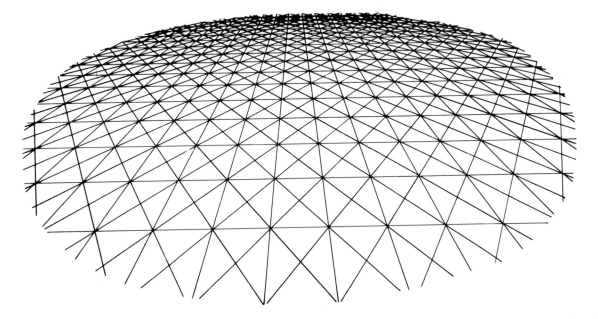

For example, in Figure 1-29 it is easy to see which of the cross bars intersects the vertical line at right angles. Yet, the same set of crosses is normally interpreted differently when accompanied by information about depth, as in Figure 1-30

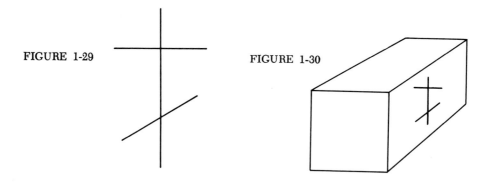

FIGURE 1-29

FIGURE 1-30

Impossible organizations. Another way of demonstrating the operation of the attempt to put objects into three dimensions during their interpretation is to construct pictures whose parts cannot be fit together to make a logical story. Here are some bits and pieces of a picture.

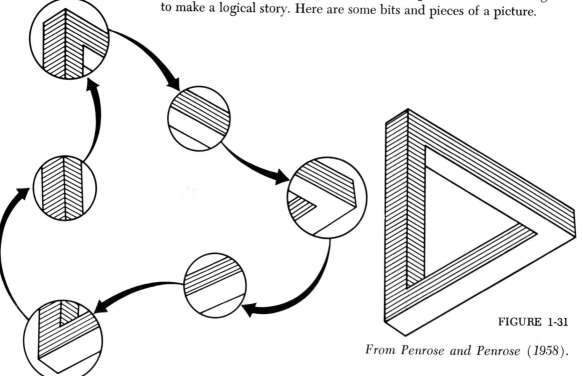

FIGURE 1-31

From Penrose and Penrose (1958).

They look like corners and sides of some three-dimensional object. Now we put them all together.

What happened? The pieces do not quite fit; the figure is impossible. But there is nothing inherently impossible about the collection of lines and angles that make up the drawing. The individual features conflict with the global interpretation. Here are some more examples to mull over.

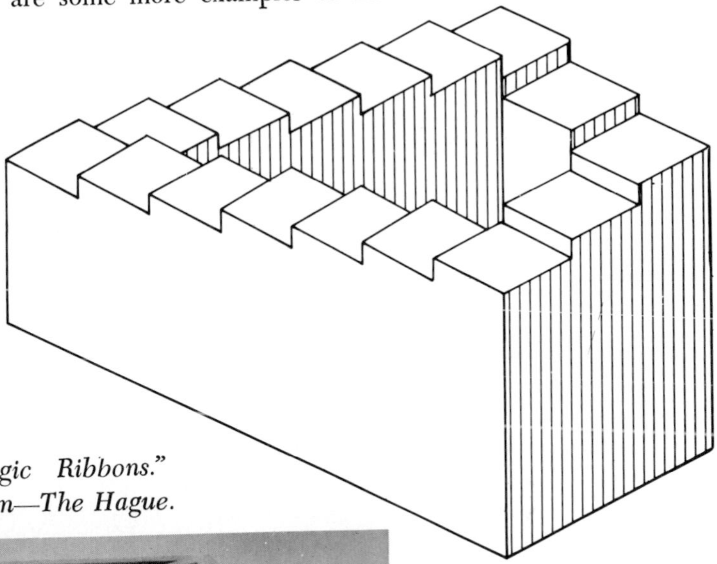

FIGURE 1-32

From Penrose and Penrose (1958).

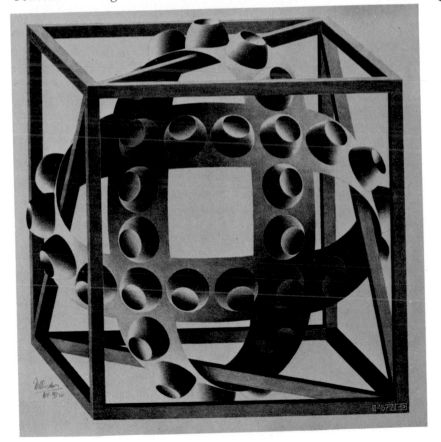

FIGURE 1-33

M. C. Escher, "Cube with Magic Ribbons."
Collection: Haags Gemeentemuseum—The Hague.

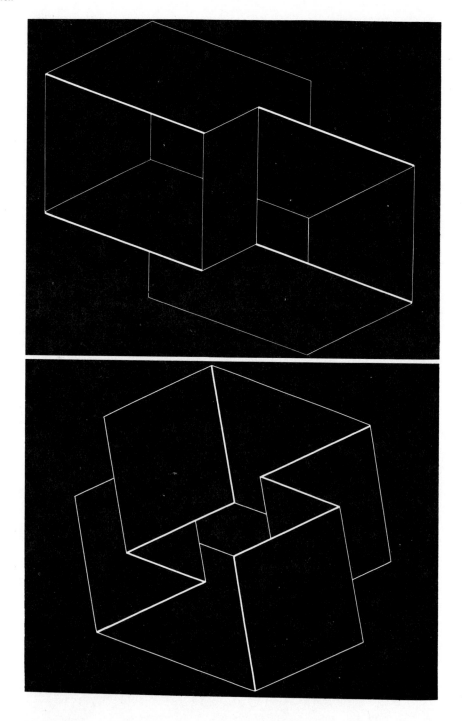

FIGURE 1-34 *Josef Albers, "Structural Constellations." 1953–1958. From* Despite Straight Lines, *pp. 63, 79. Courtesy of the artist.*

Nothing is dealt with in isolation. All the information must be integrated into a consistent overall interpretation of the visual scene. The three barrels in Figure 1-35 obviously have different sizes. Yet, it is easy to change their apparent relative sizes; just add information that provides the appropriate context.

The importance of context

FIGURE 1-35

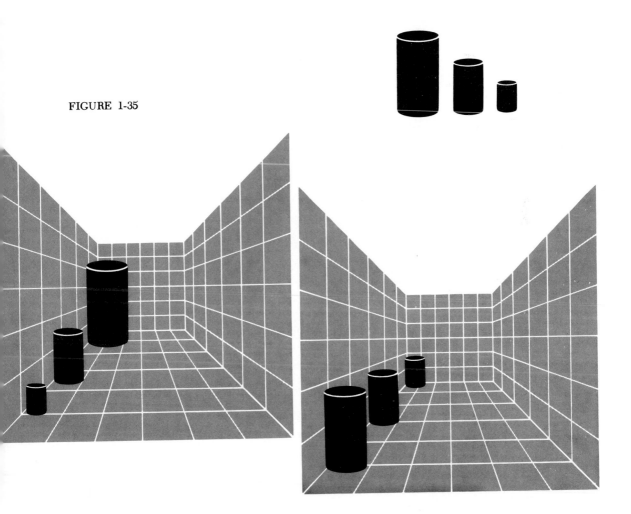

Again, the effects of context do not depend on working with familiar objects. Subtle effects seem to be present even in the meagerest of line drawings.

Normally, all contextual information fits together. As objects move away, their image size changes by just the right amount. The relative sizes and distances are what they should be. Neither the artist nor

FIGURE 1-36a

FIGURE 1-36b

FIGURE 1-36c

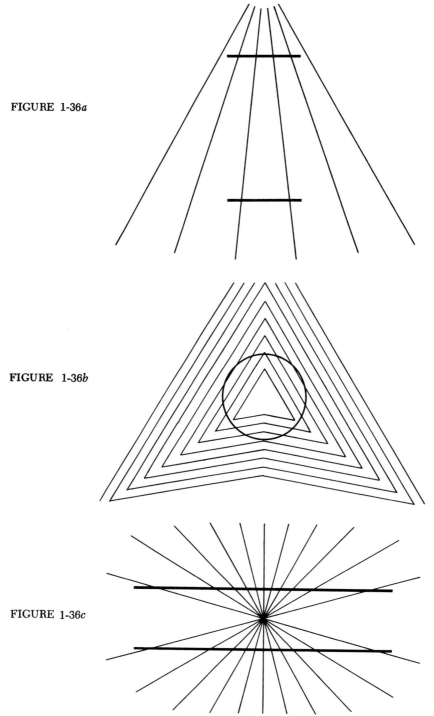

The two horizontal lines of Figure 1–36a are the same length. Figure 1–36b contains a perfect circle. The two horizontal lines of Figure 1–36c are parallel. From Luckiesh (1965).

the psychologist, however, is constrained to studying real-life situations. The surrealist delights in discovering and intentionally violating the rules for constructing logical perceptions.

René Magritte, "The Listening Room." Collection: Mr. William N. Copley.   FIGURE 1-37

We could accommodate the apple if we could assume the room was very tiny. Magritte has been meticulously careful to portray a lifelike room and apple so that neither can be easily scaled down in size. He violates the rules to provide an interesting image.

All these phenomena suggest that when piecing together sensory information, a consistent image of the world must be produced. In the laboratory, we can construct situations in which the information seen is ambiguous or incomplete. Thus, in the folded paper trick, the information about the true orientation of the figure was eliminated by viewing the object with one eye closed from a relatively stable head position. Only once the perceptual illusion had been achieved was it possible to move the head again, adding new depth cues. This time, however, the motion cues were interpreted in terms of the novel perception. As long as the interpretation was still possible (no matter whether it was unique or unfamiliar), the illusion was maintained.

FEATURE ANALYSIS   The last section concentrated on the interpretation of sensory features, on the rules of perception. But what can we say about the features themselves? What information does the nervous system extract from the signals arriving at the sense organs? Again, we make progress by looking for anomalies of perception. Actually, in studying the operations of sensory systems, it is possible to use physiological recording techniques and measure the operations of the nerves themselves. The evidence from investigations of this type will be presented in Chapter 6. But before going into the nervous system, it helps if we examine some of the more general properties of the feature extraction scheme by looking at their effects on perception.

Examine Figures 1-38 and 1-39. In Figure 1-38, there is a tiny gray spot at the intersection of all the white lines, with the exception of the intersection at which you are looking. In Figure 1-39, the inner gray squares look to be different shades of gray: In fact, they are all the same. These two figures illustrate one principle of sensory analysis: Neural cells interact with each other. Thus, the receptors at one part of the visual image are affected by the operation of neighboring receptors. Neither of these effects would occur if the receptors were independent of one another so that they simply sent a pure, uninterrupted signal to the brain. Indeed, in the one spot in the eye where the receptors do not interact much with one another, the darkening of the intersections does not take place: the small area right at the point on which the eye is focused. (This area is called the *fovea*—more about it in Chapters 2 and 3.) Figure 1-40 shows a similar result. See the faint diagonal lines running between the squares? Well, they are actually not there. The neural interaction adds them to the image.

Here in simple demonstrations are strong influences of the feature extraction system, but these demonstrations do not tell us how they operate. It is possible to obtain more information about the operation of the feature extraction mechanism through two psychological procedures:

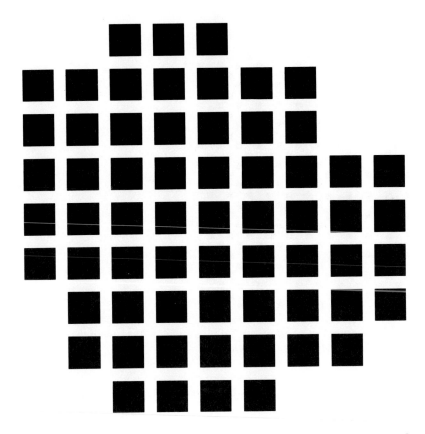

*The Hering grid: Gray spots appear at each intersection, except the one   FIGURE 1-38
you are looking at.*

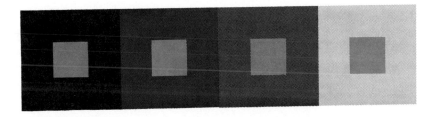

*Simultaneous contrast: The small squares all have the same intensities.   FIGURE 1-39
From Cornsweet (1970).*

FIGURE 1-40   *Springer lines: the appearance of faint, diagonal lines (which are not actually there) was discovered by Robert Springer.*

- First, the eyes are in constant motion. If that motion is stopped, the images seen by the eyes disappear. The way in which the visual image fades away when the eye is stopped suggests some of the properties of the feature extraction mechanism.
- Second, prolonged viewing of an image leaves its mark on future perceptions. The effects of these afterimages provide another clue to the operations of the visual system.

Stopping the image   The image on the eye is in constant motion, not simply because of movements in the environment, but because of a continuous tremor in the eye—small jiggling movements called *physiological nystagmus*. In fact, there are a number of different types of eye movements which go on without our noticing them. One is very small and fast: The eye moves in an angle of about 20 seconds of arc, 30 to 70 times each second. (There are 60 seconds of arc to each minute and 60 minutes of arc to a degree—thus, 20 seconds is $\frac{1}{180}$ of a degree.) Another is a large, oscillatory motion. Still another is a slow drift of a few visual minutes one way or the other. And finally, there are some rapid jerks, with an amplitude of about 5 minutes of arc, often correcting for the slow drifts. You can see the effect of these eye movements with this demonstration.

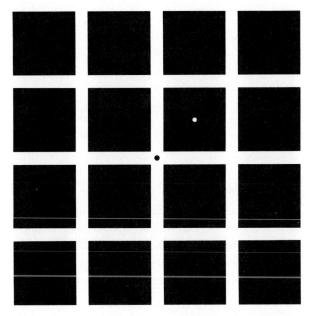

From Verheijen (1961). FIGURE 1-41

Look at the black fixation point of Figure 1-41 steadily (the dot in the center of the figure), trying to keep your eyes as still as possible. Keep looking until the black and white parts of the picture appear to shimmer (about 30 sec). Then move your gaze to the white dot. You should see a set of white blocks on a dark background, superimposed on the picture itself. The afterimage of the grid will continually shift about on the pattern, no matter how carefully you try to hold the image steady. This is physiological nystagmus.

What is interesting, however, is not so much that the eye is in continuous motion, but that if all movements are stopped, the visual image disappears. This phenomenon gives us some basic information about the way the receptor and sensory analyzing systems are working.

Movements of the visual image across the surface of the retina can be stopped using several techniques (Riggs, Ratliff, Cornsweet, & Cornsweet, 1953). One of them is shown in Figure 1-42. Here a small mirror is attached to a contact lens on the eye. The image to be seen by the subject is projected at this mirror, which bounces it off onto the viewing surface. With this system, when the eye moves to the right, the mirror does too, and thus the image is displaced to the right. With careful calibrations, it is possible to make the image move through exactly the same visual angle as the eye, so that the image seen at the retina does not change its position, regardless of eye movements.

FIGURE 1-42

From Riggs, Ratliff, Cornsweet, and Corn-sweet (1953).

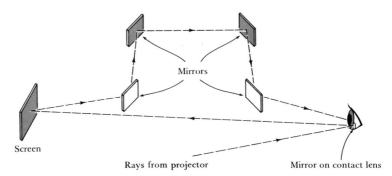

When a visual scene is viewed through such an apparatus, after a few seconds, the patterns begin to disappear. Gradually, nothing is left but a blank, homogeneous field. Figure 1-43 shows how it looks. The leftmost figure in each of the four rows shows the original image. The other four figures in each row show how things disappear. The image disappears in a peculiar way. It does not simply fade away. It disappears in meaningful chunks. Whole segments go at once, leaving other parts still visible. The more meaningful the image, the longer it lasts. The part of the image that is consciously attended to lasts longest of all. You can try this experiment for yourself by looking steadily at Color Plates I and V (in the insert following page 121). If you stare for 60 to 90 seconds without moving

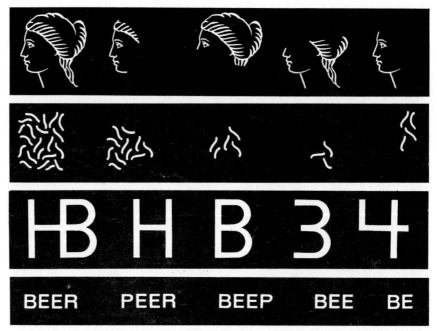

FIGURE 1-43   *From R. M. Pritchard, Stabilized images on the retina. Copyright 1961 by Scientific American, Inc. All rights reserved.*

your eyes, the lines in those plates will disappear, not gradually, but in segments.

Color Plate II is a reproduction of a lithograph, *Looking Glass Suite No. 9* by the English artist Peter Sedgley. Notice some of the characteristics of the picture. The edges of the concentric circles are blurred. That is deliberate. In fact, it is one of the secrets to its operation. Now, stare at the center of the picture from close up without moving your eyes. Stare for awhile; it takes time. What should happen first is that the middle circle will go away. Then parts of the circles will be eliminated, not gradually, but in large segments. Finally, both circles will disappear, leaving only a constant, homogeneous yellow field. If you move your eyes even slightly, it will return. (Do not be disappointed if it takes you a long time to make the picture go away. There is a practice effect: The more you do it, the easier it becomes. The first time is sometimes extremely difficult. But the experience is worth the trouble.)

Notice that when the circles disappear, the yellow field fills in to take their place. Whenever the neural circuits cease to operate normally, their absence is not noted. In this case, the evidence for the circles is not present, but the color information is: Hence, we see only the latter.

What accounts for these effects? The most popular explanation is that perception of the pattern depends on the activity of very complex feature detectors, neural circuits that detect lines, edges, angles, and perhaps circles. So long as enough information is being provided by the neural receptors in the eyes, the complex feature detector continues to respond, and the pattern can be seen intact. When the eye stops its movements the receptors in the eye cease their responses. When there are no longer enough responses coming from the eyes to drive the complex detector, it ceases to respond and the pattern disappears as a whole. Hence, the relatively long life of complex images compared with simpler ones; hence the abrupt way in which whole segments of the image fade in and out of view; hence the distortions of complex images that occur when the fading sensory signal causes the perceptual mechanisms to err in their interpretations of those data that are still available.

Two questions remain. One, do other senses behave in this way: Does a constant auditory tone become inaudible after awhile? Two, why did Sedgley's circles disappear even though no special equipment was used to stop the eye movements? The answer to the first is easy. A constant auditory signal does not exist. Even tones which appear to have a constant pitch and loudness are, in reality, a continuously changing pattern of air pressure. Auditory signals have their motion built in: The visual system must add it artificially. Other systems, such as taste and touch, do adapt. The band of a wrist watch is no longer felt after a few minutes. You notice it only when it moves. A constant taste sensation or odor disappears after awhile. All sensory systems seem to require changes in stimulation in order to maintain perception. Stop the image, and you stop the perception.

What about the second question? The picture disappeared because it was cleverly constructed with blurred edges. Even though the eye did move slightly as the picture was viewed, the resulting vibratory pattern on the retina of the eye was of a blur moving across the receptors (see Figure 1-44). The transition from one color to the next was done so smoothly that the movement of the blur was not sufficient to cause the receptor cells to note the change in stimulation.

One must be very cautious in making deductions about neural mechanisms from behavioral data such as these. Alternative explanations should be carefully considered. The disappearance and reappearance of the patterns may be due to technical difficulties in the apparatus, such as slippage of the lens. Maybe the image is not perfectly stopped. Perhaps you only think that the disappearance occurs in meaningful components, because these are the only changes in perceptions that can readily be described.

These questions should not, of course, be taken as grounds for dismissing the phenomenon, but rather as spurs toward further research. The work on stopped images provides a potentially useful bridge between our perceptual experiences and the neural mechanisms underlying human vision.

Aftereffects A second important source of information about human perception comes from a consideration of the aftereffects of strong stimulation. If one stares at a brightly colored light for a while and then looks at a smooth, white surface, the image is seen, but in the complementary color. If the original light was red, the afterimage is green. If the original was blue, the afterimage is yellow: If it was black, the afterimage is white.

Similarly, if you stand in a doorway and push hard against the doorjambs with your arms as if you were trying to raise them up over your head, you discover when you move away and let both hands relax normally, your arms slowly rise up in the air, as if of their own accord. Again, the aftereffects of intense stimulation make themselves felt in ways that tell us something about the internal functioning of the system.

Motion aftereffects. A particularly compelling aftereffect involves motion. Watch a moving object for a while. The classical object is a waterfall, but many other movements will do. The important thing is that you be able to stare fixedly at one spot, being careful not to move your eyes for several minutes while the motion takes place.

Now if you shift your gaze to a textured object (a wall, or better,

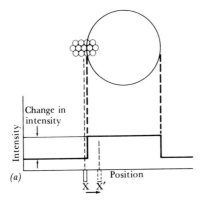

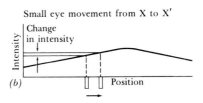

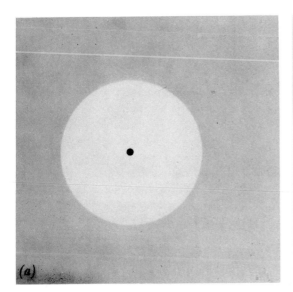

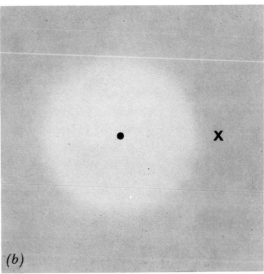

Top: *An explanation of why the blurred disk disappears, but the sharp one does not. Involuntary eye movements (nystagmus) produce strong intensity changes on the retina when the sharp disk (a) is fixated, but the same eye movement produces only a slight change in intensity with the blurred target (b).*

   Is this the explanation for the disappearance of the rings in the picture by Peter Sedgley (Color Plate I)?

   Bottom: A demonstration of the role of abrupt changes in intensity. If you fixate the dot of picture (b) steadily (closing one eye helps), the blurred disk will disappear. It will reappear if you blink or if you shift your fixation to the X. The sharp disk (a) will probably not disappear for you.

   These figures come from Cornsweet (1969).

FIGURE 1-44

some finely textured material such as curtains or bedspreads), you will see the appearance of motion in the direction **opposite** to that of the original object. If the object was moving down, after motion moves up; if you watched a contracting spiral, the aftermotion is that of expansion. If you examine the textured surface with care, you will note that the motion is really not there: The visual image is not moving. There is the appearance of motion in the absence of a moving image.

WHAT TO LOOK AT FOR MOTION AFTEREFFECTS

An extremely effective source of motion is a moving wheel that rotates some three or four times each second. The wheel should be marked with lines of high contrast so that the movement is easily observed. The best movement effects come from watching a spiral mounted on a rotating wheel: As the spiral rotates it will appear to be contracting or expanding, depending upon the direction of rotation.

To help you view the phenomenon of motion aftereffects, we have provided you with a spiral (Figure 1-45) that can be traced from the drawing in the book and then mounted on a rotating phonograph turntable. This spiral is designed to be rotated at 33⅓ rpm. If you lack a phonographic turntable, you can try inserting a pencil in the center hole and spinning the spiral around that. But rotate the spiral slowly: about the same speed as that of a 33⅓ rpm record.

Now, stare intently at the center of the rotating spiral for at least 30 sec. Do not let your eyes wander from the center. Now look at other objects around your room, or at someone's face.

As we have mentioned, the original form of the motion aftereffect came from prolonged observation of a waterfall. If you are unable to find a waterfall and do not wish to or cannot construct the wheel, then there are still some alternative methods of finding motion. One method is to use the television set, first adjusting the image to have maximum brightness and maximum contrast, second, by carefully fiddling with the vertical hold controls, to adjust the picture so that it continually drifts up or down across the screen. Unfortunately, the television image, especially on a good set, will move jerkily, hindering the effect, so that you might have to look at the image longer (please turn off the sound).

Finally, you could simulate a waterfall by turning on the water in the bathtub or shower so as to make as big a stream as possible. Stare intently at this for at least 1 min. This method is not particularly recommended, but it does seem to work.

Color aftereffects. Examine Color Plate II (following page 121). Stare intently at the black dot in the left panel, the one with all the green

If this spiral (or a facsimile) is placed on a rotating turntable and the FIGURE 1-45
center stared at for 30 sec, a motion aftereffect will occur. From Gregory
(1970).

hearts. Keep your head and eyes steady and keep staring until the whole figure starts to shimmer. Then look at the right black dot in the figure, the one in the white area. You should see a series of red hearts (it helps to blink a few times to get the afterimage started). The afterimage that results from intensive examination of a color is the appearance of the complementary color—the opposite color, if you will. You can notice this color aftereffect with any brightly colored surface, including most of the other figures included in the color plates.

The explanation of aftereffects

Notice two aspects about aftereffects. First, the aftereffect is always the opposite or complement of the original movement or muscle pressure or color (when we discuss the mechanisms of color vision we will see why red is the complementary color to green). This suggests the operation of two antagonistic systems pitted against each other. The second point is that the aftereffect requires prolonged stimulation of one of the antagonistic systems: Prolonged exposure to one of complementary colors or continued movement in one direction. This suggests that the responsiveness of the underlying neural mechanisms can be adapted or fatigued to have a reduced sensitivity to the input.

Consider the motion aftereffect. Suppose that there were specific neural detectors for movement, with the detectors for movement in one direction paired up with those for movement in the exactly opposite direction. Suppose further that these two detectors act against each other, with the action of one causing a decrease in the action of the other. Now we need further to assume that the motion detectors are connected together to form a new detector unit, one that responds with increased neural responses when movement in one direction occurs and with decreased neural responses when movement in the other direction occurs. When there is no movement, the two detectors balance each other out and the output of the new detector unit is simply a low level, background response—one that indicates no movement.

All that is needed now is to assume that either class of detectors feeding into the circuit can be fatigued by prolonged stimulation. Then, after overstimulation (and fatigue) to movement, when a stationary object is viewed, the fatigued detectors do not make their normal contribution to balance the activity in the pair of opposed motion detectors. The circuit will signal movement in the opposite direction.

The explanation of color aftereffects follows a similar line of reasoning. Again, neural cells are paired, so that cells that respond in one way are connected with cells which respond in the other, the output of the pairing being simply the difference between the two. If a **red** receptor is paired with a **green** one, both respond equally in the presence of white light, leading to no output from the combined cells. The **red** cell fires with **red** light leading to a positive output, the **green** cell with **green** light, leading to a negative output. Normally, with white light present, both **red** and **green** respond equally, leading to no output from the combined cells. Now suppose the eye focuses upon a **red** color for some period of time. By fatigue, the **red** cell loses its ability to respond. Now if the eye looks upon a white light, the **green** responds normally, but the normal response of the **red** is inhibited. The result, of course, is that the **green** responses outweigh the **red**, and the white light is seen as **green**.

Although aftereffects indicate that fatiguing is occurring somewhere in the chain of events leading to perception, the simple existence of the effect does not give any information about what parts of the system are being fatigued. To determine where the fatigue occurs, additional data are needed. The main technique is to test whether the aftereffect transfers between eyes: Stimulate one eye until fatigue takes place, then test the other eye for the aftereffect. If the aftereffect is not observed, peripheral mechanisms are assumed to be responsible. The color after-effects just described do not transfer between eyes. Thus, they are a result of fatigue or adaptation in peripheral mechanisms, probably due to the depletion of the chemical reserves in the color receptors of the eye itself.

The exact locus of fatigue underlying the motion aftereffects is less clear. Some studies have reported transfer of the aftereffect between eyes suggesting central processes are being fatigued. Others have failed to find such transfer.

The conclusion, of course, is that these aftereffects imply the operation of specific types of neural circuits in the sensory analyzing system. They suggest the presence of specific detectors for movement and for color.

Orientation-specific color adaptation

One intriguing set of aftereffects has been found from a consideration of the possible feature detectors in humans.

We have suggested that there might be special detectors for lines: Suppose there were not only line detectors, but colored line detectors in the human visual system. How could one demonstrate their existence? Following the reasoning in the preceding section, one strategy is to fatigue one set of line detectors, then present a neutral object. If the complementary set of features exists, they should show themselves.

Suppose there are both red and green horizontal line detectors. After prolonged exposure to green horizontal lines, white horizontal lines should then appear reddish (white has equal amounts of red and green). Is this effect specific to horizontal lines, or just an overall color adaptation to green? To find out, simultaneously fatigue the red vertical-line detectors so that white vertical lines will subsequently appear green.

This is the McCollough Effect (McCollough, 1965). For 5 minutes people are alternately shown red vertical lines (Figure 1-46a) and then green horizontal lines (Figure 1-46b), each pattern being left on for about 5 seconds. Then a test pattern consisting of black and white lines at various orientations is presented (Figure 1-46c): the horizontal white lines look reddish; the vertical white lines look greenish; oblique lines look white. If the head is tilted to the side so that oblique lines now become vertical or horizontal, they too take on the appropriate coloration.

The effect has several surprises. For one thing, it is very persistent. Some people still see white lines as colored for several days or weeks: an unusually long time for such a simple perceptual phenomenon to last. The effect is not a simple afterimage of the type that makes a black square leave a white afterimage. Afterimages require prolonged stimulation without any eye movements. But most surprising of all, the effect does not agree with two intuitions about line detectors.

If the specific color adaptations were due to specific circuits for detecting lines, then one would suspect that blurring the contours between the black and white stripes of the test pattern would destroy the effect (the lines are not seen sharply). On the other hand, changing the contrast between the white and black lines on the test pattern should have no effect, since the lines would still be seen clearly. The reverse is true: Changing focus has no effect; increasing the intensity differences increases the aftereffect.

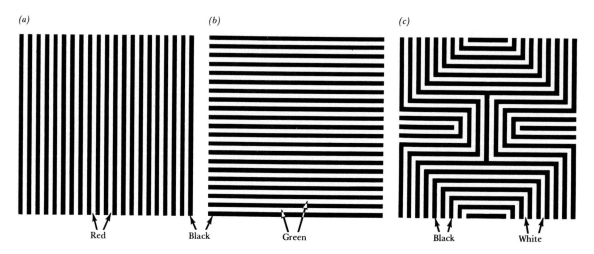

(a)   *(b)*   *(c)*

Red   Black   Green   Black   White

FIGURE 1-46   *After Gibson and Harris (1968).*

The McCollough Effect does demonstrate the operation of two complementary systems sensitive to certain patterns in the visual stimulus. And, in fact, as we shall see, a small number of colored line detectors—units which are maximally sensitive to a line of a specific color—have been found recently in the brains of monkeys. Be careful, however, in jumping to conclusions. Line detectors are far more complex than what is needed to explain the perceptual phenomenon.

Before leaving the McCollough Effect, it is interesting to note that it also works for moving images. We set up a band of horizontal stripes that can move up or down. When the stripes move up they are colored green; when they move down they are red. Each direction of movement is maintained for about 5 sec: The directions alternate while someone watches them for a total time of approximately 5 min. Now, we present a test image of black and white horizontal lines moving either up or down. When the test image moves up, the lines appear reddish; when it moves down, the lines appear to be greenish (Stromeyer, 1969; Stromeyer & Mansfield, 1970).

This is the exact analog of the McCollough Effect. All that has been changed is to substitute up and down movement for stationary lines at different orientations. Does this mean that there are color-sensitive movement detectors?

Perception without features

The work on stopped images and aftereffects illustrates some of the techniques for studying the kinds of feature detectors that may be operating in human vision. There can be no question that specific feature detectors do exist in humans. But there is doubt about the exact types of detectors operating and their overall role in human perception. There are characteristics of human perception that cannot be handled easily by an appeal to feature-detection systems.

Go back through the illustrations of this chapter. Look at the dog, or at some of the other pictures. What features are present? How do you construct a dog out of the miscellaneous blobs, where no straight lines or edges exist? How are competing organizations of the picture by Dali, or the different interpretations of the same cone shape in the picture by Magritte, explained through feature analysis?

REVIEW OF TERMS AND CONCEPTS

In this chapter, the following terms and concepts that we consider to be important have been used. Please look them over. If you do not feel comfortable with any of them, you should go back and review the appropriate sections of the chapter.

<table>
<tr><td>

*Terms and
concepts you
should know*

</td><td>

Templates
  preprocessing
  problems with templates
  receptors
Data-driven
Conceptually driven
Perceptual phenomena
  organization
  parallax
  rules for analyzing scenes
  classification of intersections
  context
Features
Stopped eye movements
Perceptual aftereffects

</td></tr>
</table>

SUGGESTED
READINGS

There are numerous sources for further information about the perceptual system. In this section we attempt to give you a rough guide to the literature. Our recommendations should act as pointers, not as absolute requirements. If you want to explore further in some topic matter, then the recommendations listed here should give you a place to start. Even if the books are not satisfactory, they themselves contain references to other places to look. Take these suggestions as useful guides to the material that is available, or comments about the works that we ourselves have found useful. But be adventurous: learn to use the tools of the library. Seek out other sources of information. Ask the people who work in the field what their favorite references are. Do not restrict yourself to the items listed here.

Perception

A good starting place is with the well-written little books by Gregory: *Eye and brain: The psychology of seeing* (1966) and *The intelligent eye* (1970). You will find his books to be interesting and easy reading. The books on *Light and vision* (Mueller, Rudolph, & Editors of Time-Life Books, 1969) and *The mind* in the Life Science Series are also excellent. The best book we have seen on visual illusions, with excellent descriptions and explanations, is by Robinson (1972).

    Gibson (1950, 1966) has done more than anyone else to emphasize the importance of the physical cues in perceptual phenomena, and his two books are filled with illustrations of his ideas. We have used some of his ideas and examples, although we disagree with some of his views about the role of cognition in perception. All in all, we have profited immensely from our written and verbal disagreements with him, and we recommend his books to you.

A good book on perception is the little monograph by Hochberg (1964). This is one of the clearer presentations of the issues and phenomena of perception. In addition, you might want to see Hochberg's article, "In the Mind's Eye" (1968), which is reprinted in the book of readings collected by Haber (1968). The readings include other interesting articles as well. Hochberg's (1972) chapter on "The Representation of Things and People" presents a number of fascinating discussions. Still another good collection of papers can be found in Vernon's *Experiments in visual perception* (1966).

There are a number of good references slightly more advanced than the ones just described. The most thorough and complete presentations are offered by Rock (1975) in *An introduction to perception* and by Kaufman (1974) in *Sight and mind.* (Rock, in his treatment of "The Perception of Form," refers the reader to this chapter of this book, so you might find yourself going around in circles.) The *Handbook of perception,* a multiple volume treatment of almost every issue in psychology that is at all related to perception, promises to become the basic source book for coming years. It is also reasonably advanced. (See Carterette and Friedman in the reference list at the end of the book.) There is a large amount of work on perception being performed within the artificial intelligence community. Much of this promises to be of great interest to psychologists, but very little has been published. One book that is available is Winston's (1975) *The psychology of computer vision.*

The journal *Scientific American* frequently publishes articles on perception. Although the general quality of psychology articles in *Scientific American* is not very good, their articles on visual perception are outstanding. Unfortunately, much of their work on auditory perception is also at a lower standard. Your best bet here is simply to go to the library and leaf through old issues—an easy and enjoyable way to keep up to date. The books edited by Held and Richards (1972, 1976) contain the best perception articles from *Scientific American.*

There are a number of technical journals in psychology that cover perception, including *Journal of Experimental Psychology: Human Perception and Performance; Perception; Vision Research; Perception & Psychophysics;* and occasionally, *Psychological Review* and *Cognitive Psychology.* These will be technical, more limited articles, but these and related journals contain the articles you must eventually read if you are serious about pursuing an interest in perception. Articles in *Scientific American,* entertaining though they may be, simply are not meant to be judged by the same high technical standards as the professional journals.

The best way of getting into the literature is probably through the *Annual Review* articles on the topic of interest: for example, Weintraub's (1975) review of perception.

A number of perceptual phenomena will be discussed in the next five chapters, so the suggested readings for Chapters 2 and 3 should be consulted for phenomena of vision, those of Chapters 4 and 5 should be consulted for phenomena of hearing and music, and Chapter 6 will present more information on pattern recognition.

Senses other than seeing and hearing are not so well understood, and so there is little material to recommend. One place to start is with the three chapters by Kenshalo, Bartoshuk, and Mozell in Kling and Riggs (1971). In addition, the *Handbook of perception* has an entire volume devoted to *Feeling, tasting, smelling, and hurting.* (See Carterette & Friedman, Volume 6, in the reference section of this book.) Also see Geldard (1973), on the cutaneous sense (touch).

Art Good classical discussions of art come from the works of Arnheim (1969a,b) and from Gombrich's book, *Art and illusion* (1960). Our emphasis on illusions, optical art, and other contemporary art comes from our own wanderings through the museums and galleries. Excellent catalogs of optical art are available both from the museums, such as the Museum of Modern Art in New York (see, e.g., *The responsive eye* by Seitz, 1965), and the Arts Council of Great Britain. (*The responsive eye* is also available as a slide set from Sandak Color Slides, Set No. 617.) Our selection of Magritte's pictures comes from one of two catalogs, one from the Museum of Modern Art (Soby, 1965), and the other from the Arts Council of Great Britain (Sylvester, 1969). Fascinating (but expensive) books are available on Vasarely (1965, 1971), and Escher's works are also available in a book, *The graphic work of M. C. Escher* (Escher, 1967). In addition, the work of Bridget Riley (de Sausmarez, 1970) and the books of Albers (1963) and Kepes (1965) should be examined by anyone who is seriously interested in the art that has been discussed in this chapter. (The figures by Albers reproduced in this chapter come from the engaging discussion of geometric illusions in Bucher's (1961) book, titled *Joseph Albers. Despite straight lines.*)

An interesting discussion of the history and development of perspective in art is provided by Pirenne's *Optics, painting, and photography* (1970). This book treats the optical properties of the eye in some detail. The book by Gombrich, Hochberg, and Black (1972) talks about related issues of art and perception.

Many excellent examples of optical art and other illusions are reprinted in *Optical illusions and the visual arts* (Carraher & Thurston, 1968).

Luckiesh's (1922) book, *Visual illusions,* provides a rich source to play with. But the best explanations are in Robinson (1972), already mentioned in the first paragraph.

The collection of optical and geometrical patterns and designs by Spyros Horemis (1970) is simply fun to look at and play with. It should be available in any quality paperback bookstore. Massaro's (1975a) book on experimental psychology presents an elaborate treatment of art in the section on visual perception. The treatment is very similar to ours; in fact, he uses some of the same pictures.

A fascinating approach to perception in music is given by Reynolds (1975) in his book, *Mind models: New forms of musical experience.*

Above all, enjoy the perceptual bases of art, tour the art galleries, visit experimental centers of art. Many artists are experimenting with very sophisticated phenomena, and the only way to discover the artists is to go and seek them out. We have found the material discussed in this chapter to be an excellent foundation for holding intelligent conversation with artists, something that formal training in art does not necessarily prepare you for.

2 The visual system

PREVIEW

This next set of four chapters examines the visual and the auditory systems in detail. The chapters come in two sets of two: the first two cover seeing, the latter two hearing. Within each set, the first chapter introduces the mechanics: the physics of light and sound, the mechanics of the eye and ear, and the basic operation of the sensory organs. These are Chapters 2 and 4: "The Visual System" and "The Auditory System." The second chapter of each set describes how the operation of that system affects our sensory experiences. These are Chapters 3 and 5: "The Dimensions of Vision" and "The Dimensions of Sound."

This chapter is the first of the two on vision. Here, we introduce you to the physics of light, to the anatomical and physiological properties of the eye, and to some of the basic visual mechanisms necessary to the proper functioning of the visual system.

You should learn how light enters the eye and gets changed into a form that the brain can use: the electrical responses of the nerve cells. You will need to know something about light, how it is measured, and what its properties are. You will need to know the parts of the eye, especially the parts that focus the light (the *cornea,* the *lens*) and the parts that are receptive to light energy and transform it into electrical activity in the nervous system (the receptors and the other cells at the rear of the eye, the *retina*). Finally, you should ask how the information from the visual world is interpreted: how colors are extracted, how movement is detected, how the location of an object is determined. This chapter emphasizes the structures in the eye and the first stages of processing in the brain. The next chapter will cover how the information is interpreted.

LIGHT

Light enters the eye and passes through the various parts—the cornea, the aqueous humor, the iris, the lens, and the vitreous body—until finally it reaches the retina. Each part performs a simple task, but each appears to have flaws. In many respects, the eye is a rather peculiar kind of optical instrument. Certainly, were optical specialists to try to design an eye, they would avoid some of the flaws found in the human eye: flaws that should make it an unwieldy and imperfect instrument. As is usual with the parts of the body, however, the eye ends up as a beautiful instrument, exquisitely tailored to the function it must perform, sensitive, flexible, and reliable.

Light is described primarily by its frequency and intensity. The *frequency wavelength* of the light wave is the primary factor in determining the color (hue) that is perceived. The *intensity* is the primary factor in determining brightness. Light waves are part of the electromagnetic spectrum.

The frequencies of the visible part of the spectrum are just above those of microwave radio transmissions and infrared and below those of ultraviolet energy and X rays (see Color Plate III following page 121). Because light frequencies are so high, frequency is not specified directly (the

Table 2–1A

Intensity (dB)	Psychological Correlate
160	
140	
120	Pain threshold
	Sun
100	
80	
	White paper in average reading light
60	TV screen
40	
	Lower light for color vision
20	
0	Threshold of vision of dark-adapted eye

Table 2–1B

Wavelength (nm)	Psychological Correlate
400	violet
450	blue
500	green
550	yellow-green
600	orange
650	red
700	red

numbers range around 10^{15} cycles per second[1]), but rather light is described by its *wavelength*, the distance traveled during the time it takes to complete one cycle. Wavelengths of visible light range from about 400 (seen as violet) to about 700 *nanometers* (seen as a red).[2]

The specification of the units of light amplitude, intensity, and energy is always a very complicated business. Because these specifications are not important for our use here, we will not use physical units. The range of light intensities that stimulate the eye is enormous: The most intense light that can be seen without pain is roughly a thousand billion times more intense than the weakest visible light (a range of approximately 10^{12}).

DECIBELS[3]

To compress the very large range of physical intensities of light we use the trick of expressing intensities in terms of how many powers of ten one intensity is greater than another. This procedure is named after the inventor of the telephone, Alexander Graham Bell, although his last name has been shortened. Thus, if one intensity is a million times another (10^6 times the other), it is 6 bels more than the other. The number of bels between two intensities is simply the logarithm of their ratios. Actually, it is not convenient to work with bels, so intensity ratios are usually specified in terms of the number of *tenths of bels* they contain, called *decibels*, and abbreviated *dB*. In the example above, the intensities are 60 dB apart. The number of decibels that separate two intensities, I and I_0, is

$$\text{number of dB} = 10 \log(I/I_0)$$

1. Doubling (or halving) the ratio of signal intensities adds (subtracts) approximately 3 dB.
2. Multiplying (or dividing) the ratio of signal intensities by 10 adds (subtracts) 10 dB.
3. If two lights are separated by $10n$ dB, their intensity ratio is 10^n. For example, a 60 dB difference in the intensities of two lights means that one light is 10^6 (1 million) times more intense than the other.
4. Since decibels refer to the ratio of two intensities, to say that a signal has a level of 65 dB is completely meaningless unless the comparison

---

[1] One *cycle per second* is called one *hertz* (abbreviated *Hz*). The unit is named after the German physicist, Heinrich R. Hertz (1857–1894), who produced and studied electromagnetic waves. We will be using the unit hertz quite often in Chapter 5, where we take up the auditory system.

[2] A *nanometer* (*nm*) is one billionth of a meter (10^{-9} meter). Sometimes, in older books, wavelength is specified in *millimicrons* ($m\mu$), *angstroms* (Å), or even *inches*. One *nanometer* equals one *millimicron*, 10 *angstrom units*, or 40×10^{-9} inches.

[3] There is another box on decibels in Chapter 4. If you have already read and understood one discussion you will only need a quick glance at the other.

level is known. Generally, whenever you see statements of this form, it means that the signal is 65 dB more intense than the standard reference level: 10^{-8} candela/meter^2 is the figure used in this book as a standard. This standard is a very low intensity of light. It is, approximately, the minimum intensity of light that can be detected by a human observer.

Decibels

Number of dB = $10 \log(I/I_0)$

I/I_0	dB	I/I_0	dB
0.0001	−40	10000.0	40
0.001	−30	1000.0	30
0.010	−20	100.0	20
0.032	−15	31.6	15
0.10	−10	10.0	10
0.13	−9	7.9	9
0.16	−8	6.3	8
0.20	−7	5.0	7
0.25	−6	2.0	6
0.32	−5	3.2	5
0.40	−4	2.5	4
0.50	−3	2.0	3
0.63	−2	1.6	2
0.79	−1	1.3	1
1.00	0	1.0	0

THE OPTICAL PATH

When light falls upon the eye, it first encounters the outside protective window, the *cornea* (see Figure 2-1). Most of the focusing of the image is actually accomplished by the bending of light at the corneal surface. Next, the light transverses a jelly-like substance, the *aqueous humor;* it then goes through the opening in the iris (the *pupil*).

The pupil

In principle, the pupil controls the amount of light entering the eye. It becomes smaller in very bright situations (to protect the eye from excess light) and bigger when it is dim (to let in as much light as possible). But consider this: The most intense lights encountered without pain are many billion times as intense as the weakest lights detectable. Given this wide range of intensities, changes in pupil size make very little difference. The widest the human pupil ever gets is about 7 or 8 millimeters (mm) in diameter; the narrowest is about 2 or 3 mm. The total change in area is not great. At its tightest constriction, the pupil lets in about $\frac{1}{16}$ the amount of light that enters when it is wide open. Changes in pupil size only reduce the intensities of signals passing through the eye by a factor of 16 (or about 12 dB). Thus, the wide range of intensities to which the eye is exposed is not much reduced.

A 10 billion to 1 range (100 dB) gets reduced to a .6 billion to 1 range (88 dB): hardly enough to make much difference.

Adjustments in pupil size are not very fast. When going from dim to bright light, the pupil takes about 5 sec to contract fully and about 1.5 sec to contract to $\frac{2}{3}$ its full size. When going from bright to dim light, it takes 10 sec to dilate to $\frac{2}{3}$ its full amount, and a full 5 min to open up completely. Clearly, the pupil does not control light intensity. Its primary function may be to restrict the light to the central regions of the lens. The lens introduces distortions, especially when light enters at the sides (see the discussion below). It also helps to maintain a good depth of field by keeping the opening as small as possible under a given lighting condition. The pupil adjusts its size to maintain a balance between depth of focus (for which it should be as small as possible) and letting in sufficient light to the retina (for which it should be as large as possible).

In addition to being responsive to changing light intensities, pupil size seems to monitor the states of the nervous system. Thus, the size

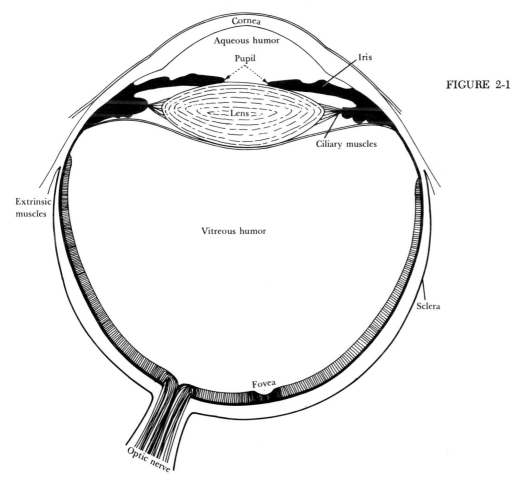

FIGURE 2-1

changes with emotional factors and even with thinking and problem solving. Some use has been made of measurements of pupil size as a way of monitoring a person's progress during the attempt to solve difficult problems, and also of emotional responses. A large pupil tends to indicate high emotional involvement.

The lens   Next in the path of light is the lens. The primary function of the lens, of course, is to focus the light coming from an object onto the light-sensitive receptors at the back of the eye. In terms of overall performance, however, biological lenses are not of particularly good quality.

The lens is composed of many thin layers of crystalline tissue wrapped together, much like the skin of an onion. The lens focuses by increasing and decreasing its thickness (that is, by changing its focal length). This is accomplished by enclosing the lens in a membrane to which the muscles that control focus are attached. The lens produces a number of distortions. Light striking the edges is not focused on the same plane as that of light striking the center of the lens, producing a distortion called *spherical aberration*. Differently colored lights are focused differently, producing a distortion called *chromatic aberration.*

In addition to these problems, the lens is continually dying, a result of a compromise in its design. All living cells need a continual supply of nutrient substances, usually carried by the bloodstream. But, obviously one does not want blood vessels running through the lens, for this would severely impair its optical quality. Thus, for its nutrients, the lens must rely on the surrounding liquids, an arrangement that is not optimal. The inner layers of the lens have difficulty getting an adequate food supply, and during the lifetime of the organism they gradually die. As the organism ages, these dead cells hamper lens functioning, in particular, focusing.

Focusing and convergence. To get a feeling for the focusing action, hold a pencil out at arm's length and focus on it. Now bring it slowly toward your nose, keeping it in focus. As the pencil comes to within a few inches of your eyes, notice that the image gets blurry and you feel a distinct "pull." As you move the pencil, two things are happening. One set of eye muscles is continuously adjusting the orientation of the eyes to keep them both pointed at (converged on) the approaching object. A second set of muscles is continuously increasing the thickness of the lens, thus bending the light rays to maintain proper focus on Figure 2-2   the retinal plane at the back of the eye.

When the pencil is moved far away from the edge, both sets of muscles relax, the lens returns to its normal elongated shape, and the two eyes point straight ahead. With this muscle action, the lens of a young person is capable of focusing on objects ranging from as close as a few inches to as far away as the stars. With age, however, the ability to increase

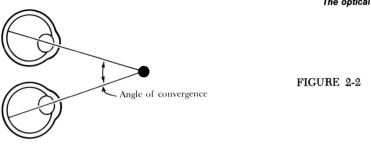

Thick lens and large angle of convergence when the object is close (pupil size decreases to increase depth of field)

Angle of convergence

FIGURE 2-2

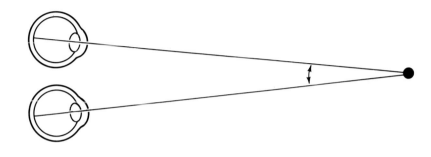

Thinner lens and small angle of convergence when the object is farther away

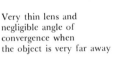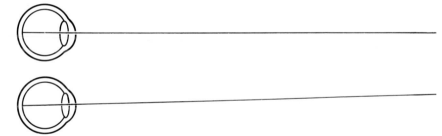

Very thin lens and negligible angle of convergence when the object is very far away

the thickness of the lens is reduced so much that an external lens (eyeglasses) is often needed for focusing on nearby objects.

Another way to feel the muscle action is to hold a finger up in front of the eyes at a distance of about 6 inches. Then, without moving the finger, concentrate first upon the finger and then upon whatever object is just above the finger (the further away, the better). You can feel the difference between changing the focus from far to near (an active contraction of the muscles of focusing and accommodation), and changing it from near to far (a passive relaxation of the muscles).

The lens in the human changes focus by changing its thickness; in optical terms, it is a variable focal length lens. In cameras and other man-made instruments and, indeed, in some species of animals such as fish, focusing is usually accomplished by keeping the thickness of the lens fixed and changing the distance between the lens and the light-sensitive elements. The change in focal length produces one interesting effect: the longer the focal length, the larger the image on the retina. This means that when we focus on objects at a distance, they are slightly enlarged in comparison to the retinal image for a nearby object in focus. The magnification is about a factor of 1.2 (the eye changes its focal length from approximately 14 to 17 mm).

One of the unsolved operations of the eye is the way it maintains focus. Just how an object is brought into sharp focus is not known. One suspicion is that the focusing system tries to maintain a maximum sharpness by maintaining greatest contrast in the image. Neural cells that are sensitive to contours have maximum output for a sharply focused image. Although focusing typically is done automatically and unconsciously, it is possible to change focus consciously. It is even possible to defocus the eyes so that no object in the line of sight is seen clearly. These conscious controls could not be exerted if the focusing mechanism were completely automatic and independent of higher brain centers.

FIGURE 2-3

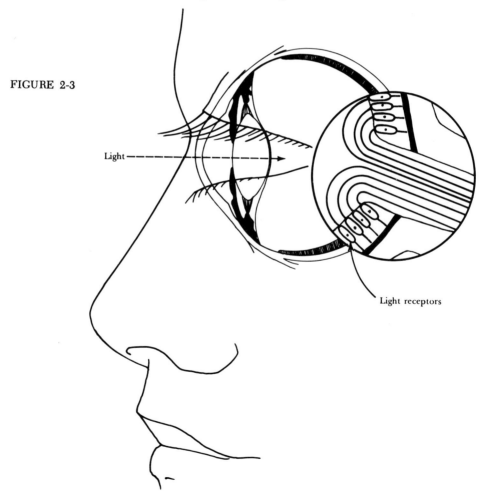

Light

Light receptors

Finally, after passing through the lens and the jelly-like substance that fills the interior part of the eye (*vitreous humor*), the light arrives at the *retina*, the part of the eye responsible for converting the light images into physiological responses. But even here there are obstacles to the light. The retina is at the rear of the eyeball, stretched out over the cup-shaped inner surface. The light-sensitive elements face in the wrong direction: They point inward, toward the brain, rather than outward, toward the light (see Figure 2-3). As a result, the nerve fibers connected to the light receptors lie in a tangled web directly in the path of the incoming light. Moreover, these nerve fibers are inside the eye, so to get out there must be an opening in the back surface. This produces a blind spot in each eye. (More on this later; see Figure 2-6.)

One of the first and most dramatic demonstrations of the eye's photo-chemical response to light was the creation of an "optogram." An animal, such as a frog, is kept completely away from light for several hours. Then the visual environment is illuminated briefly by an intense light. The frog is killed and its retinas detached and placed in a chemical solution. Afterward, the result of the light's photochemical reaction on the cells of the retina can be seen: The visual environment has been painted in vivid yellow and red onto the retina of the frog. This technique has captured the imagination of some novelists, who write of murderers identified from the optograms in their victim's eyes.

Photochemical processes are responsible for the eye's initial response to a visual signal. When the retina has not been exposed to light, it is reddish-purple in color. This characteristic color gives the chemical its name: *visual purple*. In response to light the retinal color changes, from reddish purple, to pale yellow, and finally it *bleaches* to be transparent and colorless.

Nocturnal birds and animals tend to have relatively high concentrations of visual purple, perhaps accounting for their excellent night vision. Reptiles, diurnal birds, and various species of fish have photochemical substances that bleach in the presence of light, but differ somewhat from visual purple in their sensitivity to lights of different colors. The basic method for describing these chemical reactions is to determine how much bleaching occurs for lights with constant intensity as wavelength varies. The resulting set of measurements is called the *absorption spectrum* of the photochemical substance.

The exact photochemical reaction in the eye is now well known. With no light present, there is a high concentration of *rhodopsin* (the chemical name for visual purple). When a light is turned on, a succession of changes take place, finally ending with a substance called *retinene*, which is finally reduced to *vitamin A*. The retinene gives the yellow color of the partially bleached pigment. The predominance of vitamin A after prolonged exposure to light produces the colorless appearance of the completely bleached retina.

Logic dictates that there must be some mechanisms for manufacturing or regenerating the photosensitive materials in the eye. The regeneration seems to be carried on by two separate chemical reactions. One provides a relatively fast restoration of rhodopsin levels by recombining the partially bleached products of retinene and opsin to make rhodopsin. A second, much more sluggish process produces rhodopsin from the fully bleached products, such as vitamin A.

Chemical reactions play a role in determining the general characteristics of visual sensitivity. Unfortunately, there does not appear to be a simple relationship between visual sensitivity and the photochemical reactions in retinal receptors. Under ordinary lighting conditions, only a very small percentage of the available rhodopsin is actually bleached. Moreover, bleaching only 2% of the rhodopsin concentration may change sensitivity by fifty-fold.

Despite considerable effort, the exact nature of the link between the photochemical response and the initiation of electrical impulses in the nerve fibers has not been discovered. The question of how the chemical reactions actually generate the neural impulses that carry the visual signal to the brain has yet to be answered.

THE
NEUROANATOMY
OF VISION

Figure 2-4

The retina is not a continuous surface of light-sensitive material. It is composed of a very large number of individual light-sensitive elements, or receptors, each element responding to the light energy falling upon it. In animals such as monkeys and humans, there are two different types of light-sensitive elements, one called *rods*, the other *cones*. Other animals have one or the other but not both. Pigeons have only cones, while the retina of the cat is made up mostly of rods.

Apart from the distinctive anatomy which first led to their discovery, the rods and cones have some definite functional differences. They are really two separate visual systems housed within the same eye. Each system has its own special response characteristics. Visual purple, rhodopsin, is found only in the tips of rods—not in cones. The cones contain a variety of photochemical substances necessary for color vision. A rod is about 500 times more sensitive to light than a cone, but provides no color information. In addition to all these functional differences, there are also differences in the neural arrangement that transfers the information in the two systems out of the retina to the brain.

The human eye has approximately 6 million cones and about 120 million rods: about 125 million receptors in all. This is an extraordinarily

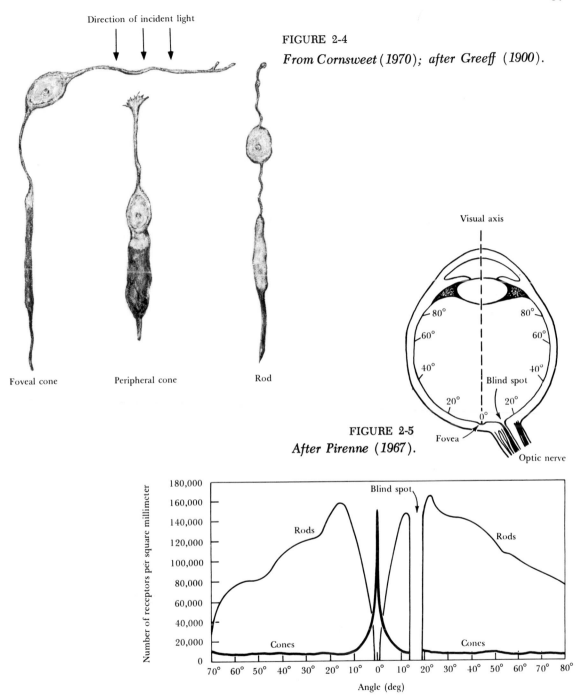

Direction of incident light

Foveal cone   Peripheral cone   Rod

FIGURE 2-4

From Cornsweet (1970); after Greeff (1900).

Visual axis

80°   80°

60°   60°

40°   40°

Blind spot

20°   20°

0°

FIGURE 2-5

After Pirenne (1967).

Fovea

Optic nerve

Number of receptors per square millimeter

Blind spot

Rods   Rods

Cones   Cones

70° 60° 50° 40° 30° 20° 10° 0° 10° 20° 30° 40° 50° 60° 70° 80°

Angle (deg)

rich density of receptor cells. The picture on a television screen, for example, has only around 250,000 independent elements. Overall, the density of packing of the light-sensitive elements is highest in the center of the eye and decreases in the peripheral regions.

Figure 2-5

Distribution of receptors on the retina is different for rods and for cones. Rods are more prevalent in the periphery, cones in the center. At the very center of the eye, there is a tiny depressed region with no rods at all, only cones. This region, called the *fovea*, has a very high density of receptors—approximately 150,000 cones per square millimeter. It is optimally located so that it receives the central parts of the image around the point at which the eye is fixating. The fovea is also the region of maximum acuity. Although most receptor elements

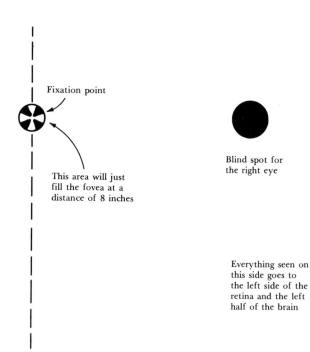

Fixation point

Blind spot for the left eye

Blind spot for the right eye

This area will just fill the fovea at a distance of 8 inches

8 inches

Everything seen on this side goes to the right side of the retina and the right half of the brain

Everything seen on this side goes to the left side of the retina and the left half of the brain

FIGURE 2-6   Instructions: *Close your right eye. Hold the page about 8 inches in front of you (see scale on left). Hold the page very straight, without tilting it. Stare at the fixation point. Adjust the angle and distance of the paper until left-eye blind spot disappears.*

- *Open your right eye—blind spot reappears (keep staring at the fixation point).*
- *Close your left eye—right-eye blind spot should disappear (you may have to adjust the paper again).*
- *When you find the blind spot, push a pencil along the paper toward it. Watch the end of the pencil disappear. (Remember to keep one eye closed.)*

do not connect directly to the brain, individual foveal elements tend to have their own private communication line to higher brain centers.[4]

The two eyes, then, collect information from the visual environment with a total of about 250 million individual receptors and send the information to the brain over about 1.6 million nerve fibers. The two different types of receptor systems complement one another. The cone system is a high resolution system capable of sending color information, but its sensitivity is limited. The rod system is very sensitive to light, but its resolution is limited and it is insensitive to color. Working together, the two systems provide an extraordinarily flexible and powerful system for carrying out the initial visual reactions to light signals occurring in the environment.

At this point, it is useful to look briefly at the processing that takes place within the eye itself. (In Chapter 6 we investigate the neural activity in some detail.) The neural cells that process information and communicate with one another are called *neurons*. A neuron consists of a cell body and an *axon* or *nerve fiber* that connects the cells to one another. Junctions between neurons occur either on the cell body itself or on spinelike extensions of the cell body called *dendrites*. The junction is called a *synapse*. Nerve fibers and dendrites can be treated like insulated conductors for transmitting the electrical signals of the neurons. In the retina, there are many cells that function primarily to interconnect adjoining areas: these cells form what is called the *horizontal organization* of the retina. The retina might be considered to be a network of neurons (the word "retina" comes from the Latin word "rete" for *net*). Some cells help carry the signals produced at the retinal detectors toward the brain: these cells form what is called the *vertical organization* of the retina. The final cells in the vertical organization are called *ganglion* cells. There are about 800,000 of them. Their axons are several inches long, and they travel from the eye into the brain.

Different types of neural cells are involved in passing the signal from the rods and cones to the brain. Signals from the receptor cells go vertically up through two synapses, first between the *receptor* itself and a *bipolar cell*, then between the bipolar cell and a *ganglion cell*. The axons of the ganglion cells make up the *optic nerve* that leaves the eye. At the same time, the analysis of the signals are performed by the horizontal organization of the retina—primarily by cells named, appropriately enough, *horizontal cells*. These horizontal cells make con-

The retinal network

Figures 2-7 & 2-8

---

[4] Most people have difficulty in remembering which cells—rods or cones—do what. Remember it this way. The **fovea** is the central part of the visual field: The *fovea* is at the *focus* of attention. This is the spot where you want to see things in color. **Cones**, in the *center* of the eye, are sensitive to *color*.

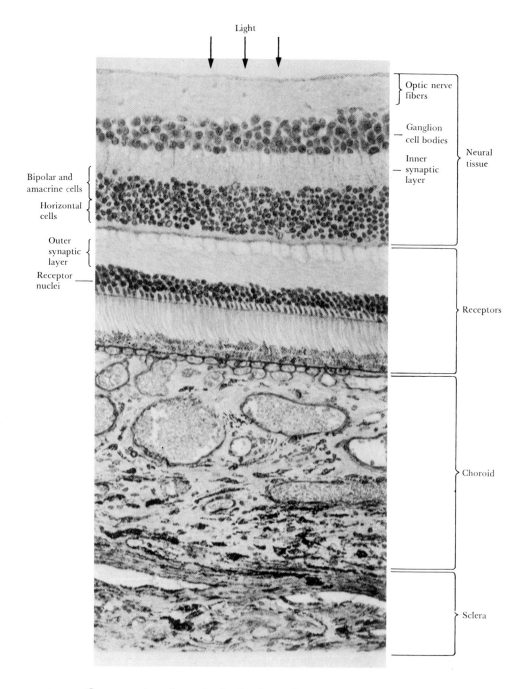

Light

Optic nerve
fibers

Ganglion
cell bodies

Inner
synaptic
layer

Neural
tissue

Bipolar and
amacrine cells

Horizontal
cells

Outer
synaptic
layer

Receptor
nuclei

Receptors

Choroid

Sclera

FIGURE 2-7   *Cross section through the back of the human retina. Magnification approximately ×150. From Polyak (1957).*

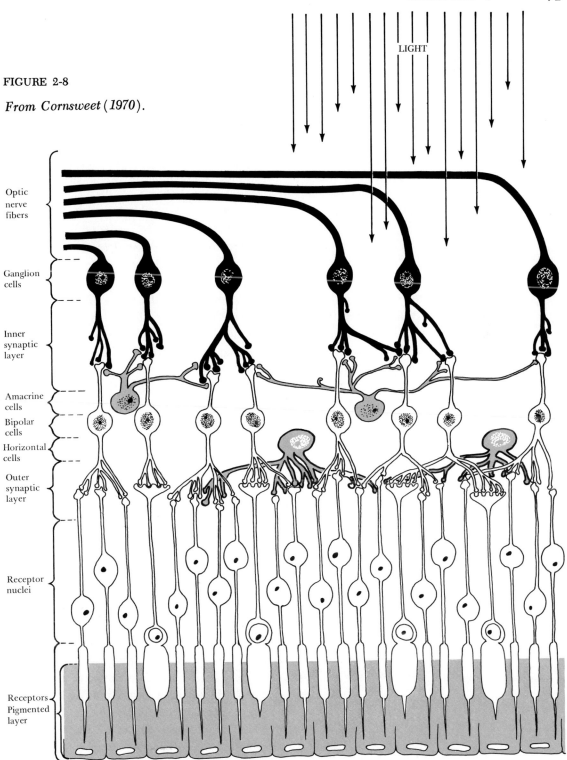

LIGHT

FIGURE 2-8

From Cornsweet (1970).

Optic
nerve
fibers

Ganglion
cells

Inner
synaptic
layer

Amacrine
cells

Bipolar
cells

Horizontal
cells

Outer
synaptic
layer

Receptor
nuclei

Receptors
Pigmented
layer

nections among the receptors themselves, modifying the activity at the junction between the receptors and the bipolar cells. In addition, there is a second level of horizontal processing performed by the *amacrine cells* at a slightly higher level. These amacrine cells modify the activity at the junction between bipolar cells and ganglion cells. These two layers of horizontal connections are the anatomical basis for the neural processing in the retinal network.

The density of interconnections varies in different parts of the retina. In the periphery, a single ganglion cell may receive information from thousands of rods. At the central foveal region of the retina, an individual cone may connect directly through a single bipolar cell to an individual ganglion cell. Direct connections of this type are usually made by smaller cells, *midget bipolar* and *midget ganglion* cells.

Why does the nervous system go through all this? It turns out that the first stages of signal processing take place right at the receptors and at the retina. The light that falls on part of the retina influences the neural responses of cells connected to other parts of the retina. We discuss the details of these interactions in considerable depth in Chapters 3 and 6, but the end result is to enhance the nervous system's response to the edges of the objects that it is perceiving, to affect the brightness that is perceived, and to affect the perception of color. In general, a region of brightness makes things around it seem darker. Similarly, dark regions make neighboring light regions seem even brighter. A patch of red will make neighboring regions look greener, and so on. The details will come in those later chapters.

THE PATHWAY TO THE BRAIN
Each ganglion cell of the retina contributes a fiber to the optic nerve. All together, the fibers number about 800,000, producing a cable about the thickness of a pencil. In the human and most higher mammals, the nerve fibers leaving each eye cross at a location called the *optic chiasma*. [The chiasma is similar in appearance to the Greek letter χ (chi), hence the name.] All the fibers from the left half of each retina go to the left hemisphere of the brain; all the fibers from the right half of each retina group together and travel to the right hemisphere of the brain.

There is no interruption in the nerve fibers at the optic chiasma: no new synaptic connections are made. As shown in Figures 2-9, 2-10, and 2-11, this regrouping at the optic chiasma splits the visual scene into two halves. The parts of the visual scene to the left half of the fovea end up at the right half of the brain; everything to the right of the fixation point ends up at the left half of the brain. (The lens reverses the visual image: Thus, an object on the left is focused on the right half of the retina and, as a result, the neural signals from that part of the image get sent to the right hemisphere of the brain.)

The primary emphasis in the processing of the visual image is concentrated upon the central part of the visual field, especially the part that falls upon the fovea. As shown in Figure 2-5, most of the cones are in the fovea. In the visual cortex, more than 50% of the neurons appear to be concerned with the analysis of the central 10% of the visual field.

The periphery of the eye is more sensitive to light than is the center, but it is not as responsive to the fine details of the scene or to color information as the fovea.

The organization scheme of the retina has some obvious advantages. But, because only a small portion of the visual scene is analyzed in great detail, the pattern-recognition system must have a way of guiding the eye to specific parts of the visual field.

The eyes move frequently, successively sampling different regions of the scene. The pattern of eye movements consists of a series of discrete jumps or *saccades* from one part of the scene to another. These may occur four or five times per second. This saccadic movement is a result

SAMPLING VISUAL INFORMATION

Eye movements

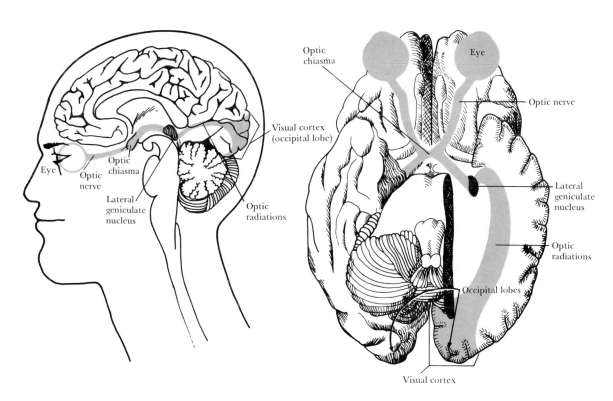

FIGURE 2-9

FIGURE 2-10

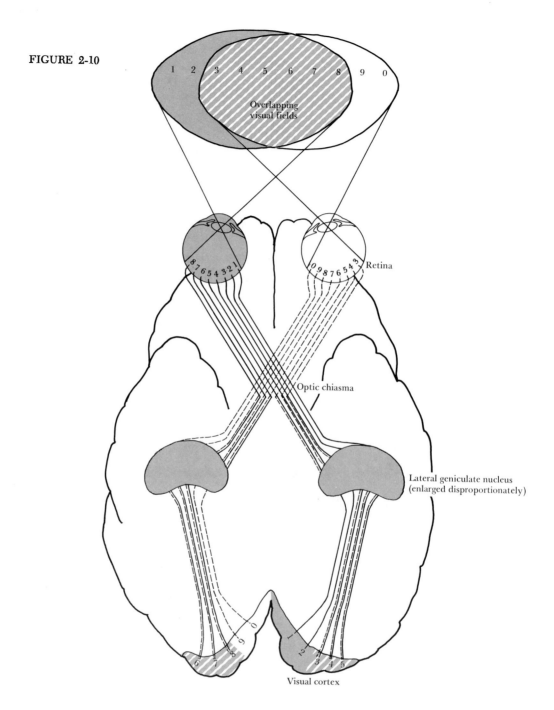

of applying full force to some of the extraocular muscles (of which there are six), producing an abrupt high-velocity change in eye position.

In humans, the eye does not move more than four or five times per second. Moreover, once a saccadic eye movement has been started, it goes to its computed end point without further correction—the movement is *ballistic*. It is not like a slow movement of the arm in picking up a pencil in which the motion is being corrected to be sure the hand arrives at the target. Rather, it is like the throw of a ball: Once the ball has left the hand, nothing can be done to alter its path.

The actual neural machinery used for the computation and control of eye position has not yet been worked out in detail: The final stages in the chain of events leading to saccadic eye movements seem to be associated with the forward regions of the brain—the *frontal eye fields*. Electrode stimulation in these regions initiates saccadic movements, with the direction and extent of movement depending on the particular location of the stimulating electrode. Generally, stimulation of the left hemisphere initiates saccadic movements to the right and stimulation in the right hemisphere produces left saccades. When both hemispheres are stimulated simultaneously, a compromise results: The direction and extent of the movement depends on the relative intensity of the stimulation in the two hemispheres.

But the mechanisms responsible for computing the direction and extent of movement from an analysis of the visual image are unknown. Some saccades seem to be relatively automatic. A movement in the peripheral parts of the visual field, for example, frequently triggers an involuntary saccade aimed at the source of the movement. For the most part, however, eye movement patterns appear to reflect a systematic sampling of environmental information based on a meaningful interpretation of the incoming sensory data. Saccades even occur during sleep. For many years now, saccadic eye movements have been the major index of dream periods (rapid-eye-movement sleep, or REM sleep) in the study of sleep.

Although the processes involved in computing the location of targets from the visual image are not well understood, recent evidence suggests that they may be carried out by a neural channel separate from the one involved in normal pattern-recognition. This might be expected. Ordinarily, the operations associated with localizing an object in the environment and those involved in recognizing it are smoothly coordinated. But an analysis designed to determine **where** things are is, to some extent, incompatible with an analysis to determine **what** things are.

The localizing channel

In **identifying** an object in the visual image—a person or a chair—exact orientation, distance, or its location in the visual field is not important. Ideally, the pattern-recognition system should ignore all these properties and concentrate only on the characteristics that are important for actually identifying the object as a chair (or person). In **locating** an object, however, identification of the objects is not important. The only relevant data are position and orientation.

Are there two independent neural channels involved in these two distinct types of analysis? The anatomy of the visual system suggests that there may be. One set of nerve fibers traveling from the eye to the brain breaks away from its neighbors and, rather than going to the *lateral geniculate nucleus* with the rest, ends up at a brain center called the *superior colliculus*.

FIGURE 2-11*a*

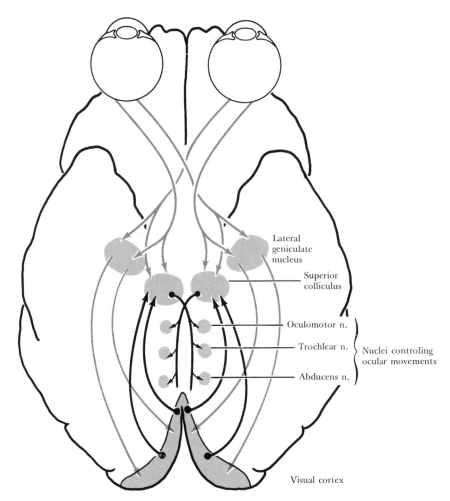

Lateral geniculate nucleus

Superior colliculus

Oculomotor n.

Trochlear n.   } Nuclei controling ocular movements

Abducens n.

Visual cortex

Like the lateral geniculate and the visual cortex, fibers leaving adjacent regions in the retina end up in adjacent regions in the superior colliculus. That is, the spatial organization of the retina is preserved. Unlike the visual cortex, however, the foveal region of the eye does not seem to be given any special treatment. The fibers leaving the colliculus appear to connect with the motor control system for eye movements, head orientation, and postural adjustments. Finally, there is some evidence for inputs into this collicular structure from the visual receiving areas of the cortex.

The anatomical organization of this collicular pathway makes it a prime candidate for a neural channel specifically concerned with localizing objects in the environment. But there is more persuasive evidence than anatomy. When neurons in this channel are activated by electrodes

FIGURE 2-11*b*

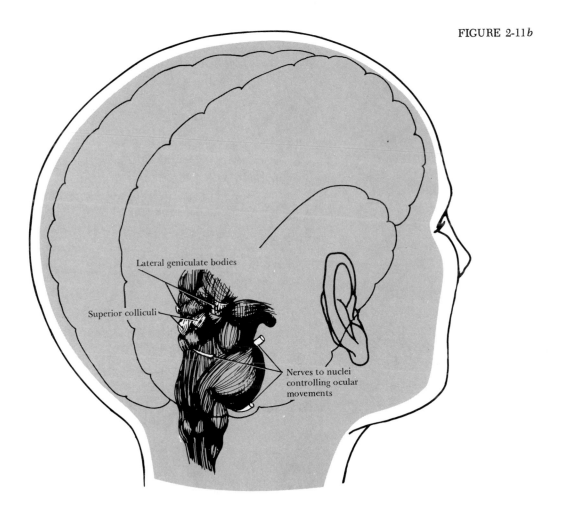

Lateral geniculate bodies

Superior colliculi

Nerves to nuclei
controlling ocular
movements

in an awake animal, some head movements and postural adjustments result. When neurons associated with a particular part of the visual field are stimulated, the animal orients in the appropriate direction, pointing to where the object would have been, had the activity been produced by normal visual conditions.

Cells in the superior colliculus are primarily activated by *moving* targets. A number of different sensory systems send information to this region: acoustic, visual, tactile. The organization of the superior colliculus seems to allow for intercommunication among the senses for information about corresponding spatial locations. Thus, this area of the brain would appear to be important in localizing objects in space, regardless of the sensory modality from which the information was received. It also seems to help control orientation of the body. Movements of the body, head, and eyes required to follow a moving object also seem to be controlled by the superior colliculus (Stein, Magalhães-Castro, and Kruger, 1975).

Whenever a neural structure associated with a particular function is identified, it opens up new experimental opportunities. What happens to vision if one or another of these two main visual channels is disrupted? Consider first the results of disrupting the channel assumed to be primarily involved in recognizing patterns.

Vision without a visual cortex

The neural channel associated with pattern recognition can be disrupted by surgically removing the visual cortex (*cortical ablation*). In cats and monkeys, ablation of the visual cortex at first appears to produce total blindness. The animals show no ability to see objects in the environment, to carry on normal visual–motor coordination, or to learn any task requiring discrimination among visual signals. Careful testing, however, demonstrates some residual visual capacities. The animal without a visual cortex can learn to make discriminations based on brightness and perhaps size.

Monkeys without a visual cortex also have some success in localizing objects. Movement seems to be important. When the experimenter holds out a choice morsel of food such as a nut, at first the monkey does not appear to notice it, but if the experimenter's hand moves, then the monkey will reach out in the appropriate direction. The monkey makes errors in estimating depth, however. The animal is never able to learn tasks that require discrimination among visual patterns.

Some degree of localization seems possible when the channel carrying pattern information is disrupted. Since the operation does not interfere with the superior colliculus, it might be suspected that this neural channel handles information about position. To prove the case, the collicular channel should be disrupted and the animal's localization ability tested.

If the two channels function independently, then pattern recognition should remain intact and localization should be severely impaired.

The experimental animal in this case is the golden hamster, whose collicular and cortical channels are particularly well separated, making it convenient for surgery. When the collicular structures are disrupted, the hamster loses all ability to localize. When offered a food (such as sunflower seeds), it is unable to perform the appropriate orientation and reaching responses. But the apparent inability to localize could really be a deficiency in pattern recognition. Maybe it simply does not recognize the food offered to it.

Vision without a superior colliculus

There is a tricky experimental problem here. If a standard experimental test is used, the hamster appears unable to learn to discriminate simple visual patterns. For example, if it must choose between two patterns located at the ends of two alleys, it never learns to select the right one in order to obtain food. Normal hamsters have no trouble with this task: They soon learn to identify the appropriate pattern and are successful at obtaining the food reward each time they are placed in the box.

Figure 2-12

But think about the task. To do this task the animal must both recognize the correct pattern and must localize it properly; but if we design the task so that no localization is required, things change. Without the requirement of localization, the hamster's behavior changes rather dramatically. It shuffles along one side of the box, and eventually it arrives at one of the patterned doors. Here it rises up on its hind paws and appears to inspect the pattern. It then enters the door or continues shuffling along the wall until it comes to the next door, where the performance is repeated. If it does not enter the second door, it may follow the edge around the entire box until it returns to the first door and begins the whole sequence again. This experiment illustrates the difference between localization and recognition.[5]

The experimental work in this area is in its early stages, and the details of the localization system have not yet been worked out. The results so far are consistent in indicating that there are two separate systems operating: one to tell us **where** things are; one to tell us **what** they are. But ordinarily two systems cannot work independently, since how could objects be matched up to their proper location? Together the two channels provide a powerful and sophisticated apparatus for sampling and analyzing the visual environment.

[5] See G. E. Schneider (1969) for details of the original experiment.

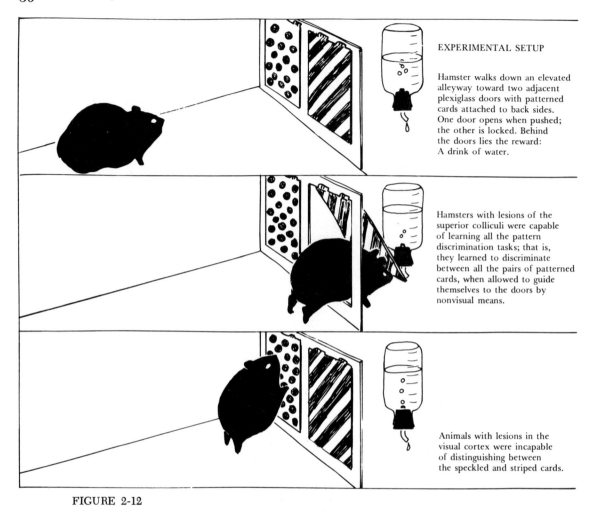

EXPERIMENTAL SETUP

Hamster walks down an elevated
alleyway toward two adjacent
plexiglass doors with patterned
cards attached to back sides.
One door opens when pushed;
the other is locked. Behind
the doors lies the reward:
A drink of water.

Hamsters with lesions of the
superior colliculi were capable
of learning all the pattern
discrimination tasks; that is,
they learned to discriminate
between all the pairs of patterned
cards, when allowed to guide
themselves to the doors by
nonvisual means.

Animals with lesions in the
visual cortex were incapable
of distinguishing between
the speckled and striped cards.

FIGURE 2-12

REVIEW OF TERMS
AND CONCEPTS

In this chapter, the following terms and concepts that we consider to be
important have been used. Please look them over. If you are not able to
give a short explanation of any of them, you should go back and review
the appropriate sections of the chapter.

*Terms and
concepts you
should know*

Light
  intensity
    decibels (dB)
  wavelength
    nanometers

The eyes
 cornea
 aqueous humor
 pupil
 vitreous humor
 retina
 fovea
 accommodation (focusing)
 convergence
The organization of neural structures on the retina
 rods
 cones
 visual purple
 horizontal organization
 vertical organization
Neural system
 neurons
 synapse
 ganglion cells
 horizontal cells
 amacrine cells
 optic nerve
 optic chiasma
 lateral geniculate nucleus (LGN)
 superior colliculus
 visual cortex
Vision
 the blind spot (what causes it?)
 eye movements

SUGGESTED READINGS

Because both this chapter and the next treat the operation of the eye, the Suggested Readings section for Chapter 3 should be consulted for a more complete list of readings. At this point, we give only a brief set of references. The best spot to begin for a general treatment of the eye and the visual system (as well as a treatment of the topics of Chapter 1) is Gregory's pair of books, *Eye and brain* (1966) and *The intelligent eye* (1970). For more advanced treatments we recommend four books. Two of them are the volumes of the *Handbook of perception* titled *Biology of perceptual systems* (Volume III) and *Seeing* (Volume V). Volume III treats the functions of the eye and Volume V covers the psychological properties of perception (Carterette & Friedman, 1973, 1975). The third book is Cornsweet's (1970) text, treating many of the same phenomena discussed by us in this chapter, as well as some advanced ones. Finally, if you are really serious about the study of the eye, the extraordinary book by Rodieck (1973) contains 1044 pages of information about the visual system, mostly about the retina.

A review of the role of the visual cortex can be found in Teuber's (1960) chapter, "Perception." Excellent sources for reviews come from articles in the *Annual Review of Physiology* and the *Annual Review of Psychology*.

The distinctions between localization and pattern recognition (and the implication that one is done in the colliculus and the other in the visual cortex) come from several recent sources. The experiment on the hamster, plus a considerable amount of supporting evidence, is reported by G. E. Schneider in a *Science* article, "Two Visual Systems" (1969). A number of relevant articles are collected in an issue of the German journal, *Psychologische Forschung* (1967 and 1968, Volume 31). (The relevant articles are printed in English.) Some of the important articles you might wish to look at are those by Held (pp. 338–348), Ingle (pp. 44–51), G. E. Schneider (pp. 52–62), and Trevarthen (pp. 299–337).

Again, more suggested readings are found at the end of Chapter 3 (and Chapter 6, for the physiological basis of seeing).

3 The dimensions of vision

PREVIEW

This is the second of the two chapters on the visual system. Here we talk about what you actually experience: brightness, contrast, flicker, and color. These phenomena may not sound like much when named in cold scientific vocabulary, but they are at the heart of visual perception. Brightness, you will immediately discover, does not simply vary with light level. As light intensity goes up, it is quite possible for the brightness of an object to go down. When you turn on more lights in a room, some objects will get brighter, but others will probably get darker. The visual system works in such a way that what is seen in one part of the scene affects how you see the rest of the scene. A bright object can make surrounding objects look darker; a green object can make surrounding objects look redder. In fact, the way an object looks to you is determined in part by what you think it is.

This chapter combines the basic phenomena of visual perception with the knowledge gained from the previous chapters to explain how some of these experiences might come about. Some of the explanations must wait until Chapter 6 for a discussion of neural circuits. Some of the explanations cannot be given at all, because they are simply not yet known. This chapter provides a good starting point for anyone interested in visual perception: it gives some answers, but it also presents a large number of important problems that still await solutions.

The chapter is really divided into two parts: first there is a discussion of black and white vision, and then there is a discussion of color. Under black and white vision, we introduce a lot of the basic principles that apply to color as well.

The first important point is to realize that there is a difference between what *is* "out there in the world" and what you *experience* as being out there. The first is the *physics* of the situation, the second is *psychology*. We are interested in the psychology and also in the relation between the physics and the psychology (which is an area of study sometimes called *psychophysics*).

Next, we treat a phenomenon discovered by Mach and therefore known as *Mach bands*. One of the fundamental things to learn from this chapter is that what is seen in one part of the visual scene affects what will be seen in adjoining parts. Understand *Mach bands* well: we will make much use of them later.

The analysis of the visual world by spatial frequencies is becoming more and more important. Read the section on this type of analysis, look carefully at the figures, and do the simple experiment requested of you. You should try to understand what this analysis is all about, for it is really quite important.

In the study of color we do two things. First, we attempt to put together a story that explains the ways in which colors are perceived to combine. In general, this is a messy area, and the technical papers and books on the topic tend to be completely unintelligible, even to the people who work in the field. The principles are relatively simple, and that is all you need to learn from this section. These principles of color will be different from what is usually taught in art classes.

We will also study how color information is processed in the brain and look at some of the psychological mechanisms that are involved. Here we take the information from the previous chapter, coupled with some of the principles that we learned from the study of Mach bands, and put together the steps of the color system.

SENSORY EXPERIENCES

When speaking of sensory experiences, such as those of seeing and hearing, it is important to distinguish between the physical light and sound waves that exist in the environment and the psychological experiences that are in the mind. The physical aspects of light and sound are easily studied, defined, and measured. A physical wave can be accurately specified by its waveform—the description of its energy or pressure variation over time—or by its spectrum—the description of how much energy is present at each frequency. The psychological aspects are not so easily specified. With sound, the two most obvious psychological dimensions are loudness and pitch, but there are also other experiences of sound quality—timbre, dissonance, consonance, and musicality. Similarly, with light, the most obvious psychological dimensions are brightness and hue, but other distinctions are possible.

With the simplest of physical waveforms, a pure sine wave of the type produced in light by a laser or in sound by a simple, smooth whistle or by an electronic oscillator, the physical aspects can be described in terms of its frequency and intensity. It is tempting to associate these simple physical variables with the psychological experience of hue and brightness or of pitch and loudness: To do so is incorrect. For one thing, the relations are not directly linear: Doubling the intensity of a physical wave does not double its perceived brightness or loudness. For another, they are not independent: Varying the frequency affects both the perceived brightness or loudness as well as its hue or pitch. And, finally, they are not constant: The perception of the hue and brightness of a light or the pitch and loudness of a tone depends not only upon its frequency and intensity, but also upon the context in which it appears, the nature of the other lights and sounds that may also be present at the same time. Even the simplest of physical dimensions is subjected to a complex analysis by the nervous system. Do not make the mistake of confusing the **psychological** perceptions of loudness, brightness, pitch and hue with **physical** properties of intensity and frequency. They are different things.

Figure 3-1 & Table 3-1

In the study of the relationship between the physical and the psychological, it is possible to measure exactly the physics, but we have only our private impressions to guide us in determining the psychology. To study psychological impressions, it is necessary to ask people to tell something about their sensations. Simply asking people to say what they are perceiving is a dangerous game. What we are told is determined as much by the subjects' knowledge of language and their expectations of what they think they should be saying as it is by the actual responses of

FIGURE 3-1

their sensory systems. Many years of studying the introspections of observers has led to an understanding of some of the difficulties of this direct approach. If care is exercised, however, it is possible to learn about perceptions with little risk of misinterpretation. The important thing is to ask the right questions.

Table 3-1

Physical Variables

Psychological Variables	Of Primary Importance	Of Secondary Importance
Seeing		
Brightness	Light intensity	Wavelength of light, adaptation of the eye
Hue (color)	Wavelength	Spectral composition, intensity and hue of surrounding lights
Saturation (richness of color)	Spectral composition	Surrounding lights
Contrast	Intensity, wavelength, surrounding lights	—

A good technique for getting at sensory impressions is to restrict the subject's task to elementary decisions—has a signal occurred; are two signals the same or different—to the operations of detections and comparison. Instead of asking a person "What do you hear?" ask "Do you hear anything at all?" Instead of asking for descriptions of the sensation, ask "Are these two things the same or not?" By asking such straightforward questions in carefully designed experiments, it is possible to learn a great deal about the basic mechanisms of sensory-information processing.

THE PERCEPTION OF BRIGHTNESS

The visual image present at one part of the retina affects the perception of an image seen in neighboring locations. Horizontal neural connections (the horizontal and amacrine cells) interlinking the retinal receptors cause interactions among neighboring regions in the retina as the information passes through the eye. This interaction plays a major role in the processing of visual inputs and accounts for some basic perceptual phenomena. The neural machinery involved is discussed in some detail in Chapter 6. At this point, we concentrate on some of the psychological experiences that are produced by these underlying interaction networks.

Brightness contrast

Examine the interior squares in the illustration shown in Figure 3-2. All of the inner squares are printed identically: The same amount of light comes from each. Yet the perceived brightness of the inner squares varies depending upon what surrounds them. The inner square on the far left appears brighter than the one on the far right.

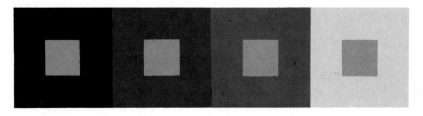

FIGURE 3-2

*From Cornsweet
(1970).*

Normally, one expects that as physical intensity increases, so too will the psychological perception increase. Thus, the brightness of an object ought to increase whenever more light is reflected from it, just as the loudness of a sound increases whenever the intensity of that sound increases. But the brightness of a target depends on the surrounding field. As the intensity of the light falling on a surface is increased, the perceived changes in brightness depend on what else is present. Look at the left pair of squares in Figure 3-2. Call the inner square the *target* and the outer area the *surround*. If the overall illumination is increased, the intensity of both the target and the surround will increase proportionally and the physical contrast between the two will remain exactly the same. The brightness of the target, however, does not necessarily increase when the illumination is raised. It may get brighter, or it may remain the same, or it may even appear to decrease in brightness. It all depends on the relative intensities of the center and surround.

The way that the brightness of the target changes with increased illumination is shown in Figure 3-3 for different ratios of contrast between

FIGURE 3-3

*From Stevens
(1961b).*

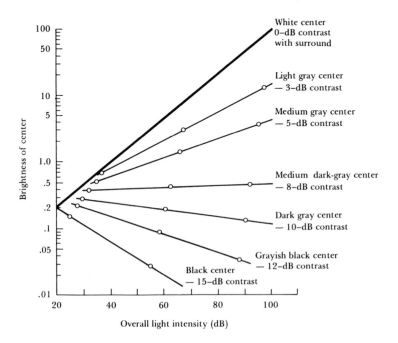

the center and the surround (the contrast ratio is specified in decibels).[1]
When the center is the same as the surround (a 0-dB difference in contrast), then the judgments of the center brightness increase smoothly and consistently with light intensity, as shown in the upper heavy line. As the contrast between center and surround increases, the brightness of the center does not increase as rapidly as the overall light level. With a medium dark-gray center (a contrast difference of around 8 dB), there is perfect brightness constancy: The perceived brightness of the center remains the same even though the illumination levels are increasing. With higher contrast, an interesting effect takes place: The more light added, the **darker** the center appears.

It is possible for you to try this experiment yourself, using the squares in Figure 3-2. To do this, you need a dark room with some way of varying the light intensity without also varying the color of the light. In the normal living quarters there are only two ways to do this. One method is to go into a closet, shut the door, and then slowly open the door. The amount of light entering the closet can be controlled by how far the door has been opened. (Careful, if the outside room is reasonably well lit, you need open the closet door only a fraction of an inch to get sufficient light.) A second method is to use a television set as a light source. Turn on the television set in an otherwise dark room and tune it to an unused channel. The brightness control of the set now acts as a way of controlling the room light. (You may wish to have the contrast control set at minimum to avoid the random dots that would normally appear on the screen.)

Now look at the squares. As you increase the room illumination from its lowest value, the right target square will get darker and darker. When you try the same thing while looking at the target on the left, it will get lighter as the room light gets brighter. Remember that all the target squares are identical: The differences in the way you perceive their brightness come from the differences in the surround. (**Note:** Do **not** try to vary illumination using a light dimmer: The color of the illumination will change and you probably will not be able to dim the lights to a low enough level.)

Although at first the fact that a target appears to become darker as the illumination is increased seems strange, it is quite apparent that it must be true. In conditions of minimum illumination, when there is absolutely no light falling upon the eyes, the resultant perception is of gray, not black. The neutral state of the perception of brightness appears to be gray. When some light is present, then we are able to see

---

[1] These brightness measurements were done using the technique of magnitude estimation as described in Appendix A of this book. The experiment was reported by S. S. Stevens (1961b).

blacks, but only if there are some brighter surfaces to inhibit the black-appearing areas.

A simple example of this phenomenon comes from considering the screen of a television set. When the set is turned off the screen is a neutral gray in brightness. If the set is turned on, some areas on the screen show intense blacks, much darker than the gray of the screen when the set was off. Yet the television set can only intensify the screen: The electron beam that impinges upon the phosphor face of the tube can only cause light to be emitted, it cannot absorb light. The apparent darkening of the screen comes about as a result of the simultaneous contrast mechanisms of the eye.

Mach bands   One of the most interesting effects of spatial interactions is a phenomenon of brightness contrast named after the Austrian scientist Ernst Mach. In his early investigations into sensory physiology (in the 1860's), Mach noted that he could see bands of darkness and brightness where there were no corresponding physical changes in the intensity of the light.

The phenomenon is as follows. A gradation in a visual image from a dimly illuminated area to a more intensely illuminated area (as shown in Figures 3-4 and 3-5) is perceived as a much sharper change in light intensity than actually exists. In fact, dark and light bands can be seen on either side of the gradation; these are *Mach bands*.

Artists, especially children, sometimes outline their pictures. Suppose that you have a picture in which all the bright areas are outlined in white and all the dim areas in black: this is something like the Mach band phenomenon. In fact, the phenomenon is so striking that for many years people thought that the real scene must have these outlines, and all sorts of errors in measurement occurred because scientists thought that the bands they were perceiving were really there on the objects that they were examining through their microscopes and telescopes. (The fascinating story of Mach bands is told by Ratliff in his book on the subject—see the "Suggested Readings" at the end of this chapter for details.)

Mach bands present the classic case for the need to be careful in distinguishing between the psychological and the physical aspects of sensation. Look at Figure 3-6. The dashed lines show the physical situation—the light intensity. The solid lines show the psychological perception of the situation—the perceived brightness. The peak in brightness, shown at point β, is only present psychologically: it is not present in the physical signal. Similarly, the band of relative darkness, shown at point γ, is only present psychologically: it is not in the physical signal. Figures 3-4 and 3-5 show two ways of producing Mach bands.

These interactions are also responsible for the way in which the vertical bands of Figure 3-7 are perceived. Although each band has constant

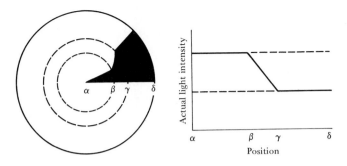

FIGURE 3-4

White disk with black sector, when rotated rapidly about the center (at a rate greater than 1800 rpm), produces the mean light density shown in the graph, which gives the appearance shown in Figure 3-6: Mach bands. From Ratliff (1965).

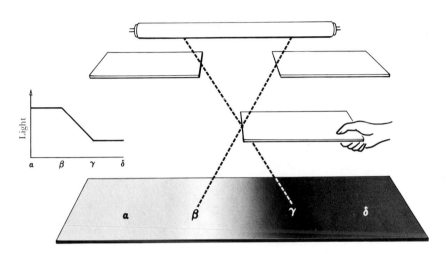

Simple method for producing Mach bands. If the lamp is about 1 foot above the white paper, the height of the card should be 1 to 2 inches. Slight side-to-side movements will enhance the visibility of the bands. The lower diagram shows what the bands look like, although this diagram is constructed artificially. From Ratliff (1965).

FIGURE 3-5

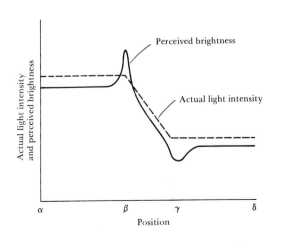

FIGURE 3-6

From Ratliff (1965).

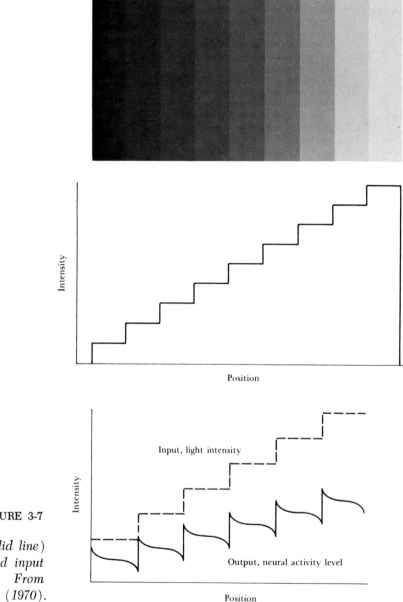

FIGURE 3-7

The output pattern (solid line) predicted for the dashed input intensity distribution. From Cornsweet (1970).

intensity, they are not seen as such. Rather, the perception is of nonuniform brightness. Look carefully at Figure 3-7. Notice that each band of gray looks as if it varies in brightness from the left side of the band to the right. Moreover, the borders between the bands look sharp and distinct, as if an artist had enhanced them slightly. All this results from Mach bands. In actuality, the bands of gray are of constant intensity, as shown by the graph in the figure. It is true that your perception of brightness does change in the manner just described (and as shown in the bottom graph), but this perception is created by your eye. To prove this to yourself, take two strips of paper and cover all the bands but one. Now you can see that the intensity is constant across the band: the Mach band does not appear if only one band is seen. Similarly, take a narrow piece of paper or a thin pen or pencil and cover the border between two of the bands: again, this destroys the Mach band and shows you that the perception is illusory. Much of what you see in this figure is really not there.

It is easy to think of a good reason why your perception should not be exactly the same as reality. It is important to be able to locate the boundaries of objects, even if there is not much actual difference in light intensities between an object and the things surrounding it. The enhancement of differences at the border areas should help any process of pattern recognition to pick out those borders in order to identify the objects viewed.

The neural interactions responsible for these visual experiences are very similar to the mechanisms found in other sensory modalities. In fact, this same type of sensory sharpening is found almost anywhere that individual sensory receptors are lined up next to one another—in vision, hearing, taste, touch, and smell. The interaction patterns seem to be critically important during the first stages of analysis in all sensory systems.

BRIGHTNESS AND DEPTH

Our perception of brightness is often determined by many complex factors. Consider this experiment, which demonstrates how both brightness and depth information interact to produce a perception that takes a number of different factors into account (Hochberg & Beck, 1954).

A room is arranged with some white objects placed on a table (see Figure 3-8). The observer views the room through a hole cut in the wall. Since the head cannot be shifted, everything must be seen from a fixed angle. A number of objects are visible sitting on a table lit by an overhead light. Some of the surfaces are illuminated directly, others are in shadow (see Figure 3-9).

Although the amount of light reflected by the various surfaces is different, all of the surfaces are perceived to have the same color: white. Why? The observer perceives the objects in three dimensions. Thus, some surfaces are lying directly under the light, while others are in shadows. Their orientation in space accounts for the varying degrees of reflected light and brightnesses are therefore perceived to be constant.

Suppose the piece of paper marked × is raised to stand in front of the overhead light, as shown in Figure 3-10. The paper is now in shadow and

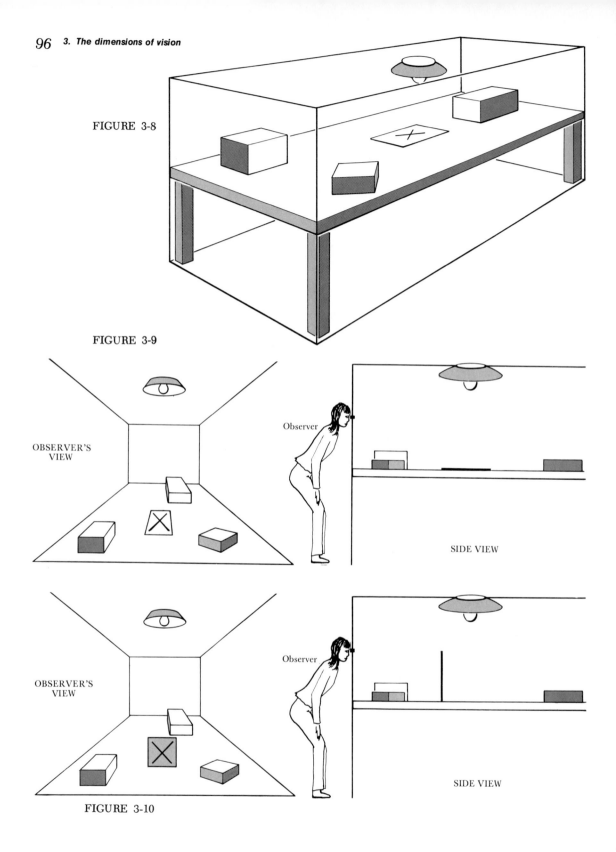

FIGURE 3-8

FIGURE 3-9

OBSERVER'S
VIEW

Observer

SIDE VIEW

OBSERVER'S
VIEW

Observer

SIDE VIEW

FIGURE 3-10

the amount of light it reflects is drastically reduced. Nevertheless it still appears just as white as the other objects. Again its perceived orientation in space is consistent with the light being reflected from it.

To change the perceived brightness, the edges of the paper can be cut to shape it like a trapezoid (Figure 3-11). When it is placed vertically in

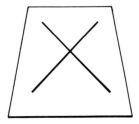

FIGURE 3-11

front of the light, the sides appear to be converging and the observer perceives the upright trapezoid as a rectangle lying flat under the light (Figure 3-12). Now, however, the paper is in fact in shadow and does not reflect

FIGURE 3-12

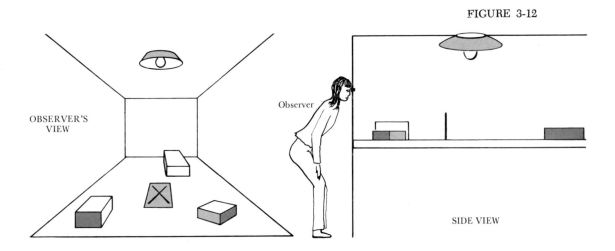

OBSERVER'S VIEW

Observer

SIDE VIEW

the amount of light appropriate to a horizontal object. Its perceived brightness therefore changes, and the paper looks much grayer than the other objects on the table. If a stick is then placed behind the paper, the depth interpretation is no longer tenable, the object is once again perceived as vertical, and it reverts to its normal brightness. In the perception of brightness, the very same visual scene can be interpreted in different ways depending upon the overall interpretation of the visual inputs.

FIGURE 3-13

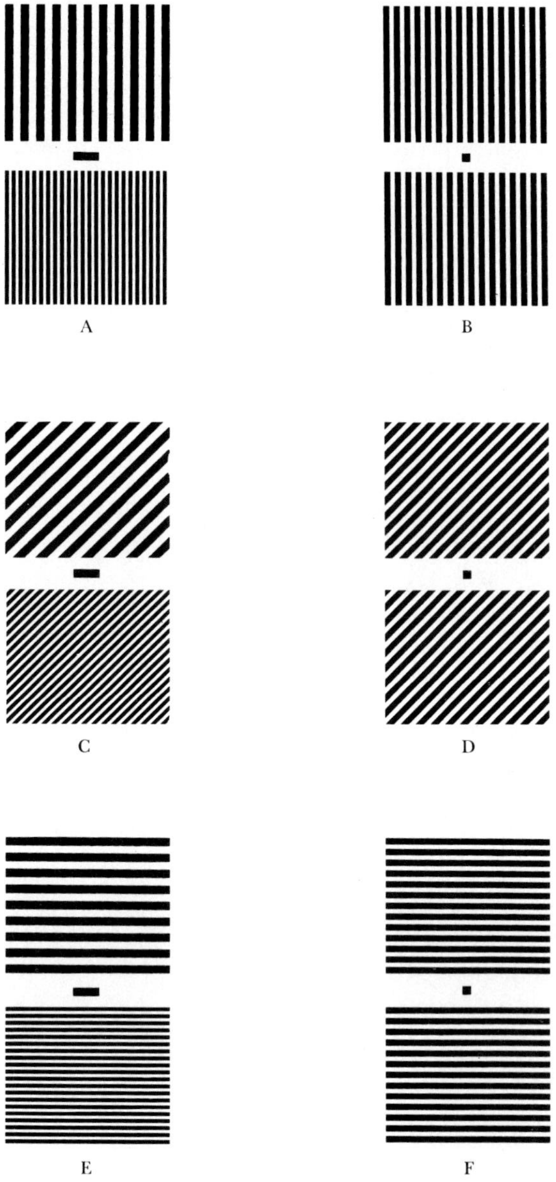

A

B

C

D

E

F

SPATIAL FREQUENCY ANALYSIS

Look at Figure 3-13. There you see a series of gratings. Do the experiments suggested in the figure legend. That is, hold the figure about an arm's length away from you (about 30 inches, or 75 cm) and stare for about half a minute at the line between the two gratings in part A. (Stare at the horizontal bar until the figure starts to shimmer.) Then quickly look at the dot between the two gratings of part B of the figure: the top grating will appear to be more finely spaced than the bottom. If you start at A again, but then transfer your gaze to D or F, you will find that staring at the vertical bars affects the perception of vertical bars, very little of

You can use this diagram, as described in the text, to demonstrate the FIGURE 3-13
perceived frequency shift. Hold the illustration about 75 cm away and,
after assuring yourself that the three pairs of gratings on the right (B, D,
F) are equal in spatial frequency, adapt for about 20 seconds to the pair
of vertical gratings (A) on the left, by looking around the horizontal bar
between the upper (low frequency) and lower (high frequency) patterns.
Then quickly transfer your gaze to the dot between the identical vertical
gratings (B) on the right. Do they still seem the same? Allow at least 2
minutes' recovery before repeating your observation, but this time adapt
to the diagonal gratings (C) and look at the effect on the similarly tilted
gratings (D) as well as upon the vertical ones (B). Finally, test the
effect on all three pairs of test gratings (F, D, B) of adapting to the hori-
zontal patterns (E). While adapting in this case move your gaze up and
down over the bar, to avoid the generation of an afterimage. Adaptation
to the diagonal gratings (C) may cause some slight disturbance in the
apparent spatial frequency of the vertical (B), but the horizontal adapt-
ing patterns (E) should have no effect on the vertical. (From Blakemore,
Nachmias, and Sutton, 1970.)

diagonals, none at all of horizontal bars. (As the figure legend suggests, similar results occur if you start out by looking at parts C or E of the figure.)

Look again at B. The vertical gratings above and below the middle dot really have the same spacing. But, after looking at the gratings of A, the perception of B changes. Looking at a wide set of gratings makes a medium set look narrower. Looking at a narrow set makes the same medium set look wider. This result is closely related to the standard results of visual aftereffects: looking at one figure for a while causes the opposite perception to appear. But this is a strange opposite: it implies that the visual system has special detectors for recognizing bars of specific spacing, and if you look too long at bars of a given spacing, detectors for that size of bars are fatigued, so when you look at a new set of bars, the perception of their spacing is shifted away from the direction of the spacing of the fatigued detectors.

If you actually brought someone in off the street in order to measure THE MEASUREMENT
visual sensitivity, the process would not go smoothly. In fact, you would OF VISUAL
probably find their behavior to be frustrating. Suppose you wished to SENSITIVITY
find their *visual threshold:* the minimum light intensity that a person can
see. A convenient way to start is with a reasonably intense test light and
then gradually reduce the intensity until the person says that it is no
longer visible. This is a rough approximation to the threshold value. Just
as you are about to record the threshold value, however, you would probably be interrupted: the light has become visible. You try reducing the

intensity again, and the same thing would happen. First the light would disappear, then a few seconds later it could be seen again. You would be trapped by the process of visual adaptation—the ability of the eye to adjust its sensitivity to changing illuminations.

To follow this process more precisely, the subject should first be exposed to an intense source of light (so that we know where the eye starts out) and then enclosed in a lightproof room. Visual sensitivity is measured by presenting weaker and weaker test lights. With the passage of time, the subject becomes increasingly sensitive to light. Figure 3-14 shows the typical changes in sensitivity as a function of time in the dark room, called the *dark-adaptation curve*.

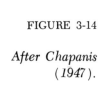

FIGURE 3-14

*After Chapanis
(1947).*

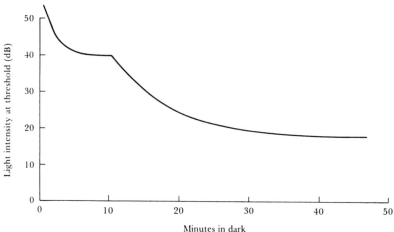

Minutes in dark

Even a casual inspection of this curve indicates that something peculiar is happening around the 10-min mark. When faced with a bumpy curve such as this, one suspects that more than a single mechanism is producing the behavior. In the case of vision, of course, there are good grounds for this suspicion. There are two separate receptor systems operating in the eye: the rods and cones that we discussed in the previous chapter. It would be nice to demonstrate that the bump in the curve results from an interaction in the behavior of these two systems.

The anatomical and functional differences between the two systems can be used to break up the dark-adaptation curve into its separate components. The rods are most dense in the periphery of the retina, the cones in the center. Restricting the test light to the periphery should produce a *rod-adaptation* curve; restricting it to the center should produce a curve based mainly on changes in cone sensitivity. Moreover, rods and cones are differentially sensitive to light of different wavelengths (as shown in Figure 3-15). Hence, the appearance of the dark-adaptation curve should depend on the wavelength of the test light. Thus, we should be able to get a rod- or a cone-adaptation curve at will. Testing at the

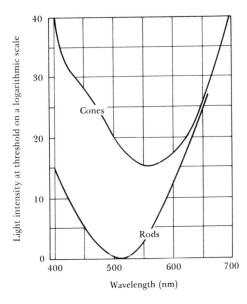

FIGURE 3-15

After Hecht and Hsia (1945).

periphery or with violet light (less than 450 nm) should yield a relatively pure rod-adaptation curve. Testing at the center of the eye or with red light (greater than 650 nm) should yield an adaptation curve based primarily on cone vision.

Indeed, all these predictions show up. For example, in Figure 3-16, a set of dark-adaptation curves is shown. The only difference among them is the color of the test light. For red test lights of very long wavelengths (above 680 nm), the dark-adaptation curve shows no sign of the kink: It is a pure cone-sensitivity curve. As wavelength decreases, the bump begins to appear and the curve for a green light (485–570 nm) is almost identical to the curve for white light. Finally, the maxi-

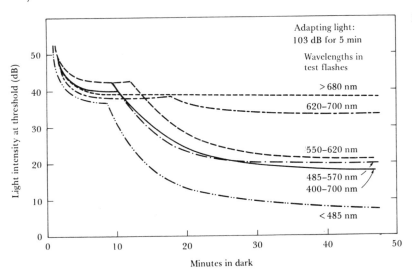

FIGURE 3-16

After Chapanis (1947).

mum sensitivity and the greatest degree of adaptations are found with the shortest visible wavelengths, a violet test light (less than 485 nm) where the rod system is carrying the main burden in responding to the visual signal. A similar set of curves results if the test light is moved from the center of the visual field toward the periphery. Light at the center will give a curve like the upper one in Figure 3-16; light at the periphery will give a curve like the lowest one.

Equibrightness contours

The eye changes its sensitivity to light as a result of the amount of light to which it has been exposed. If kept in the dark, the eye's adaptation to dark can be described by the dark-adaptation curves shown in Figures 3-14 and 3-16. Similarly, if the eye is kept exposed to a steady light, it changes the sensitivity to that light level: this is called *light adaptation.* When an eye has been light adapted, its responses to lights of different intensities and wavelengths depend upon the level of light adaptation. One useful way of examining the eye's responses to light at different adaptation levels is to expose the eye to some light intensity for a reasonable period of time and then to present a test light. The intensity of the test light is adjusted so that the subject sees it at a constant brightness level as its wavelength is varied. This procedure results in the data shown in Figure 3-17: a set of *equibrightness contours.* The set of contours shown in Figure 3-17 shows how the curves change at different levels of light adaptation. As the adaptation level changes, the equal brightness curves shift the wavelength at which they are maximally sensitive. This shift results from the different amounts of rod and cone activity present at each level of adaptation. With adaptation to a high light level (top curve), cone vision plays the major role and longer wavelengths appear brightest. With adaptation to a low light level, vision depends mostly on rods and the maximum sensitivity shifts down toward the shorter wavelengths. This was first noticed by the Bohemian physiologist Johannes Purkinje, and in fact it was one of the earliest sets of behavioral observations used to discover the difference between the rod and cone systems.

The change in sensitivity has a practical result. The relative brightness of reds and blues changes in going from bright to dim light. Thus, in bright light a red may appear brighter than a blue, but in dim light the same red may be dimmer than the blue. This phenomenon is illustrated in Color Plate IV.

If you need to keep your eyes dark adapted, yet also work occasionally in well-lit rooms, then it is convenient to maintain the adaptation level of the rod vision. This can be done by controlling the wavelength of light to which you are exposed. Wearing goggles that only allow red light through to the eyes will protect the rod system against bright lights. With red goggles, even in a well-lit environment only the cones will be

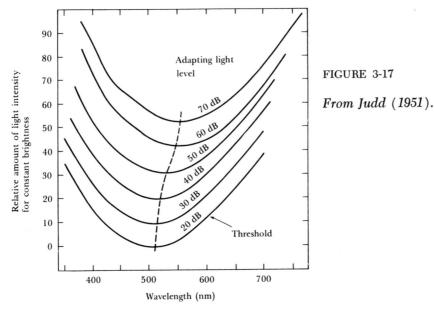

FIGURE 3-17

From Judd (1951).

exposed to light and the adaptation level of the rods is not affected. In the dim environment, when the goggles are removed, the rods will be found to have maintained their high sensitivity; even though the cones are now light adapted, they will not affect the vision. This is the principle behind the use of red goggles or rooms illuminated only with red lights for people such as radar observers who need to keep their eyes dark-adapted, even during rest breaks when they want to move about in normally lit rooms.

How long does it take to become dark-adapted? The curve in Figure 3-16 shows that the most rapid changes in sensitivity take place during the first 10 to 20 min. For most practical purposes, 30 min is sufficient for close to maximum adaptation, but careful measurements show the

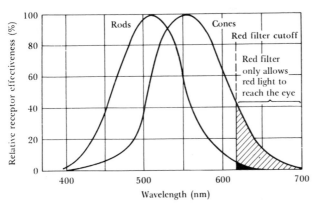

The shaded areas indicate the region where the red filter allows light to pass. Thus, almost no light excites the rods. From Hecht and Hsia (1945).   FIGURE 3-18

sensitivity continues to change very slowly for as long as 6 hours. Remember, however, that the 20 to 30 min is for a situation where the subjects are first exposed to extremely bright lights (such as a flash bulb going off in front of their eyes). With much dimmer illumination—say, the level in a fairly large room lit by several 50-watt incandescent bulbs—it may only take 5 min to become adapted to the dark. Moreover, once the eye is dark-adapted, turning on a dim light for 10 sec or so does not change the adaptation level very much; only 60 sec are then required to return to the original state. Were this not true, night driving would lead to considerable difficulties, since the lights from an oncoming car would interfere with dark adaptation, severly hampering the ability to see objects. Yet such lights have little noticeable effect on visual sensitivity.

TEMPORAL
CHARACTERISTICS
OF VISION

Integration time

Vision is not instantaneous. It takes time for the reaction to a visual image to be established and, then, once established, the reaction persists for awhile, even if the image is taken away. The chemical reactions appear to require some time to translate the light source into a neural-electric response. The retinal image fades away gradually, so the persistence can be seen for several tenths of a second (see the discussion of the visual short-term store in Chapter 8).

It is possible to perform a trade between the intensity of light and the duration that it is on. Within the response time of the eye, all that matters is the total energy presented. Thus, if the light intensity is halved and the duration doubled, a person's ability to detect a signal is unchanged. The time–intensity trade works rather well for durations up to about 20 msec. For flashes longer than 20 msec, a reduction in light intensity cannot quite be compensated for by a corresponding increase in signal duration. Once the signal flash is longer than about a quarter of a second (250 msec), the ability to detect the signal becomes totally independent of the duration, and is determined solely by the intensity of the light.

This interchange between time and intensity is, of course, not unique to the visual system. It is common to photochemical processes of all types. Suitable exposure for photographic film, for example, can be obtained with a large number of combinations of integration times (shutter speed) and intensities (aperture opening). Cameras typically provide integration times from 0.001 to 1.0 sec—a much wider range than that of the human eye. But the visual system is far more sensitive to light than the average camera film.

When flashing lights become continuous

Once initiated, the visual perception persists for a brief period after the light itself is turned off. The persistence of the visual image was first measured by an ingenious investigator in the 1700s who tied a glowing ember to a string and whirled it around in the dark. You can do the same thing with a flashlight. The speed of rotation at which the moving light appears to form a continuous circle gives the information necessary to compute the persistence of the image. The experiment gives the same result whether done with a sophisticated electronic measuring apparatus or with a flashlight or glowing ember: The estimate is about 150 msec. This value is very close to the duration of the electrical activity in the retina that is produced in response to a brief flash of light. The fact that the light pattern seems to be retained by the visual system for about 150–250 msec will turn out to be very important to our study of memory (Chapter 8).

By timing things just right, it should be possible to make lights which are actually flashing appear to be on continuously. Suppose a light is flashed. The visual response builds up and persists over some 100 msec. If a second flash is added soon enough, the response to it will build up before the reaction to the first has died away. A third flash can be added before the visual reaction to the second flash dies away. The flashing lights then, produce a continuous reaction in the visual system that is perceived as continuous light. The rate at which a flickering light appears to be continuous is called the *critical flicker frequency* (*CFF*).[2]

Critical flicker

Any factor which alters the speed of integration and persistence in the visual system also alters the rate at which flashing lights are perceived as continuous. Intense flashes produce short integration periods and, thus, must be presented at much higher rates before they fuse and become continuous. Weak flashes fuse at slow rates. Flicker is more noticeable in the periphery than in the center of the eye. You can often see the flicker in fluorescent lights and television images if you look aside so that their images are just at the "corner of the eye."

The apparent brightness of a flickering light that has fused is predictable from the integration mechanism that produces the fusion. A light flashing on and off for equal times at a rate greater than its fusion frequency appears to have the same brightness as a light that is on continuously, but only half as intense (this is called *Talbot's Law*). The visual system averages the intensity throughout the integration period, and the perception follows accordingly.

These integrational aspects of visual information-processing clearly limit the speeds at which the eye can detect and track changes in the

[2] Those of you familiar with electronic circuits will note that the temporal characteristics of the eye approximate those of a bandpass filter with an upper cutoff between 10 and 50 Hz, depending upon intensity, and with little or no direct-current response. [See Cornsweet (1970) for a discussion of the bandpass filter method of analysis.]

pattern of stimulation falling on the retina. The averaging process merges one image into the next, creating a smoothly flowing, continuous visual perception. It converts the succession of discrete pictures that are flashed on a television set or movie projection screen into the illusion of a steady, continuous visual environment.

The images on the television set or movie screen would actually flicker somewhat were not clever strategies used. Professional motion pictures are projected at the rate of 24 frames per second (sometimes 30). The light projected to the screen is interrupted during the time it takes to advance the film from one frame to the next. If this were projected normally, flicker would be seen. To avoid flicker, each frame of film is projected on the screen several times. That is, instead of a steady projection of each frame, the light is interrupted one or more times. Thus, even though only 24 frames are shown each second, the eye receives a frequency of at least 48 flashes per second, a sufficiently high rate to avoid flicker. (Some projectors interrupt the light beam twice during each frame, producing a frequency of 72 flashes per second.)

Television faces a similar problem. In the United States, a television image is painted upon the screen dot-by-dot, with the image consisting of some 525 lines, each line having a theoretical resolution of approximately 500 dots. The complete image is presented 30 times each second. If the image were painted consecutively, starting at the top left corner and working across the rows and down to the bottom right, there would be flicker because the presentation of each dot is for such a brief percentage of the time taken to present the entire picture. This is not true of a motion picture, where each element in the picture is exposed whenever the scene is illuminated.

To avoid flicker, the picture is split in half by presenting every other line of the image. This takes $\frac{1}{60}$ sec. Then, the electron beam goes back and fills in the missing lines. Thus, although the entire picture still takes $\frac{1}{30}$ sec to be presented, every area of the screen has some part of the picture presented to it every $\frac{1}{60}$ sec. This interlacing effectively eliminates flicker.[3]

---

[3] In other countries, the standards for television images differ from those used in the United States. Thus, in western Europe, most television signals have higher resolution: the image has around 600 lines, each with a resolution of approximately 600 dots. The picture is painted less frequently, however: a complete image is presented only 25 times each second. As in the United States, the picture is split into two interlaced images; thus the screen has an effective refreshing rate of 50 pictures per second. But a 50-Hz signal is sufficiently slow that flicker is often noticeable. This is especially true at the periphery of the visual field. Thus, television in Europe has better image quality but with more noticeable flicker than television in the United States.

The entertainment industry sometimes deliberately introduces flicker, providing us a chance to see what the environment would look like if our visual system did not have these integration mechanisms. The stroboscopic lights sometimes used in light shows provide a series of discrete snapshots with enough time between each that the image from one flash decays before the next appears. At these high intensities and low flashing rates, the visual system no longer merges one image into the next, and perception takes on an unreal, disconnected quality.

The start of modern theories of color vision must be credited to Isaac Newton (1642–1727) and his observations that a prism could split the light from the sun into a full spectrum of colors. From that simple fact comes the first simple theory: The color that is seen depends upon the wavelength of the light striking the eye. Like many theories, the facts are true but the theory is not (see Color Plate III following page 121).

COLORS

A prism (or the equivalent in nature, a rainbow) separates out the different wavelengths contained in white light and lays them neatly in a row, from long wavelengths to short. We perceive the spectrum as different colors laid out neatly in a row from reds to violets. Perhaps this is all there is to color vision. Maybe there is a different kind of receptor responding to each different wavelength of light (*monochromatic* light), just as there are different neurons in the auditory system that respond to different frequencies of sound.

A careful examination of color perception shows that this theory is too simple. In the spectrum of pure lights produced by a prism, some colors are absent. There is no brown or purple or pink. These colors must be created by something other than a simple monochromatic light.

When two different wavelengths of light are mixed together, we do not see two colors. Rather, we see one new color formed from the mixture. Once the lights are combined, it is absolutely impossible for the human to determine the original set of colors that went into the mixture. This is quite unlike the situation in hearing where the individual tones that make up a chord can be identified by the listener. Moreover, in color vision, mixing certain wavelengths seems to cancel out the color altogether. For example, if a bluish-green monochromatic light (with a wavelength of 490 nm) is mixed with a yellow-red monochromatic light (with a wavelength of 600 nm), and the relative amounts of the two lights are adjusted just right, the colors cancel, leaving a colorless gray. Such mixtures of lights are called *complementary* pairs.

Complementary pairs provide a clue to a useful description of human color vision. The first thing that is needed is some way of expressing the relationships that hold among all the possible perceptions of lights and colors. Ideally, it should be possible to find a descriptive system that predicts the perceived color of any mixture of lights. This is usually done by drawing a diagram in which the different possible colors and mixtures are represented, with a set of rules that describes how one predicts the results of combinations of lights. Such a diagram (and its equivalent mathematical representation) is a *color space*. Color spaces can take many forms, from a simple circle to a rather complex three-dimensional space.

The color circle   We can use the sets of complementary colors to give us the first system for describing color mixtures. The layout of colors produced by a prism describes reasonably well the perceptions caused by single, monochromatic light. It would be useful to take advantage of this description. To do so, notice two things: first, the fact that some colors are "opposites" or complements of one another; second, the two ends of the spectrum look reasonably similar—deep blue or violet at the short-wavelength end, purple at the long-wavelength end. Combining these two observations leads to a simple solution: take the line of colors given by the spectrum and draw it as a circle, putting complementary colors directly opposite each other across the diameter of the circle.

   The color circle of Figure 3-19 shows the color names and the approximate locations for the wavelengths of light that produce those colors when viewed in the spectrum. Complementary color pairs are the two colors where lines drawn through the center of the circle intersect the circle. (The region marked "purples" cannot be produced by monochro-

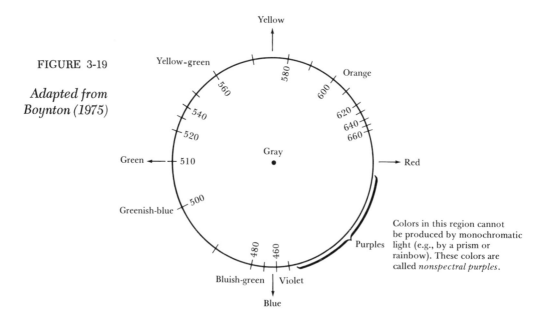

FIGURE 3-19

Adapted from Boynton (1975)

Colors in this region cannot be produced by monochromatic light (e.g., by a prism or rainbow). These colors are called *nonspectral purples*.

matic light. It will be discussed later.) Because two complementary colors form gray when mixed together in approximate amounts, *gray* is represented at the center of the circle. Thus, the center represents a point with no color, a gray. (All perceptions that do not have a color are called gray. Gray, therefore, refers to the general class of perceptions that range from black—very low brightness—through the grays, to white —high brightness. For purposes of describing color hue, black, gray, and white are all alike.) The color circle was devised by Isaac Newton as a useful way of representing color. It is not used much today, however, because it fails to capture all the phenomena of color vision, and because more accurate representations now exist.

The color circle is useful in helping to define the word **color** a bit more precisely. To represent any color, three different psychological attributes are required: *hue, saturation,* and *brightness*.

Hue corresponds to the normal meaning of color: It is what changes as wavelength changes. Location along the circumference of the circle represents hue.

Saturation refers to the relative amount of pure monochromatic light that must be mixed with the white light to produce the perceived color. All points on the circumference of the circle are highly saturated colors. Moving from the outside toward the center reduces saturation: the point labeled **gray** has zero saturation. A point midway between **gray** and **green** has an intermediate amount of saturation.

Brightness is used exactly as it was in the earlier sections of this chapter. The brightness dimension does **not** show up on the color circle. The most direct physical correlate of brightness is light intensity (with the same restrictions discussed previously).

Mixing two lights. To see how two colors combine to form a third, the first step is to locate the individual colors on circumferences of the circle, then connect the two points by a straight line. Any mixture of the two individual colors should produce a third color that lies somewhere on that line: The exact location depends on the exact amounts (intensities) of the two individual colors present in the mixture.

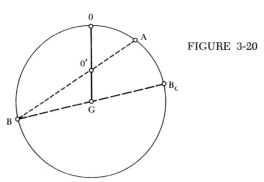

FIGURE 3-20

Suppose we mix together two monochromatic complementary colors: call them B and B_c. These two are shown on the color circle of Figure 3-20 by two points along the circumference that lie on opposite ends of a diameter. Let the mixture of B and B_c that exactly cancels be given by the point midway between the two: The point labeled G (gray) in the center of the circle.

Suppose two colors that are not complementary are mixed, say A and B. The result is some new color 0', as shown in Figure 3-20. What color is 0'? The easiest way to start is to consider the changes in perception that occur as we move from point B on the circumference of the color circle toward G. At B, there is a spectral color, one produced by a pure monochromatic light. Suppose that point B is **blue.** To move from B to G, we simply combine together two lights, one of which is gray, the other monochromatic blue. As the relative proportion of the two lights changes, we go from point B (all blue light, no gray) through some point that represents equal amounts of both lights, to point G (all gray light, no blue). The essential attribute that most people regard as **color** would not be much changed by the addition of gray; it is the saturation— the "lightness" or "whiteness"—that would change. To prove that, take any point along the line B–G (except for B and G) and ask observers to look at the spectral colors and pick out the one that matches that point most closely. They will choose the spectral color that corresponds closely to B.

Now back to the original question: what color does 0' in Figure 3-20 have? A radius drawn from the center of the circle (G) through 0' to the circumference (point 0 on the figure) specifies the hue. The distance along the radius from G to 0' specifies the saturation. The points 0 and 0' have the same hue, but 0 is more saturated. We see that mixing A and B together produced 0', a color with the hue of 0, but less saturated.

If we wish to match 0 by mixing together A and B we would fail, for the only possible results of the mixture lie on the straight line AB; the exact location depends upon the relative intensities of A and B. The more intense A is, the closer to A the resulting mixture. In attempting to match 0 by mixing together A and B, the closest that it is possible to come is 0': The same hue, but reduced saturation.

PAINTS AND LIGHTS

The color circle applies to mixtures of lights, not mixtures of paints. To determine how paints mix together, we need to consider the fact that they produce their color by absorbing light of all wavelengths except those which cause the color. The wavelengths causing the color are reflected. To see how two paints mix together, it is necessary to examine the wavelengths that the new combination absorbs. Because the absorption of colors is the most important attribute of paint, these mixtures are called *subtractive*. Mixture of lights is called *additive*.

The mixture of red and green light can produce yellow. The mixture of blue and yellow light can produce gray. (Look back at Figure 3-19.) These are the facts of color mixture, but they are contrary to all that most people learn about the mixing of colors from art classes. Why the difference? The answer has to do with the differences between the ways that two lights and two paints add together. To make a prediction of the color that results from a mixture, we should not ask what colors have been added together: That has little to do with it. The important question to ask is, what colors get to the eye?

Consider the mixture of lights. Examine Figure 3-21. Shine a blue light onto a piece of paper: Blue reflects from the paper into the eye and the paper looks blue.

Shine a yellow light onto a piece of paper. Yellow reflects and the paper looks yellow.

Shine both blue and yellow onto the paper. Both blue and yellow bounce off, and both are seen. The resulting color that is perceived is given by the mixture: gray.

Consider the mixture of paints. Paint paper blue. White light shines on the paper. The paint absorbs long wavelengths, allowing only greens, blues, and violets to reflect. The eye sees a combination of green, blue, and violet. The paper looks blue.

Paint paper yellow. White light shines on the paper. The paint absorbs short wavelengths so that only greens, yellows, oranges, and reds reflect. The eye sees these mixed together. The paper looks yellow.

Paint paper with a mixture of blue and yellow. White light shines on the paper. The blue paint absorbs long wavelengths (yellows, oranges, and reds) while the yellow absorbs the short wavelengths (blues and violets). All that is left is intermediate wavelengths: greens. Hence, the mixture of blue paint and yellow paint looks green.

The principles of color mixture learned from lights can also apply to paints. To do this, some care is needed in mixing the paints together. Suppose we wish to create a yellow by mixing red and green paints. Were we simply to mix the paints together and apply them to the paper, we would end up with some dark combination, probably reddish. This is because the paints were mixed together so that their effects on light interfered with each other. But suppose the red were painted as many small dots of paint. From a distance, it would look like a solid red. Similarly, the green could be painted as many small dots, carefully located so that the green and red dots filled the entire paper, never overlapping one another. From up close the many small red and green dots would be visible. From a distance, far enough back so that the individual dots could not be seen, the eye would receive a mixture of red and green light. The light would look yellow.

This is the principle used by a color television set to mix together its color. If you examine the screen from close up, the individual dots of color

Making paints mix as lights

MIXTURES OF LIGHTS

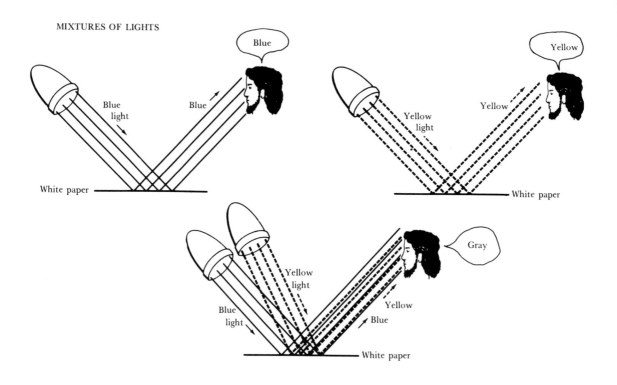

MIXTURES OF PAINTS

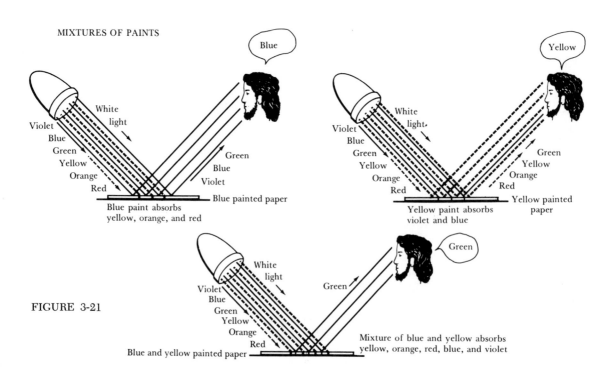

FIGURE 3-21

become visible. Long before the age of color television, the impressionist painter George Seurat (1859–1891) experimented with additive color mixtures by forming his paintings with many small individual dots of color. When viewed from a distance, the mixture of lights formed the desired colors.

By direct measurement of the color sensitivity of the cones in the human retina, three different types of cones have been discovered, each of which contains a specific pigment that is responsible for its color selectivity. The different pigments absorb light differently, each being selective to a special set of light wavelengths. One absorbs wavelengths of 445 to 450 nm best, the second has maximum absorption around 525 to 535 nm, and the last has a maximum in the region 555 to 570 nm. The overall absorption properties of the different pigments are very much like that shown in Figure 3-22. These are the three primary color receptors that control normal color vision.

COLOR SENSITIVITY OF CONES

From the description of the sensitivity of the primary receptors, it is possible to work out most of the phenomena of color vision. For example, the color circle suggests that mixture of a green (at 520 nm) and a red at 620 nm should match a yellow of 564 nm. How is that related to the cone sensitivities of Figure 3-22?

Let the vertical axis of the graph represent the amount of excitation given to each of the color receptors for a light of intensity 100 at a wavelength specified by the horizontal axis. Now consider what happens when 100 units of 620 nm is mixed with 100 units of 520 nm.

Amount of Excitation of Color Receptors

	A	B	C
Red (620 nm)	10	2	.0
Green (520 nm)	7	15	.2
Total:	17	17	.2

The total gives us the excitation that each receptor receives when excited by 200 light units: 100 from the red and 100 from the green. To use these curves, the values have to be rescaled. There is a total of 34.2 units of neural excitation. Of this, A is 17/34.2 or 50% of the total; B is 17/34.2 or 50%; C is 1%. Now go back to the curves of Figure 3-22 and find a wavelength which excites A, B, and C in these relative percentages. In this case, it is easy to find. About the only place where receptor A is excited about the same as B and excitation of C is negligible is in the region between 560 and 565 nm. The mixture will be perceived as yellow. The color circle gives the same answer.

FIGURE 3-22

From Wald *(1964).*

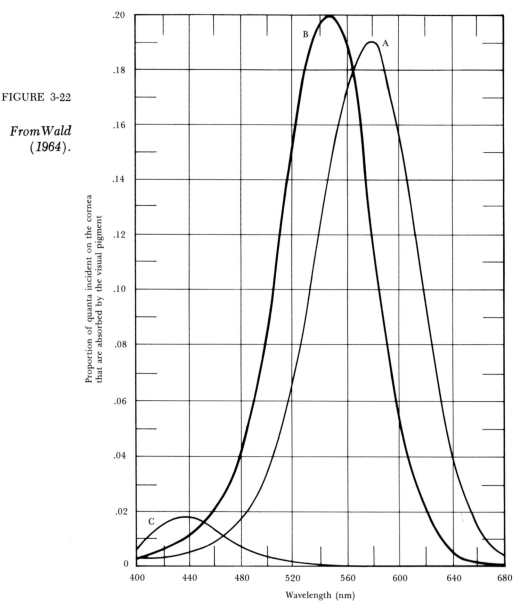

It is clear from the computations that it is a straightforward, if tedious, matter to compute for any combination of lights the relative amounts of stimulation that will occur in the three color-receptors and thus determine what other combinations of lights (or monochromatic light) will match that relative excitation.

Induced contrast   With color, much as with black-and-white, what is seen at one point affects the perception of neighboring points. This is caused by lateral inhibition: The same phenomenon responsible for increasing contrasts and for brightness constancies. Looking at a blue patch at one location reduces the sensitivity to blue in the neighboring areas; hence, more sensitivity to yellow. Looking at black increases the sensitivity to white in the neighborhood. Looking at red increases the sensitivity to green. These contrast effects are called *spatial contrast* or *induced contrast:* A color induces its complement onto neighboring regions.

The biggest effect of contrasts will occur with complementary pairs. In fact, complementary pairs of colors can be very disturbing to look at. The induced color caused by the spatial interactions can make a color look more intense, more saturated than it has any right to be (Color Plate V, following page 121).

Examine the green hearts in Color Plate II. Fixate on the black dot to form an afterimage—fixate until the colors shimmer a bit. Now look at the white surface. Yes, you see afterimages of pink hearts, but why is there any green present? It is induced.

Incidentally, now you know why the shimmering of colors occurs when you stare for a long time at a scene. The shimmering occurs at the boundaries in the picture. The small, unavoidable eye movements cause this part of the picture to oscillate back and forth so that the retinal image is not stationary but fluctuates between the two colors on either side of the boundary. Thus, as some receptors are fatigued by the steady gazing, the receptors corresponding to the boundaries are not nearly so fatigued and are more subject to contrast effects. The result is that the borders adapt differently, producing shimmering perceptions.

Opponent process color theory

The observations of color phenomena are strongly reminiscent of the Mach band phenomena, which we studied in Chapter 2. In general, they seem to illustrate a general property of the nervous system: neural components exist in complementary pairs, so that whenever there is one effect occurring, simultaneously there appears to be an opposite effect. Looking at black makes surrounding areas look whiter, looking at green makes surrounding areas redder, and so on. These sensory phenomena appear to result from the fact that one basic color receptor, when excited, opposes the operation of all surrounding receptors of the same class.

As we have seen, there seem to be three different types of cones, which we have called A, B, and C. These three basic receptors appear to be interconnected into a system that produces a set of complementary, opposing color perceptions. Perceptually, there appear to be four unique colors: blue, green, red, and yellow. (See the color circle, Figure 3-19.) The color receptors are paired so that blue and yellow oppose one another: they can never be seen at the same time (at any one place), a patch of blue makes the surroundings look yellower (and vice versa), and equal mixtures of the two cancel, producing gray. Similarly, red and green are opposing pairs. Indeed, this is the reason that the color circle of Figure 3-19 was drawn with yellow and blue at the top and bottom and with red and green at the two sides.

The opponent process color theory was first proposed in 1878 by Ewald Hering. He suggested that there were three basic opponent systems: a *blue–yellow* system, a *red–green* system, and a *black–white* system. The judgment of brightness is based on the response to the black–white system. Hues result from combinations of the two outputs of the blue–yellow and red–green systems. Saturation is determined by the amount of black–white output relative to the blue–yellow and red–green.

Although the exact details are not known, the fact that color receptors probably combine in an opponent process system is well established by behavioral and physiological investigations. For example, physiological studies of monkeys show nerve cells that increase their response rate for red lights but decrease it for green lights: exactly the type of opponent process postulated by the theory. Other nerve cells do just the opposite, increasing their response rate for green and decreasing it for red.

Blue–yellow pairings have also been found, although with far less frequency than the red–green pairs (at least in the monkeys studied to date). This is consistent with the fact that the blue–yellow system is less sensitive than the red–green one. These studies and the opponent system will be examined in Chapter 6.

Afterimages. Stare at the color patch of Color Plate II for a while without moving your eyes until the patch starts to "glow" slightly. Then look at a white surface; you will see an afterimage of the color patch. The color of an afterimage is almost exactly the complementary color of the image. Thus, the color circle describes afterimage colors: The color of the afterimage is almost directly across the circle from the color stared at.

Afterimages are reciprocal. That is, if a blue produces a yellow afterimage, then a light of that same yellow color will produce a blue afterimage. Some greens, however, produce purple afterimages, yet there is no single wavelength of light that can produce purple by itself. Purple and related colors are *nonspectral* colors, because they cannot be produced by a single wavelength from the visual spectrum. These colors can be placed on the color circle, however, by knowing their complements. They are specified by the wavelengths of their complements. If you look again at the color circle you can see that mixtures of lights will produce purple. A violet of 400 nm mixed with a red of 700 nm will produce an intense purple. Thus, the color circle not only helps explain mixtures, it also puts nonspectral colors into their rightful place.

The explanation of afterimages is simple. Prolonged viewing of a scene fatigues the receptors that have been stimulated, causing other receptors to take over when the gaze is shifted to a neutral stimulation. Thus, as with induced color, it is possible to produce "unnatural" colors with this procedure. First view a saturated green for a while, and then switch to a saturated red: You will perceive a red of supersaturation. The green receptors will be fatigued. They no longer operate to mix with the red and desaturate it. Thus, the resulting red is more brilliant than any that can be produced simply by monochromatic light.

The effect can be enhanced by adding color contrast. Look at a deep red surrounded by deep green. Then switch to deep green surrounded by deep red. You can create this easily yourself by having color slides made that are both positives and negatives of the original scene (this is easily done by your local film processor because several different color films— such as **Kodacolor**—yield color negatives which are complementary in color to the original). Project them alternately upon a screen so that they overlap. A rapid alternation is extremely effective.

In this chapter, the following terms and concepts that we consider to be important have been used. Please look them over. If you are not able to give a short explanation of any of them, you should go back and review the appropriate sections of the chapter.

REVIEW OF TERMS
AND CONCEPTS

The difference between physical and psychological variables
    intensity versus brightness
    wavelength or frequency versus color or hue
Brightness contrast
    what it is
    Mach bands (and why they might be useful)
    other influences on the perception of brightness (depth information,
      for example)
Dark adaptation—light adaptation
    the role of rods and cones in dark adaptation
    equibrightness contours (Why does wearing red goggles maintain dark
      adaptation?)
Critical flicker frequency
Color
    not all colors appear in the spectrum (or in a rainbow)
    complementary colors
    once lights (or paints) are mixed one cannot determine how the result
      was obtained
    hue
    saturation
    brightness

*Terms and
concepts you
should know*

the principles of mixing colors
> why lights differ from paints: additive and subtractive mixtures

The sensitivity to light

Induced contrast

Opponent process color theory (the details of this theory are in Chapter 6)

Afterimage color

Spatial frequency analysis
> why staring at gratings for a while changes the appearance of other gratings

The beginning part of this chapter concentrates on the role of lateral inhibition and the resulting interactions of excitation at different spots in the visual field with each other. For this topic, three books are essential reading. First, Ratliff's book *Mach bands* (1965) is an excellent introduction to lateral inhibition, to the collection of psychological data relevant to its analysis, and to a wide assortment of interesting psychological, physiological issues that result from the study of this phenomenon. Second, Georg von Békésy's book *Sensory inhibition* (1967) expands the phenomena of lateral inhibition to cover a wide variety of sensory systems, including taste and smell. This, too, is a fascinating book, interlaced with observations about the way a scientist ought to proceed in the study of any field. If it sounds like we are going overboard in our recommendations of the books by Ratliff and Békésy, you are probably correct, but it is for good reasons.

Finally, the book *Visual perception* by Cornsweet (1970) shows how to apply the mechanisms of lateral inhibition to the phenomena encountered in visual perception. Cornsweet's book is the best treatment we have yet seen on the operation of the eye at the level of the retinal processes. Moreover, he presents in very thorough and intelligible form the results of the most recent concepts of spatial Fourier analysis to the understanding of such issues as brightness constancy and critical flicker fusion. These are important issues, and the more advanced student would do well to study the latter sections of Cornsweet's book with care. (Cornsweet also provides a unique, highly intelligible treatment of color vision. It might be best, however, not to try to read both his and ours at the same time. We both use different systems to discuss this phenomenon. Although the experienced reader will be able to follow both discussions, the beginning reader will probably get confused.)

As is our custom in all the chapters that refer to perceptual phenomena, we highly recommend the *Handbook of perception*, especially Volumes III and V (Carterette & Friedman, 1973, 1975). For the basic phenomena of adaptation, the best source is still *The handbook of experimental psychology*, edited by Stevens in 1951. The book is old, but thorough, and the description of the eye's basic operation has not changed since that time. Chapter 16 of Volume III of the *Handbook of perception* also covers this material, although not as thoroughly as does Stevens. The entire book edited by Graham (1965) also treats these issues.

The experiment on the effects of depth cues on brightness originally was performed by Hochberg and Beck (1954). A more recent examination of this phenomenon can be found in the article by Flock and Freedberg (1970), and although the paper is rather technical, it is worth the effort, since it presents several alternative theories (as well as numerous references).

There are a number of fascinating studies on brightness contrast. A particularly intriguing result is given in Coren (1969), who shows how brightness contrast can change depending upon how a figure is viewed: That is, if an ambiguous figure is given another interpretation, brightness contrasts may be altered. A review of this entire phenomenon can be found in the article by Festinger, Coren, and Rivers (1970). Another important article on a phenomenon commonly known as the Gelb Effect is the analysis by Mershon and Gogel (1970). An excellent book on brightness constancy is the one by Hurvich and Jameson (1966).

Some important visual phenomena not covered in this book are discussed in Hochberg's book *Perception* (1964). In addition, the review article by Harris (1965) discussed the recovery of vision after viewing the world through distorting prisms. This is a particularly intriguing topic, and Harris not only gives a good review, but also provides relevant literature references. The work by Julesz (1960, 1964) provides a particularly novel and important introduction to some of the problems of three-dimensional space perception. His book is especially important (Julesz, 1971) and, moreover, it is thoroughly enjoyable, especially when his three-dimensional images are viewed through the colored lenses that come with the book. Enright's (1970) article on the illusion known as the "Pulfrich Pendulum" is also important here, combining as it does the discussion of a visual illusion, discussion of the perception of depth, and computations on the rate of response of the retina to visual signals. As usual, the *Annual Review of Psychology* provides a good access into material on visual perception.

Color vision is an enigma. Although it clearly is a very important topic, books which treat this in an intelligible manner are difficult or impossible to find. Cornsweet (1970) comes close, but his treatment should not be mixed with ours, as we have already noted. Graham's book (1965) contains most of the important information, but it will take a lot of

Color vision

hard work to understand it. Perhaps the best treatment is that by LeGrand (1957). Unfortunately, he does not include much of the modern work. But perhaps the best thing to do is to start with LeGrand and then work your way through the literature from there.

Kaufman (1974) gives an introductory treatment of color that might be useful to those who have trouble with the discussion in this book. Advanced reviews of the physiological responses to color are given in the chapter by DeValois and DeValois in Volume V of the *Handbook of perception,* and an advanced treatment of the psychological mechanisms of color is presented by Boynton in that same book (Volume V is Carterette & Friedman, 1975).

Spatial frequency analysis

By now, there are a number of good treatments of spatial frequency analysis, but none that really says why it is useful for the human perceptual system. A good place to start is with the *Scientific American* article by Campbell and Maffei (1974). From there, the treatment by Cornsweet (1970) in his Chapter 12 provides a good introduction to the technical aspects of specifying spatial frequencies. The chapter by Anstis (1975) reviews some of the psychological evidence and attempts to describe the utility of the approach. Volume V of the *Handbook of perception* is devoted to seeing, and we have already identified it as a useful reference. A glance at the index under *spatial frequency* and *spatial frequency analysis* verifies that this volume is valuable on this topic as well (see the chapter by Robson). The *Annual Review of Psychology* provides a useful (although technical and dry) place to start a literature search on spatial frequency. The chapters on *spatial vision* and on *perception* will be the places to look.

COLOR PLATE I   *If you stare at the center of this picture from a distance of approximately 6 inches without moving your eyes, the circles will fade away. For an explanation, see Figure 1-47. (Peter Sedgley, Looking Glass Suite, No. 9, Lithograph. Collection: D. A. Norman.)*

COLOR PLATE II   *Stare at the black dot in the left panel with head and eyes steady until the whole figure starts to shimmer. Then look at the right black dot, the one in the white area. You will see pink hearts on a greenish background. (It helps to blink a few times to get the afterimage started.) The pink is an afterimage. The green is "induced." (Modified from The Color Tree, Inmont Corporation, New York, 1965.)*

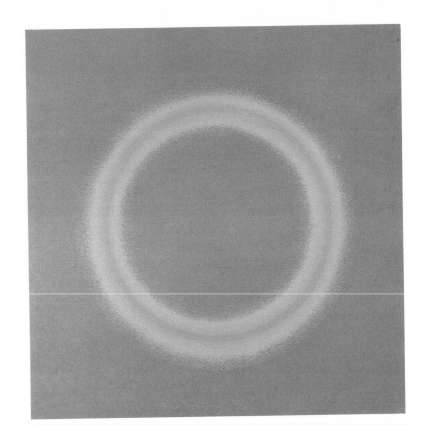

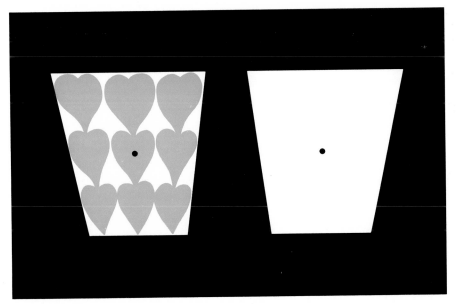

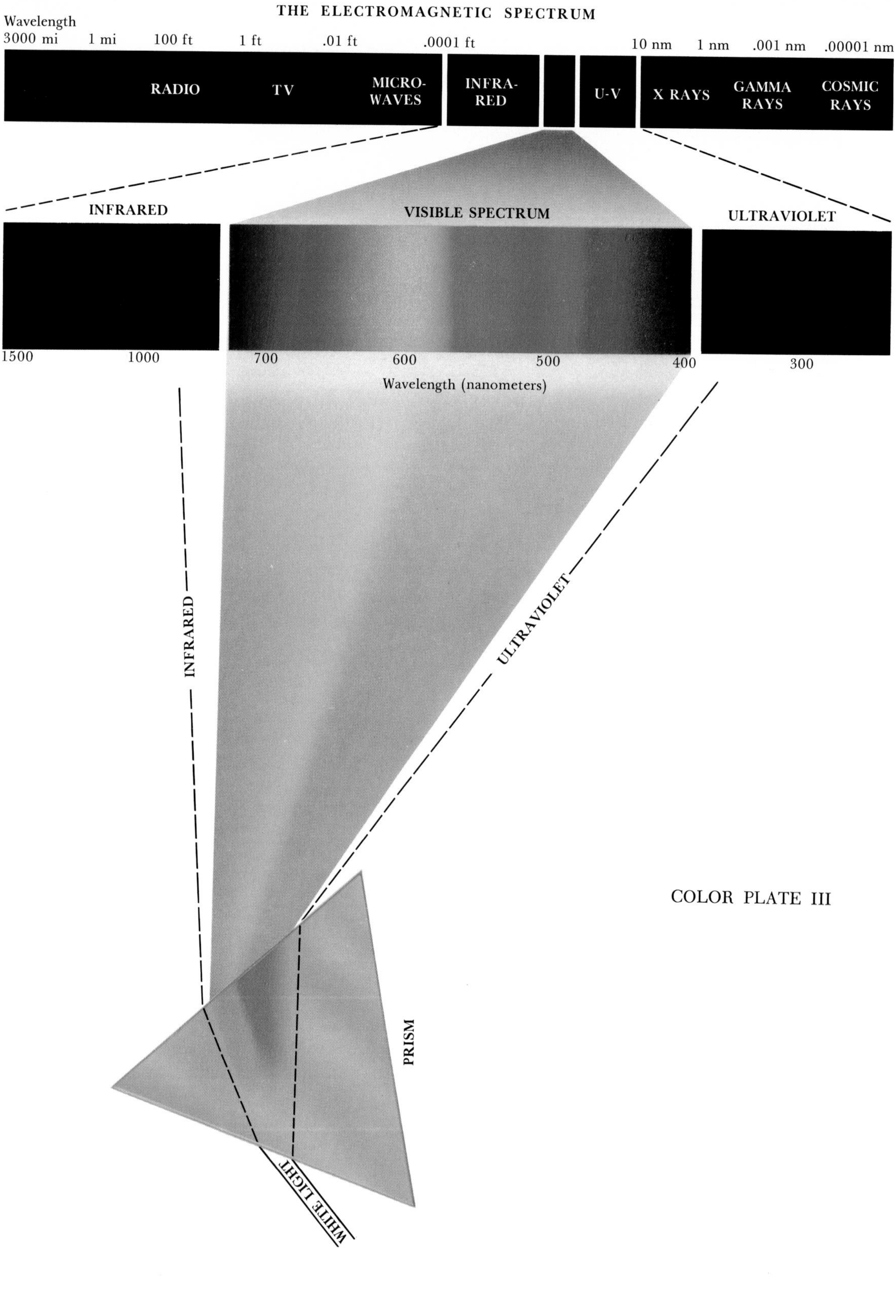

THE ELECTROMAGNETIC SPECTRUM

Wavelength
3000 mi   1 mi   100 ft   1 ft   .01 ft   .0001 ft   10 nm   1 nm   .001 nm   .00001 nm

RADIO   TV   MICRO-WAVES   INFRA-RED   U-V   X RAYS   GAMMA RAYS   COSMIC RAYS

INFRARED   VISIBLE SPECTRUM   ULTRAVIOLET

1500   1000   700   600   500   400   300

Wavelength (nanometers)

INFRARED

ULTRAVIOLET

COLOR PLATE III

PRISM

WHITE LIGHT

Purkinje Shift: *The difference between night and day visual sensitivity (rod and cone vision). Normally, the red and blue flowers are equally visible, with the red appearing brighter than the blue. The two are seen with cone vision. After about 5 min of viewing the picture in very dim light, the red flower will no longer be visible: only the blue will be seen. If the light is dim enough, only rod vision will be involved.*

    The effect can be speeded by viewing the flowers out of the corner of the visual field by fixating on the center of the red flower. In this way, the red falls upon the area of the retina with increased density of cones and the blue falls upon the area with increased density of rods. (Modified from The Color Tree, Inmont Corporation, New York, 1965.)

COLOR PLATE IV

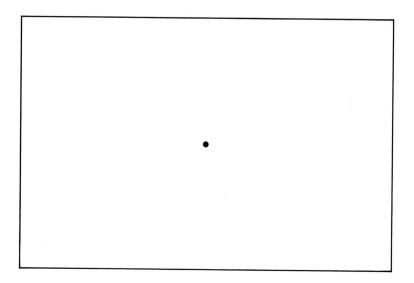

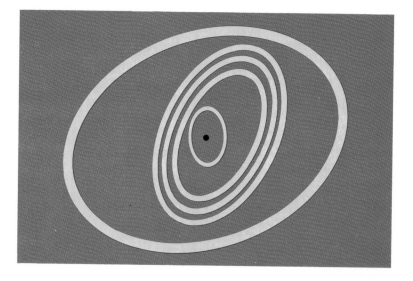

COLOR PLATE V   *Stare at the fixation point in the middle of the bottom picture. The figure will shimmer and parts will disappear. Now look at the fixation point in the rectangle above. The rings and background will be seen in complementary colors. (Modified from The Color Tree, Inmont Corporation, New York, 1965.)*

4 The auditory system

PREVIEW

This is the first chapter of the set of two on the auditory system. The ear is a fascinating piece of machinery. It is composed of tiny bones and membranes, with spiral-shaped tubes filled with fluid. When sound waves arrive at the ear, they are directed down precisely shaped passageways through a complex series of membranes and bones, which transform the sound waves to pressure variations in a liquid-filled cavity. These pressure variations cause bulges in a membrane, and the bulges act on a set of hairs that run along the length of the membrane. Each hair is connected to a cell, and when the hair is bent, the cell sends a signal along the acoustic nerve into the brain. Thus, what we hear is determined by which hairs are bent.

By comparison with the ear, all the other sensory systems are much simpler. In the eye, for example, the mechanical parts are fairly straightforward, and all the complexity resides in the interactions of the nerve cells at the back of the eye, in the retina. With the ear, the neural connections in the ear itself are relatively simple, and all the complexity is put into the mechanical structures that transform sound waves into particular patterns of bulges along the basilar membrane. (The neural circuits for hearing in the brain are quite sophisticated, of course. But the neural circuits within the ear are relatively simple.)

This chapter discusses the operation of the ear, starting with a simple explanation of the physics of sound, then describing in some detail the construction of the ear, and finally concluding with a discussion of the electrical responses to sounds. The next chapter will cover the resulting perceptual experiences of hearing.

To start with, you have to understand something of the nature of sound, of the way in which it is measured, and of the physics of sound. The concept of decibels (dB) is important, and those of you who detest mathematics should not be frightened by the concept. Decibels are pretty simple, and you really do not have to know much about them for these chapters. Decibels will not be too important in this chapter, but they will be used extensively in the next.

In reading the section on the ear, there is no need to learn all the details of the anatomy. The critical terms that you should know are listed at the end of the chapter (as usual), and maybe you ought to refer to them as you go through the chapter. You should know the distinctions among the outer, middle, and inner ear, the ear drum, the round and oval windows, and the three middle ear bones (and their associated muscles). The cochlea is important, and here you should try to understand the mechanics of the thing. Get a picture of a membrane vibrating with a bulge traveling from one end to the other. The shape and location of the bulge is very important for hearing.

The next chapter will try to piece all this information together, illustrating the applications of the details that you read in this chapter. Conceivably, you may wish to skim both chapters rapidly, then back up to read this one with more care, after you have an idea of how the concepts will be used.

THE EAR

The human ear is surprisingly complicated. From outward appearances, it consists mainly of a tube between the outside world and a small internal membrane, the eardrum. Vibrations in the air cause the eardrum to vibrate. These outermost parts of the ear, the pinna, the ear canal, and the eardrum, however, are the least important components for the ear's successful operation. The vibration of the eardrum in response to changing air pressure is only the beginning of a long chain of events, which ultimately produces our perception of sound.

The process of getting the sound through the ear to create neurological signals involves a rather intricately detailed set of steps. Examine Figures 4-1 and 4-2. First, the sound wave arriving at the ear travels down the auditory canal and causes the membrane at the end—*the eardrum*—to vibrate. This vibration is transmitted through the three small bones

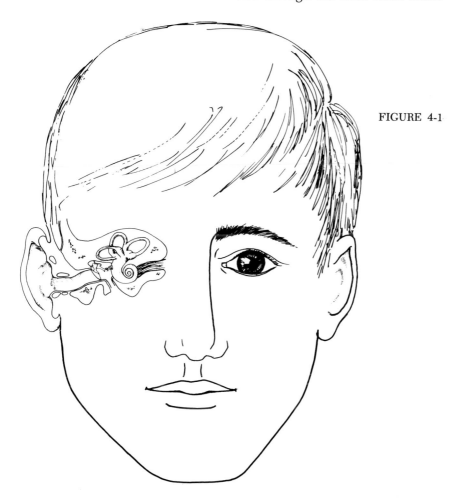

FIGURE 4-1

FIGURE 4-2

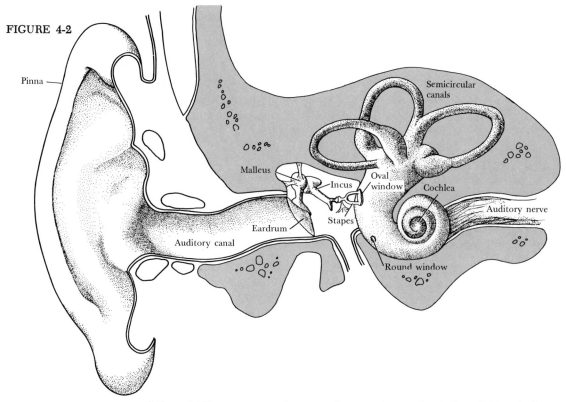

Pinna

Semicircular canals

Malleus

Incus

Oval window

Cochlea

Auditory nerve

Stapes

Eardrum

Auditory canal

Round window

of the middle ear to another membrane, the *oval window*. This window is the opening into the bony, spiral shaped structure of the inner ear, *the cochlea*. Fluids in the cochlea are set into motion by the movements of the oval window and, in turn, cause a membrane that lies along the spiral inside the cochlea to vibrate. The vibration pattern of this last membrane, *the basilar membrane*, is sensed by several rows of hairs that line the membrane, causing the cells to which they are connected to create the neural impulses that carry the acoustic information to the brain. Each component in this strange path has a good reason for its presence. Our task is to discover how each of these components contributes to the development of the neural message sent along the auditory nerve to the brain and then, how that message is decoded into the psychological experiences of sound, of music, and of speech.

THE PHYSICS OF SOUND

Sound consists of pressure variations. When an object "makes a sound" it causes pressure waves to propagate out through the surrounding medium. The sound pressures measured some distance away from the sound source create an imperfect image of the sound pressures initially generated. In part this is because the wave has been attenuated by its travel through the air and, in part, because of various types of reflections and refractions caused by objects encountered in the path of the wave.

For the simplest kind of sound, the pressure variations in the air over time produce a waveform that looks like that in Figure 4-3. To describe this waveform (a *sine wave*) three things must be specified: how rapidly it is varying (its *frequency*); how great a pressure it produces (its *amplitude*); when it starts (its *phase*). In general (with exceptions

The frequency of sound

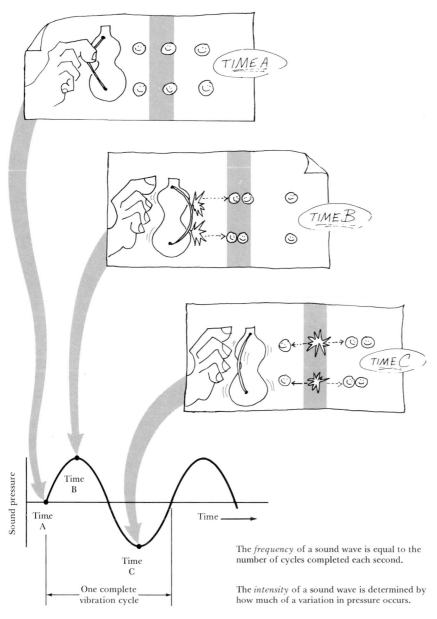

The *frequency* of a sound wave is equal to the number of cycles completed each second.

The *intensity* of a sound wave is determined by how much of a variation in pressure occurs.

The graph shows the pressure measured at the shaded (gray) area in each of the panels.   FIGURE 4-3

that will be described later), the larger the amplitude of the sine wave, the louder it sounds; the higher the frequency, the higher the pitch. A sine wave with a frequency of 261.63 cycles per second, for example, has a pitch of middle C on the musical scale. One *cycle per second* is called one *hertz* (Hz).[1]

Although the description of the variations in sound pressure with time produce a complete description of the sound, it is often more convenient to describe the wave in an entirely different fashion. Look at the sound pressure patterns shown in Figures 4-4 and 4-5. These complex

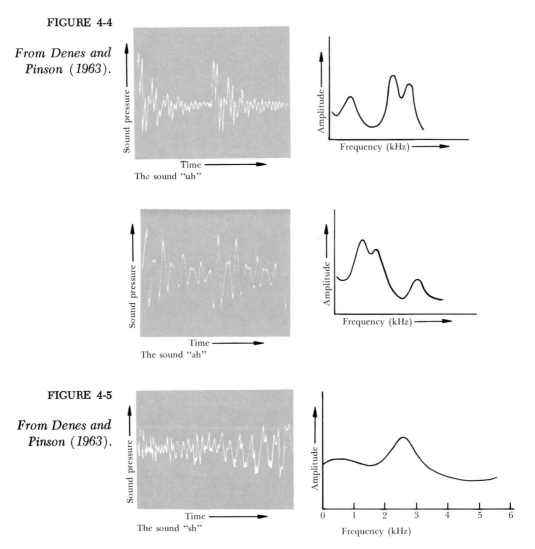

FIGURE 4-4

From Denes and Pinson (1963).

The sound "uh"

The sound "ah"

FIGURE 4-5

From Denes and Pinson (1963).

The sound "sh"

---

[1] The unit of frequency comes from the name of the German physicist, Heinrich R. Hertz (1857–1894). Frequency is often specified in *kilohertz* (*kHz*), where 1 kHz is equal to 1000 Hz.

time waves are awkward to handle. They can be dealt with more easily by breaking up the complex wave into simple elementary components, namely, the sine waves just discussed. The rationale is based on a theorem by the mathematician *Fourier* (1768–1830), who proved that any complex waveform (with certain restrictions) can be represented by a combination of sinusoidal waves of specific frequencies, intensities, and starting times: The decomposition of a waveform into its individual component frequencies is called *Fourier analysis.*

Figure 4-6

Representing complex waves by their sinusoidal components seems also to be most compatible with the way the ear actually deals with sounds. In fact, the ear appears to do a rough Fourier analysis of the incoming signal. If a 440-Hz tone (A above middle C) is played together with a 698-Hz tone (an F), it is still possible to hear the two individual notes in the resulting combination. This fact first impressed the German physicist Georg Ohm (1787–1854), and the correspondence between what is heard and the representation of sounds in terms of the separate frequency

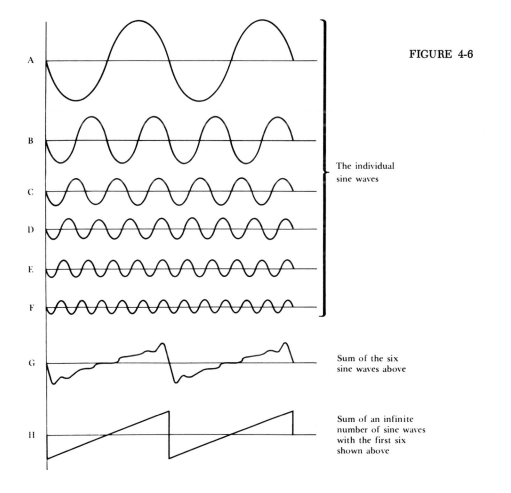

FIGURE 4-6

The individual sine waves

Sum of the six sine waves above

Sum of an infinite number of sine waves with the first six shown above components has come to be known as Ohm's Law. (This is the Ohm who proclaimed the Ohm's Law of electricity; same Ohm, different law.) Things are quite different with light. When a light of a frequency that looks red (a wavelength of 671 nm) is mixed with a light of a frequency that looks green (a wavelength of 536 nm), the resulting mixture is a light that looks yellow (a wavelength of 589 nm). Unlike the auditory system, the visual system does not keep separate the different frequencies

Table 4-1

Sound	*Intensity (dB)*
	200
Manned spacecraft launch (from 150 feet)	• 180
	160
Pain threshold	•
	140
Loud thunder: rock band	•
	120
Shouting	• 100
Conversation	• 80
	60
	40
Soft whisper	•
	20
Threshold of hearing at 1000 Hz	• 0

Sound	*Frequency (Hz)*
Lowest note on piano	27.5
Lowest note of bass singer	100
Lowest note on clarinet	104.8
Middle C on piano	261.6
Standard tuning pitch (A above middle C)	440
Upper range of soprano	1,000
Highest note on piano	4,180
Harmonics of musical instruments	10,000
Limit of hearing for older persons	12,000
Limit of hearing	16,000–20,000

impinging upon it: Visual waveforms are combined by the eye, leaving no trace of the individual components.

As is true with light intensities, the difference in sound intensity between the weakest sound that can be heard and a sound producing physical pain is immense. At 2000 Hz, for example, the most intense sound that is tolerable is about one thousand billion times more intense than the weakest detectable sound. This enormous range of intensities makes it inconvenient to describe sound intensities directly. The range is compressed by describing sound intensities in *decibels*.

The intensity of sound

Table 4-1

DECIBELS[2]

To compress the very large range of physical intensities of sound, we use the trick of expressing intensities in terms of how many powers of ten one intensity is greater than another. This procedure is named after the inventor of the telephone, Alexander Graham Bell, although his last name has been shortened. Thus, if one intensity is a million times another (10^6 times greater), it is 6 bels more than the other. If an intensity is $1/1000$ of another (10^{-3}), it is 3 bels less than the other. This is the same as having the number of bels between two intensities be given by the logarithm of their ratios. Actually, it turns out there are not enough bels in the span of sound intensities, so intensity ratios are usually specified in terms of the number of *tenths of bels* they contain. These are called *decibels*, abbreviated *dB*. In the two examples above, the intensities are 60 and −30 dB apart. The number of decibels that separate two intensities I and I_0 is:

$$\text{Number of dB} = 10 \log (I/I_0)$$

1. Doubling (or halving) the ratio of signal intensities adds approximately (subtracts) 3 dB.
2. Multiplying (or dividing) the ratio of signal intensities by 10 adds (subtracts) 10 dB.
3. If two sounds are separated by $10n$ dB, their intensity ratio is 10^n. For example, a 60 dB difference in the intensities of two sounds means that one sound is 10^6 (1 million) times more intense than the other.
4. Since decibels refer to the ratio of two intensities, to say that a sound has a level of 65 dB is completely meaningless unless the comparison sound is known. Generally, whenever you see statements of this form, it means that the sound is 65 dB more intense than the international standard reference level of 0.0002 dynes/cm². This standard is a very low sound pressure. It is, approximately, the weakest sound that can be detected by a human listener for a sound of 1000 Hz.

---

[2] Although this box is similar to the box on decibels in Chapter 2, please look it over long enough to notice the differences between the standard references for sound and light.

In this book, we will usually refer to sound levels by *dB spl*, for *sound pressure level*. This means that we are using the standard reference level of 0.0002 dynes/cm². When you read the technical literature, you might also encounter *dB sl* and *dBA*. These are measures of sound intensity designed to be relevant to the human ear: *dB sl* is *sensation level*—the reference level is the minimum detectable sound; *dBA* has the sensitivity curve of the human (Figure 5-2) built into the measuring instrument.

Decibels

Number of dB = $10 \log (I/I_0)$

I/I_0	dB	I/I_0	dB
0.0001	−40	10000.0	40
0.001	−30	1000.0	30
0.010	−20	100.0	20
0.032	−15	31.6	15
0.10	−10	10.0	10
0.13	−9	7.9	9
0.16	−8	6.3	8
0.20	−7	5.0	7
0.25	−6	4.0	6
0.32	−5	3.2	5
0.40	−4	2.5	4
0.50	−3	2.0	3
0.63	−2	1.6	2
0.79	−1	1.3	1
1.00	0	1.0	0

THE MECHANICS
OF THE EAR

The inner ear

To the psychologist, the most important part of the ear is the tiny snail-shaped bony structure in the inner ear called the *cochlea*. The cochlea is a tube, coiled up 2½ times (in the human) and filled with a saline solution. In the human, the cochlea is about the size of a sugar cube— about 0.2 inches long and 0.4 inches wide (0.5 cm long, 1 cm wide).

There are two openings in the bone that encloses the cochlea. One, a small membrane called the *oval window* is connected to the last bone in the lever chain of the middle ear. Vibrations from the eardrum via the middle ear bones pass into the cochlea through this membrane. Because the cochlea is filled with an incompressible fluid, some means must be found for relieving the pressures generated at the oval window. This is done with another small opening in the bone structure, also covered by a thin membrane. This is the opening at the rear of the cochlea—the *round window*. [You can remember which window is which by a simple mnemonic device: The *O*pening into the cochlea is the *O*val window (**O**); the window at the *R*ear is the *R*ound window (**R**).]

Figures 4-7 & 4-8

Inside the cochlea is a highly sophisticated mechanism for converting the incoming pressure variations into the electrical signals that travel along the many thousand fibers of the auditory nerve. It is easier to examine this mechanism if we unwind the cochlea (which is possible artistically, but not physically) so that you can see inside, as is done in Figure 4-9.

The two membranes running the length of the cochlea divide it into three different regions, each of which is filled with fluid. The membrane that has most importance for our discussion is the *basilar membrane*. Figure 4-10 This membrane extends all the way from the start of the cochlea (the *base*), where the middle ear bone vibrates the oval window, to very near the end of the inner tip (the *apex*) of the coil. At the apex there is a small space between the membrane and the walls of the cochlea. When stretched out, the basilar membrane is about 1.4 inches long (3.5 cm), with a width that increases from the oval window to the apex. This increase in width plays an important role in its operation. Note several things about the basilar membrane. First, it starts out by the oval

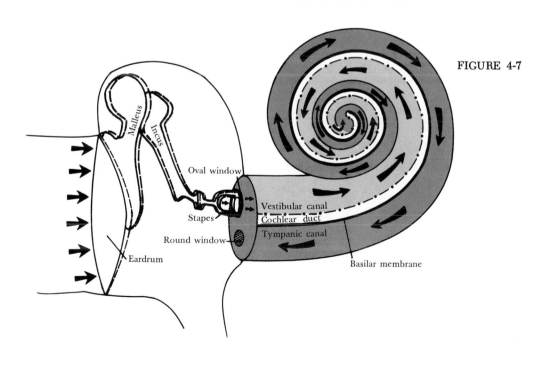

FIGURE 4-7

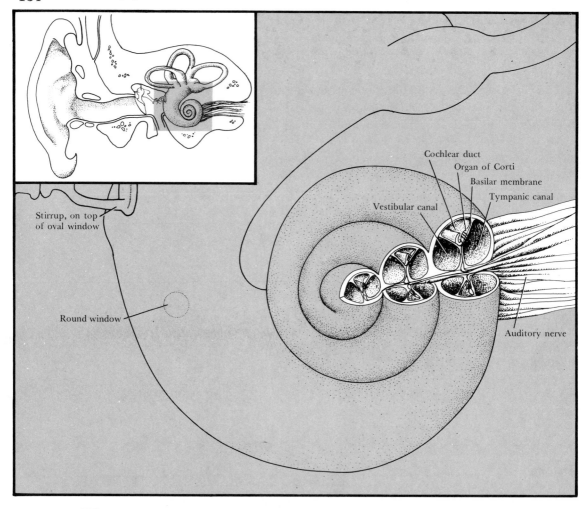

Cochlear duct
Organ of Corti
Basilar membrane
Tympanic canal
Vestibular canal
Auditory nerve
Stirrup, on top of oval window
Round window

FIGURE 4-8

and round windows, the oval window being above it, the round window below it. Thus, when we describe position along the membrane, we do so in terms of distance from the round or oval window and also distance from the apex. Second, although the cochlea itself gets narrower as it goes from the window end toward the apex, the membrane does the opposite: the membrane is wider near the apex than near the windows. Finally, the membrane decreases in stiffness towards the apex. All these factors—a widening of the membrane, an increase in mass, and a decrease in stiffness—make the part at the apex more responsive to low-frequency sounds, and the part at the oval and round windows more responsive to high frequencies.

Pressure exerted inward at the oval window produces a pressure in the fluids above the basilar membrane that is applied, essentially, instantaneously across the whole length of the membrane. (The pressure wave requires only about 20 millionths of a second to travel the length of the cochlea.) Thus, the pattern of activity produced in the basilar membrane does not depend upon which end of the cochlea is stimulated. If the system were set into motion at the apex rather than the oval window it would work just as well.

The basilar membrane itself does not react immediately to the pressure that is applied to it. As one watches the membrane where the oval window begins vibrating there appears to be a traveling wave: First it bulges at the end by the oval window, then the bulge gradually travels up the membrane toward the apex. It takes several milliseconds for the bulge to go from one end of the basilar membrane to the other. The distance it travels depends upon the frequency of the sound wave. The height of the wave is directly proportional to the amplitude of the sound: as the sound level increases there is a corresponding increase in the height of the travelling wave.

The traveling bulge results from the elastic properties of the membrane. Remember that the membrane increases in width as it goes from the oval window toward the apex and decreases in stiffness, being some 100 times stiffer at the oval window end than at the apex. These factors, combined with the geometry of the cochlea itself, cause the size of the bulge produced by a sound wave to increase gradually as the wave moves out from the oval window. The point along the membrane at which it reaches its maximum size depends on the frequency of the sound. The displacement then drops off rapidly as the wave continues on to the end of the membrane. For high-frequency tones, the maximum displacement of the basilar membrane occurs near the oval window, and there is very little activity in the remainder of the membrane. For low-frequency tones, the bulge travels all the way to the apex, reaching its peak just before the end of the membrane.

The vibration pattern converts different sound frequencies into activity at different locations along the basilar membrane. This recoding of the frequency of an acoustic signal into a particular place of vibration along the basilar membrane is what is meant by the statement earlier in the chapter, "The ear appears to perform a rough Fourier analysis of the incoming signal."

Movements of the basilar membrane

FIGURE 4-9

Basilar membrane —

Figures 4-11 & 4-12

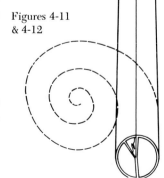

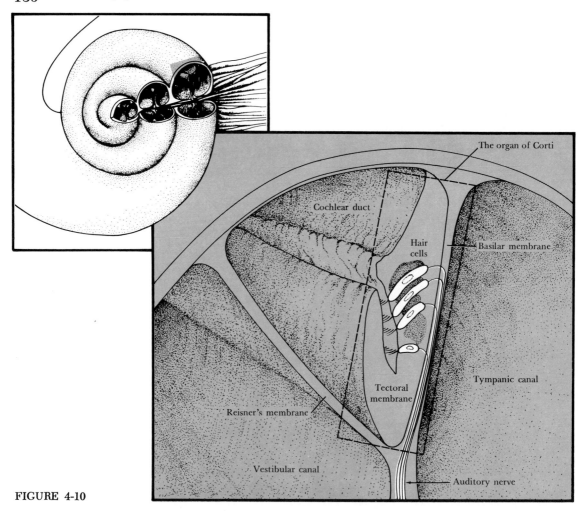

FIGURE 4-10

The organ of Corti

Cochlear duct

Hair cells

Basilar membrane

Tectoral membrane

Tympanic canal

Reisner's membrane

Vestibular canal

Auditory nerve

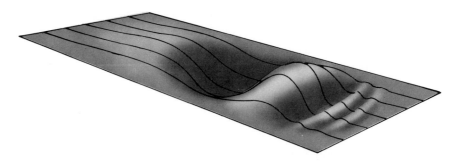

FIGURE 4-11 *After G. L. Rasmussen and W. F. Windle (Eds.), Neural mechanisms of the auditory and vestibular systems, 1960. Courtesy of Charles C Thomas, Publisher, Springfield, Illinois.*

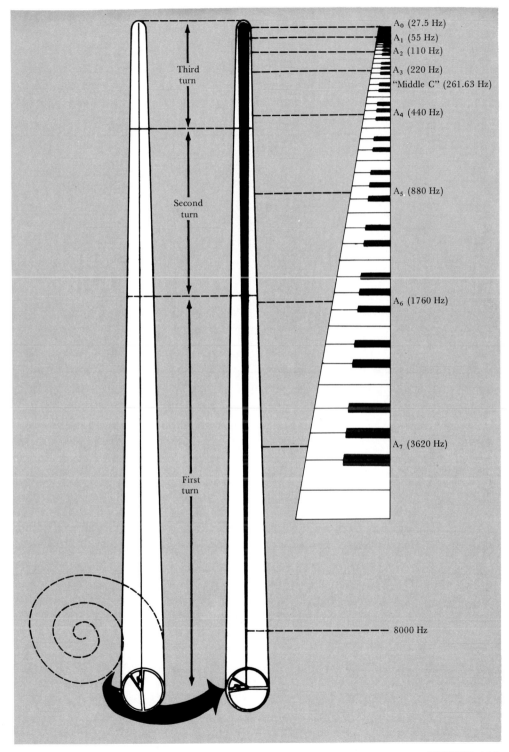

A_0 (27.5 Hz)
A_1 (55 Hz)
A_2 (110 Hz)
A_3 (220 Hz)
"Middle C" (261.63 Hz)
A_4 (440 Hz)

A_5 (880 Hz)

A_6 (1760 Hz)

A_7 (3620 Hz)

8000 Hz

Third turn

Second turn

First turn

FIGURE 4-12

The hair cells

Figure 4-13

The basilar membrane is really a piece of skin and, like skin, it has hair cells attached to it. These hair cells are part of a complex structure called the *organ of Corti*, located along the top of the membrane. In the human, there are approximately 23,500 of these hair cells arranged into two subdivisions, divided by an arch. The cells on the side of the arch closest to the outside of the cochlea are called *outer hair cells*

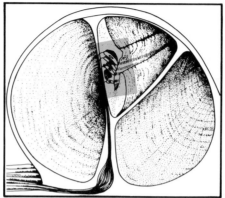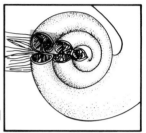

Human cochlea (sectioned)

Enlargement of section of cochlea showing position of organ of Corti and exit of auditory nerve

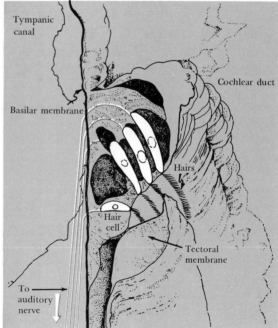

FIGURE 4-13   *Scanning electron microscope photograph of organ of Corti. ×370. Photograph from Bredberg, Lindeman, Ades, West, and Engström (1970).*

and are arranged in rows three to five abreast. The hair cells on the other side of the arch are called *inner hair cells*. They are usually in a single row. There are some 20,000 outer cells, and any given cell may have as many as a hundred hairs protruding from it. There are only about 3500 inner hair cells and about 30,000 nerve fibers that connect both inner and outer hair cells to the brain.

As you can see from the way they are sandwiched between the two membranes in the organ of Corti, any movement in the basilar membrane causes the hair cells to twist and bend. Moreover, since the membranes are anchored, there will be more movement associated with the outer hair cells than with the inner cells. The stresses and strains exerted on the hair cells initiates neural activity in the fibers connected to them, starting the flow of electrical impulses up the auditory nerve.

No matter how elegant the mechanical responses of the ear, they would be of no value unless there were some way of converting this activity into signals that can be used by the nervous system. The mechanical responses convert auditory frequency and intensity into vibration patterns along the basilar membrane. This information must now be analyzed by the nerve cells, which carry the signal along the pathway to the brain. | ELECTRICAL RESPONSES TO SOUND

In a later chapter (Chapter 6) we examine the physiological mechanisms of the brain in some detail. For the present purposes, it is only necessary to know that the various parts of the nervous system are interconnected by neurons, the cells that form the basic building block of the brain. For the moment, simply consider the neuron to be a cell that has two parts: a cell body and a nerve fiber. The fiber carries information from one neuron to another, and it can range in length from microscopic dimensions up to several feet. Nerve fibers can be thought of as wires that carry the basic signals of the nervous system from one location to another. The signals conveyed by neurons are electrical impulses that last around a millisecond in duration and have an amplitude of a few microvolts.

With a careful surgical preparation, a tiny electrode can be inserted into the auditory nerve so that it records the impulses flowing down a single auditory fiber. The first thing that is noticed is that this fiber is not quiet. Even when no sounds are presented it responds sporadically at anywhere up to 150 impulses per second. This *background* or *spontaneous* firing in the absence of any external signal is a characteristic of almost all types of sensory neurons. | *Tuning curves*

The first step in investigating the neuron is to determine what kind of signal makes it respond. We start by presenting a pure tone of moderate intensity and some high frequency, say 10,000 Hz, and then we slowly lower the frequency. At first, the neuron does not seem to notice the tone at all; it continues firing at its spontaneous rate. As the frequency comes within a certain critical range, the neuron's response will increase, reaching a peak at a particular signal frequency called the *critical frequency*. As we continue to lower the frequency, the activity of the neuron again becomes less vigorous, until it finally goes back to its spontaneous background rate. The response of the unit to different frequencies is called a *tuning curve*. It looks like this:

FIGURE 4-14

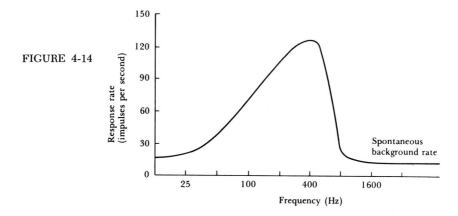

This particular unit appears to be most sensitive to a tone whose frequency is 400 Hz. For frequencies higher than 400 Hz, its response rate drops off rather rapidly. For lower frequencies, the response rate changes more slowly with changing frequencies.

This is the response pattern we expect if the neuron being monitored is reacting directly to the amount of activity in a local region of the basilar membrane. Suppose that the neuron is recording the responses of hair cells in a region about 24 mm from the oval window. The maximum vibration of the membrane occurs at this point when a 400-Hz tone is presented. But there will be some activity at this point when frequencies other than 400 Hz are presented. Here is a diagram of the amplitude of the vibration for frequencies ranging from 25 to 1600 Hz. On the right, the amplitude on the membrane is shown as a function of frequency.

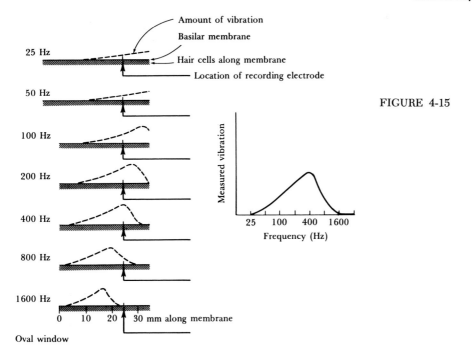

FIGURE 4-15

So far, we have been concerned only with the number of neural impulses produced by a given signal. The temporal patterns in the activity of individual neurons are also important. Consider a neural cell with a critical frequency of 500 Hz. This signal goes through a complete cycle of sound pressures in 2 msec. The impulses from the cell mirror the time properties of the critical frequency: The interval between pulses is approximately 2 msec: The cell fires in synchrony with its signal. Sometimes a pulse will fail to appear at the right time, but when it does reappear, it will again be in synchrony with the repeated cycles of the external signal. In short, a 500-Hz tone tends to produce a regular response of 500 impulses per second.

Even if the cell cannot fire as rapidly as its critical frequency, it still maintains synchrony. Suppose a cell with critical frequency of 500 Hz can only manage a maximum of 250 or 125 impulses per second. It will respond at some frequency that is a rational divisor of the signal frequency, say at 250, 125, or even 67.5 impulses per second. It will not respond to a 500-Hz tone at 73 or 187 impulses per second.

This synchronized firing might be expected from a consideration of the vibration pattern of the basilar membrane. When the membrane is moving up in response to a pressure change, it bends the hair cells

Temporal coding in neural responses

sandwiched between it and the membrane above, initiating the neural impulse. No response occurs when the membrane moves down. Upward movement is produced when the pressure in the fluids above the membrane is reduced, which happens as the oval window is pulled out by the low-pressure (rarefaction) phase of the signals.

The ability of individual neurons to follow the pressure changes of an incoming signal suggests a way of coding frequency. Signal frequency can be determined directly from the impulse rate or from the average interval between pulses. The fact that individual fibers may not be able to keep up with the pressure changes in a given signal (particularly at higher frequencies) is no problem. A large number of fibers are involved in monitoring any given region of the basilar membrane. An individual nerve may miss a few cycles, but its neighbors that are responding to the same frequency will probably respond to these missing components. When the responses of all the units are considered together, there should be a burst of impulses for every rarefaction phase of the signal.

This is precisely what is seen in physiological recordings. The activity rises and falls regularly and in synchrony with the pressure changes in the signal. The auditory nerve seems to be able to follow signals with frequencies as high as 3000–4000 Hz; such frequencies are well above the response rate that can be achieved by any individual unit. Beyond 4000 Hz, the regular cyclic response in the auditory nerve breaks down into a disorganized, continuous impulse flow.

Figure 4-16

Coding of intensity information

Responses of neurons in the acoustic nerve to changing intensities are much less complex than their response patterns to changing frequency. Basically, if the frequency is held constant while intensity increases, the response rate of the units goes up. Of course, it cannot go up indefinitely. In fact, an individual cell may start off at a spontaneous level of some 200 responses per second, increase its rate to, say, 300 responses per second when the intensity is changed by 10 dB, but show no further increases in rate with additional increases in intensity. Thus, the range over which most cells code intensity in the signal is relatively small compared to the total range of hearing. Moreover, there is an enormous variability in both the baseline rates and the reactions of individual cells to increases in the intensity of the signal.

Of course, a cell's increase in its firing rate must still maintain synchrony with the sound wave. Thus, if an individual cell has a spontaneous firing rate of 200 impulses per second, it will react to a sound first by changing the spontaneous, random firing into one synchronized

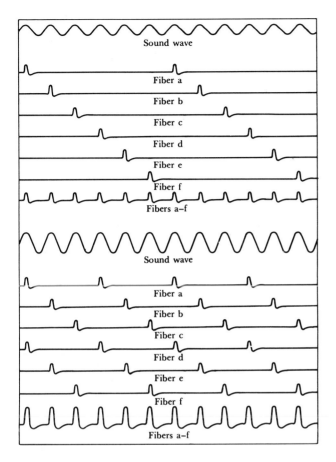

The "volley" theory. Each cycle of the sound wave elicits a response FIGURE 4-16
in at least one fiber in the array, so that the stimulus frequency is
represented in the combined pattern. At higher stimulus intensities (below), more than one fiber responds at a given cycle. From Wever
(1970).

with the signal, and then by increasing the number of neural impulses
it produces to the sound—always, however, maintaining synchrony.

When the basic frequency and intensity information has been encoded
by the auditory nerves, the signal is finally on its way to the brain.
Several different things are done as the signal makes its way up.
Specific auditory information is extracted, localization of the sound
source takes place, and a rough determination of the sound's loudness
and pitch components are extracted. A discussion of the physiological
structures and neural responses of the auditory system can be found in
Chapter 6, "Neural Information Processing."

REVIEW OF TERMS
AND CONCEPTS

In this chapter, the following terms and concepts that we consider to be important have been used. Please look them over. If you are not able to give a short explanation of any of them, you should go back and review the appropriate sections of the chapter.

Terms and concepts you should know

The parts of the ear
the outer ear
   pinna
the middle ear
   malleus (the hammer)
   incus (the anvil)
   stapes (the stirrup)
   eardrum
the inner ear
   cochlea
   oval window
   round window
   basilar membrane
   apex
   how the cochlea is unwound
the basilar membrane
   the traveling wave: what it looks like
   hair cells
   tuning curves
   critical frequency
   how frequency is represented along the membrane
   synchronization of neural impulses with the sound wave
Sound
sound waves
amplitude
frequency
decibels
hertz
Fourier analysis

SUGGESTED
READINGS

The two volumes of *Foundations of modern auditory theory* provide a good summary of much work (Tobias, 1970, 1972). Dallos (1973) provides a good description of the auditory periphery (which is also the title of his book). And Carterette and Friedman's (1976) *Handbook* volume on *Hearing* is probably the best place to start for more advanced treatments.

The works of Georg von Békésy won him a Nobel Prize for his studies of the operation of the inner ear. Anyone who intends to do work in the field of hearing will sooner or later come upon his material. Most of his important articles on hearing are reprinted in Békésy's *Experiments in hearing* (1960). Békésy's papers are delightful to read because he never sticks to a simple topic, but rather delights in demonstrating how the topic he is discussing relates to a wide variety of other phenomena.

The major readings for this chapter are listed at the end of the next; see the Suggested Readings for Chapter 5.

5 The dimensions of sound

PREVIEW

The nature of the auditory experience provides the topic for this chapter. Now, with the knowledge of the physics of sound and the operation of the ear provided by the previous chapter, we can analyze our perception of sound and make some headway toward an explanation of that experience. The two major psychological dimensions of sound studied by psychologists have been loudness and pitch, and so this chapter starts there. In addition, we cover other phenomena, most especially the localization of sound sources. In all of this, we attempt to show through laboratory analyses how these sound experiences play a role in auditory perception in everyday life.

The musician may well be disappointed by the presentation of this chapter. To the musician, our discussion of pitch will seem too simple. Moreover, we barely discuss the perception of complex sounds, of sound quality, timbre, and the other attributes so important to the musical experience. The psychologist's notions of pitch and loudness differ somewhat from the musician's. Our terms refer to a very precisely defined sensation, in particular, to how a listener matches a complex sound to the loudness and pitch of a simple, pure sinusoidal sound. Thus, a psychologist speaks of a sound as having a single pitch and a single loudness. Musicians use these terms differently, often thinking of a sound as having several pitches and several loudnesses. A full treatment and understanding of the richness of the auditory experience and the quality of the sound does not yet exist. The procedures and issues discussed in this chapter provide the tools necessary to treat musical experiences in terms of our psychological understanding. More and more psychologists and musicians are starting to explore the world of sound. As they do so, our knowledge and our perceptual experiences should expand considerably.

In this chapter we talk about how acoustical information is interpreted. You need to know the concepts about the ear and about the specification of sound (frequency in *hertz* and intensity in *decibels*) presented in the previous chapter. If you do not, you should review that chapter.

Make sure you understand the diagram that shows the equiloudness contours and understand their implications for hearing (Figure 5-2). The loudness compensator on audio sets provides a good test. If you can explain the loudness compensator—why it is needed and how it works—then you probably have a good understanding of the sensitivity of the ear.

The concept of masking is important, for it is involved in a lot of real auditory phenomena, such as why the sounds of an airplane will drown out voices, but the equally loud sound of a flute playing some music will not.

The measurement of loudness is important. At least realize that loudness only tends to double when sound intensity gets ten times as large.

The sone scale is used to indicate how *loud* something is, and you should distinguish this from decibels, which tells how *intense* a sound is. Loudness is a psychological measure of sound. Intensity is a physical measure. Loudness depends upon sound intensity, frequency, and other variables. Do not confuse loudness and intensity.

In the discussion on pitch, again it is important to distinguish among several concepts: frequency is not the same as pitch. In addition, the psychological scale of pitch (mels) is not the same as the musical scale. Here is the start of the connection between what happens on the basilar membrane and in the neurons of the ear and what is perceived. A major purpose of this chapter is to consider how the mechanisms of the ear are related to our psychological perceptions.

Two of the most important points of this chapter are how the activity in the nerve fiber and the vibration of the basilar membrane affect perception, and how pitch is perceived. Note well the rationale for place theory and periodicity theory. First we teach you these theories, then tell you they are both incorrect. Don't despair. The theories are extremely important. Although there is a tendency to complain when someone tells you to learn something that is already known to be wrong, the pitch perception theories are important, useful, and not really that far wrong. We think it essential that you understand why each theory was proposed, why it was initially thought to be right, and what the problems are.

How sound is localized is the next topic, and again there are opposing theories. But both of the sound localization theories are considered to be correct, one working at low frequencies, the other at high frequencies. Understand the reasons why. These theories should help you understand stereophonic and quadrophonic sound reproduction.

SENSORY EXPERIENCES[1]

As we discussed in the beginning of Chapter 3, it is important not to confuse the psychological attributes of an experience with the physical attributes. The physics of sound can be specified with great precision. The psychological impressions that result from exposure to a particular physical sound are not so easily specified. Moreover, the psychological impressions may depend upon the history of experiences that the observer has had. With sound, the two most obvious psychological dimensions are loudness and pitch, but there are also other experiences of sound quality —timbre, dissonance, consonance, and musicality.

With the simplest of physical waveforms—a pure sine wave of the type produced by a simple, smooth whistle or an electronic oscillator—the physical aspects can be described by its frequency, intensity, and phase (when the signal starts). If the intensity of a sine wave is increased, the sound will increase in loudness. If the frequency is increased, the pitch will increase. As a result, it is tempting to associate the psychological dimensions of loudness and pitch with the physical dimensions of intensity and frequency; however, to do so is incorrect. For one thing, the relations are not linear: doubling the intensity does not double the loudness. For another, the relations are not independent: varying the frequency of a sound will affect both its loudness and its pitch. Finally, the relations are not constant: the perception of the pitch and loudness of a tone depends upon the context in which it appears and the nature of the other sounds that are present at the same time or slightly preceding the tone. Even the simplest physical dimension is subjected to a complex analysis by the nervous system.

It is important not to make the mistake of confusing the psychological perception of sound—loudness, pitch, and timbre—with the physical properties of intensity, frequency, and spectrum. They are different things. An orchestra creates a rich auditory experience. Rock groups, music synthesizers, electronic sounds are all combined in experimental works that stimulate the listener. New recording and playback techniques provide the means of recreating for the listener the experiences of the original event, be it a conference, a speech, a musical performance, or even the special effects imagined by creative composers that cannot exist, except through recordings.

Meanwhile, noise sources pollute the environment. The noises from aircraft annoy and disturb, sometimes being simply a tolerable nuisance, other times disrupting ongoing events, sometimes even causing physical damage and mental fatigue.

---

[1] This section is almost identical to the corresponding section in Chapter 3. If you read that section, you need only skim this one.

FIGURE 5-1

Table 5-1

Physical Variables

Psychological Variables	Of Primary Importance	Of Secondary Importance
Hearing		
Loudness	Sound intensity	Frequency of sound waves (Hz)
Pitch	Frequency of sound waves (Hz)	Sound intensity
Timbre (quality)	Complexity of sound wave	—
Volume (size)	Frequency and intensity	—
Density	Frequency and intensity	—
Consonance (smoothness) Dissonance (roughness)	Harmonic structure	Musical sophistication
Noisiness	Intensity	Frequency composition, temporal parameters
Annoyance	Intensity	Frequency composition, meaningfulness

All these characteristics of sound are within the domain of the psychologist. From a knowledge of the mechanics of the ear, an understanding of the psychological dimensions of pitch and loudness, and a study of the phenomena of masking and auditory space perception, psychologists can talk about, explain, and predict many of the attributes of the auditory experience.

In this chapter, we examine some of the rich auditory experiences produced by sounds. We explore in turn four topics: loudness, pitch, the critical band, and auditory spatial perception. With each topic we introduce what has been learned from science and then deduce the practical implications. We examine the role of the four factors on the perceptions of music, speech, and noise.

LOUDNESS

The loudness of a tone depends upon both its intensity and its frequency. When frequency is constant, intense sounds appear louder than weak sounds. But when intensity is held constant, very high and very low frequency sounds seem much softer than sounds of intermediate frequency. In the extreme cases, this obviously must be true. Consider a whistle of intermediate frequency at a medium intensity level. Keep the intensity of the whistle constant but change the frequency so that it goes below 20 Hz or above 20,000 Hz (you have to do this electronically—you cannot do it by whistling). At these extreme frequencies, the sound becomes inaudible. Loudness, then, depends upon frequency, if for no other reason than the simple fact that there are limits in the range of frequencies to which the ear can respond. But loudness also depends on frequency within the normal hearing range.

Equiloudness contours

The interaction between frequency and intensity in the perception of loudness can be determined by asking people to compare two tones that have differing frequencies and intensities. Let one tone be the *standard* and give it a fixed frequency, intensity, and duration: for example, let the standard be a 1000-Hz tone with a sound pressure level (spl) of 40 dB spl presented for 0.5 sec. Let the second tone be the *comparison* tone. Make it 0.5-sec long also, but with a frequency different from that of the standard, say 3000 Hz. Now, the task of the listener is to listen alternately to the standard and the comparison tones, adjusting the sound level of the comparison until it sounds exactly as loud as the standard. When that is done, set the comparison tone to a different frequency and repeat the whole procedure. The typical result is shown in Figure 5-2: a curve describing the sound levels at which tones of various frequencies have the same perceived loudness as the standard. This curve is called an *equiloudness contour*. The level of the standard tone can be called the *loudness level* of the entire curve because it has been constructed by varying the comparison-tone frequency systematically while keeping the loudness of the comparison equal to the loudness of the standard.

Figure 5-2 shows the results of an experiment using many different standards. For each curve, the standard tone was always at a frequency of 1000 Hz, but with different sound levels. The curve labeled 40 corresponds to the example just discussed: The standard tone had an intensity of 40 dB spl and a frequency of 1000 Hz. The curve labeled 100 is an equiloudness contour obtained when different frequencies are compared against a standard tone with an intensity of 100 dB spl, but still with a frequency of 1000 Hz.

Note that Figure 5-2 shows how loudness varies with both sound level and frequency. Examine the curve in the figure labeled 50: the curve for a standard tone of 50 dB spl at 1000 Hz. When the comparison tone is around 20 Hz, it must be made quite intense (about 95 dB spl) in order to be just as loud as the 1000 Hz standard tone. As the comparison frequency is increased, the sound level of the comparison tone gets closer to the sound level of the standard. In fact, at 500 Hz, the comparison tone can be slightly weaker than the standard and still sound equally loud. Finally, although not shown on this figure, as the comparison tone goes above 10,000 Hz, it must be made more intense again to equal the standard tone in loudness.

The bottommost contour (the dashed line) shows the absolute sensitivity of the ear to different frequencies. Sounds below this line cannot

FIGURE 5-2

Equiloudness contours from data of Robinson and Dadson (1956).

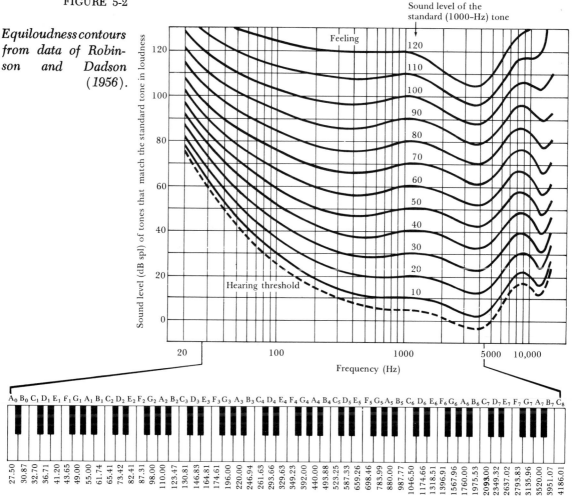

be heard. Sounds on the line are just barely detectable (and are thus also assumed to be equal in loudness). At the other extreme, the topmost contour, very intense sounds lead, first, to a sensation of "tickling" in the ear and then, as intensity is increased further, to pain. Sounds in these regions can lead to ear damage. (Damage can also occur from sounds of weaker sound levels if there is prolonged exposure.) Note that the equiloudness contour at the threshold of pain is much flatter than the contour at the threshold of hearing. If sounds are intense enough, they tend to sound equally loud, regardless of frequency.

It may come as a surprise to see where the sounds of the instruments of an orchestra lie on the equiloudness contours. The piano has the widest range of frequencies, going from about 30 to about 4000 Hz.

Listening to music

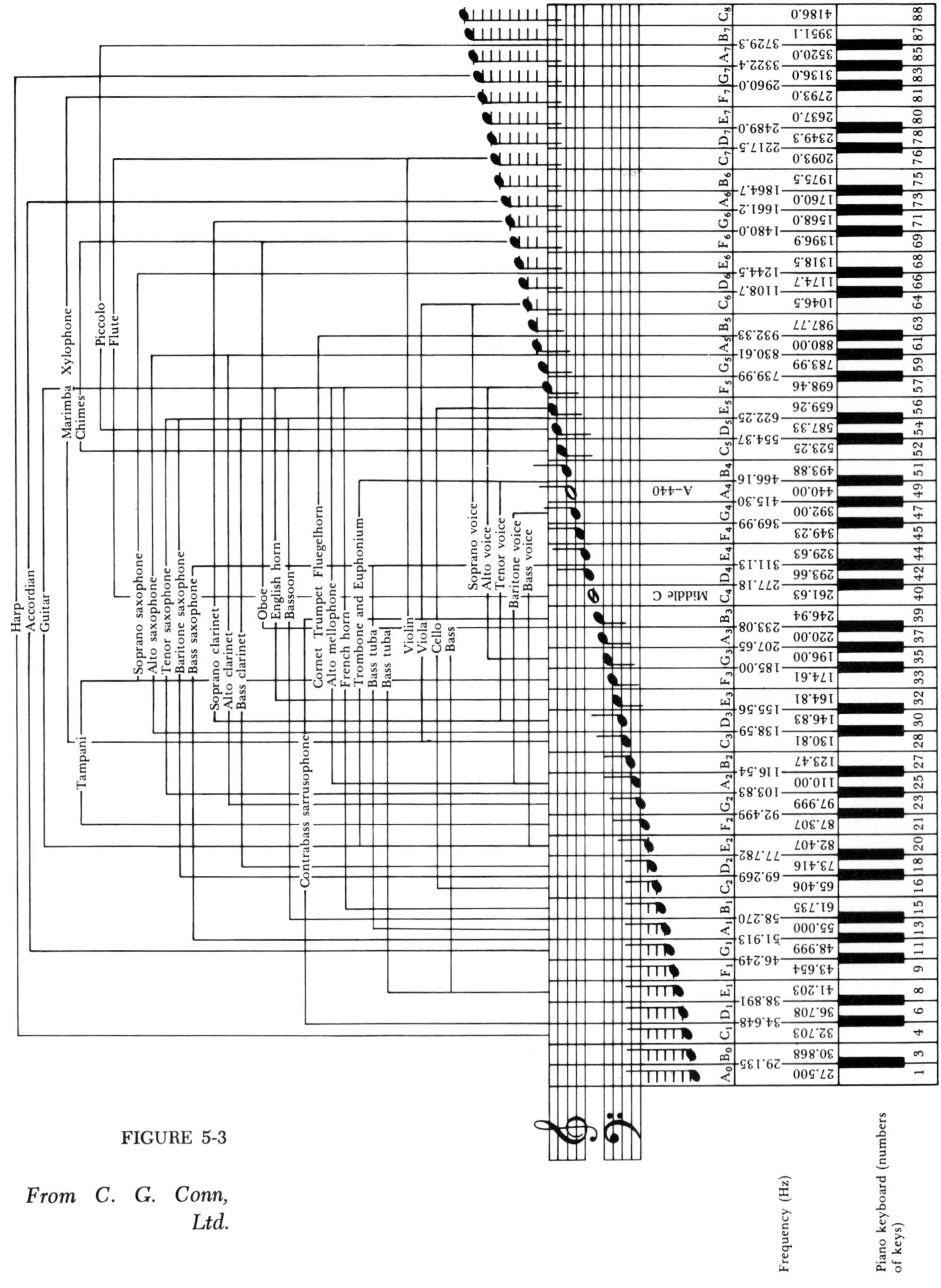

FIGURE 5-3

From C. G. Conn, Ltd.

Frequency (Hz)

Piano keyboard (numbers of keys)

Middle C $(C_4)^2$ on the piano is about 260 Hz (261.63, to be exact).

To help you see where these frequencies lie on the equiloudness contours, we show a piano keyboard in Figure 5-2 and indicate what region it covers on the curves. Figure 5-3 shows the frequency range of a number of different musical instruments. Thus, most of the sounds of musical instruments lie in the region where the perception of loudness is most sensitive to changes in frequency. This has two results: One, unless you listen to the orchestra at reasonable intensity levels, you will not hear many of the frequencies emitted by the instruments; second, the loudness relations among the instruments, so carefully worked out and controlled by the conductor, depend upon your listening to the music at the same intensity that the conductor expected for the audience. When listening to recordings of symphonic music at home, you are not likely to turn up the level on your audio equipment to recreate the intensities originally present in the hall. You hear the music on a different set of loudness contours than the conductor planned for, so that you hear a different piece of music than the conductor intended.

The problems of playing back music so that it sounds the same in the home as it did when it was recorded are well known. Consider a segment of a symphony piece which is being played so that the overall sound intensity is approximately the same at different frequencies, as shown in Figure 5-4. When a recording is played back at home, the overall picture looks similar but the intensity is reduced. Now some of the sound levels fall below the threshold of hearing. Lower frequencies that were perfectly audible at the concert can no longer be heard. Moreover, as the levels change, the relative loudness at different frequencies also changes. If an organ plays a scale at very high intensity going from low notes to high ones, in the actual auditorium all the notes would be perceived to have approximately the same loudness (at high intensities, the equiloudness contours are relatively flat). At home, however, when the scale is played back at a reasonable listening level, not only would some of the lower frequencies be inaudible, but they would now fall in the region where frequency is affecting loudness: The notes would appear to get louder and louder up to about two or three octaves above middle C, where they would start decreasing in loudness. (Note from Figure 5-2 that as frequencies decrease below

---

[2] Subscripts indicate which octave of the note is referred to. The notation is the standard used by acousticians, but not always by musicians. The first C on the piano keyboard is named C_1. All notes within the octave immediately above it are given the subscript 1: D_1, E_1, . . . , B_1. The second C on the keyboard, and all the notes within the octave above it, are subscripted 2: C_2, . . . , B_2. By this scheme, the middle C on the piano keyboard is C_4; the note on which the instruments of an orchestra tune is A_4. The highest note on the piano is C_8; the lowest is A_0 (see Backus, 1968).

FIGURE 5-4

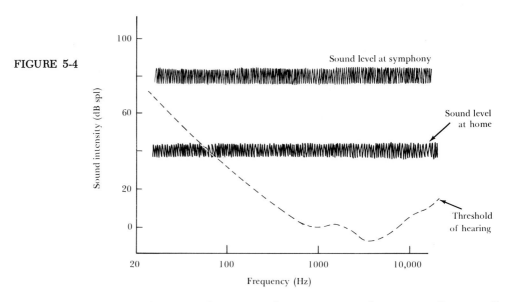

1000 Hz, they must be increased in intensity to be perceived as equally loud; thus, when intensity is constant, as frequency decreases the notes are perceived as getting softer.)

Loudness compensators. Most high-quality audio amplifiers now come with circuits that compensate for these psychological mechanisms. The control labeled *loudness compensator*, or sometimes simply *loudness*, makes the audio set overemphasize very low- and very high-frequency sounds when it is playing at low sound-levels. At high sound-levels, the loudness compensator should automatically be disconnected so that

FIGURE 5-5

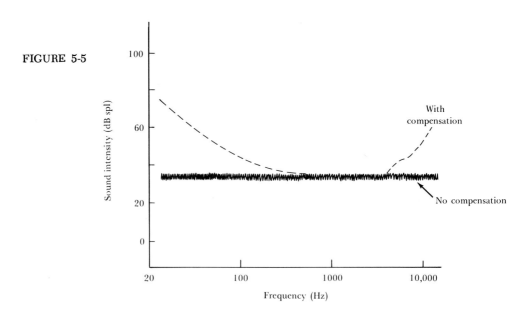

it no longer has any effect. With good playback equipment, the effect of loudness compensation on the sound levels is shown in Figure 5-5. This results in a perceived loudness that looks like that shown in Figure 5-6. Actually, this compensation can work only if everything is done just right. The compensatory mechanism must take into account the peculiarities of the acoustics of the room where the speakers are located, as well as the particular sound equipment being used.

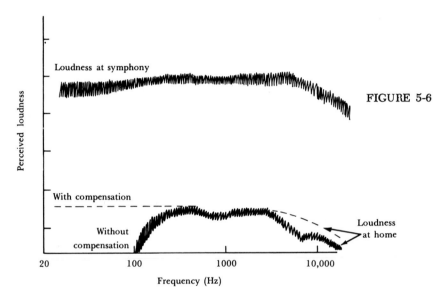

FIGURE 5-6

The loudness of a sound depends not only on its own intensity but also on other sounds present at the same time. Sounds *mask* one another: The presence of one sound makes another more difficult to hear. Rustling of papers, clapping of hands, coughing—all these tend to mask speech or music. To determine the effect of a masking, it is necessary to measure how much more intense a *test sound* must be in order to be heard in the presence of a *masking sound*. The procedure is basically similar to the one used for obtaining equiloudness contours. *Masking*

The masking experiment. One way of doing the experiment goes something like this: Two tones are presented to an observer; one is called the *test tone*, the other the *masker*. The masker is set at some fixed intensity and frequency. Then the test tone is set to some fixed frequency and the intensity value adjusted until the test tone can just barely be detected. This procedure is repeated for different values of frequency of the test tone until an entire *masking curve* has been traced out, showing exactly how intense the test tone must be at different frequencies in order that it can be detected in the presence of the masker. Once the masking curve has been determined for one particular masker, the masker itself might be changed in either frequency or intensity and a new masking curve determined.

A typical result of this experiment is shown in Figure 5-7. In this case, the frequency of the masker[3] was held fixed at 1200 Hz and the

FIGURE 5-7

From Zwicker and Scharf (1965).

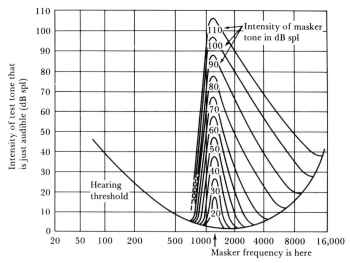

Frequency of test tone (Hz)

intensity was varied from 20 to 110 dB spl in steps of 10 dB to give 10 different masking curves.

The most striking feature of these data is the asymmetry. The masker has relatively little effect on tones below its own frequency of about 1200 Hz, but tones above this frequency are made much more difficult to hear by the presence of the masker.

The mechanism of masking. One of the explanations for this asymmetry comes from an examination of the vibration patterns of the basilar membrane. Remember the patterns shown in Figure 5-8: Low-frequency sounds tend to produce activity over much of the membrane, whereas high frequencies affect a more restricted region. If we examine these effects in more detail, as in Figure 5-9, we can compare the vibration patterns on the basilar membrane produced by the masker with those produced by the test tones. When the tone is weak and slightly higher in frequency than the masker, no part of the activity pattern produced by the tone manages to make itself felt above the pattern already caused by the masking noise. But the same weak tone at a frequency lower than the masker produces new activity in a separate nonoverlapping region. It does manage to be heard. Note that as the signal level is

[3] Actually, the masker was not a pure tone, but rather a narrow band of noise. Noise gives smoother results than does a tone. Other than this, the differences between the masking produced by a pure tone and by narrow-band noise are slight, and only of technical importance.

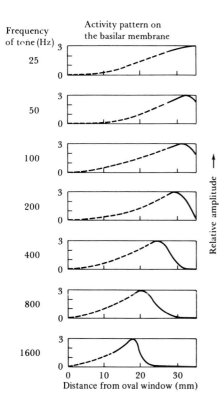

Frequency of tone (Hz)

Activity pattern on the basilar membrane

25
50
100
200
400
800
1600

Relative amplitude →

Distance from oval window (mm)

FIGURE 5-8

From Békésy (1949).

FIGURE 5-9

After Zwicker and Scharf (1965).

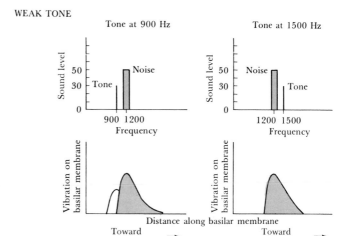

WEAK TONE

Tone at 900 Hz

Tone at 1500 Hz

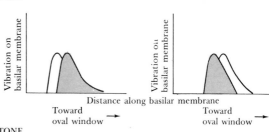

MEDIUM TONE

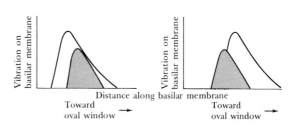

INTENSE TONE

increased, the roles of the test signal and masker are reversed. A low frequency, relatively high-intensity test tone will mask the masker.

Masking of music. Masking adds another factor to the perception of loudness and of music. Intense, lower-frequency instruments mask the sounds of weak, higher-frequency instruments. The violas mask the violins; the timpani mask the violas; the brass mask the woodwinds. But when the sounds are played back in the home, the intensity is less than when they were recorded. As a result, the masking patterns are changed. Suddenly you can follow the fine fingerings of the violin or guitar, for the sounds of the basses are much reduced in level. Is this a virtue? Not necessarily. The composer, conductor, and the players did not have this in mind; their musical intuitions took into account the effect of masking and used it assuming it would be present for the listener. To eliminate the masking effect is to eliminate the sound balance among the instruments so carefully planned according to the grouping.

The measurement of loudness

Loudness measurements are of great importance for many practical problems. Since our psychological perception of loudness does not correspond directly to measures of physical intensity, it is essential to have methods that take these differences into account.

Sones. One such procedure is based on the method of *magnitude estimation*. We present a person with two tones, both, say, at 1000 Hz, and ask him how many times louder one sound appears to be over the other. The question is a peculiar one, but people can and do answer it sensibly. (For more information and some examples you can try yourself, see Appendix A.)

The results of the magnitude estimation procedure show that loudness increases as the cube root of sound intensity. That is, the psychological Judgment of loudness, *J*, is related to the physical Intensity of the sound, *I*, by a power law of the form

$$J = kI^{0.3} \; .$$

This value of exponent (0.3) is very convenient. It works out that if the sound intensity is specified in decibels, a 10 dB increase always changes loudness by a factor of 2. Every time the physical intensity is multiplied by 10, psychological loudness is multiplied by 2, as shown in Figure 5-10.

This measurement procedure has been standardized by the International Standards Organization. The unit of loudness is the *sone*. By definition, the loudness of a 1000-Hz tone at an intensity of 40 dB spl is equal to 1 sone. Therefore, a 50 dB spl 1000-Hz tone would have a loudness of 2 sones, and a 100 dB spl 1000-Hz tone would have 64 sones.

To get the loudness of tones at other frequencies, the equiloudness contours can be used. All tones on the equiloudness contour in Figure 5-2 marked 40 have a loudness of 1 sone. Those on the contour marked 50 have a loudness of 2 sones, and on the contour marked 60 have a loudness of 4 sones. Each increase in contour by 10 dB doubles the sone value: Each decrease of 10 dB halves the number of sones.

The sone measurement describes the perceived loudness of pure tones. With complex sounds that contain many frequency components, such as voices, orchestras, or aircraft and automobile sounds, the loudness is determined by comparing them with a 1000-Hz standard. The sone value at which the 1000-Hz tone appears as loud as the complex sound is the sone level for that complex sound. The sone values for some typical sounds are shown in Figure 5-10.

Computation of loudness values in sones is fairly complex, but it is now possible to buy meters that give sone values directly. The meters incorporate computers inside them that combine the loudness values measured

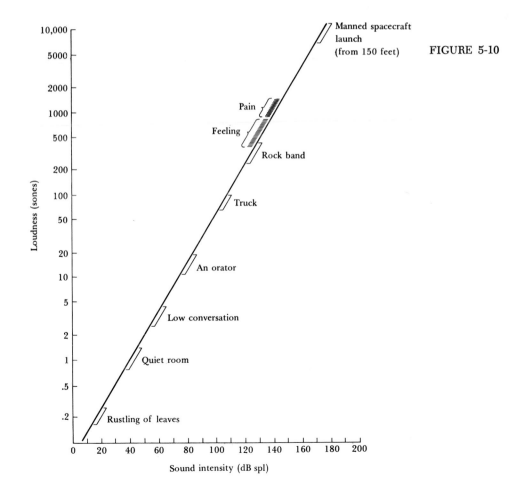

FIGURE 5-10

at different parts of the frequency range according to a formula based upon the differing sensitivity of the ear to different frequencies (as shown in Figure 5-2), as well as to the properties of the *critical band* (discussed later in this chapter). An illustration of the use of sones as a measure of loudness is shown in Figure 5-11, taken from *Consumer Reports* magazine. This figure shows a comparison of sone levels for the interior noise of automobiles when driven over different types of roads at different velocities: at 30 mph (around 50 km/hr), car 1 (the left column) is about 1½ times as loud as car 2 (the right column).

		Car 1	Car 2
¼ mi. speed at end ... (mph)			
Passing: 45 to 65 mph (seconds)		9.5	11.5
FUEL ECONOMY			
TANK MILEAGE OBSERVED ON 195-MILE TEST TRIP (mpg)		29	19
RANGE OF GAS MILEAGE TO BE EXPECTED IN NORMAL USE (mpg)		19-32	12-22
CONSTANT-SPEED GAS MILEAGE (mpg) at 40 mph		42	24.5
at 50 mph		34	23
at 60 mph		29.5	20.5
LEVEL BRAKING FROM 60 MPH			
LEVEL BRAKING FROM 60 MPH Minimum-distance stop with no wheels locked (feet)		170	180
Minimum-distance stop with some or all wheels locked (feet)		170	150
FADE TEST: Pedal effort for initial ½-g stop (pounds)		55	55
Effort for 10th repeated stop (pounds)		85	70
INTERIOR NOISE			
smooth road at 30 mph (sones)		28	19
coarse road at 30 mph (sones)		38	26
highway at 60 mph (sones)		43	33

extre... gas m......e between stop-and-go and open-road trips. Tank mileage is that actually obtained during a 195-mile trip in convoy. Constant-speed mileage is obtained by driving two ways on a substantially level road and averaging the results.

BRAKING. Minimum-distance controlled stops are shortest distance (to nearest five feet) achieved in several attempts, both without and with wheel-locking, within a 12-foot lane. (Note that wheel-locking may provoke directional instability.) Distances apply only to CU's test conditions, but the relative ranking should remain consistent under most conditions. Fade test includes 10 moderate stops at ⅓-mile intervals. Difference in pedal effort between first and 10th stops is degree of fade. Maximum Acceptable pedal effort is 150 pounds.

INTERIOR NOISE. As measured by CU. Sones are a directly proportional measure of loudness.

CONSUMER REPORTS

Ⓐ *Prices as of May 5, 1975.*
Ⓑ *Four-door model with several options.*
Ⓒ *Price includes automatic transmission, power steering, and several other options.*

FIGURE 5-11   *Sone values provide a way of directly comparing the noise levels inside different automobiles under different driving conditions. (From Consumer Reports, with permission.)*

PITCH

The musical scale

The musical scale of pitch is logarithmically related to sound frequency. Each octave in the standard musical scale is exactly twice the frequency of the previous octave. The note that orchestras use to tune their instruments, A_4 (the A above middle C), has a frequency of 440 Hz. The A's one and two octaves above that, A_5 and A_6, have frequencies of 880 and 1760 Hz, respectively. Similarly, the A's one and two octaves below have frequencies of 220 and 110 Hz, respectively. In an even-tempered musical scale, then, increasing the note by an octave doubles its frequency. Moreover, there are 12 equally spaced notes in an octave (counting all the whole and half notes). In order to divide the frequency range spanned by an octave into 12 equal intervals, each note is exactly $2^{1/12}$ times the frequency of the one before it.

Is the note of one octave perceived to be twice the pitch of the same note in the preceding octave? Our intuitions suggest yes, but experimental data indicate the answer is no. When subjects are presented with different notes and asked to judge the pitch relations among them, their perceived pitch does not follow the musical scale. Doubling or halving the frequency of the note does not double or halve its perceived pitch. (This result comes from use of the magnitude estimation procedure, described in Appendix A.) The actual relationship is shown in Figure 5-12. The unit of pitch in this diagram is called the *mel*. By definition, a tone of 1000 Hz (at 60 dB spl) has a pitch of 1000 mels.

Although this result may be incompatible with our intuition about pitch, it is highly compatible with some of the concepts in music composition. Musicians frequently debate the consequences of transposing a piece from one key to another. If a piece is written in C major and then transposed to A major, should it matter? If the change from one note to another always has the same psychological magnitude, regardless of the notes involved (equivalently, that raising a note an octave doubles the pitch), then why should it matter if the piece is transposed? The psychological distances between the notes will be the same, regardless of the key the piece is played in. But most musicians argue that transposition changes the character of the piece. The effect is subtle, but it is there. This argument is compatible with the psychological judgments

The mel scale

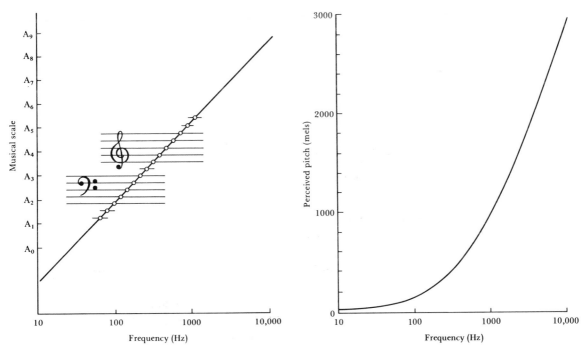

$$mels = 2410 \, log \, (1.6 \times 10^{-3} \, f + 1)$$ FIGURE 5-12

of pitch relations. The change in perceived pitch involved in going from a C$_4$ to a D$_4$ is different from that involved in going from an F$_4$ to a G$_4$ or, for that matter, going from C$_5$ to D$_5$, an octave up.

Place theory: position on the basilar membrane

To consider the question of what determines our perception of pitch, let us again return to the vibration pattern along the basilar membrane. Different frequencies set up different patterns of activity on the membrane. The location of the maximum vibration moves systematically from the oval window end of the membrane toward the apex as the frequency goes from high to low. As early as 1863, the German physicist Helmholtz proposed that pitch is determined by the position of the maximum vibration along the membrane. Although Helmholtz' reasons were inaccurate, his conclusion was sound. Psychological distance between the pitches of two tones seems to be related to the physical distance between the position of the peak activity produced by the tones. The two functions are shown in Figure 5-13. Here, location of the maximum of the vibration patterns produced by tones of different frequencies is plotted in terms of its distance from the far end (the apex) of the membrane. Perceived pitch as measured by the mel scale is also shown. The two functions are similar, not identical.

FIGURE 5-13

From Zwislocki (1965).

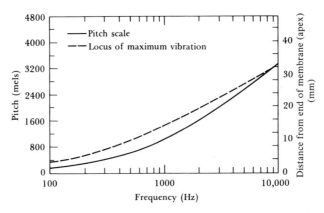

Why should distance be the critical feature? It is of no intrinsic value to the nervous system unless there are neural mechanisms to take advantage of it. The way the 30,000 fibers of the acoustic nerve distribute themselves along the membrane suggests such a mechanism. Near the oval window and for the first few turns of the cochlea, the density of the neurons appears to be constant at approximately 1150 ganglion cell neurons per millimeter. But the density of neurons decreases toward the apex. If a higher density of neurons provides more precise position information, then this distribution suggests there should be less sensitivity to changes in activity patterns in the low-frequency region—the points nearer the apex. When the curve is corrected for the relative density of the neurons, there is very good agreement: Each unit change in pitch on the mel scale is approximately equal to a movement of the vibration pattern along the membrane by 12 neurons.

The exact sensitivity of the ear to changes in frequency can be measured directly by successively presenting pairs of tones to an observer who must decide whether they have the same or different frequencies. We obtain a measurement of the *just noticeable difference* (the *jnd*) between frequencies. The ability to make such discriminations varies with frequency. At 100 Hz, a 3% change in frequency (3 Hz) is necessary before the perception of the sound is just noticeably different. Thus, at 100 Hz, the jnd for frequency is 3 Hz, or about 3% of the frequency. This percentage value steadily decreases until it reaches a minimum of around 0.2 to 0.3% at 1000 Hz. For low frequencies, the jnd for frequency is approximately constant in absolute value. Thereafter, the percentage change required to make the discrimination remains reasonably constant at about 0.3%.[4]

If the jnd for frequency is compared with the distance between the peaks in activity along the basilar membrane produced by the two frequencies being discriminated, there is good agreement in high-frequency regions but disagreement at low frequencies (Figure 5-14). But, as before, we should really take into account the way that the hair cells are spread out along the membrane. When the curve is corrected for the relative density of neurons, the match is improved: We can discriminate the difference between two frequencies whenever their peak activity is separated along the membrane by about 52 neurons.

An examination of the location of maximum vibration along the membrane, coupled with a consideration of the neural distribution, describes

---

[4] This pattern of changing discriminability is common to a number of different signal dimensions in different sensory systems. The discriminability between the intensities of an auditory signal, for example, shows a similar pattern with the jnd being approximately constant in absolute value for low intensity signals and then having an approximately constant **percentage** value as the intensities move into the middle regions of the hearing range. A constant percentage associated with discrimination is typical of many types of measuring instruments. It results from the fact that the variability in the measures being taken often depends on the level being measured, and increases with increasing levels. Consequently, the absolute size of the signal change needed for reliable discrimination will also increase. When these size increases result in a constant percentage change, the system is said to be following Weber's Law, named after the physiologist Weber (1795–1878), a contemporary of Helmholtz. If we let ΔI stand for the size of the jnd, the change in intensity that a signal must make in order for that change to be just noticeable, and I for the signal intensity, Weber's Law states that

$$\Delta I = kI,$$

where k is the relative change (100k is the percent change).

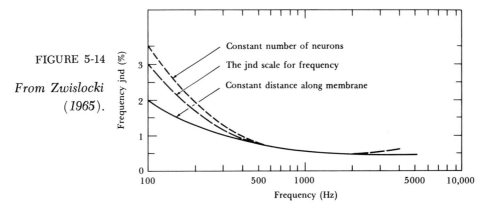

FIGURE 5-14

*From Zwislocki
(1965).*

both the subjective perception of pitch and the ears' sensitivity to changes in frequency:

- 1 jnd is approximately 52 neurons;

- 1 mel is approximately 12 neurons.

Note that a pitch change of 1 mel is less than one jnd: It cannot be detected. Pitch must change by 4 or 5 mels before an observer can detect the change. At higher frequencies (above 500 or 1000 Hz), where the density of neurons is reasonably constant along the membrane, the jnd represents a constant distance—about 0.05 mm or about .002 inches—along the membrane.

Periodicity pitch   The analysis of the patterns of vibrations along the basilar membrane describes a number of the phenomena associated with our perception of pitch. But some puzzles remain.

Loudness and pitch. The ear is not very sensitive to low-frequency sounds, yet many musical instruments produce sound frequencies in this insensitive region. Thus, a note played softly will have much of its energy lying below the threshold of hearing. What happens to our perceptions? Obviously one note played more and more softly sounds much the same, but why? Shouldn't the same piano note keep changing in pitch as it gets softer and softer and as more and more of its low-frequency components become inaudible?

Consider the piano note C_3, the C below middle C—not a particularly low note. It has the same pitch as a tone of 131 Hz (actually 130.9 Hz). But the piano note is not a simple tone. Look at the spectrum shown in Figure 5-15. Although there is more energy at 131 Hz than at other frequencies, there actually is some energy over a wide range of frequencies. As the note is played more and more softly, these low-frequency components will drop in intensity below the level that can be

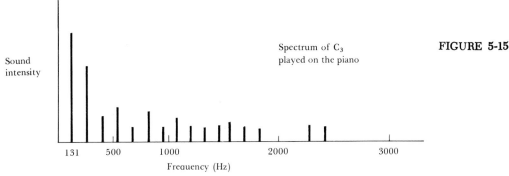

Sound
intensity

Spectrum of C₃
played on the piano

FIGURE 5-15

131   500   1000   2000   3000

Frequency (Hz)

heard. Thus, the lowest frequency present will change from 131 Hz, when the note is played at a comfortable level, to 262, to 393, and finally to 524 Hz, when the note is played reasonably softly. A pure tone with a frequency of 524 Hz matches C_5 in pitch. This is a reasonably high pitched note—it is one octave above middle C. But quite clearly, there is something peculiar going on here. A musical note simply does not appear to change in pitch in this manner as it gets softer. If pitch is determined by the location along the basilar membrane, why does the pitch of a complex tone, such as a piano note, appear to remain constant even though its frequency structure is changing? How can the piano note continue to have the pitch of its fundamental frequency of 131 Hz when the lowest frequency that is audible is 524 Hz? How do we hear the missing fundamental?

Figure 5-16

The case of the missing fundamental. To answer the question, consider a simpler situation, shown in Figure 5-17. Two pure tones, 1000 Hz (upper row) and 1100 Hz (middle row) are added to produce a complex waveform (lower row). Note that even though the only sound energy present in the system is at the two frequencies 1000 and 1100 Hz, the resulting wave pattern appears to vary at an overall rate of 100 Hz. The phenomenon in the diagram is called a *beat.* Two sinusoidal waves played together produce a beat pattern, a regular rise and fall in the sound energy at a rate equal to the difference of the frequencies of the component sine waves. On the basilar membrane, however, this beat component should not be present. There are no physical frequencies in the wave corresponding to the beat frequency. Maximums in the activity pattern should be produced only at the locations corresponding to the actual physical components of the sound—1000 and 1100 Hz. Thus, if we perceive pitch by noting the points of maximum vibration, we should perceive the 1000-Hz and 1100-Hz components, but not the 100-Hz beat frequency. In fact, we do hear the beat.

There are two possible theories to explain this phenomenon. One proposes that the perception of the beat frequency results from the

FIGURE 5-16

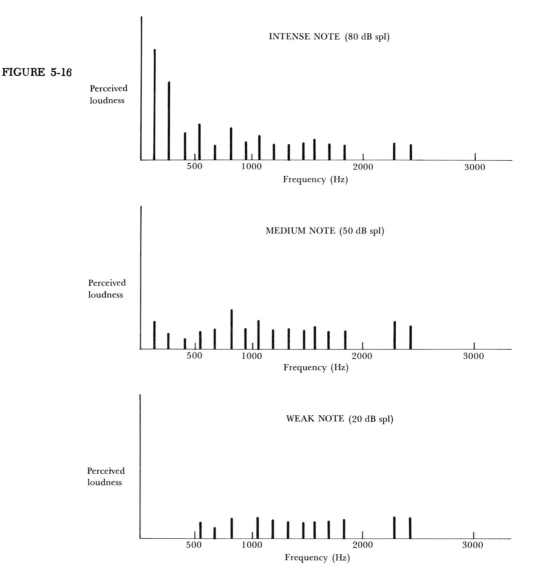

fact that the ear is an imperfect transmitter of sound: It has *non-linearities*. The mechanical structure in the ear (mainly the middle ear) actually adds extra frequencies to the incoming acoustic signal. In particular, the beat frequency is added, and thus the basilar membrane is activated in this frequency region. This explanation is compatible with the notion that a particular pitch is only perceived when there is a corresponding maximum in the vibration pattern on the membrane: the *place theory* of pitch perception.

The second theory emphasizes the importance of the synchronized firing of neurons to the changing pressures in the acoustic wave. The nerve cells reacting to the activity patterns on the basilar membrane

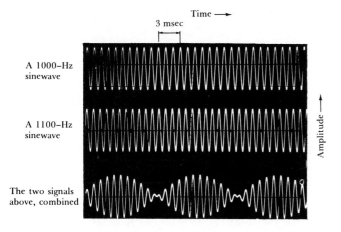

Time ———▶

3 msec

A 1000–Hz sinewave

A 1100–Hz sinewave

The two signals above, combined

Amplitude ———▶

Beats. The fluctuation in overall sound pressure which results when two sine waves of different frequencies are added together. The resulting pattern fluctuates ("beats") with a frequency given by the difference between the frequencies of the components. In this illustration, the 1000-Hz sine wave is mixed with a 1100-Hz sine wave to give a beat frequency of 100 Hz. Thus, the beat pattern repeats itself every 10 msec. Note that there is no sound energy present at a frequency of 100 Hz. We did not create a new sine wave by adding together the 1000- and 1100-Hz signals: Simply the overall envelope of sound pressures varies at the beat frequency.

FIGURE 5-17

fire in synchrony with the regular rise and fall of the beat frequency. This synchronization in the neural responses is at the basis of the perceived pitch: the *periodicity theory* of pitch perception. These are the two major explanations of pitch perception and the study of the missing fundamental is the key to evaluating them. In the next section we present an experiment that helps distinguish the two theories.

Consider a complex sound made up of the following frequencies:

| 1000 Hz | 1200 Hz | 1400 Hz | 1600 Hz |
| 1800 Hz | 2000 Hz | 2200 Hz | |

Masking the missing fundamental

If subjects are asked to adjust an oscillator so that its pitch is the same as that of the complex sound, they will set the oscillator to 200 Hz.[5] Both theories of pitch perception can explain this simple phenomenon.

The place theory explanation. The ear is nonlinear. It produces difference frequencies: The seven tones presented give six opportunities for a 200-Hz difference frequency to be added by the distortion introduced

[5] The experiment described in this section was performed by Patterson (1969).

during transmission. This difference frequency, then, is a prominent contributor to perceiving the pitch of the sound.

The periodicity pitch explanation.   The overall impulse flow in the auditory nerve is following the beat pattern of the sounds. There are nonlinearities. But neural activity is rising and falling regularly 200 times per second, and it is this activity pattern which is at the basis of the perceived pitch of the sound.

The critical difference, then, is whether the membrane is actually being activated in the 200-Hz region. The place theorist thinks that the subject perceives the basilar membrane vibrating at the 200-Hz location. The periodicity pitch theorist believes that the membrane is vibrating only in the high-frequency region between 1000 and 2200 Hz and that the nerve firings at these locations are synchronized to 200 Hz. What is the critical experiment? Disrupt the membrane in the location around 200 Hz and find out if the subject can still hear the associated pitch.

It is rather easy to disrupt the membrane in this way. One method is to add low-frequency noise to the signal—a sound that contains energy at all frequencies below some value. To be sure the noise will mask out any low-frequency activity on the membrane, add noise that contains all frequency components up to 500 Hz. How intense should the noise be?—intense enough to disrupt a real tone, if one were there. To determine this value, first present a real 200-Hz tone and have the subject adjust its

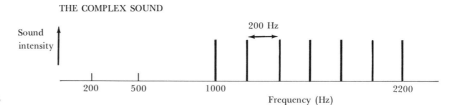

FIGURE 5-18

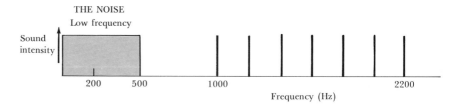

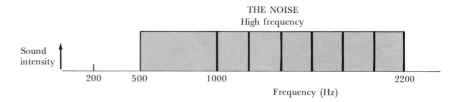

intensity so that it sounds exactly as loud as the 200-Hz tone in the complex sound. Then add low-frequency noise in an amount sufficient to mask completely the real 200-Hz tone. This noise level should be sufficient to mask any activity produced by nonlinearities. Once again, the complex tone is turned on. This time the masking noise is added. Will the 200-Hz component still be audible?

The periodicity theorist is correct: The missing fundamental is still heard when all activity in its frequency region is being physically masked by noise. Moreover, to prove that the noise does have the proper masking effect when placed appropriately, a high-frequency noise can be tested —a noise containing all frequencies above 500 Hz. The neural response pattern will be disrupted by the high-frequency noise, and the missing fundamental should no longer be heard. The result? With high-frequency noise presented, the low-frequency fundamental is no longer audible.

PITCH DISCRIMINATION WITHOUT A BASILAR MEMBRANE[6]

One way to test for the workability of a periodicity theory is to study an animal that has no basilar membrane: Can it discriminate different audio frequencies? According to place theory, if there is no basilar membrane, there can be no encoding of pitch. According to periodicity theory, pitch discrimination should be reasonably good, at least up to the point where the neural firing can no longer keep up with the signal.

The goldfish is such an animal. It has hair cells, but no membrane. The ears of most fish are rather different from those of mammals—for good reason. Not only are they evolutionarily less advanced, but the water makes a peculiar medium for sound. Water is more dense than air: Sound travels five times as fast in water as in air. Moreover, the density of the water does not differ much from the density of the body tissues and fluids. This means that the entire outer ear and middle ear are unnecessary, perhaps even harmful. Sound tends to travel right through fish, with no diminution in intensity. The ears of fish are located at the air bladders, and the distinctions found among the ears of fish seem related to the distinctions in the way their air bladders are located. What is most important, of course, is that fish—and the goldfish in particular—do have hair cells and acoustic nerves, but no basilar membrane. How, then, can they discriminate frequency?

When the goldfish is properly trained, it can indeed tell one frequency from another. The test is to hold the fish securely in a cheesecloth-padded harness and continually pair the presentation of a tone with an electric shock. Figure 5-19 The fish is presented with a series of tones of the same frequency. Then one tone is changed in frequency, and a shock follows. The fish soon learns to anticipate shock whenever the frequency changes: It shows this anticipation by momentarily stopping its breathing.

[6] The experiments on goldfish were reported by Fay (1970) and Fay and MacKinnon (1969).

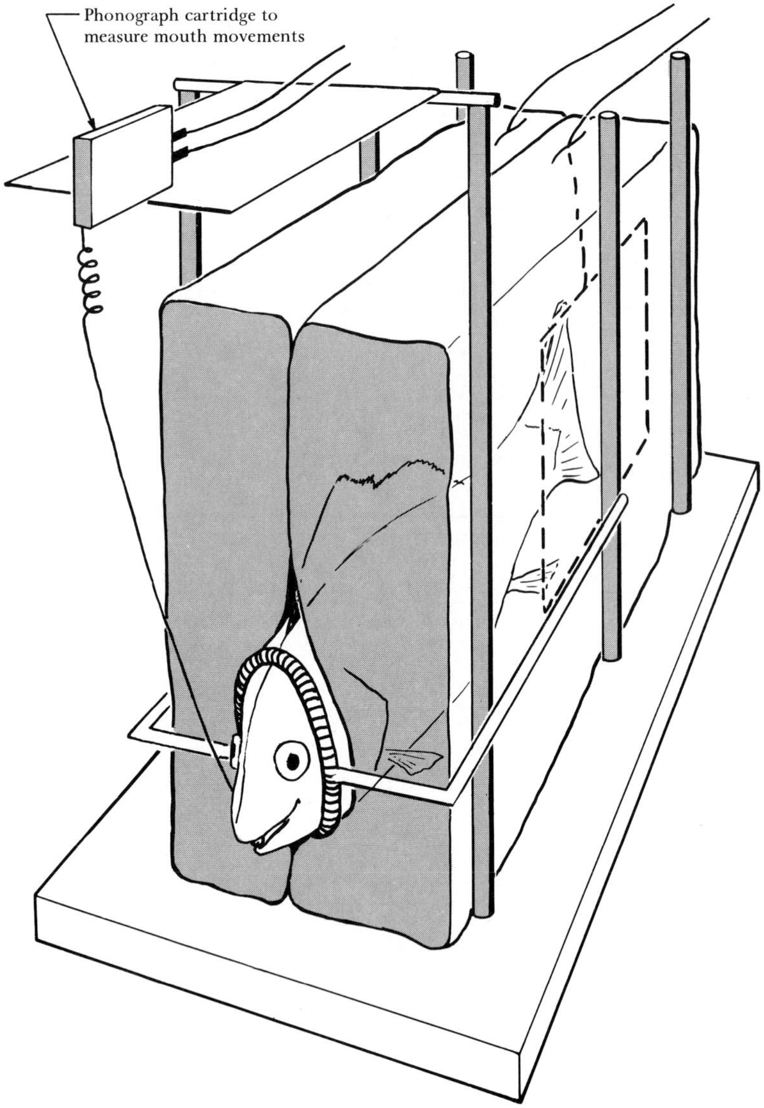

FIGURE 5-19

*From Fay and Mac-
Kinnon (1969).*

The data so obtained are shown in Figure 5-20. Note that the minimum
frequency change that can be detected by the goldfish is about ten times
larger than the minimum amount that can be detected by humans. Although
the fish is much less sensitive in absolute terms, the way its sensitivity varies
with frequency is similar to the corresponding human ability to discriminate.
The ability of the goldfish to discriminate among frequencies disappears around
1000 to 2000 Hz, exactly what one would suspect from periodicity theory.
At these levels, the nerves should no longer be able to fire in synchrony to
the auditory signal.

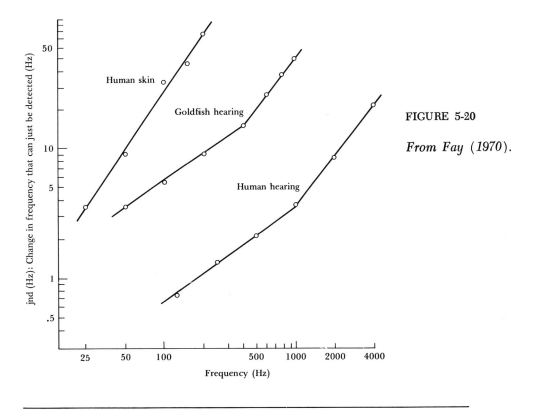

FIGURE 5-20

From Fay (1970).

Although the periodicity theory seems to fare pretty well in these masking experiments, there are two phenomena that give trouble to the periodicity account of pitch perception. One is that an individual nerve cannot respond more rapidly than about 300 to 400 times each second. How, then, can it be the basis for perceiving pitches corresponding to 4000-Hz signals? A second problem is the interesting anomaly of hearing called *diplacusis,* in which the same tone is perceived to have a different pitch with each ear. How could this be if the nerves simply fired at the rate at which the membrane was vibrating?

To answer the first criticism, periodicity theorists rely heavily on the volley principle (see page 143). Neurons fire in patterns, with a group of nerve fibers able to follow together a frequency that no single one of them could. If one nerve fires at a rate of only 300 Hz, a group of four neurons is capable of firing at a combined rate of 1200 Hz, given that everything is synchronized properly. Even so, there is no evidence that nerves, whether singly or in groups, can follow patterns of auditory frequencies greater than 2000 or perhaps 3000 Hz.

One of the strongest pieces of evidence against periodicity theory

Evidence against the periodicity pitch theory

as a complete explanation is the anomaly of diplacusis, an ailment which lends credence to the theory that pitch is determined by the location of the maximum vibration on the membrane. Someone who suffers from a severe case of diplacusis will hear two different pitches when the same tone is played to each ear. Actually, everyone perceives some small differences in the pitch of a tone heard at the two ears, especially at high frequencies. The simplest explanation is that there is not a perfect match of positions along the basilar membrane. In fact, if you consider the precision of neural wiring that would be necessary to make each pair of locations on the two membranes correspond exactly, it is surprising that this phenomenon is not more prominent. It would be surprising even if the two membranes were exactly the same size, let alone matched neuron for neuron. Moreover, as one follows the neural processing up toward the brain, it is clear that there are many places where there might be a slight mismatch between the locations of neural fibers and the critical frequencies for which they are most sensitive.

The duplicity theory of pitch perception

We have just discussed two different ways by which the auditory system might determine the pitch of a sound. The two theories are called *place theory* and *periodicity theory:* the *place* on the basilar membrane where the traveling wave has its maximum bulge, and the rate and *periodicity* at which nerve fibers respond. Whenever there are two competing theories, both with good evidence for and against them, then some other path must be sought. Perhaps both theories are correct, but in limited ranges of operation. Alternatively, maybe there is some other way of looking at the phenomena that will encompass both these theories.

Consider how we said pitch information was extracted. The location at which the maximum vibration occurs on the basilar membrane, then, would appear to be a primary determinant of pitch, supplemented by information carried by the rate at which the fibers of the acoustic nerve respond. If the fibers located at the 1000-Hz location respond at a firing rate of 1000 Hz, everything is consistent. The perception is of a pitch given by a 1000-Hz tone. If the fibers at the 1000-Hz location respond in patterns of 100 Hz, then the perception is of a complex sound, with a fundamental pitch equal to that of a tone of 100 Hz, but with a harmonic structure in the 1000-Hz region. In this case, the firing rate helps determine the pitch: The location at which the membrane is responding determines the sound quality or *timbre*. Stimulation of a location along the basilar membrane is always accompanied by a firing rate appropriate to the location. Firing rates, however, are not always accompanied by stimulation of the appropriate membrane location. From our discussion, then, both place theory and periodicity theory may be correct: maybe there should be a *duplicity theory* that combines the two.

There are great difficulties with both the place and the periodicity (firing pattern) theories. Recent work has uncovered some basic problems but not yet provided a viable substitute. The most damning evidence against place theory is that exactly the same pitch sensation can be elicited from stimulating the high-frequency portion of the membrane as from the low-frequency portion (for example, in the "missing fundamental" experiment just described). The observer can easily distinguish the sounds, but the *pitch* of that perception seems unaffected by the location along the membrane that is stimulated.

Periodicity is not an adequate explanation either, for the waveform shape can be changed dramatically without changing the perceived pitch. Indeed, there is little change in the perception of the sound with gross changes in the waveform. In a concert hall, for example, the place where you sit determines the shape of the sound waveform. Echoes, differences in the path of high-frequency and low-frequency sounds, refraction patterns, and differences that result from sound amplification systems all cause quite different sound patterns at different seating locations. Moreover, you can cause dramatic changes yourself by cupping your hands over your ears and directing the open side of the cup toward the front of the hall or toward the back. This will significantly affect the higher-frequency components of the sounds that enter the ears, dramatically altering the shape of the sound waveforms. Nonetheless, although you will be able to perceive qualitative differences in the sound, the pitches that you perceive will be unaffected by choice of seat or by the position of your hands over your ears.

A few years ago, psychologists thought the problem of pitch encoding had been solved. The leading theory was a duplicity theory that combined both periodicity and place; low frequencies were analyzed by a temporal, periodicity analysis, whereas high frequencies were thought to be analyzed by place of excitation along the basilar membrane. Today, this view is still held but with reservations. The problem of determining pitch is now regarded as quite complicated, involving the integration of complex mechanisms within the brain. There is a considerable way to go before we can formulate a comprehensive theory to explain all the mechanisms that are involved.

Current theories tend to emphasize a centralized spectral (frequency) or temporal pattern-recognition system. That is, these theories emphasize the problem of analyzing the entire complex pattern of excitation along the neural pathway, rather than one single component such as place or rate of firing. In these theories, observers get some sort of global representation of the overall sound excitation from which they extract a generalized notion of pitch. These analyses are done centrally in the brain, not at the level of the basilar membrane or the hair cells. Thus, according to this view, both place and periodicity determine pitch but the entire pattern of excitation on the membrane is taken into account.

THE CRITICAL BAND   Suppose two pure tones are presented to a subject who is to judge the loudness of the resulting sound. As the two tones move farther apart in frequency (keeping their average frequency constant), the combined sound does not change loudness until a critical frequency separation is exceeded. Beyond this, the loudness of the tone pair increases with increased frequency separation.

FIGURE 5-21

From Scharf (1970).

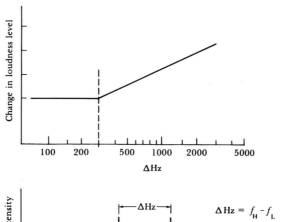

In a similar fashion, a sound containing components of all frequencies between some lower frequency f_L and a higher one f_H appears to have a constant loudness as the distance between f_L and f_H is increased, again until a critical value of separation is reached. From that point, the loudness of the sound increases as more and more frequencies are added.[7]

[7] Note that constant energy must be maintained in the sound (called *bandpass noise*, where the bandpass refers to the frequencies between f_L and f_H). To see how this is done, consider a simpler case in which a complex sound composed of separate tones is presented to a subject. If more tones are added, it is important for this task that constant total energy of the sound be maintained. Thus, if the number of tones is doubled, the energy of each tone presented must be halved to keep total energy constant. So it is with noise: The energy level at each frequency is kept proportional to $1/(f_H - f_L)$.

Consider a third example, a subject trying to detect a pure tone that is masked by bandpass noise centered around the frequency of the tone. As the distance between f_L and f_H is increased, detection becomes more and more difficult until a critical separation is reached. Beyond that point, detection is no longer affected by further increases in the width of the noise band.

All three of these examples indicate that within some critical region of frequency, sound energies are interacting with one another. As we move outside the critical region, sound energies no longer interact, although psychological attributes do add. The critical region is called the *critical band*. Its size depends upon its center frequency.

If we have two sounds that fall within the same critical band, their sound energies add. Thus, if we combined two sounds of equal energy within the same critical band, the effect is equivalent to doubling the *energy*. The resultant would be equal in loudness to a single tone that had *twice* the energy of either of the sounds. This is equivalent to a 3 dB increase in sound energy, and about a 20% increase in loudness. If the same two sounds were further separated in frequency so that they did not lie within the same critical band, then their *loudness* would add. If the two sounds had the same loudness, then when they were combined, the effect would be equivalent to doubling the *loudness*. The resultant would be equal in loudness to a single tone that had *ten* times the energy of either of the sounds. This is equivalent to a 10 dB increase in sound energy and a 100% increase in loudness.

If one looks at the pattern of excitation along the basilar membrane, it is surprisingly simple to find a correlate for the critical band similar

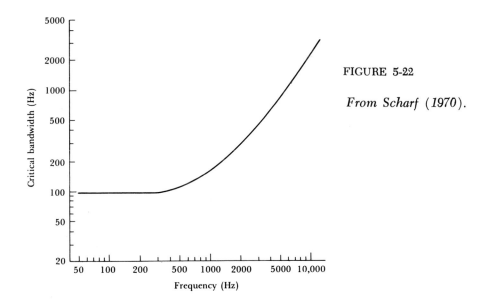

FIGURE 5-22

From Scharf (1970).

to the correlates found for the jnd and mel scales for pitch. The critical band looks as if it is simply caused by the vibration pattern. It is as if tones that vibrate nearby parts of the membrane interact differently from tones whose vibrations are further apart. Figure 5-23 shows the vibration pattern for a 1000-Hz tone and the part of the vibration pattern that corresponds to one critical band. It is interesting to note that although every part of the basilar membrane has some response to this tone, only a relatively narrow strip around the point of maximum vibration has the properties of interactions that are the characteristics of the critical band.

FIGURE 5-23

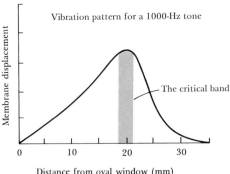

Vibration pattern for a 1000-Hz tone

The critical band

Distance from oval window (mm)

By comparing Figure 5-23 with the properties of the basilar membrane and the mel and jnd scales, the relationship among these factors can be nicely summarized:

- 1 mel is approximately 12 neurons, 0.23 jnd, and 0.009 critical bands;
- 1 jnd is approximately 52 neurons, 4.3 mels, and 0.04 critical bands;
- 1 critical band is approximately 1300 neurons, 108 mels, and 25 jnd's.

The critical band has many important properties. Beats between different tones appear to be noticeable only if the tones involved fall within the same critical band. The critical band has also been suggested as the mechanism responsible for the dissonance associated with some combinations of tones. Dissonance, it is argued, results from beats caused by two tones whose frequencies lie within a critical bandwidth of one another. Musical instruments produce complex tones, containing many harmonic frequencies. Two notes may be dissonant if any pair of their harmonics falls within the same critical band. The more audible these harmonics, the more dissonant the sound.

AUDITORY SPACE PERCEPTION

We have two ears, but we hear one acoustic world. With differences in information received by listening with two ears (*binaural*) rather than with one (*monaural*), we determine the locations of sound sources, an important factor both in adding to the enjoyment of our perceptions and in making acoustic messages more intelligible. It is difficult to appreciate the importance of sound localization because it is so seldom that we are without it: It is so common a phenomenon that we take it for granted.

With modern audio sets, however, the importance of sound localization is easy to demonstrate. Listen to a good, high-quality stereophonic recording over earphones.[8] Now, simply switch between monophonic and stereophonic modes. Listen to the difference. Stereophonic and quadrophonic reproduction not only allows the sounds to be perceived as originating from different locations in the imaginary space around you, but also gives a richer sensation of sound—one in which the various sounds are more distinct and easier to listen to.

The cues used to localize a sound source are the exact time and intensity at which the tones arrive at the two ears. Sounds arrive first at the ear closer to the source and with greater intensity. The head tends to cast an acoustic shadow between the source and the ear on the far side.

Localization

Figure 5-24

With some simple calculations, it is possible to determine the approximate maximum possible time delay between signals arriving at the two ears. The width of the human head is approximately 7 inches (18 cm). If a sound source is located directly to one side, the sound hits one ear directly but has to travel around the circumference of the head to get to the other ear. If the head is assumed to be a sphere with a radius of 3.5 inches, the extra path length is 3.5π, or 11 inches. Since sound travels at approximately 1100 feet $\sec^{-1}$ in air, it takes 76 microsec to travel an inch. For a sound to travel from one ear to the other takes around 840 microsec.

This time difference, of course, depends exactly on where the sound is located. When the sound is straight ahead, it reaches both ears at the same time. When the sound is 3° to the right, it arrives at the right ear 30 microsec before arriving at the left. This slight change—30 microsec of time difference—is detectable. It is all the change needed for an observer to detect a change in the location of the sound source. This is amazing performance, especially since the signals at the two ears must be compared with each other in order to localize the sound. The nervous system must be preserving information about the time at which a signal arrives at an ear within an accuracy of 30 microsec.

[8] You will get a less dramatic effect with speakers unless you sit so that one speaker is directly to your left and one directly to your right. The recording must be one that was recorded in the studio for stereophonic reproduction—old records or budget productions may not be very good for this. Most good rock groups or modern symphony recordings are excellent.

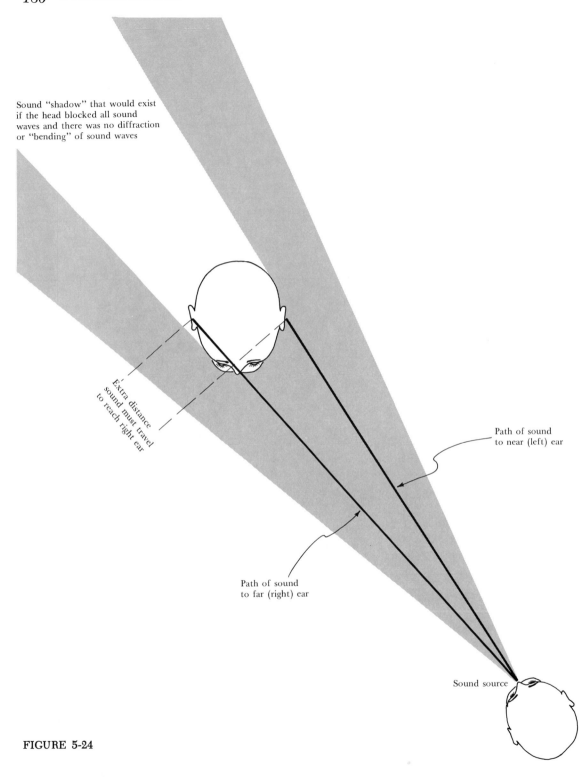

Sound "shadow" that would exist if the head blocked all sound waves and there was no diffraction or "bending" of sound waves

Extra distance sound must travel to reach right ear

Path of sound to near (left) ear

Path of sound to far (right) ear

Sound source

FIGURE 5-24

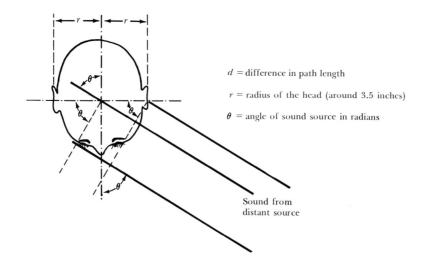

d = difference in path length

r = radius of the head (around 3.5 inches)

θ = angle of sound source in radians

Sound from
distant source

$$d = r\theta + r\sin\theta$$

IF $\theta = 30° = 0.52$ radians

$d = 3.5 \times .5 + 3.5 \sin 30°$

$d = 1.75 + 1.75 = 3.5$ inches

Time difference = $76 \times d$ microsec = 270 microsec

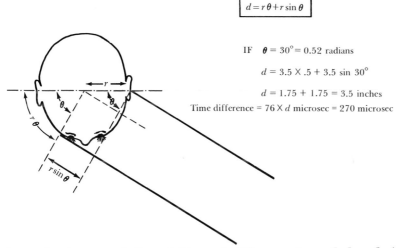

Approximate computation of binaural difference in path length for a   FIGURE 5-25
distant sound source.

The difference in the arrival time of a signal at the two ears results in a phase difference between the signals: One lags behind the other. For high-frequency signals, this time lag is ambiguous and cannot be used as a cue for localization. To see this, consider a 10,000-Hz signal. It completes a cycle of sound pressure variation every 100 microsec. When a 10,000-Hz signal is in front and to the right at an angle of 55°, the sound will arrive at the left ear some 450 microsec after it arrives at the right ear. The waveform heard at the right ear, then, is 4½ cycles ahead of the waveform at the left. But how can one tell whether two tones differ by

4½ cycles, 3½, 2½, 1½, or even ½ cycle? Alternatively, how can one tell if the source is 55° to the right or 40°, 27°, 17°, or 6°? There is no way. The longest time delay between the ears is around 840 microsec, and any sound frequency that takes less time than this to complete a cycle starts to give ambiguous location information. Time differences only provide good cues to location for sounds with frequency components less than about 1300 Hz.

Actually, localization is ambiguous even at low frequencies, since if the head is perfectly stationary, time difference alone cannot distinguish whether a sound comes from above or below, or even from front or rear. A sound in front and to one side has the same delay pattern as one in the rear in the same relative position. In real situations, these ambiguities can be removed by head movements, by visual cues, and by differences in sound quality caused by the way different frequencies are reflected and refracted by the head and outer ear.

A second cue to sound localization is the sound shadow cast by the head. With low-frequency sounds, the sound wave is diffracted and "bends" around the head, causing little or no shadow. But at high frequencies—when the wavelength is short compared with the dimensions of the head—diffraction does not take place to any significant degree. For example, a 100-Hz sound has a wavelength of 11 feet (3⅓ meters). Thus, it bends easily around the head. But a 10,000-Hz sound has a wavelength of only 0.11 feet (1.3 inches or 3.3 cm) so that it is reflected by the head, thus casting a shadow. With a source of sound at a 15° angle, the effects of the sound shadow can be measured:

Frequency	*Ratio of Sound Intensities at the Two Ears*
300 Hz	1 dB
1,100 Hz	4 dB
4,200 Hz	5 dB
10,000 Hz	6 dB
15,000 Hz	10 dB

Starting about 3000–4000 Hz, the intensity difference is great enough to be reliably discriminated, and thus provides a useful cue to localization.

Sound localization is carried out by a dual system: time differences for low frequencies and intensity differences for high frequencies. The switch between the two systems occurs in the frequency range of 1000–5000 Hz—the range of sound frequencies characterized by the largest amount of error in localization.

In determining the position of an object in space we use many different cues. So far, we have simply shown how time and intensity differences could determine the position of a sound source. But we can do more than that: we can tell the elevation (height) of the source, as well as the distance. The pinna of the ear (the skin and cartilage structure of the outer ear) plays a major role in our ability to localize sound sources. Sounds from the rear cast sound shadows because of the pinna, and the shadows affect high frequencies more than low ones. In addition, all those funny nooks and crannies of the pinna actually play an important role in determining the location of a sound, for they cause high-frequency components of the sound to bounce around a bit before entering the ear canal. This causes very slight "echoes" of the high-frequency portion of the sound wave, the exact sound depending upon the exact location of the sound source. Fill up those nooks and crannies with putty and the ability to tell the height and forward–backward direction of a sound decreases.

The distance of a sound source is judged by the reverberant nature of the sound. This cue is not reliable, but it still provides useful information, especially if the listener knows what the source would sound like from close up: then the differences in the sound can be used as a guide to its distance.

In addition to adding a spatial dimension to the perception of sound, binaural presentation also adds clarity. This is a consequence of three different mechanisms: localization, an apparent reduction in interference, and the minimization of masking.

Importance of binaural listening

Localization. Localization allows us to spread out in space many of the sounds that are heard. Suppose we are stuck with some boring people at a party. We can keep nodding and agreeing while actually attending to a neighboring conversation. Localization makes this possible. We can choose the frequency, intensity, or spatial location to which we want to listen.

When tape-recording a conversation, the result is often very difficult to understand. There are echoes and noises. The sounds of people coughing and moving about drown out the desired voice. In the real situation, we are not aware of these noises, even though they are present. Localization cues let us attend selectively only to the auditory signals of interests. A dramatic improvement in clarity comes by adding a second microphone—making a stereophonic recording. Suddenly, one can listen to **where** the voice is, tuning out the distractions. All that is needed are two microphones differentially sensitive to sound direction. They are set up properly if one is primarily sensitive to sounds coming from the right, while the other mostly picks up sounds from the left. When a person speaks from between the two microphones, he should be picked up equally on both of them. If he stands to one side, he will come through more on one than on the other.

The problems encountered in listening to a single-channel, monaural tape recorder dramatically illustrate the problems that must be encountered by individuals who are deaf in one ear. The difficulty is caused not so much by decreased sensitivity to sound, but by the reduced ability to localize sounds. If a hearing aid is used, where is the microphone to be placed? If the hearing aid microphone is worn in a shirt pocket, normal localization will not be possible. The microphone should be as close as possible to the ear. In fact, it might be best to use two hearing aids, one for each ear (even if one ear is normal), in order to recover the ability to localize sounds.

Masking level difference. The second way in which binaural reception improves clarity is by means of a phenomenon called *the masking level difference.* When trying to hear a weak voice mixed with noise presented to one ear, the addition of the same noise to the other ear will significantly improve the clarity. One ear has both signal and noise; the other ear has noise alone. One way of looking at this is to imagine the inputs to the two ears being subtracted from one another, causing the noise to be cancelled. Thus, putting the same signal and noise in both ears would do no good since subtracting the inputs to the two ears leaves nothing. An alternative way to view this is to notice that the noise being presented to both ears is lateralized in the center of the head, whereas the signal is heard only at one ear. The difference in spatial location leads to the improvement in intelligibility.

Masking. There is a third way in which binaural reception can improve clarity. Imagine listening to an orchestra with a big bass drum banging away while a clarinet plays in the low registers. If this is recorded monaurally, the very low frequencies of the drum will mask the low frequencies of the clarinet. This results from the overlap of excitation along the basilar membrane. However, if the clarinet and drum are heard in opposite ears, there can be no interaction along the membrane: Masking should not occur. Obviously, in an actual concert, sounds from the clarinet and drum will get to both ears, but differently to each ear. When two sounds are localized as originating from two different locations, the masking effect of one upon the other is much reduced. This reduction of masking makes the sounds clearer and more distinct in a binaural than in a monaural recording.

The precedence effect

In theory, localization is performed simply by using differences in the sounds arriving at the two ears. Usually, however, the initial signal is immediately followed by numerous echoes. Once all the echoes are accounted for, even a simple click can be very complicated. First the click arrives at one ear, then the other, and then parts which have bounced off the walls and ceiling of the room start arriving at the ears.

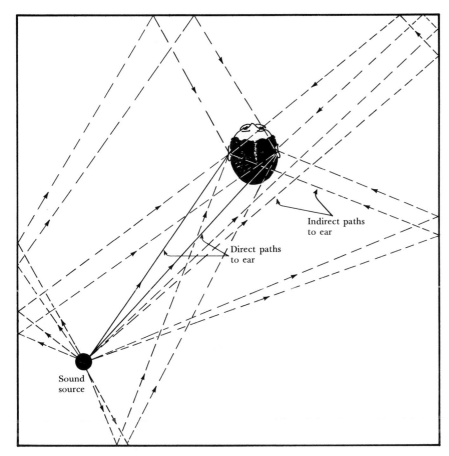

FIGURE 5-26

Indirect paths
to ear

Direct paths
to ear

Sound
source

The two ears hear a rapid succession of sounds. How can one make use of all that to localize?

Fortunately, only the first sound to arrive appears to be used. This is called the *precedence effect*. It is not completely understood. Echoes play almost no part in the psychological interpretation of the sound. Not that they are not heard. If we record various sounds, some followed by echoes and some not, it is easy to tell the difference between them. Thus, the sound information is heard, but fortunately, it is ignored by the mechanism responsible for localization.

Binaural sound. To get a recording of an event that really sounds as if you were sitting in the auditorium, it is necessary to make a *binaural* recording. To do this properly requires that a dummy of a head be placed in a seat in the auditorium, with microphones in each of the dummy's ears. When played back over earphones, binaural recording gives beautiful fidelity.

Stereophonic sound. Binaural recording is very different from the *stereophonic* recordings that are used for most records and tapes. In

Recordings

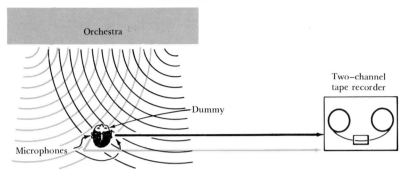

BINAURAL RECORDING

FIGURE 5-27

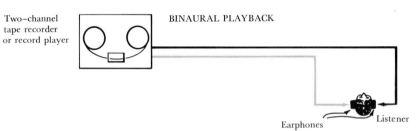

BINAURAL PLAYBACK

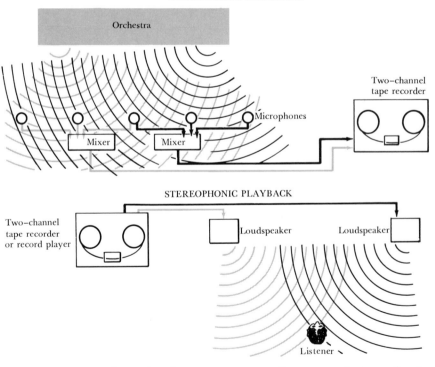

STEREOPHONIC RECORDING

STEREOPHONIC PLAYBACK

stereophonic recording, the object is to try to slice across the wavefront as it crosses some point in the auditorium and reproduce it in the listener's home. There is no way that this can actually be done accurately with only

QUADRAPHONIC RECORDING

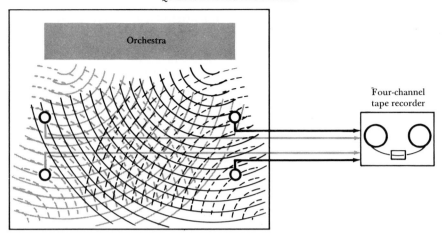

QUADRAPHONIC PLAYBACK

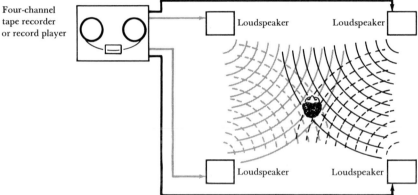

two microphones and two speakers. For this reason, four-channel sound is now being tested for home use. Ideally, with two speakers there should be two microphones spaced the same distance apart as the speakers will be. This is not very good, since it demands too much in the way of control of the playback conditions. As a result, recording engineers have learned to combine many microphones, mostly by trial and error. Pleasing results can be obtained in this manner, so that is the way recordings are currently being done. Generally, in order to make a really good recording many microphones must be scattered over the auditorium and the recording engineers determine how to combine them into two channels to give the proper effect. Psychological acoustics does not help much here. The best way to combine channels probably differs for every auditorium, for different numbers of people in the audience, and even for the way the audience is dressed.

Quadraphonic sound. As Figure 5-27 shows, the sound that we normally hear includes reflections. The feeling of spaciousness of a symphony hall comes about, in part, as a result of these reflections. Thus, stereophonic sound fails to capture all the qualities of the original sound experience, in part because the two speakers are both placed in front of the listener. This limitation is not a problem with binaural sound, because here the listener experiences exactly the same sounds as a person sitting in the auditorium. The problem with binaural sound is that it is designed for one particular position of the head: if the listener's head moves, the earphones move along with it, and so the original sound sources always appear to come from in front of the head. This gives an uncanny power to the listener. Each head movement makes it seem like the entire orchestra and room also move to keep directly in front of the head.

One technique for enriching the quality of the sound experience without the limitations presented by binaural sound recordings is to use four speakers, two in front and two to the rear of the listener. Four speakers offer a distinct improvement in the faithfulness of the situation, although it too must suffer from being only a poor approximation to the original event. With four speakers, the effect of the ears' pinnae becomes important in distinguishing sounds from the front of the head from sounds behind. The use of four speakers opens up new vistas for auditory experiences. Some composers have experimented with musical presentations aimed explicitly at being presented over four (or more) loudspeakers, with the spatial dimension of the musical experience being varied directly, in much the same way as loudness, pitch, or sound quality. (See the discussion by Reynolds, 1975, pp. 117–125.)

REVIEW OF TERMS
AND CONCEPTS

In this chapter, the following terms and concepts that we consider to be important have been used. Please look them over. If you are not able to give a short explanation of any of them, you should go back and review the appropriate sections of the chapter.

Terms and concepts you should know

The differences between:
    pitch and frequency (mels and hertz)
    loudness and intensity (sones and decibels)
Equiloudness contours
Loudness compensation
Loudness (sones)
Masking
    what it is
    how it is measured
    how it is explained
jnd
Pitch
    mels

musical scale
periodicity pitch
missing fundamental
beats
Place theory
Periodicity theory
Duplicity theory
Critical band
Localization
by arrival times
by intensity difference
ear shadow and masking

Perhaps the easiest place to start is with Volume IV of the *Handbook of perception: Hearing* (Carterette & Friedman, 1976). The two books *Foundations of modern auditory theory* edited by Tobias (1970, 1972) include several important chapters, especially on the measurement of loudness, theories of pitch, masking, the critical band, and localization.

We highly recommend the book *Mind models: New forms of musical experience* by the composer Roger Reynolds (1975) for anyone interested in contemporary uses of sound in musical experiences. Roederer's (1975) book *Introduction to the physics and psychophysics of music* is a more technical introduction to the relationship between the concepts discussed in this book and musical perception.

The chapter by Zwislocki (1965) in the *Handbook of mathematical psychology* (Volume III) is excellent, although a bit advanced. Do not be too dismayed by all the equations in the first part of the chapter. We have found that introductory students can get much meat out of this chapter if they simply skim quickly over the first few sections. The latter part of the chapter is especially valuable in discussing the relationships between the anatomy and physiology of the ear and the perception of loudness, pitch, and masking. The article by Wightman and Green (1974) is a good introduction to pitch.

The book by Kryter (1970) covers in detail *The effect of noise on man* (which is also the title). Unfortunately, although the material covered by the book is of utmost importance, the level of writing makes it very difficult for the reader.

A large amount of the fundamental advances in our knowledge of pitch was provided by the Dutch, especially the efforts of Schouten. The paper by Wightman and Green (1974) serves as an introduction to this literature, and the thesis by Plomp (1966) is especially important for an analysis of consonance and dissonance.

6 Neural information processing

PREVIEW

> Why do things look as they do? Because they are what they are?
> No, because we are what we are.
>
> . . . It seems clear to us that the answer to the broad question
> "Why do things look as they do?" will be given in an informative
> way only when the principles of neural organization are known.

[From Hurvich and Jameson, 1974, p. 88.]

This is a long chapter. Therefore, we have divided it into two parts. **Part I** deals with the basic operations of neurons, with how neurons might be interconnected to make specialized circuits, and with the study of the nervous system's operation on the retina of the eye.

Part II is concerned with the processes further along the sensory system: the processes that operate on sensory signals beyond both the retina and the inner ear, and in the brain itself.

Part I tells of the basic neural building blocks. The opening section of the chapter tells of how specialized neural cells were discovered in the eye of the frog, and the research that led to that discovery. The discovery itself is an excellent example of the way that we approach the whole problem of analyzing the parts and functions of the nervous system.

The important things to learn are the operation of nerves: what their basic parts are, how they are interconnected, and how they interact with one another. We present a very simple arithmetic model of the interactions of nerves with one another, and we consider it important that you learn how to do the computations. Once you learn how to do those computations, then you will have an excellent feel for the way in which the nervous system operates.

The interactions of nerve cells on the retina of the eye produce a number of important perceptual phenomena. We want you to understand those phenomena and to understand how the nervous system might actually operate to lead to those particular perceptions.

You should learn about the specialized nature of neural cells, especially those which form circuits for enhancing contrasts between two objects, which detect slits and lines, angles, movement, and color. The concept of neural interaction is essential to the understanding of these concepts.

Part II leaves the detailed analysis of particular neural circuits and talks instead about the general properties of sensory processing by the brain. Here, you will learn some new anatomical terms, and you will learn about even more specialized cells and about the ways by which the brain starts to put together the information received from the sensory system.

PART 1: NEURAL PROCESSES

How does one begin the study of neural information processing? What does one look for? One approach is that of Lettvin, Maturana, McCulloch, and Pitts (1959), the authors of a now classic paper on the visual system of a frog:

> We decided then how we ought to work. First, we should find a way of recording from single . . . fibers in the intact optic nerve. Second, we should present the frog with as wide a range of visible stimuli as we could, not only spots of light but things he would be disposed to eat, other things from which he would flee, sundry geometrical figures, stationary and moving about, etc. From the variety of stimuli we should then try to discover what common features were abstracted by whatever groups of fibers we could find in the optic nerve. Third, we should seek the anatomical basis for the grouping.

What should these investigators find inside the eye of a frog? From external appearances, frogs do not live in a very rich visual world. Generally, they appear to ignore most of their visual environment and show relatively little exploratory behavior. Because of their lack of active scanning and exploration they can be easily caught, provided they are approached from the rear. They seem to rely mainly on the presence of moving shadows to warn them of predators and possible danger. In fact, the only feature that stands out about a frog's use of vision is its ability to catch fast-moving flying insects. It manages this by waiting until they come within range, then lashing out quickly and accurately with its tongue.

Lettvin and his collaborators found a visual nervous system that corresponded to the frog's visual behavior. The frog's eye appears to extract only four patterns of information from the visual signal. Three of the four kinds of detectors are associated with relatively general characteristics in the visual scene: *edge detectors* that respond strongly to the border between light and dark regions, *moving contrast detectors* that respond when an edge moves, and *dimming detectors* that react when the overall illumination is lowered.

But it is the responses of the fourth class of detectors that are the most fascinating: *convex edge detectors* that respond only when a small, dark object moves into the field of vision. For there to be a response the object must be dark, must be moving, and must have a roughly circular shape. When this type of object first enters the field of view, a convex edge detector begins responding at a slow rate. As the object moves closer to the frog, the detector responds more and more vigorously. The response will continue even if the object suddenly disappears from view (but it can be stopped by a sudden change in illumination, such as that caused by an eyeblink). This, of course, is a bug detector: It provides exactly the visual information needed for efficient fly-catching behavior.

This investigation, then, suggests that the eye of the frog has in it a neural circuit for detecting bugs. The frog has an exceedingly primitive brain. By putting the bug detector in the eye, the processes needed for the precise visual-motor coordinations involved in fly-catching are simplified. But place a frog in a new environment, perhaps one in which it is surrounded by hundreds of freshly killed flies, all suitable for eating, but with no movement: The circuit fails, and the frog will starve to death. The specialization of the frog's eye marks a high point for neural efficiency and sophistication, but a low point for adaptability. This visual pattern recognition system is simply not flexible enough to adapt to new conditions.

THE ANATOMY OF DETECTORS

The differences in function of the four classes of detectors found in the eye of the frog appear to be reflected in the neural organization of the cells, as well as in their visual appearance. The four classes of receptors go to different areas of the brain; moreover, the four types of detectors also look different.

Figure 6-1 shows three things: (*a*) the predicted classification of cells by Lettvin, Maturana, Pitts, and McCulloch (1961); (*b*) the actual classification in tadpoles found by Pomeranz and Chung (1970); and (*c*) photographs of the cells found by Pomeranz and Chung.

It is not easy to determine what each type of receptor looks like. It is possible to dissect the frog's eye and examine it under a microscope. And then, indeed, four different types of cells can be seen. The problem remains: Which is which?

Some tricks were necessary to determine what type of cell corresponded to which type of detector. The main problem is that the dissection kills the cells: It is not possible to record from a cell and also to examine it under a microscope, since the normal operation of a cell will not take place unless the neural structures are undisturbed. The surgical dissections required to expose the cells for study under the microscope would interfere with their normal functioning as pattern detectors. Hence, Pomeranz and Chung resorted to some deductive logic.

The first trick was to study the tadpole instead of the frog. There seem to be only three different kinds of cells present in the eyes of tadpoles, not four. That identifies the missing cell, for if careful physiological recordings are made from living tadpoles, the edge response is found to be missing. Evidently, the *edge detector* develops only in the more mature animal.

There is only one kind of cell in the periphery of the tadpole eye. By

PREDICTED CLASSIFICATION		ACTUAL CLASSIFICATION	
Physiology	Anatomy	Physiology	Anatomy
Class 1 edge detector	Constricted tree	Class 1 edge detector	Constricted tree
Class 2 convex edge detector	E tree	Class 2 convex edge detector	E tree
Class 3 moving contrast detector	H tree	Class 3 moving contrast detector	H tree
Class 4 dimness detector	Broad tree	Class 4 dimness detector	Broad tree

FIGURE 6-1

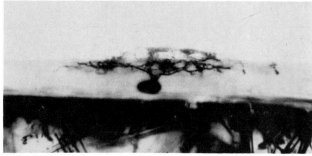

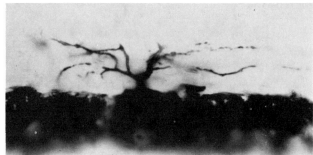

Photomicrographs (at the same magnification) of the three types of ganglion cells found in the tadpole retina. From Pomeranz and Chung (1970).

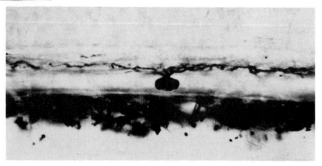

recording the responses of live tadpoles to signals presented peripherally, this detector is identified as the *convex edge detector*. Now there are two cells left to be identified: the *moving contrast detector* and the *dimness detector*. These two are determined by logical deduction. Of the two remaining cells, one has two layers, the other only one layer. Moreover, the two-layer cell is less spread out than the one-layer cell. These cues unlock the puzzle. The dimness detector has a larger receptive field than the moving contrast detector. Moreover, it clearly is a simpler circuit, so it should be the simpler cell, one layer, not two.

The study of the frog's eye illustrates the procedures and philosophy of physiological investigators. The results demonstrate that the frog has developed a highly sophisticated sensory analysis designed to extract specific information from a visual image. Of course, we do not expect to find that all animals have bug detectors. In fact, the sensory information processing performed in higher species than frogs is, in some sense, much simpler but also more elegant and flexible. It proceeds by small steps, employing simple but powerful principles for combining, rearranging and analyzing the data flowing in through the receptors from the environment. To understand it, we must understand the operation of the basic unit in the nervous system—the neuron—and the techniques for studying its behavior. We must explore how these units are put together to construct the neural circuits that analyze the information provided by the sensory systems.

PHYSIOLOGICAL PROCEDURES
The neuron

The basic building block of the nervous system is the *neuron*, the cell that handles intercommunication of information among the various parts of the body. For our purposes, a simplified schematic knowledge of a neuron is sufficient. A *neural unit* consists of several parts (see Figure 6-2): a *cell body* (also called the *soma*), a *nerve fiber* (also called the *axon*) that carries information from one neuron to another, and a terminal *junction* (a *synapse*) at which the activity of one neuron influences the electrical characteristics of another.

Junctions between neurons occur either on the cell body itself or on tiny extensions of the cell body called *dendrites*. Moreover, a single axon may send out only a few branches at its ending, or it may send out a large number of branches to make synaptic connections with adjoining cells. Similarly, the cell body may only have a few incoming connections which influence it, or may receive inputs from thousands of different neurons.

Nerve fibers can be treated as insulated conductors for transmitting the basic signals of the nervous system—electrical impulses. These elec-

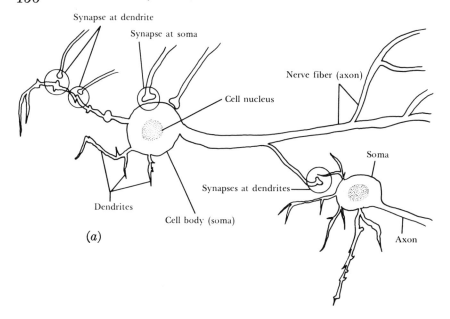

(a)

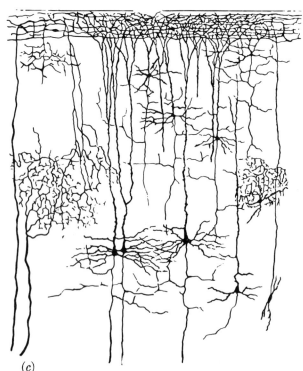

(c)

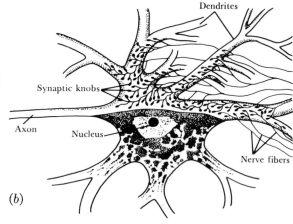

(b)

FIGURE 6-2

(a) Drawing of two neurons showing the different types of synaptic junctions. (b) Diagrammatic drawing of a neuron showing dendrites and axon radiating from the cell body. From Jung (1953). (c) Composite drawing showing the interconnections of neurons in the brain of rat and mouse. After Eccles (1953).

trical (more accurately, ionic) inputs are generated in the cell body in response to activity at the incoming synapses. At the synapse itself, an incoming impulse triggers the release of a chemical *transmitter substance,* which travels across the small gap between the axon of the arriving neuron and the receptor location of the neuron. The arrival of transmitter substance at the new cell causes a change in its normal electrical potential. If enough transmitter is received, the change in electrical potential in the cell body will be sufficient to initiate an impulse, which then travels down the axon to the next synaptic junction, where the whole process is repeated.

It is seldom the case that activity at a single synaptic connection is sufficient to generate an impulse in the receiving cell. Usually a large number of impulses must arrive at a cell before it responds with its own impulse. Synaptic junctions are of two forms: *excitatory,* in which the effect of the arriving impulse is to increase the chance that the cell will respond, or *inhibitory,* in which the arriving impulse reduces the chance that the receiving cell will respond.

A cell's response to the pattern of activity on the incoming synapses is the result of a kind of chemical vote in which the balance of excitatory and inhibitory influences determines the final activity level of the cell. The response rate of a receiving cell generally depends on the rate and pattern of the impulses arriving at the incoming synapse, but there are limitations. After emitting an impulse, a cell requires about $\frac{1}{1000}$ sec in order to recover. Thus, in theory, the most frequently any cell could respond with an impulse is around 1000 impulses per second, and in practice the maximum observed response rates are much lower—on the order of 300 to 800 impulses per second.

There are actually many different types of neural cells, each of which performs specialized functions. One important specialized cell is the *receptor* or *transducer* cell. These units are responsible for converting the energy in an external physical signal into electrical signals. The *rods* and *cones* in the eye are examples of transducers that convert the electromagnetic energy in the incoming light pattern into neural responses. Similarly, the *hair cells* of the inner ear are transducers that convert the mechanical energy in acoustic signals into electrical signals.

In order to measure neural impulses, we need to connect electrical conductors to the neurons. The device used is an *electrode.* Usually the electrode is connected to an electronic amplifier to amplify the small electrical impulses. The output of the amplifier is then fed into electronic monitors that allow the experimenter both to hear and see the neural responses produced by an external signal.

Recording neural responses

An oscilloscope is usually used to plot a picture of the voltage changes in the neuron as a function of time. Neural impulses produce brief blips or spikes on the screen when the impulse is picked up by the recording electrode. If the signal is sent to a loudspeaker, it is possible to hear a click every time an impulse is generated in the neuron. In addition, the neural response patterns are often recorded for subsequent analysis on a tape recorder, or the screen of the oscilloscope may be photographed, or the analysis may be done by a digital computer as the impulses occur.

FIGURE 6-3

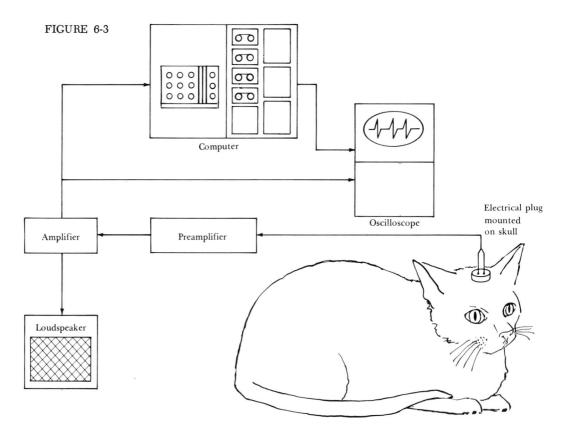

of neighboring neurons. The tip of a microelectrode is often so small that it cannot be seen with a light microscope, an electron microscope must be used.

Both types of electrodes are useful. Often, large numbers of neighboring neurons appear to be extracting similar types of information from an incoming signal, with no single fiber being solely responsible for providing the pertinent data to the brain. In this case, it is useful to study the characteristics of the average response activity of neighboring neurons with macroelectrodes. In other situations, microelectrodes are needed. Individual neurons frequently interact with one another in complex ways during the analysis and coding of sensory signals. To discover the nature of the interactions, the detailed response patterns of each individual unit must be examined.

Where should the electrode be placed? In sensory systems, the synapses of fibers carrying sensory messages tend to be clustered together in a local region called a *synaptic station* or a *relay station*. Since most of the computations carried out by the nervous system are performed at the junctions between neurons, these relay stations are profitable places to begin investigations. By studying both the input and output we try to determine how the sensory information is rearranged as it passes through a synaptic station.

The choice of experimental animal depends upon many factors. A number of the basic studies have been performed on the eye of the *Limulus,* or *horseshoe crab,* mainly because the axons of its retinal cells are relatively large and easy to monitor. More advanced animals are required if we wish to learn about systems more directly applicable to the human. Cats and monkeys are usually used for this purpose. Other animals, such as fish and, infrequently, birds, are studied when their sensory systems offer some particular advantages for investigating certain types of neural coding. Humans are only occasionally used, almost always when some brain surgery needs to be done, and the recording of neural responses is either only a very minor digression in the operative steps to be performed or is one of the procedures necessary for the operation itself.

BASIC NEURAL. CIRCUITS

In Chapter 3 we discussed how visual perception depends upon the pattern of activity that is presented to the eye. If we were to measure the response of a neuron that was connected to a particular location on the retina of the eye, and therefore presumably responsive only to light that fell at a particular point on the visual scene, we would find that it was also affected by the responses of neighboring neurons. The neurons that process sensory information interact in interesting and important ways. This interaction is responsible for the fact that a dark surface appears darker when it is next to a light surface, and lighter if it is next to an even darker surface. The interaction causes green colors to look even greener when they are surrounded by red, and for the contours of objects to be significantly enhanced—the Mach band phenomenon that we discussed in Chapter 3.

The ways in which neurons interact provide a fascinating picture of the basic principles of brain circuits. Moreover, it is relatively easy to show how simple interconnections account for some of the visual phenomena that we perceive. But to show these phenomena, we must be reasonably explicit about the ways in which the neurons interact with one another. In particular, we are going to have to devise a circuit theory for neurons and show the numerical effects of the responses of a neuron upon the responses of neighboring neurons. So, in the sections that follow, we present a very elementary simplified model of the operation of a neuron. With this basic model we can build neural circuits that perform very much like the ones that are actually encountered in the sensory systems and in the brain. Most important of all, the model makes it possible to test your understanding of the operations of neurons in explicit, systematic ways. Note that although the model we are about to present is arithmetic, the mathematics is limited to addition, subtraction, and multiplication: these simple operations are powerful enough to account for most neural interactions.

The building blocks

When we study the construction of sensory circuits, two levels of the system have to be considered: the set of cells that **transform** the external physical signals into a neural output—the *receptors* or *transducers*, and the cells that **combine** the neural signals in various ways. In the visual system, the cells that combine the neural signals are usually called *bipolar* or *ganglion cells*. We will not always be scrupulously accurate with the neurological labels. Often abstract concepts like receptors and ganglions are used when really a whole complex of elements is involved—amacrine cells, horizontal cells, receptors of various sorts, and a variety of synaptic mechanisms. But the important points of neural circuits can be made most easily by restricting ourselves to two basic types of devices: **transformers** and **combiners,** or what we call **receptors** and **neural** cells.

The receptor. The receptor reacts to external signals—sound, light, touch, taste—and puts out a neural response. The symbol for a receptor is shown in Figure 6-4. We represent the output of a receptor by a number that indicates the size of the electrical response. In general, we simplify things by ignoring the mechanisms for translating a physical intensity into a particular response value. Thus, we specify intensity of a signal simply by the amount of responses it produces in the receptor. A signal

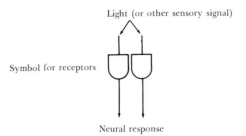

FIGURE 6-4

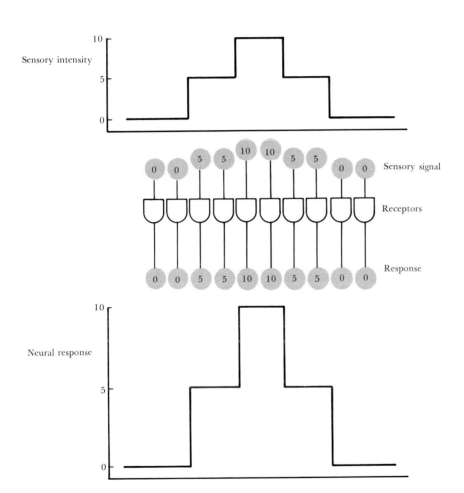

of intensity 5 means a signal with an intensity that produces 5 units worth of neural response. The figure illustrates the symbols and how they are used.

The neural cell. This is a general purpose device for mixing together neural inputs. The symbol for the neural cell is a circle. There are two kinds of connections or *inputs* to a neural cell; one is *excitatory,* the other *inhibitory.* As many inputs as necessary go to a neuron, but

Figure 6-5

FIGURE 6-5

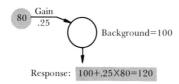

EXCITATORY INPUTS

INHIBITORY INPUTS

COMBINED INPUTS

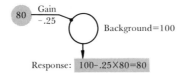

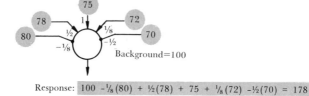

there is only one output (although it may go to several different locations).

Many neurons have a spontaneous rate of responding. That is, even when there are no signals coming in, there still may be an output from the cell. This is called the *background rate*. In the circuits that follow, the background rate corresponding to spontaneous activity is often set at 100. For particular applications this number may vary, sometimes higher, sometimes lower, and sometimes 0.

Each input to a neural cell is assigned a positive or negative number. The number is the amplification or *gain* of that input. An input with a positive (+) gain is excitatory; an input with a negative gain (−) is inhibitory. For example, suppose an input has a gain of 0.5. This means every time 100 units of neural activity is added to the input, the output of the neuron is increased by 0.5 × 100 or 50 units over its previous value. If the gain were −0.5, the output of the neuron would be *decreased* by 50 units for every 100 units input. To simplify the use of the drawings, excitatory connections are signified by arrows; inhibitory connections are signified by dots. The output of a neuron is the algebraic sum of the background rate plus the contribution of all excitatory inputs, minus the contribution of all the inhibitory units. To avoid confusion in these diagrams, all input and output values are shaded; all gains and background values are unshaded.

The basic information in a visual image is carried by variations in the light intensities striking different parts of the retinal surface. These variations may be spread out over a large part of the visual scene, corresponding to variations in the brightness of different components of the scene. At places corresponding to the contours of objects, the change in intensity may be abrupt and large. The arrangement of neural interconnections in the receptor apparatus determines how these light patterns are encoded into neural impulses by the visual nervous system.

LATERAL INHIBITION

The techniques required to discover the wiring diagram of the eye are tricky. Only a few different individual cells can be monitored at any one time. Much of the structure of the neural interconnections must be deduced by some clever experimentation.

A good deal of the basic knowledge of the eye comes from the study of the *Limulus* or horseshoe crab.

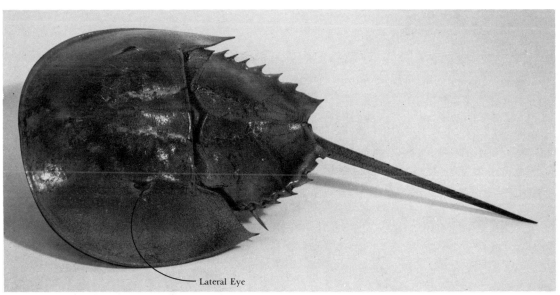

Lateral Eye

Limulus, the horseshoe crab. From Cornsweet (1970). **FIGURE 6-6**

This animal has an easily accessible eye with large, easy-to-dissect nerve fibers. The first step is to dissect the eye so that individual receptors can be stimulated directly without going through the lens and biological matter.

FIGURE 6-7

A close-up of the lateral eye of Limulus. From Cornsweet (1970).

This allows the experimenter to stimulate an individual receptor cell in the eye. Next, the electrode is placed at a ganglion cell and a light is turned on.

Suppose we watch the responses at the ganglion cell as light is directed toward the receptor labeled A in Figure 6-8. If the neural response of the ganglion cell increases, then apparently this cell is monitoring activity in receptor A.

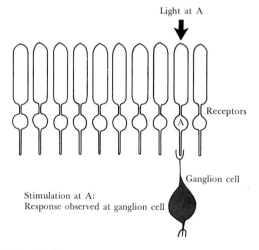

Light at A

Receptors

Ganglion cell

Stimulation at A:
Response observed at ganglion cell

FIGURE 6-8

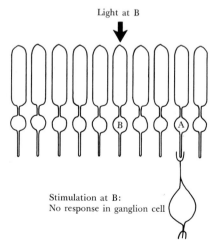

Light at B

Stimulation at B:
No response in ganglion cell

FIGURE 6-9

Suppose the light is moved to receptor B and turned on. This time, the electrode records no change in the activity of the ganglion cell. Apparently, receptor B is not influencing the ganglion cell at A. But before concluding that **only** receptor A affects this ganglion cell, consider what happens with a combination of lights. Begin again with a light at A. Then turn on a second light at B: The neural response of the ganglion cell **decreases.**

Figure 6-9

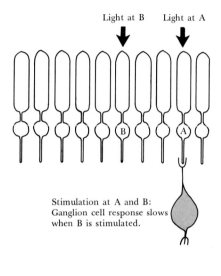

Stimulation at A and B: Ganglion cell response slows when B is stimulated.

FIGURE 6-10

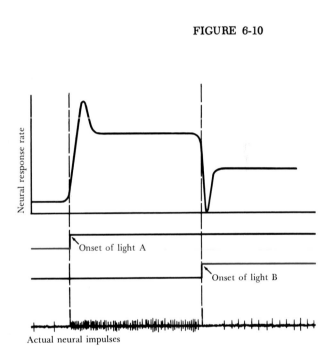

Onset of light A

Onset of light B

Actual neural impulses

Although lights on receptors other than A cannot initiate a response in the ganglion cell, they can decrease any ganglion cell activity that is already in progress.

This simple experiment demonstrates one of the most important mechanisms of sensory information processing: *lateral inhibition.* The activity in one cell is modified by the activity of its neighbors. Conceptually, the notion is simple. It reflects the operation of an inhibitory process, which causes the responses of one cell to be subtracted from the responses of another: computing the difference between two inputs. The simplicity is deceptive. It provides all the computing power needed to convert a complex light pattern falling on the receptors into the abstract rearranged sensory message that is eventually sent to the higher centers in the brain.

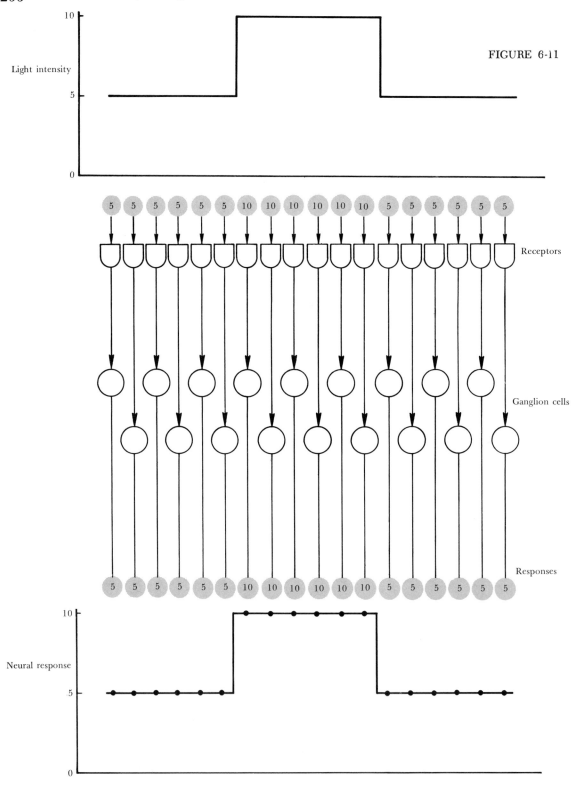

FIGURE 6-11

With the mechanism of lateral inhibition to work with, consider the basic properties of a network that extracts the contours in a figure. Begin with a one-dimensional network with the receptors all lined up in a row. A light shines on the receptors. The problem of detecting contours is to determine where the light intensity is changing. If there were a simple, straightforward connection between receptors and ganglion cells, nothing much would be accomplished. The neural response pattern would be simply a relatively faithful reproduction of the pattern of lights falling on the receptors. This is fine for some purposes, but it does not yield any mechanism for extracting contours in a figure. Something must be added to the system.

Basically, for contour extraction we would like to have relatively little response activity wherever the lights have a constant intensity and a large amount of activity wherever there are changes in illumination. One way of achieving this is to use inhibition so that responses of one receptor are modified by the receptors on either side of it. For example, suppose there is a constant light source of 10 units and we want no output at all from the ganglion cell to this light source. We need to subtract 10 units of activity, possibly by subtractions of 5 units from each side. This is easily done by setting the connection between the ganglion cell and its neighboring receptor at —.5. Now look at Figures 6-12 and 6-13. Here the figures show a system that responds only to the contours in the light pattern. In fact, if you study it carefully, you will see that it only responds when the **differences** in the light intensities striking successive pairs of neighboring cells change.

This circuit illustrates several points. First, we see the need for background activity. If there were no background rate, the negative part of the response to the input would not be observed, since a negative firing rate is meaningless. With a background rate, however, both the positive and negative responses would be observed as increases and decreases in the normal rate at which the ganglion responds. This is illustrated in the right-hand vertical coordinates of the last part of Figure 6-13 where the background rate is assumed to be 20 responses per second.

Second, this circuit responds only to the edges: It turns the world into a cartoon drawing. Differences in the overall intensity of various regions in the visual scene are not encoded. This circuit illustrates the whole point of the processing—to amplify the contours of a visual scene, thereby making further analyses easier. But this circuit has gone too far by being completely unresponsive to any part of the scene that is not a contour.

It makes sense to find a compromise between the first system which did nothing to the signal and the second which left only the edges.

Circuits for extracting contours

Figure 6-11

THE BASIC CIRCUIT

FIGURE 6-12

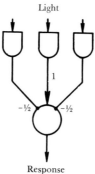

THE IMPORTANT
COMPUTATIONS

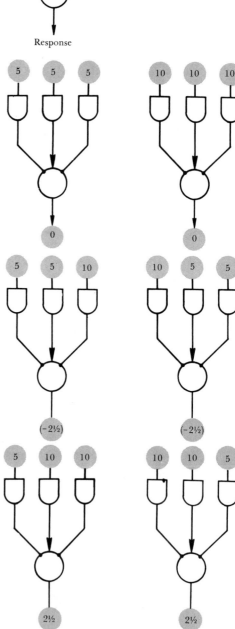

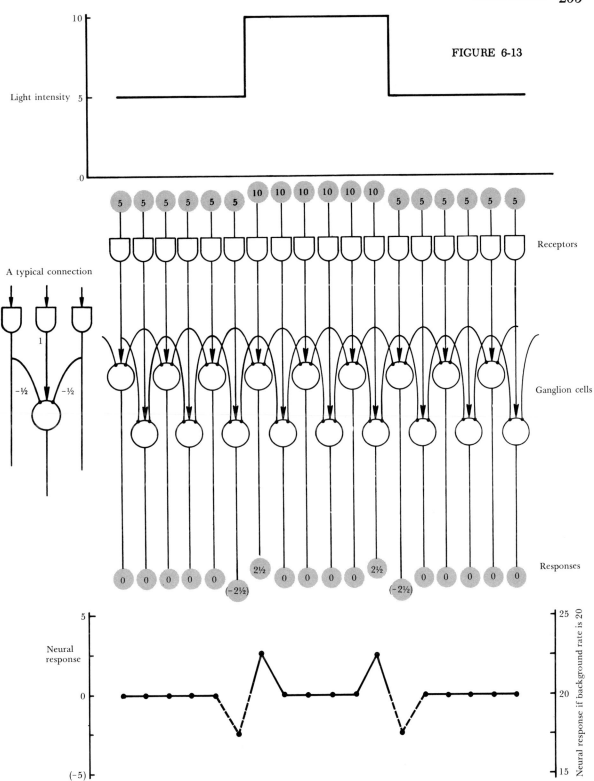

FIGURE 6-13

Light intensity

A typical connection

Receptors

Ganglion cells

Responses

Neural response

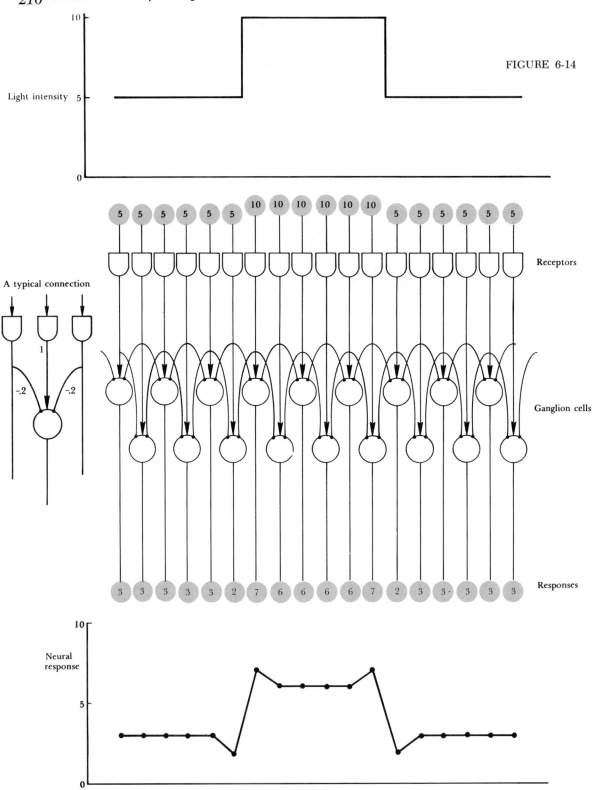

FIGURE 6-14

One way to do this is to reduce the effect of the inhibitory connections. Suppose we try a gain of —.2 (see Figure 6-14). Here is a useful result. The most vigorous response occurs at the contours, but information about the relative intensities of different regions is still preserved.

Figure 6-15 illustrates an experiment that was conducted on the eye of the crab. The photograph in Figure 6-15a shows the crab eye. A projector is focused on the eye, presenting an image of a rectangular test pattern. The test pattern is outlined in the photograph. Note that this pattern contains an intensity change: the left half is more intense than the right. The circle that has been drawn in the center of the test pattern represents the location of the recording electrode. As the light pattern was moved back and forth (as shown by the arrows), the response of the ganglion cell located at the circle was measured: the graphs in Figure 6-15b show these responses as a function of the position of the light pat-

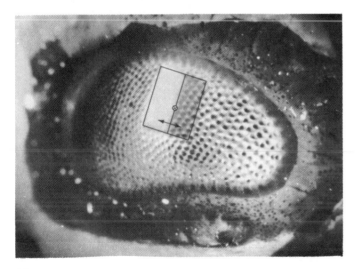

(a)

FIGURE 6-15

(a) From Ratliff (1965).
(b) From Ratliff and Hartline (1959).

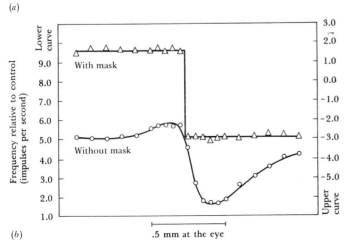

(b)

tern. Note that because the recording electrode was held fixed at one ganglion cell, to see the response caused by the test pattern, it was necessary to move the light, holding the electrode position constant. This is

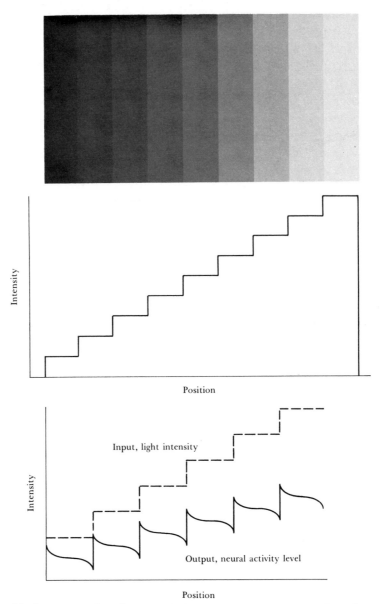

FIGURE 6-16   *Each step in the photograph has a uniform intensity, but the perceived intensity of each step is not uniform. The output pattern (solid line) predicted for the dashed input intensity distribution. From Cornsweet (1970).*

obviously easier than and equivalent to keeping the light steady and moving the electrode (or having many electrodes).

The upper graph in Figure 6-15b shows the responses of the ganglion cell when there is no lateral inhibition. This was measured by covering the eye with a mask except for the one location directly above the recording electrode. In this way, only the excitatory part of the receptive field received light. We see that when there is no lateral inhibition, the neural response gives a rather accurate portrayal of the light pattern.

To measure the effects of lateral inhibition, the mask was removed and the total light pattern shown in Figure 6-15a was presented to the eye. This allows all the inhibitory factors to operate. The resulting neural activity is shown in the bottom graph in Figure 6-15b. No longer does the ganglion cell give an accurate reproduction of the light pattern.

Figure 6-16 gives you an opportunity to experience the effects of lateral inhibition on yourself. Note that the bands of gray do not appear to have constant intensity, even though they really do (the actual intensity levels are shown in the middle part of the figure). This example is related to the Mach band phenomenon of Chapter 3. If you compute the response of the circuit of Figure 6-14 to the light intensity pattern of 6-16, you will get a pattern of neural responses similar to that shown in the bottom part of Figure 6-16 and similar to that actually perceived when you look at the gray bands.

All sensory systems so far studied appear to have contour extracting mechanisms based on the principles of lateral inhibition. Moreover, this basic mechanism has a great deal of flexibility, and can be used to perform other types of analyses of the visual image. It is instructive to try to design these circuits.

In Chapter 3 we presented an example of a visual pattern in which a dark area grew darker as illumination increased (page 91). Now we can see how this might work. Consider the neural circuit of Figure 6-17. When there is no light presented to any of the three receptors, each responds at its background rate of 50. When a weak light is presented— two areas of intensity 20 surrounding a region of intensity 10—then the neural responses for the two outside areas A and C increase with the intensity, whereas the responses for the central area B are reduced, even though more light is now falling on B than before. (In doing the computation, assume that the region of greatest light intensity extends indefinitely to the left and right.) When the light signal is increased in intensity by a factor of 4 so that the more intense outer region becomes 80 and the weaker inner region increases to 40, then the phenomenon still holds. The neural responses to A and C increase with the increased illuminations, whereas the responses to the central region (B) **decrease** still more.

FIGURE 6-17

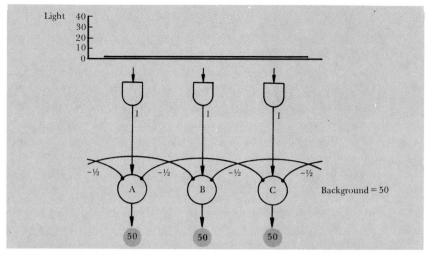

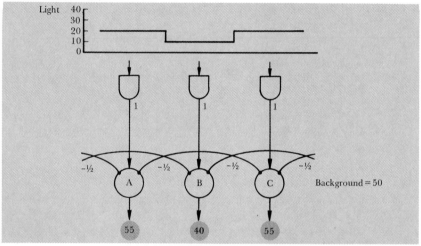

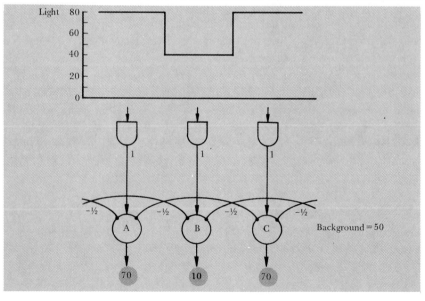

In mammals, the retinal operations differ somewhat from those of a crab, but the basic features of the analysis are similar. However, several problems arise in studying these more complex visual systems. First, an individual receptor may be connected to many different ganglion cells, making it impossible to restrict the light source so that only one ganglion cell is excited by the signal. Second, interconnectors between receptors and ganglion cells in higher organisms are both excitatory and inhibitory. In the eye of a crab, one cell can have only a negative effect on its neighbor. This is not so with other animals. Neighboring receptor cells can both increase and decrease the response of a ganglion cell.

Consider the typical recording from the retina of the cat shown in Figure 6-18. First, the electrode is placed in a ganglion cell and the responses

FIGURE 6-18

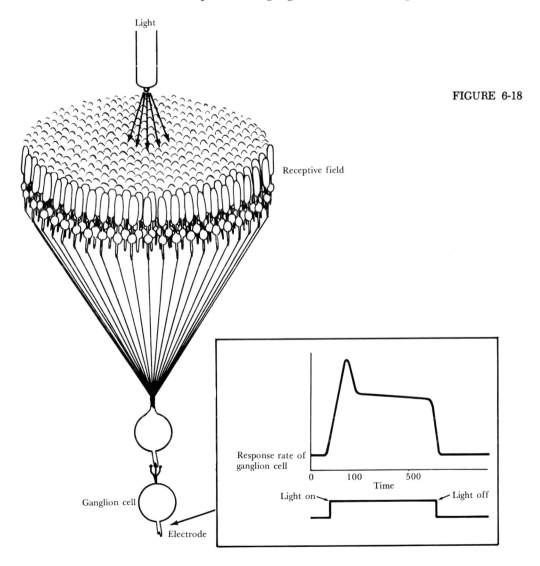

to light are recorded. Then the region of the retina where light stimulation increases the rate of responses—the excitatory area—is found by moving the spot about. The unit responds to the light shown with an initial burst of activity greater than its sustained response rate. In fact, the sustained rate after the initial burst may be barely above spontaneous activity levels.

Now the light is carefully moved around to determine the exact region of the retina that can activate the ganglion cell. Typically, the excitatory area is an elongated circle, with an average diameter of somewhere between .1 and 1.0 mm (between 4 and 40 thousandths of an inch).

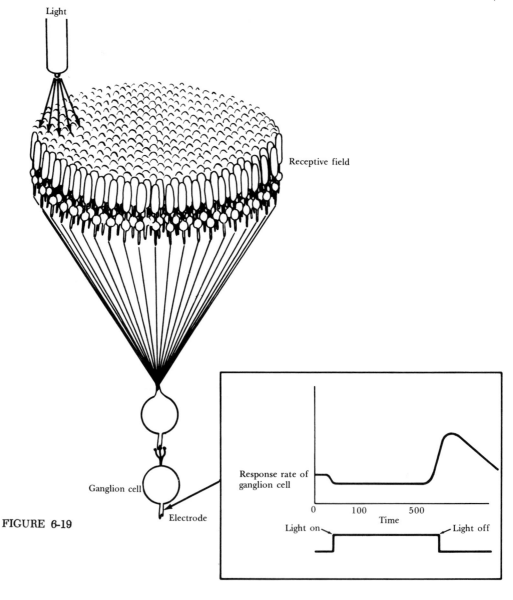

Light

Receptive field

Ganglion cell

Electrode

Response rate of ganglion cell

0   100   500
Time

Light on

Light off

FIGURE 6-19

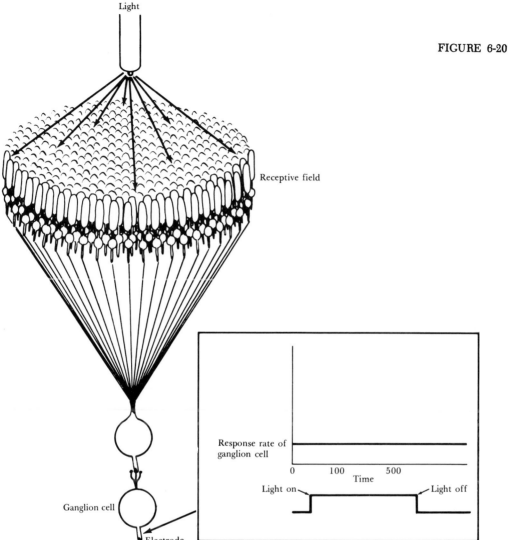

FIGURE 6-20

When the light source is placed outside the circular, excitatory region, a different type of response occurs. The light now causes a decrease in response rate. When the light is turned off, rather than simply returning to its normal background rate, the response rate substantially increases for a brief time. The region producing responses to light extinction is also circular in shape and surrounds the central excitatory area.

This ganglion unit and its corresponding receptive fields are referred to as an *on-center, off-surround unit.* Light to the center region causes an increase in the response of the ganglion; light to the surround causes a decrease in response rate with a brief burst of activity when the light it turned off. A diffuse light over the whole receptive region—both center and surround—may produce no perceptible response at all.

Figure 6-19

Figure 6-20

In general, the nervous system is quite symmetrical. Whenever one kind of neural response is found, we can also expect to find the complementary type of response. In addition to the on-center, off-surround unit, there are equal numbers of units where the response pattern is reversed: the unit is inhibited by stimulation in the central region and excited by stimulation in the surround—referred to as an *off-center, on-surround unit*.

In the retina of the cat, not all of the ganglion cells respond in the center–surround manner. The remainder of the cells show various idiosyncracies. Some may respond only to light onset or only to light extinction, but without the concentric receptive field. Many ganglion cells are of the center–surround type, but with peculiarly shaped receptive fields. Some seem entirely unresponsive to any of the standard test patterns used during typical experiments. Even the simple type of concentric receptive field can give complicated response patterns under different conditions. In Figure 6-21, the neural responses from an on-center, off-surround ganglion unit are shown. In *a*, light falls in the **on** area at two different levels of intensity: medium intensity in the first picture, low intensity in the second, and medium intensity again in the third. In *b*, the light is stimulating the **off** region and the responses to medium intensity and high intensity signals are shown. Note the **off** response burst when the light is turned off. The third row shows the response when patterns *a* and *b* are combined. The result depends upon the relative mixture of the light at the **on** and **off** regions.

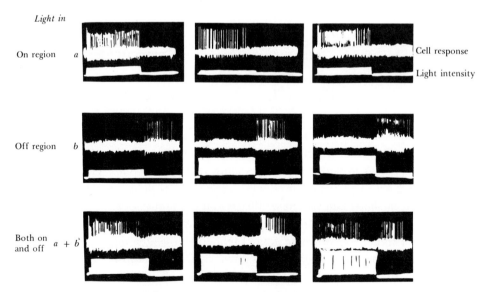

FIGURE 6-21   *From Kuffler (1953).*

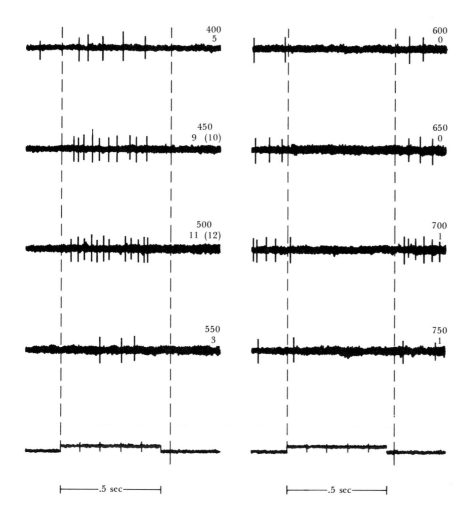

The impulses discharged from goldfish retinal ganglion cell in response to .5-sec flashes of light. Wavelength in nanometers indicated at the right-hand end of each record. From Wagner, MacNichol, and Wolbarsht (1960).

FIGURE 6-22

The basic center–surround mechanism can also operate with lights of different colors rather than for white lights in different regions. Figure 6-22 shows the responses of a ganglion cell in the retina of a goldfish to different colors of lights. The same part of the receptive field is stimulated, but the wavelength of the light is varied. The cell changes from an on-center to an off-center response just by changing the wavelength of the illuminating light. This is an important property of color-sensitive cells.

The opponent process color theory

In Chapter 3 we discussed color vision. There we saw that color vision comes about through a special combination of color-sensitive light receptors. It turns out that the combination of color receptors occurs in a way very similar to the process just discussed for the center–surround cells.

As we learned in Chapter 3, there are three basic types of cones in the retina, each sensitive to different frequencies of light. One receptor has a peak sensitivity at a wavelength of around 440 nanometers (nm), another around 530 nm, and the third around 570 nm. Researchers have given these three receptors different names: *blue, green,* and *red; short, medium,* and *long* (referring to wavelengths); and α, β, and γ. We call them *A, B,* and *C* to avoid choosing sides and to prevent confusion. Now, those three color receptors get combined into a system that feeds information to the brain as a set of complementary pairs. Essentially, the brain. receives color information along three different communication channels:

the red–green channel
the blue–yellow channel
the black–white channel

Each of these three channels specifies a continuum in the color perception space. Thus, the black–white dimension of color perception ranges from very black, through the grays, to very white. Mixing together equal amounts of black and white produces a neutral gray. The black–white channel simply signals at what point the light intensity is along this black–white continuum. A nerve fiber in the black–white channel fires at its normal background level as the light intensity becomes more black or white. Which way does the rate of firing increase? Both ways. Some *black–white* fibers increase their rate of·firing as the light becomes blacker and decrease it as the light becomes whiter. Other *white–black* fibers respond in the opposite way, increasing their firing rate as the light becomes whiter and decreasing it as the light becomes blacker. Regardless of the direction of the change in firing rate, the information content is the same: fibers in the black–white channel signal where the light intensity falls along the continuum of black to white.

Exactly the same principle holds for the red–green and the blue–yellow channels. Red and green form a color continuum (they are complementary colors). A color perception can range from a completely saturated red, through less and less saturated red, until there is complete desaturation and a neutral gray is perceived. From neutral gray it can continue to a desaturated green, and become increasingly greener up to a completely saturated green. Mixing together equal amounts of red and green produces the same neutral gray that results from mixing together equal amounts of black and white (assuming that the light energies are matched properly). Mixing a small amount of green into a large amount of red decreases the saturation of the red. It does not produce a change in hue—no greenness is added to the perception of red. Thus, the red–green channel has nerve fibers that signal where the hue falls on the red–green continuum. Just as in the black–white channel, there are actually two classes of red–green channels: one that increases its firing rate above the background rate when red light is present and decreases it when the light becomes green, and one that does the opposite.

The blue–yellow channel works in exactly the same way. Taking a very blue light and adding a bit of yellow to it simply makes it become less blue. Mixing equal amounts of blue and yellow produces a neutral gray. (When mixing lights, adding blue and yellow does *not* produce green. If you find yourself confused on this issue, please review the section on color mixing in Chapter 3.)

Figure 6-23a shows a typical recording from a red–green nerve fiber to stimulations of lights at different frequencies. Figures 6-23b and c show the average rates of responses to lights of different wavelengths for both red–green and blue–yellow channels. The increases and decreases in firing rates of the nerve fibers above the spontaneous rates are readily apparent in those figures.

What set of interconnections of cells produces these opponent processes? The answer is not yet known with certainty, although it is possible to make intelligent guesses. Two such guesses are shown in Figure 6-24. The fact that we must show two guesses rather than "the" answer is indicative of the state of the science on this topic. Essentially, everyone agrees on the fundamental principals of the operation of the color system, but there is still disagreement over the last details of the operation. Note that in the figures we have drawn two cells for each channel, with the cells receiving exactly the same inputs, but reversed in terms of whether the inputs are excitatory or inhibitory. We draw the cells in pairs to emphasize that whether the cell responds by an increase or a decrease in its firing rate is not important: the important issue is the types of light changes that lead to a change in response rate.

As we discussed in Chapter 3, the color seen at one point is affected by the colors of neighboring points. This is caused by lateral inhibition: The same phenomenon responsible for increasing contrasts and for brightness constancies. Looking at a blue patch at one location reduces the sensitivity to blue in the neighboring areas; hence, more sensitivity to yellow. Looking at black increases the sensitivity to white in the neighborhood. Looking at red increases the sensitivity to green.

Induced contrast

222

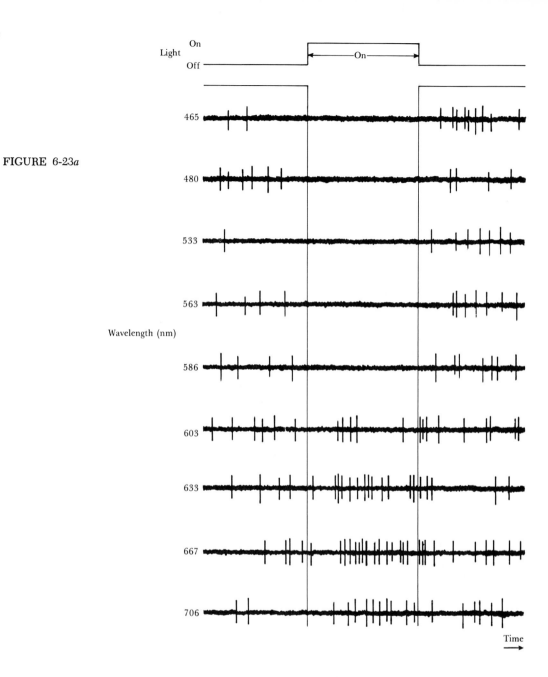

FIGURE 6-23a

(a) Responses recorded from a single microelectrode in the lateral geniculate nucleus of a monkey showing an opponent process cell; (+): responses to long wavelengths (red); (−): responses to shorter wavelengths. (b, c) Average responses of various classes of spectrally opponent cells in the brain of the monkey. The three curves in each plot are three different intensity (energy) levels, in arbitrary units. From DeValois, Abromov, and Jacobs (1966). (Parts of b and c were published in DeValois and DeValois, 1975.)

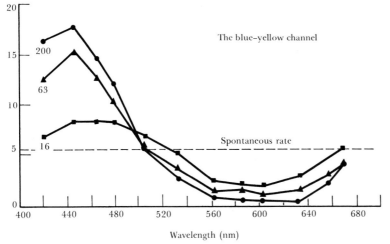

FIGURE 6-23b

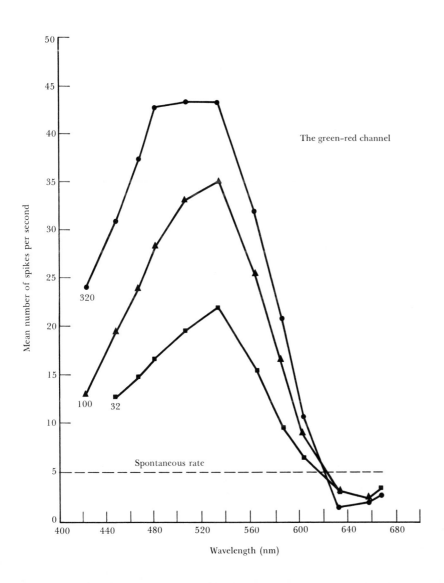

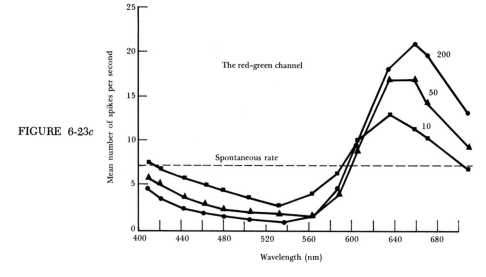

FIGURE 6-23c

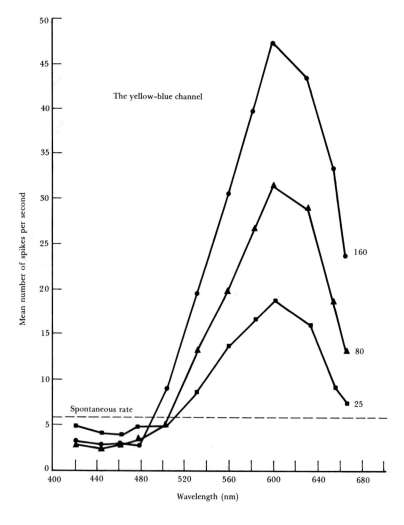

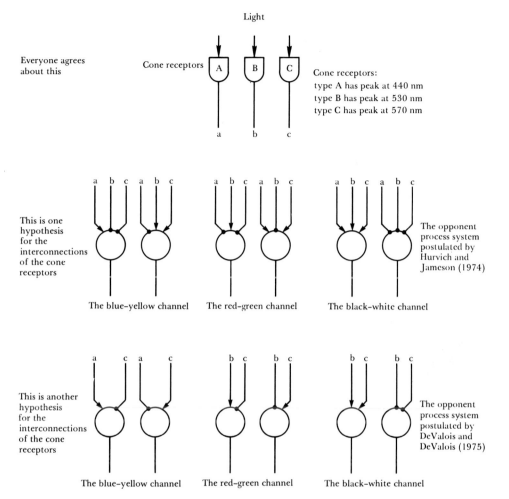

Two hypotheses about the neural interconnections that produce the op-   FIGURE 6-24
ponent process color system.

These contrast effects are called *spatial contrast* or *induced contrast* because a color induces its complement onto neighboring regions.

The explanation for induced contrast follows directly from our understanding of the neural cells. We need only assume that neighboring opponent process cells are interconnected in much the same way as the cells that exhibit lateral inhibition: when one class of opponent cell is activated, it inhibits neighboring cells of the same class. Normally, an opponent process cell has some background rate of firing. When it is activated, the rate of firing increases above the background. When its opponent color is presented, the rate of firing is decreased below the normal background rate. The color vision system can tell which color is present by determining whether the cell's firing rate is above or below the background rate. Suppose a red–green cell is activated by the presence of a spot of red light. This cell will inhibit the responses of neighboring red–green cells. The neighboring cells will decrease their response rate just as they would if a faint green light were shining on the surround. Hence, color contrasts.

RESPONDING TO
MOVEMENT

A final basic problem that the visual nervous system must solve is that of movement. Most of the receptors discussed so far are not primarily concerned with distinguishing between moving and stationary objects. Movement detectors should respond only when an object is moving, and at no other time. Ideally, they should also be selective about the direction and perhaps the speed of the moving pattern.

If we search for movement detectors in the visual nervous system, we do find them. The retinas of rabbits, squirrels, and frogs have units that are selectively sensitive to particular types of movement. Examine the data shown in Figure 6-25 from the rabbit's visual system.

FIGURE 6-25

After Barlow, Hill, and Levick (1964).

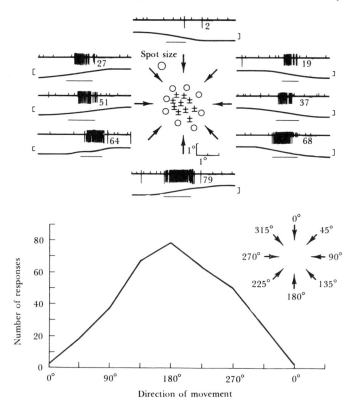

In the center of the diagram, the layout of the receptive fields is shown. The central region produces on–off responses (denoted by the symbol ±), and light stimulating the region surrounding this central part apparently produces no response (denoted by the symbol 0). The arrows show the direction of movement of a test spot swept across the receptive field: The response rates are shown for each direction. The maximum response (79 impulses) occurs to a spot moving straight up. The minimum response (2 impulses) occurs to movement in exactly the opposite direction—straight down. The number of responses produced by movement in intermediate directions is shown in the lower graph.

How does the movement detector work? A normal receptive field contains lateral inhibitory mechanisms. Two characteristics are needed to make them directionally sensitive. The first is that the inhibitory connections be asymmetrical; the second is that the lateral inhibition contain some delay. Figure 6-26 shows the basic circuit that will respond to light moving from left to right, but not to light moving from right to left.

Circuits for detecting movement

Quite sophisticated movement detectors can be constructed using this same basic design. Notice, for example, that the movement detector should respond maximally to a target traveling at a specific speed—the speed corresponding to the rate at which the inhibitory influences move

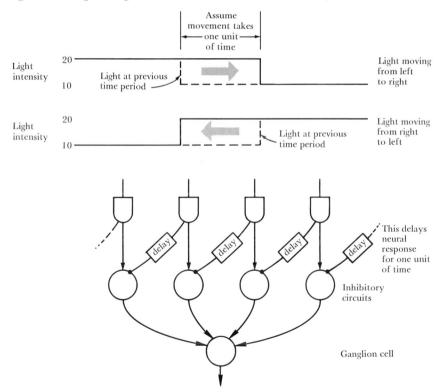

If each delay postpones the effect of the inhibitory signal for our time unit, and if the light moves at the rate of one receptor cell per unit time, this circuit will produce no response to a light moving from right to left, but it will produce a response of 20 when the light pattern shown at the top of the figure moves from left to right.

FIGURE 6-26

out across the receptive fields. And the delay of inhibition received by a given receptor region could depend on how far away the region is from the moving target. Moreover, the reaction times of both excitatory and inhibitory processes in the nervous system depend on the intensity of the signal. Thus we might expect the responses of movement detectors to depend on the intensity of a signal as well as its speed of movement.

Nothing in the circuits so far discussed would discriminate between movements caused by the head and eyes and those produced by actual movements of external objects. Somehow, higher brain mechanisms must coordinate the information provided by retinal movement detectors with the motor commands controlling the eyes and head, if it is to distinguish changes in the retinal patterns produced by head and eye movements from those produced by movements in the external world.

PART II: BRAIN PROCESSES

FROM THE EYE
TO THE BRAIN

In Part I of this chapter we analyzed basic neural processes that represent only the first levels of signal analysis. The neural signals are then conducted by the optic nerve to the more advanced stages of processing (see Figure 6-27). Now it is time to follow the trail of the visual information up into the brain.

*The lateral
geniculate nucleus*

Neural signals that leave the retina travel upward along the axons of the retinal ganglion cells until they arrive at the next relay station—the *Lateral Geniculate Nucleus (LGN)*. Here the fibers from retinal cells make synaptic connections with new cells that will carry the sensory message to the cortical receiving areas of the brain (see Figure 6-27). Fibers that come from adjacent regions in the retina terminate in adjacent parts of the LGN. Thus, neighboring regions in the LGN receive neural information from neighboring parts of the visual field.

The LGN is constructed in separate layers lying on top of each other like pancakes, three layers in the cat, six in the monkey and human. Each layer receives nerve fibers from only one eye, with alternate layers receiving information from alternate eyes. The layers are in registration so that when an object is looked at, the neural activity that results in one eye goes to a particular region of one layer of the LGN, and activity at the corresponding retinal region of the other eye goes to corresponding regions in the LGN layers directly below and above.

The elegant data-processing operations found in the synaptic junctions of the retina and the neat anatomical organization of the LGN suggest that further reorganization and analysis of the sensory information would

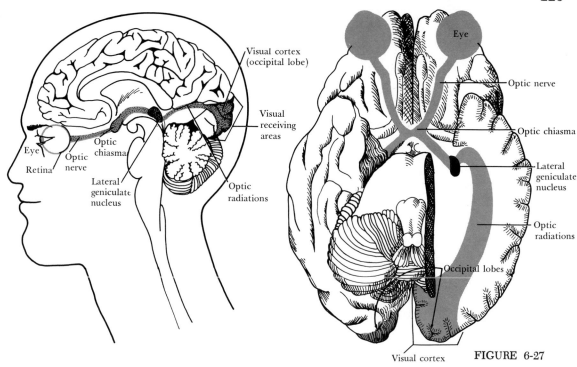

Visual cortex (occipital lobe)

Visual receiving areas

Eye

Retina

Optic chiasma

Optic nerve

Lateral geniculate nucleus

Optic radiations

Eye

Optic nerve

Optic chiasma

Lateral geniculate nucleus

Optic radiations

Occipital lobes

Visual cortex

FIGURE 6-27

occur at this higher brain center. These expectations fail to materialize. To this date, the neat anatomical layout of the LGN remains a puzzle.

What purpose could the LGN serve? Although this puzzle has not yet been solved, some possibilities seem likely. For one thing, inputs to the LGN do not come exclusively from the retina. Other parts of the brain also send signals into the LGN, in particular, a midbrain area called the *reticular formation* (we consider this neural structure again on page 675 in our study of activation). There is a suspicion that activity in these nonsensory pathways may help to determine whether the signals that arrive at the LGN are sent on to the next higher level of the system. Thus, it seems possible that the LGN may normally act like an intensity control over the visual signals traveling from the eye to the brain. This is a fascinating possibility, but it has yet to be proved.

After leaving the LGN, there are no more interruptions in the path before the visual information arrives at the *cortical receiving areas* of the brain. Here, in the *visual cortex*, there again appear neural circuits for processing the signals, some of which are similar in their operation to those found in the retina.

The visual cortex

Messages from the LGN are sent to the visual receiving areas in the cortex (the occipital lobes). At the visual receiving areas, fibers from adjacent regions of the retina end up at adjacent parts of the cortical receiving centers. The fibers leaving the visual receiving areas primarily go to the adjacent visual association areas in the visual cortex, and from there to the *temporal lobes* at the sides of the brain, an area that seems to be involved in the learning and retention of visual habits (see Fig. 11-1).

Like the LGN, the visual cortex is organized in layers, this time five of them. Counting inward from the external surface of the brain, the incoming fibers from the LGN terminate mainly in the fourth and fifth layers down. But in the cortex, unlike the LGN, there seem to be many interconnections among the layers. The analysis of a sensory message starts at the fourth and fifth layers and is elaborated through successive cortical layers until the information finally leaves the visual areas and travels to other parts of the brain.

EXTRACTING FEATURES
The general picture of cortical processing is one of a progressive rearrangement and analysis of specific aspects of the signal. The analysis is carried out region by region, with a large number of different cortical detectors responsible for the features of any particular region. Is there a contour? Is it an edge? A dark line? Does it have a light background? Or is it a slit of light on a dark background? What is its orientation? Does it extend beyond the specific region? Does it change direction? These are the questions answered by cortical detectors.

Simple cells
The lateral geniculate nucleus feeds information directly to the fourth layer of the cortex, so we start our analysis there. If we record the electrical activity at the fourth layer, carefully lowering the electrode through the top of the brain down the fraction of an inch required to penetrate the top three layers, we find cells that respond to small test lights placed on the retina. The region on the retina to which a neural cell is sensitive is called the receptive field of that cell. The receptive field is mapped by shining test lights on the retina while monitoring the responses of the cell being studied.

A typical arrangement is one in which shining the spot of light anywhere along a line increases the response of the cell. Usually, whenever such an excitatory line is found, then right beside it there is also a parallel line that causes the cell's response to decrease whenever it is excited by light. Thus, there would appear to be two parallel receptive fields, each in the shape of a straight line, one excitatory, one inhibitory.

Figure 6-28

This configuration of excitatory and inhibitory fields yields an *edge detector:* The cell responds maximally to an edge of light aligned perfectly with the axis of the fields. Any other signal pattern produces less than maximal reaction.

Other simple cells have other types of receptive fields. Another scheme, similar but a bit more advanced, is a *slit detector*. Here, there is an inhibitory zone on both sides of the excitatory region. Thus, the maxi-

Figure 6-29

RESPONSES TO A TEST SPOT

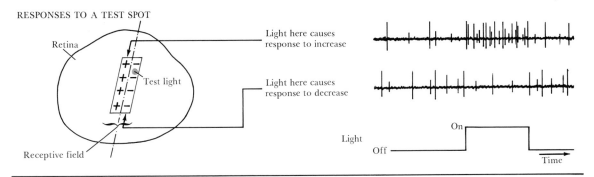

MAXIMUM RESPONSE OCCURS TO A BRIGHT – DIM EDGE

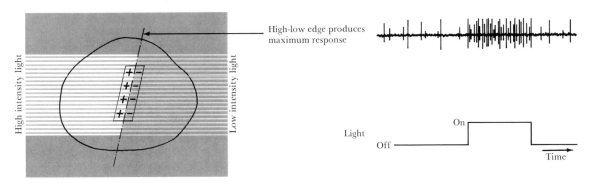

MINIMUM RESPONSE OCCURS TO A DIM – BRIGHT EDGE

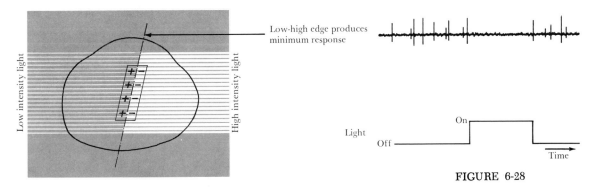

FIGURE 6-28

mum response is produced by a bright line surrounded by two dark areas; the minimum response is produced by a dark line surrounded by two bright areas. Remembering the usual symmetry of the nervous system, whenever there is one arrangement of fields—inhibitory–excitatory–inhibitory—there should also be the complementary arrangement: Indeed, there is. If the first arrangement is represented by the symbols $-+-$, then the second can be represented as $+-+$. If the former is a *slit detector,* the latter is a *line detector.*

By the way, note that information comes from the cell both when it decreases and when it increases response rate. Either reaction is informative; neither response can be considered more basic or more important than the other. The nervous system uses both increases and decreases in neural rates as signals, so it would be a mistake to assume that **on** responses are more basic or more important than **off** responses. The important point is that some change in the activity does occur.

Edge, slit, and line detectors monitor specific regions of the retina. Within a specific region, the edge or slit must be lined up perfectly to produce the maximum response. Thus, although these cells are reacting to more complex features in the visual image, they are still selective in the position and type of signal needed to produce a response.

Complex cells   At the next level of the cortical processing, things change somewhat. There are still the same basic types of features involved—edges, lines, slits, moving lines, etc.—but without some of the restrictions. In simple cells, a line detector responded only when the line was located at a very precise position on the retina. At the next higher level, the line must still have the right width and orientation but position is not so critical: It can be located any place within a rather wide region of the retina (see Figure 6-30). These cells are more complex than the ones at the lower cortical level. Hence, the convention adopted for the names of the cells: If those are simple, these must be complex.

Like the simple cells below them, complex line and edge detectors are not affected by extending the stimuli beyond the receptive field. Also, in common with the simple cells, complex cells react when the appropriate signal is moved through their receptive fields, and frequently they have a preferred direction.

For complex cells, then, the type, direction, and width of the stimulating signal still critically determine the response. The information provided by these detectors, however, is somewhat more abstract than at lower levels, since the position of the contour within the visual field is less important. Thus, the retinal areas over which complex detectors react to their preferred stimuli are considerably larger than the receptive field for simple cortical detectors.

Hypercomplex cells   More specificity about some of the features present in the signal would be useful, for example, the length of lines. The last level of cortical cells that has been investigated appears to do just this. Here there are cells even more complex than the second level—*hypercomplex cells.*

The unique feature added by these cells is that the edge or line must be terminated properly in order to obtain maximum response. Figures 6-31 and 6-32 show some examples of the response patterns of hyper-

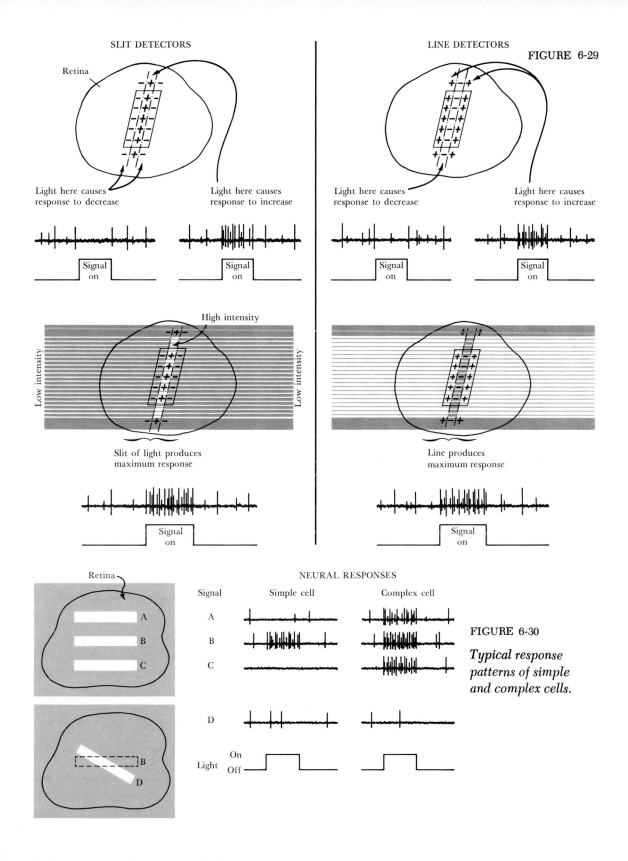

SLIT DETECTORS

LINE DETECTORS

FIGURE 6-29

Retina

Light here causes
response to decrease

Light here causes
response to increase

Light here causes
response to decrease

Light here causes
response to increase

Signal
on

Signal
on

Signal
on

Signal
on

High intensity

Low intensity

Low intensity

Slit of light produces
maximum response

Line produces
maximum response

Signal
on

Signal
on

Retina

NEURAL RESPONSES

Signal	Simple cell	Complex cell
A		
B		
C		
D		

Light — On / Off

FIGURE 6-30

*Typical response
patterns of simple
and complex cells.*

complex cells. In Figure 6-31 we have outlined the receptive field of a moving line detector. Only a horizontal line moving downward gives a response. Lines at other orientations or moving in other directions yield reduced reaction. Of course, this is a typical result of a complex cell. But note what happens when the line is extended in length beyond the receptive field: The hypercomplex cell no longer responds. This is the new dimension added at this level of processing—specificity of **size**.

The size specificity is not exact, as the details of the figure show. If the line is too long as in Figures 6-31 and 6-32, there will be little or no response. However, the same length line moved over so that one end of the line does terminate properly can cause the hypercomplex cell to respond, as in Figure 6-32.

Another innovation appears in these cells. Although the very nature of a motion detector makes it specific to movements in one direction only, hypercomplex cells can sometimes show a specificity to movement in two directions. Thus, in Figure 6-33, we see that the cell responds if the line moves either up and to the right or down and to the left. Yet, if the line is too long, the response ends.

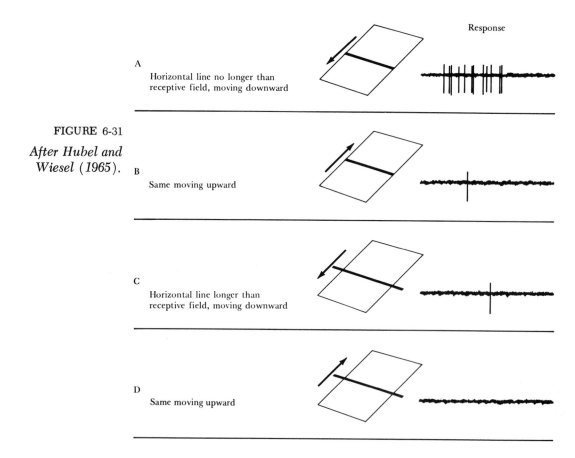

FIGURE 6-31

After Hubel and Wiesel (1965).

Response

A
Horizontal line no longer than receptive field, moving downward

B
Same moving upward

C
Horizontal line longer than receptive field, moving downward

D
Same moving upward

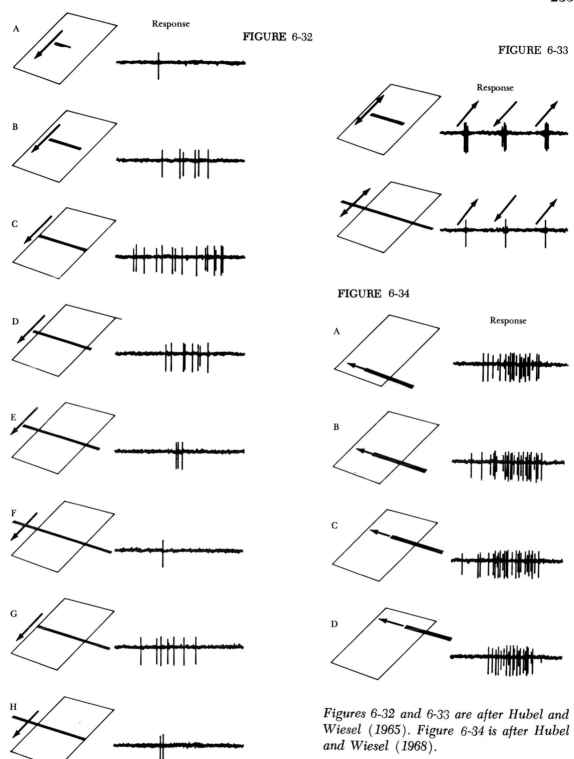

FIGURE 6-32

FIGURE 6-33

Response

FIGURE 6-34

Response

Figures 6-32 and 6-33 are after Hubel and Wiesel (1965). Figure 6-34 is after Hubel and Wiesel (1968).

FIGURE 6-36

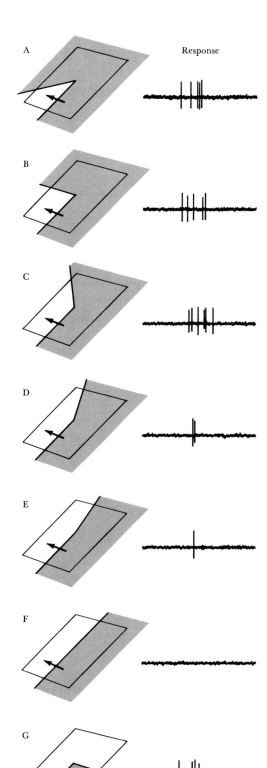

FIGURE 6-35

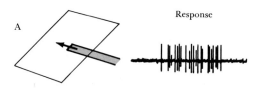

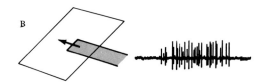

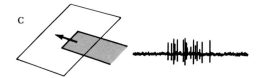

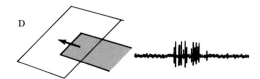

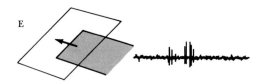

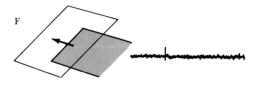

These figures are after Hubel and Wiesel (1965).

Edge detectors also show specificity of size. Figures 6-34 and 6-35 illustrate an edge detector that responds to a thin rectangle moving up into the field at any of several different locations—again, a typical complex cell response. But as soon as the rectangle is widened beyond the critical amount, the responses cease.

Still another innovation is encountered among the hypercomplex cells at this level of processing: an angle detector. Figure 6-36 shows a cell most sensitive to a right angle moving upward through the receptive field. Other angles, while giving some responses, are not nearly so effective in activating the cell.

At the end of the 1960s and the beginning of the 1970s, it was believed that there was a simple hierarchy of processing. Retinal cells were organized together into center–surround units. These units then formed simple cells, simple cells formed complex cells, and complex cells formed hypercomplex cells. Indeed, two different classes of hypercomplex cells were identified (called hypercomplexes I and II) and it was thought that the second were constructed from the first. Today we know that this view is too simple. It may still be correct in the sense that some portion of the visual analysis may follow this hierarchy, but certainly all cells do not.

W, X, and Y systems

The first clue for the interpretation of neural organization came from studying how long it took for cells to respond to stimulation of a point lower down on the visual pathway. The amount of time it took for cells to respond showed that some complex cells could respond to a signal faster than simple cells. But how could that be if complex cells were constructed of simple cells? The answer is that complex cells are not made up of the simple cells, but probably are directly connected to the LGN.

It is now thought that three different types of cells can be found on the retina: W, X, and Y cells. Of these, X and Y seem to be center–surround units. The manner by which they might be interconnected in the stages of visual processing is shown in Figure 6-37. Note that the connections shown are only speculation, and that two of the lines end in question marks indicating that not enough is known to determine where they originate.

Retinal cells of type X have small cell bodies and axons. They send reasonably slow signals up the visual pathway (about 20 meters per second). They are center–surround cells, but of small size. They tend to be located in the central part of the retina. Retinal cells of type Y have large cell bodies and axons and transmit signals reasonably rapidly (about 40 meters per second). They are relatively large center–surround units, and they tend to be located in the periphery of the retina. Type Y cells tend to be sensitive to movement and respond primarily to changes

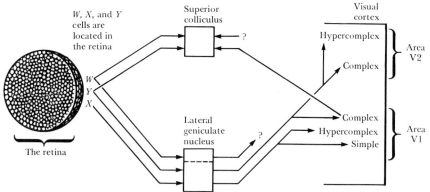

FIGURE 6-37

Visual pathways of the cat. Adapted from Blakemore (1975; also personal communication).

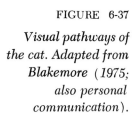

in stimulation. Type X cells tend to be sensitive to continual stimulation, to light contrasts and not to movement. Retinal cells of type W conduct very slowly (around 10 meters per second). It is thought that they have tiny cell bodies, and they do not appear to be center–surround units.

Y cells are good for detecting changes. Their large receptive fields do not lead to precise localization. X cells tell the steady-state story. They tell of the general illumination, and their small receptive fields provide good localization information (a mnemonic aid is that X marks the spot better than Y).

Figure 6-37 shows the presumed pathways of the W, X, and Y cells. We have not yet discussed the superior colliculus: this will be done in Chapter 11. However, to preview the discussions in that chapter, it appears that the visual cortex (and the LGN) are primarily concerned with the determination of *what* object has been perceived, whereas the superior colliculus is concerned with determining *where* it is (and with movements).

Spatial frequency analysis

We have just read of specialized detectors in the visual system—of detectors for lines, angles, colors, and movements. Indeed, in a few pages we will discuss detectors for the shape of a monkey's paw. Is this how the visual system works? Does the system put together the pieces of the visual scene by dissecting the parts, looking for a line here and an edge there? Are lines and edges, corners and angles the basic features of visual perception?

In Chapter 3, when we examined the visual system, we saw that there was another set of phenomena that are relevant to the ways in which visual scenes might be analyzed. If you remember, we showed you a picture of some gratings—a set of closely spaced vertically oriented black bars—and had you look at them for a while. Then, after you had stared at them for about 30 seconds you looked at a set of vertical bars with a medium spacing. These medium-spaced bars now appeared to have a coarser spacing. In Chapter 3 we suggested that the visual system might have a set of specialized receptors for bars of different spacings. What happened in the experiment that you performed on yourself was that the detectors for finely spaced vertical bars had become fatigued. This caused perception to shift so that the world became coarser, with less detail. (If you do not remember the earlier section, or if you did not read Chapter 3, go back to page 98 now and read that section.)

Spatial frequency refers to the rapidity with which the visual scene changes in space, across the page. The printed letters you are reading are sharp and crisp on the page, and this means that they have many high-frequency spatial components. Blur the image of the letters (squint, or take off your glasses) and only the low spatial frequencies will remain, and the letters become less readible. There is much speculation over spatial frequency analysis. What role does it play in the nervous system?

The analysis of visual scenes in terms of lines and angles and the analysis in terms of spatial frequency are intimately related. Suppose there is a hypercomplex cell that is specifically constructed to respond to a certain line length and width. We could also characterize the cell by saying it responded only to a specific spatial frequency. The wider the line that a cell responds to, the lower the spatial frequency that it is sensitive to. All the analyses that we have examined so far—the center–surround cells, the simple, complex, and hypercomplex cells, the W, X, and Y systems—all have straightforward interpretations in terms of cells specially designed for specific spatial frequencies.

Recall the analysis of lateral inhibition, of Mach bands, and of cells designed to amplify the neural responses to edges and contours. This chapter showed how those cells could be analyzed in terms of the patterns of light, and the effect of one cell upon its neighbor. Another way of looking at this same analysis is to say that it represents an enhancement of high spatial frequencies and a suppression of low spatial frequencies. Does it matter which description we apply to the operation of these cells? No, because these are simply two different ways of describing the action of the same cells. But then again, yes, because sometimes it is more convenient to talk about one scheme rather than another. Thus, in talking about how the eye focuses upon an image, it seems quite sensible to speak of maximizing the high-frequency components of the image. In speaking of extraction of the contours of an image, it makes sense to speak both of maximizing the high-frequency information and also of enhancing the lines and angles. Finally, in speaking of pattern recognition, it seems sensible to speak of specialized detectors for lines and segments of a scene. It is quite convenient to have two separate ways of referring to the analysis—**spatial frequencies** in discussions of the overall, global characteristics of pattern analysis, and **features** in terms of the specific details of the analyses.

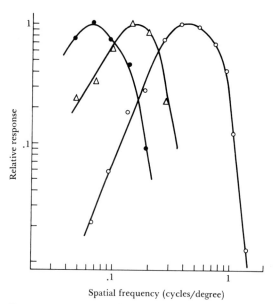

FIGURE 6-38   *Responses of cat cells to grating patterns of different spatial frequencies. (From Robson, 1975, page 108.)*

The response of nerve cells to different spatial frequencies is shown in Figure 6-38. This graph shows how three different cells in the cortex respond to gratings of different spatial frequencies. Each curve is called a *tuning curve*. Note that these tuning curves are actually not very sharp: a large range of spatial frequencies will cause some response from each nerve. Thus, although we could say that the three nerves are tuned to frequencies of around 0.07, 0.2, and 0.5 cycles per degree, in fact, each cell responds to a very wide range of frequencies.

The visual image that impinges upon the retina undergoes analysis by various neural stages before being examined for spatial frequency. The individual tuning curves of the separate cells overlap considerably. Now we are in a position to understand why looking at one spatial frequency long enough to fatigue receptors to the frequency makes the visual appearance of other objects change. The tuning curves of the individual analyzers are quite broad and they overlap considerably. Thus, whenever any particular image is viewed, a large number of curves must be activated, and the perceived frequency must be determined by the average value of spatial frequency that is involved. Thus, when one set of frequencies is taken out of the picture through fatigue, the average value that results from stimulation at another frequency will change.

ACOUSTIC INFORMATION PROCESSING   As we have seen, neurons in the visual system react to significant features in the visual signal. They detect lines and angles, movement, and color. There are numerous specialized neural detectors, from center–surround units, through simple, complex, and hypercomplex cells. But what of the auditory system? What happens to the auditory message as it makes its way from the ear to the brain?

The answer is disappointing, for very little is known of the nature of auditory neural processing. In some sense, our lack of knowledge reflects our lack of understanding of the analysis of auditory patterns. With visual signals, it is quite obvious that lines and contours, angles, and movement must play an important role in pattern recognition. But

Figure 6-39*a* & *b*

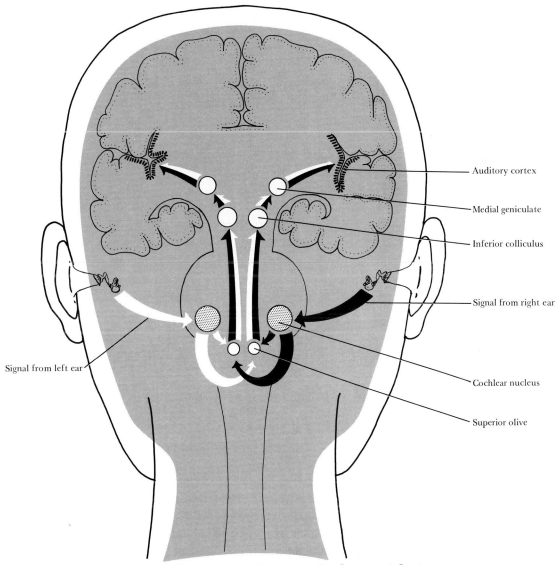

(*a*) Above: *Pathway to auditory cortex from ear. Backview of brain with cerebrum sectioned.*
(*b*) *Next page: View of brainstem, showing locations depicted in* (*a*).

FIGURE 6-39*a*

FIGURE 6-39*b*

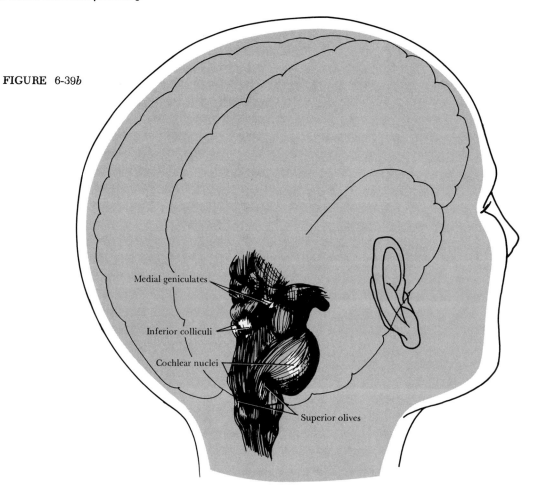

Medial geniculates

Inferior colliculi

Cochlear nuclei

Superior olives

what are the analogous features for auditory patterns? Are they pure tones or complex ones, steady sounds or changing ones? We just do not know.

The nature of human speech makes it appear reasonably definite that there are specialized sound detectors for dealing with it. The whole nature of speech seems geared to the peculiarities of the vocal and hearing apparatus, but just how speech features might be extracted by auditory mechanisms is not known. True, most physiological experiments in hearing are performed on cats and monkeys, but even though these animals do not have speech, presumably their auditory mechanisms should show some unique features of their pattern-recognition system.

It is quite clear that some sort of complex analysis must take place by neurons in the auditory cortex. Evidence of a sort comes from the fact that about 40% of the neurons there will not respond to pure tones at all, but only to more complex sounds such as bursts of noise or clicks (Whitfield, 1967). It may be that these neural units are actually designed to respond only to special, unique sounds, but the closest that we have so far been able to approach the proper sound is simply a click or noise burst.

Even the 60% of the neural units that respond to pure tones do not do so in simple ways. Some increase their rate of firing when a tone is presented (an *excitatory* response). Others decrease the rate of firing (an *inhibitory* response). Some respond only when the tone is turned on (an *on* response), others only when the tone is turned off (an *off* response), and still others both when the tone is turned on and again when it is turned off (an *on-off* response) (see Figure 6-40). These responses, of course, are similar to those found in the visual system.

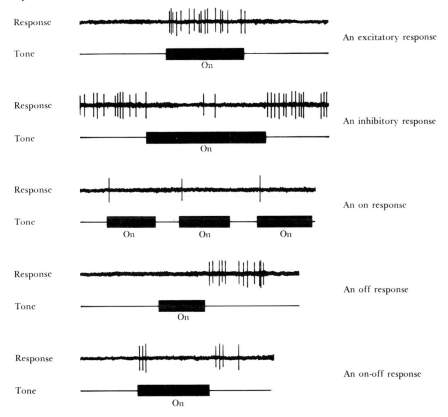

Different types of unit response to tonal stimuli obtained from the un-   FIGURE 6-40
anesthetized primary auditory cortex of the cat. From Whitfield (1967).

Some neural units in the auditory cortex maintain sharp tuning curves, others do not. Some respond only to changes in frequencies (*frequency sweep detectors*), others have regions wherein a tone at one frequency will cause the response to a tone of another frequency to cease (*interactive cells*).

Frequency sweep detectors A number of cells in the auditory cortex (of the cat, at least) seem sensitive only to **changes** in frequencies. They do not respond to a pure tone of constant frequency, regardless of how intense or of what frequency. A steady tone with constant intensity and variable frequency is called either a *frequency modulated* signal or a *sweep frequency* signal. Figure 6-41 shows a typical response of specific types of neurons to a sweep frequency signal (the frequency has been swept up and down in a sinewave pattern).

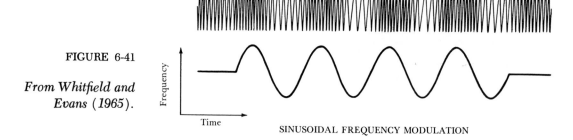

FIGURE 6-41

From Whitfield and Evans (1965).

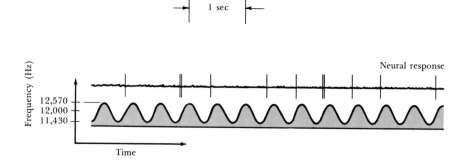

Linear changes in signal frequency produce something that looks like a ramp: a *ramp modulated signal*. A typical signal and the corresponding neural response looks like that in Figure 6-42.

Notice that the particular neural units shown here respond only to changes in frequency in particular directions. With the sinusoidal modulation, the unit shown appears to respond only to increases in signal frequency. With the ramp modulation, two different types of units are shown, one that responds only to increases in frequency, and one that responds only to decreases.

What might the neural circuit look like for these sweep frequency detectors? From a consideration of the pattern that a changing frequency

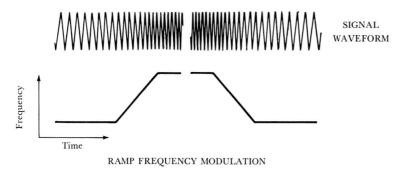

RAMP FREQUENCY MODULATION

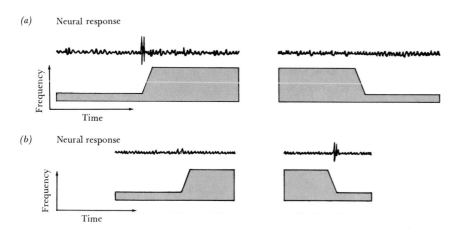

(a) The unit fires in response to a rising tone, but not to one falling   **FIGURE** 6-42
through the same frequency range; (b) the unit fires in response to
a falling tone, but not to a rising one. From Whitfield and Evans (1965).

makes on the basilar membrane, we see that a change in frequency
creates a movement in the location of maximum stimulation along the
membrane. Hence, if we were to build a movement detector for activity
along the membrane, connecting together the basic characteristic frequency cells in exactly the same manner as we connected the center–surround units earlier in this chapter, we would have a frequency sweep
detector. Just as the movement detectors were sensitive only to movement in a single direction, so should the frequency sweep detector be
sensitive to only increases or decreases in frequency, not both.

Three different types of frequency modulated units have been found
in the cat (Whitfield, 1967). They all seem to be sensitive only to frequencies within a certain region, much like the tuning curve characteristics discussed earlier. But rather than responding to any tone within
a tuning curve, they respond only to tones such that the direction of
frequency change is always either:

1. increasing in frequency;
2. decreasing in frequency;
3. upward in the low-frequency part of the response and downward in the high-frequency part.

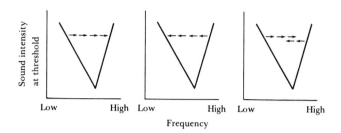

FIGURE 6-43   *Left: Units responding only to rising tones anywhere within its response area. Center: units responding only to falling tones anywhere within its response area. Right: Units responding to rising tones in low-frequency half of response area and to falling tones in a high-frequency half. From Whitfield and Evans (1965).*

What does the cat do with these sweep frequency detectors? We do not know. We know that bats have an extraordinarily large number of sweep frequency detectors. They appear to be essential to the bat's ability to navigate by echo location. By sending out acoustic signals and analyzing the echos, the bat determines the distance and direction of the objects in the environment. Do humans have and use sweep frequency detectors? Again we do not know. It is possible that such information would be useful for the very complex sound patterns that must be dealt with in order to analyze speech.

Binaural interactions   To account for the precision with which sounds are localized, the auditory system must be able to detect time differences on the order of a 10- or 20-μsec difference. Its anatomical design seems to be well suited for preserving the timing information contained in primary auditory neurons.[1] Earlier, it was noted that the neural signals leaving the ear travel only a very short distance before they arrive at the point where

---

[1] *An interesting aside:* Since the time resolution required for precise localization is the same for all animals, how does a large animal manage? The elephant has perhaps the biggest head of all land-dwelling mammals. But the various components of its auditory system are not simply scaled up proportionally in size. Rather, it has an extraordinarily long ear canal—almost 4.5 inches long. This puts the inner ears 9 or 10 inches closer together than the size of the head would imply. Without these long ear canals, the elephant would need relatively long neural cables connecting the two ears, which might increase the risk of losing the precise timing information needed for localization.

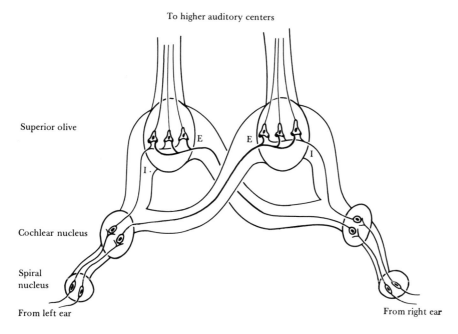

To higher auditory centers

Superior olive

Cochlear nucleus

Spiral nucleus

From left ear

From right ear

From van Bergeijk (1962). FIGURE 6-44

messages from the two ears are combined: the *superior olive*. In the superior olive, excitatory and inhibitory interactions take place between the signals arriving from the two ears—just the sort of mechanism required for binaural localization. Here in Figure 6-44, for example, is a schematic of the general types of interconnections occurring in the superior olive (E stands for excitatory, I for inhibitory). (The exact anatomy has not yet been fully worked out.) Many individual neurons in the superior olive respond differently, depending on which ear receives the signal first. If the signal occurs first in one ear, the response rate of the unit is higher than if the signal occurs first in the other ear. Different neurons seem to have different preferred sides. Moreover, in the cat, the range of time differences for which this effect is observed is about 250 μsec, approximately the time it takes a sound to go from one side of a cat's head to the other. A similar relationship is found with differences in sound intensity. The results of both these variables combine to give remarkably strong evidence that this nerve station is supplying the information that is important for the localization of sounds in the environment.

Some higher levels in the auditory system also seem to be involved in comparing the signals arriving at the two ears—for example, the *inferior colliculus*. Many units in the inferior colliculus can be activated by sounds from either ear. Some units are excitatory, some inhibitory, and some produce just the sorts of interactions needed for localization. The response patterns are similar to those found in the superior olive. Also, the colliculus is organized so that different auditory frequencies are represented in very orderly patterns. This may help in both tonal judgments and in the separation and localization of different sound frequencies.

Although we are beginning to discover some of the neural mechanisms involved in comparing and combining signals from the two ears, the problem of explaining localization is far from solved. What are the neural mechanisms that tell us that something is 37° to the right and slightly elevated? How are complicated sound patterns like several people talking at once separated out and localized? These questions lie beyond our current level of understanding.

WHAT NEXT?   So far we have restricted our analyses to the first few stages of neural processing—and with good reason. Very little is known about brain processes that follow the stages analyzed in this chapter (although see our discussion in Chapter 11). To this point, we have identified a number of different properties of the nerve cells of the cortex that deal with sight and sound. In particular, we have shown that there are a number of different types of cells, that quite often these cells have a particular degree of selectivity to the signals to which they will respond.

The specific features of the auditory or visual signal that cause these specialized cells to respond are called *trigger features*. Trigger features seem to have certain properties. In particular, as one looks further and further up the stages of brain processing, the more specific the triggers get in terms of what objects will be recognized, the less specific in terms of where that object must be located. Hence, at the first few stages of analysis, lots of different objects may trigger the cells, but these objects must be located at very specific places, and in the case of visual objects, exciting a very restricted region of the retina. Later, as we progress from simple cell to complex and hypercomplex, we find cells that are much more specific to what they will respond to: specific angles or line lengths, specific colors, specific rates and directions of movement, and then very specific combinations of even these specificities. But, at the same time, these cells are very nonspecific in their requirements as to where the signal must be. There is no contradiction in these two properties. These cells presumably combine the signals of other cells, and the combination can include inputs from cells located all over the retina or the basilar membrane, thus leading to an ability to be insensitive to the location of the signal. At the same time, by combining the features of less specialized cells, these cells can be selective, responding only if a certain combination of trigger features is present. Just how these interconnections and decisions are made is not known. Today's speculation centers around the properties of the *W*, *X*, and *Y* cells, and attempts to understand the interconnections that characterize them. One of the issues for research is whether their properties are best specified by specific patterns of light or by spatial frequencies. There is much more work to be done as this field of study has just scratched the surface of the fascinating properties of the neural system that underlie visual and auditory processing. And the other sensory systems still remain to be explored.

A few, tentative studies have been made of the response properties of visual neurons beyond the visual cortex. One set of studies concerns the area of the brain called the superior colliculus, which will be treated in Chapter 11. Some investigators have pursued single neurons in the brain areas that receive their information from the visual cortex. In these analyses, the pattern is of more specific trigger features, but with less specific reliance upon the location at which the visual object must be.

When searching for very specific trigger features, how does the investigator know what to try? How did those who studied the frog think of trying small black objects? "Well," you might say, "isn't it obvious that frogs eat flies, so isn't some signal like a fly a rather obvious choice?" Yes, that is true for the frog, but what do you try when you are working with cats or monkeys, and when all the obvious things have failed? One investigator has told us that she discovered that cells in the *visual* part of the superior colliculus were sensitive to sounds when she accidentally knocked open an air jet, causing a loud hissing sound, which in turn caused the nerve cell in the cat on which she was then experimenting to respond intensely (Gordon, personal communication—see Gordon, 1972). The accident was fortunate, but more important, the experimenter was alert to the occurrence and was able to realize its significance (which will be discussed in Chapter 11). Who would think of trying sounds on a cell thought to be sensitive to sight?

Perhaps the best summary of the frustrations and rewards of this research comes from the words of an investigator who has discovered what is perhaps the most remarkable set of trigger features to date: cells in the monkey that respond selectively only to visual signals that look like the shape of a monkey's paw, pointing upward. These were discovered in the inferotemporal area of the brain—beyond the brain levels discussed in this chapter. This "monkey-paw detector" has defied the credibility of many scientists, who although they are willing to believe the result, cannot believe the concept. (The articles by Blakemore, 1975, and Barlow, 1972, present two opposing points of view on the value of studying specific trigger features as a clue to the way the nervous system works. We present our point of view in Chapter 7.)

How does an investigator decide what signals to present to the experimental animal? How was the monkey-paw detector discovered? The report of the monkey-paw detector was made by Gross, Cowey, and Manning (1971) and by Gross, Rocha-Miranda, and Bender (1972). Here is what Gross had to say about the result:

> We often could not be sure that we had found the best possible stimulus conditions. This difficulty is underlined by our finding of a few dozen neurons with highly complex and specific trigger features which we often discovered accidentally. Among these were neurons whose best stimulus appeared to be the shadow of a monkey hand [Figure 6-45], a bullet-shaped form, the shadow of a hemostat forceps, and a bottle brush. Some neurons preferred a particular three-dimensional stimulus over any two-dimensional representation of it.

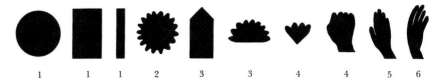

FIGURE 6-45   *Examples of shapes used to stimulate an inferotemporal unit apparently having very complex trigger features. The stimuli are arranged from left to right in order of increasing ability to drive the neuron from none (1) or little (2 and 3) to maximum (6). (From Gross et al., 1971, reproduced from Gross, 1973.)*

The existence of such cells with highly specific trigger features raises the possibility that we may never have found the appropriate trigger features for other of our cells. Thus, a (more typical) neuron that responded best to a 1° × 5° red slit oriented at 45° within its receptive field may not have been "coding" this size, shape, color, and orientation. Rather, its trigger feature might have been a far more specific, complex, and perhaps meaningful stimulus that we never used and that happened to share some of the stimulus parameters of the stimulus we did use. Thus, in searching for the adequate stimulus and systematically carrying the length, width, color, etc. of a slit we may have been like Kipling's proverbial blind men examining an elephant. [Gross, 1973, page 107]

CONCLUSION   The story presented up to this point is reasonably simple. We have seen how the rods and cones at the retina transform the optical energy they receive into electrical signals. These signals are processed by the interconnections of cells present at the retina, and then the messages are sent to the lateral geniculate nucleus (LGN) and the superior colliculus, and from the LGN to the visual cortex. Some cortical cells are specialized, being sensitive to a restricted set of visual patterns. In addition to the edge, contour, and movement detectors that we have discussed here, there are cells sensitive to color and to the spacing of light and dark areas of the visual image (that is, to the spatial frequency). Cells appear to combine these specialities, so that some are maximally sensitive only to visual signals of a particular size, orientation, color, and speed and direction of movement. The extreme case of specificity appears to be the case of a cell in the monkey cortex that would seem to be triggered best by the visual image of the monkey's paw, oriented upward (the way that the monkey would view its own paw). Although not yet so detailed, a similar story appears to hold for auditory processing.

The simplicity is illusive. From our work on the perceptual processes of recognizing patterns (in Chapter 1, and then again in Chapter 7), we would characterize the structure just described as a *bottom-up, data-driven* system. Such a system fails to handle the perceptual demands placed upon the human, for it is too rigidly tied to the exact details of the signals presented to it. The perceptual system requires *top-down, conceptually guided* processing, as well as parallel processing of signals through alternative channels. These comments apply to all sensory analysis, not only to vision. The system must be organized differently than the simple linear string implied by the current results from neurophysiological investigations of the sensory systems. Even the analysis of the retinal cells into W, X, and Y systems is not a sufficient departure from the sequential nature of the processing stages. Still, it is wise to remember that other organizational schemes than the ones so far known will undoubtedly be discovered in the next years of research.

In this chapter, the following terms and concepts that we consider to be important have been used. Please look them over. If you are not able to give a short explanation of any of them, you should go back and review the appropriate sections of the chapter.

REVIEW OF TERMS AND CONCEPTS

The concept that the frog (and most animals) has special cells in the eyes for detecting special types of visual signals.
The neuron
    axon
    cell body

Terms and concepts you should know

dendrite
nerve fiber
soma
synapse
inhibitory
excitatory
Transducers
receptor cells
rods
cones
hair cells
Electrode
How recording is done

How to do the computations for neural circuits
How to build a circuit that gives Mach bands
gain
excitation
inhibition
background rate
Specialized cells
center–surround
movement detectors
on-off cells
slit detectors
edge detectors
specialized auditory cells
simple cells
complex cells
hypercomplex cells
W, X, Y cells
The encoding of color
the opponent process system
Anatomy
retina (from Chapter 2)
basilar membrane (from Chapter 4)
LGN
cortex
temporal lobes
the auditory pathway
binaural interactions
Spatial frequency analysis
Trigger features

A good introduction to the problems posed in this chapter comes from Ratliff's book *Mach bands* (1965). A number of the illustrations used in this chapter were borrowed from that book. In addition, the reader interested in the mechanisms of neural interactions should start with the now classic papers of Barlow, Hill, and Levick (1964), the series by Hubel and Wiesel (1962, 1963, 1965, 1968), and the original, now classic paper on "What the Frog's Eye Tells the Frog's Brain," by Lettvin *et al.* (1959). Almost all the physiological information on single cells in this chapter has come from the seven references listed above.

SUGGESTED
READINGS

Georg von Békésy reviews the role of lateral inhibition in many sensory modalities in his little book, *Sensory inhibition* (1967). Basically, both Ratliff's book on *Mach bands* and Békésy's book can be considered to be required reading for anyone who has any interest at all in the material in this section. Both these books deal extensively with lateral inhibition, the primary concept involved in the construction of neural circuits. Moreover, both books are comprehensive, yet easy to read.

Cornsweet (1970) and Dodwell (1970) present a review of the neural mechanisms in a fashion very similar to that presented here. Both these books are important for several chapters of this book: Cornsweet treats many problems in visual perception in excellent and elegant ways; Dodwell discusses the general problem of pattern recognition. Deutsch (1967), an electrical engineer, presents an interesting set of neurological models in his book, *Models of the nervous system.*

There are numerous sources of information on the neurological structures discussed in this book. First, let us review the major books. Volume III of the *Handbook of perception* is concerned with *Biology of perceptual systems* (Carterette & Friedman, 1973) and makes a good review, including the sensory systems that we have completely ignored here. The volumes of the *Handbook* dealing with the specialized senses (IV, *Hearing;* V *Seeing;* VI *Feeling, tasting, smelling, and hurting*) should obviously be consulted for specific interests in these topics. The *Handbook of psychobiology* (Gazzaniga & Blakemore, 1975) is an outstanding summary of much of the important work, both in sensory systems and in higher brain structures. We recommend this book highly. *The neurosciences: Second study program* (Schmitt, 1972) and *The neurosciences: Third study program* (Schmitt & Worden, 1974) are the standard bibles for students in the field of neurosciences, and despite their high prices, are essential for any student who intends to make a career in this field. The extraordinary book by Rodieck (1973) tells you more than any one individual should ever need to know about the retina: 1044 pages of densely packed information. This book is only for those who are serious students of the eye, but for them, it may be invaluable. (It is also expensive.)

There are numerous articles on the topic of neural information processing. An excellent source of timely, informative articles is the journal *Scientific American*. Some of its articles relevant to the topics in this chapter are: Campbell and Maffei (1974) on spatial frequency analysis; Ratliff (1972) on lateral inhibition; Werblin (1973) on the neural mechanisms that control the sensitivity of the retina; and Pettigrew (1972) on binocular vision. There are many other relevant articles as well, and we recommend our favorite way of searching for material. Go to the library and get all the volumes of the journal, then leaf through them, starting with the most recent one and working backwards. Held and Richards (1972, 1976) and Thompson (1972, 1976a) have collected together the best *Scientific American* articles on perception and physiological mechanisms (respectively) and these four books are all useful for this chapter.

In the text of this chapter we recommended the papers by Blakemore (1975) and Barlow (1972) on the philosophy of neural detectors. You might also wish to see the papers by Gross (1973) for the story of specialized cells beyond the sensory cortex, and the monkey-paw detector. An interesting article on neurological circuits for motion perception is presented by Sekuler and Levinson (1974). For some nice results on the development of the specialized neural circuits that we have discussed, see the chapter by Hirsch and Jacobson (1975: in the *Handbook* by Gazzaniga & Blakemore). As usual, the *Annual Review of Psychology* and the *Annual Review of Physiology* provide good sources for further references on these topics.

7 Pattern recognition and attention

PREVIEW

Consider the problem of recognizing the signals that arrive at the sensory organs. To recognize the things in the world, we need to separate the relevant sights and sounds from among all the sensory signals impinging upon us. Once the relevant signals are extracted, we still need to determine what they represent. These are the problems of pattern recognition and attention. Both problems are intimately related.

As we attempt to piece together the mechanisms responsible for pattern recognition and attention, an apparent paradox develops. Quite often we must understand the meaning of a signal in order to analyze its parts properly, but how can we understand the meaning of a signal until its parts have been analyzed? This is like saying that to recognize something we must first recognize it. Suppose you are in the midst of a large crowd of talking people. You can choose one voice to listen to, and ignore the others. Yet if another voice mentions your name, you will probably hear it. How can you understand your name when it comes from a voice that you are ignoring?

The resolution of the paradox comes from realizing that the human mind analyzes signals by working at several levels simultaneously: the information-processing system of the mind is both *data driven* and *conceptually driven*. These two different levels of processing interact with each other, and their combined power is capable of analyzing signals that neither level could handle alone.

This chapter marks the transition from the study of relatively peripheral aspects of brain functioning to more central aspects. We are finally getting to the study of the mental processes that are called *cognition:* we are beginning the study of the mind. The purpose of this chapter is to examine how mental operations make use of information provided by the senses. Earlier chapters have covered the pathways from the eyes and ears through the parts of the nervous system that process visual and auditory information. We have seen how the information that arrives at the sensory organs is analyzed and then sent upward on its path from sensory receptors to brain processes. This direction of processing is *data driven.* Data-driven processing is initiated by the arrival of sensory data and it attempts further analyses of those data.

In this chapter we will look at how the brain begins the task of selecting relevant information from the vast number of signals that reach it and how it places an appropriate interpretation on those signals. We will discuss the need for mental processes to add their contributions, for processing to proceed by starting with conceptualizations and expectations. This direction of processing is *conceptually driven.* We will see how the combination of data-driven and conceptually driven analyses produces an efficient, intelligent system.

This chapter emphasizes the nature of the mechanisms of pattern recognition and attention. We present a model of how the system might work. Your task should first be to understand the basic phenomena, and then to understand the model that we have built. Actually, we construct a number of different models in the course of the chapter, each growing from previous ones, each attempting to remedy some of the deficiencies of the earlier models. We have decided to lead you through the sequence of models in the way they actually developed, showing how they were changed as needed to account for new phenomena. It is important to understand both how we constructed our models and why we changed them. The building and testing of models is a fundamental tool in scientific research. Even the final model of this chapter is not complete—it will be modified in coming years. It simply represents the best thinking that we can perform today. If you have thought seriously about the lessons in this chapter, perhaps you will be the first person to suggest the next stage of improvement.

You will note that the models we construct in this chapter are filled with demons and blackboards. Obviously, we do not believe that such objects reside inside the head. Each of these concepts represents some actual neurological process. By describing the operations in terms of demons, we are able to characterize the processes of pattern recognition and attention in simple, graphical terms that should be easy to understand. These demons are very simple creatures, just like the feature detectors of Chapter 6. Do not think that there is anything mysterious or complex about the demons of our models.

As you read the chapter, try to see how the phenomena that are described fit with the models that are developed. Recall the other material that you have learned in this book. Try to fit that material into the picture that we are developing. Think about your own experiences and see how they might be interpreted in terms of the models that we have presented. If you disagree with some of the statements or believe a model is unsatisfactory, try to correct the problems, remembering that your model must account for all the phenomena. It is often easy to find a problem with a model, but difficult to correct it. You might even wish to read about perceptual processing models in some of the current scientific journals. The models in this chapter are simplified versions of actual models being studied and developed. You will not find the demons that animate this introductory book, but you will find the same concepts discussed in a drier, more technical language.

RECOGNIZING PATTERNS

In Chapter 6 we studied some of the neural mechanisms underlying perceptual experiences. Are these detection systems sufficient to account for human pattern recognition? A little thought about the problem immediately raises some basic questions.

If the system is to be a model of human pattern recognition it is going to have to be quite flexible. For example, it should be able to reliably recognize a given letter even though it may appear in a variety of SIZES or *orientations.* Moreover, it should not be too disturbed by various kinds of distortions in the patterns. We can easily recognize a pattern when parts of it are missing

or when there are extra irrelevant lines

or when a variety of patterns are associated with the same letter:

A ℓ ⓐ 𝑎 𝒶 𝐀 𝒶 𝐀 A

˙uʍop ǝpᴉsdn pǝʇuᴉɹd ǝɹɐ ʇɐɥʇ sɹǝʇʇǝl pɐǝɹ uǝʌǝ uɐɔ ǝʍ 'pǝssǝɹd ɟᴉ 'ʇɔɐɟ uI

This is a formidable list of requirements. However, they must be dealt with if we are to understand perceptual information processing. Let us examine the kind of system that emerges when we try to combine the features extracted during visual processes with the power and flexibility of human perception, in an attempt to build a model of human pattern-recognition.

One possible method of using feature analysis for recognizing patterns is the system called *Pandemonium* (Selfridge, 1959). This system is composed of a succession of *demons* who work on the pattern, each performing a different job.

The first set of demons, the *image demons*, have the simplest job. They merely record the initial image of the external signal. The image is next analyzed by *feature demons*. Each feature demon looks for a particular characteristic in the pattern: the presence of a certain type of line; the presence of angles of some sort; or, perhaps, certain curves

Pandemonium

Figure 7-1

FIGURE 7-1

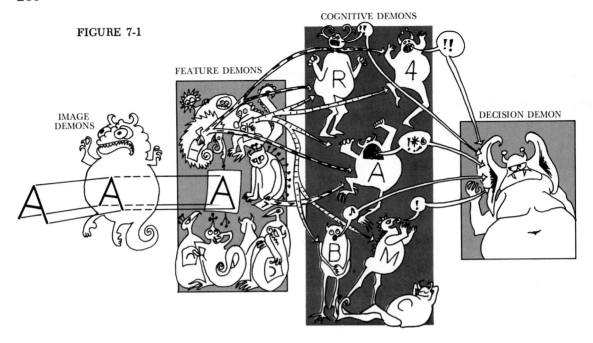

or contours. *Cognitive demons* watch the responses of the feature demons. Each cognitive demon is responsible for recognizing one pattern. Thus, one cognitive demon would be used for recognizing A; one for recognizing B, and so forth. The A cognitive demon tries to find evidence for the presence of the features associated with its particular pattern. When a cognitive demon finds an appropriate feature, it begins yelling. The more features it finds, the louder it yells. Finally, a decision demon listens to the pandemonium produced by the cognitive demons. It selects the cognitive demon who is yelling the loudest as the pattern that is most likely occurring in the environment.

In Chapter 1 of this book we discussed and illustrated a number of different perceptual phenomena. We also examined one possible mechanism by which the nervous system might recognize the signals that were presented to it. That scheme was the template scheme of *pattern recognition*. That is, we examined how a system might work if it had a set of templates or accurate images of the objects that it would experience, and when sensory signals were received, it attempted to match the templates against those signals. In Chapter 1 we showed that this scheme was too restricted and inflexible to be of much use in recognizing patterns that had any variability to them.

In Chapter 6, we examined actual neural cells that seemed to perform specialized functions, extracting special features from the sensory signals. The features that we examined in the visual system corresponded to such things as line segments of certain orientations, angles, light contrasts, movements and colors. Some neurons seem best characterized as recognizing spatial frequencies, or certain spacings of the contours of images. In the auditory system, there were analogous features. We found cells that responded to certain auditory frequencies, to pitch changes, and to the onset or offset of signals. As we went higher and higher into the nervous system, leaving the analyses performed at the sense organs themselves and going to the centers of the brain, the feature analyses seemed to be more and more explicit, being more specialized in terms of the *descriptions* of the signals to which they would respond, but being less sensitive to the locations of these features in the visual (and presumably, in the auditory) field. These cells, the ones that detect special features present in the arriving signals, are like the demons of the pandemonium scheme of pattern recognition. Each specialized neuron is a feature demon. Maybe the features are then sent to other neurons, which look for special combinations of features and which, therefore, act as the cognitive demons of the pandemonium model. Perhaps the "monkey paw detector," which we discussed briefly in Chapter 6 corresponds to one of the cognitive demons.

The pandemonium scheme is like the template scheme in some respects: there is a matching of specific sets of features for specific items that are to be recognized. But a template of features is much more powerful than a template of specific lines and angles. Pandemonium systems will recognize letters despite changes in size, orientation, and despite a number of other distortions. Pandemonium, then, describes the sequence of events needed for a feature analysis of patterns. It differs from the template scheme mentioned in the first chapter only in that the image is first recoded into a set of features rather than being matched directly against an internal replica or representation. Like the template scheme, pandemonium looks for all patterns at the same time. Each cognitive demon reports the degree to which the input matches its particular set of features. It is an appealingly flexible scheme for pattern recognition. It is possible, for example, to make it learn. Each cognitive demon could gradually learn how to interpret the various features associated with its particular pattern. It is reasonably easy to include the effects of context by adding *contextual demons* who add their voices to the pandemonium. Moreover, the feature analysis is compatible with what we know about the way the nervous system analyzes external signals. As the previous chapters have shown, individual neurons in the perceptual system have just the type of response patterns that make them useful feature demons.

Does a feature-recognition system solve the problems associated with the changing sizes, orientations, and positions of a given pattern? Not directly. It depends on the nature of the features being analyzed. Suppose H is described as having two long vertical lines plus a short horizontal line. With this set of features, any changes in orientation would pose just as much of a problem for feature analysis as it did for template matching. Pandemonium outlines how features might be used to recognize patterns; it does not in any way tell us what features are actually being extracted from the incoming sensory information.

If we were going to design a machine to recognize patterns, we would study the pattern set and try to determine the features that uniquely classify each pattern. In principle, we would be perfectly free to select any set of features we thought would reliably discriminate among the patterns. The main criteria would be that the feature set be as simple as possible; that it produce as few errors as possible; and that the features be analyzed using simple circuitry. Our task, however, is not to build some arbitrary machine, but rather to understand the pattern recognition system of the human.

How to build pandemoniums   The study of the kinds of neural responses produced by specific incoming signals suggests that the perceptual systems of most higher-level organisms extract a wealth of data about specific features in the visual image. Recall that in the brain centers which receive sensory information from our receptors, some individual neurons react only to the presence of a straight line at a particular orientation in a particular part of the retinal image. They show the same reaction regardless of the length of the line. Neighboring neurons may also respond maximally to a line of a particular orientation, but may not be so fussy about its exact location. Still others seem to be most sensitive to contours of certain shapes or to intersecting lines that form an angle of a particular size. Visual systems, then, typically extract an enormous amount of detailed information about specific features in the visual image. In fact, more information is extracted than would be needed to recognize letters on the basis of a pandemonium scheme.

The information can be condensed by applying the same principle that was used to construct templates: Simply connect together a number of cells to construct a more general feature detector. For example, neurons responding to vertical lines in different parts of the retinal image could be connected together to produce a general vertical line detector. The response rate of this feature demon would code the **number** of vertical lines in the pattern, regardless of the length, intensity or "goodness" of each line. Similarly, a general feature demon for horizontal lines and for diagonal lines could be made by connecting up the appropriate neural detectors. The same could be done with angle information: One feature demon could specify the number of right angles in the pattern; another the number of acute angles. Finally, there ought to be some information related to curves. For the present purposes, we can invent two curve demons that would be useful in a pattern recognition system: One that responds to the number of continuous curves (such as in O and Q), and one that responds to the number of discontinuous curves (D and C). After making the appropriate connections, the resulting system would look like Figure 7-2.

Table 7-1

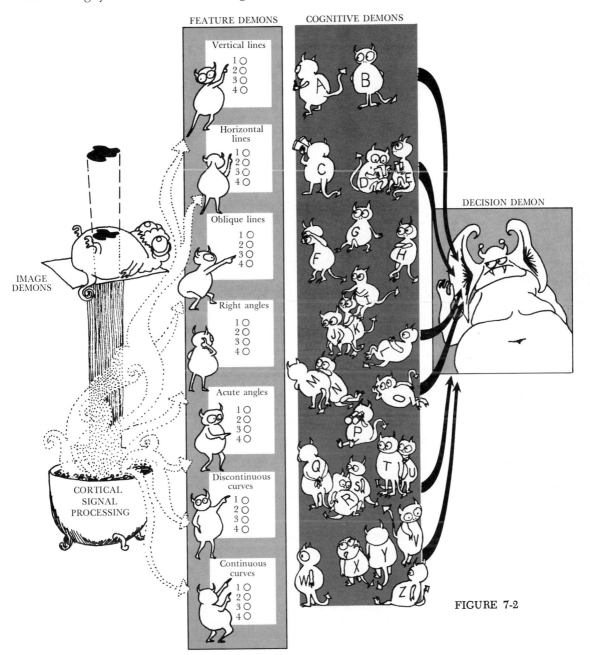

FIGURE 7-2

Table 7-1

	Vertical lines	Horizontal lines	Oblique lines	Right angles	Acute angles	Continuous curves	Discontinuous curves
A		1	2		3		
B	1	3		4			2
C							1
D	1	2		2			1
E	1	3		4			
F	1	2		3			
G	1	1		1			1
H	2	1		4			
I	1	2		4			
J	1						1
K	1		2	1	2		
L	1	1		1			
M	2		2		3		
N	2		1		2		
O						1	
P	1	2		3			1
Q			1		2	1	
R	1	2	1	3			1
S							2
T	1	1		2			
U	2						1
V			2		1		
W			4		3		
X			2		2		
Y	1		2		1		
Z		2	1		2		

Here the sensory information has been analyzed for seven general types of features. Each feature demon reports the number of a certain type of features that are contained in the pattern. The cognitive demons look for the particular values of the features that describe their pattern, and the vigor of their response is determined by the number of such features found. The proper pattern is finally selected by the decision demon, who reacts to the cognitive demon who is responding most vigorously.

One more problem must be overcome before this system can function. Some letters differ from others only in that they have **additional** features. For example, F has a vertical line, two horizontal lines, and three right angles. The letter P has all those features plus a discontinuous curve. If P is presented to the system, there is no problem: The P demon responds more than the F. But if F is presented, both the F and P demons yell equally: The decision demon will be unable to chose between them. The same problem arises between P and R, V and Y, O and Q, etc.

One way to solve this problem is to set up a standard maximum response level for all demons. A demon responds at his maximum rate only when **all** those features it is looking for are present. Both the absence of a looked-for feature and the presence of an unsought feature inhibit the demon from yelling at full capacity.

In outline, this is a prescription for a specific feature-recognition system. Will it work? The only way to find out is to test it and see how it behaves. Watch what happens when a letter is presented—say, the letter R.

Figure 7-3

First, the R is encoded by the image demons, and the information is sent on for further processing. Now the feature demons begin responding. The first feature demon records the presence of a vertical line. This is not much help in classifying the pattern. The diagram shows the cognitive demons that are activated by the presence of a single vertical line. Of the 26 possible letters of the alphabet, 13 have a single vertical line, 6 have two horizontal lines. As we follow down through the list, we see that different features activate different sets of cognitive demons. In this case, the decision demon has an easy choice, since R is clearly the most active responder. The next most likely pattern would be a P, which appears on four of the seven lists, and the third most active demon would be the D, which is matched by three out of the seven features.

The importance of errors. Notice some of the important characteristics of the behavior expected from this type of pattern recognition system. To recognize the R, for example, not all seven feature demons are needed. It suffices to note that there is an acute angle and a closed contour. The same would be true if the angle information was extracted from the pattern—the presence of the three right angles and the one acute angle uniquely characterizes the pattern as an R. For any given letter, then, the seven feature demons are supplying more information than is required. This means that some of the feature demons can fail, and the pattern recognition system would still operate correctly for some signals. All seven features are needed only when all the possible patterns are considered together. That is, if we write down the values for the features associated with each letter, we need seven different features

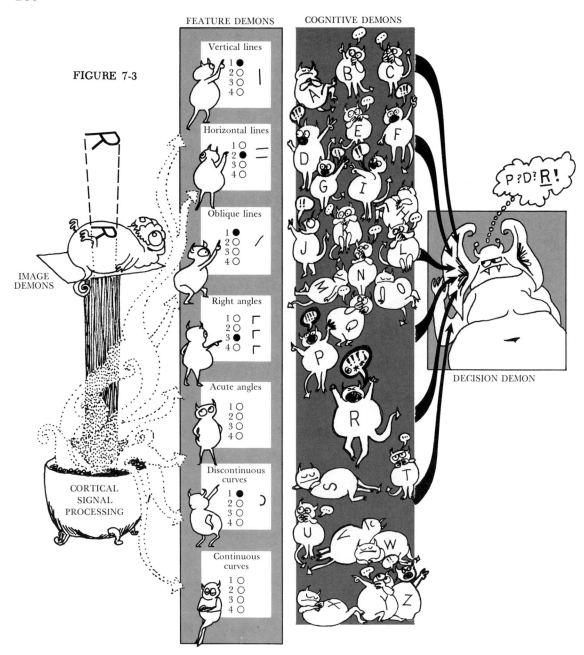

FIGURE 7-3

in order to have a unique string of numbers for every letter. If more patterns are added, more features must be used, and the nature of the features will depend on the characteristics of the additional patterns.

A second point to notice is that the particular set of features selected for the recognizing of patterns will determine the kinds of recognition errors that are made. On the average, if there is trouble identifying an R, we might expect the P to be a likely alternative choice. When the incoming signal is transformed into the feature set, P is the pattern most similar to R.

One test for the theory, then, would be to present people with the various letters under conditions where they are difficult to identify, to see what kinds of errors are made. The results of such an experiment produce a *confusion matrix* which describes the patterns of errors subjects make when trying to identify the letters. Figure 7-4 shows an example of a confusion matrix produced by flashing the various letters shown in Figure 7-5 briefly on a screen and asking people to report what they saw. (These data come from an experiment by Kinney, Marsetta, and Showman, 1966.)

Vertically, along the left, are the letters that were actually displayed. Horizontally, along the top, are the letters which the subjects reported they saw. If we follow down the left column until we come to R, then the corresponding horizontal row gives the responses made when the subjects attempted to identify this letter. Moving across that row, we find that the observers made a total of six mistakes in identifying R: Four out of those six times, they reported they saw a P.

A third point to notice about a feature recognition scheme is that the errors in identifying letters need not be symmetrical. Take the letter C, for example. If this letter were presented, only the open contour (discontinuous curve) demon would respond. Thus, when C occurs, the decision demon should have trouble in deciding whether it was a C or a G. Note the errors made in recognizing C in the confusion matrix. Subjects had more difficulty in identifying C than any other letter: 21 times they reported they saw a G when a C was actually presented. The letter C, however, will not necessarily be a frequent response when G is presented.

Responses to distorted patterns. Now that we have explored some of the characteristics of pandemonium, let us return to consider the problems produced by distortions in the external pattern. Changes in the size of the characters do not present any problem for this feature-extraction scheme. The feature demons collect information from line detectors which are themselves insensitive to the length of the lines. Right angles are still right angles, and acute angles are still acute angles, regardless of the size of the letter.

Orientation is a different story. Laying an F on its side would be very confusing to these particular demons, since it creates a pattern with two vertical and one horizontal line plus three right angles. Turning F completely upside down, however, would not disturb this particular pattern-recognition system: The horizontal and vertical line demons would make exactly the same response.

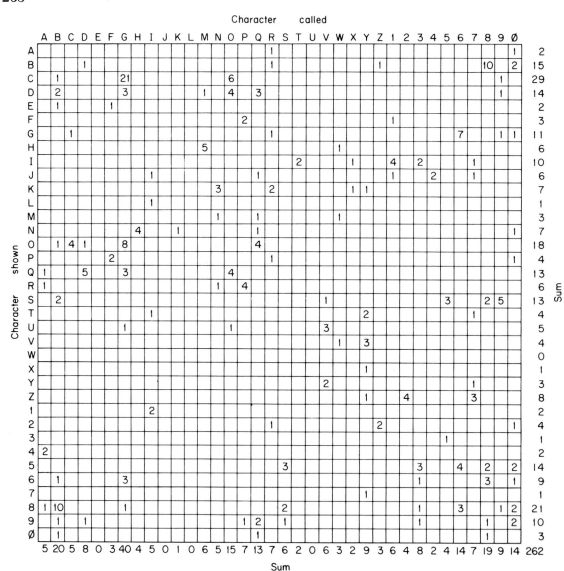

FIGURE 7-4   *From Kinney, Marsetta, and Showman (1966).*

FIGURE 7-5   A B C D E F G H I J K L M N O P Q R

S T U V W X Y Z 1 2 3 4 5 6 7 8 9 Ø

It is not too difficult to see how a feature-extraction scheme might provide a reasonable start toward a system for recognizing letters. Even a very simple set of features appears to work reasonably well for letter patterns. The story is not nearly so simple with speech. Here, the very nature of the speech waveform adds immense difficulties to the analysis.

There are three major difficulties with the recognition of speech. First, there is the problem of segmentation: The units to be recognized are not clearly demarked. Second, there is enormous variability in the physical waveforms when different people speak the same word, or the same person speaks a given word in different contexts. Finally, there is little agreement about the identity of the basic features that could be used to recognize speech, if indeed there are any.

In the analysis of printed text, each letter is clearly separated from its neighbors by a fixed amount of space, and each word is separated from neighboring words by an even greater amount of space. Thus, it is a simple matter to determine the boundaries between letters, words, and sentences—not so with speech.

The segmentation problem

When you listen to someone speaking, the words sound distinct and usually reasonably well articulated. There appears to be a well-defined separation between most words. All this is an illusion. The clear distinctions that are so easily perceived are not present in the physical signal but are a result of the pattern recognition process: They are put in by the analysis. In fact, the spoken waveform is a peculiar combination of inarticulate sounds, ill-pronounced segments, deletions, and contractions. Worst of all, there is no apparent connection between the breaks in the speech waveform and the boundaries between words. Consider the phrase **She uses standard oil.** When the phrase is spoken, there are exactly three breaks in the sound pattern, none of them occurring at a boundary between words. The breaks all occur in the pronunciation of the word **standard:** one after the *s,* one after the *n,* and one after the *r.*

Listen to someone speaking a foreign language. If you do not understand the language, the speech seems to come in a continuous stream at a rapid rate. Even the beginning student who has painstakingly learned some vocabulary of a language has difficulty finding the individual words in the apparently continuous utterances of the native speaker. In fact, the seeming rapidity of foreign languages is, in most cases, an illusion. The differences in our perceptions are due to the operation of a pattern recognition system. In the one case, the sounds can be meaningfully interpreted and the words stand out as discrete entities; in the other case, the recognition system is inappropriate, and the sounds appear as unorganized, meaningless nonsense.

There are some properties in the physical waveform that are of some use in segmenting the verbal message. None of the physical characteristics so far studied, however, provides entirely reliable clues to the boundaries between words. And in many cases it seems that the analysis system must know what the word is before it can find the proper boundaries. How can the sound pattern *ai-s-k-r-ee-m* be segmented appropriately until it is known whether the words are associated with the phrase, **When I see a snake I scream** or the phrase **Buy me some ice cream.** The pattern recognition process is circular. We need to understand the utterance in order to analyze it, and we must first analyze it in order to understand it. The system must operate at different levels of analysis at the same time.

Classifying speech sounds

Phonemes. Linguists have long tried to characterize the sound components in speech. It is clear that in printed English the syllable and the individual letter represent elementary units of a word. In spoken English, the basic units are not so easy to discern. But to the trained ear, there appears to be a small vocabulary of basic sounds from which all words are formed. A particular sound qualifies as a basic unit if it serves some functional purpose in the language. Consider the words **bat, pat,** and **vat.** Each of these words has a different meaning. The difference is signaled entirely by a change in only one sound, in this case the initial sounds "b," "p," and "v." A sound that, by itself, can change the meaning of a word is called a *phoneme*. One way to determine the phonemes of a language is to experiment, saying a word and systematically changing one of the sounds until the word changes into a different word. If a single change in sound transforms one word into another, then you have identified two phonemes: one that corresponds to the initial sound, one that corresponds to the new sound.

Consider the following experiment on the simple word **bat.** The word **bat** is called a CVC word because it consists of a consonant (symbolized by C), followed by one vowel (V), and terminated by another consonant. When we systematically try different sounds for the first consonant of the CVC, we get a sequence of different words. Each sound that leads to a new word is also a new phoneme: **bat, fat, gat, ...** This simple experiment yields a number of phonemes: *b, f, g, h, k, m, n, p, r, s, t, v, x, th, sh.* Similarly, systematically varying the V part of the word **bat** reveals the phonemes: *ee* (as in *beet*), *i* (as in *bit*), *e* (as in *bet*), *a* (as in *bat*), *aw* (as in *bought*), *oo* (as in *boot*), *uh* (as in *but*), *oi* (as in *Boyt*), *au* (as in *bout*), *ai* (as in *bait*), *oa* (as in *boat*), *eye* (as in *bite*). All in all, systematic substitution of sounds into this one CVC has revealed 26 of the phonemes of English: 14 consonants and 12 vowels. All the other English phonemes can be discovered in much the same way, using other test words. The entire set of phonemes for English is shown in Table 7-2. Because of the fact that there is no simple translation between a single English letter and a phoneme, special symbols are used to indicate the phonemes, thus avoiding the problems we just experienced in indicating the vowel sounds.

Note that every letter does not necessarily correspond to a phoneme. Moreover, the number and nature of phonemes differ from dialect to dialect in the English language. In some parts of the United States, the three words **merry, marry,** and **Mary** are pronounced identically. For most speakers of English, however, the three words are spoken quite differently. When there are severe accent differences, the recognition system fails. The various pronunciations of English spoken in Ireland, Scotland, and certain parts of New York and London, for example, differ from the "standard" so much that they may not be understood by other English-speaking people unfamiliar with those accents.

If phonemes are the basic building blocks for words, have we found the features for a pandemonium system of speech recognition? Probably not. Equating phonemes with features is not very helpful. Unlike the

Table 7-2   The Phonemes of Standard American English [a]

Vowels		Consonants			
		Voiced		*Voiceless*	
ī	as in h*eat*	b	as in *b*ee	p	as in *p*ea
i	as in h*i*t	d	as in *D*ee	t	as in *t*ea
ē	as in h*ate*	g	as in *g*ale	k	as in *k*ale
e	as in b*e*ll	v	as in *v*eil	f	as in *f*ail
æ	as in h*a*t	ð	as in *th*y	θ	as in *th*igh
a	as in b*aw*l	z	as in *z*oo	s	as in *S*ue
ʌ	as in h*u*t	ž	as in a*z*ure	š	as in A*sh*er
ə	as in sof*a*			h̩	as in *h*e
ō	as in b*ow*l	ǰ	as in *j*unk	č̓	as in *ch*unk
o	as in h*o*t	m	as in *m*ail		
ū	as in h*oo*t	n	as in *n*ail		
u	as in b*u*ll	ŋ	as in si*ng*		
oy	as in b*oi*l	l	as in *l*ee		
aw	as in *out*	r	as in *r*ail		
ay	as in h*eigh*t	y	as in *Y*ale		
		w	as in *w*ale	hw	as in *wh*ale

[a] Standard American English is one name given to the dialect of English now spoken throughout the United States but reflecting pronunciations that originally were characteristic of the American Middle West. Many dialects of English do not have all the phonemes listed above. In particular, many American dialects are missing either *o* (which comes to be pronounced like *a*) or *hw* (pronounced in these dialects as *w*). Some dialects may have more phonemes.

line and angle detectors of the visual system, there is no known way of actually analyzing and extracting the phonemes from a speech waveform. So far, only the human can recognize a phoneme in the speech wave.

Distinctive features.   The difficulties in identifying phonemes has led to other schemes for classifying speech sounds. One method is to examine how speech is produced to see whether the waveform can be described in terms of the various operations involved in generating the sounds. Speech sounds result from the complex interaction of a number of parts of the vocal apparatus. The diaphragm forces air up through the trachea. The soft palate opens and closes the nasal passages to the flow of air. The tongue, teeth, and lips all move in synchrony to determine the harmonic and temporal structure of the sound patterns produced.

Sounds can be classified according to the operation of these various components. If the air passing through the trachea vibrates the vocal chords, it produces a *voiced* sound, such as "a" or "z." When the vocal chords do not vibrate during the sound production, an *unvoiced* sound is produced, such as the "s" sound of **hiss.** Note that the only distinction between the way "z" and "s" are produced is in the voicing. You can easily experience the voicing by sticking a finger in each ear while saying the words "his," "hiss," "buzz" and "bus." Notice the vibrations during the "z" part of "his" and "buzz," and their absence during the "s" part of "hiss" and "bus." Notice also that all whispered sounds are voiceless. When whispered, *"When will the bus stop?"* sounds the same as *"When will the buzz stop?"*

Another distinctive feature is formed by the possibility of restricting the air passage somewhere in the mouth to produce the hissing, turbulent sound of a *fricative*—"sh," "s," "f," "v," "th." In other sounds the flow of air is completely interrupted for a short period of time, then released explosively to produce a *plosive* or *stop*—"t" and "d" are examples. Stops produce a definite break in the wave pattern, but unfortunately these breaks are not related to word boundaries. When we produce the word **hippopotamus,** for example, there are three distinct breaks in the speech flow.

Thus, we can recode speech sounds into the distinctive features associated with their production: Each produces a unique characteristic in the resulting sound. Table 7-3 lists one possible classification of the distinctive features for each of the phonemes in the English language.

FEATURE ANALYSIS   The analysis of speech sounds into phonemes, and then the division
IS NOT SUFFICIENT   of phonemes into distinctive features, is important for the analysis of the fundamental elements of speech perception, but it misses some of the

Table 7-3 Distinctive Feature Values for Selected English Phonemes[a]

Phonemes

Features	ī	i	ē	ɛ	æ	ʌ	ā	ō	o	ū	u	y	w	p	b	f	v	m	t	d	θ	ð	n	s	z	č	ǰ	š	ž	k	g	ŋ	h	r	l
Vocalic/nonvocalic	+	+	+	+	+	+	+	+	+	+	+	−	−	−	−	−	−	−	−	−	−	−	−	−	−	−	−	−	−	−	−	−	−	+	+
Consonantal/nonconsonantal	−	−	−	−	−	−	−	−	−	−	−	−	−	+	+	+	+	+	+	+	+	+	+	+	+	+	+	+	+	+	+	+	−	+	+
Sonorant/obstruent	+	+	+	+	+	+	+	+	+	+	+	+	+	−	−	−	−	+	−	−	−	−	+	−	−	−	−	−	−	−	−	+	−	+	+
High/nonhigh	+	+	−	−	−	−	−	−	−	+	+	+	+	−	−	−	−	−	−	−	−	−	−	−	−	+	+	+	+	+	+	+	−	−	−
Back/nonback	−	−	−	−	−	+	+	+	+	+	+	−	+	−	−	−	−	−	−	−	−	−	−	−	−	−	−	−	−	+	+	+	−	−	−
Low/nonlow	−	−	−	−	+	−	+	−	−	−	−	−	−	−	−	−	−	−	−	−	−	−	−	−	−	−	−	−	−	−	−	−	+	−	−
Anterior/nonanterior														+	+	+	+	+	+	+	+	+	+	+	+	−	−	−	−	−	−	−	−	−	+
Coronal/noncoronal														−	−	−	−	−	+	+	+	+	+	+	+	+	+	+	+	−	−	−	−	+	+
Round/nonround	−	−	−	−	−	−	−	+	+	+	+	−	+																						
Tense/lax	+	−	+	−	−	−	+	+	−	+	−																								
Voiced/voiceless														−	+	−	+	+	−	+	−	+	+	−	+	−	+	−	+	−	+	+	−	+	+
Nonstop (continuant)/stop (noncontinuant)														−	−	+	+	−	−	−	+	+	−	+	+	−	−	+	+	−	−	−	+	+	+
Nasal/oral														−	−	−	−	+	−	−	−	−	+	−	−	−	−	−	−	−	−	+	−	−	−
Strident/nonstrident														−	−	+	+	−	−	−	−	−	−	+	+	+	+	+	+	−	−	−	−	−	−

The symbol + means that the phoneme has the feature listed before the slash; the symbol − means that the phoneme has the feature listed after the slash. Thus, reading across the first row of vocalic/nonvocalic features, the phonemes ī through u are vocalic, and the phonemes y through l are nonvocalic. Unspecified features occur because for any given language, certain things are predictable. In the bottom six rows, a blank signifies an unspecified feature. For example, all English vowels are nonnasal and voiced, so the feature values for [nasal] and [voice] are left unspecified. Some languages use these features contrastively; e.g., in French, nasal and oral vowels contrast: *bon* "good" and *beau* "beautiful" differ only in vowel nasalization. Similarly, languages like Japanese and Comanche have voiceless vowels.

[a] Adapted from Noam Chomsky and Morris Halle, *The sound pattern of English* (Harper and Row, 1968), pp. 176–177 and 303.

important problems of perception. We still need to understand how words are deciphered from the speech sounds and how the meaning of utterances is determined. Moreover, as we will see, some speech cannot be understood until the meaning has been determined. Thus, the type of feature analysis that we have just been performing is absolutely essential to the perceptual process, but by itself it is not sufficient.

Feature extraction schemes break down in a number of situations that humans deal with routinely. How can analysis of features tell us whether the sounds *noo-dis-plaee* represent the words **new display** or the words **nudist play**? What features tell us that the symbols I3 are numbers when they appear in the context of I3 579 but are letters when they appear in the context I3 Y ? What does a feature recognition system do with this pattern—what features describe the cathedral in Figure 7-6?

The demons of pandemonium are really not enough. More information must be included in the pattern-recognition process to explain the tremendous power of the human recognition-system. What else is there, though, when features fail?

A matter of context   A large part of the interpretation of sensory data is provided by the knowledge of what the signal must be, rather than from information contained in the signal itself. This extra information comes from the *context* of the sensory event. Context is the overall environment in which experiences are embedded. You know many things about the material you are reading, in addition to the actual patterns of letters on this page. You know that it is written in English, that it is discussing psychology in general, and the psychology of pattern recognition in particular. Moreover, you have probably learned quite a bit about the style of writing, so that as your eyes travel over the page, you are able to make good predictions the words which you expect to see. These predictions are good enough to make you automatically fill in the missing "about" or "of" in the previous sentence,[1] or, equivalently, not even notice its absence. The enormous amount of information that is accumulated and routinely used to understand the events, we call the context of those events. The ability to use context makes the human perceptual system far superior and more flexible than any electronic pattern-recognition system so far invented.

The effects of context are easy to document. Figures are perceived more quickly and easily if they are meaningful than if they are simply decorative. The ability to read and remember letters is much more difficult if they are laid out haphazardly in a meaningless string—**sgtooeurua**

---

[1] A good example of this is our continual difficulty in keeping the predicted preposition out of the sentence. The typists and editors keep automatically replacing it.

Roy Lichtenstein, "Cathedral #5." Lithograph, $48\frac{1}{2} \times 32\frac{1}{2}$ inches.
Collection: D. A. Norman.

FIGURE 7-6

—than if the same letters appear in a meaningful order—**outrageous.** Even when the letters do make meaningful words—

inm	ull
ycr	ena
aft	rt
ors	

—they are difficult to perceive unless they are in a format consistent with the normal mode of dealing with them.

Wet socks. A number of experimental techniques have been used to demonstrate the effects of context on the perceptual analysis of incoming signals. In one example (an experiment by Miller, 1962), subjects listened to a string of words like **socks, some, brought, wet, who.** The words were mixed with noise so that each individual word could be correctly identified only about 50% of the time. In a second test, the words were then rearranged, so they appeared in a meaningful order—**who, brought, some, wet, socks,** and again the subjects attempted to identify them. When the words were spoken in a grammatical order, the recognition performance of the subjects improved dramatically. In fact, the contextual cues improved recognition an amount equivalent to decreasing the noise intensity to 50% of its previous value. The physical information is the same in both cases. It was the context that produced such a dramatically improved accuracy in the perception of an identical physical signal.

Consider what happens when a word is heard without any context, such as the **brought** in **socks, some, brought, wet, who.** It sounds like a hissing gurgle in the background of noise. Perhaps a few features are extracted. Perhaps the "b" sound is recognized and it is noted that the word is one syllable long. The two features are sufficient to rule out words such as **hospital, Mississippi, bananas,** and **boondocks,** but there are still a large number of possibilities left—words such as **brought, boy, brings, brags, buys, bought, bit, bones.** Let us use these eight words as our best possible selections. Without additional information, no decision can be reached. A guess at this point would be correct about 1 out of 8 times, $12\frac{1}{2}$%.

Now, suppose the same word is embedded in the phrase, **who b____ some wet socks,** the second condition in Miller's experiment. The context allows the possible alternatives to be reduced considerably. The unknown word is probably a verb, so out go **boys** and **bones** as possible alternatives. It must be able to take an object: You cannot "brag" socks, so another possibility is eliminated. It must have some plausible meaning. "Who bit the wet socks" is an improbable statement, so out goes **bit.** Now there are perhaps four alternatives left: **brought, brings, buys,** and **bought.** With just a little extra information about feature, we can narrow down the choices even more. Was there a hissing sound of "s?" If not, the word is either **brought** or **bought**: only two possibilities. Even by guessing, there is now a 50% chance of being right, a great improvement over the $12\frac{1}{2}\%$ guessing chances without the aid of contextual information.

The power of context is clear. Rules can be used to reduce the number of possible alternatives that are to be considered at any moment. This does not imply, of course, that perception requres a conscious trial-and-error approach to determine the alternative that best fits the contextual information. We do not know exactly what mechanisms underly the use of contextual information, but we do know that context plays a major role in our perceptions. It supplies the rules underlying the construction of our perceptual world, tells us what to expect, and gives plausible interpretations of what we are perceiving.

Note that to take full use of contextual information, perception must lag behind the information received by the sensory systems. The perception of the word **brought** was aided not only by words appearing before it (**who**), but also by words that appeared after (**socks**). This lag between the intake of sensory information and the final interpretation of a message is an important part of the structure of our perceptual analysis. When reading aloud, for example, the eyes scan the words well ahead of the part of the text being spoken. A skilled typist reads the text far ahead of the place being typed. We move forward to gather as much contextual information as possible before actually executing the responses required by the task we are performing. The more we know about what is to come, the easier it is to perceive what is at hand.

The structure of language seems to be designed to complement the ability of the human to piece together the meaning of a communication from a few isolated fragments. Language is highly redundant. We say and write many more words than are really needed in order to be understood. Omit much words make text shorter. You not have trouble understanding. One scheme for estimating redundancy in the language is to mutilate the text in systematic ways and ask a person to reconstruct the missing sections. The ease with which this task can be done gives a measure of redundancy of the language. Thxs wx cax rexlaxe exerx thxrd xetxer xitx an x, axd yxu sxilx maxagx prxttx wexl. Thng ge a ltte tuger f w sipl deet th lete.[2]

The importance of redundancy

If the language were more efficient, or if humans were less able to use contextual information to guide their perceptions, then communication would be a painful and hazardous process. We would have to attend very carefully to every word spoken: one word missed, one dis-

---

[2] The complete versions of the sentences read: "Thus we can replace every third letter with an x, and you still manage pretty well. Things get a little tougher if we simply delete the letter."

torted syllable, and the whole meaning of a sentence might be lost or misperceived. We could not afford to relax for an instant. Even the slightest noise could lead to disaster. The redundancy of the language, then, allows us to attend selectively to bits and pieces of a communication, to anticipate what will come next, and to look selectively for the key words and phrases that convey the basic meaning of the message. As a result, we can relax, confident that we can miss much of the details of speech or print, yet not miss the intended meaning.

DATA-DRIVEN AND CONCEPTUALLY DRIVEN PROCESSING

The sequence of operations we have been discussing can be characterized as data driven. A signal first arrives at the image demons, who then pass on their results to higher levels. At the next level of analysis, critical features are probably identified—the distinctive features that characterize phonemes. These features are sent to the cognitive demons, who act upon them. Finally, a decision demon selects the alternative that has the strongest evidence. The analysis of the signal thus proceeds in a straightforward way from the receipt of the signal itself, up through successive layers of processing, until at last a decision is reached. In the illustrations of pandemonium, this is characterized by a flow from left to right through the diagrams. We call this system of analysis *data driven,* because all activity in the system is started by the arrival of sensory data. Data-driven processing starts with sensory data and systematically works its way through successive stages of analysis.

At this point we have pushed the data-driven analysis about as far as it can go. We have seen how the sensory systems operate and how the first stages of pattern recognition might operate. We have seen something of the power of feature analysis. The pandemonium model of pattern recognition puts together our knowledge of the sensory systems and neural processing. Unfortunately, we also see that there are phenomena that this system of analysis cannot handle, phenomena that seem to require information about the nature of the items that are to be recognized in order that they can be recognized.

Expectations and conceptualizations must play a major role in the analysis. Our memory system maintains a record of past experiences, a general knowledge about the organization and format of the events we experience, and knowledge about the structure of language. The information from memory must become combined with the information from the sensory analysis. Just as the data-driven part of the analysis must play an important role, so too must a *conceptually driven* analysis become a part of the processing cycle.

Conceptually driven processing starts with general knowledge of the events that are being experienced and with specific expectations generated by this knowledge. The expectations are really simple theories or hypotheses about the nature of the sensory signals that are expected to occur. These expectations guide the stages of analysis at all levels, from getting the language analyzing system alerted (if the input is expected to be language), to setting up the feature detectors for the specific inputs that are expected, to directing the attention of the system to the details of the particular events. Conceptually driven processing is just the reverse of data-driven processing. Whereas data-driven processing starts with the signals and ends with the interpretations, conceptually driven systems go in the other direction. We have argued in this chapter (and in Chapter 1) that *both* data-driven and conceptually driven processes are required. Neither alone is sufficient; both must be present. But how can both of these discrepant processes operate at the same time? How do they communicate with one another? How do they avoid conflicts?

The solution to the problem of combining data-driven and conceptually driven processing turns out to be rather simple. After all, we have already seen how we can model the sensory analysis by using demons, each of whom is responsible for some particular task, each of whom then reports the results of the analysis to some other set of demons. This system seems to be a good description of our understanding of sensory analysis so why not let the conceptually driven processing system work in much the same way? Let there be specialized demons for context, expectations, sentences, and phrases. Let there be demons for syntax and semantics, as well as the demons we already know about for phonemes and features. In fact, we no longer need to distinguish between demons that do data-driven processing and those that do conceptually driven processing. The system can work by having a large number of specialized demons who do their particular tasks on whatever relevant data exist at the moment. There is one critical new concept however: all of the demons must be able to communicate with one another.

Specialist demons

At this point, we cannot simply patch up the old analysis. It is best to start over. We need a system organized around the specialist demons that provides them with a method to communicate with one another. There are a number of ways by which this might be accomplished. We symbolize the central communication process by imagining it taking place on one centrally located *blackboard* to which all demons have access. Each demon watches the blackboard, looking for information that it can analyze. As soon as information relevant to a particular demon's speciality is put onto the blackboard, that demon gets to work. Most important of all, when each demon finishes its own specialized task, it writes the result on the blackboard for some other demon to pick up.

In this way, no individual demon needs to know about the other demons. Each demon simply watches the blackboard for information that it can analyze; each demon adds its analysis to the blackboard for other demons to analyze.

Note that if sensory information gets added to the blackboard just like any other information, then there is absolutely no need to distinguish between data-driven and conceptually driven processing. It all happens automatically. If new sensory data arrive, they are placed on the blackboard, thereby setting off the sensory specialists who are capable of handling them: this is the start of a data-driven process. If some demon believes that the next word that will arrive over the sensory channel is "peppermint," it adds this information to the blackboard. This would cause specialized demons to look for the individual letters and features of those letters: this is conceptually driven processing. But note that as far as each demon is concerned, it is simply watching the blackboard for relevant information, adding what it can to the analyses that are going on. At any given moment, a demon might be part of either a data-driven chain or a conceptually driven chain. The demon does not know and does not care.

The blackboard and the supervisor

With all the specialized demons running around, each doing its own particular analysis, each searching the blackboard for new information and adding its own contributions, there must be some way of supervising the general activity. People have limited processing capability; a person cannot analyze everything that appears at the sensory system. In terms of our system of specialized demons, all scurrying around, this means that there must be some limits on what can be accomplished. There are two obvious sources of limitations. First, there is a limited number of demons. A specialist demon working on one set of data cannot simultaneously be working on another set. Second, the blackboard is probably of limited size: not every possible analysis can fit. (Indeed, the blackboard is probably closely related to the sensory information storage and short-term memory systems discussed in Chapter 8. These memory systems have limited time durations and capacities for holding information.)

To avoid conflicts in the demands upon demons and to ensure that a promising direction of analysis is carried out (while unpromising directions are stopped), some general supervision of the effort is required. So, to our system we add a general overall *supervisor*, who guides the specialist demons in a cooperative effort. The job of the system is to put together a logical interpretation of the newly arriving sensory signal, using all sources of knowledge to which it has access. The supervisor makes sure that the demons do not get in one another's way, that a promising path does not get ignored because the needed specialist demon is busy at some other task, and that the blackboard does not get so crowded that relevant information is covered over or lost.

The supervisory demon takes its guidance from what it sees on the blackboard and from the distribution of activity of the specialist demons. The supervisory demon is really just another specialist demon, the only difference being that it can direct the efforts of the others. Note that the supervisory demon bases its instructions on the analyses it sees on the blackboard: it can make mistakes. (We discuss the limits on processing capability later in this chapter. The role of the supervisory demon is also discussed in more detail in Chapter 15.)

To see how the blackboard system operates, let us look at the process of interpreting a written sentence. We need an illustrative sentence. Take this sentence as an example. Figure 7-7 shows the system in the midst of the analysis of **TAKE THIS SENTENCE AS AN EXAMPLE.** At the point shown in the figure, the sensory analysis is working on the third word of the sentence. The features that have been extracted so far are shown on the right-hand side of the blackboard. Some specialist demons have already started to put together the sentence, and from their analysis of the words **TAKE THIS** they have suggested that the newly arriving word should be either an adjective, adverb, or noun. Other specialist demons have enhanced that prediction by suggesting a set of possible words that also make sense in the context of the sentence. All these predictions are present on the blackboard.

The analysis of a sentence

Meanwhile, the feature analysis demons have been at work, adding to the blackboard. One of the letter specialist demons who has been watching the blackboard has decided that the first letter must be an **S.** Now the appropriate demons can start restricting the set of possible words. Some specialists have deleted all words from the blackboard that do not start with an **S.** Other specialists have matched the length of the possible words with the apparent length of the word under analysis, thereby rejecting all the suggested words, except for **SEQUENCE** and **SEN-TENCE.** Finally, a specialist demon working on **SEQUENCE** decides that its features are not compatible with the sensory features that are on the blackboard. This leaves only one possible interpretation. The word is **SENTENCE.**

This analysis could have been wrong. Note that with the exception of **S** no other letter was analyzed or recognized in isolation. Note also that the list of possible words being considered on the blackboard does not exhaust the real set of possibilities. We have shown a situation in which the analysis proceeds smoothly, combining the information provided by context with the actual information present on the printed page. The

On the power and weakness of the specialist system

FIGURE 7-7

sentence being analyzed was actually used in the text, where it followed a discussion for the need to consider how contextual information might be used in the analysis of a sentence. Thus the words of the example sentence fit naturally into the processing of that sentence. But suppose we take this harpsichord sentence as an example. Now, the preceding sentence is one that does not conform to the rules. The word "harpsichord" makes no sense in the sentence. You certainly would not have predicted its occurrence. Nevertheless, every reader should have been capable of reading the word "harpsichord."

The human pattern recognition system operates most efficiently when contextual and sensory information combine, each contributing some part of the overall analysis. Whenever this happens, then neither the sensory analysis nor the contextual analysis alone need be carried out completely. As soon as the combined information yields an unambiguous interpretation, processing can stop. Thus, in Figure 7-7 we showed how the word **SENTENCE** could be recognized even before the feature analysis task had been complete. The human can also succeed when either source of information is deficient. When the sensory information is weak, then the contextual information must compensate (as we will illustrate shortly). When the contextual information is weak, as in the "harpsichord" example, then the feature analysis must compensate. In this case, the identification of the words can not be performed until the feature analysis has been completed. Thus, although we fully expect that all of you were able to read the "harpsichord" sentence, we suspect that some of you had some difficulty. The word "harpsichord" should have taken longer to read than the other words of the sentence. Some of you might have been so biased by your expectations that you did not even perceive the word "harpsichord" until the discussion in the text indicated that you must have missed something as your eyes skimmed the page.

Here we have a pattern recognition scheme that continuously constructs and revises expectations about what it is perceiving as it proceeds to interpret a sensory message. It does not rely exclusively either on its own internal models or on the evidence of its senses. But the two sources of information must match before it concludes it has successfully interpreted the incoming signal.

This type of pattern-recognition system requires the ability to construct and test hypotheses simultaneously at several different levels. The rules embedded in the grammar and meaning of the language lead to expectations. Within this general context, a small set of specific words match both the context and the sensory evidence that has been interpreted so far. These expectations in turn generate predictions about the specific pattern that is currently being deciphered. As soon as the appropriate specialist demons begin reporting, the whole complex of expectations will be simultaneously matched, and the system can move on to the next segment.

At the other end, the sensory system must supply a number of different levels of sensory evidence. Sensory data regarding the general length and shape of the word is combined with the contextual information to narrow down the set of alternative possibilities. Information about the approximate sizes and shapes and number of surrounding words is probably used to decide on what to interpret next. In addition to these general features, a small part of the message is being simultaneously analyzed in detail.

The great virtue of this jointly data-driven and conceptually driven process is that it allows a selective sampling of environmental information, so that only the amount of evidence needed to interpret a signal unambiguously need be collected. The synthesizing process guides attention to the most pertinent parts of the message and, within the focus of attention, to the most pertinent features in the pattern. It can form incorrect hypotheses and make errors in predicting the sensory events, but it has many built-in safeguards. Suppose that when all of the evidence is in, the sensory data fail to match one of the expected letters. The smooth flow of processing must be temporarily interrupted until the ambiguity can be resolved. But consider the options for such a system in detecting and correcting errors. Letters can be skipped; spot checks can be made. Do the new sensory data fit with current expectations? If there is a successful match now, the previous mismatch could be due to a malformed or improperly detected input. When this happens, the system can still carry on. If it does fail, then it must go back and recheck to see if it began on the wrong track. Maybe houseboat a word has appeared entirely out of context, so that contextual constraints must be relaxed to let the sensory information play a more dominant role in guiding the interpretations. A word that is out of context in a sentence can be understood, although it may cause the system to do a "double take." Even words never seen before can be analyzed, although obviously no meaning will be found for such a malidrotful input.

Note how this system was able to recognize the word **SENTENCE** despite the fact that only one of the letters in the word could be distinguished from the features that had been extracted. To see that this result is commonplace, consider how the sequence of symbols shown in Figure 7-8*a* might get analyzed. Not one single letter can be identified. Yet, if that sequence is presented in the proper way, embedded within the sentence shown in Figure 7-8*b*, then it can usually be deciphered. In Figure 7-8*b* we have an apparent ink spot overlaying the exact same symbols seen in Figure 7-8*a*, yet now it is but a simple matter to read off the sentence **THE WORK MUST GET DONE.** The perception of the noisy segments of the **W** helps us perceive the **R,** just as the perception of the noisy parts of the **R** helps us perceive the **W.** Each part of that sequence of symbols helps the perception of the other parts. Even though no single segment can be seen clearly, the whole word is reasonably easy to read. Here then, is an example of a sequence of symbols that cannot be analyzed letter-by-letter, but must be analyzed as a whole. Moreover, the perception of each part is helped by the context provided by the

(a)

(b)

FIGURE 7-8

other three parts—again, even though no single part is clearly perceived.

Before completing our analysis of the processes of pattern recognition, we should consider some further phenomena related to the more global aspects of signal processing. An important part of the specialist–blackboard system is the part that determines which message will be attended to or analyzed at all: this is, in part, the role of the supervisor. In the next section we take up the study of selective attention. Of particular interest will be whether the data we find related to selective attention will fit easily into the model we have developed so far.

Imagine yourself at a crowded, noisy party. You are standing with a group of people with other groups all around. To which conversation will you listen? Despite all the noise, you can decide which of the many conversations you wish to listen to—you could eavesdrop on the conversation behind you, or on the one to the right or left. But any conversation you listen to causes the loss of the others. This, then, is the selectivity of attention. It is possible to stand in the room and select which of several conversations is to be followed, but it is not possible to take part in two or more different conversations simultaneously. Yes, several conversations can be monitored by following a few words from each and perhaps keeping track of who is where. But if the conversations are at all serious, the sense of each gets lost when you try to do too much. It is possible to be selective in extracting sense out of all the noise of the party, but there is a limit on the ability to understand different conversations simultaneously.

Attention is somewhat of a two-edged sword. On the one side, it gives the desirable attribute of allowing us to follow the one set of events that may be of interest from among many going on simultaneously, even though each tends to obscure the others. Without this selective ability life would be chaotic, since we could make no sense

THE PHENOMENA
OF ATTENTION

out of the events of the world unless each occurred in isolation without competition or interference from others. But, on the other side, attention limits our ability to keep track of all the events that do occur. Often it is desirable to keep track of several things simultaneously. Even if only one set of events is of immediate interest, it is undesirable to follow it with such concentration so as to be unaware of the occurrence of other events that are potentially more important than the one on which we are concentrating. It is desirable to be able to concentrate on one event to the exclusion of others only so long as we will be interrupted from that concentration whenever something more important occurs. For this to happen, some way must be devised of monitoring even those events to which we are not attending, separating out the irrelevant aspects and interrupting our concentration for the pertinent aspects.

Selecting messages   Let us start with an experiment. In the passages that appear in the figures for this section, two different messages are printed together. Your job is to follow one message (a relevant message) and ignore the other (an irrelevant message). Read the shaded message aloud as rapidly as possible and ignore the other. Make sure you read as quickly as possible only the shaded message. Try it now with Figure 7-9 before reading on.

FIGURE 7-9

In performing an experiment like this one on man attention car it house is boy critically hat important shoe that candy the old material horse that tree is pen being phone read cow by book the hot subject tape for pin the stand relevant view task sky be read cohesive man and car gramatically house complete boy but hat without shoe either candy being horse so tree easy pen that phone full cow attention book is hot not tape required pin in stand order view to sky read red it nor too difficult.

Without looking back, what did you notice about the unshaded words? Do you remember any of them? Did you notice that each word appeared twice? Probably not.

This is the first piece of informal evidence about the cues used in selecting messages. You can be reasonably successful at limiting attention to a single, relevant passage. Physical characteristics of the message, shading in this case, can be used to separate the relevant message from the irrelevant one. It is as if you had some internal switch which allowed messages with the right physical properties to pass but rejected the rest.

But how far did you go in analyzing the irrelevant material? Did you really reject it solely on the basis that it wasn't shaded? If nothing is remembered about the rejected message, then perhaps the first theory of attention is that irrelevant material is only analyzed far enough to determine its general physical characteristics. Then the processing of irrelevant material is discontinued.

This initial hypothesis is clearly too simple. Consider the task illustrated in Figure 7-10. Once again read aloud the text that is shaded as fast as you can, just as before. Ignore the unshaded material.

> It is important that the subject man be car pushed house slightly boy beyond hat his shoe normal candy limits horse of tree competence pen for be only in phone this cow way book can hot one tape be pin certain stand that snaps he with is his paying teeth attention in to the the empty relevant air task and hat minimal shoe attention candy to horse the tree second or peripheral task.

FIGURE 7-10

Notice what happened here. All of a sudden the shaded sentence dissolved into a series of unrelated words. The sentence itself continued in the unshaded print—the print you were supposed to ignore. Now, if you can reject irrelevant material solely on the basis of its general physical characteristics, then you should have had little difficulty in continuing to read the shaded words. In fact you should not even have noticed that the sentence was continued in unshaded print. Most people, however, will start to read the unshaded letters, thus following the meaning of the material rather than obeying instructions and processing only the information with the correct physical properties. [3]

Physical cues are useful in separating relevant from irrelevant information. But more than physical cues must be involved in selecting which words to read, or there would be no tendency to switch to the unshaded words when they fit into context. The problem, then, is to figure out just what is being attended to and what is being ignored. It is obvious that to do this, we need a better way of controlling attention. Did you really attend only to the shaded message, or did you cheat a bit (inadvertently) and look at the other message to see what it said? If we want to find out the limits of the attention capacity, we must make sure that all attention is devoted to one task. Failing that, at the very least, we must be able to measure how much attention is applied to the relevant information. Only then can we start to discover how much can be extracted from irrelevant material.

Shadowing. To determine the type of information that gets extracted from an unattended message, we need an experimental task that allows us to tell whether the subject is truly occupied with the attended task.

---

[3] Unfortunately, this example does not work too well because it is possible to move the eyes so that they are centered only on shaded words: The nonshaded words never fall on the fovea. In the actual experiments, the words are all spoken, and therefore, both messages are treated equally by the sensory system.

One popular task is to ask subjects to *shadow* material presented to them. In a shadowing task, a series of words is read to the subjects and they are asked to repeat aloud (to shadow) each word as they hear it. This is difficult to do, especially if the material to be shadowed is presented at a reasonably quick rate. Thus, subjects are forced to devote a substantial portion of their attentional capacities to the task of shadowing. As experimenters, we can tell how well the subjects are attending to the shadowing task by how accurately they repeat the words presented to them. In general, it is wise to select the difficulty of the material being shadowed and the rate at which it is read so that the subjects make a small percentage of errors, perhaps 10%. In this way, we can tell whether their attention to the shadowing task changes by whether or not their error rate changes. (It is important that the subjects not be able to shadow perfectly, for if they can do the shadowing without making any errors, the task might also be easy enough that they have some spare time to do other things.) Thus, in a typical experimental session, each subject is asked to shadow some selection of material (usually played through a tape recorder) that is presented over earphones to one ear. Then, the test material is presented in the other ear (or sometimes, visually). After the session, the subject is questioned on the contents of the material to see what aspects can be remembered.

FIGURE 7-11

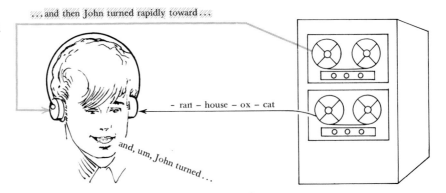

You should try the shadowing task. Get together two other people. Have one sit directly to one side and read aloud from this text or from a magazine at a reasonable rate. You try to shadow it. The passage should be read in a flat, unemotional voice. Repeat each word as it is said—do **not** hang back waiting for phrases or sentences to be completed. After you have had some practice at shadowing, then have the other person sit at your other side and read a second message as you are shadowing the first (perhaps the random words of Table 9-1). Try to attend to this second message, but without disrupting your shadowing performance on the first. The person who is reading the material that you are shadowing should tell you (poke you in the ribs) if you falter. Try different kinds of material for both messages and see if it makes any differences in the difficulty of the task. What do you perceive or remember about the second message? It is reasonably simple for you to replicate most of the studies involving shadowing that we discuss here.

When fully engrossed in a task, whether it be the result of shadowing or by the semitrance that accompanies the reading of a good novel, the watching of a good play or film, or even daydreaming, the subjective impression is that of being completely enveloped by the material on which we are concentrating. It is as if a switch disconnected all signals from reaching consciousness except those to which we were attending. Suppose we daydream in midst of a lecture. The sounds of the lecturer reach our ears, but leave no impression in our mind. The words spoken are not understood. By conscious exertion of willpower, the daydreaming can be stopped and the lecture attended to. Even though there need be no movement of muscles or parts of the body in changing from concentration on the daydream to concentration on the lecturer, there is quite a difference in perception. In both cases we "hear" the lecturer, but in one case we follow the words; in the other we do not. At what point is the bottleneck? Where does the analysis of the lecturer stop?

The simplest theoretical position is that the signals from the environment pass through the sensory systems and the analyzing mechanisms found there. This must be true, since we do "hear" the unattended sounds, even if they are not understood. At some point, however, there must be a switch that passes the signals to which we wish to attend and blocks the rest, as in Figure 7-12.

Processing the rejected message

FIGURE 7-12

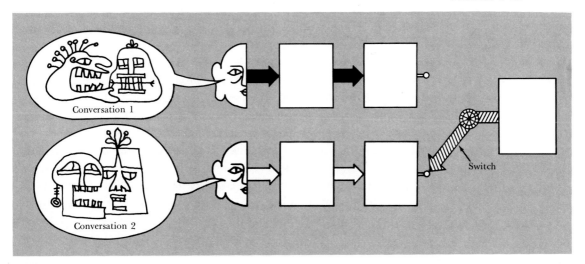

Conversation 1

Conversation 2

Switch

Even a simple study of attention soon shows that some aspects of material that is not being attended to can be noticed. When people are kept busy shadowing material, they still show the following recollection of material that they are not shadowing:

They are able to

- remember whether a voice was present at all,
- tell whether the voice changed from a man's to a woman's,
- notice signals, such as a whistle.

They are not able to

- remember the contents of the message,
- recognize the language of the message,
- tell if the language changed during the course of the experiment,
- distinguish speech from nonsense sounds.

These results indicate that people notice only the gross physical characteristics of signals to which they are not attending: is something present; is it a man or a woman? They fail to notice things that require interpretation, such as the meaning of the words, the identification of the language, or even whether the sounds form a meaningful language.

Although relevant material seems to undergo a rather complete analysis, the analysis of all other incoming signals seems to stop very early. It would appear that a selection mechanism examines the incoming features and selects the relevant material from the irrelevant by the physical features present, then controls a switch that allows only the relevant signals to get through to further analysis.

Although you may sometimes feel that when you are concentrating deeply upon something you have indeed thrown a switch that disconnects the rest of the world, this model of processing is wrong. The problem is not that there could not be a switch inside the head, but simply that the switch model does not account for all the data.

Remember the example in which you were asked to read the words in shaded print while ignoring the unshaded ones? Suddenly the meaningful sentence formed by the shaded words turned into gibberish, but the sentence itself continued in the unshaded words—the ones you were asked to ignore. When the experiment is actually performed as a shadowing task with subjects asked to shadow only the material heard in the left ear and to ignore everything else, they are quite likely to switch the ear they are shadowing when the sentence material switches (see Figure 7-13). The context and meaning of the messages cause errors (although the subjects will often become aware of their error and then stop and apologize). Many variations of this experiment have been performed, and all lead to much the same conclusion: there is some awareness of the material in the nonshadowed channels. Thus, it often happens that subjects will notice their own name when it is spoken in the ear to which they are supposedly not listening. They will pick up words that fit sensibly within the task that they are performing. They will not do well at picking up material from the nonshadowed ear, but neither will they miss everything, as the switch model might imply.

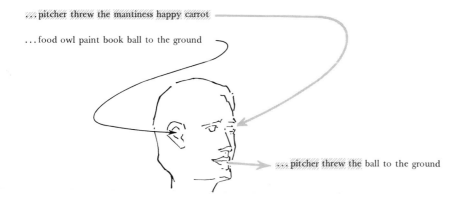

FIGURE 7-13

One last obligation remains—to go back and make sure that the picture of pattern recognition that we developed earlier is consistent with our understanding of the process of attention. This is the major obligation of any scientific theory: to be able to account for all the relevant phenomena. A theory can often be devised to account for one restricted set of things. The test of a theory comes in its ability to account for a wide range of phenomena. This is a very important point. A full understanding of the mechanisms of the mind will not come about until different aspects of people's behavior are related to one another. The current situation is a good example: the phenomena of sensory analysis, perceptual analysis, pattern recognition, and attention are all intimately related. One theory should be capable of encompassing them all.

    Let us return to our final model of pattern recognition (see Figure 7-7) and ask how well it fares when asked to account for the phenomena of attention. The answer is that it is satisfactory, which is no surprise, since that model was constructed using our understanding of both pattern recognition and attention. Still, let us look at it in terms of a problem in attention.

Specialist demons and the supervisor

Figure 7-14 illustrates our final model. Specialist demons are hard at work attempting to understand the sensory evidence arriving at the sense organs. The demons look for relevant data and then add their analyses to the blackboard. Two different messages arrive at the same time, however, and so the demons are split, some of them picking up the features from one voice and others the features resulting from the second voice. In this particular illustration, we simplify the task for the two demons by using voices from a man and a woman. Thus, once the features of the speech stream have been analyzed by the appropriate specialist demons, it is possible to direct the others to work only on features dealing with the woman's voice. In this way, the supervisory demon can watch over the blackboard and direct most of the specialists to work on the one speech train considered most relevant. This allows contextual and meaningful analyses to be concentrated on that one line of speech.

We assume that the specialist demons do not restrict their attention to one section of the blackboard: they watch the whole thing. Thus, were the other voice to produce a sound relevant to the main analysis, it would be likely to be picked up by a specialist. Still, in relatively simple attentional situations, where the several sensory inputs are easily segregated by spatial location or by physical features in the voices, it is unlikely that the analyses get far enough along on the irrelevant channel that specialist demons have much to contribute.

Whenever the different messages are not so easy to separate, however, as when several people are all speaking from the same location with similar voices, then the division of effort can only be made after each train has been analyzed far enough to see whether it is relevant to the major analysis. Here, the supervisory demon plays a major role in directing specialist demons to work on the major analysis. In Figure 7-14, in the relatively simple case where the voices can be distinguished by their physical characteristics, we see that the structures being constructed for the female voice are far more elaborate than for the male voice. The more difficult the task of separating out the relevant message from the irrelevant ones, the less difference there will be in the structures built for each message. But the more effort that goes into building structures for the interpretation of irrelevant channels, the less well analyzed will be the relevant one. This, then, is the trade-off in attentional capacity. There is a fixed amount of effort that can go on, and processing on any one task may detract from the processing that is possible on another.

Remember the experiment shown in Figure 7-13? The listener was asked to shadow material presented to one ear, but suddenly the material being presented to that ear was switched to the other ear. In such cases, people often repeat the words that correspond to the continuation

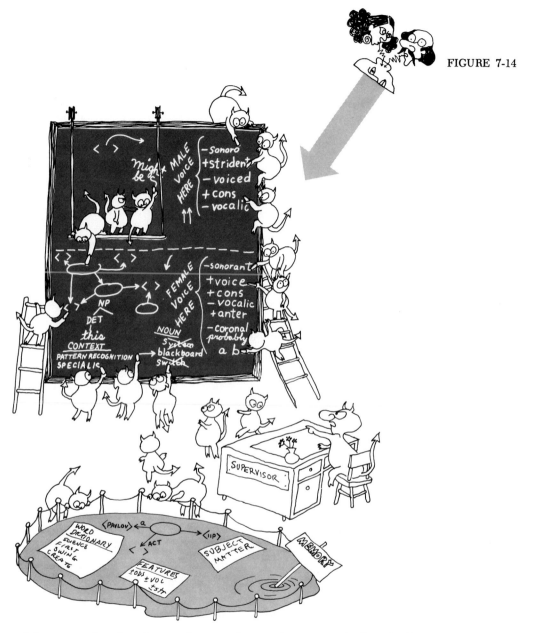

FIGURE 7-14

of the material, rather than sticking to the ear they were asked to shadow. This happens when the structures built up for the material being shadowed are well developed. Even when the information starts appearing on the other ear, the specialist demons still pick it up because it fits the expectations and existing structures so well. This experiment neatly demonstrates that it is not possible to turn off completely the analysis of any single sensory channel. All sensory data get entered onto the blackboard, and any specialists relevant to those data will work on them. There is data-driven analysis of all incoming information. Exactly how far each sensory channel will be analyzed or how much weight will be given to the results, however, depends upon the interplay between the demands placed upon all the demons and the analyses that have been put on the blackboard.

Figure 7-14 fulfills our goal of constructing a single model that incorporates all that we have discussed about pattern recognition and attention. The model is both data driven and conceptually driven. Specialist systems at all levels of analysis are free to contribute their interpretations. The general knowledge of the topic matter and of the previous structures gives conceptual guidance; the sensory information that continually arrives provides data-driven guidance. Both directions of analysis complement one another.

CONCLUSION   We see that the processes of pattern recognition and attention require a combination of all levels of processing, from sensory feature analysis to the interpretation of the meaning of the passages. For this reason, the areas of pattern recognition, perception, and attention have been central topics of concern to psychology. The mechanisms discussed in this chapter will apply to much of the work in the remaining chapters of the book. To conclude this chapter, let us return to some of the phenomena of perception that we discussed in Chapter 1. The difference is that now we should be able to understand them.

Figure 7-15 shows a normal picture, one in which both data-driven and conceptually driven analyses are consistent. But now look at the simple line drawing of Figure 7-16. The features are present, the expectations are almost met—but not quite. As a result, our perception of the image fluctuates as we try to force one or another set of rules onto the interpretation. If there are only features, with no expectations, then the whole perception fluctuates radically, unable to form a stable interpretation. In Figure 7-17, there are distinct features present, but no constraints on the interpretations, so that it is possible to view the scene as patches of shifting, triangular networks, as rectangular tubes extending in depth either vertically or horizontally, or as other variants.

Finally, recall the picture of the dalmation dog (Figure 7-18). Here there are no features to speak of, only interpretation. Once given the basic framework of the dog, however, the conceptually driven process matches the specks of light and dark in the picture to that of the image of the dalmation dog, unambiguously and correctly identifying the photograph. Without the interpretation process, this picture is unintelligible.

Robert Glasheen (photographer), "La Jolla." Copyright 1966, Glasheen   FIGURE 7-15
Graphics.

With the interpretation process, the dog stands out distinctly and clearly.

To understand the process of pattern recognition, we must understand many different steps in the analysis of information. The patterns of energy that strike the sensory organs can be interpreted as meaningful signals only through the combination of sensory analysis, memory processes, and thought.

The blackboard model represents a system that works at the task from all possible angles. It attempts to convert the sensory evidence into an interpretation consistent with our knowledge about the world. It is continuously constructing, testing, and revising hypotheses about what is being perceived. When the predictions fail or the context is lacking, it proceeds slowly, relying heavily on the sensory data. When operating

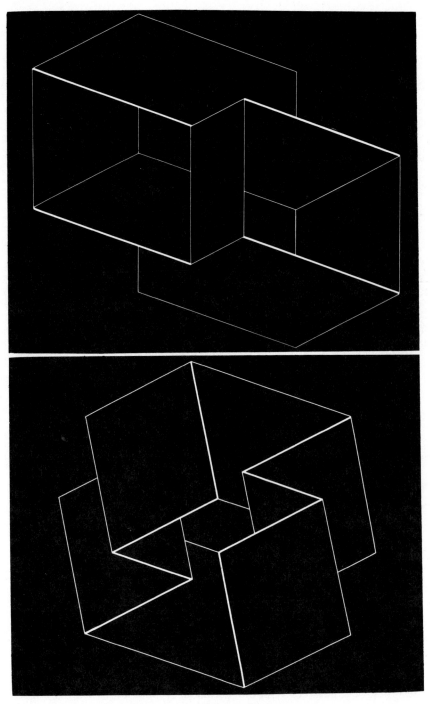

FIGURE 7-16 *Josef Albers, "Structural Constellations" 1953–1958. From Despite Straight Lines, pp. 63, 79. Courtesy of the artist.*

FIGURE 7-17

From Carraher and Thurston (1968).

in a familiar and highly predictable world, it can move quickly and efficiently, sampling only enough data to confirm current expectations and reconstructing what it does not see according to the rules of its internal model. Moreover, the prescription for conceptualization imposes some interesting demands on memories and on cognitive functions. There must be a temporary memory to record the results of the analysis to date. It must be able to retrieve the pertinent information from the permanent memory structures rapidly and efficiently. It must be able to work with different types of information at different levels of analysis at the same time, to integrate sensory, cognitive, and memory processes smoothly. It is a complicated mechanism, but so is the human brain.

FIGURE 7-18   *R. C. James (photographer). Courtesy of the photographer.*

REVIEW OF TERMS
AND CONCEPTS

In this chapter, the following terms and concepts that we consider to be important have been used. Please look them over. If you are not able to give a short explanation of any of them, you should go back and review the appropriate sections of the chapter.

*Terms and
concepts you
should know*

Why template models fail
Pandemonium
   the role of
    image demons
    feature demons
    cognitive demons
    decision demons
    confusion matrix

Speech recognition
   the segmentation problem
   phonemes
   distinctive features
The problems with feature analysis
The role of context
The role of redundancy
The specialist model
   the role of specialist demons
   the role of the blackboard
   the role of expectations
   the role of feature analysis
Data-driven and conceptually driven processing
   what the terms mean
   why each is necessary
   why each is unsatisfactory when used alone
Attention
   shadowing
   features on nonattended channels that are ignored or processed
   the problems with a switch model of attention
   how the specialist model applies to attention
   the role of data-driven and conceptually driven analysis in attention

SUGGESTED READINGS

Much of the material in this chapter is covered in more depth in *Memory and attention* by Norman (1976, 2nd edition). The books by S. Reed (1973) and Dodwell (1970) cover a good deal of the psychological literature on pattern recognition: we recommend starting with Reed. (They do not cover the work on blackboard-type models.) Much of the literature on pattern recognition comes from the engineering and computer sciences, but most of this work is rather technical. Good introductions are provided in *The psychology of computer vision* (Winston, 1975) and *The thinking computer* (Raphael, 1976).

Feature analysis, confusion matrices, and in particular the pandemonium model from the first edition of this book for the recognition of printed letters of the alphabet are discussed in some detail in Chapter 6 in Massaro's (1975b) *Understanding language*. His entire book is quite relevant to the issues on pattern recognition that are covered in this chapter. Massaro also considers the specific features that might be applicable to speech recognition, the role of language (grammar), and the pattern of eye movements in reading.

Our blackboard model of pattern recognition and attention has been inspired by the work of the speech-recognition group in the Computer Science Department at Carnegie-Mellon University. A good, but advanced, collection of papers on speech recognition is the set edited by Reddy (1975), which includes discussions of blackboards and other systems of speech recognition. An excellent treatment of the theoretical issue of pattern recognition, including reading and related issues, is given by Rumelhart (1977). His book is meant for the junior or senior student in psychology.

Good articles on speech perception can be found in several places. We recommend the chapter by Stevens and House (1972), in which they discuss two types of models: linear and analysis-by-synthesis. These two models correspond roughly to our distinction between data-driven and conceptually driven processing. Useful discussions of speech can be found in *Cognitive theory* edited by Restle, Shiffrin, Castellan, Lindeman, and Pisoni (1975). Section I of the book contains four chapters (by Studdert-Kennedy, Cooper, Wood, and Pisoni), all devoted to contemporary issues in speech perception.

Fromkin and Rodman (1974) provide an introduction to the phonetic and phonemic analysis of language. The classic work on speech analysis is *The sound pattern of English* (Chomsky & Halle, 1968). However, a professor of linguistics who reviewed this chapter warned us not to list it in our suggested readings. She said, "Although Chomsky and Halle is the best book for the analysis of speech, it is much too advanced: it is even too advanced for graduate students."

The major recent books on attention are Broadbent's (1971) *Decision and stress,* which reviews a huge body of literature; Kahneman's (1973) *Attention and effort;* Moray (1970); and Norman (1976).

Some important papers on pattern recognition and attention have appeared. Two important symposia were organized by Solso, and the chapters in the books that resulted provide a good review of this area (Solso, 1973, 1975). One good place to start would be the chapter by Weisstein (1973) titled—are you ready?—*Beyond the yellow Volkswagen detector and the grandmother cell: A general strategy for the exploration of operations in human pattern recognition.* The chapters by Shiffrin and Geisler (1973) and by Winston (1973) in the same book (Solso, 1973) have much more conventional titles and cover some issues in visual recognition, including some issues of how the lines that are perceived in the world are used to infer the three-dimensional objects (Winston's chapter). The book reporting on the second symposium (Solso, 1975) contains chapters by Estes (1975) on letter identification, Mayzner (1975) on visual information processing, and Posner and Snyder (1975) on attention and cognitive control.

Posner has studied a number of different issues related to the discussions of this chapter. Two papers of special interest are his review of psychophysiological aspects of attention (Posner, 1975) and the paper by Posner and Snyder (1975) on cognitive control. Posner, Nissen, and Klein (1976) discuss the dominant role of visual inputs over other sensory information. A thorough review of the physiological measurements of attentional states is presented by Hillyard and Picton (1977).

One important and fascinating topic concerns abnormalities of attention. Possibly the best introduction is the book by G. Reed (1972). McGhie's book (1969) is perhaps the standard one on the pathology of attention.

8 The memory systems

PREVIEW

All intelligent systems require a memory. Memory plays a critical role in our functioning. To speak, write, read, listen, walk around the streets— all require memory. Whether brushing our teeth or eating, whether engaged in creative processes that are profound or trivial, we need an active memory system that can guide our actions and make a record of our accomplishments.

The human memory system is capable of a rich variety of operations. At one extreme, it holds a highly detailed record of sensory images long enough to permit the identification and classification of sights, sounds, odors, tastes, and feelings. At the other extreme, memory records our experiences for use throughout our lifetime. Yet, despite their power, our memories can fail in frustrating ways. We can remember what we ate for dinner yesterday, but not the name of the person we have just met at a party. Some things seem easy to remember, others seem almost impossible.

In the next chapters of the book we discuss different aspects of memory. We will see how memory is used in thought, in language, and in decision making. We will examine the neurological basis of memory and the representation of knowledge within memory. This present chapter provides an overall picture of the systems of memory: sensory information storage, short-term memory, and long-term memory. Here we cover both their purposes and operations.

In reading this chapter, the most important thing to learn is the distinctions among different types of memories. In this chapter we talk about three memory systems: sensory information storage, short-term memory, and long-term memory. You should learn the properties of these three systems and understand the evidence that has been used to deduce their existence.

The next chapter will cover how memory is used, including some techniques for learning new information. The material in this chapter is essential for the understanding of the next one: the structure of the memory systems forms the basis for our future discussions. The next chapter will build upon the discussions here, with emphasis on long-term memory and on the process of acquiring information into long-term memory. In addition, there will be some reinterpretation of the information given here.

THE STORAGE SYSTEMS

Memory is not a unitary process. At least three different aspects of its operation can be identified. One aspect is primarily important for the proper operation of perceptual processing, including the mechanisms of pattern recognition. Thus, we appear to have a memory system that maintains a detailed image (for a few tenths of a second) of the sensory information that has arrived at a particular sense organ. This memory system is called *sensory information storage*. A second aspect of memory maintains information for a few seconds, perhaps a few minutes. This is the *short-term memory* system. But short-term memory is not like sensory information storage, for now the information is already encoded, already categorized by pattern recognition mechanisms. Short-term memory is also the stage where we maintain information that we need temporarily for a few minutes or that we are trying to organize and store permanently. The third aspect of memory is the *long-term memory* system. Here is where permanent records of our experiences are maintained. This memory phase has essentially unlimited capacity. Thus, the major issues in the study of long-term memory are the organization of the information during the storage process and the search operations required to retrieve information at a later time.

In addition to the parts of memory that maintain information for various amounts of time, other parts of the memory system are concerned with control—with the overall selection and supervision of the memory operations. The control processes determine how information is transferred among the various forms of memory, and they determine the operations that will be performed by the memory system. These aspects of memory are discussed in Chapter 9.

FIGURE 8-1

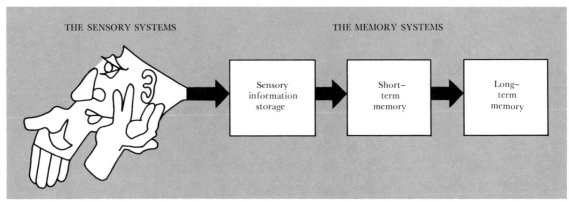

THE SENSORY SYSTEMS   THE MEMORY SYSTEMS

Sensory information storage → Short-term memory → Long-term memory

Sensory information storage system

We start with the *sensory information storage* system. This system maintains a rather accurate and complete picture of the world as it is received by the sensory system. Its duration is short—perhaps 0.1 to 0.5 sec.

- Tap four fingers against your arm. Feel the immediate sensations—note how they fade away so that at first you still retain the actual feeling of the tapping, but later on only the recollection that you were tapped.
- Close your eyes, then open them for as short an interval of time as possible before you close them again. Note how the sharp, clear image that you picked up stays for awhile and then slowly dies away.
- Listen to some sounds, say the tapping of your fingers or a few whistled notes. Notice how the distinctness of the image in your mind fades away.
- Hold your clenched fist out in front of you. Rapidly open your hand, extending two fingers, and then close your fist again. But see the shadowy trace of the fingers remain for awhile even after your fingers have again formed a fist.
- Wave a pencil (or your finger) back and forth in front of your eyes while you stare straight ahead. See the shadowy image that trails behind the moving object.

This last demonstration is the most important, for with it you can estimate how long the image lasts. Change the rate at which you wave the object back and forth. Note that if you go too slowly, you lose the continuity of the image between the endpoints of the movement. At what rate does the shadowy image just barely maintain its continuity? You should discover that it takes about 10 cycles every 5 sec to maintain the continuity of the afterimage. This means that the moving object passes in front of your eyes 20 times in 5 sec, or four times each second—the visual trace lasts about .25 sec (250 msec).

The characteristics of the visual sensory-information store are closely linked with the characteristics of the response time of the visual system studied in Chapter 4 There we suggested that the duration of the system could be measured by watching a flashlight rotate in a circle: The rate of rotation that allows the trail of a full circle to be seen gives an estimate of visual response time. Does this estimate agree with the one from the "shadowy image of a waving pencil"?

The *short-term memory* (STM) system holds a different form of material *Short-term memory* than the sensory information store. Here the information retained is not a complete image of the events that have taken place at the sensory level. Rather, short-term memory seems to retain the immediate **interpretation** of those events. If a sentence has been spoken, you do not so much hear the sounds that made up the sentence as you remember the words. There is a distinct difference here between remembering an image of the events and remembering the interpretation of those events, a difference to be described in more detail later.

Things like the last few words of the sentence you have just heard or seen, a telephone number, or a person's name can be retained in short-term memory, but capacity of this memory is limited. Only about the last five or six items that have been presented can be retained. By conscious effort, by repeating the material to yourself over and over again, you can maintain the material that is in short-term memory for an indefinite amount of time. The ability to keep things active in short-term memory by this **rehearsal** of the items is one of the most important characteristics of the memory system. Information in the sensory information store cannot be rehearsed. It lasts only a few tenths of a second and there is no way to prolong it. In short-term memory, a small amount of material can be retained indefinitely by the act of rehearsal.

Long-term memory There is a clear and compelling difference between the memory for events that have just occurred and the memory for events long past. The one is direct and immediate; the other is tortured and slow. Events that have just occurred are still present in the mind—they have never left consciousness. Time and effort is required to insert new material into *long-term memory* (LTM). Past events have to be dredged up with effort. Short-term memory is immediate and direct; long-term memory is labored and strained. From short-term memory:

What were the first few words of this sentence?

From long-term memory:

What did you eat for dinner last Sunday?

Long-term memory is probably the most important of the memory systems, and it is also the most complex. The capacity of the sensory information store and short-term memory systems is very limited—one by a few tenths of a second, and the other by a few items, but there appears to be no practical limit on the capacity of long-term memory.[1] Everything that is retained for more than a few minutes at a time obviously must reside in the long-term memory system. All learned experiences, including the rules of language, must be a part of long-term memory. In fact, much of experimental psychology can be considered to be concerned with the problems of getting material into long-term memory, keeping it there, retrieving it, and interpreting it properly.

The real difficulties associated with long-term memory stem mainly from one source: retrieval. The amount of information contained in

[1] Obviously, there has to be some limit: The brain is a finite device. But there are approximately 100 billion (10^{11}) neurons in the brain, each capable of storing a reasonable amount of information. For all practical purposes, then, we can consider that the memory capacity of the human brain is unlimited.

the memory is so large that it should be a major problem to find anything. Yet things can be found rapidly; even in so prosaic an act as reading, the meanings of the symbols on the printed page must be interpreted through direct and immediate access to long-term memory. The problems associated with being able to get to the one correct item from among the millions or billions that are stored dictate much of the overall structure of all the stages of the memory system. We devote Chapter 10 to the study of the organization of long-term memory.

These are the memory systems. We begin the study of memory by examining the initial two stages of memory: the *transient memories*—sensory information storage and short-term memory. Each memory serves a different function, stores a different form of information, has different capacity limitations, and operates according to somewhat different principles. Let us consider how each of these transient memories functions.

The job of extracting the features of a sensory message in order to determine what that message represents may take time—more time than the duration of the actual signal allows. The *sensory information storage* system (called SIS) plays the logical role of giving the feature extraction and pattern recognition systems time to work on the signals arriving at the sensory organs.

SENSORY INFORMATION STORAGE

After a visual input, a visual image remains for several tenths of a second. This image is the visual sensory information store. This means that it is possible to work on a sensory event for a duration of time that is longer than the event itself. This storage is useful in situations where an image is exposed very briefly: in viewing motion pictures and television, in maintaining a continuity of perception during the time it takes to complete an eye movement or eye blink. In fact, for brief exposures to a signal, the duration of time for which the visual image is present is almost irrelevant: The controlling duration is the length of time material stays in the SIS.

Not only does the SIS seem to retain a good image of the sensory events that have occurred during the past few tenths of a second, but there is more information stored there than can be extracted. This discrepancy between the amount of information held in the sensory system and the amount that can be used by later stages of analysis is very important. It implies some sort of limit on the capacity of later stages, a limit that is not shared by the sensory stages themselves. The limitation shows up during the attempt to remember the material presented. The tremendous amount of information carried in a sensory image is usually of no importance for interpreting its meanings. In fact, for many purposes, too many details just make the job harder. Computer devices which attempt to read printed text, decode spoken speech waveforms, or even read printed music are easily thrown off the track by trivial details in the input that are never even noticed by the human doing the same task. Tiny dirt spots, or breaks in printed letters confuse the computers. But with the human, even gross errors such mispellings often go unnoticed.

The sensory system must maintain an accurate image of everything that arrives at the sense organs, since although most of that information will turn out to be useless, the sensory system has no way of determining what aspects of the input will be of value. Only the systems that recognize and interpret the signals can do that. The SIS would seem to be ideally suited for its purposes. It holds everything for a short duration of time, giving the processes of pattern recognition time to pick and choose.

VISUAL DISPLAY EXPERIMENTS

The tachistoscope   The apparatus most frequently used in the study of human visual processes is the *tachistoscope*. Basically, this is simply a device to present visual images for very brief periods of time. It was invented in the 1880s, and although today the instruments can be fully controlled by electronic circuits (and even computers), the principles have not changed since about 1907.

The basic tachistoscope is a lightproof box, often simply a long, enclosed rectangular tube made out of some lightproof material. The subject looks in at one end. The object that is to be seen is placed at the other end (see Figure 8-2). Initially, however, everything is dark, so nothing can be seen. When a light is flashed inside the box, whatever is at the end of the tube can be seen. By using special lights, usually gas-filled bulbs that are ionized by the application of a high potential between electrodes, it is possible to control the light duration accurately to fractions of a millisecond.

FIGURE 8-2

Often, the experimenter wants to control the viewing of several different objects. This can be done by adding mirrors to the box. Special mirrors are used, with the surface of the glass only half-silvered, so that half the light hitting the mirror goes through it and half gets reflected. With the arrangement shown in Figure 8-3, the subject can see into three different locations. If only light A is on, only stimulus A can be seen. Similarly, light

B allows stimulus B to be seen, and light C stimulus C. Thus, information can be presented at any or all of three locations. All that is needed is to control accurately the times at which each of the three lights is on.

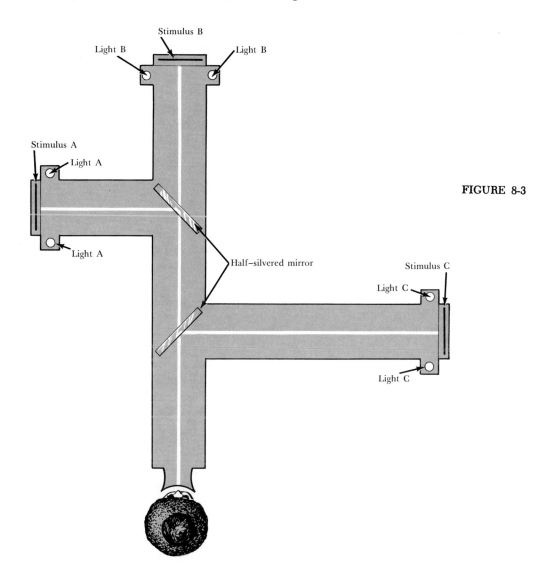

FIGURE 8-3

This particular tachistoscope, called a *three-field tachistoscope,* is the type of instrument used in many of the experiments discussed in this chapter, Some tachistoscopes make one modification, however. The quality of the image seen by the subject depends upon the number of mirrors the image has bounced off and gone through. In the instrument of Figure 8-3, more light can come from C (the path only involves one mirror) than from B or A (the path involves two mirrors). Thus, tachistoscopes add dummy mirrors and filters so that the images from each of the fields will (as much as possible):

1. Travel exactly the same distance in going from the location of the stimulus card to the subject;
2. Pass through the same number of mirrors;
3. Be reflected off of the same number of mirrors.

The oscilloscope and CRT displays   It is possible to generate a visual image directly from a computer or micro-processor. In these cases, the computer controls the operation of a cathode ray tube (CRT) or an oscilloscope tube in which light is emitted by an electron beam hitting a phosphor coating on the rear of the visible part of the tube. A television screen is an example of a CRT. Two types of display systems are in common use. In one, the computer controls the exact points of illumination of the CRT. It can typically control the electron beam to go to any one of about 1,000,000 locations on the tube face by specifying the horizontal and vertical coordinates of the desired point with an accuracy of 1 part in 1000. In addition to points, lines and shading can sometimes be directly controlled. In the other display system, the computer controls the generation of a television signal, which can then be viewed on a regular television set. Here the resolution is limited by that of television: in the United States, this is the equivalent of points on a matrix 500 points high by 500 wide: 250,000 locations on the screen. In most laboratory situations the resolution is only 250 points by 250 points: 62,500 locations.

These computer-controlled display systems are replacing the tachistoscope in a wide number of applications. But these displays are not as good as those in the tachistoscope for several reasons. First, the intensity and contrast of the image is severely limited. Second, the quality of the image is not very good, for even an image created from 1,000,000 points cannot compare with a high-quality photograph. Third, it is difficult to get good color display with CRTs. Fourth, it is not possible to control timing accurately. When the computer directly controls the construction of the image, the time it takes to create the image is often as long as the time one wishes the display to last (to plot 100,000 points, even at the rate of 10 points per microsec, would take 10 millisec). When the computer controls a television image things are even worse. Here one is limited by the television system in use: In the United States, each image takes exactly 1/60 sec to produce, and in Europe, it takes slightly longer, 1/50 sec. (In both the United States and Europe, these times are for every other line of the television image.) It is for all these reasons that the computer-generated display has not yet completely replaced the tachistoscope.

The capacity of SIS   It is easy to demonstrate that the SIS initially contains more information than the stages of analysis that follow are able to use. Suppose a complex visual image is presented briefly. The observers will only be able to extract a small amount of the information present in the image. They will claim that they did not have enough time to "see" it all. But if they are told to look at only one particular part of the image, they can concentrate their attention on that part and report on it with high accuracy. This basic phenomenon indicates that the restriction on our ability to deal with sensory inputs comes during the analysis process.

The experiment. It is important to examine this experiment with some care, since it is the central technique used in the study of sensory information storage systems. In one form of the basic experiment, the card of Figure 8-4, containing nine letters arranged in three rows of three letters each, is exposed in a tachistoscope for 50 msec. Typically, the subject will manage to read only four or five of the nine letters. Even if more letters are presented or the exposure duration varied, the number of letters reported remains nearly the same: about four or five.

To find out what subjects can actually see, we should not ask them to report everything. Maybe they see them all, but then forget some. To test this idea we can ask for a **partial report** of the letters presented. That is, present the group of nine letters as before, but mark off one of the letters from the rest with a marker and ask only for the marked letter. The subjects never know which of the nine letters is going to be marked until **after** the exposure (see Figure 8-4).[2]

Now, if they can always report any randomly marked letter, they must really be able to see **all** nine letters in the flash. If they do not know which letter is to be marked until after the exposure, they must have all nine in SIS, be able to search for the marker, and then report the letter.

The results of the experiment are shown in Figure 8-5: the subjects almost always correctly identify the marked letter. Thus, they see more than they can report. Evidently, in the original experiment, all the letters were in SIS, but by the time they had processed three or four of them, the others had faded away.

Figure 8-6

The bar-marker technique is a valuable procedure for the study of perception. The next important use of the technique is to delay the marker, make it so that it does not come on immediately with the other letters. This should tell us what the SIS looks like. The general results of this manipulation are easy to determine, even without doing the experiment. First of all, the subjects normally can recall only about four or five of the letters presented to them if there is no marker. Second, they can get any of the marked letters if the marker appears at the same time as the letters. Thus, if the marker is delayed for a very long time—long enough so that the visual image has completely faded away and the subjects report that they cannot "see" the letters any more—then according to Figure 8-5 the subjects should remember only about half (four or five) of the nine letters. The chance that they will remember one particu-

---

[2] These experiments were performed by Sperling (1959, 1960). Sperling actually signaled the letters to be recalled with a tone, rather than with a bar marker. This led to slightly different results than those shown here, but the difference *is* slight and the principle demonstrated here is correct.

THE STIMULUS CARD

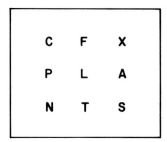

FIGURE 8-4

THE BAR MARKER

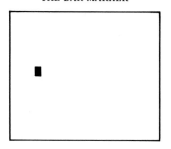

WHAT THE SUBJECT IS SHOWN

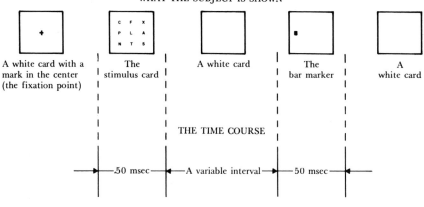

FIGURE 8-5

From Sperling (1959).

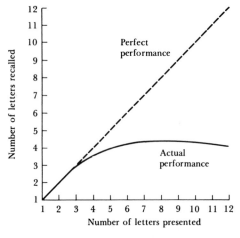

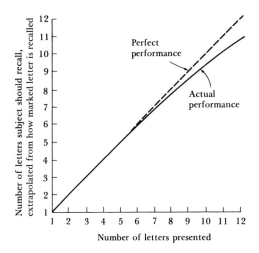

FIGURE 8-6

Data from Sperling (1959).

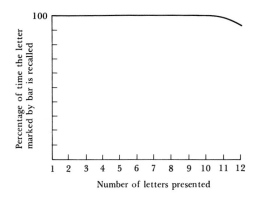

lar letter of the nine, the one that is indicated by the marker, is therefore about 50%. As the delay in the marker is increased, then, the performance will range from about 100% correct to about 50% correct.

Typical results of the experiment are shown in Figure 8-7 The ability to report a randomly designated letter decreases smoothly as the marker is delayed more and more, with the performance leveling off after about 500 msec (.5 sec). It looks as if the SIS consists of an image of the signal that decays in time such that little remains of the image after about .5 sec. (Alternatively, the decay of the memory image looks like an exponential process with a time constant of approximately 150 msec.)

A strange thing happens with certain types of markers. In the early studies of the visual information storage system, a circular marker was used and the subjects' task was to report the letter that appeared within the circle. Unlike the situation with the bar marker, when the circle comes on shortly after the letter set, it seems to "erase" the letter that it surrounds.

Figure 8-8

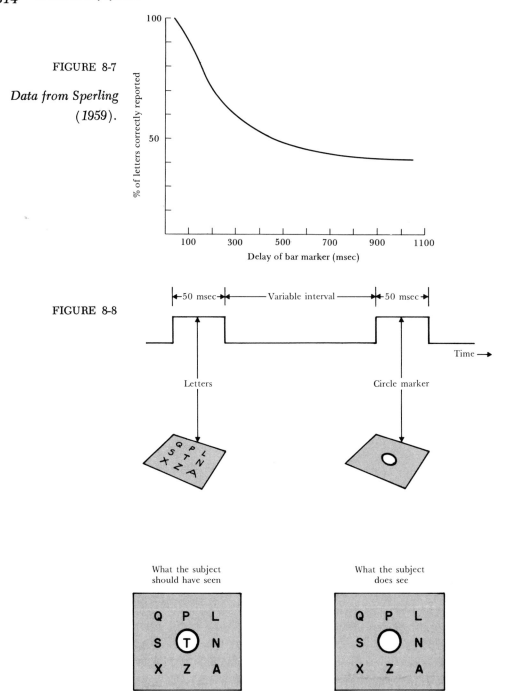

FIGURE 8-7

*Data from Sperling
(1959).*

FIGURE 8-8

This phenomenon of erasure is both intriguing and important. It is a potentially useful tool in controlling the duration that the SIS maintains the image.

Whenever one signal is presented after another, two different things seem to happen. First, there is a summation of the trace of one signal with the image of the other. This can lead to a reduction in the contrast or clarity of the fading image of the first figure, thus reducing the amount of processing on that figure. Second, there can be disruption in the processing of the first if a second image is presented before the first has been fully analyzed. Which of these two processes predominates depends on the particular image sequence presented: Both are always present, but sometimes one is more important than the other.

Regardless of how the phenomenon of erasure is explained, it is an important tool, for when the second stimulus (the masker) is presented, it effectively stops the processing of the first (the signal). Thus, even though the SIS lasts for some time after the signal has been presented, the time available for processing the signal can be precisely controlled by presenting a masker at the desired time.

It is now common practice that when material is to be exposed tachistoscopically to subjects, it is followed by a masking stimulus. Without the masker SIS maintains the image, so it is not possible to know exactly how long a period of time the subjects spend processing the material. With the masker, the time is controlled precisely by the experimenter.

In 1954 two psychologists at the University of Indiana, Lloyd Peterson and Margaret Peterson (1959), tried a very simple experiment, but with surprising results. They asked subjects to remember three letters and then, some 18 sec later, asked them to recall the three. The task sounds absolutely trivial. The interesting thing is that the subjects were not able to remember the three letters. What is the gimmick? Simple. Between the time the three letters had been presented and the time they were to be recalled, the subjects had to do some mental work. They had to count backward, by threes, at a rapid rate.[3]

SHORT-TERM
MEMORY

This simple experiment illustrates the central property of the short-term memory system. But there is more, a change in the material that is to be remembered produces surprisingly little change in the memory, so long as the number of items is constant. Look at Figure 8-9. This shows the rate at which subjects forget things. The curve labeled "three consonants" is the experiment just described. In the figure, the horizontal axis tells the time in seconds between presenting the three letters (all were consonant letters) to the subjects and asking them to recall them. (Remember, all during this time the subjects are busy counting

[3] To "count backward by threes" the subjects start at a randomly selected three-digit number, such as 487, and then say aloud the sequence of numbers formed by subtracting three from each previous value, e.g., 487, 484, 481, 478, 475, ... The subjects are required to do this counting at a rapid rate, either simply "rapidly," or in time to the clicks of a metronome. Try it: The task is harder than it would seem.

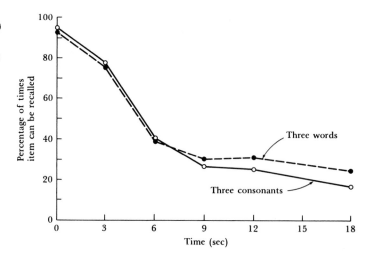

FIGURE 8-9

*After Murdock
(1961).*

backward by threes.) The vertical axis shows the percentage of times that the subjects could recall the material when tested at any particular retention interval. Thus, if there is as little as 6 sec between presenting three consonants and testing for their recall, only 40% of the subjects can recall all three of the consonants.

What do you think should happen if the subjects are given three **words** instead of three **consonants?** How different should the memory for **house–apple–book** be than for **C–X–Q?** Compare the curves labeled "three consonants" and "three words." They are nearly the same.

What possible mechanisms could produce such a memory system? It is a memory that appears to have a very small capacity and a very short life. But the capacity is not too sensitive to the length of the items stored. Obviously, this is not the SIS of the previous section, since there, memory lasted only a fraction of a second. But neither is it the long-term memory system, since there material is retained indefinitely. In this memory, material lasts only a short time: Hence, it is short-term memory.

*Errors in recall
from short-term
memory*

Start with a sequence of **visually** presented material, such as letters of the alphabet. To test memory for these letters, ask the subjects to **write** down as many of the letters as they can remember. When the subject makes an error trying to recall the letter **F**, it is much more likely to be reported as an **X** than as an **E**. Although **F** and **E** share common visual features, **F** and **X** share a common initial sound. Similarly, a **C** is more likely to be recalled as a **T** than as an **O** When the subject makes an error, it is most likely to be by producing a letter that **sounds** similar to the correct one, not one that **looks** similar.

For the pattern-recognition system in Chapter 7, exactly the opposite types of errors were made: **C** and **O** might be confused, certainly not

C and **T**. This difference results from the fact that short-term memory is a later stage in the human information processing system. When the visual input is at the first stages of pattern recognition, then visual errors can occur. These errors indicate that in the process of encoding the visually presented information into short-term memory, it has gotten into an acoustic form. Yet nowhere in the experiment was a spoken representation required by the subjects: They **saw** the letters when they were presented, and they were asked to **write** the answers.

Acoustic confusions. The whole concept has set off a plethora of experiments and theoretical interpretations. At first, the observations seemed natural and obvious. Most people can "hear" themselves saying the things they read. If you say things to yourself, isn't it natural that you should remember the sounds rather than the sights? But just what is this "saying?" Although you can hear yourself, it is a mentalized hearing that is involved—an inner, silent speech.

Is inner speech absolutely necessary for verbal processes? Must all visual words be recoded into inner speech? If so, what of people who are born deaf? They manage to read, yet clearly without the need to transform visual words into auditory ones.

And what about this: Are the confusions really among the **sounds** of the spoken words, or are they perhaps **articulatory** in nature? That is, so far we have implied that visually presented words are encoded by matching the letter patterns to the **sounds** made when those words are pronounced. This would lead to **acoustic** confusions. But it is also possible that the recoding is not into sounds, but rather into the sequence of muscle patterns necessary to speak the words. In this case, sounds that are **produced** in similar ways would be confused: *articulatory confusions.* Several of the theories on how humans recognize speech require one or the other of these modes. It would be valuable to be able to distinguish between the two, but no one yet knows how to do so. The problem is that any two patterns of speech that sound similar are also going to be produced in similar ways. With minor exceptions, the patterns of confusions of similar sounds are almost the same as the pattern of confusions from similar articulations.

On top of all these issues comes yet another question: Why is acoustical coding necessary at all? (From here on, the words "acoustical coding" are used to indicate that the visual representation is changed to something related to the sound or production of the words; no favoritism is implied for acoustical over articulatory theories.) Why can't people simply read a passage of printed text without transforming the words into some acoustical format? This is exactly what some speed reading courses promise to teach.

Look to your right, now to your left. While looking toward the left, try to recall what you saw on the right: Does it make sense that you do this acoustically, by recalling a verbal description of the scene? Of course not. Think about performing some action, perhaps washing your hands (with soap). Again, an acoustical format for the remembrance seems far-fetched. Clearly, one can carry acoustical encoding too far. The evidence for its existence is restricted to studies of the memory for verbal information, that is, for information that requires the use of language: letters, words, or sentences. But for these materials the evidence is quite strong. There does appear to be an acoustical representation for items, even when it might seem unnecessary.

It is patently obvious that everything seen does not need to be transformed into words. But there is good sense to the notion that material input to the system does get transformed into a common format. Certainly, it would be silly to store the minute patterns of each individual input. It is not important whether a sentence is spoken slowly or in haste; whether the printed text is viewed from straight on or rotated at an angle. These are trivial physical variations: It is the meaning of the words, not their appearances that should be remembered. Similarly, a sentence means the same whether it is spoken or read—why should the differences be preserved? Does it not make sense that the same mechanisms that eliminate such trivial variations of the input as the angle at which letters are viewed might also eliminate other aspects?

The problem of determining the meaning of the sensory signals is very difficult, as the analysis of Chapter 7 has shown. But it is clear that thought processes must operate on some internal coding—a coding that reflects the meaning of the material being thought about, not its physical realization. In order to make most efficient contact with the storage of information in the long-term memory, it would be useful for all information to be transformed into the same common form.

Note, however, that in transforming information into some common format we do not necessarily discard information about the physical nature of the signals that have arrived at the sensory system. You probably can remember quite a bit of the physical details of this book, including the part of the page on which some of the statements or illustrations were presented, possibly including some of the details of the look of the printed page. It is a common experience (which has been verified experimentally) to remember on what part of a page you read something. If we simply transformed information into acoustical fragments, such detailed physical information would be lost.

REHEARSAL   When dealing with language, why should the common format not be acoustical, whether the language material is read, heard, or thought? Suppose you are given a list of names to learn or a telephone number to dial. Most people do this by saying the items over and over to themselves.

In general, whenever it is necessary to retain information for more than a few seconds of time, some of the information is lost unless it is consciously repeated over and over again. This silent mental repetition of the material that is to be learned is called *rehearsal.* Later, we will see that there are at least two different forms of rehearsal. One form seems primarily to help maintain information within short-term memory (and is therefore called *maintenance rehearsal*). The other form of rehearsal seems to help integrate the material being rehearsed into the structures of long-term memory (and so it is called *integrative rehearsal*). We will discuss integrative rehearsal later (in Chapter 9), when we discuss some of the properties of the organization of material within the long-term memory system.

Retention of material in short-term memory through rehearsal can only come about if the amount to be retained is sufficiently small. Although rehearsal is capable of keeping material alive, it cannot increase the capacity of the memory system. It is as if the maintenance rehearsal process simply took the weak, decaying trace of the signal and refreshed it, thus effectively reentering it into short-term memory. Hence, we show this rehearsal process in Figure 8-10 as a loop leaving and entering short-term memory. If too many items are to be rehearsed, however, then the rehearsal of them all will not be completed in time. The last item will decay away before the rehearsal process can get to it.

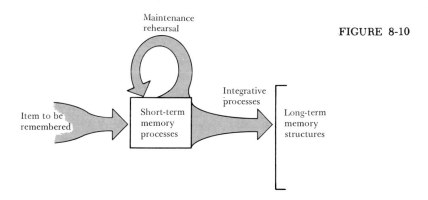

FIGURE 8-10

How fast can rehearsal be done? Silent speech takes place at a rate very close to the rate of spoken speech. To measure the rate of silent speech, pick up a pencil and count mentally (and therefore silently) as rapidly as you can from 1 to 10. As soon as you reach 10, start over again, simultaneously making a mark on the paper. Do this for exactly 10 sec, and then count the marks. How far did you count? If you got to 82, then you rehearse 8.2 digits per second. You can confirm this by trying other material: Try the alphabet. Note that the number of items you can keep in short-term memory through maintenance rehearsal is a function of how long it takes to say those items.[4]

Forgetting   How is material lost from short-term memory? There are two possible ways: Forgetting could result from interference from other material or simply as a result of the passage of time. Let us examine the implication of each possibility.

Forgetting by interference.   In this mode of operation, the short-term memory is assumed to have a limited capacity for the number of items it can retain. There are several ways in which you can think of this. For example, short-term memory could be treated as though it were simply a set of slots somewhere in the brain. Whenever something is presented, it goes through the standard processing by the sensory system and is identified by the pattern-recognition stages. Then, the meaningful representation of the item presented is inserted into one of the empty short-term memory slots. If there is a limited number of slots—say, seven—then when the eighth new item comes in, one of the previous seven would have to go.

This basic formulation of a limited capacity short-term memory suggests that forgetting is caused by interference from newly presented items, because each new presentation causes one old item to be lost. (This, of course, only happens after short-term memory has become filled.) This particular version of the slot model is too simple to work well: It says, for example, that an exact number of items should always be remembered, never more, never less; it also says that an item is either remembered perfectly or forgotten altogether. But it is not too difficult a task to modify the structure to take care of these objections.

One way is simply to realize that the memory need not be entirely present or absent: It can partially exist. Think of trying to understand a soft voice in the midst of other voices—the louder the voice, the easier it is to understand, the softer the voice, the more difficult, until it is so weak that it is not even possible to tell whether the voice being listened for is present or not. If the voice is the **signal** and the background voices the **noise**, then it is the ratio of signal level to noise level that determines the ability to understand the voice. So it could be with memory. The representation of an item in the memory is its *memory trace*. It is the **signal** we are trying to recall against the back-

---

[4] It is instructive to try **visual** rehearsal: Go through the alphabet visually, as rapidly as possible, mentally imagining the image of each letter before going on to the next. You will discover that visual rehearsal is slower than acoustical rehearsal. To prevent yourself from cheating as you go through the letters, say aloud **yes** or **no** whether each capital letter has a horizontal line. Hence, the first five letters yield: **Yes, Yes, No, No, Yes.** (This technique was introduced by Weber and Castleman, 1970.)

ground of other memories, the **noise.** The stronger the memory trace, the easier it is to decipher; as the memory gets older it fades away, until finally its trace is so weak as to be undecipherable.

There is an analogy, then, between deciphering a weak signal in noise and remembering an old memory. Newly presented items have high strength; older items have weak strength. Just as there will be mistakes in interpreting a voice which has a low ratio of signal to noise levels, so too there will be errors in retrieving memories that have low trace strength. And, in retrieving from short-term memory, these errors will tend to be acoustically related to the words that were stored.

Now how do the memory traces get weaker? According to this theory, the strength of the memory depends on the number of items that have been presented. Suppose that initially when something is presented into memory it gets a trace strength of, say, *A*. Each time a new item is presented, it causes all the trace strengths of previous items to decrease by some constant percentage of their previous value. If the fraction of the memory trace strength that remains after each new item has been presented is represented by the forgetting factor *f* (*f* is obviously a fraction between 0 and 1), then we can follow the fate of an item (call it the *critical item*) as more material is presented.

Figure 8-11

When the item is first presented, its trace strength becomes *A*.

When one more item is presented, the trace strength of the critical item drops to *Af*.

When a second new item is presented, the critical strength drops to $(Af)f$ or Af^2.

In fact, if *i* interfering items have been presented after the presentation of the critical item, the strength of the critical item is Af^i—a simple geometric decay of memory trace strength with the number of items that has been presented.

Forgetting by time decay. The second way by which the capacity of short-term memory might be limited is by a time-dependent process, one in which the longer an item stays in memory, the weaker it gets, until finally it disappears entirely. Here, time alone is sufficient for the disappearance of material from memory, much like the role that time plays in the loss of electrical charge from a capacitor or in the decay of radioactive substances. Aside from this, however, the description is very much like the one for item decay.

For the time theory, assume that each instant of time causes a reduction in the trace strength of previously acquired items to some fraction of their previous values. That is, each instant of time in the time-decay theory acts much as each presentation of a new item in the interference theory. Simply place the *i* for the number of items with *t* for the amount

SENSORY
PROCESSING

PATTERN
RECOGNITION

SHORT–TERM MEMORY

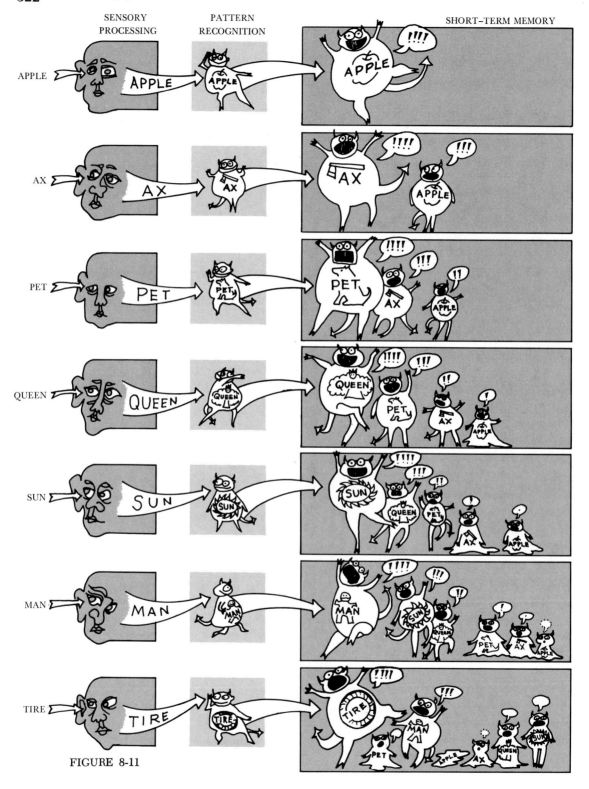

FIGURE 8-11

of time. If t seconds have elapsed since the presentation of a critical item, its trace strength will have decayed from its original value of A to a value of Af^t.[5]

Forgetting: time or interference? The critical test of the two competing theories requires some way of first presenting material to subjects and then having them do nothing until tested for their memory of the material. The time decay theory predicts a loss of memory: The interference theory predicts no loss. The problem with this critical experiment lies in the difficulty of getting subjects to "do nothing." If they truly have nothing else to do, then they rehearse the material presented to them. A perfect memory in this experiment is equally well explained by the rehearsal or by the lack of interference: The experimental results prove nothing. If rehearsal by the subjects is prevented by giving them some other task to do, then that other task can cause interference, so a poor memory after this experiment also proves nothing: The loss in memory could be equally well explained by a time decay or by the effects of interference.

One way of doing the experiment is to devise a task so difficult that the subject is unable to rehearse the memory material, yet so different from the memory task that it should not add any interference. One such task is that of detecting a weak signal in noise. Thus, if the subject is first presented with a set of letters to learn, then with a difficult detection task for 30 sec, then tested on memory for the letters; there is the possibility that neither rehearsal nor interference has taken place.

This experiment is very difficult to do, and the results so far have been inconclusive. After the first attempts, it was thought that the results showed that the interference theory was correct. There appeared to be no loss in memory for as long as 30 sec. One major difficulty with these experiments, however, was determining whether or not subjects might have secretly rehearsed during that 30-sec time interval. Originally, it was believed that they had not rehearsed. Now, however, more sophisticated analyses of the results of newer experiments, including a closer look at what the subjects claim they were doing, indicates that surreptitious rehearsal probably does take place during this time interval. Although not fully established, it appears that unless subjects perform surreptitious rehearsal, they do forget.

As is often the case when there are two competing theories to explain a phenomenon, the truth probably lies somewhere in between. Evidently,

---

[5] Those of you who think that exponential functions should be expressed by the value of e can translate this expression to its equivalent form:

$$Af^t = Ae^{-kt},$$

where $k = -\ln(f)$.

forgetting in short-term memory comes about through both a decay in time and through interference from the presentation of other material.

Attributes of memory

Now let us return to the question of the basic unit of storage. What is the nature of these memory traces in short-term memory? One previous datum yields quite a bit of information: the fact that acoustic confusions occur in short-term memory.

Consider the word **hose.** The goal is to determine just how this word is represented in the short-term memory. Suppose that it is **attributes** that get stored, not words. For example, assume for the moment that each sound is an attribute. This is, of course, a gross oversimplification of the truth, but it is sufficiently accurate to illustrate the concepts.[6] Suppose the item **hose** is to be stored. It is not put away simply as a single unit. Rather, the single memory-unit contains the three basic attributes: the sounds of **h, o,** and **z.** Thus, each attribute of **hose** can be forgotten independently. When the word is to be retrieved from memory, this is done by retrieving however many attributes are still present and then attempting to reconstruct the word they must have represented.

- If the **h,** the **o,** and the **z** are remembered, then the word recalled will be **hose.**
- If only the **o** and **z** are remembered, then the word recalled might be **doze, rose,** or even **hose.**
- If only the **h** and **z** are remembered, then the word recalled might be **his, haze,** or even **hose.**
- If only the **h** and **o** are remembered, then the word recalled might be **hole, hope,** or even **hose.**

When a single attribute is lost, then the possible words that can be reconstructed from what remains (plus the knowledge that there is a total of three components) is rather limited. All, obviously, are acoustically similar to the original. Note that the correct item will be remembered a reasonable percentage of the time simply by lucky reconstruction from what is left. With two attributes lost—so that all that remains is the sound **h, o,** or **z,** then there are many more possible items that fit in with the information that is retained and a very small chance of being lucky enough to get the correct word. With all three attributes gone, nothing remains to guide the reconstructive process.

The reconstruction process of memory. Let us now examine the reconstructive nature of short-term memory. We have just seen how acoustic confusions are produced during the reconstruction of partial information. This is one positive piece of support for the idea that at-

---

[6] For verbal information, attributes are most likely to be the phonemes or distinctive features described in Chapter 7. For visual information (pictures and visual perceptions) they are probably the visual features discussed in Chapter 6.

tributes are stored. If it is attributes that are stored, then clearly the longer the name of the item presented, the fewer the items that can be retained. Let us see how the nature of the items themselves determines how much can be recalled.

Suppose this list of letters is to be remembered:

L
B
X
K
F
M

The complete set of phonemic attributes of these letters is:

e,l
b,ee
e,ks
k,ai
e,f
e,m

We know that the capacity of short-term memory is limited. For the present example, assume that short-term memory can hold only six attributes. How many letter names can be remembered? It depends upon what six attributes were retained. If they had distributed themselves this way:

_____,l
b,_____
_____,ks
k,_____
_____,f
_____,m

probably all six of the letters could be recalled correctly, simply by reconstructing what must have been present. After all, what letter besides **X** ends in "ks"?

Suppose the memory for the six attributes was scattered, one attribute per letter, in this way:

e,_____
_____,ee
e,_____
_____,ai
e,_____
e,_____

Even then, the reconstructive process would still do reasonably well. Look at the four cases where the items are "e_____." How many possible letters are there that start off with the sound "e"?

F, L, M, N, S, and X.

Six possible letters, and the reconstructive process must select four. Thus, anywhere from two to four of the letters starting with the sound "e" would be recalled correctly just by chance alone.

Similarly, when the memory for the other attributes is considered, recall would always be reasonably accurate simply by guessing. On the average, three to four of the letters can be correctly recalled from any sequence of six attributes.

The important point of this demonstration is that there is more to the short-term memory process than simply counting up how many attributes are retained. There is also a reconstructive process that pieces together the information available into the most likely description of what has been presented. With skill and some luck, it is quite likely that with only six attributes in memory we could remember all six letters—a feat that would require all twelve attributes if there were no reconstruction of the possible letters from the information that had been retained.

The reconstructive process is not always so successful. It is possible to create sequences of words that give the process difficulties. Consider the memory for the sequence:

> BEE
> SEE
> PEE
> LEE
> MEE
> FEE

Here, the attributes are

> b,ee
> s,ee
> p,ee
> l,ee
> m,ee
> f,ee

As before, suppose only six were remembered. With luck, all six items could be reconstructed:

b,_____
s,_____
p,_____
l,_____
m,_____
f,_____

But, with an equally likely choice of attributes, the reconstructive process would face severe difficulties:

_____,ee
_____,ee
_____,ee
_____,ee
_____,ee
_____,ee

From these six attributes, what were the original items? You cannot tell. In fact, on the average, fewer items could be recalled from this latter list than from the first one. In the first case, with the letters **L, B, X, K, F,** and **M,** we could always recall between three and six of them, depending upon which attributes had been retained. This is an average of four and a half letters. But when the items were BEE, SEE, PEE, LEE, MEE, FEE, between zero and six can be recalled, depending upon which attributes had been retained. This is an average of approximately three. Moreover, in the first case we would remember the correct **order** of the letters, but certainly not in the second case.

This discussion has made several different points. The number of attributes in memory does not immediately tell how many items can be recalled. To determine that, it is necessary to know something of the reconstruction process. Some material will be easier to reconstruct from the attributes that do remain in the memory than other material. In general, it is possible to recall more items that are **acoustically different** from one another than items that are **acoustically similar.**

Memory for very long words, words such as the names of states, does not pose any particular problems for this scheme. Suppose the memory list had been

CONNECTICUT
MASSACHUSETTS
PENNSYLVANIA
CALIFORNIA
ALABAMA
MISSISSIPPI

At first, it might seem that it should be more difficult to remember long names with such large numbers of attributes. Not necessarily so. Granted that it does take many attributes to encode CONNECTICUT— *k-uh-n-e-t-i-k-uh-t*—only a few of these attributes are needed to reconstruct it. After all, there simply are not very many words that are as long as CONNECTICUT and that have attributes in common. When an item in memory is reconstructed from only a few of its attributes, there can be errors caused by generating other words that share those same attributes. But since there are fewer long words than short ones, there is much less chance of confusion with long words: even a few attributes readily lead to constructing the correct item.

Note that regeneration of a word from its attributes requires the use of long-term memory. The selection of words that fit the attributes within short-term memory obviously comes from information that is kept within long-term memory. You might have noticed that some other attributes have quietly sneaked in. For one, we suggested that the length of the word might be a useful cue in attempting to reconstruct the original item: this implies that one of the attributes in short-term memory is word length. There is often other information available as well. For example, if it were realized that all the words to be learned were the names of states, then the task of reconstructing each word from its attributes becomes even easier, since the set of possible items is now very much reduced. But information such as "these are all state names" brings up issues that we will get to later when we talk about long-term memory.

Selective interference: A useful experimental tool We can study some of the properties of STM by using a technique that we call *selective interference*. Let us begin by examining this technique. We have already suggested that information is retained within STM in the form of *attributes*. When the information to be retained is words, we believe that the attributes are related to the phonemic (or distinctive feature) structure of the words. When a person attempts to recover information from STM, then there is some reconstructive process, attempting to determine just what item might have been presented that would be consistent with the set of attributes still in STM.

Consider the following *interference experiment* designed to demonstrate the reconstruction of items from the attributes in STM. The experiment has three parts to it:

> presenting the *stimulus material*—the items that are to be remembered;
> presenting the *interference task*—a task specifically designed to interfere with the retention of the stimulus material;
> *testing*—determining what has been retained of the stimulus material.

In the Peterson and Peterson experiment, which we discussed earlier, three letters were presented to the subjects, who were then asked to count backward by threes. After some period of time, they were asked to stop counting and to recall the three letters: the letters were the stimulus materials, the counting was the interference task, and the recall was the test.

Now consider another task we discussed earlier, learning a list of words that sound alike. Suppose the words were:

BEE   TREE
SEE   GLEE
PEA   KEY

These are the stimulus items. Now, after presenting these items to the subjects, we quickly present an interference task: we make the subjects write down the following six words while also saying them aloud:

SHE   THREE
KNEE   TEA
FREE   PLEA

The subjects are told that the words in this interference list are not to be remembered, but as you can imagine, the words will interfere anyway. Obviously, the attributes of the interference list are so similar to the attributes of the stimulus list that when the time comes to retrieve the stimulus items, there will be a lot of confusion.

Now consider a variation of this experiment, this time with a different interference task. This time the words the subjects are asked to write down and say aloud are:

ESKIMO   VIOLIN
BUFFALO   PENCIL
TELEPHONE   WINTER

This second list has been chosen so that their attributes differ from those of the stimulus list items. Accordingly, we would expect the subjects to have a much easier time recalling the stimulus items in this second experiment than in the first, even though the stimulus lists were the same in both experiments.

The technique of selective interference we have just illustrated is a useful tool in determining the properties of the memory system. By determining the nature of the items in the interference list that cause the most difficulties with the retention of the items in the stimulus list, we can determine the nature of the attributes of the memory system. This technique has been applied to studies of all three memory systems: SIS, STM, LTM.

One conclusion from these studies is that there are differences in the retention of visual and verbal information. A dramatic example of this is presented in the accompanying Box: *Are there separate short-term memories for words and visual images?* Other studies have shown different effects for visual and spoken word presentations, and for retention of words and of pictures. Work on memory for other sensory systems (and for the memory of motor actions) has not progressed far enough yet that definitive statements can be made about their properties. One thing is certain, however: whatever the modality or the task, there seems to be a special status for the memory of the stimulus items most recently presented and for the actions most recently performed. This special status is what we have characterized as *short-term memory,* and it plays an important role in the normal processing activities of humans.[7]

ARE THERE SEPARATE SHORT-TERM MEMORIES FOR WORDS AND VISUAL IMAGES?

The technique of selective interference can be used to illustrate a dramatic feature of the memory system: the lack of interference between information that is represented in different sensory modalities. Perhaps the most interesting set of experiments on this topic has been performed by Lee Brooks, and the easiest way to present his work to you is simply to reprint part of a paper in which he explains the types of experiments that he did. Basically, Brooks was attempting to show that when people had to do tasks that involved keeping information within STM, the memory could be selectively interfered with by the nature of the task the person was required to perform on the material. Here is a case where the interference task is actually some operation that is to be performed directly on the stimulus material.

Let me give a short demonstration of this kind of experiment. I will read a short sentence such as "There is the low friend who stole the child's candy." What I would like you to do is to say "yes" for each word in the sentence that is a noun and "no" for each word that is not. In this case you would say "no, no, no, no, yes, no, no, no, yes, yes." Try this *from memory* on the following sentence: "A bird in the hand is not in the bush." It turns out to be a surprisingly difficult task, one in which it is very easy to omit a word or lose track of your place. The difficulty is substantially removed by using a different method of signalling your decision. For example, try categorizing the same sentence, but instead of saying "yes" and "no" tap your right hand if a word is a noun and your left if it is not. When these conditions are run in a formal experiment, virtually every subject takes longer and makes more errors with vocal signals than with tapping (Brooks, 1968). In both cases, the sentence must be reproduced inter-

---

[7] Note that although all researchers agree about the special status of newly presented items or just performed activities, not all wish to separate the short-term and long-term memory systems. Some scientists believe that there is simply one large memory system, and that the special status of some items simply reflects the types of attributes for those items and the nature of retrieval from the memory system. There is no disagreement about the phenomena, however. We return to this issue when we discuss "depth of processing."

nally and the same decisions made with the same amount of response uncertainty. The only variable which could account for the difference in difficulty is the mechanism or process used in producing the response. A tempting conclusion is that some portion of the mechanisms which are producing the overt yesses and noes is also being used in the internal production of the sentence or decisions.

This interpretation is made more convincing by showing that a comparable conflict can be produced with a visual referent. For example, look at the block letter **F** in Figure 8-12. The dots on each of the corners can be treated as items to be categorized just as were the words in the sentences. Study the **F** for a minute and then *from memory* work around clockwise from the asterisk deciding whether each dot is on the top or bottom, or is in-between. That is, work around saying "yes" for each dot that is on the top or bottom and "no" for each dot that is in between. You may have some small difficulty recalling the figure, but the conflict experienced in saying "yes" and "no" to categorize the sentence in the previous example does not seem to be present. This difference would be expected if the difficulty with the sentence had resulted from the overloading of some verbal or articulatory mechanism by saying "yes" and "no" and internally producing the sentence at the same time. The **F** is experienced as being visualized and consequently could be expected to be involved in conflict only if you were trying to do something with the visual system at the same time. Such a conflict can easily be arranged by signalling your decisions by *pointing* to and therefore by necessity looking at printed yesses or noes. To demonstrate this point, try using the array in Figure 8-13 first for the sentences and then for the **F**. For the sentence "A bird in the hand is not in the bush," you would point to the N (no) in the first row of Figure 8-13, the Y (yes) in the second row, the N in the next two rows, the Y in the next row, and so on down the list. This manner of signalling your decisions turns out to be very similar to the tapping task; it seems quite easy to say the sentence to yourself and signal the decisions at the same time. But using this output device for the **F** is quite another matter. Try it quickly for top-bottom dots on the **F**. That is, once again thinking of the **F** as a sequence of dots, work down Figure 8-13 pointing to a Y for a dot on the top or bottom and an N for one in-between. Most people report real difficulty after the first few categorizations. They point to the first three Y's, then a couple of N's, but then look away from the page reporting that they are having trouble keeping their place. The response time and error data that we have collected supports the impression that the difficulty when dealing with the **F** comes in trying to look at anything else at the same time.

This demonstration that I have been describing was combined into an experiment with two types of referent (sentences and line diagrams) and three types of response output (pointing, tapping, and speaking). The longest times for categorizing the sentences occurred when the spoken response (yes, no) was used; the longest times for categorizing the line diagrams occurred when the pointing response was used. No one of these

FIGURE 8-12

FIGURE 8-13

Y   N

Y   N

Y   N

Y   N

     Y   N

Y   N

Y   N

Y   N

    Y   N

Y   N

response modes was the most difficult overall. Rather it seemed that the difficulty arose from the combination of trying to say "yes" and "no" while thinking the sentence or from making a visually guided response while visualizing the diagrams. In this situation then, when a person claims that he is visualizing, he apparently really means that he is doing something visually; he is visualizing in the sense that he is less free to do anything else visually at the same time. When he claims that he is thinking words, he is apparently saying something to himself in the sense that he is less free to say anything else at the same time. [Quote from L. Brooks (1970). *Visual and verbal processes in internal representation.* Talk presented at the Salk Institute, La Jolla, California. With permission of the author.]

What do we conclude from this set of demonstrations? Are there separate STM systems for visual and verbal materials? Do the control signals for arm movements reside in yet a different STM system? Or is there perhaps only one STM system but so designed that when the attributes of the items within the system differ radically from one another, there is no interference among them? As yet, there is no agreement: nobody knows.

If you think carefully about the differences between the two alternatives we just posed, there is actually little *functional* difference. One alternative is that there are many different STMs, perhaps in different places. The other alternative is that there is just one STM, but that it can contain different types of attributes that do not interfere with one another. If you are only interested in how people perform the tasks that they do, then it really does not matter which explanation is correct: for your purposes, the two explanations predict exactly the same behavior. Therefore, they are functionally equivalent. If you are a physiological psychologist, interested in how the STM is constructed, then you do care about the differences in the explanations, for in the one case you must find many different STMs, and in the other, you need only find one. In psychology, as in all sciences, the type of explanation that is useful depends upon the type of question that is being asked.

This discussion of the different forms of interference that occur with different types of tasks makes a convenient place to pause in our study of the memory systems. This chapter has introduced you to the major issues and concepts. The next chapter reviews these issues, introduces the study of how information gets acquired by the long-term memory system, and emphasizes how memory is used. The material in this chapter forms the background for the discussions of the next.

REVIEW OF TERMS AND CONCEPTS   In this chapter, the following terms and concepts that we consider to be important have been used. Please look them over. If you are not able to give a short explanation of any of them, you should go back and review the appropriate sections of the chapter.

Sensory information storage (SIS)
  its duration
  possible purpose
  its capacity
  the probe technique for measuring SIS capacity
  masking
Tachistoscope
Short-term memory (STM)
  its capacity
  the use and function of counting backward by threes
  acoustic confusions
Rehearsal
  maintenance rehearsal
  integrative processes
  theories of forgetting: time and interference
  attributes
    their role
    their possible composition
  the reconstructive nature of memory
  selective interference
Long-term memory (LTM)

Terms and concepts you should know

Because Chapter 9 covers the use of the memory systems described in this chapter (with special emphasis on the relationship between STM and LTM), many of the references described in the Suggested Readings for that chapter are highly relevant here as well: see that section of Chapter 9.

SUGGESTED READINGS

The early work on the sensory information storage system was done by Sperling (1960) and by Averbach and Coriell (1961). All the experiments on SIS in this book come from the work of Sperling. An excellent review of the work on SIS systems can be found in the review article by Dick (1974). Note that Dick calls this storage system *iconic memory*. It has sometimes also been called *visual short-term memory*. Chapters 4 and 6 of the book by Massaro (1975b) present excellent discussions of SIS, with particular emphasis on its role in the understanding of language, especially in reading.

One phenomenon not discussed in this chapter is that of "photographic" or "eidetic" visual memory. This is a strange and puzzling phenomenon. Most of what we know is contained in a small number of articles. Perhaps the best place to start is with the paper in *Scientific American* by Haber (1969). From there, one could go to the monograph by Leask, Haber, and Haber (1969). The best review of the whole topic is provided by Gray and Gummerman (1975), and the most intriguing result is described by Stromeyer and Psotka (1970), with a more elementary description in *Psychology Today* by Stromeyer (1970).

Weber and Castleman (1970) did the experiment which measured how long it takes to visualize the letters of the alphabet. Brooks (1968) has examined the manner by which visualizing auditory events interferes with visual processing, and vice versa. Experiments on the decay of memory were performed by Reitman (1971, 1974) and also by Atkinson and Shiffrin (1971). Sperling and Speelman, in Norman's *Models of human memory* (1970), discuss at an advanced level the notion of attributes in memory and the reconstructive process. Similarly, a very advanced treatment is given by Norman and Rumelhart in the second chapter.

The original work on acoustic confusions was performed by Conrad (1959) and Sperling (1959, 1960). Further work has been done by numerous people, so the best source now is a review article or book; for example, Neisser's 1967 book *Cognitive psychology* or Kintsch's 1970 book on memory; the articles by Wickelgren and Sperling and Speelman in Norman's (1970) *Models of human memory*. An extended series of discussions on the implications of acoustic confusions on the form of storage for verbal material (especially printed matter) is contained in the book edited by Kavanagh and Mattingly (1972). This book reports the results of a conference that discussed reading and language, and the discussions among the participants (also reported in the book) are perhaps more important than the papers themselves.

Peterson's article on short-term memory which appeared in July 1966, issue of *Scientific American* is relevant here. Peterson and Peterson did the original experiment in which subjects were asked to count backward by three's after receiving a simple item which they were asked to memorize. Some studies on memory of nonhuman primate (that is, monkeys) are reported in Jarrard's book (1971).

9 Using memory

PREVIEW

In the previous chapter we examined the memory systems: sensory information store, short-term memory, long-term memory. In this chapter, we examine some of the operations that can be performed upon memory and some memory strategies useful for learning. These are practical issues. In addition, we will be concerned with the mechanisms that oversee the use of memory mechanisms that we call the *interpreter* and the *monitor*. This chapter starts to lay out the fundamental principles of mental processing.

When someone asks you a question, the answer depends partly upon why you think you were asked the question. In general, you do not tell people anything you believe they already know (unless you are taking examinations, in which case you tell the instructors only what you think they already know). It is the monitor system of the memory that selects the appropriate response to a question. One important point of this chapter is the simple yet powerful observation that memory is more than a mere warehouse of information from which one simply looks up the answer to questions. Quite often the easiest task of memory lies in finding an answer: the more difficult task is to determine how to use the answer.

There are two major issues discussed in this chapter. First, there is the study of how information gets into long-term memory. Actually, the problem in learning new information is not in getting the information into memory; it is in making sure that it will be found later on, when it is needed. Thus, the task for the person who is attempting to acquire new information is to integrate it appropriately with the material that is already within the memory system. In the first parts of this chapter we examine the findings of psychologists on the process of acquiring new information, examine the role of attention and of what we call *integrative processes*, and then conclude that the depth to which information is processed is an important factor in determining how well it will be retrieved at a later time. Finally, we conclude the first topic with some useful instructions on mnemonic techniques: systems for learning new information in such a way that it can be retained. We present some of the secrets of the memory courses that you may have seen advertised. These mnemonic systems do two things for you. First, they illustrate the practical application of the principles of this chapter. Second, they really do work: if you learn them and use them, you will improve your own ability to remember.

In the last part of the chapter, we examine the overall properties of the memory system—the operation of the memory system, with special emphasis on the types of supervision given by the interpretive and monitoring processes. We describe the answering of questions and the search for old memories. Both require extensive problem solving and decision making on the part of the memory system. You should appreciate the issues and understand some of the problems. (You should also realize that these same principles must play an important role in social interactions, thus preparing yourself for the discussion in Chapter 16.)

This chapter allows you to consider your own use of memory. How do you answer questions? Ask other people questions: see how they decide to respond. Try recalling the names of friends you have not seen for three or four years: What processes are you using? This chapter is designed to start you on the path toward understanding memory.

FROM SHORT-TERM MEMORY TO LONG-TERM MEMORY

The major task in the learning of new material is to integrate it properly within the structure of information already present within long-term memory. Material that is to be retained must be structured in a way that allows its retrieval later on. This means, among other things, that there must be some path in memory from the starting point of the retrieval effort to the item being sought. The integrative processes that occur during learning are not yet well understood. Sometimes these processes occur naturally, with little conscious awareness of their operations. Sometimes the integrative processes require a deliberate mental effort, working through an elaboration of the material with great care.

As we go about our daily activities, we seldom exert any effort to retain a memory of them. At the end of the day, however, it is possible to recite such experiences as the foods we ate, the clothes we wore, the places we went, and perhaps the people we met. The recall attempt at the end of the day flows naturally and easily. But although the daily recall indicates retention and integration of the activities, there will not be good retrievability of these same events after a passage of several weeks. To recall what was eaten at the most recent meal is relatively easy. To recall what was eaten the day before yesterday is difficult, and to recall the meals of a week or a month ago is usually not possible unless something exceptional occurred then. The problem arises in *differentiating* the knowledge of today's events from all the past ones. The problem of item differentiation arises whenever there is learning of two types of similar material. This problem poses some interesting speculative problems about the memory system: Why can you not remember the meals of exactly one month ago? Is the information still within the memory, but with no access, or did the information gradually fade away as new experiences with meals were encountered? Current theoretical views favor the first interpretation over the second, but the matter is still under debate.

Often, learning new material can be a special, conscious activity. Trying to learn the names of people to whom one has just been introduced, or a telephone number, or vocabulary for a foreign language, are typical examples that usually lead to a period of deliberate memorizing. For a short time the material that is to be learned can be retained within short-term memory by recycling the information that is to be retained— by *maintenance rehearsal*. But maintenance rehearsal alone does not lead to good memory retention. Some sort of integrative processes must be brought to bear on the material.

In the next sections of the chapter we examine some of the factors that lead to retention of information in long-term memory. We start with the more classical experiments—experiments on the retention of simple lists of words. These experiments demonstrate the dual role of short- and long-term memory, and they are thought to reflect the role of maintenance rehearsal. Then, we examine the nature of integrative activities that can be performed in order to learn newly presented information. This leads to a discussion of some theoretical issues, as well as to the study of special memory techniques. These special techniques—mnemonic systems—should also be useful things to know, for if you learn and use them, you can considerably improve your memory skills.

Learning lists Suppose you look up a telephone number or meet a person at a party, you know the number or name for a few seconds, but then you lose track of it completely. The material gets stored perfectly in short-term memory, but it never seems to make it to long-term memory. The difference between the accurate memory for material that is still in short-term memory and the meager, impoverished memory for other material can easily be demonstrated.

You are asked to learn a list of unrelated words. One at a time, each word that is to be learned appears before you, either flashed on a screen or spoken clearly and distinctly. You are allowed exactly 1 sec to attend to each word before the next is presented. Finally, after 20 words have been presented to you, you are asked to recall as many of them as possible. Try the experiment using 20 words from Table 9-1. It will help the discussion that follows if you try the task, giving yourself some feeling for what it is like to be in such an experiment.

When most people do this task they find it advantageous to recall the last words that were presented as quickly as they can, first, before trying to remember anything else. The last words are in a type of "echo box," a temporary memory from which the words can be recalled with ease only if nothing else happens to interfere with it. If there is some conversation, or if the person tries to recall other words first, then the contents of the "echo box" disappear. This "echo box" is, of course, the short-term memory. Most subjects quickly learn to empty their short-term memory immediately before going on to other items.

One way of examining the results is to number the words according to the position in which they were represented, and record the chance that a word will be recalled as a function of its position in the list. This analysis produces the *serial position curve* shown in Figure 9-1. Here, the length of the list was 30 words, the percentage of times each word was recalled is shown for the words in each position of the list. This particular set of data comes from a classic experiment conducted by Murdock in 1962. In this study, 19 subjects listened to a list of 30 unrelated words presented at the rate of one word each second. At the end of each list, they were given 1.5 min to write down all the words

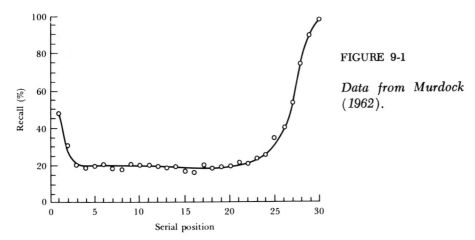

FIGURE 9-1

Data from Murdock (1962).

they could remember in any order they wished. Five to 10 sec after they finished writing, a new list was presented. This same procedure was repeated 80 times (on four separate days, so only 20 lists were learned in any one session).

The serial position curve is an important tool of psychologists. But it is really not a single curve. It should be separated into the two parts shown in Figure 9-2. The last part of the list is remembered better

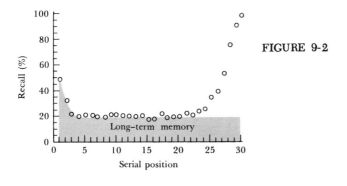

FIGURE 9-2

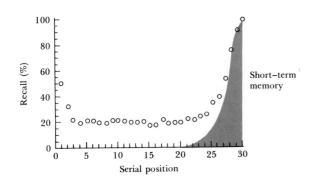

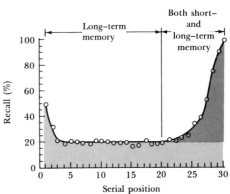

than the rest: The last item is recalled about 97% of the time. This later part of the curve represents recall from short-term memory. The rest of the curve reflects a different memory process—the retrieval of information from long-term storage.[1]

FIGURE 9-3

Data from Murdock (1962).

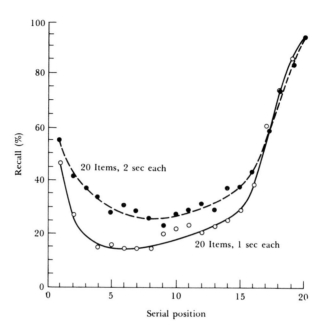

How do we know this? Well, for one thing, some operations affect one of the memories and not the other. For example, if presentation of the words is slowed up to allow 2 sec on each word rather than one, the results look like those shown in Figure 9-3. There is no change in the short-term memory portion of the curve. There is an improvement in long-term memory. (These data were also collected by Murdock, the only difference being that the lists were 20 items long and each item given for 2 sec.) Evidently, the added time gives subjects more

[1] In Figure 9-2, the percentages for long-term memory cannot simply be added to those from short-term memory to give total recall. Rather, we assume that an item is recalled **either** from long-term memory **or** from short-term memory, but not both. Thus the percentage recall is given by the sum of the **percentage** of words recalled from short-term memory plus the **percentage** of those words from long-term memory that were not already recalled from short-term memory. If R is percentage recall,

$$R = \text{STM} + \text{LTM}\left(1 - \frac{\text{STM}}{100}\right)$$

time to do maintenance rehearsal and work on the material, thus getting more information into long-term memory, but having no effect on short-term memory. In fact, varying both how many items are presented in the list as well as how fast they are presented produces a family of curves (Figure 9-4), which again show that the short-term memory component of each curve is the same for all, while the long-term memory sections differ.

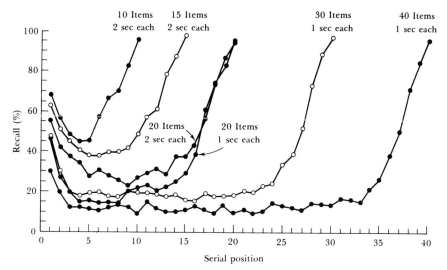

FIGURE 9-4

Data from Murdock (1962).

It is possible to show the opposite: factors that affect short-term memory and not long-term memory. One obvious way of doing this is to prevent subjects from immediately recalling the words from short-term memory at the end of the experiment. That is, we do exactly the same experiment as before, but this time, at the end of the presentation, the subjects are given a three-digit number and asked to count backward by threes—the task described in Chapter 8 for the short-term memory experiments (see page 315). Short-term memory recall should disappear. And so it does. The easiest way to convince yourself of this is to try it. Take 20 words from Table 9-1 and read them at the rate of one word per second. As soon as you get to the end of the list, start counting backward by threes from some arbitrary number, say 978. Count as rapidly as you can for approximately 20 sec. Your short-term memory will be wiped clean. The experimental results from an experiment just like this are shown in Figure 9-5. Notice that the last parts of the curves are perfectly flat: no short-term memory for the words is left.

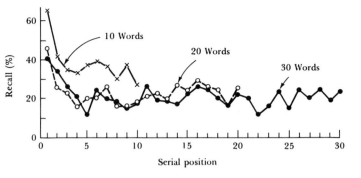

FIGURE 9-5

Data from Postman and Phillips (1965).

Table 9-1

	A	B	C	D	E	F
1.	REAM	TIME	CROW	IDES	CLOVE	SQUAB
2.	LATCH	STAB	BORE	TROOP	THUS	QUIP
3.	HOT	SOLVE	WILT	KEY	PLAY	SPREAD
4.	SKIRT	HOUSE	PLATE	HERS	COO	GRADE
5.	JAB	MUFF	JAZZ	STUB	SQUILL	RARE
6.	CLOG	DRAFT	DEAR	GOAD	CLOY	TRIED
7.	MARE	SAY	FAN	CHART	CLING	SHOAL
8.	ELSE	OFF	WRENCH	BATHE	MAID	HAT
9.	WAGE	BOIL	POLE	TEACH	PLATE	QUICK
10.	JOWL	COURT	HERB	BED	PRATE	SHOW
11.	CHAP	SLOT	LAUGH	SCALD	WALL	TRILL
12.	TROUT	HAND	FIT	CAPE	LET	PLAY
13.	BLOT	DIRT	GRILL	THRONE	RAW	SOP
14.	REEK	CLOT	SWIRL	GNAW	WOOD	SAGE
15.	TAPE	OUT	COAST	NET	SWARM	BLONDE
16.	DUSK	GREET	SNACK	SWAM	ELK	TELL
17.	LIST	PENT	SNOW	PRICE	HOWL	JADE
18.	SMUG	STALE	DRAPE	SWEPT	SHOP	IRE
19.	DUCK	STONE	SNAIL	BLANK	PEN	MOON
20.	BIG	DICE	RAGE	SPRAY	ROCK	SLEIGH

TESTING MEMORY

It would appear to be an easy task to study memory. Simply ask a person what can be remembered. But a little bit of thought will show that things are not quite so simple. First of all, it is important to know whether or not the item being tested for was ever actually learned. Second, if the item was learned, you must know how well it was learned. It seems likely that something learned very well will be retained differently from something learned poorly. Third, one must select the type of memory test with some care, for different types of tests get at different aspects of memory storage and retrieval. Items that do not appear to be remembered by one type of test might very well reveal themselves with another type of test.

As part of the experimental investigation of memory, psychologists often attempt to control the amount of original learning by doing the teaching themselves. In order to see how well one can remember events over a three-month period, the experiment would last at least three months. But in the study of memory for events over long time periods—say over a 20-year span—it is the rare investigator who can maintain contact with subjects, so other techniques may have to be used. One technique (used by Linton, 1975) is to study memory for significant public events culled from newspaper headlines over the time period of interest. Another technique (used by Squire, Slater, & Chace, 1975) is to study memory for the stars of television and radio shows, using subjects who have viewed significant amounts of television during the time period under study. Both of these techniques are fraught with difficulties (see Linton's 1975 account of some problems), but at least they guarantee testing events that can be verified. Asking a subject to generate instances of personal experiences or the names of acquaintances from some long-past period leads to the problem that there is usually no way to verify whether the subject's recollection is accurate. Subjects make up logical sounding stories, which they themselves believe, and so it is essential that the experimenter have an independent check on the information. The reconstructive nature of memory makes the invention of events (confabulation) a natural outcome of memory retrieval, and the person doing the recall may be absolutely convinced of its accuracy, even when one can prove that the alleged event could not have occurred.

Controlling the original learning of material

To minimize the potential difficulties, the experimental psychologist can turn to the laboratory. Things are much simpler in standard laboratory experiments. Here, the experimenter presents a list of items—pictures, sounds, words, stories —to the subjects and controls the amount of study of each item. Then, after a precise time interval during which the activities of the subject are carefully controlled, tests can be given for the memory of the items.

The two basic methods for testing memory are recall and recognition tests. In addition, there are numerous variations on these techniques, such as forced-choice, prompts, and other modifications.

Types of memory tests

Recall. In recall, a person is asked to retrieve the items that were learned with no other helpful information except the particular instructions of the experiment:

"Recall the list of words you just learned."
"What was the next-to-last word in the list?"
"Who is the prime minister of Japan?"

A recall test is thought to require a reasonably extensive search of memory, first to find the appropriate context for the information sought and then to retrieve the particular item itself. In general, recall tests show the poorest performance among memory tests. As a result they can often reveal memory weaknesses sooner than other methods. A person may fail completely at the recall of an item, even though there is indeed some knowledge of that item within their memory system. It could be that the memory search has not reached the appropriate region, or it could be that the memory is not complete enough to allow the subject to regenerate the item sought.

Recognition. In a recognition test, one presents the subject with the item of interest and asks whether or not it is recognized: "Is this one of the items you were asked to learn?" Recognition tests of memory are generally thought to be more sensitive measures of how much a person has stored than are other methods, because more information is presented to the person, and the only task is to decide whether the presented information matches what is already in memory. In most situations, the task is more complex than might seem at first glance. For example, if we ask whether the word MINNESOTA appeared in the list of state names discussed in Chapter 8 (in the section on attributes of short-term memory), this is a recognition task. But you are *not* being asked to decide whether the word MINNESOTA is in your memory system. We suspect that it is, especially if you live in the United States. Recognition tests usually require a person to decide whether a particular event occurred in a particular context, and this can require considerable decision making. More on this later in the chapter.

Memory and attention

There is a conflict between trying to remember the information that arrived moments ago and the processes involved in understanding the sensory data now arriving. That is, we have a choice: either we can mull over the implication of what we have just experienced or we can take note of what is currently happening. Consider a typical lecture in the classroom. Thinking about what has just been said prevents full attention to what is now being said. There is no way out of this dilemma.

The reason for the conflict comes from the limits on processing capability of the human that we discussed in Chapter 7. Mulling over the information that has been presented, thinking through implications, and following new paths within the memory are all *top-down, conceptually driven* processes. They require the operation of the conceptual mechanism. But the pattern recognition process also relies upon conceptual guidance, and the effort expended upon one is effort that cannot be given to the other. Look back at Figures 7-7 and 7-14. There is a limited number of processing resources (there is a limited number of demons in the figures). The resources are not sufficient to do everything, so some choice has to be made about where the effort will go.

The description presented in this chapter of the flow of information from the sensory receptors through the various memory systems is a description of the *data-driven* aspect of memory processing. Once we get to rehearsal mechanisms, however, we are starting to talk about conceptually driven aspects. When we start discussing integrative rehearsal, we are addressing the need for higher order analysis of the information, considering its implications and how it fits within the existing memory structure. Data-driven aspects of processing tend to occur automatically, requiring little conscious attention: They are triggered automatically by the arrival of sensory data. Conceptually guided processing, however, is quite different. The resources required to do any conceptually driven process take away from resources required for others. Whether the conceptually driven task is relevant or irrelevant to the task at hand does not matter, it takes its share of resources away from the total amount available. Daydreaming can completely halt all learning. Taking notes in a lecture can tie up so much of the processing capacity that no conceptual processing of the material can be performed. A student must continually choose between taking complete notes or understanding and remembering what was said.

What happens to memory in the absence of attention? To study this, we have subjects do several tasks simultaneously. The goal is to adjust things just right so that all of the subjects' attention must be devoted to one of the tasks. Then they are tested to see what they know about the things that happened in an entirely different task going on simultaneously. In one experiment of this type, the subjects had to shadow words presented over earphones to one ear while common English words were presented to their other ear, each word occurring as many as 35 times. When the experiment was over, their memory for the words presented to the unattended ear was tested: There was absolutely no memory for these words. Evidently, the attention required to do the shadowing task completely disrupted the ability to deal with the information presented to the other ear.

Memory without attention

This result is not unexpected. The subjects certainly had no time to rehearse or organize the English words. But did the subjects actually hear the words? How far did the unattended information get? Did it get as far as short-term memory?

To discover whether material that is not being attended to gets into short-term memory, it is necessary to interrupt the subjects immediately after the material has been presented to them, and ask whether they remember anything. When the experiment is done in this way, subjects can in fact retrieve the last few items presented from their short-term memory. But if there is a delay as long as 30 sec between presenting the material and testing for its recall, the subject cannot remember any of the unattended words. When attention is concentrated elsewhere, additional incoming information seems to get as far as the short-term memory. But then it can dissipate without a trace. If the test of memory is given immediately, some of the information is still in short-term memory, and can be retrieved.

Note the similarity between the tasks of shadowing (in Chapter 7) and of counting backward. In the counting-backward task, attention is occupied by the counting immediately **after** the items have been presented. For shadowing, the attention is also occupied **during** the time the information is coming in.

There is another way of demonstrating the effects of attention on long-term memory. Suppose subjects are given a list of words to remember, and suppose they are tested immediately after each list is presented. Their recall will follow the standard type of serial position curve, such as that shown in Figure 9-6a. The experiment continues until 50 different lists have been tested. Then, without any warning, the subjects are asked to recall as much as they can from **all** of the earlier lists. What happens?

One plausible answer is that their performance should look something like that shown in Figure 9-5: That is, it should be the same as Figure 9-6a, but with the short-term memory component gone. This, however, is not what happens. Instead, the subject shows no memory whatsoever for the items presented last in each list, even though many of the first items can be recalled (see Figure 9-6b). Why is there absolutely no memory for the last items in the lists of the experiment of Figure 9-6, whereas there is some in the experiment of Figure 9-5?

One possible explanation is that the subjects use different strategies in allocating their attention in these two experiments. In the experiment that produced the results shown in Figure 9-5, the subjects knew full well that they were later to be tested on their total recall. But in the experiment shown in Figure 9-6 (performed by Madigan and McCabe, 1971), the subjects had no idea that they were later to be tested on all of the lists. During each list they may have concentrated most of their attention on the early items, since those are indeed the hardest to retain. They paid no attention to the last item, relying on the fact that if that information were recalled immediately, it could be retrieved correctly from short-term memory without having to spend much effort on it. This strategy is perfectly adequate for the initial part of the experiment, but it showed up as a disadvantage on the later, unexpected test.

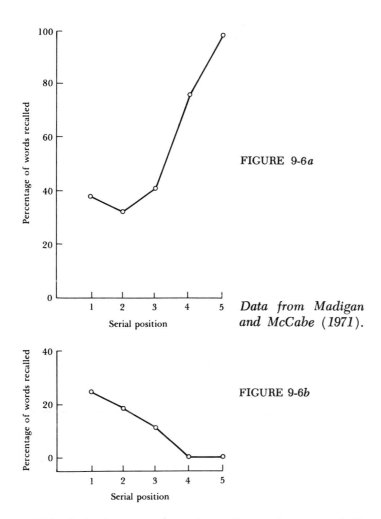

FIGURE 9-6*a*

Data from Madigan and McCabe (1971).

FIGURE 9-6*b*

In both shadowing and simple-recall experiments we find evidence that complete lack of attention to incoming material can allow both a normal short-term memory for that material and also a complete lack of long-term memory storage.

Consider how someone might learn a simple set of facts. Take as a simple illustration an example from Chapter 2: the names of the two types of cells on the retina of the eye—*rods* and *cones*. Neither name is a new word. They are simply being used in a new way. We can use their old meanings to help us. The names were originally assigned to the cells because their appearance was thought to be similar to rods (long, cylindrical objects) and cones (circular, tapered objects). In addition to remembering the names, you also ought to remember where they are located and what they do. In Chapter 2 (in footnote 4) we noted that *cones* were located in the *center* of the retina and were sensitive to

INTEGRATIVE PROCESSES

color. That is, we formed a memory aid (a mnemonic) by linking the location and function to the cell name with the first letter of each word. This takes care of the cones: what about the rods? How can you remember that they are primarily in the periphery of the retina and not color sensitive? You might think of *rods* as being the "reverse" of cones. If cones are in the center, rods are not. If cones are used for color vision, rods are not. If rods are very sensitive to light, cones are not. All of these strategies make for effective retrieval aids.

Now consider all that we just went through only to learn some simple aspects about two things. All that elaboration appears to be useful. The human memory system works best when it has an organization for the material that is to be learned. To do this it is sometimes helpful to use accidental relationships among the items (such as the common first letter of cone, center, and color), since additional relationships make it less difficult to retrieve something from memory. Notice the reconstructive nature of the memory. The names of the cells in the center of the retina might be recalled by retrieving some of the relationships and deriving the names. Here is a mythical example of how someone might use the memory aids:

> *"Let's see, what were the cells called? One is in the center—center; it's sensitive to color; "c"—"kuh"—"cone." The other one is not in the center, it's the reverse, rear, r, rrr—rods! Rods and cones, that's what they're called."*

Notice what has happened. We established a logical, connecting structure between the material to be learned and other things we already knew. Note why some structure must be imposed upon material that is to be learned. Recall the immense capacity of human memory, with sufficient storage to record a lifetime's worth of experiences and thoughts—tens or hundreds of billions of items. Human memory must have some organizational structure to it or else once something was stored away it would never be retrieved again.

The need for organization   Consider a large library, one with perhaps a million books. In such a library, organization is the key to efficient use. Each book is catalogued by its title, author, and subject matter. When a book is improperly placed on the library shelves it might as well not exist at all. Anyone trying to find that book will go to the spot listed in the library catalog and, if the book is not very close to the proper location, it becomes a hopeless task to search for it.

Notice how much of a library is devoted to aids for retrieving information. First, there is the card catalog, a reasonably large set of cards that list the contents of the library by the titles of the books, by the content matter, and by the names of the authors. If there are one million books in the library, there will be at least three million cards in the card catalog. In addition, libraries usually have a shelf index, a list of all of the books organized by the order in which they appear in the shelves: that makes at least four million items in the catalogs. But this is not all. Many of the books in the libraries are simply guides to the contents of the library. There are all sorts of abstracts, publications such as *Chemical abstracts* and *Psychological abstracts* that summarize publications in the fields they cover and refer the reader to the appropriate books or journals. There are yearly review books, such as the large number of *Annual review of —— view of ——*, each reviewing the literature of a particular field for a given year. And then there are all sorts of cross-referencing devices, including computerized referencing services, all designed to help the user thread through the maze of information that exists in the library to the appropriate location where the exact information that is being sought might be found.

If the need for comprehensive organization is so great in a library, it is even greater in human memory. Humans encounter huge amounts of information as they go through their lives, and one never knows just how and when that information will be needed later. There must be something analogous to library catalogs and indexes and abstracts. At the very least, information that is stored within the memory system must be interconnected so that it is possible to trace a path among related items. In this way, whenever any item close to the desired one is found, then it should be possible to trace through the interconnections to get to the proper place in memory.

Forming interconnected structures: An example. To emphasize the need for integrating the material that is stored into a closely knit structure, consider the following story taken from Bransford and Johnson (1973). Read the story one time only, aloud. Do not re-read any part of it. After reading say the alphabet backward once, aloud, to minimize any short-term memory retention of the story. Then recall the story aloud. Simply retell it as accurately as you can.[2]

Title: **Watching a Peace March from the 40th Floor**

The view was breathtaking. From the window one could see the crowd below. Everything looked extremely small from such a distance, but the colorful costumes could still be seen. Everyone seemed to be moving in one direction in an orderly fashion and there seemed

---

[2] Better yet, try to do this with your friends. Have them read the story aloud. Then have them say the alphabet backward (or count backward by threes for awhile). Then have them recite the story for you.

to be little children as well as adults. The landing was gentle, and luckily the atmosphere was such that no special suits had to be worn. At first there was a great deal of activity. Later, when the speeches started, the crowd quieted down. The man with the television camera took many shots of the setting and the crowd. Everyone was very friendly and seemed glad when the music started.

STOP: DON'T GO ON UNTIL YOU HAVE RECALLED THE STORY, EITHER ALOUD TO SOMEONE ELSE OR BY WRITING IT DOWN.

When you recalled the story, what did you do with the sentence:

The landing was gentle, and luckily the atmosphere was such that no special suits had to be worn.

When this same experiment was actually done by Bransford and Johnson, only 18% of the subjects recalled at least one idea from the sentence. Even when subjects were given the cue sentence

"The landing_____and luckily the atmosphere_____

so that all they had to do was to fill in the blanks, only 29% recalled at least one idea from the sentence. Obviously, the sentence is a peculiar one. It does not fit into the structure of the story. By itself, the sentence is perfectly understandable, but it has no associations to the story, so it is usually not retrieved.

A dramatic change takes place when the story is organized differently. We have talked about the story as a description of a person's view of activities while on the 40th floor of a building. But suppose the title is changed:

Title: **A Space Trip to an Inhabited Planet**

Now the previously discrepant sentence fits into the memory structure with ease.

When Bransford and Johnson had people read the story and recall it (just as before), with the *space trip* title, 53% of the subjects were able to recall at least one idea from the sentence about the atmosphere and the suits. Giving subjects the cue sentence increased the score to 82%. (Obviously, these were different people than had read the story with the other title.) Try it yourself on some friends. The simple change in title makes all the difference. Unless new material that is experienced fits within the existing organizational framework of memory, there is apt to be little or no recall of it later.

We can describe the implications of the peace march/space trip example by borrowing from the techniques we will explain in the next chapter. Suppose we draw a picture of the knowledge within human memory by showing how the information within the mind is interconnected. We do this by drawing diagrams of information *networks*. This will be described in detail in the next chapter, but for now simply note that we can represent the concepts in memory by means of the dots, brackets, and circles of Figure 9-7*a* and the interrelationships among

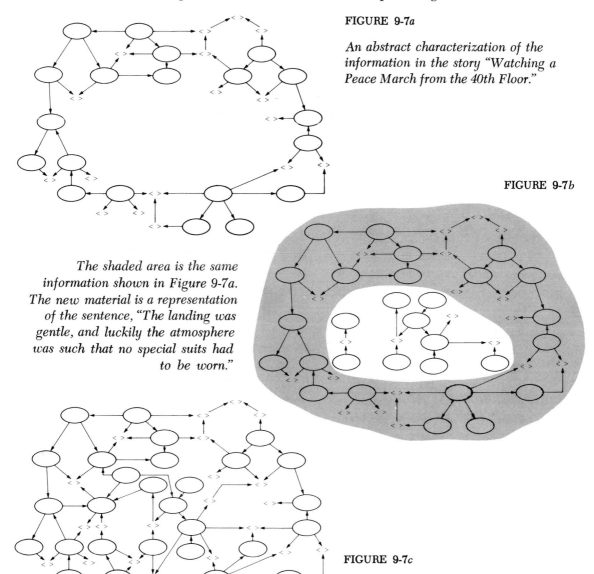

FIGURE 9-7*a*

An abstract characterization of the information in the story "Watching a Peace March from the 40th Floor."

FIGURE 9-7*b*

The shaded area is the same information shown in Figure 9-7a. The new material is a representation of the sentence, "The landing was gentle, and luckily the atmosphere was such that no special suits had to be worn."

FIGURE 9-7*c*

An abstract characterization of the information in the story "A Space Trip to an Inhabited Planet."

these concepts by the arrows of the figure. Suppose that Figure 9-7*a* shows the knowledge content of the story "*Watching a Peace March from the 40th Floor*." Now, look at Figure 9-7*b*. The area that is shaded is simply the exact same information that was shown in Figure 9-7*a*. But we also show the discrepant sentence, *The landing was gentle, and luckily the atmosphere was such that no special suits had to be worn.* The point, of course, is that this sentence sits in the middle of the structures created by the story, but is not connected to them. In fact, the one sentence forms two separate structures, neither of which has relations to the other. Thus, *The landing was gentle* has no relationship to *Luckily, the atmosphere was such* . . . , at least not within the context of a peace march. If a person recalls the story by going to the structures and simply following the links and arrows until all the information has been found, the discrepant material is likely to be left out.

But now consider what happens when someone learns the story "*A Space Trip to an Inhabited Planet*." The memory structures for this story are again represented by the nodes and arrows, but this time the special sentence can be directly interrelated within the structures. The result is shown in Figure 9-7*c*. Indeed, the material is so well integrated that only a careful comparison of Figure 9-7*c* with Figures 9-7*a* and 9-7*b* will make it possible to distinguish that sentence from all the rest of the material. In this situation, the retrieval of the special sentence should be equal to retrieval of any of the other material from the story.

Depth of processing   At one time it was thought that the major factor that determined how well something was learned was the amount of time that it resided in short-term memory or, perhaps, the amount of time that it was rehearsed. More recently, this view has been superseded by the understanding that neither time nor rehearsal alone plays a critical role. Material that is rehearsed for long durations can still fail to be retrieved later, while other material that was processed more quickly can often be retrieved later without difficulty. The difference in the retrievability of the material appears to be related to the level of processing that each has received.

Suppose you are asked to learn a list of 20 words, perhaps being given five seconds to study each word. Just saying the sound of the word over and over again for the five-second period will have little effect; memory will be poor. Examining each word for semantic judgments, perhaps by looking at each word in turn and then thinking of a word that means just the opposite, will make a marked improvement in later recall. Trying to string the words together into a meaningful fashion, perhaps forming a mental image of each successive pair of words, will improve memory even more. In fact, if you can create a story that incorporates each of the 20 words in turn, you are quite likely to be able to retrieve all 20 with perfect accuracy at the time of the test. The rule would appear to be that the more deeply the material is processed—the more effort used, the more the processing makes use of associations between the items to be learned and knowledge already in the memory—the better will be the later retrieval of the item.

Recent research on memory indicates that the operations a person performs on material to be learned are critically important in determining how well that information will be retrieved later. Interestingly enough, it does not seem to matter whether the person is trying to remember the material or not. Evidently, people do not really have a good idea of how their memory systems work or of what they should do in order to learn something.

How do you go about learning anything? Suppose you are given a shopping list to learn. Try it: Here is a list of items. Learn them:

Bread
Eggs
Butter
Salami
Corn
Lettuce
Soap
Jelly
Chicken
Coffee

Only ten items: that should not be very hard. Come on, spend fifty seconds trying to learn them: five seconds an item.

Most of you probably will attempt to learn the items by rehearsal, by saying them over and over again to yourselves. This is maintenance rehearsal, and it is indeed quite effective in maintaining items in short-term memory (except that you probably cannot do it fast enough to maintain ten items in STM). But the problem with maintenance rehearsal is that it does not establish any useful links in memory. There are no new paths. There are no new structures that will get you access to the items that have been rehearsed. To see this, simply recall the ten items: write them down. How many can you recall? A list of ten things should not be hard to retain, especially when they are all common names of grocery products. But most of you probably could not recall all ten of the items.

Some of you, however, undoubtedly did recall all ten items. And it is quite likely that instead of maintenance rehearsal, you performed integrative rehearsal. That is, instead of simply saying the items over and over again, hoping thereby to "burn them in," if you had thought of useful stories or relations among the items, made up images of the items and the shelves of the grocery store, or of the parts of your home, then you probably were able to recall the items.

Forming mental images turns out to be a very effective way to learn things. To help you understand what we mean, consider what you could have done with that list. You could have gone through the ten items and as you came to each, made up a picture in your mind of some typical thing you would do with it. Then, when you had finished with the picture and had gone on to the next item, you could have made the picture for the next item relate to the previous picture. Suppose you were learning the items of the grocery list in this way:

> Imagine getting a fresh, unsliced loaf of **bread** and ripping off a big piece with your hands. Put the **bread** down on a plate with two **eggs.** Now, think of the **eggs,** think of cooking them in your favorite style, and then eating huge portions of the **eggs,** mopping up the plate with the **bread.** Put generous hunks of **butter** on the plate. Think of cutting a hunk of **butter**—then a hunk of **salami.** Slice a big hunk of **salami.** Think of holding a big piece of **salami** in your hands, having it turn into an ear of **corn,** which you now hold in your hands and proceed to eat . . .

We leave the generation of the rest of the story to you. Later on in this chapter we discuss a systematic set of things that can be done to enhance the retention of information. For now, let us simply note the distinct differences in structures that resulted from the integrative operations just performed and from simple repetition of the items over and over again.

Levels of analysis. Suppose we give people a list of words to examine. Some words are long, some short. Some are printed in yellow ink, some in green, some in red, and some in blue. Half are nouns and half are verbs. We ask different people to do different things as they examine the words. We could ask them to look at each item and:

> say what color ink it is printed in
> say how many letters it contains
> say how many letters rhyme with the word "see"
> say whether it is a noun or verb
> give a word that rhymes
> give a word that means the opposite
> make a mental image of the item
> make a story that incorporates both the current item and the previous one

The operations in this list are ordered roughly in terms of the amount of analysis of the words that are required. To say what color ink an item is printed in does not even require that the words be read: it only requires examination of the physical features. Similarly, to determine the number of letters, one needs only to count. Neither color naming nor the counting of letters requires much pattern recognition or memory. To say how many letters rhyme with "see" does require more analysis. Each letter must be examined, and its pronunciation compared with that of the word "see." To recognize letters and to extract their pronunciation requires pattern recognition processes and the use of memory. But so far, none of these tasks requires understanding the words.

The task of determining whether a word is a verb or a noun is the first that requires looking at the word as a whole. But even this task does not require any more than a superficial, dictionary-like look up, checking the grammatical classification of the word. To determine a word that rhymes with the word on the list requires still more processing, this time to examine the sound patterns and to search memory for other words that have similar sound patterns: more analysis than any other task so far, but still no need to examine the meaning of the words. Finally, the last three tasks in the list start to require interpretation of meaning: "Give a word that means the opposite," "make a mental image of the item," "make a story that incorporates both the item and the one previous." These all require considering the meaning of the words in increasing degrees. Making up a story that incorporates two of the words is clearly the hardest of the tasks. This task involves the most use of memory structures, and therefore the most processing.

The ordered list of tasks demonstrates an increasing *depth of processing*. Each task requires a different *level of analysis*. Each successive task goes deeper into the semantic, meaningful interpretation of the items. It turns out that if we had asked different groups of subjects to do the different tasks and then at the end asked them to recall as many of the words as possible, we would find that the different levels of analysis produced quite different memory performances. The deeper the processing required, the better would be the recall. And this would be true despite the fact that each group spent equal amounts of time at the tasks, and despite the fact that no group was told that they would later be asked how many of the words they could recall. (It turns out that being told that there will be a later test of memory makes almost no difference in the results, presumably because people tend to do maintenance rehearsal when they are told to learn a list of words. The tasks that require a high level of analysis are really much more effective memorization strategies than is maintenance rehearsal.)

STRATEGIES FOR
REMEMBERING

Let us now look at some particular types of integrative processes. In particular, let us look at the strategies that have been developed for efficient memorization of material. An examination of these strategies can prove useful for two reasons. First of all, they are of practical use. They provide simple procedures that you can learn to apply for routine memorization. Second of all, examination of the common principles behind techniques for improving memory performance can tell us more about how the memory systems work. Experimentation with different strategies can help determine the properties that are effective and those that are not, and this in turn can help the scientist who is attempting to piece together the workings of human memory.

Throughout the ages there has been considerable concern about techniques for memorizing information. The ancient Greeks had formal courses on the "art of memory," and the strategies for memorizing material were considered an important part of the techniques of orators. Today, the practice of memory skills is not so well known, and good memories are not as important as they used to be, most likely because the influence of books, reference works, note-taking, and tape recorders has made reliance on one's own memory less crucial. Still, most people wish they could remember better than they do. Practitioners of the ancient skills of memory are still much in demand for their courses, for exhibiting their talents on the stage and on television, and even for writing best-sellers on the art of memory.

The basic strategies for improving memory are well known and relatively easy to apply. Nothing seems to come for free, however, and the development of a good system for remembering things requires study, effort, and practice. The trick to every method for the development of memory systems lies in learning how to organize the things that are to be learned so that they can be found again when they are needed. Organization is the essential feature of any large data retrieval system, and the human memory is no exception. Human memory is a highly interconnected system: any single item within the memory is connected to many other items. Most memory systems capitalize upon the interconnections, teaching techniques for the deliberate formation of associations between items that will be effective in guiding the later retrieval of specific information.

Mnemonics

"I before e except after c."

"The shape of Italy is like a boot."

"I can remember the streets because they are arranged in alphabetical order."

"If I want to remember an item I simply imagine it sitting on top of my head. Then the next time I want to remember it, I simply look mentally at the top of my head and there it is."

Mnemonics is the ancient art of memory. To remember things we sometimes need to go through some weird mental contortions. Surprisingly enough, if we do these contortions properly, they work. The examples above illustrate some of the techniques: in the order given, they are rhymes, visual imagery, simple rules, and the method of places.

There are many other tricks to memory. All of them require that the items to be learned be connected in some meaningful way. The difficulties arise when the things we wish to learn do not appear to have any meaningful connection. The mnemonic systems are designed especially to impose meaning upon otherwise unrelated items. Let us look at three of these methods.

Method of places. With the method of places, you memorize some geographical locations and then use them as cues for retrieving the items. Often, you can use places you already know: the floor plans of buildings, the paths you take between classes, or the inside of your living quarters.

Let us illustrate the method of places with that shopping list again:

Bread
Eggs
Butter
Salami
Corn
Lettuce
Soap
Jelly
Chicken
Coffee

To remember the list, we will simply visualize the places along some path and then mentally put one item at each place. Consider the set of places that lie along the path that one of us takes every day in going to the university where he teaches. A fanciful figure of that path is shown in Figure 9-8.

Now, learn the list of ten grocery items by picking up the items one at a time and visualizing them along the path. The first item is *bread*. Put a big loaf of bread right in front of the front door of the house. Make it a huge loaf, completely blocking the door. Imagine having to force your way out of the house. Do not worry if the picture is not logical. Make it absurd: just make sure that the bread is clear and distinct. Now do the same thing for the other nine items (see Figure 9-9):

1. A very large loaf of **bread** is blocking the front **door** (the bread is bigger than the door).
2. The **sailboat** on the beach is filled with **eggs.**
3. The **railroad train** is carrying a stick of **butter.**

FIGURE 9-8

4. The **street** of the town is covered with slices of **salami.**
5. The **sand** on the beach is made up of kernels of **corn.**
6. Giant heads of **lettuce** are rolling down the **hill.**
7. The **trees** are all standing in deep pools of **soap** suds, only the very tops are visible.
8. There is a big pool of **strawberry jelly** on the **golf course.**
9. **Chickens** are sitting in the **gliders,** acting as pilots.

10. A huge **coffee** pot is hanging over the **Psychology Building** at the university, pouring coffee into the building.

This is the method of places. To recall the items you wanted to learn, simply go back over the places—mentally retrace the route from "home" to "university." You can do this by following Figure 9-8, looking at each of the ten locations in turn and repicturing the objects that you placed there.

FIGURE 9-9

Normally, of course, you would not use someone else's set of locations, but rather your own set. If you used the rooms where you live, you need to traverse the area mentally, looking at the locations in each room where you placed the objects. If you used a familiar path, simply retrace that path.

It is important to have a special set of target places on which you put the items you are trying to remember. If you put the items arbitrarily along your path, you will probably fail to look in the right places, thus neglecting some of the items. The items have to be noticeable also, or else you might not see them when you look.

Method of associations. There are other ways to learn lists. One way is to find simple associations between each of the items so that they can all be connected into a meaningful story. For example:

> *In the morning I woke up, washed my hands with* **soap,** *and started the* **coffee** *for breakfast. I had* **corn** *flakes for cereal and* **eggs** *with* **bread** *and* **butter,** *I looked for* **jelly** *but there wasn't any. Then I made a* **salami** *and* **lettuce** *sandwich for lunch and got the* **chicken** *ready for supper.*

This method, making up a story, is closely related to the method of places. The story gives a framework to anchor the otherwise arbitrary collection of items. It provides a single meaningful tale that is easy to remember. Once the story is started, the events flow logically in sequence, therefore recalling the items that are to be remembered.

Method of key words. This procedure serves somewhat the same purpose as the preceding ones. Here again, the problem is to link together otherwise unrelated concepts. This technique uses *key words,* words that are associated with numbers. Learn the following pairs of numbers and words:

> **One** is a **bun**
> **Two** is a **shoe**
> **Three** is a **tree**
> **Four** is a **door**
> **Five** is a **hive**
> **Six** is **sticks**
> **Seven** is **heaven**
> **Eight** is a **gate**
> **Nine** is a **line**
> **Ten** is a **hen**

Notice that this sequence itself uses a simple mnemonic device: The words rhyme with the numbers. Hence, it is easy to learn. Now, let us turn to our shopping list. To learn that list by the method of key words, simply pair each item with one of the key words to form some image— meaningful, bizarre, absurd. For example:

> One is a bun, a big hot dog bun with an even bigger loaf of **bread** in it, sticking out at both ends. Two is a shoe, filled with **eggs.** Three is a tree, growing in a tub of **butter . . .**

Later, to recall the items, simply go through the numbers in order, recall each key word, recreate the image, and there is your item.

When more than ten items must be strung together, there are more systematic ways of getting key words. Here is one standard system, in use for several hundred years. Each digit from zero through nine is associated with a unique sound—always that of a consonant.

number	sound	rule
0	s or z	(s or z for cipher or zero)
1	t or d	(a t has one vertical bar)
2	n	(an n has two vertical bars)
3	m	(an m has three vertical bars)
4	r	(the word four ends in r)
5	l	(L is the Roman numeral for 50)
6	ch or sh	(no rule, just learn it)
7	k or ng	(if you work hard, a 7 can be made to look like a k)
8	f or v	(the script f looks like an 8)
9	p or b	(9 looks like a twisted, rotated p or b)

How do you use it? Do you need a key word for 307? Well, that is the sounds of m–s–k: that makes up the word *mask.* How about 71? Try *cat.* The important thing about a key word is the sound, not the spelling. Hence, *cat* is pronounced *kat,* yielding the digits 7 and 1. This is the famous number–consonant alphabet, used since the early 1600s. It appears frequently in secret mnemonic methods. Surprisingly enough, it is always the same old set of letters, even when the proponent of the system claims it to be new and unusual and even in Spanish, German, and English. Table 9-2 shows a list of 100 key words derived from the number–consonant alphabet.

Once you have learned the number–consonant alphabet, then you have some powerful tools at your disposal. First of all, you can learn any sequence of numbers: dates, telephone numbers, license plates—whatever you need to learn. Simply change the digits to consonants and then form words. Actually, it is quite difficult to find words that fit, so to help, people have made up many sets of standard key words, such as the set

Table 9-2   100 Key Words from the Number–Consonant Alphabet[a]

1	HAT	21	KNOT	41	ROAD	61	JET	81	FOOT
2	HEN	22	NUN	42	RAIN	62	GIN	82	FAN
3	HAM	23	NAME	43	RAM	63	JAM	83	FOAM
4	HAIR	24	NEAR	44	ROAR	64	JAR	84	FIRE
5	HILL	25	NAIL	45	RAIL	65	JAIL	85	FILE
6	SHOE	26	NICHE	46	RICH	66	JUDGE	86	FISH
7	HOOK	27	NECK	47	ROCK	67	JACK	87	FIG
8	HOOF	28	KNIFE	48	ROOF	68	JOVE	88	FIFE
9	HOOP	29	KNOB	49	ROPE	69	SHIP	89	FOB
10	DICE	30	MOUSE	50	LACE	70	GOOSE	90	PIZZA
11	DEED	31	MAT	51	LADY	71	GATE	91	POT
12	DOWN	32	MOON	52	LAWN	72	GUN	92	PEN
13	DAM	33	MOM	53	LOOM	73	GUM	93	POEM
14	DEER	34	MARE	54	LIAR	74	GEAR	94	PEAR
15	DOLL	35	MAIL	55	LILY	75	GALE	95	PAIL
16	DISH	36	MATCH	56	LASH	76	GASH	96	PATCH
17	DECK	37	MUG	57	LOCK	77	KICK	97	PICK
18	DOVE	38	MUFF	58	LEAF	78	GOOF	98	PUFF
19	DOPE	39	MAP	59	LIP	79	CAB	99	PIPE
20	NOSE	40	RICE	60	JUICE	80	FACE	100	DOSES

[a] Modified from M. N. Young and W. B. Gibson. *How to develop an exceptional memory.* Copyright 1962 by the authors. Reprinted, with modifications, by permission of the publisher, Chilton Book Company, Radnor, Pennsylvania.

of 100 in Table 9-2. Most professional practitioners of memory have learned a dozen different key word lists. Notice that the key words are relatively easy to learn once you learn the number–consonant alphabet.

The key word technique lets you do two things. First, you can remember an arbitrarily long string of items (such as grocery lists) by numbering the items and then associating each item to be learned with an image of the key word for that number. Thus, if you have a list of items with **outboard motor** as item number **14,** you simply picture an **outboard motor** mounted on the back end of a **deer,** propelling it swiftly through the water. To remember the items, you mentally go down the list of numbers. The numbers lead to the key words, which yield the images, which give you the items.

Second, key words let you remember a string of digits—simply change the digits to consonants, change the consonants to key words, and there you have it. Do you wish to remember the telephone number of the White House: (202) 456-1414? Picture the White House with a big **nose** (20) sticking out of it. A fat **hen** (2) has bitten the end of the nose. The hen is sitting on a big **rail** (45) that is suspended in the air, and a **shoe** (6) is hanging on the end. The shoe is swinging, and it knocks against the **door** (14) twice (which makes it 1414). If you learn this sequence of images, whenever you think of the White House, the **nose** sticking out being bitten by the **hen** will remind you of the rest of the image and then the number. True, it seems a bit ridiculous: but it works.

What mnemonics do. All of these techniques provide an organizational framework for the material to be learned. All of them require effort. Some, such as making up a story, require quite a bit of effort at the time of learning. Others, like the key word technique, require both a good deal of concentrated effort over a period of months to learn the system and then some additional effort at the time the items are to be learned. That is one secret of these techniques: they force attention to the material. In addition, they impose organization onto otherwise unrelated items. Finally, by being systematic, they provide a specific set of methods for storing new material in memory and for starting the search for previously learned information.

How to remember. What should you do when you need to remember something? The answer varies with what you want to remember and with your own unique abilities. In general, however, there are several rules that ought to be applied.

1. *Work.* Memory seldom comes easily. It requires attention to the material, effort, and some skill.
2. *Understand.* Know what you are trying to do. Try to paraphrase the material. Know how it is related to other things.
3. *Organize.* Divide the material into small pieces. Fit each piece sensibly with the others. Try to combine it with what you already know. Things in isolation are hard to remember. Look for structure in the material itself. Use mnemonic aids where possible.

A good example of the difficulty of learning new information can be observed during introductions at parties. "I always have trouble remembering names," claim many people, but how hard do most people try? When introduced to someone, a new name is seldom attended to beyond the length of time it is spoken in. To learn someone's name you must first make sure that it has been heard properly—what better way than simply to repeat it fully? But this is usually not enough, and if no further effort is exerted, the name will disappear forever.

One problem is that the name is in STM for a short while, and because it seems available then, people are fooled into thinking they have learned it. To ensure that a name makes it past STM, wait about 30 to 60 seconds and then try to recall it. Say it aloud. If you fail, it is not too late to ask for the name again. (If you ask within a few minutes of being introduced, you need not feel embarrassed—it is only the next day that everyone expects you to have remembered their names.) Moreover, try to link characteristics of the name with features of the person to whom you are introduced. The standard memory courses always suggest that if, for example, the person is named Sharon Fisher, you should match her face up with a fish. This is the correct principle, but it is seldom so simple. Usually, we must struggle with the name as best we can. Try to make a point of using the name right away, a few times, during the conversation. It is interesting how well such a simple principle helps.

THE STUDY OF
LONG-TERM
MEMORY

Query: **In the place you lived in two places ago, as you entered the front door, was the doorknob on the left or right?**

Here is a question that requires information from long-term memory. There seems little doubt that you must have the information, but how do you find it? What is the retrieval process like? Try to answer the question stated above: on which side was your doorknob? You will find that the task seems more like that of solving a problem than of retrieving something from memory. If you persevere, you will almost definitely be able to come up with the proper answer. To do the task, first, you must back up through the places you have lived to find the proper one. Then you must recreate the front door. Try coming up on it from different angles. Sneak up quickly, with your hands filled with packages—see whether you shift the load in order to free a hand for the knob. Or think about the inside of the door: which way did it open? Is there anything behind the door? A closet, an obstruction? Work on the task: the answer will appear.

Studies of remembrance, problem solving, thinking, and mental operations have much in common, since there is little to distinguish among them. A person recalling material seems to be solving a problem. First, the question is analyzed to decide whether it is legitimate. Then, a quick decision is made about the information required for the answer. Is the information likely to be known? How difficult will it be to find? If recall of the information is attempted, then there must be selection of a strategy. As the retrieval process proceeds, the information in the request must be combined with partial solutions to form new questions that guide the search. The retrieval path seems to be organized around prominent events, landmarks in the memory that stand out above the myriad of stored details. An analysis of a successful recall indicates that much of the recollection appears to follow from logic and a reconstruction of what must have been.

The study of long-term memory is the study both of this problem-solving process and of the structure of the memory on which it operates. The things we remember are organized into a complex structure that interconnects the events and concepts built up by past experience. The act of remembering is the systematic application of rules to analyze this stored information.

The study of long-term memory is more than the study of how we remember. It is also the study of the mental strategies and mechanisms that guide much of our behavior. In this chapter we talk of three aspects of memory: the storehouse of information (which we call the *data base*), *interpretive mechanisms* that operate upon the data base, and a *monitor* that oversees the operations, deciding when they are productive and when they are not, exercising an overall guidance to the operation of the system (see Figure 9-10). Note that these three mechanisms play major roles in all intellectual functioning: learning and retrieving information, problem solving, decision making, and guiding a person's interactions with the world and with other people. This chapter introduces these concepts, but they play important roles in all the remaining chapters of the book.

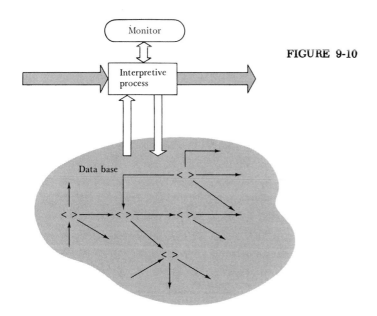

FIGURE 9-10

Perhaps nowhere else is the power of human memory so clearly exhibited as when people answer questions about what they know. Consider what is required to answer a question. First, it is not sufficient just to have the pertinent information stored in memory. It is necessary to search out and find all the stored information that is relevant, to evaluate any contradictory data, and finally to put it all together to form the best answer, given the information retrieved.

Answering questions

The human brain is not the only system faced with the problem of answering questions based on large amounts of information. There are numerous examples of systems that are capable of holding vast amounts of data: They range from such traditional devices as libraries to modern computer-based systems. When working with such memories, the first thing that is discovered is that getting information into the system is usually not a basic problem. The difficulties arise in trying to get it out.

Regardless of the memory system we contemplate—be it the human brain, a library card-catalog, a large collection of file folders, or a computer mass-storage device—there are types of queries for which the organizational structures of the memory (including its indices and abstracts) are inappropriate. Yet an omniscient outside observer might declare that the information required to answer the query does, in fact, exist in the system, if only the user would ask the correct questions and then put together the results sensibly. How can the system be designed so that, after we have gone to all the trouble of collecting information, we can find the information we want? What kinds of retrieval strategies are required? If the questions to be asked are known beforehand, the problem may not be too difficult. It is relatively easy, for example, to design the census system so that it can quickly find out how many people are under the age of 30, if you know you want that information before you store the data. But what about questions that were not anticipated? Is it possible to build a data-processing system that, like the human memory, can answer almost anything that comes to mind?

The key to any large-scale memory system, then, is not its physical capacity for storing huge amounts of information. Rather, it lies in its ability to retrieve selected pieces of data on request, its ability to answer questions based on the information stored. We can learn a great deal about the nature of the data-processing operations involved in human memory by thinking about the kinds of questions people can answer and of the mechanisms and procedures necessary to answer them. The operation of the monitor and the interpretive system are as important as the actual storage of information in memory.

Monitoring the response.   How do you answer questions asked of you? One thing is certain. There is more to answering questions than simply finding the relevant material and presenting it to the questioner. Social rules dictate what you can and cannot say. Courtesy, honesty, deceit, fear, pride—all affect the form of the responses you actually give to questions. These issues are discussed more fully in Chapter 12 on language and Chapter 16 on social interactions, but let us consider some simple illustrations here.

Query: **Where do you live?**

This would seem like a straightforward request, but the answer depends upon what you think the questioner knows. Suppose you (like one of us) lived at 402 Ocean Front, Del Mar, California. Then each of the following answers is correct, yet each is suited for a different purpose:

Answers: **In the United States.**
In southern California.
Just north of San Diego.
In Del Mar.
On Ocean Front, by 4th street.
In the house with the strange shape and no windows.

The answers cover a broad range of assumptions about the knowledge and interests of the person asking the question. Suppose you are in Europe, at a beach on the Adriatic Coast, and the person the next blanket over asks you, in heavily accented English, where you live. The first answer might apply. Suppose you are on the Del Mar beach just off 4th street, and the person on the next blanket over asks where you live. Now the last answer applies. Moreover, if you gave one of the first few answers, it would be considered rude.

This example shows some of the requirements of the *monitor,* which oversees the operation of the memory retrieval. It is not enough just to get the answer. There must also be a consideration of the purpose of the conversation, some thought to how the other person intends to use the information.

Query: **Where were you the night of the crime?**

Suppose that the world famous detective, M. Peerout, has just asked this query of the actual criminal. Here the monitor function is rather obvious: The criminal dares not state the truth. Instead, an answer must be fabricated, but the fabrication must be of a very special form. It must be plausible, it must hold up even under extensive scrutiny, it must not be contradicted by any other information that M. Peerout might have, and it must not reveal too much knowledge of the crime itself. The fabricated answer must then itself be kept in memory, for it will almost certainly be used again. We are sure that you can carry this scenario on and on. Again, the point is that monitoring the retrieval of information is an ever present process, whether the purpose be that of selecting an appropriate answer from the set of correct information or of manufacturing an answer to avoid revealing the actual information.

When to retrieve information.   Suppose you are asked:

Query: **What was Beethoven's telephone number?**

What is your answer to this query? Nonsense, you say. Beethoven died before telephones were invented. But suppose we ask about someone who had a telephone?

> *Query:*   **What was Hemingway's telephone number?**

You still refuse to try to retrieve the number. You don't know. How do you know you don't know? What about:

> *Query:*   **What is the telephone number of the White House?**
>
> **What is the telephone number of your best friend?**
>
> **What is your telephone number?**

The principle being illustrated is that, when asked to recall something, you do not start off blindly searching the data base. Rather, the monitor instructs the interpretive processes to analyze the question to see whether you are likely to find anything. On the basis of this preliminary analysis, you may conclude that there is no sense in even attempting to recall the data. Maybe the information does not exist. Maybe the information exists, but you know it is not in your memory. But what information do you use to decide that you do not know Hemingway's phone number, even if he had a phone? Maybe you think you might be able to retrieve the information if you tried, but it would require too much effort to be worth the bother. Are you really sure you could not produce the White House number if you worked on the problem for awhile? After all, did we not just teach you a method for learning the number?

When we ask questions of human memory we discover that there are procedures that analyze the message to determine if the relevant information exists, whether it is likely to have been stored, and the effort required and probable success of an attempt at retrieval. This whole sequence of operations seems to be carried out rapidly and unconsciously. We are only vaguely aware of the complexity of the rules involved.

Clearly, such a system is a great advantage for a large-scale memory. It does not waste time looking for things it does not know. It can judge the cost of retrieving information that is difficult to find. When faced with a continuous bombardment of sensory information, it is very important to know what is not known, since it lets us concentrate on the novel, unique, important aspects of events in the environment.

Retrieving an image

> *Query:* **In the rooms you live in, how many windows are there?**

This time, retrieval should proceed smoothly. First you conjure up an image of each room, then examine it, piece by piece, counting the windows. You then move to the next room and continue the process until you finish. The task seems easy. Yet, apart from the fact that people can have and use images, very little is known about the nature of internal images, how they are stored or how they are retrieved.

It is clear that our memories contain a large number of images of past experiences. An image can be retrieved and examined at will: the face of a friend, a scene from our last trip, the experience of riding a bicycle. This record of visual experiences suggests some important principles for the analysis of retrieval strategies. Saving some form of a replica of the original information provides a great deal of flexibility in being able to deal subsequently with questions about experiences. It is unlikely that you thought about the possibility of someday being asked for the number of windows. There is no need for you to take note of this fact whenever you are in your room. As long as you save an image of the rooms, you can worry later about retrieving particular pieces of information when they may be required.

We do not always deal with visual information by storing it all away. Often we analyze and condense incoming information, throwing away irrelevant details and remembering only what seems important. Try to recall what we have said so far in this chapter. You do not conjure up an image of the pages and read off the words. You recall a highly abstract version of your visual experience, reorganized and restated in your own terms.

An adequate model of human memory, then, will have to describe when incoming events are saved in their entirety and when only the critical features are extracted and stored. Recording a replica of the information uses up considerable memory space, makes subsequent retrieval more complicated and time consuming, and tends to clutter up the memory with irrelevant details. Reorganizing and condensing the information to save only the central features runs the risk of failing to record information that might subsequently be important. It limits the range and variety of ways in which past experiences can be used and the types of questions we can answer. Maybe it would be optimal to save both a complete record and a reorganized, condensed version, or maybe there are more sophisticated ways of dealing with rote records. Are there general rules for recording and reconstructing images that simplify the storage problem without sacrificing details? After all, houses have lots of things in common, such as roofs and walls. Perhaps the human memory system capitalizes on these similarities.

Regardless of how the information is actually stored, it is important to have both some form of an image of the rooms and a procedure for counting the windows. During retrieval, these two processes interact: One retrieves and constructs the image; the other analyzes and manipulates the retrieved information. Just as for problem solving, retrieval requires the active construction and analysis of information through the application of rules or procedures. This constructive aspect of human memory comes out more clearly when the system is presented with yet another kind of question.

Retrieval as problem solving

Query: **What were you doing on Monday afternoon in the third week of September two years ago?**

Don't give up right away. Take some time to think about it and see if you can come up with the answer. Try writing down your thoughts as you attempt to recover this information. Better still, ask a friend to think out loud as he tries to answer the query.

The type of responses people typically produce when asked this kind of question goes something like this:

1. *Come on. How should I know?*   (Experimenter: Just try it, anyhow.)
2. *OK. Let's see: Two years ago. . . .*
3. *I would be in high school in Pittsburgh . . . .*
4. *That would be my senior year.*
5. *Third week in September—that's just after summer—that would be the fall term. . . .*
6. *Let me see. I think I had chemistry lab on Mondays.*
7. *I don't know. I was probably in the chemistry lab. . . .*
8. *Wait a minute—that would be the second week of school. I remember he started off with the atomic table—a big, fancy chart. I thought he was crazy, trying to make us memorize that thing.*
9. *You know, I think I can remember sitting. . . .*

This particular protocol is fabricated from several actual ones to illustrate how the memory system works on this kind of retrieval problem. First, the question is whether or not to attempt the retrieval at all. The preliminary analysis suggests it is going to be difficult, if not impossible to recover the requested information and the subject balks at starting at all (line 1). When he does begin the search, he does not attempt to recall the information directly, but breaks the overall question down into subquestions. He decides first to establish what he was doing two years ago (line 2). Once he has succeeded in answering this question (line 3), he uses the retrieved information to construct and answer a more specific question (line 4). After going as far as he can with the first clue, he returns to pick up more information in the initial query, "September, third week." He then continues with still more specific memories (lines 5 and 6). Most of what happened between lines 7 and 8 is missing from the protocol. He seems to have come to a dead end at line 7, but must have continued to search around for other retrieval strategies. Learning the periodic table seems to have been an important event in his life. The retrieval of this information seems to open up new access routes. By line 8, he once again appears to be on his way to piecing together a picture of what he was doing on a Monday afternoon two years ago.

Here memory appears as a looping, questioning activity. The search is active, constructive. When it cannot go directly from one point to another, the problem is broken up into a series of subproblems or subgoals. For each subproblem, the questions are: Can it be solved; will the solution move me closer to the main goal? When one subproblem gets solved, new ones are defined and the search continues. If successful, the system eventually produces a response, but the response is hardly a simple recall. It is a mixture of logical reconstructions of what must have been experienced with fragmentary recollections of what was in fact experienced.

Retrieving long-past names. Retrieving information that has been within the memory for a long time can be a difficult, time-consuming task. Suppose you were asked to retrieve the names of the people with whom you went to school three to twenty years ago—what do you think would happen? Williams (1976) asked people to do this task, and kept his subjects at the task for days and days—in some cases months—continually attempting to retrieve names. The longer the subjects tried to remember, the more they could remember. The progress of one subject at recalling the names of classmates is shown in Figure 9-11.

The process of retrieving names is actually a process of reconstruction, very much like the construction process described in Chapter 8 for the retrieval of items in short-term memory given the attributes that were available. Williams found that his subjects had to reconstruct the entire context of the retrieval. For example, when subjects said aloud the things they were doing, it was possible to see the search strategies. Here is an actual transcript from one of the subjects (the names of the people mentioned by the subject have been changed to protect their privacy):

> *Subject:* I was trying to think of Carl's last name but I just can't think of it. Umm, okay, let me see if there's any other neighborhoods that I haven't gotten to that I can remember where people my age lived. Um . . . humm. There is no one that lived way up on the end . . . And now I'm trying to think of of the Sunset Cliffs down on Cal Western 'cause a lot of people always used to go there and go tide pool picking and just run around and go surfing. I'm trying to think of all the people that perhaps went surfing or even tide pool picking that were in my grade. Um . . . if I could see them lined up against—there's this one cliff down at Newbreak Beach they always used to line up with their boards and sit down and look at the waves, and then I go down the row and see if there's anybody I haven't already named. There's Benny Nesbit, I already named him, and Dave Culbert and they used to go surfing, and um there are a lot of older people too. Um, Joe Nate, I already named them, all those guys used to go surfing. Um, he was older—he was older—

and older—he was younger. A lot of those guys were older. Let me see, him and him . . . Okay I was just going down the list and I don't see anybody that I haven't already seen and there was this one girl who always used to be down there, but she was younger. I already named the people that she hangs around with. Um, is there anybody else that I know that used to . . .

This protocol illustrates a number of the properties of retrievals from long-past memories. Most important of all, in this example, is the estab-

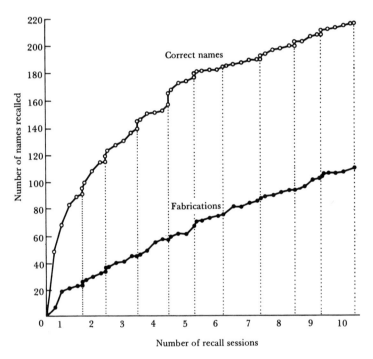

FIGURE 9-11   *Names recalled versus time. The subject was directed to "think out loud" while recalling the first and last names of everyone who graduated from high school with her. Her progress was studied in 10 sessions of approximately one hour each. Each session is marked by the vertical dotted lines. At the beginning of each session, she reported any names that she had inadvertently recalled between sessions (thus occasionally producing two data points for one time). "Correct names" are defined as those from the subject's yearbook in the twelfth grade. The total number of possible correct names is approximately 600. Fabrications are false responses, usually the names of actual people, but not members of her high school class.*

lishment of a *context*. The subject spent considerable time recreating the actual setting where the experiences took place. Then, she systematically went down the list of people that she could imagine in that context, checking the names that are retrieved, or searching further when a person is noticed but for whom the name is not immediately available.

One interesting property of retrievals is what Williams calls *overshoot*: the continual recollection of information about a person, long after their actual name had been retrieved. The overshoot appears to have two purposes. First, it acts as a check on the validity of the name. Overshoot provides the information needed to confirm that the person whose name was recalled actually was one of those being searched for. Second, it helps generate a new context, thus getting to new pockets of names.

Here is another protocol that illustrates the grouping of information. In this example, the subject goes from one context to another, picking up groups of people at each. Again the establishment of the context appears to be the critical step in getting access to the names. (As before, this is a real protocol, except that the names have been changed.)

Subject: Umm I was picturing the people that I knew, and trying to see if there was anyone missing. I'm pic—picturing a familiar place and I just located two more. There's Mike Peterhill and um (tapping) Larry Atkinson. I located them at their house, or at Larry's house where they work on cars.

Experimenter: Mm-hm.

Subject: OK? And that was next door to Arlene and next door to Bill, um OK, and then oh um, there was my old girlfriend (laugh). I wonder why I remembered her. Um, I remembered her because I remembered the, I was thinking about the house where Larry lives, and was remem—remembering going to visit him once while he was working on this old, uh car, Pack, old Packard and Mary was there, so that's her, and then her friends now are Jane and, uh . . . What was her name? She didn't have too many friends, she was like—her friends were all spaced out in different places—um, to get back. That's not a valuable list. I'll only get one more name off it.

Now, people I knew through my sister—hm—I didn't know them very well, they were just acquaintances, there's Leanne, and don't even remember his name, and let's see, don't remember her name. I'm re—I'm remembering now people, uh, who were friends of my sister's whose names I've forgotten, but who—or who I don't remember right now, but who I can remember situations where they were at—and what they looked like partially—uh—Oh, wow, OK, I just lo—located a storehouse of people. There was an afterschool thing where I used to go all the time, and there was lots of people there, and I have a whole building full of people, but I can't remember a lot of those names. There's Ruth Bower, Susan Younger, Sue Cairns— oh, wow, Jeff Andrews, Bill Jacobsen, I just located a whole another group of people—whew (laugh) wow—um—

One problem with the reconstructive process of memory is that it may lead to *false constructions* or *fabrications*. Sometimes the name that was recalled was wrong. Sometimes the recall is similar to the correct one, sometimes it is an actual name, but of a different person than is being thought of. Sometimes the name belongs to the person, but that person was known elsewhere, not as a student in that school. When Williams checked the school records and verified the names, he found that a substantial number of the recollections were indeed fabrications. At first, fabrications were limited, but as recall continued, the rate of false retrievals increased substantially. By the tenth hour of recall, almost 50% of the newly generated items were false. The number of fabrications are also shown in Figure 9-11.

Metamemory: Knowledge about your own memory system. An interesting issue, little explored, is how much people know about their own mental processes, and how much they know of their own memory. Actually, as we have seen, there are two different issues in the study of memory. One is the knowledge of the system, the roles of STM and LTM, and the operations that can be performed, such as maintenance and integrative rehearsal, or mnemonic strategies. The other is knowledge of one's own knowledge: knowing what is contained within the data base.

By the time most people reach adulthood, they have developed a good intuitive feeling for the properties of their memory. People generally do different things when they wish to remember something for future use than when they never expect to need the same thing again. Sometimes the activity is mental, as in laboriously repeating a person's name over and over again in hopes of retaining it. Sometimes the activity is external, as in writing a note on a piece of paper in order to remember a date or a shopping list. Sometimes the activity is a mental note of an external aid, as in determining who are the authorities on a topic rather than learning the topic itself.

Similar phenomena exist in attempting to retrieve information from memory. In attempting to retrieve the name of a person who has not been seen for several years, one might deliberately attempt to relive some of the activities of those years, hoping thereby to reexcite the sought-for name. Sometimes one engages in deliberate cueing strategies, such as going through each of the letters of the alphabet in turn, hoping that the appropriate letter will cue the sought-for item. Sometimes one tries to remember where to look for the answer—in a book, or in a file, or even to remembering who else might know. And sometimes one simply decides the information is not known or that it is not possible to retrieve it, and so gives up the task.

All of these activities of memory storage and retrieval illustrate activities that are concerned with how much people know about their own knowledge. We call this knowledge about memory *metamemory*. Several investigators have studied just how a person's metamemory develops with age (see, for example, Flavell and Wellman, in press). For instance, when children are shown a set of items, children at the age of 4 do not seem to distinguish between "looking closely" at them and "memorizing them." At the age of 7, the children understand the difference, but do not seem to know how to make use of that understanding. By the age of 11, the children do different things when they memorize and when they look.

When we discussed the role of rehearsal and of special mnemonic strategies earlier in this chapter, we noted that most people are not very good at learning things. If they are asked to memorize a list of items, they will most likely perform maintenance rehearsal, an ineffective procedure. Thus, people seem to be aware of some of the properties of their memory system, but they appear to confuse the activity generated by rehearsal with useful actions. In addition, we suspect that they confuse the fact that an item currently in STM is easy to retrieve with the expected ease of retrieval at a later time. There seems to be the belief that if information is so readily available, it must be learned.

In this chapter we have discussed knowledge of the contents of the data base as an important determiner of memory retrieval. When people do not believe they know some information, they will not spend time attempting to find it. Often, of course, these judgments about one's own knowledge will be false. Most instructors have had the painful experience of trying to convince students that they really do have the proper information within them, if only they would relax a bit and search their memory data bases intelligently.

Usually, one gains knowledge of one's own mental structures only by experiencing them. The exceptions come only when a deliberate effort is made to study mental capacities and systems—as in the study of this book. Because most people do not get formal training in the development of memory skills, it is no wonder that development of metamemory is stretched out over the entire preadolescent period. In fact, the development of memory skills is usually incomplete, for most people do not know of powerful memorization techniques that have been developed over the years. As we saw in this chapter, some memory strategies can be very powerful.

REVIEW OF TERMS
AND CONCEPTS

In this chapter, the following terms and concepts that we consider to be important have been used. Please look them over. If you are not able to give a short explanation of any of them, you should go back and review the appropriate sections of the chapter.

Terms and concepts you should know

The study of memory
   the serial position curve
      primacy
      recency
   the difference between recall and recognition
   some standard techniques of studying memory
   the role of attention in memory processes
      data-driven and conceptually driven processing
Long-term memory (LTM)
   maintenance rehearsal
   integrative processes
   the difficulties of retrieval: the library analogy
   depth of processing
   levels of analysis
   mnemonics
      rhymes
      key words
      places
      associations
The role of the monitor, the interpretive processes, and the data base
   the interrelation between these three concepts and
      SIS, STM, LTM, maintenance rehearsal, integrative processes, and memory strategies
What it means to consider memory retrieval as problem solving
   the role of reconstructive processes in retrieval from LTM (and the relationship to the reconstruction from memory attributes in STM— discussed in Chapter 8)
   overshoot
   false constructions (fabrications)
   setting a context
Metamemory

SUGGESTED
READINGS

There are a fair number of texts and chapters that deal with the material covered here. In addition, the psychology journals are filled with papers that add new evidence or enrich our understanding of the various issues of human memory. We believe that a good set of introductory texts are the books written by Norman (1976) and by Rumelhart (1977). Norman's book is considerably easier than Rumelhart's, so it should be examined first. There are several other good introductions: Klatzky (1975) and Loftus and Loftus (1975).

Work in these areas is so active that perhaps it is best to go directly to the psychology journals and to browse: it will not take long before you are deeply involved with the studies. As usual, the *Annual Review of Psychology* provides a convenient spot to start, for it has reasonably frequent comments upon the literature in memory. The suggested readings in Norman (1976) also provide suggestions of where to read. Almost nothing is available concerning the operations of the interpretive system and of the monitor: this area of research is much too new.

An important collection of articles on the nature of short-term memory and depth of processing is the three chapters by Bjork, Craik and Jacoby, and Shiffrin, in the book *Cognitive theory* edited by Restle, Shiffrin, Castellan, Lindeman, and Pisoni (1975). Shiffrin (in press) reviews the literature and theories on information processing and memory. The major important article on depth of processing is by Craik and Lockhart (1972).

A fascinating description of a person with an anomalous memory is given in Luria's *The mind of a mnemonist* (1968). Luria is an important Russian psychologist, and in this book he describes someone who has an extraordinary memory capacity: Is S. just an anomaly, or does he represent some important issues that we have missed in our laboratory studies? Hunt and Love (1972) talk of a similar person in the United States.

To learn more about mnemonic systems, perhaps the easiest way is to get one of the standard books written by practitioners of the art. We recommend Lorayne and Lucas (1974) or Young and Gibson (1962). For the scientific literature on mnemonics, see Bower (1970). Atkinson (1975) has an interesting paper on the application of "mnemotechnics" to language learning.

The retrieval of long-past memories has not been thoroughly studied. The protocols of subjects that were in this chapter were from the Ph.D. thesis of Williams (1976), which at the time this book was written, had not yet been published (but check the *Psychological Abstracts* to see if it has been published since). Linton (1975) and Bahrick, Bahrick, and Wittlinger (1975) describe two other studies of the memories for long-past events. Linton is studying herself over a five-year period, writing down the events that she experiences and periodically testing herself. Bahrick, Bahrick, and Wittlinger looked at how well people recalled the names of others after a lapse of five years.

10 The representation of knowledge

PREVIEW

A critically important topic is the study of how information is represented within the memory data base. Most of this chapter is devoted to the presentation of one powerful tool in the study of memory representation: the *semantic network*. The principles that govern the semantic network are relatively simple. Human knowledge is extremely extensive and everything seems to be related to everything else. Thus, when we describe human knowledge, the result can quickly appear to be complicated: the drawings look like cobwebs woven by aberrant spiders but do not be dismayed by the complexity of the diagrams in this chapter. The complexity is apparent, not real. We believe that the principles used to develop semantic representations are so important to the study of memory processes that it is essential that you work through them. When you understand the fundamental principles of the semantic network representation, you will have two things. First, you should gain in some understanding of your own memory systems. Second, you will have made an excellent start toward the understanding of the technical literature on both human and artificial memory (as studied in the field of artificial intelligence).

The discussions of semantic networks are quite important. You should learn to draw the networks, learn to read the diagrams. The same system described here for representing knowledge within memory will also be important in later chapters, especially in the chapter on language. Make sure that you understand the diagrams.

We conclude the chapter with a discussion of some issues related to the representation of knowledge, including some of the current controversies over the form of the representation. In particular, we discuss the role of images both as a way of maintaining information in memory and as a useful means of viewing one's knowledge. Unfortunately, although most people would agree that mental images play important roles in human cognition, not much is known about them. Thus, this part of the chapter can only suggest the properties of mental images. We cannot deal with images in the same extensive manner as we can with semantic networks.

REPRESENTING INFORMATION IN MEMORY

We have seen something of the structure of the memory system, the monitor, and the interpretive system. Now it is time to examine the data base and, in particular, the nature of the information that is retained within memory. At this point, let us examine one possible representation for material within the data base of human memory. The goal is to put together a model of memory, one that has the characteristics of human memory, with special emphasis on the way that concepts and events might be represented and on how the relations among different items in memory might be represented.

The structure of concepts Human memory contains an enormous variety of concepts that can be retrieved and used at will. People have concepts of houses, dogs, cars, politicians, and astronauts. Large amounts of information associated with any given concept can be produced on demand. The first job, then, is to decide how to represent concepts in a memory system.

Think of a word, say, **teapot.** Ask a friend to explain what it means, or explain it to yourself out loud. What kinds of information do you produce when describing its meaning? A typical explanation looks something like this:

> **Teapot,** *n. A container something like a kettle, made of metal or china.* [*The Golden Book Illustrated Dictionary for Children*]

Or

> **Teapot,** *n. A container with a handle or spout for making or serving tea.* [*The Thorndike–Barnhardt Comprehensive Desk Dictionary*]

Similarly, for other words, say, **tapestry, tart,** and **tavern,** the dictionary states that

> a **tapestry** is *a piece of cloth with figures or pictures woven into it;*
> a **tart** is *a small, baked crust or pastry filled with fruit jelly or jam;*
> a **tavern** is *a place where beer, wine, or other alcoholic drinks are served.*

These examples remind us that the definition of a word consists of other words. Typically, a definition starts off by saying, "Concept A is really something else, namely concept B"; a tapestry is a piece of cloth, a tart is a pastry. It then goes on to specify the restrictions on the concept. Unlike other places, taverns serve beer and wine. The unique thing about a tapestry is that it has figures or pictures woven into it. A teapot has either a handle or a spout and is used for tea.

Another form of information that is often used in explaining a concept is an example. If you were explaining a **tavern** to a friend, you would probably point out some specific examples. If we look up **place** in a dictionary, we might find little else but examples.

> **Place,** *n. A city, town, or area.*

(Notice that the dictionary did not mention **tavern** as an example of a place.) Similarly,

> **Container,** *n. Anything with the property of holding something, such as a box, barrel, can, or jug.*

It seems, then, that if a person or dictionary is questioned about what a word means, all that is produced is other words. For some reason, this does not seem to disturb us. The hoax only becomes apparent if you persist and ask for the definitions of words that are used to define other words. A little experimentation with dictionaries soon reveals the shallowness of their definitions. Words that seem especially circular in their definition are family terms: **father, mother, parent, child.** For example, *Webster's New Collegiate Dictionary* defines **son** as a *male offspring of human beings* and **offspring** as *the progeny of an animal or plant.* So far, so good. But when we look up **progeny** we discover that it is given in terms of **offspring:** *progeny—the offspring of animals or plants.*

An important part of the meaning or comprehension of a concept, then, must be embedded in its relationships to other concepts in the memory. On examining the format of typical definitions, a rather small number of relationships seems to predominate: the *class* of concepts to which it belongs, the *properties* which tend to make that concept unique, and *examples* of the concept. A standard definition, then, can be summarized schematically as in Figure 10-1.

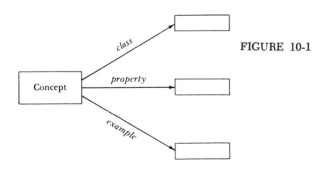

FIGURE 10-1

FIGURE 10-2

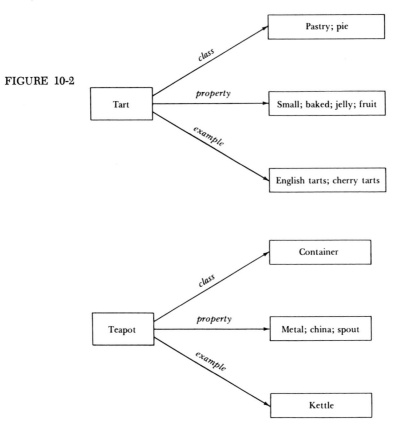

Filling in the blanks with some of the above definitions produces Figure 10-2. Moreover, the words used in the definition are themselves concepts, and therefore defined in the same way. The result is an interlinking structure that may not be apparent when looking up definitions, but that certainly becomes obvious when the structure is shown graphically, as in Figure 10-3.

To represent concepts in the memory the diagrams show two kinds of things: boxes and arrows. The boxes represent the concepts. Notice that the arrows have two important properties. First, they are **directed**. That is, they point in a specific direction. We can follow them in either direction, but they mean different things. Second, they are **named**: there are three kinds of names so far—*property*, *example*, and *class*.

Semantic definitions   So far we have concentrated on dictionary definition. Obviously, we do not really care about how a dictionary defines terms: we are interested in how concepts are represented in human memory. But the dictionary examples indicate several important aspects we must consider. In par-

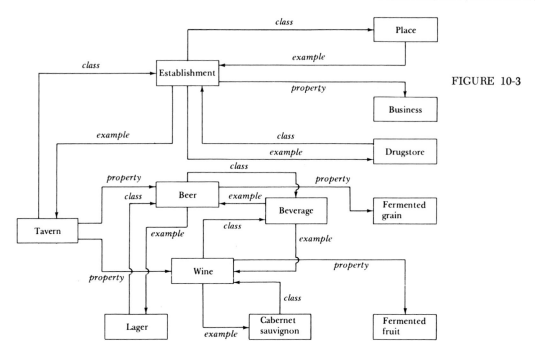

FIGURE 10-3

ticular, knowledge contained within human memory forms an interrelated web of concepts and actions. Knowledge of one topic is related to knowledge of others. The human memory system makes possible the tracing of the relationships among the knowledge within the data base.

Let us examine how information might be represented within human memory. Three properties are needed. First, the system is capable of recording individual concepts and events. Second, it is capable of interrelating these to one another. Third, it provides some way of getting access to the information.

If we call each basic unit in the memory system a *record*, we see that each record must contain *pointers* or *references* to other memory records. Moreover, the pointers that relate the individual records with one another differ in their meanings, so the pointers must be labeled. Thus, in Figure 10-3, the boxes are memory records and the arrows indicate the relations among the records.

To illustrate the representation, consider how information about *dogs* might be represented. What is a *dog?* A child might define it something like:

> *Child:* A dog is an animal. It has four legs and it barks and it eats meat. It's about *this* big.

A child really knows more about dogs. Consider the following possible conversation:

Us: Do you know many dogs?
Child: Oh yes, Gretchen and Bingo and Taco.
Us: Does Bingo bark?
Child: Of course, silly, Bingo is a dog, isn't she?
Us: I have a dog named Pavlov. Does Pavlov bark?
Child: You mean when it's angry or hungry? Sure.
Us: Which is the biggest dog—which is the smallest dog?
Child: Well, Gretchen is bigger than me, really big, and Taco is tiny: I can hold him in one hand.
Us: But I thought you said dogs were *"this* big."
Child: Well yeah, dogs are, but Gretchen is bigger and Taco is littler.

This conversation illustrates several things. People have general knowledge about dogs that can be used to infer the properties of specific dogs. Thus, the child believes that Pavlov probably barks, even though it has never met Pavlov. The general knowledge that dogs bark is thought to apply to all dogs. But some general knowledge is applied differently. Thus, dogs can vary in size.

Our memory systems must contain both general knowledge and specific knowledge. The definition of dog is a *generic* definition. The knowledge about Gretchen and Taco is knowledge about particular instances of the general concept. The generic definition applies generally to all dogs, but with some flexibility. Basically, people seem to use generic definitions as a *prototype:* it describes the typical characteristics of dogs, but any particular individual dog need not follow the generic definition exactly.

Thus, the typical dog barks, has four legs, and eats meat. We expect all actual dogs to be the same. Despite this, we would not be too suprised to come across a dog that did not bark, had only three legs, or refused to eat meat. If we had to say how big an unknown dog was, we would think of some typical size. But we know that all dogs do not have the same size. It is important to know the typical values of things. When we say that one dog is "large," another "tiny," and a third "average," we are making use of the typical size. The words "large," "big," "tiny," and "average" are *relative* terms: they require some standard. When we say, "Taco is tiny," we really mean to say, "Compared to the typical sizes of dogs, Taco is tiny (but if Taco were a mouse, he would be big)."

Semantic networks   Our memory representation must have two important properties. First, there is a need for generic information about concepts that provides general knowledge, letting us deduce the properties of instances of the concept, even if we have not experienced those instances. Second, the generic knowledge is prototypical: it specifies typical values, but we are not surprised if particular instances of the concept differ from some of the generic properties.

In the memory data base, we must have some way of distinguishing the individual instances, yet some way of relating them so that we can deduce the general properties when we need them. Figure 10-4 shows a set of memory records that start to meet these requirements. (Each record

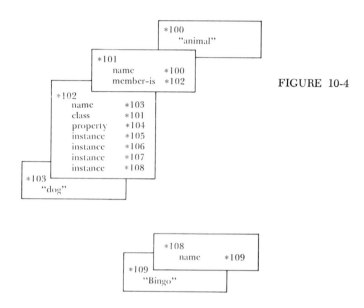

FIGURE 10-4

is given a number for purposes of identification: a typical number is *108, pronounced "star 108.") The figure shows the interrelations among the records. Thus, record number *102 contains in it references to record numbers *101, *103, *104, and others. Record *103 contains the information about the English names of the items referred to in *102, namely, the word "dog."[1]

Nodes and relations. Another way of diagramming the same information shown in Figure 10-4 is shown in Figure 10-5. You should convince

---

[1] Actually, because you can sometimes have a word "on the tip of the tongue," where you are able to remember the starting sound but not the entire word, we know that a single record probably does not contain the actual letters or sounds of the name, but rather itself refers to the individual elements that comprise the name. Thus, a person seeking the English word that describes a concept may be able to find the record that states the starting sound and the length, but might be unable to retrieve all of the records necessary to specify the actual word.

yourself that all of the information in Figure 10-4 iş present in Figure 10-5 (we have added some additional information to Figure 10-5). We find Figure 10-5 somewhat easier to use. Diagrams such as Figure 10-5 are called *semantic networks:* they illustrate the net of interconnections among meaningful (semantic) components in memory. Semantic networks are drawn to have *nodes* that are interrelated by pointers or *labeled relations.* The nodes correspond to the records of Figure 10-4. In Figure 10-5 some nodes are represented by black dots, some by angle brackets, and some by ovals. The different symbols for the nodes are for our convenience in talking about them. The symbols correspond to different types of information within the records. Nodes represented by black dots correspond to generic records. Nodes represented by angle brackets correspond to instances of generic concepts, or nodes that contain some particular values of information (such as size or sensory information). Nodes represented by ovals correspond to *propositions,* particular statements that apply to the other nodes in the network. The relations among the nodes have names associated with them to distinguish the different meanings of the relations, just as we illustrated earlier in our discussion of dictionary concepts.

isa. Figure 10-5 has some important properties. Note the relation labeled "isa" that goes between particular instances of a concept and the generic node of the concept. The word "isa" should be read as the phrase "is an instance of." Thus, node ●110 represents an instance of ●102: ●110 is the thing called "Bingo," ●102 is the thing called "dog." Thus, Bingo is an instance of "dog," which in turn is a member of the class "animal." Any property of dogs is likely to apply to Bingo, and any property of animals is probably applicable to dogs. Thus, because ●101 indicates that animals all breathe air and eat food, we infer that so too do all dogs (●102). Similarly, because ●102 indicates that all dogs bark, eat a specific food (meat), and have a typical size (indicated by node ●192), we infer that individual dogs such as Bingo eat meat, bark, and have that size. In addition, we know that Bingo is female, a property that obviously does not apply to all dogs. The important point is that the semantic representation gives us a way of inferring the properties of particular concepts from the properties of generic concepts.

Default values. The information contained in the generic nodes can be considered to be the value for typical instances. These values are *default values.* That is, if you know that some concept (say Pavlov, ●112) is an instance of the generic concept for dog (node ●102), then if you are forced to guess some of the properties of Pavlov in the absence of specific information, you use the default values. By default, Pavlov barks, breathes air, eats meat, and is a typical size dog. We may later need to modify these statements, but meanwhile they are useful assumptions.

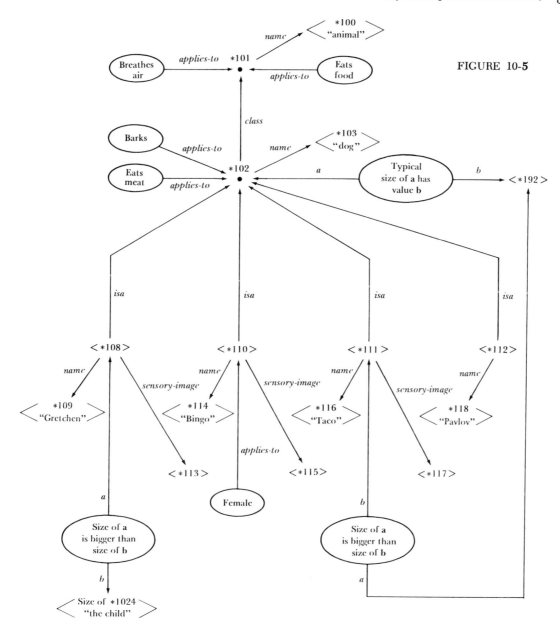

FIGURE 10-5

Propositions. Figure 10-5 also shows how one can represent the statements that Gretchen is bigger than the child we spoke to, Taco is small (for a dog), and Bingo is female. The ovals in the figure stand for *propositions:* statements that characterize the properties that apply to the nodes of the network. The propositions play a critical role in the representation, and in fact, all of the information now contained in the nodes represented by dots and by angle brackets can also be represented by propositions. Sometimes semantic networks are called *propositional representations.*

Propositions often represent reasonably complex ideas. Propositional statements may concern the particular properties of things, they may actually be instructions that can do things to the memory or that can control a person's movements and activities, or they may represent the events and episodes that have been experienced. Because propositions are so rich in structure, we have given them labels that describe the function they play in the diagrams. Thus, one of the propositions in Figure 10-5 is labeled *"size of a is larger than size of b."* Obviously, we do not believe that the propositions and concepts in memory are specified by verbal descriptions of this sort. The description is solely for your benefit: so that you can understand the role that they play in the diagrams. Actually, the propositions themselves are probably decomposable into a rich, interlocking structure of more fundamental concepts. We shall discuss a little of this in the chapter on language: further discussion can be found in the books by Norman, Rumelhart, and the LNR Research Group (1975) and by Schank (1975).

Sensory images and motor control images

In considering the representation to this point, you may have been bothered by the apparent circularity: things get defined in terms of themselves. The circularity of definitions is true of dictionaries, but not of human memory. Dictionaries are constructed of words, and so words must be defined in terms of other words—there is no way of avoiding the fundamental circularity of the definitions. But the human has sensory systems, arms and legs, and muscles that are capable of controlling the body and performing actions. Sights, sounds, feelings, tastes, movements, actions—all these are part of the information within memory. All this information adds specificity to the data base. Thus circularity of the information is avoided by providing reference to real sensory events and real actions that can be performed. In Figure 10-5 we indicate that part of the semantic definition of nodes *108, *110, and *111 (Gretchen, Bingo, and Taco) are the *sensory images* of these dogs. (Note that *112, Pavlov, does not have any sensory image, for if Figure 10-5 represents the data base of the child with whom we had that earlier conversation, Pavlov has only been introduced by name, never experienced.)

Just as there must be sensory images that record the perceptual experiences, there must also be images for recording the responses that people make: their actions. The systems that control the muscle movements in the human are called the *motor control systems.* Accordingly, the representations of the control processes for these movements are *motor control images.* We will meet motor images again in Chapter 13, where we discuss the possibility that a child's first knowledge of the world is built up from its own movements and their effect upon the world: hence, motor images form the foundation of the representation of information within the memory data base.

Very little is known about just what information from the perceptual experience is contained within a sensory image and just how the control of motor (muscle) movements is represented within the motor image. The concepts are essential, however, for any complete theory of the memory system, and so you can view their inclusion in diagrams such as Figure 10-5 as reminders that this information must exist and as goads to those who study memory to attempt to learn more about these important issues.

Note that much of our knowledge is probably encoded in combinations of network representations, sensory images, and motor control images. Thus, a concept such as "eat" must contain information about the acts of chewing and swallowing, and the senses of feel, temperature, and taste that result. Thinking of eating a marshmallow brings to mind a different set of images than does thinking of eating a gelatin dessert, or peanut butter, or honey, or a very hard or tough piece of food.

Because the sensory and motor control images form such an essential component of the memory representation, we sometimes combine the two types of images into one, making them *sensorimotor control images* (they will be called *sensorimotor schemas* in Chapter 13). The inclusion of information about the motor movements and the sensory impressions allows the human memory system to avoid the circularity that is found in dictionaries. Human memory representations are not circular because eventually they refer to real motor actions or to real reference objects in the world. Actually, we can find the counterpart of sensory images in dictionaries: dictionaries attempt to avoid the circularity of their definitions by including illustrations in their text and by attempting to describe the sensory images that they believe their readers to have.

In considering how to represent various kinds of information in memory, an important problem comes up. Suppose we are trying to remember the information:

PRIMARY AND SECONDARY CONCEPTS

Leo, the hungry lion, has a sore mouth.

The difficulty here comes from the way in which we add the fact that the lion has a sore mouth. Figure 10-6 shows one way of representing the sentence. Note that **sore** has to apply to **mouth**, not **Leo.** If **sore** applied to **Leo,** then all of **Leo** would be sore, not just his mouth.

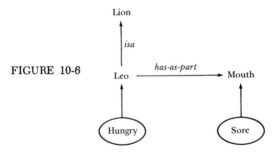

FIGURE 10-6

By the way, note that Figure 10-6 illustrates some shortcuts in drawing these diagrams. We simplified things by writing the name of each node directly on the node, rather than laboriously pointing to the name with an arrow labeled *name*. Second, we did not bother to write the word *applies-to* on the relations between the propositions (ovals) and the nodes to which they apply. Both deletions simplify diagrams, but without changing their structure. You should still remember the earlier, more complete form: the name of a node really is not part of the node; the unlabeled relation is really called *applies-to*. Figure 10-6 also introduced a new relation, *has-as-part*. This indicates that the node pointed to forms part of the other. Thus, the body of a person *has-as-part* arms and legs; a house *has-as-part* doors, windows, walls, and roof. Neither *isa* nor *class* is an appropriate label for this relationship.

The description shown in Figure 10-6 is satisfactory only if this is going to be the only time the concept of mouth is mentioned in the data base. But suppose **Joan is a person who has a big mouth.** Adding this information to the data base would produce Figure 10-7. This is wrong. This diagram only has one mouth, and it is both big and sore.

FIGURE 10-7

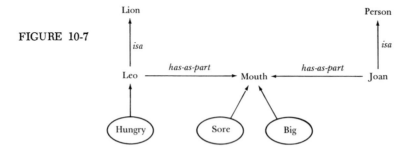

Although we need only one generic definition for the concept of mouth, we need to have many instances. In other words, we want only one *primary* or *generic definition*, but many possible *secondary* or *instance definitions*. We represent secondary concepts by enclosing them in angular brackets like this ⟨**mouth**⟩. This can be read as "this mouth." This primary–secondary distinction is invaluable, as Figure 10-8 shows.

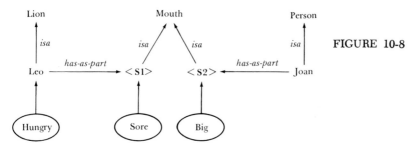

FIGURE 10-8

Secondary concepts usually do not have names, and their definition can always be found simply by following the *isa* arrow, as illustrated in Figure 10-8. The secondary node labeled **S1** is that of a **mouth,** in this particular instance, a **sore mouth.** Secondary node **S2** is also that of a **mouth,** but in this instance it is a **big mouth.** When retrieving information, we can automatically substitute **sore mouth** for **S1** and **big mouth** for **S2** to recover the correct information in each case.

To introduce the idea of a data base for storing information and its interrelated structure, we have restricted ourselves so far to descriptions of concrete nouns and basic kinds of relationships. These concrete concepts are an important part of the human memory, but they represent only part of the information people normally encounter. What about events? What about the memory for the plot of the last novel you read? How can actions be represented in such a system?

Remembering events

Using the same basic strategy, it is rather easy to add different types of information to the data base. Only two more steps are required, one very simple, the other rather complicated. The easy step is simply to expand upon the allowable types of arrows that can interconnect concepts. Before letting these arrows proliferate freely, however, it is important to decide on the types of arrows that might be connected to events.

The problem is to represent an event in the memory system. We do that by adding a new type of node to the memory, an *event* node. Thus, in the situation

The dog bites the cat.

we wish to add the description of that event. To do that, consider an event as a *scenario,* with actions, actors, and stage settings. All the information must get encoded, with each part of the scene properly identified to its role in the event.

Consider again the situation **The dog bites the cat.** Here the sentence that describes the event can be broken down into three parts: a subject (**dog**), a verb (**bites**), and a direct object (**cat**). But we do not really wish to determine subjects, verbs, and direct objects, for these are often misleading. Take the sentence, **The cat is bitten by the dog.** What do you call the subject? **cat** or **dog**? We want it to be **dog.** The instigator of the action is **dog,** so it is **dog,** not **cat,** that is our subject.

To record events, some new concepts must be defined. Consider how an event is described. What we want to do is to break it down into a set of simple relationships that describes the basic concepts of the event. Events can often be described in sentences, but the sentence must be analyzed with some care. Linguists are very careful to distinguish among several levels of language. One, called *surface structure,* represents the part that is visible: The actual sentences people speak. The other level is called *deep structure* or *semantic space,* and it represents the meanings that underlie the sentences. Clearly, the important thing for memory is deep structure, or semantic space. Some sentences can look very similar to one another at the surface structure, but mean completely different things at the semantic level. Consider the sentences

Patrick is cooking.

Supper is cooking.

These two sentences look very much the same, but they mean quite different things. In one case, Patrick is standing at the stove cooking something. In the other, we can hardly imagine supper to be standing in the kitchen cooking something: It is supper that is being cooked, perhaps by Patrick:

Patrick is cooking supper.

To discover the basic structure of an event without being misled by the surface structure of the sentence that describes it, we always start by ignoring the details of the sentence and by identifying the *action.*[2] The first step in the analysis is to decide what the *scenario* is: What is the action? Next, find the actors and the things being acted upon. The actors, who cause the action to take place, are called *agents.* The things being acted upon are *objects,* and the person who receives the effect of an action can be called a *recipient.* Here are some examples:

Patrick is cooking.

   Action: cooking

   Agent: Patrick

   Object: none

---

[2] These examples and analyses come from Fillmore (1968)

Supper is cooking.

> *Action:* cooking

> *Agent:* none

> *Object:* supper.

Patrick is cooking supper for Cynthia

> *Action:* cooking

> *Agent:* Patrick

> *Object:* supper

> *Recipient:* Cynthia

Identifying things this way simplifies life considerably.

Now we see how to represent events in the data base. The entire event centers around some action, so the action becomes the central node: We represent it in diagrams as a node, drawn as an oval around the word (usually a verb) that describes the action. Then the actors and objects that comprise the scenario are attached to the event node by arrows that identify their role: The basic format is shown in Figure 10-9.

Thus, the sentences

> **Patrick is cooking supper for Cynthia.**

and

> **Cynthia's supper is being cooked by Patrick.**

are both diagrammed as the same scenario—that of Figure 10-10. Although the sentences look quite different from each other (they have different surface structure), they have the same meaning (the same deep structure), so they are drawn the same in terms of the information recorded in the memory. Moreover, there is the strong implication that the cooking is being done somewhere (a *location*), with something (an

FIGURE 10-9

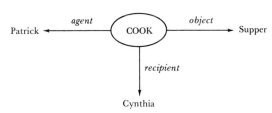

FIGURE 10-10

instrument), and at some specific time (*time*). These unstated concepts are simply added to the event node whenever they become known. No new structure need be created for them.

Other *cases* (that is what things like *agents*, *objects*, and *recipients* are called) that are useful are such things as

> *time:*   when an event occurs, often specified simply as past, present, or future, or conditional. (*Louise*kissed *Jack: Time is* **past**).

> *location:*   where an event takes place (*Bob hit Jack* **on the head:** *Location is* **head**).

> *instrument:*   the thing involved to cause the event (*Bob hit Jack on the head* **with a rock:** *Instrument is* **rock**).

> *truth:*   whether the event was true or false (*I* **did not see** *Dolores: Truth is* **not**).

A partial list of the cases used to describe events is given in Table 10-1. The event

> **Yesterday, at the beach with my new camera, I photographed the house on Ninth Street.**

is analyzed as

> *action:* photograph
>
> *agent:* I
>
> *object:* house on Ninth Street
>
> *location:* beach
>
> *instrument:* my new camera
>
> *time:* yesterday

This analysis can be broken down even further. The *object* can be analyzed as a *concept* (house) plus a *location* (Ninth Street). The *instrument* is a specific camera, namely mine. Hence, the final structure is as shown in Figure 10-11.

Now we have sufficient tools to add a rich set of events into our data base. Figure 10-12 serves as an illustration of many of the concepts that we have just discussed. It will also be useful later when we need a data base to use as an example. Figure 10-12 was constructed by taking the general information shown in Figure 10-3 and adding to it the information contained in the following sentences:

> **Luigi's is a tavern.**
> **Louise drinks wine.**

Bob drinks wine.
Mary spilled spaghetti on Sam.
Al owns Luigi's.
Bob likes Louise.
Al's dog, Blackie, bit Sam because he yelled at Mary.
Mary likes Bob.

These sentences (plus the information that is in Figure 10-3) allow us to construct a reasonably rich data base, as shown in Figure 10-12. You should make sure you understand this figure: it will be used later on.

Table 10-1   The Parts of an Event

Action	The event itself. In a sentence, the action is usually described by a **verb:**
	The diver was **bitten** by the shark.
Agent	The actor who has caused the action to take place:
	The diver was bitten by the **shark.**
Conditional	A logical condition that exists between two events:
	A shark is dangerous **only if** it is hungry.
	Linda flunked the test **because** she always sleeps in lectures.
Instrument	The thing or device that caused or implemented the event:
	The **wind** demolished the house.
Location	The place where the event takes place. Often two different locations are involved, one at the start of the event and one at the conclusion. These are identified as **from** and **to** locations:
	They hitchhiked **from La Jolla to Del Mar.**
	From the University, they hitchhiked **to the beach.**
Object	The thing that is affected by the action:
	The wind demolished the **house.**
Recipient	The person who is the receiver of the effect of the action:
	The crazy professor threw the blackboard at **Ross.**
Time	When an event takes place:
	The surf was up **yesterday.**
Truth	Used primarily for false statements:
	No special suits had to be worn.

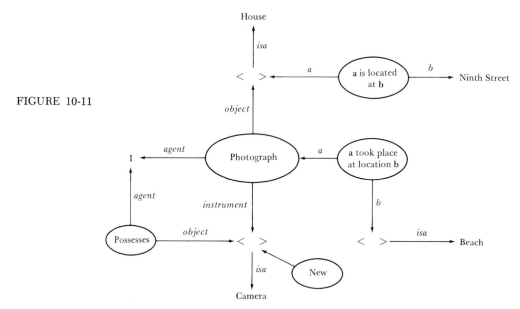

FIGURE 10-11

FIGURE 10-12

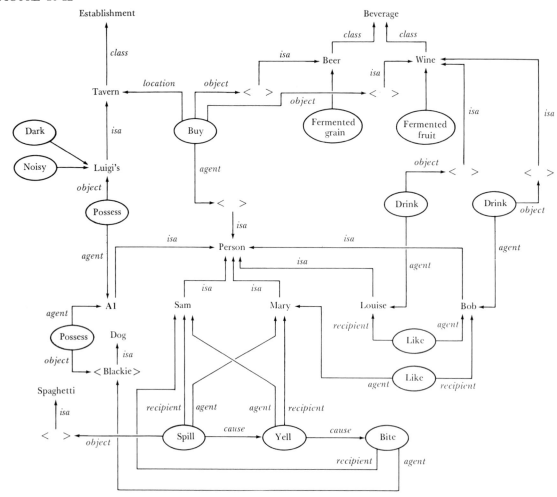

The representation shown in Figure 10-12 is not complete. It does not show the meanings of the actions such as *spill, yell,* and *bite.* It does not indicate fully where all the actions took place, and it does not show the exact time sequence. Presumably, full descriptions of semantic networks must show all these details (and they do—consult the references described in the Suggested Readings).

We now have the basic design for the data base underlying human memory. The memory system is an organized collection of pathways that specify possible routes through the data base. Retrieving information from such a memory is going to be like running a maze. Starting off at a given node, there are many possible options available about the possible pathways to follow. Taking one of these paths leads to a series of crossroads, each going off to a different concept. Each new crossroads is like a brand new maze, with a new set of choice points and a new set of pathways to follow. In principle, it is possible to start at any point in the data base and, by taking the right sequence of turns through successive mazes, end up at any other point. Thus, in the memory system all information is interconnected.

Figure 10-12 shows two different classes of information intermixed. First, there are the *definitions* of terms, such as parts of the diagram showing that a tavern sells beer, which is a class of beverage made from fermented grain. Second, there are the representations for specific *events,* for the episodes that have occurred—that Mary spilled spaghetti on Sam, causing Sam to yell at Mary, causing Blackie to bite Sam.

Episodic and semantic memory

The term *semantic memory* has been used to refer to the class of information characterized by the definitions that people have within their memory. The term *episodic memory* has been used to refer to the second type of information—information about particular *events* that have been experienced. The distinction between the two classes of information was made by Tulving (1972), and it has proven to be useful in discussing human memory. Both semantic and episodic memory are related; both are contained in the same data base of knowledge.

Semantic memory usually develops from information stored in episodic memory. Consider how the part of semantic memory that encodes the fact that dogs (and other animals) usually have tails might have developed. Your first experience with dogs might have come from a pet, or a stuffed toy dog. Then the tail might have simply been a convenient play object, something to be pulled. The concept of tail would be incorporated within the episodic memory for your experiences with tails. Over the years, however, you would have encountered many different dogs, many different animals, and therefore many different tails. Your knowledge of dogs and tails would become more general, less dependent upon particular instances. Gradually, you would come to realize that most dogs have tails, and the result would be semantic knowledge. Eventually, you would lose track of the fact that most of the information within semantic memory originated as particular episodes.

It is convenient to distinguish between semantic and episodic memory because the form and access of information is quite different in the two systems. Concepts in semantic memory are accessed readily, without apparent search or effort. In speaking or listening in your native language, the meanings of frequently used words and concepts come readily to mind, seldom with any feeling of effort or difficulty.

It is often difficult to remember episodic information. To recall exactly what events took place at Luigi's, or what was eaten for dinner exactly one week ago, takes effort, often accompanied by slow, deliberate searches of memory. Differences in the access of the two forms of memory make it convenient to speak of them separately at times, despite the fact that the two are intimately related, that one probably derives from the other, and that it is not possible to draw a sharp boundary line between the two different forms.

Using the data base   In the past sections we have described some of the basic principles underlying the representation of knowledge within the data base of long-term memory. Now it is time to discuss some of the ways in which the memory system is used.

Remember the overall structure of the memory system discussed in the previous chapter. There we suggested that there were three major components that had to be considered whenever someone actually used memory:

> the data base
>
> the interpretive system
>
> the monitor

Whenever an actual question is asked of memory, it is up to the monitor to guide the interpretive system in its examination of the data base. Basically, the monitor sets up the strategies that will be used to assess information, and the interpretive system actually performs the examination of the data base structures. Think of the interpretive system as sitting above the data base and examining it by following the relations between the nodes.

Viewing the data base. How much of the data can be seen at any one time by the interpretive process? So far, we have been drawing the networks so that everything is visible at once: It is not a difficult task to see just how things are interconnected. But it is quite possible that things are not so visible to the interpretive system. One way of thinking of this is to assume that the interpreter views the network by shining a flashlight at it. The only part visible is the part illuminated by the light. The question is, then, how wide is the beam of light produced by the flashlight? Figure 10-13 illustrates different views of the data base that result from different flashlight beam widths.

We can see from the diagrams that there are many possible levels of visibility possible. (Note that the flashlight analogy is not completely accurate in that we show the network as getting more or less visible in terms of the number of arrows and concepts that can be seen, not in terms of physical diameter.)

The limitations in what the human retrieval process can "see" at any one time may be really a limitation of **short-term memory**. It is very likely that short-term memory holds the information on which the interpretive process is working. The capacity of short-term memory is measured in items, in psychological units. Now we can speculate about the nature of that unit. Perhaps a unit in short-term memory is a node. It is quite likely that the restricted number of nodes that can be retained in short-term memory may put some basic limitations on the ability of the interpretive processes to search out and evaluate information stored in the data base (long-term memory).

Try this thought experiment. Consider the incident at Luigi's, described in Figure 10-12. Imagine the scene. Luigi's is a dark, dim tavern, with customers sitting in booths in dimly lit corners. The owner, Al, is a friendly, personable chap. His dog, Blackie, is always around. Suddenly, among a group of people in the corner, a scuffle erupts. Sam can be heard yelling at Mary. Blackie bites Sam, and there seems to be spaghetti over everything. Imagine the entire scene in your mind. Is the whole thing clear? If so, what kind of a dog is Blackie? How long is its tail? Now look at its collar. What do the identification tags dangling from the collar say?

Most people find that as they imagine the scene, there is a limit to how much detail can be brought in at once. Originally, when they imagined the scuffle at the tavern, they claimed it all to be sharp and clear in their minds. Yet, when they are queried about the details of the dress of any of the participants, the color or length of their hair, or even the details of the tavern itself, they discover that it really is not quite so clear. When you are asked to examine the dog, the image of the dog fills your conscious awareness, and the rest of the incident. while still there is some sense, fades from its central location in the thought process. This can go on indefinitely. When you are asked to examine the dog in detail, it too turns out to be not so clearly noted. Examining the collar causes the rest of its body to fade from view. In fact, examining the tags hanging from its collar causes the collar itself to disappear into a haze.

Interpretive process

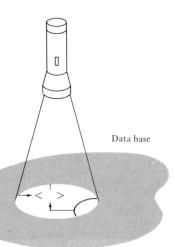

Data base

FIGURE 10-13

A medium beam

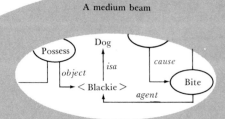

The narrowest beam

A reasonably wide beam

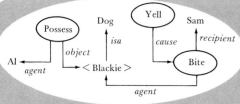

A narrow beam

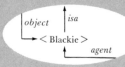

It is tempting to argue that we can bring only a limited number of nodes into the short-term memory at one time (alternatively, into the illumination afforded by the flashlight). Thus, there is probably a central secondary node that refers to the entire incident at Luigi's (not shown in the diagram). This can be examined, but it is a general concept of the event, and it does not contain any details. When any of the details are followed, such as the node that represents any of the individual participants, then the other nodes that represent the details of the event are no longer visible. Although not shown in the diagram, presumably Blackie points to a complex set of interrelations that define the appearance and exact details of its existence as a dog. When any of those nodes are examined with care, then the ones around it are no longer quite so visible, and the ones distant (such as Blackie's role in the incident at Luigi's) are far removed from consideration.

Generalization. Another important aspect of the use of memory is the generalization of knowledge. Here, the interpretive system plays a critically important role. Figure 10-14 shows a picture of the concepts that might be encoded within the data base of someone's memory. To simplify the discussion, no events are portrayed, simply concepts related to **Mary, Bob,** and **Sam.**

Given the kind of information shown—that **Mary** is **short** and **friendly,** that **Bob** is **red-haired** and **radical,** and that **Sam** is **smart**—what kind of conclusions can be drawn by thinking about the relationships that exist? After all, as more and more information accumulates about concepts, it is perfectly reasonable to stop now and then to ask what has really been learned.

Query: **Tell me about person.**

For this query, the memory system should respond with a list of people, and then the properties of those people. But in the process,

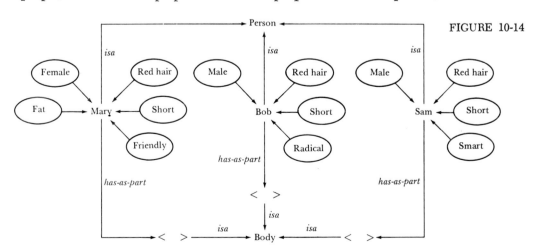

FIGURE 10-14

it might learn some interesting things. For example, consider this hypothetical output from the interpretive processes:

> Mary, Bob, and Sam isa person. Mary is friendly, fat, and short. Mary has red hair. Hmm, Bob has red hair. Sam has red hair. All persons have red hair. Bob is short. But look at this. Bob, Mary and Sam are short. All persons are short. . . .

From the information stored in this data base, **all persons** are short, red-haired, and have a body. Thus, the concept of **person** can be generalized by putting together common information.

The system for generalizing is rather simple. First, examine all instances of a concept for information held in common. Whenever the same information is found stored at all concepts, generalize the knowledge of these concepts. Do all people have bodies? The data base only has three examples of people, and each of them does indeed have a body. The obvious thing to do is to add the property of body to a common location, as the information **person has body.** When we do this we get the generalizations shown in Figure 10-15.

FIGURE 10-15

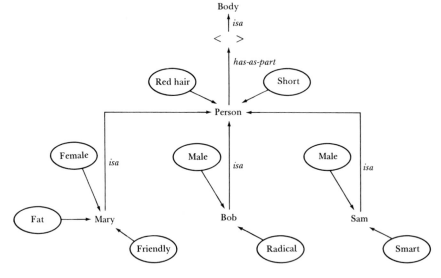

These generalizations of Figure 10-15 are peculiar: All people have red hair, are short, and have bodies. We would agree with the last, but not the first two. But, in part, this is simply because the memory that is illustrated only knows three people. You disagree that all people have red hair, but this is because you have encountered hundreds or thousands of people, and many of them did not have red hair. For the system illustrated, having red hair and being short is just as accurate a characterization of people as is the fact that they all have a bodies.

We have now explored some of the varieties of information stored within human memory, talked of some of the complexities of the use of memory, and talked of the variety of informational storage that might apply to the way things are represented within memory. The structure of memory discussed here has emphasized its dynamic and integrative nature. The system is continually modifying itself through active interaction with its environment. Thus, our understanding of a concept continues to be elaborated and embellished, even though the concept may never directly be encountered again. Such an evolution is a natural property of the type of memory system we have been examining. As more information about the world is accumulated, the memory system's understanding continues to grow and become elaborated. As an automatic by-product of this changing structure, our knowledge continually changes.

The continual evolution of the stored knowledge within the memory system has very profound effects on the way that new information is acquired. It suggests that there must be a tremendous difference between the way a message is encoded into a child's memory and the way the same information is encoded by an adult. For children, each concept encountered has to be built up from scratch. A great deal of learning must take place during the initial construction of the data base: understanding is only slowly elaborated as properties are accumulated, as examples are learned, and as the class relations evolve. At first, most of the concepts in memory will only be partially defined and will not be well integrated with the other stored information.

Later in life, when a great deal of information has been accumulated and organized into a richly interconnected data base, learning should take on a different character. New things can be learned primarily by analogy to what is already known. The main problem becomes one of fitting a new concept into the preexisting memory structure: Once the right relationship has been established, the whole of past experience is automatically brought to bear on the interpretation and understanding of the new events.

For models of this type, the development of individual differences and idiosyncratic systems should be the rule, rather than the exception. Understanding evolves through a combination of the external evidence and the internal operations that manipulate and reorganize the incoming information. Two different memories would follow exactly the same path of development only if they received the identical inputs in the identical order and used identical procedures for organizing them. Thus, it is extremely unlikely that any two people will evolve exactly the same conceptual structure to represent the world they experience.

Be careful to note what is at the basis of this idiosyncratic development. We expect that both the basic structure of memory and the processes for manipulating and reorganizing information are similar from individual to individual. However, even though this basic machinery is the same, its operation will not necessarily generate the same memory products. What people believe depends on what they have experienced and what sequence of inferences and deductions has been applied to the stored information. Even very subtle differences in the environment can produce different memory products, despite the fact that the underlying machinery for interpreting and remembering information may be common to all people.

The possibility that a basic set of processes can be used to deal with a variety of environmental contexts is, of course, a very adaptive feature of the memory system. But we might expect that the flexibility with which it can deal with new information would continuously change as the structure is built. It is seldom that an adult encounters an entirely novel event—one that is totally unrelated to existing conceptual structure. Almost everything that is experienced can be related to what has been encountered in the past. Even when one experiences clearly discrepant information, the conceptual structure is made up of such a complex and interdependent set of relationships that it resists revision. Thus, an adult is more likely to reject a discrepant input or change its meaning than to modify or change beliefs. With children, the conceptual structure is not nearly so elaborate or so highly interconnected as that of adults. New experiences can be taken in stride, since contradictions seldom arise.

Perhaps the most interesting of the areas left unexplored is the interactive aspect of the human mind. People ask questions: They explore their own knowledge, they read, think, daydream, and act. The model we have described here hints at these processes, but it does not do full justice to them. We have suggested some ways by which the memory system might ask for confirming evidence about the deductions and inferences it makes, but we have only scratched the surface of this very important area. The main problem at the moment is that there are no systematic tools for analyzing the natural exploratory behavior of people at work and play. But a start has been made.

PROTOTYPES   A problem with the semantic memory structures that we have just been discussing is that all instances of a class are defined in much the same way as one another. In principle, this is a good idea. Some simple observations of people's knowledge structures, however, reveal problems. For example, if we ask people to respond *true* or *false* to each of the following statements as quickly as possible, we get different times for the different statements:

> **A canary is a bird.**
> **An ostrich is a bird.**
> **A penguin is a bird.**

Everyone seems to respond *true* to all these statements, but it usually takes much more time to answer about the penguin and ostrich than about the canary. These results pose a problem. The fact that people can answer the questions properly indicates that they have information about all of the birds within their memory structures. But why, then, is there a difference in decision time?

According to the principles that we have just been studying, the three different birds are represented in the data base something like the structures shown in Figure 10-16. According to Figure 10-16, if asked whether a canary is a bird, all the interpretive system has to do is go to the memory location for the word "canary," see what node that corresponds to, and then see if that node *isa* bird. Indeed, going to the node for the word "canary" in the data base shown in the figure would direct the interpreter system to node *497. Node *497 does indeed have a relation labeled *isa* that leads to the node for "bird." Hence, the interpreter would conclude that a canary is a bird. In a similar fashion, the word "ostrich" would lead to node *1763 and the word "penguin" would lead to node *1428. Both of these starred nodes have relations labeled *isa* leading to the node for "bird." Thus, according to the diagram of Figure 10-16, it should take exactly the same amount of time to say that any one of those three names is an instance of bird.

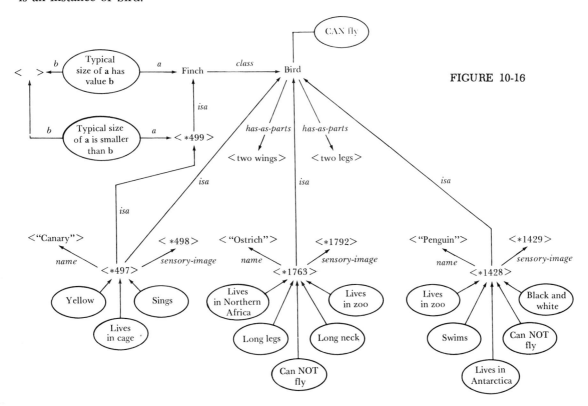

FIGURE 10-16

It seems quite clear that people do not answer these simple questions by searching for the *isa* link between nodes. In fact, if we simply think back and reflect upon our own mental processes, we can find some hints of the decision mechanism. A canary (or a sparrow, robin, or pigeon) is a reasonably typical bird. It is about the right size, it looks like a typical bird, and it does the things one expects of birds. But an ostrich and a penguin are not respectable types of birds. Why, they cannot even fly— what kind of a bird cannot fly? If we were to judge canaries and ostriches and penguins on how well they fit our conception of a typical, proto- typical bird, then we are not surprised to find canary fitting well and the others being discrepant. Perhaps we make the "true" and "false" judg- ment by comparing our idea of a bird with our knowledge of the par- ticular instances being tested: the more typical the instance, the faster the response.

Perhaps the memory representation for a bird consists of an example of a prototypical bird, perhaps by an image, perhaps by a list of the features commonly thought to be a part of birds. One theory suggests that there are two types of features: *defining features* and *characteristic features.* Defining features must be true of all instances of the class. Characteristic features help distinguish among the different varieties, and they need only be possibly true. Thus, for a bird, some defining features would be that it has wings, has feathers, lays eggs, and builds nests. In addition, it has a beak, two eyes, legs, and ears, and it flies. Characteristic features include such things as its size, color, call, and activities. For most people, the general concept of "bird" reminds them of something like a sparrow or robin. Hence, the closer the item that is to be judged to this proto- typical bird, the faster will be the judgment. An ostrich is just not a typical bird: it is too big, its legs are too long, and it does not have the proper shape or proper wings.

This picture of memory representation suggests that we remember con- cepts in terms of prototypes or typical instances. Thus, a typical animal for most people is something about wolf size, with four legs and a tail. This does not mean that when a person is asked to think of an animal that a wolf comes to mind. Certainly, when thinking of animal in general, one does not imagine a fully detailed image of a particular wolf, with grin- ning mouth, drooling tongue, and shaggy fur. The idea is that the repre- sentation of "animal" that is excited within memory is most likely to include features of a four-legged, wolf-sized mammal, and least likely to include concepts like wings or gills.

This is an easy point to demonstrate. As quickly as you can, say aloud YES or NO whether the following are *animals:*

COW
TAIL

CHAIR
LION
CAR
AMOEBA
GIRAFFE
PENCIL
LOBSTER

It is a crude experiment, for as you can readily imagine, both the particular order in which the words are presented and the level of experience you have with the task make a difference in the speed of the response. Yet you should have noted that you took longer with YES answers to *amoeba* than to *lion* and *cow* (assuming that you did say YES to an amoeba). An amoeba (or a grasshopper, spider, or lobster) is not like the prototypical animal, at least not to most people.

Whatever the interpretation one wishes to place on these observations, certainly the type of model we talked about for semantic networks cannot be the entire story. The interpretive system does not appear to determine whether an "amoeba" is an animal by looking at the node for "amoeba" and determining whether or not it is connected to the node for "animal" by the relation *class* or *isa*. Rather, it appears that the interpretive system looks at the node representing the concept and determines what features are stored with that node. Then the features are compared with the features for "animal": the more similar the features of the comparison node to the features at "animal," the easier the judgment.

Figure 10-17 shows what the memory structure might look like if we deleted the relations labeled *isa* and *class*. Now, to tell whether a canary, ostrich, or penguin is a bird, there is no choice but to compare the features at the nodes with the *prototype* node for "bird." According to the information shown in Figure 10-17, it is unlikely that the possessor of this particular data base would judge a penguin or an ostrich to be a bird. Presumably, most of us have richer information at our nodes, and so we are capable of answering the questions properly. Nonetheless, the penguin and the ostrich probably differ sufficiently from our prototype view of a bird that we take longer to admit that they really are birds.

The solution shown in Figure 10-17 is not really very satisfactory. The relations named *class* and *isa* are much too important to be discarded. They serve a variety of purposes, and it does not seem reasonable to discard them simply because of this one set of experimental findings. Nonetheless, the experiments are important and the question becomes how to keep the *class* and *isa* relations and also account for the experimental results?

Whenever different evidence seems to lead to opposing viewpoints, it is likely that the correct theory will be a combination of the conflicting systems. So it is in this case. It is still too early to know what the final

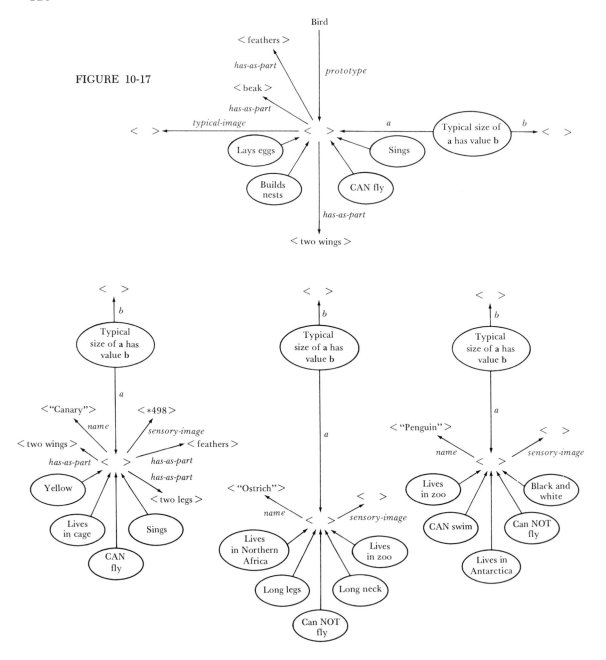

FIGURE 10-17

resolution of this particular discussion will bring—the work reported here is still in its infancy. One obvious solution is to suppose that the interpretive system does some tasks by comparing features, others by following *class* and *isa* relations. It appears that judgments about how typical an item is usually involve a perceptual task. Perhaps perceptual judgments are performed by feature comparisons while semantic judgments follow *class* and *isa* relations. This suggestion does not solve all the problems, but it does suggest why people tend to classify whales as fishes and bats as birds, even though they have been taught that whales are actually mammals and that bats are rodents. If perceptual features are used to make the judgments, then whales and bats get classified with fish and birds. If semantic information is used, they get classified correctly.

We see, therefore, that it is possible that the data base of memory can be used in many different ways. It can be viewed as a semantic network, where nodes represent concepts and actions, with the relations among the nodes creating an interconnected memory structure. Alternatively, the memory might be considered a collection of concepts, each associated with a list of features.

MENTAL IMAGES

We would like you to close your eyes and imagine yourself at the following imaginary concert (do not simply recall a real one). Imagine that you are sitting in the middle of a large auditorium with people all around you. The stage is ahead, slightly below the level of your seat. It is brightly lit, and the musical group is playing while standing. Now spend a few moments trying to imagine the scene.

Imagined scenes have much in common with real perceptions. In the concert scene that you just imagined, you probably had many details available to you. Despite the fact that the scene was imaginary, you could probably answer many questions about it.

How far were you from the stage?

How high above it?

Were you directly in front of the stage or off to one side?

How loud was the music?

How bright was the stage?

How many performers were there?

Were there microphones on stage?

Did all the performers hold their instruments in their hands?

Was there sheet music or not?

If there was a conductor, did you see a back or a front view?

How did you answer those questions? Did you have a vivid picture of the concert? Could you hear the music, see the people, see colors? Different people will have different impressions of what they did. Some people will have had visual and auditory images. Others will deny having any images at all. Yet most of you will be able to answer at least some of the questions, especially the first few.

Most people will admit to having some form of mental images, although there is wide variation among those images. Some people claim to have very detailed images, with color and sound, and sometimes odor and touch. Other people claim to have only vague, incomplete images, and sometimes deny the existence of any images. Visual and spatial images are the strongest for most people. Kinesthetic (motor movements) images are also usually fairly strong. Auditory imagery is not so common as visual imagery, and mental images of taste, touch, and smell are not so common.

What is an image? Is it like the real perception of something? Probably not. The normal individual does not confuse mental images with reality. Whenever there is such a confusion, it is classified as an abnormality, a hallucination. But the fact that hallucinations do occur—and with reasonable frequency—indicates that the perception of images might have a lot in common with the perception of reality, enough that it is possible to confuse the two.

An experiment Imagine an elephant standing against a blank wall. Now imagine a dog
on images   standing next to the elephant. Can you see the dog's ears?

Imagine a fly standing next to a blank wall. Now imagine a dog standing next to the fly. Can you see the dog's ears?

Kosslyn (1975) discovered that people took 200 milliseconds longer to evaluate properties of animals that were imagined standing next to elephants than properties of the same animals that were imagined standing next to flies. A dog next to an elephant is relatively tiny. A dog next to a fly is relatively large. Kosslyn reasoned that his experimental subjects formed mental images of the animals and then verified the existence of ears or other features by mentally looking at the image for the features, as in Figure 10-18.

These results suggest that we form mental images in a restricted space. That is, it is almost as if we have a fixed-size screen in the head, and if we put two animals on the screen to scale, one an elephant, the other a dog, then the elephant will fill up the screen and the dog will be small. But if the two animals are a fly and a dog, the dog will fill up the screen and the fly will be small. In the second case, with a large image of the dog, the ears would be easy to see. In the first case, the image of the dog would be relatively tiny and the ears difficult to see.

Kosslyn also varied the size of the mental image directly, by telling his subjects just how large to make their mental images (showing them four different sizes of squares, and instructing the subjects to make their imagined animals the same size as a particular square). The results are shown in Figure 10-19.

FIGURE 10-18

FIGURE 10-19

Graph from Kosslyn (1975).

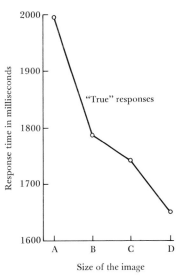

Do we store images in the head—do we have pictures stored in memory? Hardly. We do not have real sounds cooped up inside the brain, nor actual pictures, smells, and tastes. But clearly we recognize tastes and smells and sounds (to say nothing of the sights of friends and belongings). So we must have some representation of those perceptual experiences stored in a manner that the pattern recognition mechanisms can make use of them. These perceptual representations are probably used in a wide range of situations, from the simple experiments in imagery described here to all mental processing. We need to imagine the rhythm and sounds of utterances to compose poetry, and to imagine tastes to do creative cooking. We need to imagine sounds to compose music. We need visual images to do visual tasks and motor images to do motor skills. When the tennis instructor says to keep the arm parallel to the ground, you need to be able to imagine the appropriate set of motions in order to do that properly.

Are images stored in the head? Yes and no. What is an image? Is it a photograph or a tape recording? If so, the answer is no—we do not appear to have photographs or recordings within memory, fortunately. Can you imagine trying to find something if we had accurate tape recordings of all the sounds we had ever experienced? Imagine that you actually had mental recordings of all the conversations and lectures you ever heard. The problem is not to find room; there is plenty of storage space in the brain. The issue is one of organization. If the brain did contain an accurate recording of all the sentences ever heard, how would you ever find the one you wanted? Then again, how would you ever visualize an imaginary tiger if all you had stored were photographic-like pictures of tigers?

No, we do not have accurate pictures or tape recordings in the head. But clearly we have the information necessary to recreate the sights and sounds of our experiences to a degree sufficient to let us recognize those sights and sounds when we again experience them, and to let us manipulate mental images of them when we need to. The examples of semantic networks presented in this chapter were designed to account for the organizational properties of the memory system, to show how information might be classified and related to each other. Thus, if you wished to retrieve an image of a tiger, you could start with animals and trace your way through the *class* and *isa* relations until you found the information sought. If you wanted an animal with stripes, you could start both at stripes and at animals, seeing what memory structures had stripes applied to them while also having the appropriate relationship to animals. In either case, the organizational structures of memory are critically important in allowing you to find the information that was sought.

Just how information is represented within the data structures of human memory remains a mystery. In this chapter we have introduced you to one of the major theoretical attempts to specify the representation of knowledge. In addition, we have discussed a few of the outstanding issues involved in the representational discussions, especially the problems of prototypes and of mental images.

The information in this chapter is not the final answer. There will be many new ideas developed in the future that will expand our understanding of the human memory system. The direction of research at the current time in the field of cognitive psychology is heavily influenced by these methods of representing information, and the journals and conventions are filled with debates about the merits of images versus networks. The field of cognitive science is of critical importance, and research efforts are producing exciting developments.

A FINAL COMMENT

In this chapter, the following terms and concepts that we consider to be important have been used. Please look them over. If you are not able to give a short explanation of any of them, you should go back and review the appropriate sections of the chapter.

REVIEW OF TERMS AND CONCEPTS

Semantic networks
  class
  property
  example
  record
  nodes
  pointers
  labeled relations
  generic definition
  instance
  relation labels
    isa
    class
    applies-to
    sensory-image
    motor-control-image
    has-as-parts
  prototypical knowledge
    default values
    propositions

Terms and concepts you should know

primary concepts

secondary concepts

surface versus deep structure

case relations, the most important being:

    agent

    object

    recipient

    time

    instrument

    location

Episodic and semantic memory

Generalization

The argument for prototypes or features: how a network can be used if it
does not have *isa* and *class* relations

Mental images

SUGGESTED
READINGS

The representation of knowledge is an important issue, both to those who
are interested in psychology and also to those interested in the construction of computer systems and the study of artificial intelligence. Here,
several good books exist. The two standard works in psychology on semantic networks are the books by Norman, Rumelhart, and the LNR
Research Group (1975) and the book by Anderson and Bower (1973).
The former book is (obviously) most closely related to the approach
described here, but the serious student will have to consult both. Kintsch's
(1974) book takes a slightly different approach, but it is a very important
contribution to the study of these issues. The books edited by Bobrow
and Collins (1975) and by Cofer (1976) present important collections
of papers on topics relevant both to psychology and to artificial intelligence. Bobrow and Collins is more relevant to artificial intelligence, Cofer
more relevant to psychology.

Rosch's studies of the representation of information are quite important.
Perhaps most important for the issues discussed in this chapter is her
analysis of *basic categories* (Rosch et al., 1976). Other papers of hers that
are useful to examine are Rosch (1973a, 1973b, 1975). Tulving (1972) is
the source of episodic memory. Further studies of semantic networks and
a few, closely related means of describing the representation of knowledge within human memory can be found in the papers by Collins and
Loftus (1975), Rips, Shoben, and Smith (1973), and Smith, Shoben, and
Rips (1974). Rumelhart and Ortony (1976) summarize a number of
these issues.

Just how images of sights and sounds are represented within memory
is not known. Palmer (1975) speculates on some of the issues. Paivio's

book (1971) and paper (1975) discuss the ideas of imagery, and the paper by Pylyshyn (1973) argues against the storage of uncoded images. To get some insight into the fierceness of the arguments, see Kosslyn and Pomerantz (1977). Probably the easiest way to get into these issues is through the chapter on the representation of information in Norman (1976).

As you might imagine, studies of how information is represented within the mind are of fundamental importance. The area of study is fairly new, however, and although it has been growing rapidly, the problems are so complex and the tools that we have to use so modest that progress has been slow. You can expect the coming years to bring new developments. So, skim the major journals in the field. The ones most likely to cover issues about representation are the theoretical journals: *Cognition, Cognitive Psychology, Journal of Cognitive Science,* and the *Psychological Review*. In addition, there will be new books.

11 The neural basis of memory

PREVIEW

This chapter continues the examination of memory, this time emphasizing the neurological basis of memory. Because we still do not know much of the brain structures concerned with the higher-order processes of thought and memory, this chapter must be viewed as just a beginning to the formal study of these processes.

We start with a discussion of the brain mechanisms that might be responsible for memory and then move to a discussion of neurological findings relevant to memory studies. Studies of patients with memory difficulties have provided a good deal of valuable information about memory. The studies of electroconvulsive shock therapy and the stories of the patients H.M. and N.A. help us to reach a better understanding of the properties of the nervous system. After reading these sections, it would be a good idea to sit back and consider the implications of the phenomena. Most important, attempt to tie in the discussion of the role of the interpretive system and the monitor from Chapter 9 to the difficulties in retrieval faced by these patients.

The chapter concludes with a special topic, one not directly related to the study of memory: specialization of the hemispheres. The brain is approximately symmetrical, with the right half being almost identical to the left half. It is thought that the two halves of the brain perform different functions, each half specializing in different aspects of behavior. In particular, the left hemisphere (for most people) is thought to control language. We examine some of the evidence for this specialization of brain function in the latter part of the chapter. Nobody really knows the full extent of brain specialization. Some of the issues raised in this section cannot yet be resolved. Further discussion of the implications of the specialization will occur in Chapter 15, where we discuss the mechanics of thought.

In reading the section on the control of brain function and the roles played by the two halves of the brain, ask yourself how the brain can operate with two different processing systems. How does the left half of the brain know what the right half is doing? Does it matter? Why would the brain have evolved in this fashion? Does it really make sense that the two halves of the brain might control different modes of thought? If so, where do you remember things? If both halves of the brain think about the same things (but in different ways), then both need access to the same memory records, to the same experiences and knowledge. Do we have two memory systems, one for each side of the brain, or do both halves have equal access to the same memory structures? The last section of the chapter is very much like the standard cliché that can be found at the end of many scientific articles in the technical journals: these studies raise more questions than they answer.

STORING INFORMATION

Despite years of research, much of the brain remains a mystery. An anatomical examination of the brain shows that it is divided into a number of distinct regions. Seen from the top, the human brain appears as two masses of convoluted tissue split down the middle. The two halves are called the *hemispheres, left* and *right.* Together they form the *cortex,* the most advanced part of the brain (sometimes called the *cerebral cortex*).

FIGURE 11-1

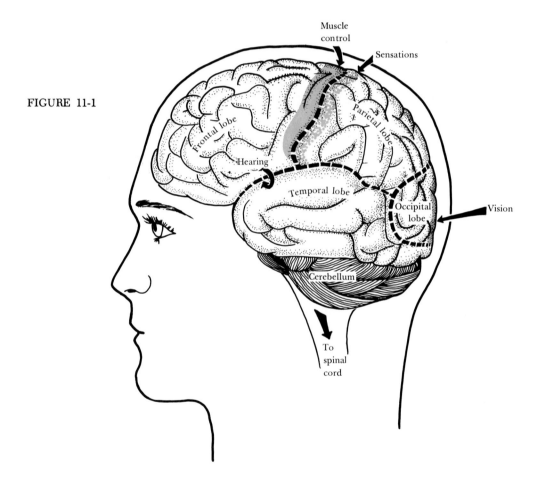

The different sections do differ anatomically so they have been given different names. The front parts are called the *frontal lobes,* on the sides are the *parietal* and the *temporal lobes* (actually tucked under somewhat), and to the rear are the *occipital lobes.* The brain is symmetric and so there are two each of these lobes—one on the left hemisphere, one on the right. (As with the rest of the body, the symmetry is not exact. The left half of the brain is usually slightly larger than the right, just as the right hand and foot are often slightly larger than their mates.)

Some structural or chemical changes in the brain must occur as a result of the acquisition of new knowledge. Somehow, cortical neurons alter their reaction patterns to the external events the organism comes to recognize and remember. There are a number of popular theories of how this comes about, all of them highly speculative. We are a long way from having a truly accurate or complete description of the way in which the nervous system stores information. The theories are important, even if incomplete, for they serve as useful guideposts as we follow the trail of the memory system.

There is reasonably good agreement that permanent storage of information takes place either through chemical or structural changes in the brain. There is little or no disagreement that the immediate, ongoing activities of thought, conscious processes, and the immediate memories—sensory information store and short-term memory—are mediated through electrical activity. This means that the two processes must make contact with one another: Somehow the chemical or structural changes in the brain must affect the electrical activity. Moreover, if the immediate memory systems are the result of electrical activity, then we should be able to show that neural circuits can indeed be constructed that have the capability of acting as a memory. Let us start the study of the memory systems with the problem of devising circuits that remember.

Neural circuits of memory

The main requirement of a memory circuit is that the effects of an input persist after the input has ceased, since this is the definition of memory. But more is required. A memory circuit must be selective. It should show a preferential response to a certain pattern of inputs and little or no response to other patterns. We begin by putting together some simple circuits that can qualify as memory. But first, for those readers who have not worked through Chapter 7, a paragraph of review of neural circuits.

Figure 11-2

A review of neural circuits. The electrical impulse conveyed by the *neuron* travels from the *cell body* through the *axon* to the next cell body. The place where the neural axon makes contact with the cell body is called a *synaptic junction.* There may be many thousands of synaptic junctions on a single cell body. In diagrams, the basic neuron is represented by a circle and a line. The circle is the cell body, the line an axon connecting the neuron to others. There are basically two kinds of synaptic connections, *excitatory* and *inhibitory.* An excitatory connection means that if a signal (neural impulse) comes along an axon to an excitatory connection, it tends to make the neuron on the other side of that synapse respond with its own neural impulse. That

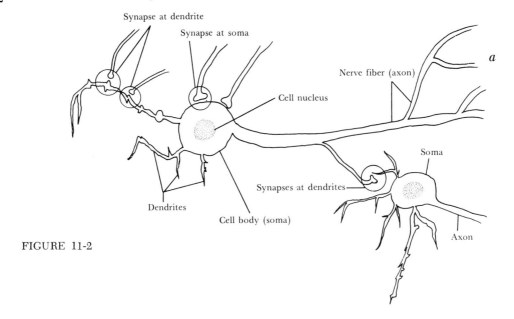

Synapse at dendrite

Synapse at soma

Nerve fiber (axon)

a

Cell nucleus

Dendrites

Synapses at dendrites

Cell body (soma)

Soma

Axon

FIGURE 11-2

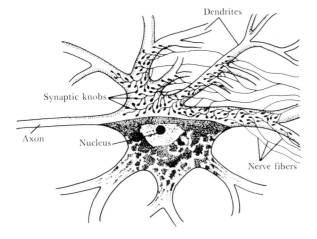

Dendrites

b

c

Synaptic knobs

Axon

Nucleus

Nerve fibers

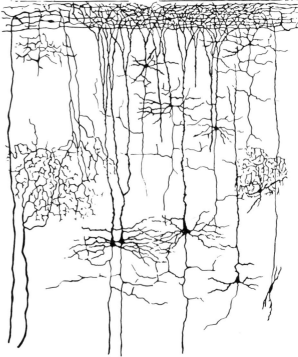

These figures are after J. C. Eccles, Possible ways in which synaptic mechanisms participate in learning, remembering and forgetting. In D. P. Kimble (Ed.), The anatomy of memory. Vol. I, Palo Alto, California: Science and Behavior Books, 1965.

is, an excitatory connection tends to make the new neuron *fire*. An inhibitory connection tends to prevent firing. In the nervous system, a rather large number of impulses arriving at excitatory connections may be required to make a cell body fire: One is seldom sufficient. For the present analysis, however, we shall suppose that a single neural response arriving at an excitatory synaptic connection can make the new cell respond. Although this is inaccurate, it is only wrong in terms of numbers. The logic is sound and the story is easier to follow in terms of single neural impulses.

FIGURE 11-3

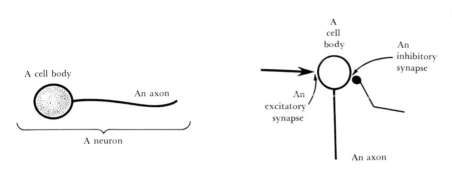

Consider the problem of maintaining a memory for a sensory input. Suppose that the printed capital letter **A** has been presented, that the various stages of pattern recognition have taken place, and that the **A** has been recognized. There are at least three different ways in which the nervous system could respond to the presence of the **A**.

There could be a *unique cell* that encodes the presence of each item, so that whenever the pattern recognition system discovers the presence of **A**, the unique "A" cell responds.

There could be a *unique pattern* of cells that responds to each item, so that the presence of an **A** is designated by the unique configuration of neural cells that respond.

There could be a *unique code* for each item, so that the letter **A** is specified by a special pattern of neural firings.

Whichever of these possible codes is present, there still must be some way of **remembering** that the **A** occurred. Let us examine one simple scheme for constructing a memory.

Physiological mechanisms of short-term memory. The effects of neural activity upon a nerve cell often outlast the duration of the activity. Current research on the mechanisms responsible for short-term memory has tended to concentrate upon studies of the neural sensitivity of the single cell. Some events are known to depress the sensitivity of a cell for

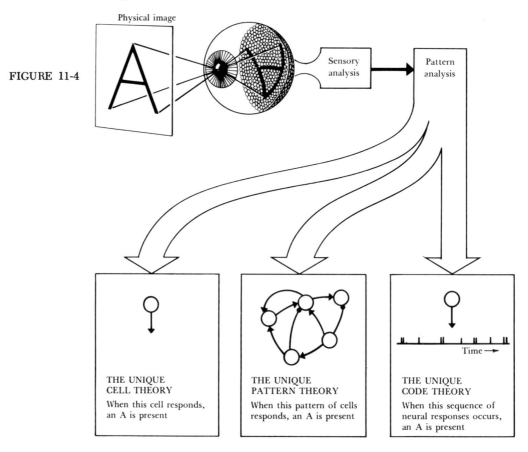

FIGURE 11-4

Physical image

Sensory analysis

Pattern analysis

THE UNIQUE CELL THEORY

When this cell responds, an A is present

THE UNIQUE PATTERN THEORY

When this pattern of cells responds, an A is present

THE UNIQUE CODE THEORY

Time →

When this sequence of neural responses occurs, an A is present

periods as long as an hour. During this time stimuli that would normally cause the cell to generate neural impulses do not do so. Other events can increase the sensitivity so that events that would not normally lead to the generation of neural impulses will now do so.

The animal called the "sea hare" or *Aplysia* is a type of snail (with no shell) that inhabits tidepools. The typical animal is between 5 and 12 inches long and has a siphon that takes in water and passes it through the gills. If the siphon is disturbed by being touched or squirted with water, the gills will retract. If the disturbance is repeated over and over again, the animal will *habituate* to the disturbance and will no longer withdraw the gills. The term "habituation" means a decrease in a response with repeated stimulation. Once the gill withdrawal is habituated it stays habituated for several minutes, even in the absence of further stimulation. It is possible to *dishabituate* the response: squirting water on the *neck* will cause gill withdrawal even on a habituated animal.

Habituation and dishabituation of *Aplysia* may seem like a strange place to begin the search for memory mechanisms in humans, but there are some good reasons for looking at phenomena such as these. The primary justification is based on evolutionary principles. The neural components of the nervous system of different animals are strikingly similar. Thus, the operation of nerves, including their structure, synaptic mechanisms, and biochemistry seems to be much the same in both invertebrate and vertebrate nervous systems. It is quite possible that the behavior seen in lower animals is the precursor to the more complex behavior of higher animals. In addition, *Aplysia* represents an ideal candidate for neural research. Its neurons are relatively easy to work with. One of the nerve cells is actually large enough to be seen with the unaided eye— about 1 mm in diameter. It is possible to identify and name the individual neurons so that scientists around the world can all find and work with the same neurons. *Aplysia* is a simple enough animal that it may eventually be possible to diagram the entire neural system and understand in detail how it works.

Figure 11-5 shows the specific neural connections in *Aplysia* from the sensory neurons to the motor neuron that controls the gill withdrawal (the neuron that neural scientists call L7). We can tell where habituation occurs. Touching either the siphon or the region called the purple gland of *Aplysia* causes gill withdrawal. Repeated touching of the siphon will habituate responses to the siphon. But when the purple gland is touched, the gill will withdraw again. The same is true in the other direction: habituating the gill withdrawal response to touching the purple gland does not habituate responses to the siphon. This means that the habituation is not taking place within or after L7. The habituation must occur prior to the synaptic junctions on L7. If it were L7 that habituated, then habituation to stimulation of either the siphon or the purple gland would also cause habituation to the stimulation of the other. It does not. Now look at dishabituation. When you touch the neck or head region of a habituated animal, the result is dishabituation of both the purple gland and the siphon. Evidently, the stimulus that causes dishabituation increases the sensitivity of all synapses, thus overriding any habituated synapses.

The changes in sensitivity seem to result from changes in the chemical composition at the synapses, either on the outside of the neuron (presynaptic), or just inside the neuron, possibly at the neural membrane itself (postsynaptic). One possible mechanism for the increase in synaptic efficiency has to do with the rapid flow of sodium ions into a neuron with each neural impulse, and the slower pumping action required to get the positive sodium ions out of the cell again. These ionic changes affect electrical potential at the cell membrane, which can act together with a regulation of calcium ion activity to improve the release of transmitter substance across the synaptic gap.

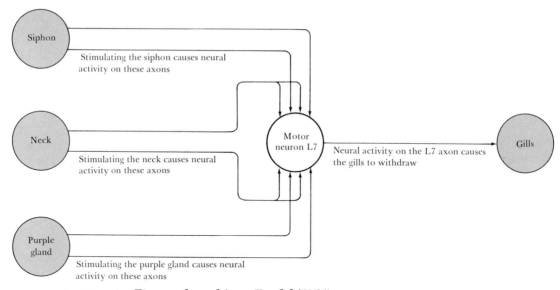

FIGURE 11-5   *Figure adapted from Kandel (1974).*

The details of the mechanisms are important, but not relevant for our purposes. The important result for us is that these mechanisms provide candidates for the temporary maintenance of neural excitation or depression at single nerve cells. A natural thought is that these temporary changes at cells might account for short-term memory phenomena. It is premature to draw conclusions about this possibility. Given the extreme complexity of the human nervous system with its billions of neurons, it is unlikely that a single simple mechanism will account for something as complex as short-term memory. Nevertheless, events as simple as those of a single cell can affect the behavior of simple organisms such as *Aplysia* and may be related to the more complex memory structures of the human.

Long-term memory.   There are numerous candidates for the neural mechanisms of permanent change in the human brain. Most interest today is centered upon investigation of the protein structure of neurons and synaptic junctions. Protein synthesis seems necessary for the formation of long-term memory. Drugs that inhibit protein synthesis also seem to disrupt the formation of long-term memories in the animals into which the drugs are injected. The memory information could be encoded within the protein molecules, or it could be encoded at the synaptic level, with the new protein making long-lasting changes to the synaptic efficiency. Protein synthesis requires time, in part because the molecules involved are very complex. Moreover, if the synthesis of protein occurs in the cell body, the newly synthesized proteins then have to be physically moved down the axon to the nerve endings where they might have some effect. There is indeed a constant movement of nutrients and chemicals down the axons, but the flow takes time. Several minutes might be required to move proteins to nerve endings.

A current view of the neurological basis of memory suggests that the initial specific neural excitation creates temporary changes at synapses. These temporary changes react in short-term memory. Possibly these are the processes discussed in the previous section. Long-term memory processes result from the creation of new proteins that modify the permanent responsiveness of the neuron. During the time that it takes to create the long-term changes, the information is maintained in the short-term memory (see Figure 11-6). Thus, both short- and long-term memory represent different phases of the activity that occurs at a neuron. Both memories might affect the very same structures, the only difference between the two being the permanence of the effect. Note that there is a time period during which only temporary (short-term memory) exists, and the long-term, permanent trace has not yet been established. The establishment of permanent traces from temporary ones is called *consolidation:* the time it takes to form the permanent traces is called the *consolidation* period.

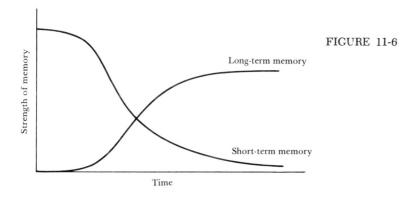

FIGURE 11-6

The description of the chemical nature of memory just provided is highly controversial. A large number of investigators are studying the problem, and new results get announced with increasing frequency. The nature of the consolidation process is under debate. One strange aspect of consolidation is that it does not appear to present any noticeable behavioral result. We do not notice any particular change in our memories as they are supposedly switching from one method of storage to another.

The roles of the biochemical processes are under continual scrutiny. Are memories stored at single cells? Do short- and long-term memories use the same synaptic junctions? Is long-term memory permanent? Are there perhaps several phases of long-term storage, each more permanent than the one preceding it? Are genetic mechanisms the same as memory mechanisms? The issues go on and on. Research into the physiological mechanisms of memory is currently an exciting developing field.

DISORDERS OF
MEMORY

Evidently, the short-term memory is necessary to hold information for the time period required for consolidation. During the period of electrical activity after the occurrence of an event, the memory for it becomes consolidated into long-term storage. Thus, it should be possible to interfere with the permanent memory of events by interfering with this electrical activity. This turns out to be true. The application of large amounts of electrical current to the living brain disrupts short-term memory.

Electroconvulsive shock

As the name implies, *electroconvulsive shock* (ECS) is the application to an animal of an electrical voltage of such high magnitude that it produces convulsions. In a typical experiment with rats, the ECS is applied to the animal shortly after it has made its response: the question under study is the effect of the ECS on the learning of the response.

The best experiments to date on ECS and learning have involved what is called the *pedestal* condition. Basically, the experimental task is this. A rat is placed on a raised pedestal that is too small for comfort. The grid below the pedestal is electrified. When the rat steps down, which is its natural response, it receives a mildly unpleasant shock to the legs. Under normal conditions, a rat exposed to this condition learns very quickly, usually on a single trial, to remain perched on the pedestal. But the application of ECS can change this result. Note that although ECS is an electrical shock, it is not the same one as the shock applied to the legs: it is only coincidental that electric shock is used both for the grid and for ECS. In the experiment, as soon as the rat steps down, it receives a small electrical shock to the feet. Then, with a minimal delay, it receives a huge electrical shock to the brain—the ECS treatment. Rats who receive the ECS immediately after stepping down do not seem to learn to stay on the pedestal. Thus, the ECS appears to destroy the memory for the foot shock. The longer the delay between the response of stepping down and the administration of ECS, the less likely the memory will be affected, and the less likely the animal will step down, despite the ECS.[1]

The pedestal experiment avoids several problems. Suppose a different task were studied: Suppose the animal were trained simply to go down a particular alley of a maze in order to obtain food, and suppose it were given ECS after each learning trial. It might very well avoid the alley containing the food because of the unpleasant experience of the shock. That is, it would not be possible to distinguish between an inability to remember where the food was and attempts to avoid the ECS shock. In the pedestal experiment, however, it continues to make a response that results both in a foot shock and ECS. If the rat remembered any un-

---

[1] There have been many studies of the relation of electroconvulsive shock to retrograde amnesia. A critical review and bibliography of these experiments can be found in the paper by Deutsch (1969).

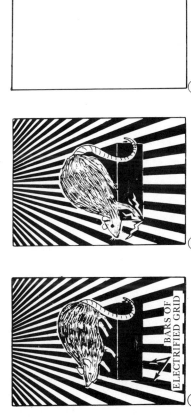

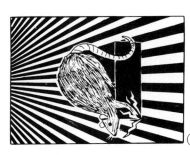

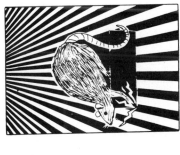

① Rat is placed on pedestal above an electric grid

② Rat steps down from pedestal and receives mildly unpleasant electric shock

③ Rat removed from pedestal

④ Rat replaced on pedestal

⑤ Rat does not step down

① Rat is placed on pedestal above an electric grid

② Rat steps down from pedestal and receives mildly unpleasant electric shock

③ Rat removed from pedestal and given electroconvulsive shock

④ Rat replaced on pedestal

⑤ Rat steps down

BARS OF ELECTRIFIED GRID

FIGURE 11-7

pleasantness due to the ECS it should show an increased reluctance to step off the pedestal. This does not happen, so the animal appears to forget both the unpleasantness of the shock as well as the unpleasantness of the ECS.

Amnesias   Electroconvulsive shock can disrupt learning in animals, and may create an amnesia in humans, at least for very recent events. These amnesiac effects are interesting in themselves and offer some guidelines for the study of memory. A common form of amnesia is called *retrograde amnesia*. It usually is brought about from some severe jolt to the brain, either by a fall, a crash, by being hit on the head or, of course, by electric shock. The victim of retrograde amnesia appears to forget events prior to the accident. Strangely enough, however, the victim does not forget events that occurred far in the past. Rather, it is as if there were a simple line in the memory extending in time. When the accident occurs, the line is erased, starting with the time of the accident and extending backward for a duration proportional to the severity of the wound.

As the patient recovers, old memories return first:

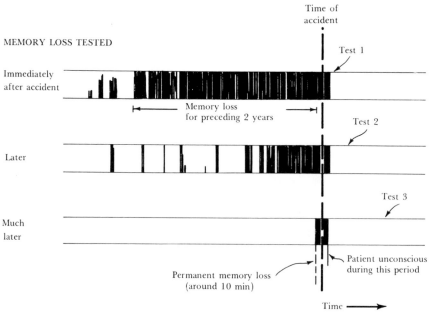

FIGURE 11-8   *Hypothetical recovery phase after retrograde amnesia. After data of J. Barbizet,* Human memory and its pathology. *W. H. Freeman and Company. Copyright © 1970.*

Thus, memories were not really erased: Rather, they were simply covered over. The process of recovery appears to be that of uncovering the memory line, starting with the very distant past and working its way forward to the present. How much is eventually recovered depends upon many factors, but almost everyone recovers. (The scenes you see in the movies in which memory is lost for years and years seldom happen, and when they do, they are likely to be caused by psychological factors rather than by physical brain damage. That is, the patient is deliberately—albeit, unconsciously—suppressing certain memories. They can all be retrieved after sufficient psychiatric treatment.) The last few minutes prior to the accident never seem to be recalled. It is as if these events were only in short-term memory at the time of the accident and never made it to long-term memory. This fact is often used as support of the time period required for the consolidation of a memory.

The pattern of forgetting and recovery in retrograde anmesia has some important implications concerning the way memories function. First, notice that only the memory for events that have occurred in the past is affected. Other kinds of stored information—information about the comprehension and use of language—remains intact. We will see later that some kinds of brain damage appear to affect only language functions without disrupting the memory for the past.

Electroconvulsive shock with humans. Electroconvulsive shock is used as therapy for mental disorders, especially in cases of extreme depression (when ECS is used as therapy it is called ECT—electroconvulsive therapy). It is not known exactly how shock treatments work to change mental functions. One recent hypothesis is that the shock itself does not directly have an effect, but that it stimulates chemical changes that do modify neural behavior. Whatever the effects of electroconvulsive therapy on mental disorders, the application of ECT does affect memory.[2]

Because ECT is currently in use as a therapeutic technique, it is important to determine its effect on such processes as memory. As a result, some valuable studies of the effect of ECT on memory have been performed on patients who were going to receive the ECT anyway.

How does one test a person's memory for long-past events? To do an adequate test one must know exactly what events the person has experienced. It is not adequate simply to ask a person what is remembered of

---

[2] We are not sympathetic with the use of ECT as a therapeutic treatment. The mechanism by which ECT operates is unknown. The effectiveness of the treatment is debatable. Moreover, it is known that ECT can produce changes in other systems such as memory. The reason ECT is used is that psychological and psychiatric clinicians have the problem of attempting to alleviate the real, difficult ailments of their patients. The patients are suffering now, they cannot wait for years until more effective chemical or psychological treatments are developed. ECT does appear to help some patients. Nonetheless, treatments that have the possibility of causing permanent, irreversible changes in brain functioning would appear to be very undesirable. Certainly, ECT should be restricted to one hemisphere at a time (unilateral ECT) for, as we discuss later, this causes much less disruption on memory than does ECT applied to both sides of the brain (bilateral ECT).

the past. Questions like this are guaranteed to provide misleading accounts of a person's memory, for it is not possible to test the accuracy of the report and it is not known how characteristic the things remembered are of the actual memories the person has.

Several techniques have been devised for these studies. The best method seems to be testing for the remembrance of pubic events. This way, it is possible to verify the results. Two sources of public events are the newspaper headlines for the years being tested and such widely experienced events as television shows.

Squire, Slater, and Chace (1975) have studied patients' memories for the names of television shows. They studied shows for which they could both determine the year in which the show's name was learned and also be reasonably sure that the show had indeed been noticed. They selected only shows that met the following criteria:

1. The shows had to be presented only during "prime time" (between 6 PM and 11 PM).
2. The shows had to be shown nationally.
3. The shows had to be shown for only a single season.
4. The shows must all have been watched by approximately the same percentage of viewers in the country.

This yielded the names of 80 programs that had been shown from 3 to 17 years prior to the memory test. The shows were randomly divided into two groups. Questions about one set were given to the patients before bilateral ECT and questions about the other set were given one hour after the fifth ECT treatment. (Treatment was given three times a week.) The results are shown in Figure 11-9. It is clear that the ECT affected the memory of names from 1 to 4 years prior to the treatment but had no effect any further back than that. Recovery of memory after this ECT treatment seemed to be complete. The lower part of Figure 11-9 shows the data reported for other groups of patients who were tested for their memory of the television shows 1 hour, 2 weeks, and 6 months after the completion of ECT. By 6 months, performance at all years was the same as for patients who did not have ECT.

Recovery from retrograde amnesia. Testing for the memory of television show names does not provide a careful test of memory, but it does provide a start. Moreover, these results are consistent with the general clinical literature on memory disorders. In both ECT and amnesia, the memory does gradually recover after the traumatic experience, so the information cannot have been wiped out by the shock, but simply made inaccessible. Thus the actual storage of information must be separate from the processes that retrieve stored memories.

Consider again the strange pattern of recovery from amnesia. Older memories are both the least likely to be lost and also the first to come

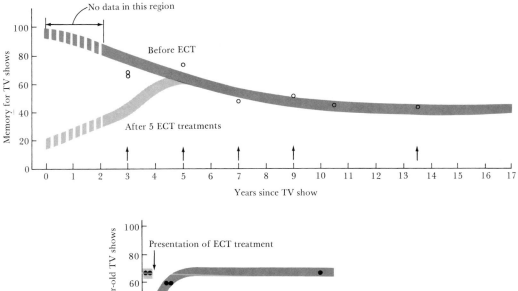

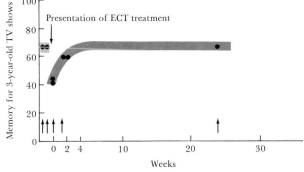

*Effect of ECT treatment upon memory for TV shows. Top graph shows   FIGURE 11-9
normal performance (heavy shading) and performance tested 1 hour
after ECT. Bottom curve shows hypothesized course of recovery of memory for names of 3-year-old TV shows. In both graphs, actual data are
available only for points indicated by arrows. Data are from Squire,
Slater, and Chace (1975).*

back. The recovery proceeds in time from the distant past to the present.
This suggests two things about the nature of memory. For one, information about **when** an event occurs must be an important cue to its subsequent retrieval. Otherwise, why would the recovery pattern be so
closely connected to the time an event happened? Second, this patterning
would tend to imply that older memories are stronger than newer ones:
Memory may somehow be automatically strengthened simply with the
passage of time. Otherwise, why should the oldest memories be most
resistant to the effects of traumatic shock and the recent memories the
most vulnerable? But this interpretation also goes against all common
sense. Certainly, we have greatest trouble in retrieving old memories;
if they are the strongest, should they not also be the easiest to use?

The very difficulty of getting to older memories may be the clue
to their apparent resistance to amnesias. Maybe the event only affects

stronger and more accessible memories. Maybe the trauma spreads from the present—certainly the most available of our memory experiences—to the past through the trail of the long-term memory structure. Is this because older memories are stronger, or simply because older memories are not as immediately accessible as new memories and, therefore, are harder to destroy? How does one tell?

The fact that the events of the last few minutes before the brain injury are never recovered is consistent with the earlier results concerning the effects of ECS.[3] Disruption of short-term memory seems to interfere with the storage of the events in long-term memory. This does not mean that so long as short-term memory is functioning properly, the information will be automatically recorded in long-term memory. We remember the events that just happened for a brief period of time, apparently without effort. But to record a more permanent memory of the events seems to require active effort. Something more than short-term electrical reverberation seems to be necessary in order for the storage of long-term information to take place.

The cases of H.M. and N.A. Consider the memory disorder suffered by a patient whom we shall call N.A. He was stationed at a rather boring military base, so, to pass the time, he used to fence. One day the protective tip of the foil used by his opponent came off, and N.A. was wounded; the tip of the weapon passed through the rather weak bone structure of the nostril and penetrated slightly into the brain. Several months after the incident, to the casual observer, N.A. appeared to be fully recovered. He walked about and acted normally. He could hold normal conversations. There was one striking feature about his behavior: He did not appear to be able to retain any new knowledge for more than a very short time.

A good illustration of his difficulties comes from this anecdote.

One of the psychologists studying N.A's memory difficulties was Dr. Wayne Wickelgren, then at the Massachusetts Institute of Technology. As Professor Wickelgren tells the story:

> I was introduced to N.A. in a small coffee room in the Psychology Department at M.I.T. The introduction went approximately as follows. N.A. heard my name and he said,
>
> "Wickelgren, that's a German name, isn't it?"

[3] There is a disconcerting discrepancy here between the times associated with short-term memory in animals and in humans. The ECS work with animals suggests that short-term memory lasts for as long as an hour. In some animal studies, anything retained during the first 24 hours after an event is considered to come from short-term memory. With humans, short-term memory typically refers to time measured in seconds. As we saw in Chapter 8, human short-term memory may persist only for a period of some 20 to 30 sec.

I said, "No."

"Irish?"

"No."

"Scandinavian?"

"Yes, it's Scandinavian."

After having about a five minute conversation with him, I left to go to my office for perhaps another five minutes. When I returned, he looked at me as if he had never seen me before in his life, and I was introduced to him again. Whereupon he said:

"Wickelgren, that's a German name, isn't it?"

"No."

"Irish?"

"No."

"Scandinavian?"

"Yes."

Exactly the same sequence as before. [Wickelgren, personal communication]

Although each conversation with N.A. appeared to be perfectly normal, whenever anything occurred to break the continuity of the session, then things started all over again as if they had never occurred before.[4]

What is life like for someone with this impairment? Another patient who has been studied extensively is H.M., who had severe epileptic

[4] Incidentally, this makes it very difficult to do experiments with these patients. One of us had been working with Professor Wickelgren studying short-term memory in Harvard and M.I.T. students. On one of N.A.'s visits to M.I.T., we thought it would be valuable to test N.A. on our experiments, since this would allow us to compare N.A.'s memory with that of our other subjects. We were never able to get beyond the instructions. N.A. would listen to our explanation of the experiment, nod his head and say, "Fine, let's go." Then we would turn around to start the tape recorder and other apparatus. Just as the first experimental material was to be presented, we would say, "Are you ready?" Invariably, the reply would be something like, "Ready for what? Do you want me to do something?" Later on, Wickelgren was more successful, but our initial difficulties illustrate the fact that, although such patients appear to provide extremely useful information about memory, it is extremely difficult to obtain the necessary data. In addition, they suffer from other problems caused by the neurological deficit, problems which are unrelated to memory but which also cause motivational and emotional difficulties in doing these studies.

For a more complete description of the tests one performs on such patients, see the series of six papers which appeared in *Neuropsychologia*, 1968, **6**, pp. 211–282, which discusses the two individuals, N.A. and H.M.

seizures. When he was 27 years old, he was no longer able to work, and because of his desperate condition, both of his medial temporal lobes were surgically removed. (These are the lower side lobes of the brain.) Afterward, his severe epileptic seizures disappeared, his IQ measured at 118 (compared with 104 before the operation), but he could not learn new things. Here is how some of the scientists who have studied H.M. describe his life:

> During three of the nights at the Clinical Research Center, the patient rang for the night nurse, asking her, with many apologies, if she would tell him where he was and how he came to be there. He clearly recognized that he was in a hospital but seemed unable to reconstruct any of the events of the previous day. On another occasion, he remarked, "Every day is alone in itself, whatever enjoyment I've had, and whatever sorrow I've had." He often volunteers stereotyped descriptions of his own state by saying it is "like waking from a dream." His experience seems to be that of a person who is just becoming aware of his surroundings without fully comprehending the situation, because he does not remember what went before. [Milner, Corkin, & Teuber (1968)]

Once again, the type of impairment suffered by these patients poses some interesting implications about memory. Their memory systems appear to work properly in every respect but one: the ability to use newly acquired information. The entry and retrieval of information from short-term memory seems to be unimpaired. The patients can hold a conversation and thus must be able to retrieve word meanings from their permanent memory. They are capable of using the system—they simply cannot use it for any new information.

This is an important distinction. How can a patient carry out the complex retrieval processes needed to comprehend and use language, yet be unable to use newly acquired material? Even H.M., the patient most severely affected by his disorders, had undisturbed comprehension of language: "He can repeat and transform sentences with complex syntax, and he gets the points of jokes, including those turning on semantic ambiguity." (Milner *et al.*, 1968).

Previously we found it was important to distinguish between the information that already resides in memory and the processes responsible for retrieving it. Remember also that we distinguished between maintenance rehearsal and integrative processes. These patients can set up temporary memories—both the normal short-term memory and whatever "working memories" are required to keep track of the information as it is retrieved from long-term memory. But the integrative processes responsible for making this temporary material permanent have been selectively disturbed. Evidently newly acquired information is not properly integrated with previously learned material.

What can these patients learn? The answer to this question is not easy to obtain. It is clear that some things can be learned: H.M. could not describe his job in the state rehabilitation center (mounting cigarette lighters on cardboard frames for display), even after 6 months of daily exposure. But he did become "dimly aware" of some things—his father's death, the assassination of President Kennedy. Does this slight residual memory capacity tell us something about the nature of the memory processes, or is it simply an indication that the neurological deficit is not complete? Patient N.A., for example, has continued to improve his memory ability slightly during the period following his accident, so that when one of us tested him at the University of California some 5 years after the incidents described earlier, he had improved somewhat in his ability to learn things. However, attempts to try to improve his memory still further through training in mnemonic techniques met with dismal failure. Patient H.M. has not improved in his memory skills with time.

Patient N.A.'s memory skills have continued to improve slowly. It is now over 10 years since the accident, and N.A. can drive by himself from his home to the hospital where he is being treated, a distance of approximately 30 miles. N.A. can therefore remember some things. But the drive is relatively simple, consisting of a straight trip south along major highways. He has been unable to learn more complex trips, such as the delivery route followed by his mother on her job.

When N.A. was tested on his memory for the names of television shows, his recall was normal for shows in the 1950s (25 years earlier), below normal for the 1960s (15 years earlier), and very bad for the 1970s, despite the fact that N.A. spends a good deal of time watching television. On tests for names of well-known people currently in the news, N.A. can get only 3 or 4 correct out of 20 names; normal people get 14 or 15. But these tests are for *recall*—N.A. is asked to generate the names himself. When tested for the *recognition* of names, he performs at a normal level.

Studies of patients with memory disorders are starting to reveal a pattern in the disruption. When the first studies were reported, it was believed that they indicated an inability to learn new material: to transfer information into long-term memory. Today, that interpretation is being increasingly questioned. Sensitive tests reveal some memory for recent information (usually recognition tests). Many scientists now believe it is the retrieval mechanisms that are the cause of the memory deficit, not the storage mechanisms.

There has been increasing interest in the study of people with amnesia. *Other studies* The most common cause of amnesia appears to be that resulting from the *of amnesia* *Korsakoff syndrome*, an ailment often encountered in the chronic alcoholic and thought to result from lesions in the brain (perhaps a result of vita-min deficiency from too large a dependency upon alcohol in the diet).

Korsakoff patients exhibit many of the symptoms described for N.A. or H.M. They seem unable to learn new information, but are quite able to talk about events that occurred prior to the onset of the amnesia. Even after years of treatment in a hospital, some cannot find their way down the corridor along a route followed daily.

Kinsbourne and Wood (1975) have suggested that amnesiac patients may be especially deficient in their retrieval of *episodic events,* but nor-mal in retrieving *semantic events* (see the distinction discussed in the previous chapter). Thus, in asking an amnesiac patient to give an inci-dent relating to particular words, they got back definitions or general uses of the words, not incidents. Normal subjects however, are quite capable of giving incidents. For example, when Kinsbourne and Wood attempted to get a description of an episode by asking a patient to give a personal memory for *flags* or *flag,* they got back only a general descrip-tion: *"Of course, I remember flags. Flags are for waving in parades, lots of times in parades."* When the patient was asked to state a specific mem-ory of any particular parade or flag that he had ever seen, he continued to say that he had seen flags in parades because they were very common things in his life. He was unable to describe any specific flag or parade that he had ever seen.

From all these studies, some of the general characteristics of memory are starting to emerge. For a brief time after their occurrence, events seem to persist in short-term memory. Long-term memory seems to re-quire time to be established. It is possible to disrupt long-term memory by electrical shock, chemical agents, and direct manipulation of the brain by physical shock, disease, injury, or surgery. These disruptions seem to affect the retrieval of information. As we saw in earlier chapters, the organizational properties of the memory system are critical, for with any large memory, the problems of getting access to the information far outweighs the problem of storage.

The disorders of memory seem to affect the integrative processes neces-sary for incorporating newly acquired material into the information already present within memory and the interpretive and monitoring processes necessary for guiding the retrieval of old information. Specific events seem lost for some types of ailments, recently experienced events seem unavailable for others. Information in semantic memory—the ge-neric definitions of concepts and the structures that allow the use of language and daily functioning in the world—appears least susceptible to damage. These patients can speak and understand speech. They can hold apparently normal conversations, provided the topic matter does not require them to retrieve material affected by their ailment. Such performance could not be possible without a considerable amount of normal functioning of the memory system.

Studies of neurological disorders are still in their infancy. The experiments are difficult to perform, and our knowledge is still sketchy. This is a valuable area for future research: studies of memory abnormalities may not only teach us more about memory but also lead to therapy for those who are afflicted.

Where in the brain do particular functions get performed? The first information regarding localization of brain function came from gross observations of patients with brain injuries. Thus, it was quickly noted that destruction of the areas to the rear of the skull caused visual deficits, while destruction of parts of the frontal areas tended to produce emotional and motivational deficits. In addition, destruction of the left half of the brain affected speech, especially for right-handed individuals. Hence the first general statements of localization of function.

LOCALIZATION OF BRAIN FUNCTION

But there is a complication. To the surprise of everyone, both people and animals can sustain huge injuries that destroy large portions of the brain without any apparent disruption in their memories. In fact, it seems to be almost impossible to eradicate specific memories absolutely once they have been established. About the only rule that emerges is a very general one: The greater the damage to the brain, the more it affects the patient.

This last statement, known as the *Law of Mass Action,* originates with the pioneering work of the psychologist Lashley (1931, 1950). Lashley sought the *engram,* the neural trace of a specific memory. He taught various tasks to his experimental animals, and then surgically destroyed parts of their brains, hoping to discover just which part contained the memory for the task. Lashley failed to find any evidence whatsoever that a specific memory is stored in a specific part of the brain. Instead, he found that the memory for the task was disrupted in a manner roughly proportional to the amount (weight) of the brain tissue destroyed—the Law of Mass Action.

This same result is mirrored by the types of memory losses typically encountered in patients who suffer from neurological damage, whether by accident or by surgery. It has never been possible to show that specific memories are destroyed. It is possible to lose memories of a restricted time period, as in amnesias, but a specific memory for a specific event, once well established, cannot be surgically erased. Granted, a patient may not be able to recall specific events, he may have great difficulties with his memory, being unable to distinguish new events from old ones, but there is no evidence that this is any more than damage to certain retrieval functions, making old recollections difficult to get at.

What is the general conclusion from this? One possibility is that memories are not stored in specific locations, but rather they are scattered about as patterns throughout the brain. In this case, any specific memory would involve large sections of the brain, with no one section being absolutely necessary, but the more sections that join in, the clearer the recollection. Thus, some scientists suggest that incoming events are impressed upon the continuing activity over much of the brain, and memory consists in an alteration of this complex diffuse pattern of ongoing activity.[5]

Despite Lashley's failure to find memories for specific activities located in specific parts in the brain, many neuroscientists do believe strongly that brain *functions* are specifically located. As we saw in the chapters on seeing and hearing, the sensory system projects onto well-specified, precise locations of the cerebral cortex. Any injury to the sensory areas produces precise, well-documented disturbances in sensory and perceptual functioning. This is true for all sensory systems, including touch, taste, smell, and kinesthetic senses. In a similar way, the motor control of muscles is also governed by precise locations in the cerebral cortex. Thus, the input and output controls of the body are controlled by precisely located, specialized sections of the brain. But as we move toward broader, more cognitive mechanisms, knowledge about their locations becomes poorer.

Much of our evidence on the localization of brain functions comes from the study of patients with neurological deficits, sometimes caused by genetic defects, sometimes caused by surgical procedures, but most often the result of accidental injury and of stroke (the destruction of brain tissue resulting from rupture or blocking the blood vessels that supply the brain). Different sites of injury lead to different deficits. There are specific types of language disorders (aphasias) and memory disorders (amnesias) resulting from specific areas of damage. The language disorders are particularly interesting, because initially they appeared to provide a useful research tool. Some patients lose the ability to name objects, others seem to have receptive difficulties. For example, some patients are unable to understand spoken language although their hearing appears to be normal and they can read, write, and speak. Others can write, but not speak (although perhaps they can sing), and so on. The

---

[5] Those of you who know about the way that a visual image is recorded on a *hologram* will immediately recognize the analogy. Unfortunately, the analogy is too simple. There are many more facts about human memory that must be explained than simply the Law of Mass Action. Hologram models have not yet been applied to sufficient numbers of problems of human memory to allow them to be evaluated.

search for a useful means of classifying aphasias has not been too success-ful, however. The disorders suffered by patients do not come in neat and simple packages. This is probably related to the fact that the brain dam-age itself is usually widespread, rather than limited to a single region. The most common brain damage is caused by an impairment in the blood supply—a stroke—and strokes tend to damage large areas of the brain that cut across regions thought to be specialized for different functions.

Perhaps the most important reason for the failure to find precise locali-zation for the performance of cognitive functions or for memory is that no single mechanism is critically responsible. Language involves the interactions of different knowledge systems: the acoustical and visual processing of incoming information; the control of the lips, tongue, vocal chords, and breathing muscles; the deciphering of the words; the under-standing of the language structure; the meaning of the words; the inter-action of the words with the situation; and pragmatic and social knowl-edge. Similarly, memory for a real event, such as eating a meal, involves memory for the activities, the sights, sounds, tastes, and movements, memory for the concepts and for the actions, memory for the individuals present at the event and for the topics discussed (and the topics dis-cussed may themselves involve other memories). It is no wonder that neither memory nor language can be localized at a specific, single place in the neurological brain tissue. Even if a specific part of the brain is damaged, human cognitive behavior is determined by such an interlock-ing structure of knowledge and mechanisms that there may be no notice-able deficit. When brain damage is severe enough to have a noticeable effect on cognitive performance, then it has probably affected a variety of functions.

The body is symmetrical. We have two arms, two legs, two eyes, and two ears. We also have two brains, or at least two halves that are almost exact duplicates of one another. Each half has its own centers for receiv-ing auditory, visual, and tactile information and for control of muscle movements. The two cortical halves of the brain communicate with each other by means of a massive set of nerve fibers called the *corpus callosum.*

Specialization of the two hemispheres of the brain

Figure 11-10

The symmetry in the anatomy of the two halves of the brain imme-diately raises the question of whether or not they could work inde-pendently of one another. Certainly, the anatomical evidence does not rule out such a possibility. Each sensory organ sends its information to both halves of the brain. But are there two separate memory systems? Does each half of the brain store the same information, providing re-dundancy in case of breakdown? Or do they divide the load, with one half doing some things and the other half others? Or, possibly, does one half loaf, doing little or no work, being completely superceded by the other, functional half? The answers to all these questions appear to be yes: a cautious and guarded yes, with if's, but's, and maybe's, but yes.

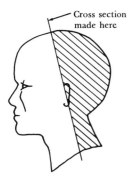

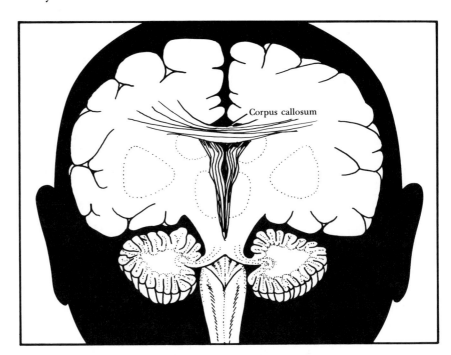

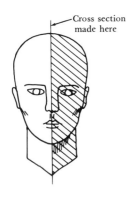

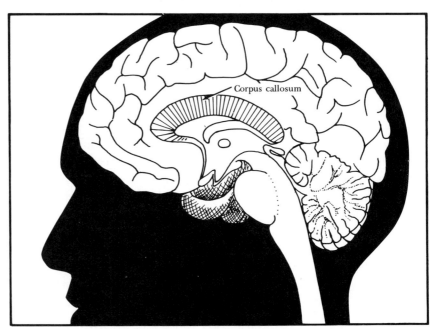

FIGURE 11-10

The visual system provides the best test of the function of the two hemispheres. With the visual system, everything at the left half of the retina gets sent to the left half of the brain. Everything on the right half of the retina gets sent to the right half of the brain. This is true of both eyes. (Remember that the lens of the eye reverses the image, so that when you look straight ahead, objects to the left end up on the right half of the retina and, thus, at the right half of the brain.)

Split brains in animals

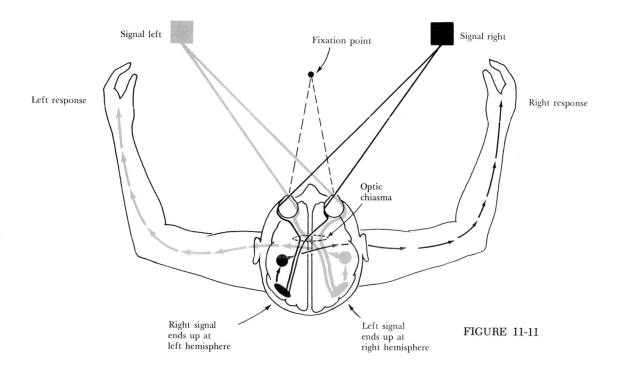

FIGURE 11-11

Yet, when looking straight ahead, there is not a vertical line going down the center of the field of view. How is the information arriving at the two hemispheres coordinated to give a single, coherent perception and memory?

The first question, then, is how does the information arriving at one side of the brain interact with the information arriving at the other side? One way to get at this issue is to train an animal on some task where only one side of the brain receives the sensory information. Then do tests under conditions where only the opposite side, the untrained hemisphere, can see the test stimulus. Can the animal perform the task properly?

Figure 11-11 shows the optic fibers going from the eyes to the brain, meeting and crossing over at the location called the *optic chiasma* (see Chapter 2). If a surgical cut is made through the middle of this structure, then the left half of the brain receives information only from the left eye and the right hemisphere receives information only from the right eye. This is the first test. With the optic chiasma cut, the animal is trained with the left eye open and a patch over the right eye. After it has learned the task it is tested with the patch over the left eye and the right eye open. Does the right half of the brain know what the left half learned? The answer is yes. The animal is perfectly able to perform the task even though the right hemisphere has had no direct experience with the information before.

The left and right halves of the brain seem to be aware of what each is doing. How does this happen? Two answers come to mind. One, each hemisphere sends incoming information it receives to the other side as soon as it comes in and this duplicates memory records in both hemispheres. Since both halves of the brain are remembering the information, it doesn't matter which is subsequently tested on the learning task. Two, the material presented to the left hemisphere is stored only in that hemisphere. During testing, the right hemisphere may simply have complete access to the information stored in the left. Again, obviously, this system would be able to perform the experiment just tried.

Clearly, the key is the communication channel between the two halves of the brain. Suppose an experiment starts out exactly as before with the optic chiasma cut and the animal trained on a task using only the left eye. This time, after training but before testing, a cut is also made through the corpus callosum, severing the communication lines between the two hemispheres. The animal is then tested with the right eye. Now the right hemisphere no longer has access to the left and can't use any information that might be stored there. Unless duplicate memories have been built up, the animal should be unable to perform the task. The task can sometimes be done just as well with the right eye as with the left. Apparently both hemispheres have stored information relevant to the learning experience.[6]

Hemispheric specialization in humans Unlike animal brains, the two hemispheres in the human brain seem to be specialized in the kinds of information they store. The left hemisphere usually contains the information necessary for processing language symbols. This raises some interesting questions: What memory

[6] There is actually a good deal of debate on this point. Some researchers believe that only "simple" tasks get stored in both hemispheres, with "complex" tasks residing primarily in one (see Myers, 1962). See Chapter 5 of Gazzaniga's book *The bisected brain* (1970) for a more complete discussion of this issue.

functions can be performed by the mute half of the brain? Can it recognize anything? Can it memorize?

Consider the typical behavior of a patient who has undergone surgery to arrest epileptic symptoms. The operation is similar to the one for animals. The corpus callosum is sectioned, severing cortical communication between the two halves of the brain. (However, the optic chiasma is not cut, as it is with animals.)

From casual observation, the patient appears to be perfectly normal after the operation. (In fact, some people have been born with this split and lived for many years without problems.) Careful experimental procedures are needed to detect any peculiarities in behavior. The key is to test the patient when the sensory input is restricted to a single hemisphere of the brain. By controlling which hemisphere receives the sensory information and asking appropriate questions, we can probe the memory capabilities of each half of the brain.

First of all, the patient responds normally to any object presented to the right hand or to the right visual field. That is, if the patient is shown or handed a pair of scissors on the right side, the response is, "Those are scissors." This is to be expected, since the sensory input in this case reaches the left hemisphere and therefore makes normal contact with the language centers. Objects presented to the left visual field or to the left hand have an entirely different effect. If the patient is asked what is being held in the left hand, the answer is that the left hand feels numb. If a visual image is presented to the left visual field, the flash can be seen but without details.

Figure 11-12

What is the problem here? At first, it appears that nothing can be recognized with the right hemisphere. But if an object is first put into the left hand, then removed and put in a bag with other objects, the patient is quite capable of retrieving the correct object with the left hand when asked to do so. Moreover, if after an object is presented to the left hand, a series of pictures is flashed to the left visual field, the patient can point to the appropriate picture, but only with the left hand. In addition, although objects cannot be *described*, their *functions* can be demonstrated by gestures. For example, if shown a knife, the patient might make cutting gestures. If shown a key, he or she might place it in an imaginary keyhole. Finally, the patient can draw with the left hand a picture of what can be seen in the left visual field. In all of these cases, the person is totally incapable of describing the object verbally.

Even after a patient has successfully retrieved an object from a bag or has pointed it out in a picture, or has demonstrated its use, it still cannot be named. If asked what has been drawn with the left hand, the answer will be wrong. For example, if a picture of "$" is presented to the left visual field and "?" to the right visual field, a "$" will be drawn with the left hand, and "?" with the right. If the word "key" is presented to the left visual field and "case" to the right, the patient will claim not to know what has been seen, but nevertheless can search with the left hand and find a key. When asked what is being held, the patient may say that it is a case of some sort, such as "a case of beer" (Sperry, 1968).

What do these phenomena indicate? They suggest that when communication has been cut between the two hemispheres of the brain, the person appears to act like two separate people; the left hand truly does not know what the right hand is doing. Since the left half of the brain is the only one that can use language, the person is incapable of verbalizing or writing about anything the right half of the brain is monitoring. But the right half of the brain is still capable of object recognition and memory as well, for it can search for and find an object that was presented and then removed. Furthermore, it is evident that the classification of information in the right half of the brain involves rather sophisticated conceptualization. Suppose the patient is presented with a picture of a clock in the right visual field and asked to pick it out of a pile of objects with the left hand. If there is no clock but only a wristwatch in the pile, the wristwatch will be selected. The watch is functionally the same as a clock. Moreover, the watch is chosen even when other objects in the pile are physically more similar to a clock. In other words, although the right half of the brain cannot use language normally, it can use concepts. The right half of the brain, then, while independent of language, is nevertheless still capable of intellectual tasks.

One rather startling result is that while the right half of the brain cannot speak, it can obey spoken commands and can recognize written words. Thus, it is not quite accurate to say the right half of the brain is working entirely without any language function.

The right half of the brain is incapable of language **production,** but it is capable of language **recognition.** The left hand (controlled by the right half of the brain) cannot write the name of an object flashed in the left visual field (this is language production). Yet, the right brain can recognize a written name of an object flashed in the left visual field (this is language recognition). To demonstrate that recognition had indeed occurred, the patient is asked to push a button when the specific name is presented or to use the right hand to pick out an object from among many objects in a bag.

The right half of the brain is limited in its ability to recognize language. It is very good at comprehending concrete nouns, but somewhat less good at comprehending verbs or nouns derived from verbs (such as "locker," "clipping," or "fall") (Gazzaniga, 1970, p. 119). For example, the patient is incapable of moving either hand appropriately to commands such as "knock," "squeeze," "point," when they are presented

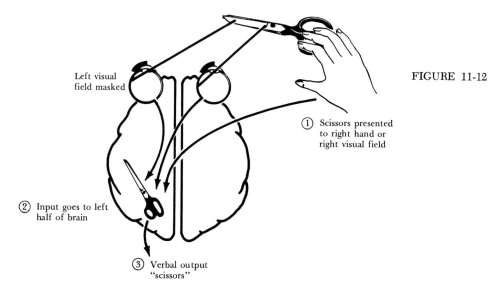

FIGURE 11-12

Left visual field masked

① Scissors presented to right hand or right visual field

② Input goes to left half of brain

③ Verbal output "scissors"

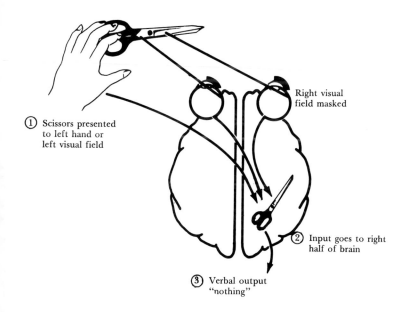

Right visual field masked

① Scissors presented to left hand or left visual field

② Input goes to right half of brain

③ Verbal output "nothing"

to the right hemisphere. A simple control test demonstrates that this inability to respond is due to problems of language comprehension rather than of motor control. The patient is perfectly capable of using the hand to perform the appropriate movement if a **picture** of the movement, rather than a verbal command, is flashed to the right hemisphere.

The brain of higher organisms, then, seems to consist of two fully equipped central processing systems, tied together by a massive set of communication lines. Ordinarily, each system receives only part of the sensory information arriving from the various sensory receptors. The left half of the brain receives visual information from the right half of the visual field, tactile information from touch receptors in the right half of the body, and the bulk of the auditory information from the right ear. The right half of the brain receives the complementary set of sensory data. The communicating fibers of the corpus callosum seem to be used to transfer the missing parts of the message to each cortex, so that each half of the brain has a complete representation of the environment. Normally, the two hemispheres appear to build up duplicate memories in a learning task, even when the sensory messages may be restricted to one half of the brain. When the two processing systems are disconnected, they are capable of functioning independently. Each half can acquire and store the information needed to perform a learning task. The fact that each hemisphere is receiving only part of the environmental information does not seem to be a serious handicap. Congenital brain damage affecting the corpus callosum in humans does not produce any serious impairment of perceptual or intellectual abilities.

The fact that the two halves of the brain in a split-brain patient function independently of each other does bring up certain problems in decision making, as the following excerpt from Gazzaniga's book illustrates.

> Case I . . . would sometimes find himself pulling his pants down with one hand and pulling them up with the other. Once, he grabbed his wife with his left hand and shook her violently, while with the right trying to come to his wife's aid in bringing the left belligerent hand under control. Once, while I was playing horseshoes with the patient in his backyard, he happened to pick up an axe leaning against the house with his left hand. Because it was entirely likely that the more aggressive right hemisphere might be in control, I discreetly left the scene—not wanting to be the victim for the test case of which half-brain does society punish or execute. [Gazzaniga (1970), p. 107]

Since there are two brains controlling the same organism, duplicating memories seems to be a straightforward way of coordinating the activity of the two systems. It avoids the possible conflicts that might arise if each half of the brain were learning different things. This duplication of memory, however, may be a luxury that can only be afforded by lower organisms for whom the demands of the environment seem unlikely to strain their learning and memory capabilities. In humans, the situation is not so simple. The extraordinary perceptual learning, memory, and motor demands imposed by the human's language system seem to have led to some degree of specialization in the functions performed by the two hemispheres. One of the hemispheres, usually the left, seems to develop most of the functions needed for language production. Only brain damage to this "dominant" hemisphere appears to affect a person's ability to cope with language.

In addition to raising problems in coordinating information, having two brains that can function independently has its advantages. First, it gives great flexibility to the operation. With two symmetrical halves of the brain, either can take over, should emergency arise. When children receive severe brain injury at an early enough age the other side of the brain can take over, compensating for the damage. Is the compensation complete? It is difficult to tell. To tell would require a control, some way of knowing how the person would have developed had the brain been normal. Whether or not it is complete, the compensation is amazingly good.

Two brains: fixed or flexible

The brain does not retain this flexibility, however, as the organism grows older. The younger the child when the damage occurs, the greater the chance that the unimpaired hemisphere can take over the duties of the injured one. Whether the dependence upon age has to do with maturation or simply with the learning of language is not known, but certainly it seems safe to generalize and say that the more language has been developed, the harder it will be to have one hemisphere take over for the other. Language is a strange and complex behavior that requires an immense amount of storage and computational ability. Humans may be unique in having a complex language, one in which the ordering of symbols determines their meaning and in which sentences can be transformed from one form to another without changing meaning. Although some animals have means of communication (and although chimpanzees can be taught a limited language), none has yet shown that it has a language of anywhere near the complexity of human language. Certainly the complexity of the language is related to the complexity of the brain structure.

Figure 11-13

Thus, when a language has been well started with a reasonably large vocabulary and reasonable comprehension of grammatical rules, then it makes sense that the brain structures have become organized around the language, whether by biological or chemical changes or simply by acquiring a large, complex data base of information. And with this complex organization, the ability to transfer to a new hemisphere should the old one become damaged is also lost. In fact, after puberty, should

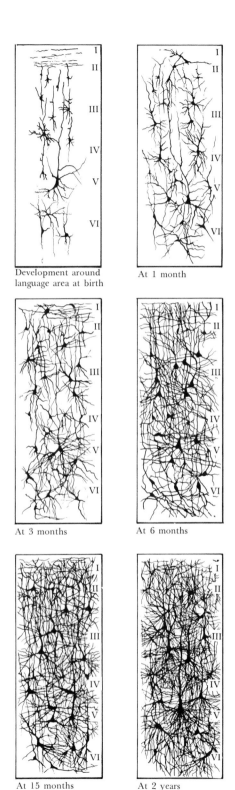

Development around
language area at birth

At 1 month

At 3 months

At 6 months

At 15 months

At 2 years

FIGURE 11-13

Neurons in the VI layers of the cerebral cortex as a function of age. After photographs of Conel (1939–1963) and graphs of Schadé and van Groenigen (1961) and Lenneberg (1967).

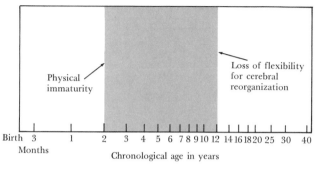

FACTORS WHICH LIMIT THE ACQUISITION
OF PRIMARY LANGUAGE SKILLS

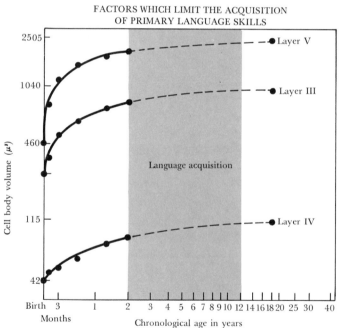

the language hemisphere become damaged, it is very unlikely that the other will be able to take over the function.

It is not known why the left hemisphere usually controls language. The two hemispheres seem to start off the same, and from appearances there is no reason why one should be better suited for dealing with language than the other. Yet, language usually develops in the left half, nonverbal skills in the right. Most people are also right-handed, although there is no logical reason why this should be so: Why should not 50% of the population be left-handed? It is thought that there is a connection between the left-hemisphere dominance of language and right-handedness. Left-handed people seem to have a tendency to use the right hemisphere for language. But this is not always true. Many left-handed people have language processes specialized in the left hemisphere. The stronger the trait of left-handedness in a family, the greater the likelihood that the hemispheres are reversed. Thus, the daughter of two left-handed parents, especially if some of her siblings are also left-handed, is likely to have language centered in the right hemisphere.

One result with important implications for the treatment of patients comes from the same set of studies on the effect of electroconvulsive therapy (ECT), which we discussed earlier. Squire and Chace (1975) studied the effects on memory when patients were treated with shock to both hemispheres of the brain simultaneously (bilateral ECT) or treated with shock to only a single hemisphere (unilateral ECT). There seems to be a different effect upon memory for each. Bilateral ECT is more severe in its effects upon memory. The results of the experiments show that in either case there is full memory recovery after 6 months, but the initial effects of the treatment are more severe for those with bilateral than for those with unilateral ECT.

Although the experimental results failed to find any deficit in memory performance six months after the bilateral treatments, the patients do not agree. Patients who received unilateral shock believed their memories had not been affected by the treatment. But patients with bilateral shock "believed that they sustained continuing difficulties even six-to-nine months after treatment." As you can imagine, determining whether a person's memory for long-past events is normal can be a difficult task. To do it correctly, you must know what the patient has experienced earlier, and you must also compare the actual performance with how well the same patient would have remembered those experiences had there not been the ECT treatment. Patients who still believe their memory to be impaired could be correct, for they might have more information about their own memory processes than our experiments can provide. But we do not know, since metamemory is not all that accurate.

People do not know how to learn things effectively, and it can take weeks to recall some information. Patients might simply be reacting to their long hospitalization and to their general difficulties and expectations when they believe their memories still to be impaired. This is a point that deserves careful, serious research: such research is slowly progressing.

Now we can relate the work on bilateral ECT to the discussions of hemisphere specialization. If memories are encoded in one side of the brain only, then why would bilateral ECT be worse than unilateral (assuming, of course, that the unilateral ECT was applied to the hemisphere that contained the memories)? There are two possible explanations. First, memories may be present in both hemispheres. Second, there is the problem of transfer. Information in one hemisphere often gets transferred to the corresponding locations in the other hemisphere: the corpus callosum keeps the two hemispheres in communication. But with bilateral ECT the communication has no effect, for both hemispheres are temporarily nonfunctional.

Specialized hemispheres— specialized thought

The artist peers intensely at his painting, critically analyzing the structure, the balance, the conflicts. He paints a bit of color on a convenient piece of cardboard and holds it up next to the area of the painting that bothers him. Scowling, he adds some green, some white, some cyan. He tries again and again, until the floor is littered with the scraps of test colors. Finally he is satisfied, and he applies paint to the canvas itself.

The scientist props the graphs on the desk, pushes away the calculator and stands up. She backs off and looks at the graphs from a distance. The floor is littered with books and papers, products of a fruitless search for an explanation. Finally, she gives up and leaves the office. The next morning, while showering, the play of light, shadows, and water droplets on the walls catches her attention. Suddenly something clicks into mind, and without further thought, she understands the pattern of her data: a new theory has been devised.

Two modes of thinking: one cool, intellectual, analytic—carefully calculating the best among alternatives, often experimenting to find the right possibilities. The other mode haphazard, unplanned, free—leaving things to chance, to subconscious processes, to the random strike of inspiration. Usually one thinks of the scientist as an example of the former, and the artist as an example of the latter. But, as these examples illustrate, each can have moments of careful, planned thought, and each can have hunches, wild guesses, or inspired ideas.

In searching for explanations of the specialization of the two brain hemispheres, some people have argued that each hemisphere controls different modes of thought. One hemisphere—usually the left—is claimed to be specialized for the performance of analytical or logical thinking. This is also the hemisphere that usually controls language. The other hemisphere—the right for most people—is claimed to be specialized for nonanalytical, continuous, or synthetic modes of thought. The right hemisphere is regarded as the nonscientific hemisphere, unfettered by conventional logic or reason, but rather rhythmic, artistic, creative in style.

These are strange claims. What is the evidence? Part of it comes from the clinical studies we have just reviewed, evidence from the division of talents exhibited by the two hemispheres of patients who have had the corpus callosum surgically divided. Another part of the evidence comes from experiments with normal subjects. Here, it has been shown that with most right-handed people, verbal material can be remembered slightly better if presented to the right ear than to the left. Music, however, appears to be remembered better if presented to the left ear rather than to the right (see Kimura, 1961, 1964). (Remember, each ear, like most sensorimotor systems, sends most of its signals to the opposite side of the body.) Usually with normal subjects, to show hemispheric dominance the task must be difficult and both hemispheres must be stimulated. Thus, to demonstrate that someone can hear words more clearly with the right ear than the left, it is necessary to put extraneous sounds to the other ear at the same time. The apparent reason for this is that otherwise the unoccupied hemisphere can analyze the signals received by the other hemisphere, perhaps by monitoring the signals received by the other hemisphere across the corpus callosum. Alternatively, since each ear does send signals to both hemispheres, unless one stimulates both ears, there is nothing to stop both hemispheres from performing the task, thus completely eliminating any difference due to the ear at which a sound is received.

The same problem occurs in vision, even though all of the scene to the right of where the eye is fixated is analyzed by the left hemisphere. The corpus callosum still sends the sensory signals from the right and left visual fields across to the other hemisphere, so just as in hearing, stimulation of both sides of the eyes is necessary to get maximum effect.

The Stroop phenomenon. An interesting demonstration of the specialization of the hemispheres has been conducted by Cohen and Martin (1975). Their experiment makes use of the phenomenon first noticed by Stroop (1935; therefore called the *Stroop test*). The Stroop phenomenon occurs whenever the analysis of sensory information contains a conflict in information. To experience the effect, go down the list of boxed numbers shown in Figure 11-14 as rapidly as possible. For each box say aloud how many items it contains. For example, a box like this

```
┌─────┐
│ 3 3 │
│ 3 3 │
└─────┘
```

should receive a response of "four."

You should have found occasional conflicts between the number that you were supposed to speak (corresponding to the number of elements in the item) and the numeral of which the item was composed. The conflict occurs only if you read the numerals, something you are not asked to do. But Stroop demonstrated that reading is done quite automatically, and it is difficult or impossible to prevent it (in the words of Chapter 8: reading is a data-driven process). Thus, the number that is generated internally through reading conflicts with the number generated through counting.[7]

Cohen and Martin performed an auditory analog to the Stroop phenomenon. The pitches were low or high: the subjects had to respond by saying either the word "high" or the word "low." But, as illustrated in Figure 11-15, the notes were generated by someone singing the words "high" and "low." The word "high" was sung at both high and low pitches, and so was the word "low." The sung words corresponded to the pitch

FIGURE 11-14

```
┌─────────┐
│  2 2 2  │
└─────────┘
┌─────────┐
│ 2 2 2 2 │
│  2 2 2  │
└─────────┘
┌─────────┐
│   9 9   │
└─────────┘
┌─────────┐
│  6 6 6  │
│   6 6   │
└─────────┘
┌─────────┐
│    3    │
└─────────┘
┌─────────┐
│ 1 1 1 1 │
│ 1 1 1 1 │
└─────────┘
┌─────────┐
│  7 7 7  │
│  7 7 7  │
│  7 7 7  │
└─────────┘
┌─────────┐
│ 5 5 5 5 │
└─────────┘
┌─────────┐
│ 6 6 6 6 │
│   6 6   │
└─────────┘
┌─────────┐
│  3 3 3  │
│  3 3 3  │
└─────────┘
┌─────────┐
│ 7 7 7 7 │
└─────────┘
┌─────────┐
│  2 2 2  │
└─────────┘
┌─────────┐
│  3 3 3  │
│  3 3 3  │
│  3 3 3  │
└─────────┘
┌─────────┐
│  1 1 1  │
│   1 1   │
└─────────┘
┌─────────┐
│    7    │
└─────────┘
┌─────────┐
│ 3 3 3 3 │
│  3 3 3  │
└─────────┘
┌─────────┐
│  2 2 2  │
└─────────┘
┌─────────┐
│ 7 7 7 7 │
│ 7 7 7 7 │
└─────────┘
┌─────────┐
│  8 8 8  │
│  8 8 8  │
└─────────┘
┌─────────┐
│ 4 4 4 4 │
│  4 4 4  │
└─────────┘
```

FIGURE 11-15

[7] Actually, Stroop experimented with a task of color naming. The names of colors were printed in colored inks, so that the word "blue" might be printed in red ink, the word "red" in green ink, and so on. The subjects were asked to name the ink colors as rapidly as possible. This task produces dramatic results, much more dramatic than for the example shown here: Subjects usually get through 3 or 4 names before they start sputtering, stumbling, and usually giggling. The only way to do the task efficiently is to prevent reading, which can be done by trying to look only at the corners of the words, or by defocusing the image (or taking off one's glasses).

half of the time. (If you try this experiment, be sure to have an equal number of matches and conflicts of words and pitches.)

When Cohen and Martin did the experiment monaurally, presenting the sung words to the right ear (or the left ear) alone, they found only a slight effect of hemisphere dominance. Subjects were equally accurate to tones presented to either ear, but slightly faster with the left ear when the words were in conflict with the pitches.

Then Cohen and Martin did the experiment with the sung word presented to one ear while a story was read into the other. As before, the subjects was simply asked to respond as quickly as possible with the pitch of the sung word. In addition, to make sure they listened to the other ear, they were quizzed on the contents of the story. To ensure left-hemisphere dominance for language, only strongly right-handed subjects were tested. This time, the results were more dramatic. In fact, only half the subjects tested could even do the task. As you might imagine, it was all very confusing.

In order to understand what is happening in this experiment, it is necessary to keep in mind which side of the brain is doing the tasks, as well as which side of the brain originally receives the information. Figure 11-16 illustrates the situation when the story is presented to the right ear of the person and the tones to the left. Basically, the things to remember are:

> words are interpreted by the left hemisphere;
> tones are interpreted by the right hemisphere;
> sounds presented to the left ear are initially processed by the right
>   hemisphere;
> sounds presented to the right ear are initially processed by the left
>   hemisphere.

FIGURE 11-16

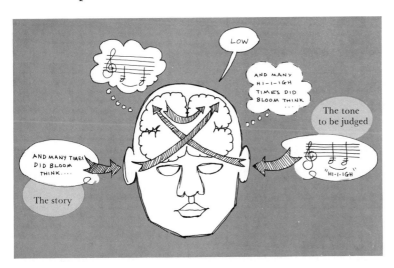

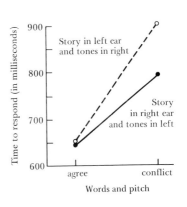

When the story is presented to the right ear (as in Figure 11-16), it is processed initially by the left hemisphere—which is appropriate for the task. The word that is sung, however, has to be sent from the right hemisphere to the left. Because the sung word has to undergo this extra step, the determination of the pitch can usually occur before the interpretation of the sung word. As a result, there is a minimal Stroop effect: minimal confusion between the sung word and the actual pitch.

When the story is presented to the left ear and the tones to the right, things change. Now, the story originally arrives at the inappropriate hemisphere and must be sent over to the other side. Similarly, the tones are initially processed by the inappropriate hemisphere. But the sung word that also arrives at the right ear is initially sent to the left hemisphere, where it can be interpreted. The sung word gets a headstart in interpretation over the determination of the pitch. As a result, there is more possibility of interference between the verbal analysis of the sung word and the determination of the pitch of the note: the Stroop phenomenon.

As the graph in Figure 11-16 shows, in both conditions subjects take considerable time to report the pitch of the sung tones. But when the tones are in the right ear, and when there is conflict in the sung word and the actual pitch, subjects take almost ¼ sec longer (250 millisec) to respond than when there is no conflict. There is over 100 millisec difference between hearing the tones in the right ear and hearing them in the left ear when the pitches and words conflict.

Cohen and Martin suggest that verbal analysis and pitch analysis are being performed independently by the different hemispheres and that there is a race in processing between the right and left hemispheres. If conditions favor the verbal analysis, then there is the possibility of a response conflict, and the system is slowed down.

CONCLUSION   When we consider attempts to locate the brain mechanisms responsible for learning and memory, we find that it is very difficult for the scientist to proceed. The brain appears to be an enormously complex structure, with many of the parts working together. Human behavior is determined by multiple causes and sources. No single component seems to be solely responsible for even simple acts. This means that a relatively large amount of the brain is used for almost any task. Moreover, more parts are operating than are logically necessary. This provides tremendous versatility and resilience to the brain and to human behavior. The brain can sustain extensive damage without totally incapacitating the whole organism. The human brain is an elegant structure whose parts work in harmony with one another to produce individual behavior. Thus, although our studies have not succeeded in discovering the location of any specific functional components of memory, they have provided a compelling picture of the neural mechanisms and their operations.

The studies of neural mechanisms responsible for memory provide hints of the structure of the brain, but much more work must still be done. The studies of the deficits suffered by patients who for one reason or another suffer anomalies of memory offer a potentially rich source of information about the memory system and about the brain. They are valuable for improving both the level of general understanding and therapeutic techniques. Again, much more work remains to be done.

The studies of the two hemispheres of the brain indicate that there are differences between them and that they appear to be specialized for different tasks. But we do not yet know where this observation leads. The differences that we note in the normal person are small and can be observed only under special conditions. The only solid scientific evidence we have about the differences in hemispheric functions deals with rather simple processing tasks. We do not know enough about the mechanisms and processes of thought to be able to test hypotheses like those presented at the beginning of this chapter—that the two hemispheres control radically different styles of thought, that some people may be dominated by one hemisphere and thus exhibit different thought patterns from other people. These hypotheses are sheer speculation. There is to date no scientific evidence that can support (or disprove) conclusively such speculative statements. Thus, these studies have served mainly to raise questions; much more research remains to be done.

In this chapter, the following terms and concepts that we consider to be important have been used. Please look them over. If you are not able to give a short explanation of any of them, you should go back and review the appropriate sections of the chapter.

REVIEW OF TERMS AND CONCEPTS

Cortex
    left and right hemisphere
    corpus callosum
    (you do not need to know the following terms, but you should recognize them:
        frontal lobe
        temporal lobe
        parietal lobe
        occipital lobe)
Nerve cells
    soma

Terms and concepts you should know

cell body
synapse
   excitatory and inhibitory
axon
dendrite
Unique cell theory
Unique pattern theory
Unique code theory
Habituation
Dishabituation
Consolidation
ECS and ECT
   unilateral and bilateral
   the pedestal experiment
Retrograde amnesia
   time course of recovery from amnesia
Implications from studies of H.M. and N.A.
Law of mass action
Studies of split brains
   specialization of the hemispheres
The Stroop phenomenon

SUGGESTED
READINGS

General

There is no easy source for the work on the biological and neural bases of memory. An excellent introduction to physiological mechanisms is presented by Shepherd (1974). Perhaps the best advanced source for material related to this chapter is *The handbook of psychobiology*, edited by Gazzaniga and Blakemore (1975): In that book, see Chapter 7 on the biochemical basis of memory, Chapter 16 on the neurological study of learning, and Chapter 19 on hemispheric specialization. In addition, the other chapters of this handbook will certainly be of interest to many of you. The *Annual Review of Psychology* and the *Annual Review of Physiology* will provide a quick reference to recent research, and the last four or five years of the reviews ought to be examined. (Beware that the annual reviews are usually pretty dull; their purpose is to tell you where to find the interesting and important work, not to make you excited over the subject.)

Memory
mechanisms

Deutsch's (1973) book, *The physiological basis of memory*, contains a set of interesting papers. We also recommend Mark's (1974) book, *Memory and nerve cell connections*, which presents his arguments for a memory system related to the normal system that guides the developing organism. He presents some interesting arguments about synaptic mechanisms. The work on *Aplysia* reported here is partially taken from the chapter by Kandel (1974) in *The neurosciences study program* (1974), and as we indicated in the suggested readings for Chapter 6, the whole study program provides a wealth of important information on all phases of physiological mechanisms (see Schmitt, 1972; Schmitt & Worden, 1974). Thompson's search for the site of memory is described in his paper of 1976(b). An excellent review of the theories of physiological mechanisms of short-term memory is provided by Squire (1975) in the book edited by Deutsch and Deutsch (1975) on short-term memory: the last six chapters of Deutsch and Deutsch are also highly relevant to the discussion of this chapter.

There are a number of good books on amnesias and memory pathology. *Memory deficits* Talland (1965, 1968) covers mostly the Korsakoff syndrome, patients who have memory deficits as a result of acute alcoholism. More general books are the articles collected by Talland and Waugh (1969) on general memory pathologies and some laboratory research, Barbizet's *Human memory and its pathology* (1970), and the book, *Amnesia*, by Whitty and Zangwill (1966). (See especially the chapter by Williams on the effect of ECS with human patients.) The classic study of amnesia from head trauma is by Russell and Nathan (1946). It clarifies the relationship between anterograde and retrograde amnesia. Studies of amnesia related to the analysis of STM and LTM can be pursued in the reviews by Kinsbourne and Wood (1975), Squire (1975), Warrington and Weiskrantz (1973), Baddeley and Warrington (1970, 1973). Our source for the work on ECT has been the work of Squire (1974) and Squire, Slater, and Chace (1975). A thorough treatment of ECT is given in the book edited by Fink, Kety, McGaugh, and Williams (1974).

A fascinating report of the effect of a brain wound on a patient's thought patterns is described in the book *The man with a shattered world* by the noted Russian psychologist Luria (1972). (While we are at it, Luria's (1973) *The working brain* is an excellent introduction to the entire topic.)

The studies of patients H.M. and N.A. were reported in a series of six papers that all appeared in the same issue of *Neuropsychologia*, 1968, **6**, pp. 211–282. A summary of the behavioral results of brain injury can be found in Rosner's *Annual Review of Psychology* (1970) article, "Brain Functions."

Lashley's work is of great importance in the study of the localization of specific memories, even though some recent experiments are shedding some doubt upon its generality. Three important papers by Lashley that ought to be examined are 1931, 1950, and perhaps most important, his famous and influential paper on the problem of serial order (1951).

The best way to start is with the book, *The neurophysiology of Lashley* edited by Beach *et al.* (1960). Lenneberg's book (1967), *Biological foundations of language* presents important information about memory disorders that affect the development of language, as well as a discussion of *aphasia,* a language-specific impairment that results from brain injury. The articles by Geschwind (1970, 1975) are good summary articles on aphasia and apraxia.

Some very recent studies carried out in England (reviewed in Warrington & Weiskrantz, 1973) indicate that there are alternative explanations to the problems suffered by some amnesic patients. It may not be that they are unable to enter new information into long-term memory; rather they may simply be unable to retrieve it properly from among all of the various items they have acquired since their deficit. In addition, the existence of a novel patient with a very much impaired short-term memory but with no apparent deficit in acquiring new material raises some interesting puzzles. It is too early for these results yet to be evaluated. Some idea of the scientific debate on the interpretation of amnesia can be seen in the interchange between Gold and King (1974) and Miller and Springer (1974).

Hemispheric specialization   The literature on split brains and their general implications ought to be examined by starting first with the articles of Sperry (1961, 1968). The literature is reviewed very nicely in Gazzaniga's *The bisected brain* (1970), and the references contained in that book will send you to the rest of the literature. One additional source is Mountcastle's book on cerebral dominance (1962). More recent reviews are Sperry's (1974) and Chapter 19 in Gazzaniga and Blakemore (1975).

The bilateral symmetry of the brain has interesting implications for behavior, among them a possible explanation of the difficulty faced by children (and some adults) in distinguishing left from right. These issues are discussed in an article by Corballis and Beale (1970). You might enjoy the discussion by Levy (1969, 1974) on the evolution of specialization. An important experimental study on patients with severed hemispheres is provided by Levy, Trevarthen, and Sperry (1972). Gazzaniga and Hillyard (1973) describe how the two halves of the brain can apparently work independently to increase the capacity of each half alone. Kinsbourne (1973) describes some novel problems and issues dealing with control structures for the two hemispheres.

12 Language

PREVIEW

There is more to language than words. *How* something is said is as important as *what* is said. Subtle social conventions govern conversations and writings. To be an effective user of language one must take into account the characteristics of the listeners: their knowledge, their social background, the reasons they have for taking part in the communication. Quite often the meaning that is conveyed is quite different from the one implied by a literal interpretation of the words that are spoken.

Analyzing what is spoken is not a trivial task. Although our analysis of sentences proceeds effortlessly, a complex set of processing mechanisms is involved. Language understanding and production is perhaps the most complex activity performed by a human. Remember that although you read these sentences with ease, not everyone can do so. Most ten-year-old children cannot read this book, even though they have had at least eight years of language experience.

This chapter is organized around a simple principle. The purpose of language is to communicate information from one person to another. Information in the mind is represented by an interlocking network of constructs—the knowledge representations that we discussed in Chapter 10. Speakers and writers have the job of communicating the structures in their minds to the minds of their listeners and readers. But the structures in the mind are complex, intertwined, multidimensional assemblages. And language is conveyed by a relatively slow, linear string of words. Somehow, the words, spoken and written one at a time, must allow the recipient to construct the proper mental structure. For these reasons, language conveys much of its intended meaning through social conventions, shortcuts, and heavy reliance on the powerful processing machinery that the speaker expects the listener to bring to bear on the problem. Thus, more is conveyed than is said.

This chapter starts with an analysis of some of the nonverbal aspects of language: the rules by which people interact with one another. You should be able to expand upon the principles mentioned in the first part of this chapter simply by observing yourself and your friends during the course of the day. Many of the subtle aspects of the interactions you will observe convey a considerable amount of information.

The second part of the chapter deals with the rules of language—in particular, the grammatical structure of English. Here you should be concerned with understanding something of the rules, but most important, with the reasons underlying these rules. Language must be deciphered by the people who receive it, and without an implicit set of rules beneath its structure, it might be impossible to understand what was meant. In examining the structure of language, think about how that structure guides the listener or reader to reconstruct the mental structures that are intended. The discussion of the problem of reference is a good example of the problem of making sure that all users of language share a common set of mental ideas.

Finally, the last part of this chapter deals with the psychological mechanisms that might actually analyze the spoken and written words and reconstruct the intended psychological meaning structures in the memory system. Here, you should understand the roles of the grammatical analysis of language, the conceptually driven guidance system, and the data-driven guidance system. The analysis of language is one of the most important aspects of human intelligent behavior, and it is important to get a good understanding of the mechanisms that are operating.

LANGUAGE AND COMMUNICATION

Language is for communication. That is what it is all about. But if language is to communicate, the people who are communicating must know quite a bit about each other. There is a lot more to the business of communication than the stringing together of words. One cannot study language simply by looking in dictionaries for the meanings of words and looking in grammar books for the rules by which to connect them together.

One might suppose that a professor lecturing to a class is the prototypical example of the communication of meaning. The professor knows the subject matter, the students do not. The professor's job is to transmit his or her knowledge to the class. But there are many different ways of transmitting the knowledge. Consider the tone of voice adopted by the professor. The teacher can be jovial or stern, condescending or demeaning, friendly and open, or distant and aloof: these differences can affect how much is learned. Suppose a student fails to understand the material: Can the student say, "Excuse me, I was daydreaming. Would you explain that again?" Obviously not, not even if true. Such a statement would be taken as an insult by the instructor, and as humorously out of place by the other students. But why? Everyone daydreams. Even professors daydream, sometimes right in their own lectures. (We know.) But we are not allowed to admit it. Strong social norms control the communication among people, and one fundamental rule is to be attentive to another's words. It is not usually considered proper to admit otherwise.

Participants in conversations make assumptions about the other people. These assumptions have been called *conversational postulates* and they reflect the tacit agreement that speakers share with one another about the social rules governing conversations. Conversational postulates vary from one group of people to another, from one culture to another. They depend upon the actual people speaking too, so that the rules that govern speech between two children are different from the rules that govern speech between two adults, or between a professor and a student, or between the Pope and a visitor. Some rules are universal, such as

Conversational postulates

Only one person speaks at a time

but other rules vary, such as the way by which a person signals a desire to speak. Among social equals, one person can start speaking as long as the other has paused for a long enough period of time. If one does not wish to let the other speak it must be signaled by filling the pauses with sounds such as "*ah*," "*umm*," or deliberately never finishing the sentence by ending each utterance with "*and . . .*" or "*but the umm . . .*" Among social unequals, the socially superior person can interrupt the junior people just by speaking—all the others will usually stop.

Communicating knowledge structures

When people talk to one another they share ideas in common. One communicates by building upon the common structures of the speakers, adding information that is novel, but yet related to what is already known.

FIGURE 12-1

Communications tread a path between repeating what the listeners already know—thus leading to boredom—or stating ideas so new and unfamiliar that the listeners have no means of incorporating them into their knowledge structures. Teachers find this narrow path extremely frustrating, for whenever one person attempts to teach a classroom of students it is almost guaranteed that some students will be bored and others completely lost. (The only exception is when everyone is bored or everyone is lost.) Even in a two-person conversation it is difficult for the two participants to keep at the right level.

Suppose in a casual conversation Al asks Bob

Where is the London Bridge?

(Assume Bob really does know and Al does not.) How should Bob respond? The problem with answering questions is that there are many possible answers. To know how to answer the question properly Bob must know

Why was the question asked?
How much does the asker already know?

Some postulates state that in normal circumstances, the speaker is assumed:

to be sincere
to be relevant
not to say to others that which they already know
not to be superfluous

All these postulates imply that a speaker takes into account the knowledge structure of the listener. Indeed, in a conversation there are three aspects of importance:

The knowledge structure of the speaker
The speaker's understanding of the knowledge structure of the listener
What the speaker believes the listener believes to be true about the knowledge structure of the speaker

All these aspects get used by the participants. Bob could respond by saying any of the following:

It's at Lake Havasu.

It's in Arizona.

It's in the western part of the United States.

It's in the United States.

or even stating where it is not:

It's not in London anymore. It got bought by some eccentric American.

Which of these answers is wanted all depends upon why Al asked. If the question had been asked when Al and Bob were both in London, the last answer would probably be correct. But if the question had been asked while Al was sitting in an automobile in Las Vegas, Nevada, map in hand, then the answer should probably be very detailed:

Take route 95 south about 100 miles to Needles, California. Then take 40 east for about 20 miles into Arizona till you hit 95, the road to Havasu. It's another 15 miles south. You can't miss it. There's nothing else there. The bridge doesn't even go anywhere.

To answer questions in a manner that is informative you have to know what information the askers seek. You certainly are not being very helpful if you tell someone something that they already know. So to answer a question you have to make assumptions about a person's knowledge. Sometimes the proper way to answer a question is to find out more about the asker, thus returning a question with a question. Answering a question by asking a question can be carried out to extreme measures, but usually the flow of conversation goes quite naturally, as in this example:

1. Claudia: *Can you come to my party tonight?*
2. Doreen: **I don't know. I have some visitors from out of town.**
3. Claudia: *How many?*
4. Doreen: **Two.**
5. Claudia: *Bring them along.*
6. Doreen: **Are you sure you won't mind?**
7. Claudia: *Of course not. I would like to have you.*
8. Doreen: **O.K. That's a good idea. I'll ask them if they want to come.**
9. Doreen: **I'll call you later and let you know.**

Here, as the indentation shows, there are at least three levels to the conversation. First, on line 1, Claudia asks the original question about the party. Doreen's answer, on line 2, introduces a new topic, the visitors. This, in turn, generates a third level of conversation, Claudia's question about the visitors. The answer to this question, line 4, pops the conversation back up a level to the topic of the visitors. But at line 6, Doreen asks a new question, pushing the conversation down another level again. This level gets resolved at line 7, which allows Doreen to give a two-part answer, responding (at line 8) to the second-level suggestion of line 5, and finally (at line 9) responding to the original question asked in line 1 of the conversation.

The exact conversational rules that are followed can vary with the situation. In very polite conversation the rules are often quite different: the purpose of some polite conversations is to pass sounds back and forth and no meaning is intended. When a teacher talks with a student (or a parent with a child) the rules are different also, because the purpose of the conversation is different. Thus, if the teacher asks the student a question such as

What is the difference between an agent and a recipient?

the student had better ignore the usual rule of conversation that states

Do not tell someone what they already know.

into a rule something like

You must tell teachers exactly what they already know.

ON TELLING LIES

The act of lying uses many of the subtleties of language and communication. For most of us, telling an outright lie is a difficult and emotional task. There are a large number of moral and cultural rules that must be violated and the willful violation often reveals itself in stress and emotion on the part of the person telling the lie. You may notice this yourself: your heart rate increases, your breathing becomes a bit labored, and your sweat glands secrete a bit more fluids. Indeed, these emotional overtones of lies are so powerful and pervasive that they form the basis of lie detectors (polygraphs), devices that primarily measure galvanic skin response (GSR—a function of how much sweating goes on), heart rate, breathing, and sometimes muscle tension and blood pressure. These emotional factors also create stress that can overload the cognitive system, causing you to say things you otherwise would not, or to forget the things you had so carefully planned to say or do.

Other difficulties involved in the telling of lies have to do with the way people receive and interpret information. If you wish to tell a lie, you are telling a story that is not true, but that will be believed as true. To do this, you need to take into account what people will believe and what they will not. This requires you to consider what your target group knows about the world, about you, and about the things of which you are lying. Thinking about telling a believable lie is a useful demonstration because it forces you to consider many of the aspects of communication that you ordinarily ignore.

What do you do when you lie? First, there must be some purpose to the lies, some motive that underlies the telling of a falsehood. In most cases lies are told either to impress the listeners, to prevent the listeners from knowing something, or sometimes to protect the listeners from discovering something about themselves that the teller thinks they would be better off not knowing. (Lies that are told to protect the hearer are called "white lies" and they are one of the few types of deceit that our society permits, and sometimes encourages.)

When telling a lie one has to draw a careful line between what will be believed and what will be impressive. Suppose you are talking to a very dull and tiresome teacher whom you are trying to impress because you would like to get a decent grade. You have been talking for five minutes, which is about all you can stand. How do you make an excuse to get away? You cannot simply say

"I'm getting bored. I want to go."

The truth could harm you. Certainly such a blunt statement will win no friends. You could try to be ambiguous:

"Oh my goodness, it's late. I must go."

But what if you are asked why you have to go? Then you need a reason. The reason has to be impressive enough that it will make an impact on your listener, as well as being a sufficient reason to let you leave. But if it is too impressive, it might not be believed. Thus, you could say

"I have an appointment with a friend."

But if you are trying to impress the teacher, saying you need to talk to a friend does not get you very far. No, you should need to talk to an important person, thereby implying that either you are friendly with such people or that you yourself are important enough to have to talk to important people. So here are the sorts of options one has:

"I have to go talk with a librarian."
"I have a meeting with Professor Simpson."
"I have a meeting with the head of the Psychology Department."

Each of these possibilities increases in prestige value. But if meeting with the head of a department is impressive, why not go further:

"I have a meeting with the president of the university."
"I have a meeting with the President of the United States."

Somewhere along the line the story simply is not going to be believed. Indeed, suppose you really did have a meeting with the President of the United States. Then you face exactly the same problem, the only difference being that now you are attempting to make people believe something that really is the truth. The problem is to pick a level that is impressive yet still believable. Moreover, it cannot be something where you can be found out. Suppose you convinced your listener that you were off to see Professor Simpson but then it became known that she was in Kyoto at the time. Of course, there is a similar problem with the truth. Suppose you really did have a meeting with the President of the United States. How would you convince your friends?

THE RULES OF
LANGUAGE

When we talk about language, we distinguish between the words that are used to communicate ideas and the ideas themselves. The words are all that are measurable in language behavior: They can be seen or heard. Hence, we call the actual sentences that are written or spoken the *surface structure* of language. The meanings conveyed by words are not visible: They depend upon the memory structure of the people involved in the communication. Hence, we call the meaning communicated by message the *meaning structure*.

Given that language consists of words, not the circles and arrows that we have used to illustrate memory structures (in Chapter 10), then some conventions must be devised to indicate which spoken relations correspond to concepts, which to actions, and what relations apply between the concepts and actions. Note that for any given meaning structure there is a wide variety of possible sentences that can be used to describe it. Moreover, the entire structure need not be communicated if the receiver of the information can already be assumed to understand certain basic concepts.

THEY ARE WORKING STUDENTS

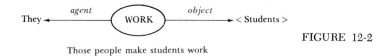

Those people make students work

FIGURE 12-2

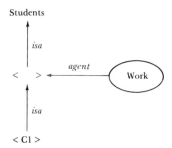

C1's are students who work

Just as it is possible to represent one basic underlying structure by many different surface structures, it is possible to represent different meaning structures by the same surface structures. Consider the sentence:

They are working students.

This sentence has two possible meanings (at least). Each meaning translates into a different meaning structure, as is shown in Figure 12-2.

The grammatical rules of a language specify the ways by which a meaning structure can be converted into a surface structure. In speaking or writing, people must go into their own meaning structures and apply the relevant grammatical rules to form legitimate sentences. In listening or reading, the reverse operations must be applied. People must try to disentangle the words spoken to them and recover the meaning structures.

It is important to keep in mind, however, that meaning and grammatical correctness are related but they are far from being the same thing. The sentence

Eat apple

is ungrammatical, but in context, it is perfectly meaningful: the relational and conceptual information is unambiguous. Some grammatical distortions may also make the message uninterpretable. If they destroy the information that specifies roles of the various participants, part of the meaning is lost:

Tickle Don Julie

Finally, a sentence may be perfectly grammatical, yet still raise interpretive problems because some of the information needed to encode it unambiguously into memory is missing:

They are working students.

Visiting professors can be boring.

A psychological study of grammar is concerned with the cognitive processes that translate between surface structure and meaning. Whether or not the message follows the rules of correct speech is not a reliable indicator of whether these cognitive processes will break down during its interpretation. Thus, many sentences that seem to have ambiguous surface structure are actually quite intelligible because only one possible meaning can be intended by the particular choice of words. Thus

Kiss John tiger

is both ungrammatical and unintelligible, while

Shoot John tiger

is ungrammatical, but can be interpreted if necessary: Only one word, **John,** can serve as the obligatory human **agent** of **shoot** and the remaining word, **tiger,** is a satisfactory (and even likely) **object.**

Language provides clues for its analysis. People speak to one another in ways that guide the interpretation of the meaning conveyed by the language. Sentences are constructed of phrases, and the order in which the phrases and words are put together conveys part of the information about their intended composition. In addition, prepositions are important clues to the listener about how the phrase that follows is to be interpreted.

All languages face similar problems in conveying meaning, and the solutions take on different forms in different languages. In English, adjectives and modifiers of a noun always appear before the noun: In many other languages the adjectives and modifiers appear after the noun. In English, the order of the words adds important information: The two sentences

The dog bit Joyce.

Joyce bit the dog.

mean quite different things. In other languages, word order might be important only for emphasis, and the roles of the different parts of the sentence are signified by changing the form of the word to indicate their case. The important point is that all languages must signify the relationships that the components of a sentence have with one another and the only possible signals are through the ordering of the words, through the use of special function words, or by changing the form of the words themselves.

English sentences are composed of several different kinds of sentence parts, linked together according to formal grammatical rules. In this book, we have been primarily concerned with the meanings of sentences rather than the exact surface structure, but in fact, the two are closely related.

English grammar

According to traditional grammar, the normal, simple English sentence is composed of a subject and predicate, or subject, verb, and object. As we have already seen, these kinds of distinctions are of little use to us: we need to dissect the sentence differently.

Consider the sentence

The very old man eats oysters.

We can decompose this sentence in several ways. First, the phrase, **the very old man** is a *noun phrase* (*NP*). Second, the phrase, **eats oysters** is a *verb phrase* (*VP*), and third, we see that the verb phrase consists of a *verb* (*V*) plus a noun phrase. Hence we get a simple set of rules for decomposing this form of sentence.

$$1. \quad S \rightarrow NP + VP.$$

$$2. \quad VP \rightarrow V + NP.$$

(These can be read as: 1. A sentence *goes to* a NP plus a VP. 2. A VP *goes to* a V plus a NP.)

A noun phrase can be dissected further.

3. NP → Art + N.

4. N → Ad + N.

Rule 3 allows a noun phrase to be replaced with an *article* (*Art*) plus a noun. Rule 4 says that there may actually be a string of modifiers in a noun phrase, so that a N can continually be replaced by an *adjective* or *adverb* (*Ad*) plus N. Rule 4 allows the phrase **The very tired big fat hungry dirty old man.** These rules are optional, so that any or all might be applied to the analysis of the sentence. An example of this is Rule 4, which is not used in the phrase **the man** (Art + N), is used once in the phrase **the old man** (where the N of Art + N has been replaced by Ad + N), and is used twice in the phrase **the very old man** (where the N in the Art + Ad + N has itself been replaced with Ad + N, giving Art + Ad + Ad + N).

If we add some rules for transforming the results of these rules (V, N, Art, Ad) to words, we have completed the analysis of the sentence, **The very old man eats oysters.**

$$S \rightarrow NP + VP$$

NP	**VP**
NP → Art + N	
N → Ad + N	VP → V + NP
N → Ad + N	NP → Art + N
Art → The	V → eats
N → man	Art → (deleted)
Ad → very	N → oysters
Ad → old	

The application of these rules is shown in tree-structure format in Figure 12-3 along with a picture of the meaning structure for the same sentence.

The grammar as written so far cannot handle prepositional phrases, such as used in the sentence

The very old man lives in the tree house.

The phrase **in the tree house** is a *prepositional phrase* (*PP*) and it consists of a *preposition* (*Prep*) plus a normal noun phrase. The preposition in this sentence (**in**) signifies that the noun phrase that follows specifies location. To handle these phrases we simply need to expand Rule 2:

2A. VP → V + NP.

2B. VP → V + PP.

2C. PP → Prep + NP.

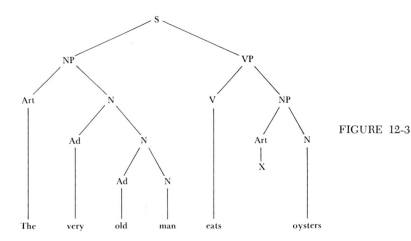

FIGURE 12-3

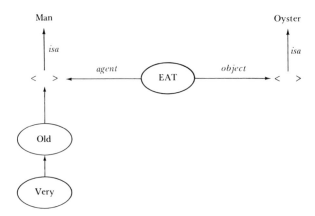

Clearly in any given situation, either Rule 2A or 2B is applied: not both.

Now, with the addition of a dictionary, we can apply these rules to the new sentence, as shown in Figure 12-4. The dictionary looks like this:

$$V \rightarrow \text{lives, eats, sings, ...}$$

$$N \rightarrow \text{man, tree, house, limerick, oyster, ...}$$

$$\text{Art} \rightarrow \text{the, a, an, ...}$$

$$\text{Ad} \rightarrow \text{old, many, few, very, tree, ...}$$

$$\text{Prep} \rightarrow \text{in, on, at, by, to, ...}$$

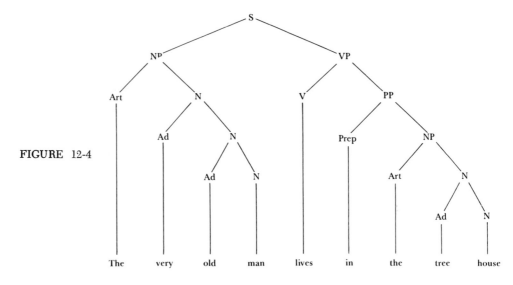

FIGURE 12-4

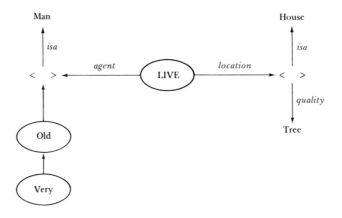

Figures 12-3 and 12-4 show in diagram form the derivation of sentences. Because these rules all revolve around phrases, they are called *phrase-structure rules* (or sometimes *rewrite rules*), and the complete set of rules determines a *phrase-structure grammar*. (The several rules shown here are far from complete.) *Transformational* rules must be added to these phrase structure rules to account for the way that these phrases can be rearranged in the actual surface structure of sentences. For example, consider the passive sentence:

The tree house is lived in by the very old man.

A passive sentence requires a rearrangement of the phrases of the sentence. Thus, in this example, the original sentence had the phrase structure:

$$NP \quad + \quad V \quad + \quad PP$$
(**The very old man**) + (**lives**) + (**in the tree house**)

The passive sentence construction rearranges this in the format:

$$PP \quad + \quad V \quad + \quad NP$$
(**In the tree house**) + (**lives**) + (**the very old man**)

This sentence framework, although perfectly intelligible, is not normally considered to be grammatical, except in certain stylistic conventions such as in poetry:

> *In the tree house lives*
> *the very old man*
> *who constantly eats oysters*
> *as fast as he can.*

Normally, passive constructions are signaled by special construction of the verb. Moreover, the agent (or instrument) of the verb is signaled by the preposition **by.** Hence, some more modification of the sentence must occur: The initial PP has its preposition deleted, leaving a NP; the verb has an auxiliary added to it; the terminal NP is preceded by the preposition **by** turning it into a PP; the Prep deleted from the PP is reinserted after the verb. In successive stages, the changes are:

(The very old man)	*(lives)*		*(in the tree house)*
(NP_1) +	(V)	+	(PP)
(PP) +	(V)	+	(NP_1)
$(Prep + NP_2)$	+ $(Aux + V)$ + $(Prep)$ +		$(by + NP_1)$
(NP_2)	+ $(Aux + V)$ + $(Prep)$ +		(PP)
(**The tree house**)	(**is lived**)	(**in**)	(**by the very old man**)

These are *transformational rules,* since they allow the various segments of the sentence to be shuffled about or transformed. Syntactical cues to the reshuffling are added, however, presumably to enable the person who reads or hears the transformed sentence to reconstruct the original version, although, as the poetry example shows, this is not always necessary.

It is possible to build up complex sentences from more simple ones. Thus,

The very old man who lives in the tree house eats oysters.

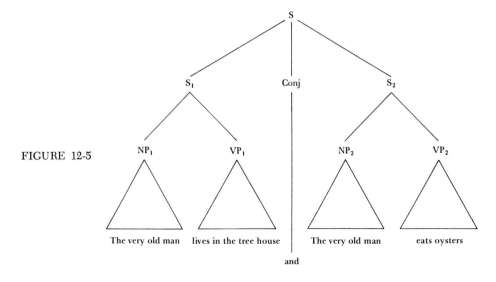

FIGURE 12-5

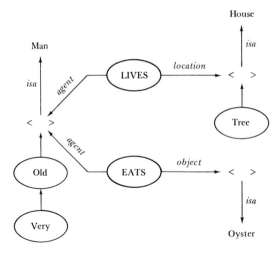

is composed of the two sentences we have been discussing. A slightly different way to combine sentences is with *conjunctions* (*Conj*):

1A. S → S + Conj + S.

1B. S → NP + VP.

Conj → and, but, because, or, . . .

Thus, by Rule 1A, our two sentences can be combined this way:

(**The very old man lives in a tree**) *and* (**the very old man eats oysters**)

This sentence is diagrammed in Figure 12-5.[1] By looking at the sentence, the outline of the sentence, and the diagram for the meaning structure, we see that NP_1 is both the same as NP_2 and also plays a role in S_1 analogous to NP_2 in S_2. Normally, whenever this happens, we apply a *deletion rule,* allowing NP_2 to be eliminated:

The very old man lives in a tree and eats oysters.

Deletions often cause difficulties in the analysis of sentences because, once the item is deleted, it is difficult to tell what was there originally. Thus, deletions are often signaled by replacing the deleted phrase with a pronoun:

The very old man lives in the tree house and *he* eats oysters.

I saw the girl you saw talking to John yesterday and *she* waved at me.

The problem of reference

One major problem in communication is to ensure that both speaker and listener have the same concept in mind. If we remind you of a discussion from a previous chapter, we must identify that discussion precisely enough that you will recall the proper one. The problem of specifying a concept is called the *problem of reference.* All languages provide mechanisms for letting the speaker point out to the listener just what concepts are under discussion. In English, the simplest mechanisms to use for signalling information are the *definite* and *indefinite articles:* the words *the* and *a.* (These words are also called *determiners* because they *determine* the status of the phrase that follows them.) When the word *the* occurs in a sentence, it usually means that the speaker believes that the listener will know what is meant, or that it will be explained shortly. The listener, therefore, uses the word *the* as a signal that the concept that follows should already exist in his or her own memory structures.

Language is not really quite this simple. Although *the* is a signal, it sometimes has other meanings, for there are a lot of subtle situations that arise in the specification of a concept. Moreover, the speaker and the listener often are not so closely calibrated that one really knows what the other person's knowledge structures look like. But still, in general, words like

the, those, these, this, that, them, their,
he, him, his, she, her, hers, . . .

---

[1] Note that we have introduced a new symbol into the diagram: the large triangle. This is simply a shorthand for the tree structure that would normally be drawn for the expansion of the NP's and VP's into the final words. The actual structures that the triangles have replaced are shown in Figures 12-3 and 12-4.

refer to particular concepts that the listener is expected to already know. On the other hand, words like

a, an, some, any, . . .

refer to concepts that are either just being introduced or where it does not really matter whether the listener and speaker agree exactly. Sometimes, when the word *the* is used, the explanation follows in the very same sentence, **as in**

The cat that howled all night on the fence outside my bedroom window . . .

Here, the phrase *the cat* is not meant to be understood without the clarification that follows. The clarification is contained in a *clause,* signalled with the word *that.* The *that clause* explains **the cat:**

Which cat? Why, the particular cat that I am about to tell you about—the cat *that howled all night on* **the fence.**
What fence? Why the fence *that is right outside my bedroom window.*

Once all these concepts have been introduced, the speaker can continue simplifying the sentence tremendously by using *pronouns* such as:

It *didn't stop until I threw both my shoes at* **it,** *but then* **it** *must have eaten* **them** *or something, because this morning I couldn't find either* **one.** *So* **that's** *why I'm barefoot today.*

The words *it* and *them* are *pronouns* that provide us with simple ways to refer to concepts. Thus the pronouns *it, them,* and *that* refer to the cat, the shoes, and the entire story, respectively. Pronouns are not always easy to decipher. Many problems occur in communication because one person erroneously believes the other understands which concept is being discussed.

Figure 12-6

Different languages—different rules. Most of the discussion in this chapter is based on an analysis of English. What happens in other languages? Actually, the story is much the same but the details change. The basic problems of reference, of conversational postulates, and of communicating ideas and structures are similar for all languages and all cultures. The differences are more in the manner of the details than in the principles.

Studies of all languages, from those such as English, French, Russian, and Japanese, to others such as Arabic and the American Indian languages show that all have similar mechanisms. Sometimes referents are given by changing the form of words, sometimes by the order of the words in the sentence. Pronouns can often be eliminated by setting up specific spatial locations for the concepts that are to be talked about.

FIGURE 12-6

Thus, in sign language, a signer telling of an incident that involved two people and some object might "place" one person to the right, the other to the left, and the object in the middle. Then, by turning to the right or to the left while making the signs, or by gesturing to any one of the places, the appropriate reference is automatically indicated, yet without using any specific word or sign. In all languages the basic problem of reference remains the same, so each language must have some specific way of dealing with it.

The similarities across languages are not accidental. There must be common factors operating in all languages. Communication among people requires information about memory structures to be passed back and forth among them. Language is only the vehicle for the transmission. The basic problems of communication reflect the problems of making mutual contact among diverse ideas, of explaining the concepts held by one person to another, and of finding some sort of common mutual understanding about the concepts being communicated. Moreover, all people have the very same mechanisms for seeing, hearing, speaking, and gesturing. All have the same processing mechanisms of perception, pattern recognition, and memory structures. Thus, although each language and each culture has evolved special methods, they all share common purpose and common information-processing capabilities. Often, of course, the languages and the cultures have evolved specialized procedures, tailored to the types of interactions that are common and the sorts of topics that are discussed. Hence, when people with different languages or different cultures attempt to communicate, there can be problems, especially when a person interprets something according to one cultural rule, when in fact it might mean something quite different according to the rule used by the other.

THE POWER OF WORDS

The power of words is the power of infinite flexibility. Language labels are arbitrary. Each language community has some degree of freedom in the way it carves up perceptual experiences in assigning names. Any set of examples can be linked together through a common label and thus force a specific pattern of generalization and differentiation on the developing conceptual structure of the child. A person from the Philippines must develop a conceptual organization for 92 different terms for rice; the Eskimo discriminates more than half a dozen different types of snow. The symbols that are used by any given language community reflect the perceptual and symbolic structures that are most useful to them. But perceptual capabilities are not altered by the acquisition of a language. Any person, regardless of the language spoken, can distinguish among the varieties of rice that receive special labels in the Philippine community, even if they cannot be named. The differences can be described symbolically—one type of rice is smaller, perhaps more oval-shaped, and slightly darker in color. As language begins to interact with conceptual development, words become the anchor points of conceptual structures. Once we have words as names of objects and events, we can think by manipulating the words, often a far easier task than that of manipulating the concepts themselves. But does the use of language labels alter the way we think? Does it affect what we see, what we attend to, or what we remember?

Memory for simple perceptual experiences is directly related to the ease with which the language can communicate that experience, since the efficiency with which an experience can be encoded into memory depends upon the previously acquired symbolic structure in the data base. The way in which a given language refers to perceptual experiences can have a considerable effect on the encoding and retention of sensory information. Recall that there is considerable evidence that incoming information is often encoded into its acoustic label on its journey into memory. These labels can provide a potential filter for the information that is remembered about an event.

Each language community seems to develop its own labeling patterns that determine the ease of encoding, remembering, and discussing specific perceptual experiences. Events and perceptions that are important to a community tend to be expressible in a few words. The words themselves seem to be governed by a similar principle (called Zipf's Law). In most languages the most frequently used words are also the shortest. Notice, for example, the length of English prepositions: **in, of, at.** We will see that this is a special class of words that is used very frequently, since they communicate general relations among concepts. Abbreviations follow the same rule. New technological events introduced into a culture, such as the **automobile** or **television** tend initially to have relatively long descriptions associated with them. As they become frequently used in the language, the pressure toward communication accuracy and efficiency sets in: **automobile** becomes **auto** or **car; television** becomes **TV ; telephone** becomes **phone.**

People from all language groups can communicate all types of perceptual events that are communicable in other languages, although some may be more difficult than others. Each different language may affect the way experiences are normally structured and remembered, but it does not affect the underlying cognitive machinery that builds these structures.

The ability to use a simple word or phrase to describe a concept does have far reaching implications on a person's ability to think and to interact with others. Labels have two important properties. First, they are a shorthand notation, allowing a single item to represent what might actually be a complex experience. Second, they represent the shared concerns of the community of language users. If thought processes are limited by the amount of information that can be maintained within short-term memory at any one time, then use of a shorthand notation increases the power of the memory by letting a few items stand for a complex set of thoughts. In science and mathematics the powerful use of symbols is well known: When we use the single term *STM* or *DNA* or the single symbols Σ or H to stand for the complex ideas of memory, genetics, summation, or entropy, we increase the ease with which we can think or speak about these concepts. This, in turn, aids the ways by which the concepts can be manipulated and transformed into new ideas and new formulations.

Language could not serve as a means to communicate unless it were able to take advantage of the shared experiences of the community of language users. The word "entropy" has quite different meanings for different people. It means one thing for someone whose primary concern is thermodynamics, a different (although related) thing for someone who studies information or communication, and yet a different (although still related) thing to someone interested in philosophy, or art, or the relationships among the concepts of orderliness, energy, and communication. Words like "home," "friends," and "love," all depend upon a shared set of experiences for their meanings to be shared. Different people share similar meanings for words only inasmuch as they share similar cultural and learning experiences. The use of language requires the shared meaning structures of words and a shared cultural background.

Words and morphemes   Words are not the smallest unit of meaning: Words themselves are composed of parts. The part of a word that contains the basic unit of meaning is called a *morpheme*. Many words are also morphemes, such as

> house, car, but, and, of, hospital

But words can have prefixes added or subtracted and the prefixes themselves are morphemes. Thus, the morpheme *-s*, when added to the end of some nouns, indicates plurality:

> psychologist + s = psychologists

The morpheme *-en* can change some adjectives and nouns to verbs:

> dark + en = darken

Similarly, we have prefixes and suffixes we add to words that expand upon their meaning:

> anti-, pre-, re-, dis-, un-, -ed, -ing, -en, -ism, -ment, -ly,

illustrated by that favorite word of children:

> anti + dis + establish + ment + ar + ian + ism
> = antidisestablishmentarianism

Actually, English is remiss in the construction of new words from morphemes, at least compared to most languages. The German who reads this discussion will wonder what the fuss is all about: the construction of new words by putting together old ones is done routinely in German.

When someone says

> I borrowed a book on juggling from Lucy.

an enormous range of implications are conveyed by the words in that sentence. At the simplest level of analysis, the words themselves convey more than single concepts. The word "borrow" for example, is a reasonably complex concept. Consider the phrase:

> *Person P borrows object O from donor D.*

This sentence can be translated into the following sequence:

> *Person D had possession of object O.*
> *Person P wanted possession of O for a limited amount of time.*
> *P wanted O because some of the properties of O were desirable to P.*
> *Person D did not need the desirable properties of O, at least not for
>   the limited time that P wished to have O.*
> *D knows that P has O.*
> *P asked D if D would give possession of O to P for a limited time.*
> *D gave permission for P to have O.*
> *P promised to return O after some time. (That is, P entered into a
>   social obligation with D, that if D gave O to P, later P would give
>   O to D.)*
> *Possession of O was transferred from D to P.*

This analysis may seem a bit far-fetched, but if anything, it is not complete enough. You can convince yourself that all these implications result from the sentence by trying a few experiments. For example, consider the results of adding some *but* conditions afterwards. Each *but* adds a new interpretation to the sentence that violates one of the inferences, thereby making the inference visible. Here is a sequence of *buts,* in the same order as the list of inferences. Notice how each condition violates an inference of the sentence.

> I borrowed a book on juggling from Lucy,
>> **but** she didn't have one.
>> **but** I don't intend to give it back.
>> **but** I haven't the slightest interest in juggling.
>> **but** she was using it continuously to learn the three-ball cascade.
>> **but** she doesn't know that I have it.
>> **but** I asked her for a book on history.
>> **but** she said I couldn't have it.
>> **but** then she wouldn't let me take it.

In a similar fashion, one can imagine the person who was told the sentence about the borrowing of the juggling book to respond with a series of questions.

> *Can I see it?* (implying that physical transfer of the book took place)
>
> *I didn't know that Lucy knew anything about juggling.* (implying that Lucy wouldn't have had the book unless she had read about its topic matter)
>
> *I'm surprised she would give it to you, of all people.* (implying that Lucy wouldn't be expected to give this particular borrower permission)

Language understanding may start with the simple analysis of the words and grammatical structure of the sentences that are uttered, but it certainly does not stop there. The implications of the utterances go far beyond the words: tremendous amounts of general knowledge about the world and about social conventions are implied as well. Much of the structure is carried by the hidden meanings of the words. As we have just seen, even the simple word "borrow" is quite complex, and it implies a lot of underlying structure. The analysis of a word into its underlying structure is called *lexical decomposition.*

Lexical decomposition is an important tool for understanding the psychological process of language understanding. Language comprehension simply will not take place without lexical decomposition that is coupled with inferential processes. Look at that long list of related concepts we produced for such a simple sentence as "I borrowed a book on juggling. . . ." At the moment, however, the need for this analysis creates a puzzle. If all these inferences are required, if the single word "borrow" requires such a lengthy analysis, how do we manage to understand the sentences we read and hear as quickly as we do? Do not all these analyses take an exorbitant amount of time?

At the present time, this whole line of research is much too young to have reached any definite conclusions. Lexical decomposition might get postponed until the time that it is needed, rather than being done automatically, with the receipt of each new sentence. A number of researchers, for example, have been unable to find good evidence for lexical decomposition, despite the fact that they agree that it is a logical necessity.

It is most likely that only partial decomposition is performed at the time that ideas are received. Probably some concepts are fully decomposed, others only partially, and some not at all. Decomposition has its deficits both in the amount of processing effort it takes to do all the analysis and also in the amount of memory load it imposes. Think of the horrible load on short-term memory structures if every time someone wished to think of Amy borrowing that book on juggling from Lucy they had to keep in mind all the various implications. How much tidier to use the single, simple concept of "borrow," adding the underlying components only when necessary. Since short-term memory is quite limited in capacity, filling it up with the aftereffects of the analysis of a single word would be an extremely inefficient way to perform language processing.

The psychological mechanisms of language understanding have a number of constraints upon their operation. For one thing, they must work sufficiently fast that they can keep up with the speech. A little bit of introspection reveals that the mechanisms just barely keep up. In normal conversation, especially the polite, relatively meaningless conversation that takes place formally, the language mechanisms have no difficulty. Indeed, there is so much time left over that it is sometimes possible to listen to two or more conversations, simply by time sharing—switching attention rapidly among them. In lectures, however, or when encountering a rapid speaker, the mechanisms often fail to keep up with the analysis of the meaning. The analysis of how the sentence is put together (the syntactic analysis) seems to get finished, but a full understanding of the message lags behind. This leads to the feeling that "I understood the words, but I certainly didn't understand what was said."

PSYCHOLOGICAL MECHANISMS OF LANGUAGE UNDERSTANDING

A second constraint is that the analysis of the sentence must proceed primarily in the same order as the words are spoken. At first, this requirement might seem obvious, but in fact, we will see that some parts of the language analysis cannot really be completed until a good deal of the sentence has been heard. It is sometimes more efficient to analyze sentences backwards, from the last word back to the first. Students of German often are taught to look at the printed sentence until they find the main verb and then to work backwards from there. The person listening to the language does not have this flexibility, however. The only way one could perform the analysis of spoken language backwards would be if the words not yet analyzed could be maintained temporarily in a memory system until the language mechanisms were ready for them. But the size of short-term and sensory memories is simply not sufficient to allow this. (Note that in those languages that seem to require backward processing—such as German—the written form of the language is usually much more complex than the spoken form. Literary German may indeed have to be understood by going through the sentences backwards, but this can be done because the printed page serves as a memory for the words. Spoken German is not as complex as written German.)

A final constraint upon the language-analyzing mechanisms is that they must be robust, tolerant of errors and missing information. It must be possible to understand spoken language even when the speaker makes a mistake or when the listener lapses in attentiveness now and then. Language understanding allows these errors, so whatever the language understanding mechanisms, they must not be overly demanding about receiving perfect linguistic utterances.

Understanding sentences The mechanisms responsible for our understanding of the printed and spoken language are very closely related to the mechanisms of perception and pattern recognition (studied in Chapters 1 and 7). This is no surprise, for the problems are very closely related. Indeed, the difficulties of deciphering the visual and auditory symbols that comprise language are precisely problems in perception. And, as in perceptual processing, we find that language is analyzed by a combination of data-driven, bottom-up mechanisms and conceptually driven, top-down mechanisms.

Data-driven and conceptually driven processing. In our discussion of pattern recognition, we saw that two different directions of processing were important: *data-driven* and *conceptually driven* processing. Data-driven processes are those that respond to the signals arriving at the sensory systems: the eyes and ears in the case of language. In data-driven processing, the sights and sounds are deciphered, probably into sensory features. These features are recognized by specialized sensory-analyzing mechanisms. When appropriate combinations of features occur, they are recognized as the component parts of particular items. Finally, the collection of items present at any moment (and the interrelationships among them) yield an interpretation of the visual or auditory scene. This direction of analysis is also called *bottom-up* analysis (because it starts with the "lowest" level of information—sensory data—and works its way up the chain to the "highest" level—meaning structures.)

Conceptually driven processing moves in the other direction, starting with the expectations and contextual cues that are always present. Are we talking about language understanding?—then expect to find words referring to grammar, to memory structures; expect to find the demons of Chapter 7 popping up at any moment. These expectations work at many levels. At the highest level of conceptualization, the general nature of the memory structures that you are building as a result of the sentences you attend to is used to guide the lower level of analysis. You expect to get information that will fill in the details of the structures and add the missing pieces. So, conceptually guided processing helps structure expectations about the topic matter that is being discussed, about the particular type of information that will be provided, and then about the specific content of the arriving sentences. Moreover, from experience in reading the book or listening to the particular person who is speaking you expect a certain style of speaking, certain grammatical classes of speech, particular vocabulary, and even a particular type style or accent. This flow of analysis is conceptually guided processing: it works from the highest level of general conceptualizations of the topic down to more and more specific information, finally to the expectation of particular words, visual images, and sounds. Conceptually driven processing is also called *top-down* analysis (because it starts with the "highest" level of analysis—meaning structures—and works down toward the "lowest" level—the arriving data).

Both data-driven and conceptually driven processing must take place together: each is necessary, neither alone will usually suffice. In this section, we demonstrate how the different sources of information present can interact to yield an understanding of language. To illustrate this, we bring back our old friends from Chapter 7, *demons*. Demons are imaginary creatures that we have constructed to aid you in understanding what might go on in the mind. Each demon is actually a reasonably simple device for carrying out some specific operation. A demon has a set task, and it sits around inside the mind waiting for the opportunity to do its job. Whenever it sees an appropriate set of conditions, it does its assigned task, signalling its activity either by attracting the attention of other demons or by sending its results to other demons, who determine if they should take any actions. We illustrate this sending of data by having demons write their results on a *blackboard* that is viewed by all other relevant demons. But do not think there is anything mystical about them: they represent simple, straightforward operations.

The basic strategy is simple. Different demons are specialized for different purposes. There are demons for

words (such as bus, horse, the, caution)

grammatical classes (such as determiner, noun, preposition)

sentence components (such as noun phrase, verb phrase, prepositional phrase)

In addition, some demons look out for special grammatical situations, attempting to piece together the components discovered by others into intelligible ways. And other demons specialize in meanings, hunting through the data base of memory for the implications of the information coming in.

A SYSTEM FOR
UNDERSTANDING
LANGUAGE

Demons

Some demons drive the system from the data, stating what features are actually being perceived and presenting the data that must be accounted for in the analysis. Sentence and meaning demons work from the top down, suggesting hypotheses to account for the data that have arrived. These conceptually based demons make the system powerful, fast, and relatively insensitive to errors made in the sensory analysis. But the conceptual guidance itself makes errors, telling the system to expect things that never happen. The data-driven demons must correct the conceptually driven demons. The system must always hedge, always be willing to back up and try a new path.

Understanding a particular sentence

Let us follow the process of understanding a sentence. Take as an example:

Kris rode the horse with caution.

Follow the analysis shown in Figure 12-7. When the demons involved in language mechanisms hear the word *Kris*, they identify it as the proper name of a person: assume that *Kris* is a friend, a person already known. If so, the demons can find the structure in memory that corresponds to *Kris*, an important first step in building the appropriate understanding of the sentence.

The second word of the sentence is *rode*. The sounds of the words *rode* and *road* are the same, but they mean quite different things. We must determine which word is meant. We do this quite simply by the context: Sentences often start out with a proper noun followed by a verb, less often with a proper noun followed by a noun, Hence we expect the verb interpretation—*rode*.

The analysis of the words *Kris rode* has set the conceptually driven processing to predict a set of possible continuations.

Kris rode a bus.
Kris rode to work.
Kris rode a bicycle.
Kris rode in . . . *any moving object large enough to carry a person, but most likely to be a vehicle.*

These expectations could be wrong, the sentence could actually be

Kris rode quickly.

The next word turns out to be *the*, a definite determiner. As we have already discussed, *the* is a special word. First, it signifies the start of a noun phrase. More important, however, it is a signal that the phrase that follows may be one that the speaker believes the listener already knows about, or that will be explained in the rest of the sentence.

FIGURE 12-7

Suppose that the sentence prior to the one being analyzed was

> There was a horse with a saddle (but no owner) walking all around the university yesterday. Kris said she would take it to the football field. Kris rode the . . .

Now, not only does the word *the* signify that the next phrase will be something already known but, because the previous sentence has been about a horse, and because the verb *ride* signifies the sort of thing one can do to a horse, the listener has every right to believe that the next word will be horse, or related to horse, as in:

Kris rode the strange new horse . . .
Kris rode the ownerless horse . . .

or as in the actual sentence:

Kris rode the horse with caution.

This sentence fits the expectations. Note that the phrase introduced by *with* adds further information to the description, in this case specifying the *manner:* how the action was performed. The preposition *with* usually specifies a qualification on some action. Other possibilities for this sentence would be:

Kris rode the horse with
    care.
    Glen.
    the aid of a book on how to ride horses.
    one hand tied behind her back.

Still other possibilities exist, as in:

Kris rode the horse with the cropped mane.

In this particular case, however, the sentence is interpreted properly, with conceptually driven processing interacting smoothly with the data-driven analyses to determine the final structures. The conceptually guided processing provided the guidance necessary to avoid the potential ambiguity over the sound of the word *rode,* and it helped predict the form of the rest of the sentence. But the conceptually guided processing was never sufficient. It never was able to predict the exact words that actually occurred: the data-driven processing was necessary to get the system started and to keep it running smoothly on a proper interpretation. Neither the data-driven nor the conceptually driven processing alone would have done the task as easily as the joint combination of efforts made possible.

Garden path sentences   The analysis of sentences does not always proceed as smoothly and directly as the example of Kris riding the horse illustrated. Sometimes context and expectations can set up the system in deceptive ways. It is instructive (and fun) to collect examples of sentences that can be interesting to analyze: Consider the meaning of the sentence

I saw the pigeons flying to the statue.

This sentence is quite straightforward: no particular problems are encountered in reading it. The related sentence

I saw the Grand Canyon flying to New York.

is quite different. This is an example of a *garden path sentence.* It usually causes the language analysis system to go astray, down the wrong garden path, suddenly brought up short with the realization that the Grand Canyon cannot suddenly sprout wings and fly through the air. We deliberately set you up with the sentence

I saw the pigeons flying to the statue.

In actuality, the second sentence is the same as

I saw the Grand Canyon while I was on my airplane trip to New York.

Such garden path sentences are useful in demonstrating how the language understanding system sometimes makes erroneous hypotheses about the sentence structures. If you liked that example, try these (the correct interpretations are provided in the Suggested Readings section):

The boat sailed past the pier sank.
The old man the boats.

Language is a means that people have evolved to communicate their   SUMMARY
ideas to each other. Language enables people to encode the structural
networks inside their memory systems and to express them through
spoken or written symbols. The speaker or writer of language must always take into account the capabilities and knowledge structures of the
listener or reader. In turn, the listener (or reader) must attempt to
decipher the utterances, interpreting what each utterance could mean,
and asking why each one might have been produced.

Language systems are formal mechanisms for transmitting information
among people. For human beings, language is perhaps the most important cognitive function that they perform. It is little wonder then,
that the study of language processing is a fundamental part of the study
of human information processing.

In this chapter, the following terms and concepts that we consider to be   REVIEW OF TERMS
important have been used. Please look them over. If you are not able   AND CONCEPTS
to give a short explanation of any of them, you should go back and
review the appropriate sections of the chapter.

*Terms and
concepts you
should know*

Conversational postulates
   for normal conversation
   among social equals and unequals
   in being very polite
   in answering questions
   in telling lies
Surface structure
Deep structure
English grammar
   noun phrase, verb phrase, prepositional phrase
   phrase-structure grammar
   transformations
   tree structures
Reference
   determiners
   pronouns
Words as symbols
   language and STM processing load
   morphemes
   lexical decomposition
Understanding sentences
   role of conceptually driven and data-driven analyses
   word demons
   the role of the blackboard in communicating among demons
   the analysis of sentences
   garden path sentences

SUGGESTED
READINGS [2]

There are a number of excellent references on the study of language. Perhaps the most pleasant is the book by Peter Farb (1974) entitled *Word play: What happens when people talk.* This is a general introduction for the nonscientist that discusses many of the different issues involved in language understanding, including some good chapters on conversational postulates and related issues.

All the works on language presented here owe an immense debt to Noam Chomsky, whose work on the study of grammar revolutionized

---

[2] The two garden path sentences discussed earlier in the chapter should be interpreted to mean:

1. The boat that was sailed past the pier sank (later in the day).
2. In case of shipwreck, the young and the old should leave the ship first and enter the lifeboats. The young huddle in the center, the old should man the oars. Hence, the old man the boats.

linguistic theory. Most of the papers that we have referred to above will credit Chomsky extensively. But most of his papers are very advanced and not easy for the beginner to read: perhaps the best place to start with Chomsky is in the appendix that he wrote for Lenneberg's (1967) on *Biological foundations of language* (Chomsky, 1967).

The work described in this chapter uses concepts by a number of modern linguists. The case grammar comes from Charles Fillmore (1968, 1969). The books in which the Fillmore articles appeared contain other papers highly relevant to the linguistics used here. Bruce (1976) provides a good review of different work on case grammar. The text book by the linguists Fromkin and Rodman (1974) provides an excellent introduction to the formal analysis of language and recent work by linguists.

The book *Explorations in cognition* by Norman, Rumelhart, and the LNR ·Research Group (1975) contains a report of the work that has guided much of the discussion in this book. Chapter 3 of the LNR book deals with conversational postulates· and the problem of reference, and is perhaps the easiest spot to begin the search for more information on these topics. Chapter 4 is an introduction to modern literature in linguistics on the meaning of sentences, and it too provides a rapid guide to that literature. Chapters 5, 6, 7, and 8 discuss how language is understood and present a description of a mechanism for language understanding called the *Augmented Transition Network* (ATN) which forms the basis for our demons. Finally, Chapters 9 and 10 discuss the problems of lexical decomposition and, again, provide good introductions on these topics.

An important contribution to our understanding of language is provided by the work of Schank, most especially his notions of lexical decomposition and causality: he calls his work *conceptual dependency theory*. The most complete presentation of Schank's ideas are found in his book (Schank, 1975), although his *Cognitive Psychology* article is also a good starting point (Schank, 1972). The work by Winograd (1972) presents an excellent description of the problems of machine understanding of language and describes the development of a computer system for understanding language. Winograd's later book (in preparation) is an excellent introduction to modern computer-based analyses of language.

Anderson and Bower (1973) provide an important psychological analysis of language processing, and Anderson's later book (1976) provides many advances. Anderson also discusses how a child might acquire language. Miller and Johnson-Laird (1976) do a thorough analysis of language in their book, which is an important contribution to our understanding.

A fascinating look at language analysis as a guide to psychotherapy, showing how a deep underlying understanding of language might help the therapist get at the problems facing the patient is provided by Bandler and Grinder (1975). Fromkin's (1973) *Scientific American* article on slips of the tongue is amusing, but also a demonstration of how an analysis of these errors can provide important clues to how speech is organized in the human. In a more traditional vein, Lindsley (1975) has experimentally examined how simple utterances are planned, demonstrating that in many cases we select the verb of a sentence before deciding upon the other words.

The literature on the psychological study of language (psycholinguistics) is large. A good entry to the field is through the *Annual Review of Psychology* articles: See Johnson-Laird (1974). The chapter by Bever (1970) has been an important source of some basic strategies that might be used in the understanding of language. Volume 7 of the *Handbook of perception* is entitled *Language and speech* (Carterette & Friedman, 1976). Fodor, Bever, and Garrett (1974) cover a good deal of ground in their book *The psychology of language*.

Further studies of language are presented in the next chapter, where we discuss some issues involved in the child's learning of language, and so you should consult the Suggested Readings for Chapter 13.

13 Learning and cognitive development

PREVIEW

The ability to learn the consequences of one's actions is fundamental to the adaptive behavior of all organisms. Much of the study of intelligent behavior can be characterized as the study of the ability to learn about the contingencies of the world.

There is little formal distinction between learning and memory. Studies of learning tend to emphasize primarily the acquisition of knowledge: Studies of memory tend to emphasize the retention and use of that knowledge. Clearly, the two are so interrelated that the study of one must necessarily be a study of the other. Thus, we have already discussed the principles of learning in the several extensive chapters on memory. A major omission, however, has been how the knowledge within the memory system is acquired: How the relationships that exist among the environmental situations, the actions of the human, and the resulting outcomes are established. When an outcome cannot occur unless either a specific set of environmental conditions are satisfied or a specific action is performed, then we speak of the *contingencies* that operate among environmental conditions, actions, and outcomes (for example, the outcome, rain, is contingent upon certain atmospheric conditions). The major emphasis of this chapter is the way by which knowledge of contingencies is acquired: The problem of *contingency learning*.

The chapter starts with a discussion of the laws of learning: they form the foundation for the rest of the chapter. Following that, we turn to the development of the child, heavily influenced by the work of the Swiss psychologist, Jean Piaget. The important thing to get out of this section is some understanding of the concept of a sensorimotor schema, of the way that layers of knowledge interact, with each layer forming a foundation for the knowledge that is yet to be acquired. This layering of prerequisite concepts and structures makes it appear as if the child progresses in stages, continually enriching its abilities to do mental operations.

The acquisition of language is obviously an extremely critical part of the learning structures of a child, and a major portion of this chapter is devoted to that topic. We emphasize the problem faced by the child in acquiring language concepts and the principles that must be involved.

The chapter ends with a discussion of how the principles of the chapter apply to other areas, especially to the daily learning that people experience. Throughout all these discussions, the emphasis is on the principles that the learner uses to develop appropriate memory structures.

COGNITIVE LEARNING

Experimental studies of learning suggest that a simple, yet powerful principle is at the basis of intelligent behavior. Both perception and behavior appear to become organized by observing the consequences of actions. In the language of one of the foremost investigators of cognitive development, Jean Piaget, the organism learns by constructing sensorimotor schemas.[1] It extracts the relationship between the information picked up by its sensory system and its actions (motor activities). A *sensorimotor schema* is a plan (a scheme) for performing an organized sequence of actions to perform some specific act, coordinating the information picked up by the sensory system with the necessary motor (muscle) movements. The acts of eating, walking, or riding a bicycle require their own well-developed sensorimotor schemas. In order to construct these schemas the organism must be particularly sensitive to certain kinds of consequences, such as those associated with a desirable and necessary outcome, like food. But, in the human infant at least, any change in the external world may attract its attention and serve as the basis for learning about the contingencies between actions and outcomes.

Our goal is to describe the underlying conceptual schemas that result from the learning process. Our view of learning is the same as our view of memory: when new information is learned, it is added to preexisting meaning structures within the memory system. The problem facing the learner is to determine the conditions that are relevant to the situation, to determine what the appropriate actions are, and to record that information properly.

Laws of learning   Perhaps the most powerful description of the controlling factor of behavior is the *Law of Effect:*

> **An action that leads to a desirable outcome is likely to be repeated in similar circumstances.**

This law is simple: it is an attempt to state the basic condition that underlies much of learned behavior. It was first postulated by the psychologist Thorndike in 1898, and it has been studied extensively. Those of you who have had other introductions to psychology will recognize the law of effect as a central guiding statement of learning. To cause an organism to learn (usually the organism is a laboratory animal), make certain that each time it performs the desired act it immediately gets a reward. Traditionally, there are two different types of learning: *classical conditioning* and *instrumental learning*. The investigation of operant conditioning has been heavily influenced by the work of B. F. Skinner, who began

---

[1] *Schema, schemas,* and *schemata.* Technically, the word *schema* has *schemata* as its plural. We prefer the simpler term *schemas.*

studying learning processes in the early 1930s. The term *operant conditioning* comes from the emphasis on the study of behavior that *operates* upon the environment in order to produce some outcome. The field of operant learning is a part of *instrumental learning*—the acquisition of responses that are *instrumental* in obtaining some reward. Operant behavior is today a major influence in the study of animal and human learning, and it emphasizes the nature of the reinforcements that are given to the organism as a result of its behavior patterns.

Our concern in this book is with human learning, with the way that people acquire and use new knowledge. As such, we are interested in the way that new structures are acquired into memory and are coupled together with the appropriate actions that need to be performed in any situation. The path we follow is to examine the development of a memory *schema:* the basic organizing unit of information in memory. An important organizing principle will be the combination of schemas for motor control (muscle movement) and for sensory images. We call the schema that combines sensory and motor information a *sensorimotor schema.* We view learning as the construction of knowledge structures.

For our purposes, the law of effect is not a sufficient explanation of learning. In our opinion, it suffers the problem of attempting to describe the phenomena of learning by simple description of the events and responses of the organism, without any consideration of the internal information processing that must also be taking place. As a result, the law gets into serious difficulties in attempting to explain the real behavior of complex organisms. The problems result from several sources. First, the law of effect is vague about the temporal conditions that are involved. Second, it ignores the necessity for causal relationships between the actions and the outcome. Finally, the law of effect emphasizes the desirability of the outcome, known as its *reinforcing* value. We believe that the important part of an outcome is its *information.* The outcome serves as a signal to the organism about the result of its acts.

A critical assumption in our analysis concerns the role of *causality.* The organism must recognize the causal relation between its actions and the events of the world. Indeed, if there were no causal relation, why would there be the law of effect? In order to understand the phenomena of learning, we need three laws that state the relationships between an organism's actions and the apparent effects of those actions.

The Law of Causal Relationship:

> **For an organism to learn the relationship between a specific action and an outcome, there must be an apparent causal relation between them.**

The Law of Causal Learning:

For desirable outcomes:
The organism attempts to repeat those particular actions that have an apparent causal relation to the desired outcome.

For undesirable outcomes:
The organism attempts to avoid those particular actions that have an apparent causal relation to the undesirable outcome.

The Law of Information Feedback:

The outcome of an event serves as information about that event.

Note that there is an important distinction between *actual* causal relationships and *apparent* ones. The laws just stated are all based upon *apparent causality*. The animal does not necessarily know the way in which the world really operates.

The difference between real causality and apparent causality is related to the distinctions we made in the chapters on hearing and seeing between physical variables and psychological ones. Real causality is a statement about the world, about the physical conditions that operate there. But humans can only infer the operations of the world from their observations. There is a strong tendency to infer a causal relation between an action and an outcome that follows shortly thereafter. There are strong tendencies to infer causal relations among actions and outcomes that appear to be logically related (from other considerations) and to infer a lack of causality among the actions and outcomes that do not appear to be related. But the apparent causality may not reflect the real causality that operates in the world. Sometimes real and apparent causality will be the same. Sometimes humans will infer causal relations where there are none. Sometimes, they will not notice causal relations that actually do exist. Unless humans are capable of performing scientific experiments that can reveal the actual causal relationships, they must deal with inferred or apparent causal relationships between their actions and the outcomes.

Humans sometimes do act as if they are testing their ideas. In social situations, people attribute reasons for the actions of others, sometimes attributing the acts to environmental causes, sometimes to the personality of the person. Most people seem to believe that they get angry only when forced to by outside events, but that other people often get angry or "lose their tempers" because "that's the way they are—it's their temperament, they're always like that." The attribution of causes and purposes to the actions of oneself and of others makes an interesting subject of study, and in Chapter 16 we examine this issue (called *attribution theory* by social psychologists).

One important result of apparent causal relationships between responses and outcomes is the phenomenon known as *learned helplessness.* Animals and humans will not perform actions that would get them out of unpleasant or painful situations if they have come to believe that there is no causal relationship between their actions and the outcomes in a situation. In humans, such beliefs can apparently be a major contributing factor to the clinical abnormality called mental depression.

Learned helplessness

Consider the following experimental situation. A dog is placed in a *shuttle box,* an apparatus that has two compartments separated by a barrier. Its task is to learn to jump across the barrier from one compartment to the other at a particular time. The experiment is designed to produce a painful situation for the dog, one that it will attempt to avoid (or at least, to escape). The traditional technique used in psychological experiments has been to apply electric shock to the animals: a painful event that the animals will attempt to terminate.[2]

When the dog is in one compartment, the grid on the floor is electrified, presenting a shock to its feet. It quickly learns to *escape* the shock by jumping the barrier into the "safe" compartment. Usually the arrival of shock is preceded by a cue: ten seconds before the shock, a signal light comes on. The dog learns to *avoid* the shock by jumping the barrier during the ten seconds between the light cue and the shock. These two procedures are called *escape learning* and *avoidance learning,* respectively.

Notice what is learned with the avoidance procedure. Once the avoidance response has been learned, and the animal has learned to avoid the shock by jumping the barrier when the light comes on, its behavior is extremely difficult to extinguish. Even when the shocking apparatus has been totally disconnected from the shuttle box, the dog will continue to jump the barrier when the light comes on for hundreds of trials. To the animal, the contingency in operation is that it will not get a shock if it jumps the barrier. Disconnecting the shocking apparatus does not affect

---

[2] These studies grew out of a long series of research projects studying the fundamental properties of learning. The use of animals makes it possible to control the experiments to a greater extent. Electric shock has proven to be the most effective noxious stimulus in the study of particular types of behavioral situations. The results have led to a greater understanding of human behavior and have some application in developing clinical treatments for depressed patients. It is important to realize that important scientific discoveries often result from studies that were thought to be so fundamental that they had no foreseeable application.

this contingency. When the light comes on the animal jumps and does not get shocked. As far as the animal is concerned, its action has led to the result that was expected, so no change in behavior is warranted.

Now consider a situation in which a different dog is placed in a shuttle box, again with electric shocks. This time, however, there is no barrier, and no response that it can make will allow escape or avoidance of the shocks. There is no correlation between actions and outcomes. After the dog has acquired some experience with this condition, the experimenter changes the situation. Now, the barrier is again introduced and the situation changed so that it is possible to escape or avoid the shock by jumping the barrier at the appropriate time. Unlike the dogs in the earlier experiments, dogs that have first experienced the situation with zero correlation find it difficult to learn that they can now escape shock. Some dogs never learn, even if the experimenter carries them over the hurdle in an attempt to demonstrate what the dogs should do (Seligman, Maier, & Solomon, 1971). These dogs seem to develop a hypothesis of *helplessness*. Unfortunately for the dogs, once such a hypothesis is established, it is difficult to eradicate. During the period of inescapable shock, the dogs presumably learn that all the responses in their repertoire lead to shock. Each time the dog receives a shock, it also receives a confirmation of its hypothesis: the expectation being confirmed, the dog is even less likely to do something on the next trial.

Some insight into the situation comes from performing an analogous experiment on humans, the advantage being that we can then ask why they fail to learn the escape response once the conditions change. In one such experiment, of the subjects who never did learn to escape, 60% reported ". . . that they felt they had no control over shock, so why try. These subjects reported that they spent the majority of their time in preparation for the upcoming shock. Approximately 35% reported that they, after pushing one or two buttons (the appropriate response, if done at the proper time), abandoned the idea of escape [Thornton & Jacobs, 1971, p. 371]." Subjects who did not learn the zero correlation situation responded quite differently. Not only did they learn to escape, but more than 70% of them ". . . reported they felt they had control over shock, and their task was to find out how." The power of an inappropriate hypothesis is found in the behavior of subjects who had decided that shock was not under their control when, in the condition where they could actually escape, they "accidentally" did manage to escape. These subjects would sometimes ". . . escape or avoid shock on one or more trials, but on subsequent trials would again take the full (3 sec) shock. It appeared that these subjects did not associate their responding with the reinforcement."

One of the difficulties faced by the animal or human subject in the experiment on helplessness is that there is little to differentiate the condition of zero correlation from the new, changed situation. This is a common phenomenon: when the situation changes, but without any particular signal or noticeable way of telling, the animal or human will persist in the old behavior, even if it is now inappropriate. Why not? If a fearsome sea monster suddenly appears off the coast, eating four bathers and chasing numerous others, would you not hesitate to go swimming there? And if that sea monster now goes away, finding humans to be untasty and preferring the quiet comfort of the ocean depths, how are the bathers to know? If there is no signal that announces the departure of the sea monster, there is no way of deciding whether it is safe to enter the water. The prudent course of action is to swim elsewhere, preferably places not connected to the coast. People will therefore avoid swimming in the bay for a long time after the actual danger has passed.

The situation in which a person (or animal) apparently learns that no response will be effective in avoiding an unpleasant experience has been termed *learned helplessness*. This is another example of *metaknowledge*: the knowledge of one's own capabilities. In this case, the meta-knowledge is knowledge of one's own competence or control of a situation.

Seligman (1975) has suggested that the early learning experiences of a person help determine the amount of confidence that person has in his or her own abilities at a task. If two people are taught a series of skills, one by a competent instructor, the other by an unsatisfactory one, then it is likely that the person with the good training will learn the skills and the other will not. So far, no surprises. But this initial experience may generalize to other situations. The person who is now skilled has probably acquired self-confidence in a whole area. The person who failed may have generalized that feeling of failure into one of incompetence in the general area of those skills. This general feeling of either competence or incompetence can have important overall implications for an individual's behavior. In severe cases, the belief of inability to do things successfully can generalize to a belief of inability to deal with the normal situation in life. This, suggests Seligman, can lead to the general abnormality of mental behavior known as depression.

In the discussion of learning, a reinforcement helped the organism to acquire the response that just preceded. But reinforcement is also a signal, signifying to the organism just which conditions are the desirable ones and which are the undesirable ones. Thus, one would expect that a reinforcer would have its optimum signaling properties only if it is unambiguous; that is, it should not lead to any confusion about which specific action is being reinforced. To maximize this signaling property, one of two conditions must be met. Either the reinforcer must occur rapidly after the appropriate action so no confusion results from the

Reinforcement as a signal

performance of other, irrelevant actions and also so the action can still be remembered within the short-term memory; or, alternatively, if there is a delay in the outcome, the relevant event must be distinct enough to be identified within the long-term memory for events.

Normally, to teach an animal something, the outcome must follow the action within about 5 sec. This limit on the delay of reinforcement has been variously interpreted, but a simple interpretation, certainly, is that the outcome must occur soon enough to guarantee that the action to be reinforced is still within short-term memory. There are exceptions to this 5-sec finding. Animals seem capable of discovering (and thereby avoiding) dangerous foods, even though the illness that results from the ingestion of such foods may not occur for many hours (Garcia & Koelling, 1966). The association between the specific food and the illness appears to be a result of both an innate strategy and the appropriate use of the long-term memory structure. That is, the animal apparently automatically associates any feelings of nausea with the last novel food that it has eaten, and therefore will avoid that food. This would seem logical enough: it is reasonable to assume a causal relation between eating and nausea. This assumption will not work, however, unless the memory for the most recent meals is relatively complete and relatively accessible. But, interestingly enough, this appears to be true. Consider yourself. Although you probably made no special attempt to remember what you have eaten, you can probably remember with ease the things eaten for your last two meals. Usually, the strategy of avoiding novel foods eaten just prior to sickness is sufficient to prevent recurring food-caused sickness. The innate character of this strategy is shown by the fact that if an animal is made nauseous by some nonfood treatment (X-rays, for example), it will still shun the last novel food. The causal relationship between eating and health seems to be fundamental. There is no apparent causality between lights, buzzers, and nausea. Even if animals are placed in a situation in which a buzzer or light signals the arrival of heavy radiation (which causes radiation sickness), they will not learn to avoid the lights and buzzers. Rather, they tend to associate the cause of the sickness with the last novel food that they have eaten, even if the intake of food was several hours prior to getting sick, and even when the food itself had nothing to do with the sickness.

There are lots of anecdotes one can tell about similar situations with humans: someone getting sick after eating a new food often develops an intense dislike for the food, even if it is known that the sickness has nothing to do with that food. Similarly, a food that is eaten just prior to getting well seems to become well liked. Thus, in some cultures, a sick child is continually fed freshly made, home-cooked chicken soup. Because the child does eventually get better, it also develops a liking for the chicken soup. Later, when the child has become an adult, it may realize that the soup has nothing to do with the recovery from illness, but every time he or she becomes ill, there comes that craving for a bowl of homemade chicken soup.

A major theoretical issue for many years has been the question of whether or not learning can occur without awareness. This is a very difficult question to answer, as the length and fierceness of the dispute will testify. People who claim that there need not be awareness, often claim this to prove that an outcome must serve as a reinforcer, not as a signal in a learning experiment. The laws of learning that we have presented in this chapter will be bitterly contested by some psychologists, for they seem to imply conscious awareness of the causal relationship between an animal's acts and the environmental outcomes. But, as we shall see in the chapters to follow, human thinking does occur without the immediate awareness of the person, and certainly does occur without retrospective awareness. For example, one can be aware of the clue used in solving a problem or of the contents of a dream at the instant it is occurring, but have forgotten it within minutes afterward. Therefore, when quizzed by an experimenter, there would appear to have been absolutely no awareness of the event. The possible short life of the awareness of an event hampers the experimental search for an answer to the issue. But even if an answer were possible, there would appear to be no reason why memory schemas and hypotheses could not be developed and tested subconsciously, without the awareness of the person involved.

Learning and awareness

A contingency learning system geared simply to extract correlations among the environment, actions, and outcomes has a fatal flaw. It cannot separate out those aspects that actually cause the outcome from those that just accidentally happen to be correlated with it. A gambler may believe that crossing the fingers will ensure winning. A parachutist may believe that a good luck charm guarantees safety. A chimp may believe that standing on its left leg is essential in order for it to get grapes. This phenomenon is termed *superstitious behavior*. It is easily demonstrated in the laboratory. It suggests that once contingencies of an event have been established, the animal is strongly inclined to repeat past actions whenever it encounters a similar context. This aspect of contingency learning describes well many superstitious rituals, from rain dances to knocking on wood.

COGNITIVE
DEVELOPMENT

Humans, however, have a protective mechanism. Even a very young infant is not blindly driven by contextual cues, mechanically producing responses that are associated with sensorimotor schemata built up from

Learning by experimentation

past experiences. Rather, the infant appears to vary its actions intentionally in order to observe the similarities and differences in the consequences that result. Here, for example, is Piaget's (1952) description of his son Laurent's experimentation at the age of 10 months:

> Laurent is lying on his back but nevertheless resumes his experiments of the day before. He grasps in succession a celluloid swan, a box, etc., stretches out his arm and lets them fall. He distinctly varies the position of the fall. Sometimes he stretches out his arm vertically, sometimes he holds it obliquely, in front of or behind his eyes, etc. When the object falls in a new position (for example, on his pillow), he lets it fall two or three times more on the same place, as though to study the spatial relation; then he modifies the situation [p. 269].

An infant experiments with its world. In this way, it discovers how its actions affect the environment, and is protected against coincidental relationships between responses and external consequences. This strategy separates causes from correlations. (In some case, of courses, the principle is difficult to follow: parachutists do not leave their good luck charms at home just to test the relevance of their actions to the outcome. Nonetheless, experimentation is a crucial aspect of the intellectual development of human beings.)

The importance of expectations   *Goal-directed behavior.* Evidence that the infant is anticipating that specific consequences will result from its actions begins to appear at a very early age. Before an infant is 6 months old, it seems mainly to be reacting to external signals: it responds to events when they occur; it does not initiate them. If it sees an object, it may reach out for it or suck on it, but does not seem to be unduly perturbed when it disappears from view.

By about 6 months of age, however, it starts to show indications that it has specific expectations as it interacts with its environment. They appear first in its searching behavior. Before the age of around 6 months, attempts to retrieve objects that cannot be seen are rather primitive, perhaps only a brief groping or visual search for an object that has disappeared from view. But soon the infant shows a systematic exploration of the probable hiding places—under the covers, behind obstacles, in the closed fist of a parent. Finally, deductions about the location of an object from observations of the external events become a routine part of its search behavior.

The most complex aspects of goal-directed behavior emerge when we consider how the infant applies sensorimotor intelligence to solving practical problems. Examine again the behavior of Piaget's child, Laurent:

> At 16 months, 5 days, Laurent is seated before a table and I place a bread crust in front of him, out of reach. Also, to the right of the child I place a stick about 25 cm long. At first Laurent tries to grasp the bread without paying any attention to the instrument, and then he gives up [p. 335].

Laurent has a problem. His habitual response of reaching for an object fails to achieve the desired goal, so some new response must be tried. But how is the new response selected: Is it random; is it blind trial-and-error; is it based on things he has done at the table before?

> I then put the stick between him and the bread; it does not touch the objective but nevertheless carries with it an undeniable visual suggestion. Laurent again looks at the bread, without moving, looks very briefly at the stick, then suddenly grasps it and directs it towards the bread. But he grasped it toward the middle and not at one of its ends so that it is too short to obtain the objective. Laurent then puts it down and resumes stretching out his hand towards the bread. Then, without spending much time on this movement, he takes up the stick again, this time at one of its ends (chance or intention?), and draws the bread to him. . . . Two successive attempts yield the same result.
>
> An hour later I place a toy in front of Laurent (out of his reach) and a new stick next to him. He does not even try to catch the objective with his hand; he immediately grasps the stick and draws the toy to him [p. 335].

Somehow, Laurent has discovered that an action–consequence sequence must be modified to achieve a particular goal. But how did he learn the new schema? He had never before used sticks to retrieve objects. What was guiding his selection of responses and what precisely did he learn from his initial failure? Did he learn that his arm was not long enough so that he must search for an "arm extender?" How does he know that? How does the environmental context—the presence of sticks, for example—help satisfy his search for a solution to the problem?

Learning that a stick can be used as a tool for reaching something may sound like a primitive task, but it is a surprisingly difficult one. This level of problem solving is beyond the explanatory capabilities of any existing theories of contingency learning, since this is very sophisticated learning, despite its apparent simplicity. In fact, it seems to represent the intellectual limits of nonhuman organisms: Only the very highest species of animals—some species of primates and man—are capable of solving the "stick problem."

The cognitive capability of the human changes radically during the years from its birth through adolescence. Starting at first with the minimum ability to learn of the correlations of the world, it slowly develops an awareness of concepts and events and, then, simple sensorimotor schemas. During the first years of its life, a chimpanzee has a faster and more advanced intellectual development than does a human infant in the same time period. But around the age of 2, there are dramatic changes in the human infant's cognitive capability. For one thing, it learns to internalize its thoughts, so that it is no longer so dependent upon external events. For another, it is starting to develop language, a symbolic skill that will allow it to advance rapidly in the acquisition of knowledge.

The development of the human can be characterized by the several stages through which it passes. The person who has done most to study the intellectual development of the child and specify its progress has been the Swiss scientist, Jean Piaget. We have already discussed some of his ideas (and briefly met his child Laurent). Now let us examine Piaget's several stages of development of the intellect.

Piaget has identified several periods, subperiods, and stages in the cognitive growth of the child. The first period is that of *Sensorimotor* development: It lasts from birth through the age of about 18 months to 2 years. The second period is that of *Preoperational Thought*, running from the end of the sensorimotor period (age 2) through about age 7. This leads to the *Concrete Operations* period which lasts until about age 11. Finally, there is the period of *Formal Operations*, (starting around 11 years and lasting through adolescence), in which the final aspects of adult intelligence emerge.

Sensorimotor learning
We have already discussed the basic features of sensorimotor learning. To review, during that period, the child acquires an understanding of objects and actions. It learns that it can pick up and manipulate objects, that it can move about in the world and initiate events. The infant has learned that it is separate from its environment and that objects have permanence: It has learned about space and time and form, but it still lacks a good internal representation of the world. At the end of the period, imagery is just beginning, language is just starting.

THE DEVELOPMENT OF IMAGES

A central part of contingency learning is the organization of perceptual features into clusters based on their association with an action sequence. The child must construct an internal image of the external events.

The ability to organize perceptual information according to response contingencies is probably *innate*, present at birth. The resulting development of the internal images is crucial to the cognitive growth of a child. Presumably, the first concepts developed in the infant's brain are of the objects it experiences. Initially, however, these concepts may have meaning only in terms of its own actions (that is, only *motor meaning*). In fact, at first, the infant may not even recognize that external objects exist independently of actions. Piaget has suggested that in the first sensorimotor schemas that develop, perceptual features are not distinguished from the actions themselves. For example, Figure 13-1 shows a possible sensorimotor schema: The event of **move arm** causes a pleasant sound, but no separable concept of a prerequisite object has yet emerged.

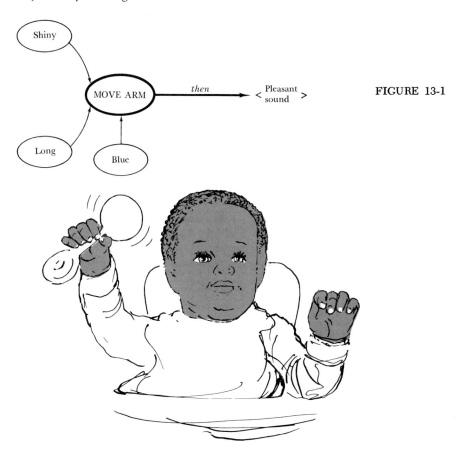

FIGURE 13-1

Gradually, as the child continues to manipulate the objects in its environment, the sensory components become separated from the action and begin to achieve an existence of their own. This is a critical beginning step in the child's acquisition of knowledge. Once the appropriate set of features is linked together in a separate, independent image, the memory system can recognize the object when it appears, allowing it to deal with the internal cluster of information—the memory node—as a unit.

FIGURE 13-2

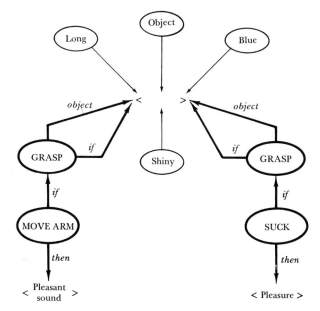

The same mechanisms continue to operate as the infant matures, but the problems associated with organizing perceptual information in a learning situation change. As the repertoire of images builds up, new objects must be integrated into existing perceptual structures through the processes of generalization and discrimination, since most of the things the infant encounters will have both similarities and differences compared to the things it already knows.

Preoperational thought

From the ages of roughly 2 through 7 the child begins to use an internal representation of the external world. This is a first major step toward adult thinking: the performance of mental experiments. Now, for the first time, the child can predict the course of an event without actually having to experience it, and can answer the question, "What would happen if . . . ?"

In the beginning, however, there are still severe limitations on the ability to internalize events. The child is mostly restricted to concrete actions and does not form abstractions or generalizations. Moreover, once a mental sequence of actions is started, it proceeds systematically, step-by-step, with little or no opportunity for flexibility.

Some of a child's apparent peculiarities in forming abstractions and generalizations can be seen in its classification behavior. Suppose you present a child with a set of pictures of objects that differ along a variety of dimensions and ask it to put together the pictures that seem to belong together. Faced with this task, an adult will usually select some physical dimension or combination of dimensions and systematically sort the objects according to the selected criteria. The child's behavior (during the preoperational stage) is quite different. Similarities and differences in physical characteristics only seem to be used if there is no other choice. In dealing with familiar objects, the child tends to group them according to their connection with a common environmental situation. Pictures of a stove, a refrigerator, a bowl of cereal, and a doll for Mommy may go into one pile; or it may build up a pile based on a barnyard or farming scene. Moreover, unlike the adult, it is not too fussy as to whether everything fits together nicely.

In some respects, an adult, confronted with an experimental task in concept formation, behaves quite similarly to the child. If college students are requested to subdivide a pile of cards into two groups by whatever rule they wish, a common strategy is to select a single dimension and try using it as the basis for making responses. Thus, they may pick all cards with red borders for one pile, blue borders for the other. When a card comes along that does not fit the rule, a new rule is selected and tried. In a complicated task, the subjects may not remember the rules they have tried before, and may repeat themselves. Like children, adults find rules that require them to combine several dimensions simultaneously more difficult to deal with than classifications based on a single dimension. If dimensions must be combined, then the simple *conjunction* of dimensions seems easiest (to belong to a class, an object must have **all** the attributes: for example, it must both be red **and** large). *Disjunction* is harder (the object must have any **one** attribute: for example, it must be either red **or** large). Concepts based on contingencies among the dimensions are hardest of all to learn (if the object is red, it must be large; but if it is blue, it must be small).

Overall, however, some of the characteristics of a child's classification behavior are distinctly different from the adult's. The most important feature seems to be that the child's induction mechanisms tend to deal with only a restricted range of the available information. The child tends to focus on only the dominant characteristics of an event. Moreover, it seems to require only local consistency across examples rather than consistency that spans a full history of the relevant information. A child is likely to group a bat with a ball (because you play with them), then a tomato with the ball (because they are round), and then put a rose with the tomato (because they are red). An adult does not do this. Rather, adults insist on finding one single rule that applies to all objects.

The preoperational child tends to be egocentric, centering its internal representations around itself. That is, it seems completely unable to take or to understand another person's point of view. This affects language behavior and it also has strong implications for a child's ability to learn by communicating with others or by mentally picturing a scenario from some other perspective.

In addition to all these limitations (or perhaps, as a necessary result), thinking processes seem to be irreversible. Although it can imagine the outcome of a certain sequence of operations, it cannot return to the initial state. It is as though the mental performance of the imagined event had the same characteristics as the real performance of an actual event—once done, it cannot be undone.

The most famous example of irreversibility is Piaget's *water glass problem*. Take two glasses, one tall and narrow, the other low and wide. Fill the low, wide glass with water. Now, with the child watching closely, pour the water from the wide glass into the narrow one: Obviously it rises to a much greater height than it had before. Now ask the child whether the new glass has the same amount of water in it as did the old glass; a child in the preoperational stage will respond **no**, the narrow glass has a different amount in it. Some children will say there is now more (the level is higher) or that there is less (the width is thinner), but whichever mode of operation they focus on, they believe that the amount of water is changed. The child does not yet have a concept of *conservation of volume*.

Concrete operations   Around the age of 7, the child enters the stage of concrete operations. Now the problems of conservation are no longer troublesome and the child passes the water glass test with ease. It has learned both that matter is conserved and also that one dimension (height) can compensate for another (width). Although still limited to concrete reasoning about objects, the child nonetheless has acquired broad new powers of thought such as the rules of manipulation, of number and space, of simple generalization, and of simple abstraction. But still, during this stage, the child's thought remains rooted to concrete objects and events, centered primarily on things that exist, and lacking any true notions of abstraction.

The development within this stage of concrete operations can be seen by giving the child two small balls of modeling clay of the same size and weight. One ball is then shaped like a long sausage. Before the age of 7 (before concrete operations), the child believes that the amounts of matter, weight, and volume have all changed. At 7 or 8, it believes that matter is constant, but that weight and volume still change. Around 9, the child recognizes that both matter and weight are unchanged, but still thinks volume differs. It is not until the age of 11 or 12 that all three concepts are seen as stable.

Finally, starting around the age of 11, the child begins the last stages in the transition to the full logical power of the human brain. During the early years of adolescence its language powers will become perfected, logical operations will appear, the laws of propositional arguments and implication will be learned, and it will begin to demonstrate abstract, hypothetical reasoning. (See Table 13-1.)

Formal operations

Table 13-1   Piaget's Periods of Intellectual Development in the Child

Approximate age (years)	Description
0–2	**Sensorimotor Development** Development of sensorimotor schemas. Learns of object permanence and actions. Limited to operations that actually affect the world
2–7	**Preoperational Thought** Language development starts. Learns to activate sensorimotor schemas mentally, without actually performing actions—mental experiments possible. Limited to concrete actions primarily dealing with events of present. Operations are egocentric, irreversible
7–11	**Concrete Operations** Logical deduction starts. Can manipulate concrete ideas. Still egocentric (but less so), still limited to possible events. Concepts of conservation, reversibility, and compensation are developed
11–15	**Formal Operations** Development of implication, abstraction, propositional logic, capable of mental hypothesis testing

A note of warning. Do not place too much emphasis on the stages; do not take the particular ages as absolute firm figures. Piaget has always stressed the developing enrichment of the child's knowledge structures. He has criticized American psychologists for overemphasizing the notion of stages and of ages. Piaget states that before a child can solve one type of problem, it must have first developed the appropriate prerequisite mental schemas. This means that knowledge will develop sequentially, with certain types of operations not possible to the child until it has acquired a sufficient background of mental schemas. This causes the appearance of stages. Moreover, because of the great similarities of the educational process in many of the industrialized nations of the world, the ages at which these prerequisite knowledge structures are acquired tend to be the same. But the notion of formal stages is wrong: some children can perform some tasks that appear to be from higher level stages before they can do others. This means that the special prerequisite knowledge for those tasks has already been acquired. Moreover, different cultures can have different rates of development.

Thinking A prerequisite of the ability to think is the construction of internal representations of external events. The processes involved in organizing and structuring perceptual information into sensorimotor schemas are invaluable aids to higher mental processes. Once internal structures are available, the thought processes are freed from dependence on the environment. With an internal representation of the world it is not necessary actually to execute an action in order to determine its consequences. Instead, the entire sequence of events can be anticipated through a mental simulation: mental simulation is the essence of thought.

Consider some of the advantages of working from an internal representation. Human thinkers can start with some desired goal and mentally work backward through their internal structures, hoping thereby to discover the possible actions that lead to the goal.

The internal sensorimotor schemas can provide a selective filter for attention and perception: They tell a person what to look for, they lead one to examine the features of the environment that are available, as well as to discover those that are missing. Missing conditions can be treated as subgoals, thus providing a method of discovering the sensorimotor schemata that might be appropriate for obtaining them. Expectations can play a central role even when failures occur. They can specify the crucial information that is needed for the intelligent selection of a new response action whenever an old one fails to produce the desired result.

Do lower organisms have the capabilities to plan? We do not know for sure. Certainly they are capable of following through relatively complex chains of actions, but the extent to which the anticipation of future events governs their current responses is difficult to determine. In the first 2 years of life, the human infant is developing sensorimotor intelligence, and shows only the beginnings of such planning activities. For the most part, animals and infants below the age of 2 seem to rely largely on trying out responses to see what will happen, rather than starting with a distant goal and working out a strategy for achieving it.

Thought requires the ability to simulate whole scenarios mentally, to hypothesize new possibilities, and to manipulate them symbolically. The same basic abilities required for the development and manipulation of sensorimotor schemas are pertinent to all levels of thought. In our study of problem solving and decision making in adults (in Chapter 14), we shall see that the solutions to the problem situations involve a series of real and mental actions and consequences, with various choice points arising during progression through the problem.

One major learning task faced by the young child is that of acquiring language. Here, many of the issues discussed in this chapter come fully into play. Language systems are large and complex. Although no one yet understands the structure of language or how it is acquired, we can introduce the problems and some of the suggestions and hypotheses. Let us begin by characterizing the initial problem faced by the young infant. Here, we speak of infants in their second year of development—12 to 15 months of age.

LEARNING A LANGUAGE

For the young child, learning the vocabulary of its first language is a difficult task. Simple names of objects and actions start to be learned early, usually when the child is between 1 and 2 years old. Some verbs are acquired early, but others require considerable development on the part of the child. Thus, verbs such as "want" and "go," "all-gone" and "do" are learned very early, followed by words such as "give" and "take." By the age of 2, most children have developed a vocabulary of about 50 words. A verb like "pay" or "trade" is not usually learned until the age of 5 years, and a verb like "sell" may not be fully understood until about 8 years. Other words take even longer: indeed, most people learn new words throughout their entire lifetime.

Learning the vocabulary

The problem in learning words is not a result of lack of exposure to them. Consider the meaning of the phrase "lexical decomposition." You can hardly be blamed for not having learned this phrase when you were 5 years old, because you might have come across it for the first time while reading this book. But a child of 5 will not be able to understand that phrase even if exposed to it, certainly not in the rich meaning that we intend it to have. To understand phrases such as "lexical decomposition" or words such as "prediction" or "assimilation," much more is needed than exposure to the words: a large body of knowledge must first be accumulated. After all, a word is simply a label for a set of structures within the memory system, so the structures must exist before the word can be considered learned.

The problem faced by the child

We start with the real objects in the world. Objects have names, and the relationship between the arbitrary sound pattern that we call a spoken name and an object is something that is not particularly obvious to a young child.

To understand the problems faced by a child, you should imagine yourself in a completely novel environment. Imagine that you are on a strange new planet. The environment is unlike anything ever experienced before: strange shapes and colors surround you, some stationary, some moving, seeming to make continuous, fluid transformations of shape, size, consistency, and color. Weird sounds are all around.

A bright circular illuminated region has hovered within 3 feet of your head ever since you started to explore the planet. At first you paid little attention to it, except to wonder at its existence. But when you turn on your flashlight to illuminate some shadows, suddenly the region starts to move about. When you flash your light on and off, you discover that the region mimics your light flashes. Now when you stop flashing for a moment, the region moves systematically from you toward various odd-shaped rocks, stops at the rocks, and then always undergoes the same systematic change in colors. It returns to you and then repeats the whole process. Slowly, you realize that this illuminated region is the intelligent organism of the planet: it is trying to teach you its language, starting with the name of an object.

At first, you most likely did not pay much attention to the rocks, but now you see that the ones pointed to by the region of light have something in common (they all have projecting proboscises) and they all differ from the other rocks (which have no proboscises). Joyfully, you mimic the region's flashing with your flashlight. You even name the region: *Region,* or *Reej* for short. With each flash that you make, Reej becomes animated, moving all around in colorful display. But, then you note that Reej's movement changes at times. When you flash your light alongside rocks, Reej shows great movement, but the same sequence of flashes alongside others provides quite a different response: you discover that you *overgeneralized.* You thought that any rock with a proboscis got the same sequence of flashes. Now you see that the rocks differ: the number of proboscises matters.

As you can now see, learning the language is going to be a difficult task. Moreover, language learning cannot take place until you have figured out what the objects and actions are on that planet. The child on our planet is faced with an analogous problem. There is a bewildering array of moving and stationary objects, looming faces that make strange noises, and different sights and sounds, not always correlated with one another. Before the child can hope to associate any particular sound sequence to a particular class of objects, it is going to need:

- *The concept of object:* a distinction between objects and backgrounds.
- *Some concept of object constancy:* the notion that an item is the same object despite the fact that it can appear at different times in different locations, different distances, and different rotations (thus having different sizes, shapes, and locations on the retina).
- *Knowledge that attributes differ in importance:* milk bottles may come in different shapes and styles, but the different-looking items are the same class of object. A mother or father may change clothes or hairstyle, but still be the same person. With people, the important attributes that remain constant are their facial features.
- *Coordination of space and object, of things felt, seen, heard, tasted, and smelled:* to learn that the parent's sounds are correlated with presentation of a particular object, one must realize that the sound came from the parents, and that the object is always associated with that sound.

In addition to all this, there are a bunch of unresolved issues relating to the child's perception and generation of speech sounds: Is speech something very special for the human, so that there are innate mechanisms for detecting speech sounds and for attempting to correlate them with experience, or must these aspects of language be discovered also? How does the child organize the sounds themselves? How does the child separate words from one another and from random, irrelevant sounds, such as coughs and scrapes, barks and meows? And what about production of sounds: How does the child come to control the complex set of muscles necessary for synchronizing the diaphragm, the vocal cords, the tongue, lips, and cheeks so that speech can be generated?

Learning words

Despite all the problems, one can see how a child might come to learn the names of objects. Objects are solid, substantial things. They exist, they can be pointed at, touched, manipulated. But what about events and actions? How does one name those?

Consider first the learning of a word like "bring." One way to teach such a word is to give different objects to the child, each time saying the phrase: *Bring X.* Thus, suppose the child has learned the words for "milk," "rattle," and "ball." Now, the parent brings each in turn, saying:

> *Bring ball.*
> *Bring milk.*
> *Bring rattle.*

The hope is that the child can extract the constancies in these sentences and actions, recognizing that the second word varies while the first always remains the same, and also recognizing that the basic acts vary in many ways, but share the common feature of a new object appearing each time. Moreover, the new object is the one named by the second word. If this set of constancies can be extracted, then the child has both acquired words for the actions and objects and also a simple grammar: *a verb is followed by an object.*

The word *bring* is actually too complex for a starting point. Children usually start by acquiring some of the simpler features of verbs. Thus, a common initial verb for children is "all-gone" as in *all-gone milk.* The word "all-gone" refers to the final state of the object, and many of the complications of the verbs that describe how the object got to that state can be ignored:

All-gone milk.	(The child drank the milk.)
All-gone Daddy.	(Daddy walked from the room.)
All-gone Mommy.	(Mommy went to work.)
All-gone ball.	(The child dropped the ball.)

In our discussion of learning, we stated that the laws of learning must include the notion of causality:

> **For an animal to learn the relationship between a specific action and an outcome, there must be an apparent causal relation between them: the action must be an apparent causal factor for the outcome.**

Almost the same exact principle must apply for language learning. A child will not learn the definition of a word like "bring" unless it is in some way capable of perceiving the causal relationship among the parent's actions and the appearance of the object, as well as the relationships between the words uttered by the parent and the actions.

Remember the argument we raised about a child's initial learning of sensorimotor schemas? There we suggested that at first the child did not distinguish among actions and objects: everything centered upon the motor movements. Knowledge is acquired through action. This is Piaget's position about the original acquisition of knowledge by the child. It has strong implications about language learning as well. The Piagetian position argues that original language learning occurs by learning names for actions. Objects are not separated from the events that have caused them to be perceived, and it is only later that the child realizes that different agents can perform similar actions upon objects, and that there is indeed a separation between motor movements and objects (see Sinclair-deZwart, 1973).

There is considerable evidence that the first words learned by a child do not separate the actions and events from the concept of object. After all, what kinds of language does the child first experience? Primarily, the child is talked to by adults or older children about its experiences: the separation between events and objects is not clear. If Piaget's notions about the inherent stage of developments are correct, with the child first learning about sensorimotor schemas, slowly learning to internalize concepts about the world, then one would expect language to mirror this developmental sequence. Thus, even if the child learns the word "ball," it might associate a whole host of features and events with the concept, including the rolling, bouncing, unstable characteristics of the object. Thus, although the term "ball" might appear to be applied correctly to round, ball-like objects, the child might actually be using it to represent the actions of the item.

The important point is that words are labels for concepts within a person's memory structures, so the initial concepts developed in a language must mirror the initial concepts developed by the child. In learning the meaning of a term, a person must somehow determine the appropriate memory structures for that term, and there is no direct way to determine whether the structures used by one person match those of another. This problem is especially acute with the child, for the child only has a limited set of memory structures and probably little or no awareness of the possible conflicts in the development of appropriate labels for structures. The words used by a child must reflect the initial concepts that have been developed by that child.

Remember our encounter with Reej, the illuminated region of light from the distant planet? A problem that we had in determining the names of objects was figuring out the relevant attributes of those objects: When Reej repeats a given flash in front of two or three different rocks, how do we decide which rocks are named by that sequence of flashes and which are not? Similarly, with actions, how do we know just what component of an action goes by the name often spoken along with it? The answer is that we do not know, at least not until there has been considerable experience with names, objects, and events.

Overgeneralization and overdiscrimination

The young child has the same problem. Indeed, we can imagine two different scenarios of language acquisition, one leading to the phenomenon called *overdiscrimination*, the other leading to the opposite phenomenon, *overgeneralization*.

Overgeneralization. Consider the child exposed to the family's pet dog. Whenever the dog is nearby, the parents are apt to say "doggie." What concept does the child develop for that word? One possibility is that the child relies upon the perceptual properties that it perceives:

a dark object the same size as a baby that moves about close to the floor. These perceptual features then comprise the child's knowledge structures for the concept of "doggie." To the child, any object that has these features is a "doggie." Thus, another dog might be called "doggie," but so too might a cat, a person crawling on hands and knees, or even a large movable toy (say a large toy cart). The resulting confusion is called *overgeneralization:* The use of a word is generalized to situations that have some features in common with the correct situation, but for which the use is inappropriate.

FIGURE 13-3

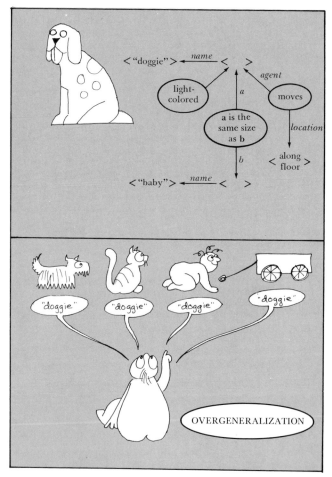

It is relatively easy to find examples of overgeneralization. For example, most infants initially call all people "da-da" or "ma-ma." Clark (1973) has collected some of the evidence for overgeneralizations from children of different language groups (some examples are given in Table 13-2).

Table 13-2   Examples of Overgeneralization [a]

The original item	The child called it by the name	The child used the name for these items
Sciseaux (French for scissors)	Sizo	All metal objects
Dogs	Bow-wow	First a toy dog, then a fur piece with an animal head, then other fur pieces
A baby	Bebe	Other babies, then all small statues, then figures in small pictures and prints
Dogs	Bow-wow	First a fur piece with glass eyes, then father's cuff links, then pearl buttons on a dress, then a bath thermometer
Moon	Mooi	Cakes, then round marks on window, then writing on window and books, then round shapes in books, then tooling on leather book covers, then round postmarks, then the letter O

[a] From Clark (1973).

The extracts of children's speech behavior reported by Clark show how variable the features can be that are used to encode the concepts. Thus, we apparently find the word "moon" taken to mean "a small round shape" and the word "scissors" to mean "a bright object." "Dog" (labeled by its sound, "bow-wow"), in one example seems to be associated with "furriness," and in a different child's example, seems to mean "small shiny items." One presumes this peculiar definition resulted from exposure to a dog with bright shiny eyes.

Overdiscrimination. In overgeneralizing, the child picked up some perceptual features of the concept, but not enough to distinguish it from lots of other things. Hence, the child overgeneralized, calling many different things by the same name. But suppose the child picks up too much, or too specialized a feature? Then the child will *overdiscriminate*, calling an object by a name only if it meets exactly a particular set of requirements.

Consider a child who again is told the name "doggie." Suppose the first encounter is with a large, spotted, glassy-eyed, droopy-eared, panting dog. If the child picks up all these features, then that concept of "doggie" is going to be so specialized that almost nothing will ever satisfy it. Cats and people certainly will not be called dogs, but neither will other kinds of dogs. Indeed, even if the first dog is seen again, but with its mouth shut (and therefore with no visible tongue), it too will not be called a dog. This is overdiscrimination.

FIGURE 13-4

Overgeneralization is much easier to observe than overdiscrimination. When a child overgeneralizes, it makes an observable error, calling specific objects by the wrong name. But when a child overdiscriminates, it is likely not to say anything at all. This makes it diffcult to tell whether the child has overdiscriminated or whether it simply wishes to remain quiet.

Note that the processes responsible for both overgeneralization and overdiscrimination are useful. A child must learn that all animals have properties in common, that there are general rules that apply to a variety of situations. Similarly, the child must learn to discriminate. It must be able to pick up the features that allow it to distinguish one individual from another.

You might not be aware of the extreme difficulty faced by the child. How is it to learn just when it should generalize and when it should discriminate? In learning the distinctions among people, the child must attend to the critical features that cause one person to look different from another, usually facial features, and ignore those features that are irrelevant, such as clothes. That is fine for learning to distinguish Mother from Father, or Julie from Joyce, but what about instances where the child must generalize? Consider how the child learns about firefighters, or police: These groups are identified by the clothes they wear, and the facial features and other discriminating information must be ignored.

There are similar examples with verbs. In the game of baseball, when one player throws a ball to another it is called a "throw" or "toss"—unless the two players involved are the pitcher and catcher, in which case it is called a "pitch." When one person runs after another, the only thing that distinguishes between the two acts of "fleeing" and "chasing" is the relative position of the participant (or the causes of the action). The child faces a severe problem in trying to make all the appropriate distinctions at the proper times; there are no easy rules to follow.

Learning to speak

From birth, the child is bombarded with a mixture of well-formed grammatical sentences, ill-formed fragments of sentences, utterances that are anticipations, questions, and baby-talk imitations of its own attempts to communicate. Out of this mish-mash of verbal utterances, it must somehow extract the rules for transmitting conceptual and relational information. An English-speaking child must learn that adjectives precede the noun that they modify. But how exactly does it pick this up? In actual speech, the same two words can appear in many different orders. Consider a simple example: The child is learning colors. It asks for the color name of milk and is told *"The color of* **milk—white.**" Here the noun and its adjective appear in reverse order, although with a slight pause between the noun and the color name. How does the child learn from examples like this to say **white milk** in sentences such as:

I don't want the white milk, I want the pink (strawberry) **milk.**

Folklore has it that a child learns to speak properly because its parents continually correct his errors. In fact, this is simply not true. Sometimes the child's speech is corrected, but usually it is either ignored or answered. Table 13-3 shows an example of the role of a mother in commenting on the speech of her child. In an analysis of numerous utterances (some of which are shown in Table 13-3), Brown and Hanlon (1970, Chapter 1) found no evidence whatsoever that mothers corrected grammatical mistakes with sufficient frequency to account for the fact that their children did learn the grammar.

Table 13-3   Examples of Utterances Approved and Disapproved[a]

Approval

Adam	Draw a boot paper.	**Adam's Mother**	That's right. Draw a boot on paper.
Eve	Mama isn't boy, he girl.	**Eve's Mother**	That's right.
Sarah	Her curl my hair.	**Sarah's Mother**	Um hmm.

Disapproval

Adam	And Walt Disney comes on Tuesday.	**Adam's Mother**	No, he does not.
Eve	What the guy idea.	**Eve's Mother**	No, that's not right. Wise idea.
Sarah	There's the animal farmhouse.	**Sarah's Mother**	No, that's a lighthouse.

[a] From Brown and Hanlon (1970, Table 1.12, p. 49).

Imitation   Imitation clearly speeds up for the child the acquisition of solutions to the practical environmental problems it faces. A child can learn simply by watching how things are manipulated and used. Indeed, it seems quite capable of building complicated action schemas out of observations. Imitation may also play a major role in the social development of the child. The family, the cast of characters on television shows, and friends all provide models for personal interactions. From such observations, the child learns the social behaviors that are appropriate in various social encounters. The models become translated into behavior.

Could imitation be a primary mechanism for learning language? This seems unlikely. The whole developmental pattern of language acquisition argues against the proposition that the child learns to comprehend and use language by imitating what is heard. The first words are only the crudest approximations to the appropriate sound patterns, yet a child makes no attempt to practice and refine each word before going on to acquire new ones. At no time during the progression of a child's language from one-word utterances to adultlike speech does the speech pattern really appear to be an imitation of what is heard. On the contrary, the most striking thing about children's speech is its novelty to adults. If children learned by imitation, why would they say **goed** for **went, doed for did, sheeps,** or **you naughty are**?

In fact, it is difficult to decide what the child would imitate even if it wished to do so. The hallmark of language is its infinite variety of expression. The child who is learning a language seldom encounters the same sequence of words more than a few times. Moreover, children born with congenital defects in their speech apparatus comprehend language perfectly even though they cannot speak and, thus, cannot imitate what they hear. The pattern of development seems to reflect the struggles of the child's induction processes as they attempt to extract the system of rules underlying language.

Parentese. Children do get assistance from their parents in acquiring language. Mothers and fathers speak differently to their children than they do to other adults. The special language has been called "motherese" and "fatherese": we will call it "parentese." Parentese is not the same as baby talk, but parents do simplify the structure they use, attempt to make their speech clearer and more distinct, and reduce the length of their utterances. It is possible to see if this has an effect on children's speech by recording the language spoken by parents to children in the home and attempting to determine how the type of language learned by children over a six-month period is related to the kinds of speech produced by the parents. One such study has been carried out by Newport (see Newport, Gleitman, & Gleitman, in press). She found that mothers' speech contained a lot of statements referring to particular objects in the environment:

That's a lamp.

That's an ashtray.

There's a boat.

The frequency with which its mother uttered such sentences determined the child's growth in ability to use noun phrases and vocabulary. Phrases that did not have a specific referent, or that did not provide a name, such as:

What's that?

did little to affect the child's development.

The structure of the utterances of the mothers also made a difference. Thus, mothers who asked **yes–no** questions of the form:

Are you going to the store?

Do you want a cookie?

Can you sing a song?

in which the first word is an auxiliary verb affected the child's development of auxiliaries. Sentences such as

I wonder if you can sing a song?

differ from **yes–no** sentences in that the auxiliary "can" is buried in the middle, whereas it is the first word in a **yes–no** question. Children seem unable to pick out all the words in a string, so there is a likelihood that the first few words of a sentence will be understood better than later words.

Language as communication

If we consider language to be a device for communication, how well does the young child do? The answer is **well**. Let us consider a few sample sentences from the repertoire of the 2-year-old:

Baby highchair	**Mommy eggnog**
Sat wall	**Mommy sandwich**
Pick glove	**Throw Daddy**

Do these utterances make sense? Probably not to you, since they are much too truncated to specify the exact nature of the relationships of the words to the actions. But consider when they were uttered. In general, the phrases of the child are perfectly understandable to the mother, since the context in which they were uttered leaves almost no possible ambiguity. Brown and Bellugi (1964), who recorded the preceding examples of child's speech also recorded the Mother's expansions of those sentences:

Baby is in the highchair.

Mommy had her eggnog.

Mommy'll have a sandwich.

He sat on the wall.

Throw it to Daddy.

Pick the glove up.

The child's speech seems to be composed of a telegraphic rendering of the full adult sentence. Function words are omitted. Complex grammatical relations are not yet discernable. But the adult can often expand the child's sentences with ease, simply using contextual information to determine the intended meaning and then adding the functor words and whatever else is necessary.

A good illustration of this comes from Eve's mother's expansion of the statement, **Eve lunch.** Roger Brown reports that Eve said this on two occasions, separated by about 30 min. For the first, Eve's mother was making lunch, so she expanded the utterance to **Yes, Mommy is going to fix Eve's lunch.** In the second, Eve said the utterance while sitting at the table eating, so her Mother expanded it as **Yes, Eve is**

eating lunch. The first expansion puts Eve in the possessive relation toward lunch. The second expansion makes Eve an agent of the action **eat** and lunch an object. The fact that the same utterance is so easily interpreted by the mother in two different ways argues for the satisfactory use of language as a vehicle of communication by Eve, even though her grammatical skills were quite limited.

One concludes, therefore, that a child's language is based on meaning rather than grammar. It would appear to reflect the underlying conceptual base that has been acquired about the world. Hence, the study of language development should be performed along with the study of general development.

When a child begins to use language, it has already acquired some of the basic structural information it needs through interactions with the environment. It must still learn how to communicate symbolically. The child's first attempts to communicate seem to be almost a direct statement of the internal memory structure. All of the function words that explicitly communicate relational information are missing: as a result, the child's speech is telegraphic. But there are more limitations. The child's memory span seems much reduced from the adult's, the child does not know all the phrase and transformational rules (if it knows any at all), and it also does not yet know what information must be specified and what can be deleted. Word order appears to be the only specific relational information that is systematically communicated in beginning speech. If an agent is included in the child's utterance, it does tend to appear before the verb. For other types of relations, however, it is difficult to determine whether or not the child is using the appropriate order. In adult English, if the **agent** is missing and there is only an **instrument** and an **object** mentioned in a sentence, then in an active sentence, the **instrument** must come before the verb and the **object** after:

Performance limits

The **key** *opens the* **door.**

    instrument   object

If the child simply shortened this sentence, it should say **Key open.** Instead, it will say **Open key.** Why? Evidently the child has in mind a difference sentence, one with an agent, such as:

Daddy *opens the door with his key.*

In this case, the abbreviated sentence **Open key** is correct.

In English the basic sentences have the form *Subject–Verb–Object* (SVO). Children follow this basic word order in putting together their first utterances. Thus, even while they are in the age group where they are only producing two-word sentences, when they wish to construct a sentence about a subject, a verb, and an object, they are likely to produce a two-word sentence in the appropriate order. Thus, if a child is expressing the concept that **Daddy** *should* **give** *it* **milk,** the possible statements are

Daddy give.   (SV—Object deleted)

Daddy milk.   (SO—Verb deleted)

Give milk.   (VO—Subject deleted)

The child is *not* likely to say any of the other three combinations of words: **give Daddy, milk Daddy,** or **milk give.**

Thus, even the shortened, abbreviated structures of young children follow sensible grammatical rules. Evidently, the child does understand the concepts of *agent, recipient, object, instrument*—the case structures of Chapters 10 and 12—at an early age, and the grammatical constructions of the child use those cases and word order appropriately.

One puzzling question is why the initial utterances of a child are so short. When a child can say each of these three fragments:

Daddy give.

Give milk.

Daddy milk.

then it must be capable of understanding the entire sentence:

Daddy give milk.

Why can the child only say two out of the three words?

Some people have suggested that a child's short-term memory capacity is limited, and so the processing effort necessary to put together strings of words quickly exceeds its capacity. Thus, although the child may indeed have the underlying structure of its father causing it to get milk, it cannot hold the entire three-word string within its memory. Upon closer examination, however, it turns out that there is no need to postulate that children's memory sizes differ at all from that of adults. Instead, one needs to determine how the child makes use of its memory. The child does not have a good understanding of the strategies available to it for memorizing things, for organizing material, for improving the use of its own memory structures. The child must develop the use of its own memory, just as it must develop the use of its other capabilities. In Chapter 9, we discussed the concept of *metamemory:* one's knowledge about one's own memory structures. A child has a badly developed metamemory.

There is another problem in the development of language that tends to restrict the length of an utterance: for efficient use of memory, the items that are to be maintained must be well learned, integrated concepts. Give an adult a task as complex as that faced by the child attempting to put together a sentence and you will have the same memory limitations. For example, consider what happens to an adult who is learning a foreign language. Here is how one of us reported upon his progress in a French course. This report was written after one week of French lessons, with about 6 hours of class, 3–4 hours of listening to tape recordings of French, and 1–2 hours of study of the textbook.

Language learning is a slow, painful business. It is difficult to understand the instructor when she talks (she speaks no English during 2 of the 3 hours of each lecture). It is difficult to repeat the phrases.

In listening to the other students, it is amazing how the memory span drops to 2 or 3 syllables with unfamiliar sounds.

Attentional overloads are everywhere. Once, when we were all taking turns answering and asking a simple question ("What is your name?"), I carefully rehearsed the four-word answer and the four-word question for about 2 minutes prior to my turn to speak. When it was my turn, I managed the first four-word phrase perfectly, with a good accent: *Je m'appelle Monsieur Norman*—hardly a difficult phrase, considering that half of it is my own name, although pronounced in French. The instructor then interrupted to praise my accent, which caused me to forget entirely the second phrase (which should have been *"Comment vous appelez-vous?"*).

When the instructor asks simple questions, or asks us to generate simple transformations of phrases ("Change *Pierre mange* to *Il mange* . . ."), the time required is huge—10 seconds is not uncommon.

Most of the students in the class seem completely bewildered, complaining after class of frustration and feelings of inadequacy. Yet, the instructor is excellent.

My guess is that there is a severe motivational problem, for the task of learning the language is so difficult that you don't get much feeling of accomplishment. No matter how well you do, there is always something that is wrong, and there is so much more to learn. It takes a child years to learn a language—about 4 years to be adequate, 8 years to be fairly good, 12–14 years to be excellent (I am starting these estimates from age 2). Adult learners complain of the speed of learning, but adults actually do quite well compared to children.

LEARNING AS
ADDITIONS TO
KNOWLEDGE

The learning that we have studied in this chapter illustrates only one of the many kinds of learning situations. The situation you are in now, reading this chapter, is also learning, but the activities in which you are engaged differ radically from those described in the chapter. We emphasized activities such as that of a child exploring the environment, actively attempting to discover the relationships between actions and outcomes. It was an exploratory, trial-and-error situation. Adult learning sometimes has these same characteristics, but more often it consists of the acquisition of new knowledge or new skills under the guidance of an instructor or a book.

Book learning, or instructed learning, no longer requires painstaking exploratory efforts at determining the relationships among environmental situations and actions: the role of the instructor or book is to point out the relevant issues and to guide the acquisition of the important knowledge. Most adult learning can be characterized as an attempt to fit the new knowledge that is being presented into the memory structures already present—to use the existing memory schemas to guide the formation of new schemas. We have already discussed some of the issues of this form of learning in our chapter on memory, and we will discuss other issues in the chapters on thinking and applications. Most important here is the realization of the tremendous amount of knowledge that is required for a person to learn most topics.

Think of how much time and effort it takes to learn a topic. Almost any topic that is worth learning takes years to learn well. A good way to characterize such topics is by the existence of experts: whenever a topic is rich enough or important enough that there are expert practitioners of it, then it will be a situation in which many years are required to attain expert knowledge. Think of a topic: history, automobile repair, mathematics, skiing, art, baseball, languages—even psychology. All these topics require years of study to master. Note that we have mixed two different types of knowledge into one list. Tasks that require accurate motor skills (baseball, skiing) are mixed with those that seem more cognitive (history, mathematics). But the distinctions among these fields are less important than one might think. Notice that topics such as art and automobile repair are already mixtures of types, requiring considerable amounts of knowledge, but also considerable manipulative skills as well. We claim that topic matters are actually very similar in terms of the organization of knowledge and the procedures necessary for learning them. The topics do differ in the types of skills that are involved: Some require graceful, controlled hand movements, some require good memory abilities or abstract reasoning, others require spatial judgments, and still others require body coordination. But all require large amounts of knowledge organized together in ways that make the relevant knowledge accessible rapidly, efficiently, and at appropriate times. The secret of learning complex topic matters lies in the appropriate organization of information within memory.

Consider what it takes to become knowledgeable about some subject matter. This book, for example, clearly requires a considerable amount of time to read. Yet the book is just the surface. On the one hand, you could not start this book without already having acquired a reasonable background of knowledge about the world, about science, mathematics, art, and music. Even if you believe yourself to be weak or deficient in these topics, you probably have studied each for several years during the course of your schooling. This book, if taught completely, with some depth, has about a year's worth of material: yet the book is just an introduction. To understand any single one of the topics discussed here requires intensive thought and study: one or more advanced courses could be designed to expand upon any of the topics covered here. Indeed, we do not know of a single person in the world who is an expert on all of the topics covered in this book.

Consider any sport or performing act. Professional concert artists learn their instrument at very early ages—long before the teenage years, and they typically practice 4–5 hours a day, every day, for the rest of their lives. Professional athletes have devoted similar amounts of time, and they too find they must continually practice or lose their skills. It takes many years to be skilled at a foreign language, and lack of use of that language will cause the ability to deteriorate. Skilled knowledge of history or mathematics or literature all require enormous amounts of time and study, and no matter how much has been learned, there is always still more to acquire.

This list leaves out more than it encompasses, but the story seems to be the same for every complex topic: thousands and tens of thousands of hours of learning and practice are required to master complex topics. Indeed, there is no evidence that one ever reaches peak performance: no matter how much time has gone into learning, more study and learning can further improve performance. Only the physical effects of aging upon the body (especially for motor skills) or a loss of motivation to continue seems to control the ultimate amount of knowledge that is acquired.

One common set of instructional methods requires the learner to develop strategies and hypotheses about the material to be acquired. This is especially true of systems called *discovery learning* or the *Socratic dialogue* method of tutorial instruction. Here, the instructors answer questions either with questions or with demonstrations, and students are taught to ask and then answer their own questions, to discover by themselves the important relations among the material they are learning. With clever guidance from the instructor, students "accidentally" come across and (most importantly) notice the critical information. Other instructional methods are more directed toward the sheer presentation of knowledge, practice at using that knowledge, and tests to ensure that the knowledge has really been acquired and that it can be used at appropriate occasions.

Most learning by adults can probably be characterized as consisting of many small steps, each one simple and direct, but with inevitable complications and difficulties arising for two reasons:

1. New knowledge must be properly integrated within the memory structures of previously acquired knowledge.
2. There must be a suitable set of background knowledge and memory structures before any particular new knowledge can be properly acquired.

Many difficulties in learning new things can be attributed to failure of one of these two aspects of learning. When something is considered to be difficult or complex, perhaps unintelligible, it usually means that Reason 2 is involved: the learner does not yet have sufficient background knowledge. When something seems to make sense yet is later unavailable for use at an appropriate time, it is usually Reason 1 that is faulty: the new knowledge was not properly integrated with existing knowledge. Even when information has indeed been acquired, if it is unavailable, it might as well not be present at all.

Studies of the learning process—especially the learning that takes place in the acquisition of complex topic matters—are in their infancy. In part, this is because the recent developments in the study of memory have not yet made much impact on studies of learning. Studies of the learning of complex topic matters are themselves complex, and not much headway has been made into the development of experimental and analytical tools for the task.

The learning of complex topics can probably best be characterized as consisting of three types of operations on memory structures: *accretion,* *restructuring,* and *tuning.* Basically, if you consider human memory to be organized into memory schemas, then knowledge that is acquired must either be fit into existing schemas or new schemas must be acquired. To learn a topic, initially there must exist some basic amount of information about it. This information consists of the facts and background material for the topic; it is gradually accumulated or *accreted* into the memory structures.

When the topic matters being learned are novel, the existing memory schemas will be inadequate to characterize the newly accreted information, so *restructuring* of schemas must occur. Restructuring is probably the fundamental process in the learning of new information. Old schemas are modified or *restructured,* and new ones created. Then, the information already existing within memory must be fit into the newly created structures, and new information can enter directly into the new schemas. It is unlikely that the newly structured schemas are completely appropriate for the material: they must be adjusted or *tuned* to fit the exact conditions of use. For most complex topics, the stages of learning—accretion, restructuring, and tuning—probably occur over and over again, perhaps never ceasing during the many years that it takes to learn any complex material.

Thus, the learning of complex material can be analyzed as consisting of repetitive instances of three different phases of learning:

    accretion: the acquisition of new information;

    restructuring: the formation of new schemas with which to organize the knowledge;

    tuning: the adjustment of the memory schemas for adequacy and efficiency.

In this chapter, the following terms and concepts that we consider to be important have been used. Please look them over. If you are not able to give a short explanation of any of them, you should go back and review the appropriate sections of the chapter.

REVIEW OF TERMS AND CONCEPTS

Contingency learning

Schema (schemas, schemata)

The law of effect: the laws of causal relationship, causal learning, and information feedback

The difference between actual causality and apparent causality

Learned helplessness
   escape learning
   avoidance learning
   helplessness

Specific taste aversion: why is this important?

The role of reinforcement

Learning by experimentation

Expectations and goal-directed behavior

Sensorimotor schemas

Stages of development
   sensorimotor
   preoperational
   concrete operations

Terms and concepts you should know

SUGGESTED READINGS

General issues in learning

Several books on learning are relevant in this chapter. In particular, we recommend Saltz (1971), *The cognitive bases of human learning.* A more traditional approach to learning is contained in the books by Horton and Turnage (1976) and Hulse, Deese, and Egeth (1975). Hilgard and Bower's (1975) book is organized around the traditional major people who have studied learning, and it is only in the latter chapters that there is much overlap with the material presented here (make sure you use their latest edition). The issues on learning and awareness are discussed in Brewer's (1974) chapter on the topic.

Work on learned helplessness is most easily approached through the book by Seligman (1975), which covers the exciting clinical literature of human ailments related to helplessness (namely, depression); also see the paper by Maier and Seligman (1976). The experiment on humans was done by Thornton and Jacobs (1971). Work on aversion to specific tastes has primarily been performed by Garcia and his colleagues (see Garcia, Hankins, & Rusiniak, 1974; Revusky & Garcia, 1970; Rozin & Kalat, 1971).

Development

Two good books on developmental issues, especially of topics not covered in this chapter, are by Bower (1974), which emphasizes the child's development of perceptual skills, and the more general text by Turner (1975), which covers a wider variety of topics. By far the most important influence on the study of intellectual development has come from the laboratories of Jean Piaget in Geneva. A prolific investigator, Piaget has turned out scores of studies spelling out the stages of development that a child must pass through on its way from early infancy to adulthood. It is clear that anyone wishing to pursue the topics developed in this chapter must read Piaget. But how? Piaget does not make life easy for his readers. His writings (in French) are difficult to follow. Even when he is translated into English, his books are often rough going. Moreover, there is an enormous quantity of them: One bibliography (Flavell, 1963) lists 136 books, chapters, and articles by Piaget in the period between the early 1920s and early 1960s. We have found it useful to approach Piaget in easy steps.

The easiest introduction that we have found is the small book by Ginsburg and Opper (1969). From there, you might wish to go to the collection of six essays collected together into a smaller book (Piaget, 1967: paperback). This is an especially good introduction to Piaget, since it gives him to you directly without benefit of interpretation. Moreover, the editor (Elkind) and the translator (Tenzer) have been especially good at making his writing easy for the reader. The only quarrel we would have with this book is that it does not give the full flavor of Piaget's approach to the study of psychology, since it leaves out the lengthy, small-print records of the speech and actions of the children that he is observing, which play so prominent a role in his books. Nonetheless, it is a good start. The best, most complete treatment of Piaget is given in Flavell's book (1963). This is a very thorough book on Piaget's works and various theoretical positions, and although it is technical enough that you may wish to work up to it by reading the two books we have just mentioned first, it is an excellent treatment. Piaget himself seems to approve of the book, although he views Flavell's emphasis on experimentation—and the critique of his methods—with some disfavor, treating it as a typical response of the experimentally oriented American psychologist. (See the foreword by Piaget in Flavell's book.)

If you have come this far and still wish to know more about Piaget, then it is time to read his works directly. The works mentioned so far should give you ample bibliographical sources for reading Piaget, but we found for ourselves that his single most important book is *The origins of intelligence in children* (1952). A good number of Piaget's works are available, translated in English, and in paperback, published by Norton and Co.: Piaget's *The child's conception of number, The origins of intelligence in children,* and Piaget and Inhelder's *The child's conception of space.* The book by Evans (1973) contains an interesting discussion of Piaget, including conversations with him about his ideas and some good summary articles.

Flavell and his colleagues have studied extensively the development of role playing in children, and especially the child's egocentricity (Flavell,

1966; Flavell, Botkin, Fry, Wright, & Jarvis, 1968). Smedslund has a series of six papers on the child's acquisition of conservation and reversibility (Smedslund, 1961a–f). A different view is presented by Bruner (1964). A thorough source for the studies in the development of children is in the *Handbook of child psychology,* edited in two volumes by Mussen (1970). Some of our material on children's reasoning and thinking was taken from the chapter by Berlyne (1970) in that handbook.

First language learning

There are numerous sources for the study of the development of language in children. The best general book is probably *Language development* by Dale (1976). Lenneberg (1967) provides an excellent treatment for the biological foundations of language, including the survey of physiological changes that take place in the brain of a child as it matures. We have profited much from the works of Roger Brown, and we have relied extensively on his book *Social psychology* (1965) for much of the work on development of intelligence and of language (a very excellent 150 pages of discussion: pp. 197–349). We recommend this set of readings to you highly. In addition, we recommend Brown's paper (1973a) and later book (1973b).

The book edited by Moore (1973) presents an important set of papers on acquisition of language, including the paper by E. Clark (1973) that formed the basis for the discussion on overgeneralization and overdiscrimination. A contrary view to Clark's is proposed by Nelson (1974, 1975). The work on parentese came from that of Newport, reviewed in Newport, Gleitman, and Gleitman (in press).

A major set of studies on the fundamental mechanisms of language acquisition is reported in J. Anderson (in press). How a child acquires verbs of possession is examined by Gentner (1975) in a study based around the notion of lexical decomposition (as discussed in the previous chapter). Chimpanzees are now learning to communicate in sign language. For some discussions of the issues involved here, see Fleming (1974: a sympathetic review) or Brown (1970: a critical review).

Work on the study of how children use their memories and on the general use of memory capacity and its apparent changes with age can be traced in the papers by Olson (1973) and Huttenlocher and Burke (1976). Metamemory is discussed by Flavell and Wellman (in press) and Kreutzer, Leonard, and Flavell (1975). The child's use of memory structures for comprehension is examined by Paris (1975). Hagen (1972) discusses the development of memory strategies, and the entire book in which Hagen's chapter occurs is highly relevant (Farnham-Diggory, 1972).

Studies of general learning processes relevant to the topics discussed in the last part of this chapter are rare. See Rumelhart and Norman (in press) and the article by Norman, Gentner, and Stevens (1976). The book edited by Klahr (1976) contains a few relevant starts. Also see the *Annual Review* article "Models of Learning" by Cotton (1976) for general guidance to the literature.

Learning complex topics

14 Problem solving and decision making

PREVIEW

This chapter starts the study of thinking. Here we set the framework for the systematic, analytic study of cognitive processes involved in thought. We begin by analyzing a problem: the DONALD + GERALD crypt arithmetic problem. It is important that you appreciate the mental operations that we are discussing, and the only way to do this is by first trying to work the problem for yourself. As you attempt to solve the problem, observe yourself. Note what you are doing, note the types of difficulties you have and the parts of the problem that give you clues to the solution. Indeed, we do not care if you ever solve the problem, we only care about your own observations of your mental behavior as you try. (If you are already an expert at solving these crypt arithmetic problems, then observe some friends who are trying to solve it, asking them to think aloud as they go through the process.)

Several points are made in the chapter about the stages of problem solving. One of them concerns the ways by which psychologists attempt to analyze what people do. Try to appreciate the *problem behavior graph* as a means of diagramming the solution to problems such as the DONALD + GERALD task. Another point deals with the sufficiency of a person's comments as a basis for understanding what is really happening. In both this chapter and the next you will see that you do not necessarily know what you are thinking, and the reports people give of their thoughts are not always complete or accurate.

The crypt arithmetic problem takes some people a long time to solve, yet in principle it can be done very quickly (as we demonstrate). One major reason for the difficulties lies in the limited capacity of the short-term memory system. Note the analysis of tic–tac–toe: a complete analysis of the game is more complex than you can do in your head, unless you are experienced in the game. Experience changes the nature of a problem-solving task.

In the section on decision making, there is similar concern with the limitations of human short-term memory that change the nature of decisions. One important point in decision making is the distinction between the psychological value of things (utility) and the economic value. Trying to make a choice among complex issues involves combining one's psychological impressions of the issues and comparing those impressions. Just how the impressions are formed and compared determines the resulting decision, and the same person can arrive at different decisions simply by comparing the same things in different orders. These arguments describe an important aspect of human behavior.

The notions of risk, of probability, and of subjective probability should be studied with care: probability is an important concept in actual day-to-day experiences. Again, we note how the availability of information from memory plays a large part in decision making.

THE ANATOMY OF THE PROBLEM

Just what must be done in order to solve a problem? In this section we examine the strategies and procedures that people use. Problems come in two broad classes: problems that are well defined and those that are ill defined. A well-defined problem is one that has a clearly stated goal. Thus:

- What is the best route to the other side of town when all the main streets are closed because of the parade?
- What is the solution to the chess problem from last night's paper: white to checkmate in four moves?
- What were you doing 16 months ago?

These problems have well-defined attributes: a definite goal, a definite way to tell whether the problem solving is proceeding in the correct direction. Ill-defined problems are, perhaps, more frequent.

- Direct the filming of the most meaningful movie of the century.
- Make something significant of your life.
- Create a permanently lasting work of art.

We concentrate our study on the well-defined problem for good reason. The goal is to understand the processes people use in working through to the solution of a problem. We wish to understand how they construct internal models of the problem, what strategies they use, what rules they follow. We want to see how they assess their progress as they move toward a solution. The results of these investigations should apply to all problem-solving behavior, be the problems ill or well defined.

Some of the basic principles of problem solving behavior have already been introduced. In the study of sensorimotor intelligence, we discussed the notion of selecting behavior based on an expected goal, of following through a chain of sensorimotor schemata to discover the end result of a possible action sequence, of starting with the final goal and working backward to form a plan for achieving that goal. We were exploring how these strategies were applied to practical environmental problems. Now we shall see the same procedures emerge as we study how people attempt to solve abstract conceptual problems.

Perhaps the best way to begin is to examine a problem. It will help in the analysis if you have an idea of the steps and operations that are being discussed. Attempt to solve the problem described below. Working on the problem will give you a feel for the tactics you use and the decisions involved, even if you cannot solve it. *Think aloud* as you work, saying all the thoughts that come to mind. Spend at least 10 min at the problem, even if it does not appear that you are making progress. Remember, the important thing about this analysis is to discover the types of mental operations that people do. It really does not matter whether the problem ever gets solved.

$$\begin{array}{r} \mathrm{D\,O\,N\,A\,L\,D} \quad \mathrm{D} = 5 \\ + \mathrm{G\,E\,R\,A\,L\,D} \\ \hline \mathrm{R\,O\,B\,E\,R\,T} \end{array}$$

This is a problem in crypt arithmetic. In the expression, there are ten letters, each representing a different, distinct digit. The problem is to discover what digit should be assigned to each letter, so that when the letters are all replaced by their corresponding digits, the arithmetic is correct.

Please speak aloud all that you are thinking as you attempt to solve the problem. You may write down anything you wish.

Protocols   The first step in the investigation of any phenomenon is to observe the behavior associated with it. The obvious difficulty in studying human problem solving is that much of what goes on is not directly observable: People go through their internal mental operations quietly by themselves. One way of getting around this difficulty is to have people make their thought processes available to others by asking them to describe aloud what they are doing as they attempt to solve a problem. The result is a word-by-word compilation of their verbalized thought processes, a *verbal protocol*. Clearly, although there are difficulties in interpreting these protocols, they provide extremely useful initial information about the thought processes involved in problem solving.

We shall analyze a small part of the verbal protocol of a subject who was attempting to solve the DONALD plus GERALD problem. This particular subject was a male college student at Carnegie–Mellon University, who was given instructions about the problem similar to those given here, and then asked to think aloud as he attempted to find a solution. The complete transcription of his verbal descriptions consisted of some 2200 words produced over the 20-min problem-solving period. This was the first time this subject had tried to solve this type of problem.[1]

The protocol from   **Each letter has one and only one numerical value—**
DONALD +
GERALD   (This is a question to the experimenter, who responds, "One numerical value.")

---

[1] The problem, the analysis, and the quotations that follow all come from the work of Newell (1967).

There are ten different letters and each of them has one numerical value.

Therefore, I can, looking at the 2 D's—each D is 5; therefore, T is zero. So I think I'll start by writing that problem here. I'll write 5, 5 is zero.

Now, do I have any other T's? No. But I have another D. That means I have a 5 over the other side.

Now I have 2 A's and 2 L's that are each—somewhere—and this R—3 R's. Two L's equal an R. Of course, I'm carrying a 1 which will mean that R has to be an odd number because the 2 L's—any two numbers added together has to be an even number and 1 will be an odd number. So R can be 1, 3, not 5, 7, or 9.

(At this point there is a long pause, so the experimenter asks, "What are you thinking now?")

Now G—since R is going to be an odd number and D is 5, G has to be an even number.

I'm looking at the left side of this problem here where it says D + G. Oh, plus possibly another number, if I have to carry 1 from the E + O. I think I'll forget about that for a minute.

Possibly the best way to get this problem is to try different possible solutions. I'm not sure whether that would be the easiest way or not.

The analysis. These words, then, are our data. What principles can be discovered from them? The first impression from such a protocol is that this problem solver does not proceed in a straightforward, direct manner. Rather, he accumulates information by various hypotheses to see where they take him. He frequently encounters dead ends, backs up, and tries another tack. Look at the protocol. He starts off energetically and discovers first that $T = \emptyset$. (we write zero as $\emptyset$ to avoid confusion with the letter O).

Therefore, I can, looking at the 2 D's—each D is 5; therefore T is zero. So I think I'll start by writing that problem here. I'll write 5, 5 is zero.

He then looks to see if his knowledge that $T = \emptyset$ and $D = 5$ can be of any use elsewhere in the problem. He looks for a T.

Now, do I have any other T's? No.

This failed; how about D?

But I have another D. That means I have a 5 over the other side.

Having noted this fact, he finds another spot in the problem that seems promising.

Now I have 2 A's and 2 L's that are each—somewhere—and this R—3 R's.

Two L's equal an R. Of course, I'm carrying a 1 which will mean that R has to be an odd number. . .

Even though he has now deduced that **R** is an odd number, he then goes back over that again, as if to check the reasoning:

. . . because the two L's—any two numbers added together has to be an even number and 1 will be an odd number.

But this time he pursues his reasoning a little further and explicitly lists the possible numbers:

So R can be 1, 3, not 5, 7, or 9.

He abandons this route, however (after a long pause), evidently because there is no obvious way of selecting the particular value for **R** out of the possible candidates. Once again he returns to the basic idea that **R** is odd; does this give any information about **G**:

Now G—since R is going to be an odd number and D is 5, G has to be an even number.

This brief analysis of the first few minutes of the protocol is enough to reveal some general patterns in the subject's problem-solving behavior. He knows the overall goal he is trying to reach. The first thing he does, however, is to break down the final goal into a number of smaller steps. He then proceeds by successively trying out a variety of simple strategies, each of which he hopes will yield some information. Some strategies work, and so more and more data are accumulated. Other strategies do not seem to work; in this case, the subject backs up and tries a different line of approach.

This is a description that applies to a wide variety of problem solving and cognitive tasks. The same general principles appeared in the application of sensorimotor intelligence to practical problems. But our description so far leaves us with a set of unanswered questions. What is involved in breaking the overall goal down into a set of smaller, simpler steps? How does the subject know what kinds of strategies will be useful in solving the problem? How does he choose a particular strategy to apply at a particular moment? How does he know whether the strategy he is using is moving toward the solution rather than up a blind alley? To answer these questions, we need a better procedure for analyzing protocols.

Verbal protocols are clumsy to deal with. To study the problem-solving process in more detail, we need some method of representing the events that take place. A useful technique is to construct a visual picture of the sequence of operations going on during problem solving. One such technique available for this purpose is the *problem behavior graph,* a method developed by Allen Newell and Herbert Simon of the Carnegie–Mellon University of graphing the subject's progress through a problem (see Newell & Simon, 1972).

The problem behavior graph

States of knowledge. We noted from the protocol that the subject gradually accumulates new information about the problem by applying rules or strategies. He operates on his existing knowledge and the statement of the problem to add to his knowledge. All the information the subject knows about the problem at any moment is called his *state of knowledge.* Each time he applies some *operation* to some new fact, he changes his state of knowledge. A description of his problem-solving behavior, then, should trace out this progression in the subject's states of knowledge. To do this in the diagram, represent a state of knowledge by a box, and the operation that takes the subject from one state of knowledge to another by an arrow, as shown in Figure 14-1.

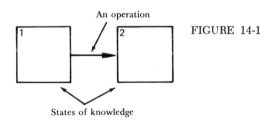

FIGURE 14-1

The protocol then is represented by boxes and arrows that describe the path taken by the subject through successive states of knowledge. To illustrate this, consider again the protocol for the DONALD + GERALD task.

The graph for DONALD + GERALD. For the first few statements, the subject simply is verifying that he understands the rules of the task. The first actual deduction does not occur until the statement:

Therefore, I can, looking at the 2 D's—each D is 5; therefore, T is zero.

The subject clearly is processing the information in a single column, the one that reads **D + D = T.** Call this operation *process column 1.* (Number the six columns of the problem from right to left.) The operation moves the subject from his initial state of knowledge (where he knows that **D = 5**) to a new state, state 2, in which he also knows that **T = Ø** (we write zero as **Ø** to avoid confusion with the letter **O**). Does the subject also realize that there must be a carry into column 2, the next column on the left? So far, from the information in this protocol, we cannot tell. Looking ahead, however, we see, **Of course, I'm carrying a 1,** so he does know this fact. The problem behavior graph up to this time shows two states of knowledge, as shown in Figure 14-2.

FIGURE 14-2

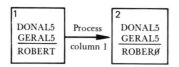

The next several statements in the protocol are concerned with the act of writing down what has been learned so far. Then there is an attempt to get a new column, either one with **T** or one with **D.** The first operation to **get new column (T)** is unsuccessful, the second succeeds in finding another **D.** The problem behavior graph has progressed slightly, as shown in Figure 14-3 (the old states are unshaded: The one added since the last diagram is shaded).

FIGURE 14-3

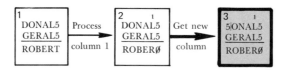

At this point, the subject again chooses to get a new column, trying first column 3, then 2.

> **Now I have 2 A's and 2 L's that are each—somewhere—and this R—3 R's.**

This gets him to the point where it is worthwhile to *process column 2,* moving him from state 4 to state 5, where he concludes that **R is odd.** The progression is shown in Figure 14-4.

FIGURE 14-4

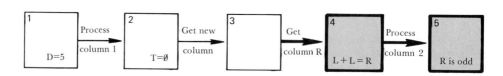

Backing up. Now the subject backs up. Notice this sequence. First, at state 5 he says

> Two L's equal an R. Of course, I'm carrying a 1 which will mean that R has to be an odd number . . .

But then, he decides to generate the actual possibilities for numbers, and to do this he backs up to state 4 and tries a new approach.

> . . . because the 2 L's—any two numbers added together has to be an even number and 1 will be an odd number. So R can be 1, 3, not 5, 7, or 9.

To illustrate the backing-up process, the next state, state 6, comes off of state 4. This is done in Figure 14-5 by showing the transition to state 6 by a vertical line from state 4. State 6 is simply the same as state 4, only at a later point in time. At state 7, the subject has again regenerated the fact that **R is odd**, and in state 8, he methodically tests all odd numbers.

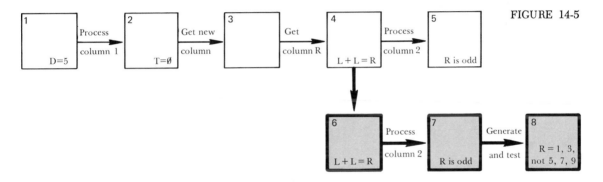

FIGURE 14-5

Note that when the subject generates the candidates for **R**, he does a thorough job and does not exclude the values already used. Thus, he explicitly generates and then rejects the possibility that **R = 5**. He did not simply skip over that possibility.

The next part of the record illustrates the experimental difficulties of getting protocols. The subject did not say anything, so the experimenter was forced to interrupt and ask him to speak. The result is that there is no evidence about how the possible values of **R** have been used. Rather, the process seems to have backed up again, this time going to column 6 with the fact that **R is odd** and that **D is 5**, concluding that **G** must be even. This takes us to state 10.

> Now G—since R is going to be an odd number and D is 5, G has to be an even number.

This deduction is not correct, but nevertheless, at the point represented by state 10, it describes the actual state of knowledge of the subject (see Figure 14-6). The possibility that **G** need not be even is recognized rather quickly in this case.

> I'm looking at the left side of this problem here where it says **D + G. Oh, plus possibly another number, if I have to carry 1 from the E + O. I think I'll forget about that for a minute.**

This last statement indicates another start at processing column 6, ending up at state 12 and the knowledge that there may be a carry, and then the decision to back up once again and forget about the value for **G**. This concludes our analysis of this segment of the problem. This segment of the problem behavior graph is shown in Figure 14-6.

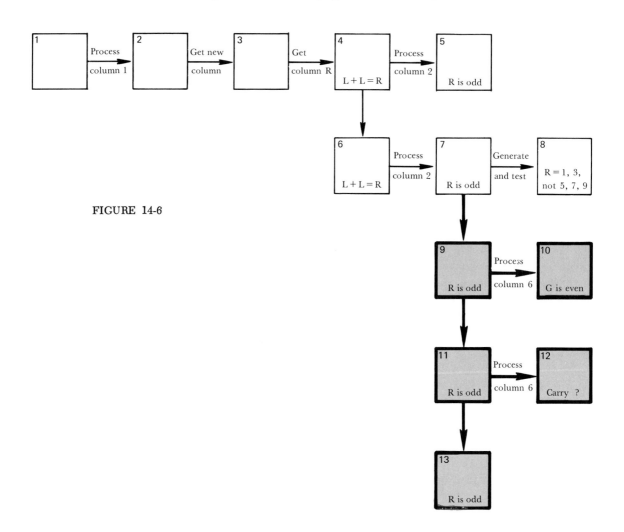

FIGURE 14-6

The short segment of the protocol just analyzed illustrates a method for decomposing and representing the steps involved in solving a problem. Figure 14-7 gives, in schematic form, what the entire graph looks like when the protocol for the complete 20 min the subject spent on the task is represented.[2]

In analyzing the complete protocol, the same rules appear. The subject seems to have only a very small set of strategies, which he used repeatedly. In the full analysis of this subject, there were over 200 transitions among states of knowledge, yet only four different operations were needed to describe how he got from any one state to the next.

The problem-behavior graph is one method of dissecting the stages of problem solving, decomposing the process into a series of small steps. It graphically illustrates the mixture of successes and failures that go on in a problem-solving task. This general form of analysis and pattern of behavior seems to apply to a wide variety of problem situations. Certainly, the specific rules a subject uses depend on the particular nature of the problem he is solving, but the overall structure of his problem solving behavior is quite similar. The subject reorganizes the overall problem into a set of simpler subgoals or subproblems. At any given time, his progress can be summarized in a state of knowledge. It represents the information he has accumulated up to that point. He proceeds from one state of knowledge to the next by attempting to apply a particular operation selected from a small set of operations. If successful, he obtains new information, and thus moves to a new state of knowledge. His course is erratic, involving continual trial-and-error, testing the effectiveness of various operators, backtracking when a sequence of operations leads to a dead end and beginning once again. To describe his behavior, the notions of goals, states of knowledge, and operators have been introduced. Let us consider how these notions apply to problem solving in general.

STRATEGIES OF PROBLEM SOLVING

If the puzzle you solved before you solved this one was harder than the puzzle you solved after you solved the puzzle you solved before you solved this one, was the puzzle you solved before you solved this one harder than this one? [Restle, 1969]

[2] *Using the graph.* To read these graphs, always start at the upper left-hand box and go horizontally to the right. When the end of that line is reached, back up to the first downward line and go down one level. Then again go horizontally to the right. Keep doing these steps, careful never to repeat, until all the paths have been covered. The rule: **Follow the graph as far to the right as possible, then back up to the first new vertical line and go down one step. Repeat as many times as necessary.**

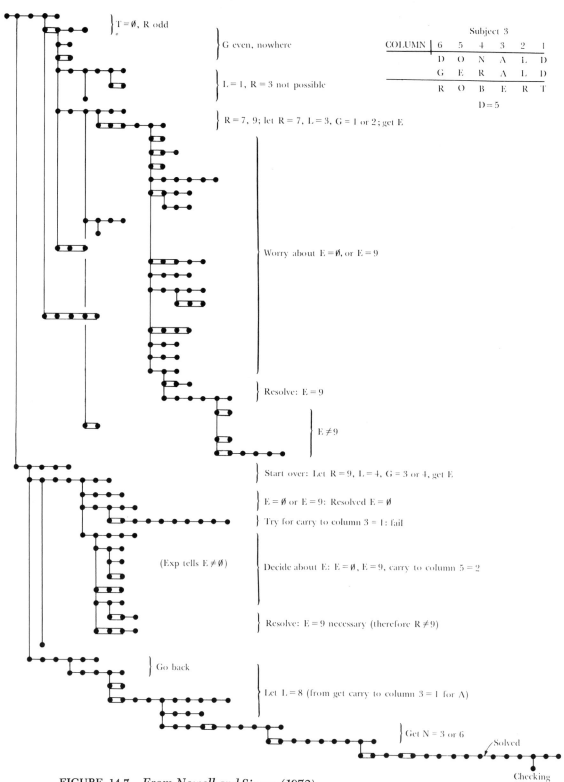

FIGURE 14-7   *From Newell and Simon (1972)*

The **final goal** of this puzzle is clear: to produce an answer, yes or no. But if we simply start off working forward through the sentence from beginning to end, we quickly get bogged down in the complex linguistic structure. A *forward search* for a solution is not going to work. What about a *backward search?* Start at the goal—to answer yes or no—then ask what is needed to achieve that goal. Clearly, one strategy that should be helpful is to break the problem up into *subgoals,* so that it becomes manageable. For example, a specific subgoal might be simply to try to understand each phrase in the statement. Now what would be a good operator for achieving this subgoal?

One way to proceed is to attach labels, such as a different letter, to represent each different puzzle. Then any phrase that refers to a puzzle could be relabeled by the appropriate puzzle letter. The phrase, **this one,** is clearly equivalent to the phrase, **this puzzle,** or, to give it a name, **puzzle A.** Hence,

> **this puzzle = this one = puzzle A**

and by making the substitutions, the problem can be restated as

> **If the puzzle you solved before you solved puzzle A was harder than the puzzle you solved after you solved the puzzle you solved before you solved puzzle A, was the puzzle you solved before you solved puzzle A harder than puzzle A?**

That worked pretty well, so try it again. Transform every occurrence of the phrase, **the puzzle you solved before you solved puzzle A,** into the phrase **puzzle B.** This substitution gives a new version of the problem:

> **If puzzle B was harder than the puzzle you solved after you solved puzzle B, was puzzle B harder than puzzle A?**

One phrase still remains to be interpreted: **the puzzle you solved after you solved puzzle B.** According to the previously used transformation, the puzzle prior to A must be puzzle B. Hence, by reversing the transformation, the puzzle that followed after puzzle B must be puzzle A. Thus, the phrase, **the puzzle you solved after you solved puzzle B,** should be labeled **puzzle A.** Now the problem is trivial:

> **If puzzle B was harder than puzzle A, was puzzle B harder than puzzle A?**

This example demonstrates some of the basic strategies humans apply in their attempts to solve problems. Most problems involve some aspect of **forward search.** That is, first one simply tries out some method of

Searching for solutions

attack and then decides whether progress has been made. If so, you keep going from where the previous step left off. The process is something like the way a stream of water meanders down the hillside. The water simply starts to flow in all downward directions: the unique configuration of the land determines the exact path the water follows. The important aspect is that the search progresses from the start to the finish, using simple, direct steps. In this particular puzzle, a simple forward search did not work.

A second approach is to **work backward.** Here one looks at the desired solution and asks what the previous step must have been to have arrived there. Then, from that step, the one just prior to it is determined, and so on, hopefully back to the starting point given in the original specification of the problem. Working backward is very useful in some visual problems, such as looking at a map in order to decide the route from one location to another.

In working backward, progress is made in small steps. A **subgoal** is defined, and an attempt is made to solve the subproblem. At this point, a strategy, perhaps the most powerful one, enters in: the *means–ends analysis.* In the means–ends analysis the desired subgoal—the end—is compared with the present state of knowledge. The problem is to find an operator—a means—that will reduce the difference. In the puzzle problem, the end was to understand a phrase in the sentence; the state of knowledge was a complex linguistic structure. The means of reducing the difference between the two was to simplify the phrases by labeling them appropriately. This is only one example of the means–ends analysis. The same strategy is applicable to many varieties of problem solving behavior, often with unexpected success.

Selecting operators   How did we come up with the idea of relabeling a complex phrase with a letter in order to simplify the puzzle problem? Clearly, one of the main problems for a human is finding the particular operators that will work in a situation. Breaking up the overall problem into subgoals is useful for setting the problem up. The means–end analysis is useful for evaluating whether a given operator will make some progress toward the solution. But none of these tactics tells us which operator we should be considering.

Heuristics.   The mathematician Polya (1945) suggests that to solve a problem:

> **First, we must understand the problem. We must clearly understand the goal, the conditions imposed upon us, and the data. Second, we must devise a plan to guide us to the solution.**

But the crux of the matter is to devise the appropriate plan, the operators that will, in fact, guide us toward a solution.

In the study of problem solving, plans or operators are divided into two types: *algorithms* and *heuristics*. The distinction between the two is whether the plan is guaranteed to produce the correct result. An algorithm is a set of rules which, if followed, will automatically generate the correct solution. The rules for multiplication constitute an algorithm; if you use them properly, you always get the right answer. Heuristics are more analogous to rules of thumb; they are procedures or outlines for searching for solutions which are relatively easy to use and are often based on their effectiveness in solving previous problems. Unlike algorithms, however, heuristic methods do not guarantee success. For many of the more complicated and more interesting problems, the appropriate algorithms have not been discovered and may not even exist. In these cases, we resort to heuristics.

A very important heuristic device is to find **analogies** between the present problem and ones for which the solution is known. Often, this requires a bit of skill in recognizing the similarities and a bit of subterfuge in ignoring obvious differences. Solution by analogy is extremely valuable, even if the analogy is far-fetched. The danger, of course, is that one can think there are similarities where in fact there are none, causing much wasted time and effort before the error is realized and a new approach tried.

Heuristics come into play in any complex, problem-solving situation. In fact, much of the study of thinking and problem solving involves a search for the kinds of heuristics people use. The role of heuristic strategies is best understood by considering a specific example.

Chess playing. Chess manuals do not give a prescription guaranteed to lead to success. Rather, they contain heuristic rules:

> **Try to control the four center squares.**
> **Make sure your king is safe.**

In fact, the differences among chess players seem to lie mainly in the power and efficiency of the heuristic schemes they employ while playing the game (see Simon & Simon, 1962). A good place to examine the operation of these rules is with the last few moves of a game, just before a checkmate (an attack on the opponent's king from which it is impossible to escape).

If we consider all the possible moves and counter moves that are available at any given stage in a chess game, there are about a thousand combinations that could conceivably take place. The number of possible sequences of eight moves, then, would be 1000^8 (a million billion billion, if you care to spell it out). Were we to try to devise an algorithm for evaluating the best one of these possible combinations, we would have to explore literally billions of different possibilities. The sheer effort involved would overload even the largest high-speed computer.

Chess players clearly do not try to follow through all possible combinations to their conclusions. They selectively consider only those moves that would seem to produce important results. How do they know which of the millions of possibles moves should be considered in detail?

Several studies of chess experts—those who have reached the internationally recognized level of *Grand Master*—suggest that chess masters use a number of heuristic rules to examine and select moves. The rules are ordered in terms of importance, and this order is used to discriminate among promising moves. A sample of some of the heuristics used by chess Grand Masters gives an indication of how their search for appropriate operators is guided:

- Give highest priority to *double checks* (moves that attack the king with two or more pieces simultaneously) and *discovered checks* (moves that take one piece out of another's line of attack).
- If there is an alternative, use the most powerful piece to make the check (the power of a piece depends on the flexibility of moves that can be made).
- Give priority to moves that leave the opponent with the least possible number of replies.
- Give priority to a check that adds a new attacker to the list of active pieces.
- Give priority to a check that takes the opponent's king farthest from its base.

These are simple rules. When they are applied to a number of standard chess ending situations (taken from one of the standard books on chess), they succeed in a large number of cases. Of more importance, they succeed without requiring too much memory capability on the **part** of the player: only 9 to 77 possibilities need to be considered in the *exploration phase* of reaching the solution, and 5 to 19 possibilities in the *verification phase* (to check that the combination of moves is indeed valid and sound). Since the solution of some of these problems might take a chess Grand Master some 15 min to discover, they would not seem to require a great mental capacity at any one time. In fact, the task would appear to be equivalent to that of spending 15 min in memorizing a grammatical English selection of 75 to 100 words (the preceding three sentences, for example). The different levels of ability among chess players seem to result more from the efficiency of the selective heuristic schemes they have developed, rather than from sheer mental capacity.

By starting with subjects' verbalizations of their thoughts while problem solving, we have been able to discover quite a bit about the nature of the processes involved. Moreover, protocol analysis need not be limited to pure problem-solving situations. When a clinical psychologist attempts to evaluate a patient, the procedures followed are based on a somewhat less formal analysis of the patient's protocol, but the philosophy is quite similar. The clinical psychologist tries to deduce the nature of the internal operations in the memory structure by following the paths the patients or clients take as reflected in their descriptions of their thoughts.

Limitations of protocol analysis

 There are dangers that result from too heavy a reliance on the protocol generated by the subject. An example of the problem comes from one of the earlier studies of reasoning (Maier, 1931). In this experiment two cords hung from the ceiling of a room. The subject's task was to tie the strings together, but it was impossible to reach both at the same time.

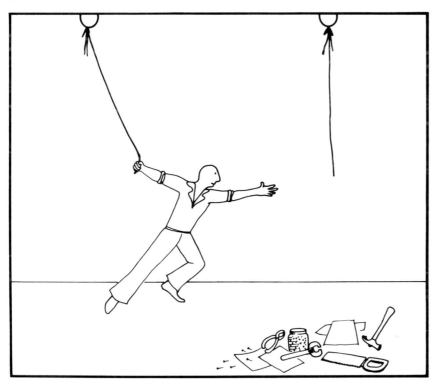

FIGURE 14-8

A number of solutions were possible by clever use of the various objects scattered deliberately but inconspicuously throughout the room. Only one solution was of interest to Maier, however, and he explored the hints needed to get his subjects to come up with it. (We deliberately will not tell you the answer, so that you can try the task yourself.) The experimenter (who was in the room with the subject) used two different hints.

Hint 1. The experimenter walked about the room, and, in passing the cord which hung from the center of the room, he put it in slight motion a few times. This was done without the subject knowing that a suggestion was being given. The experimenter merely walked to the window and had to pass the cord.

Hint 2. In case hint 1 failed to bring about the solution within a few minutes, the subject was handed a pair of pliers and told, "With the aid of this and no other object, there is another way of solving the problem." [The description of the hints is Maier's, as outlined in the original article (1931).]

Maier divided the subjects who successfully solved the problem after receiving the hints into two groups—those who appeared to solve the problem as a whole ("The solution just came to me; I don't know how"), and those who seemed to go through a series of steps to the solution ("Let's see, if I could move the cord, . . . throw things at it, . . . blow at it, . . . swing it like a pendulum . . . aha!"). The interesting difference between these two groups, from our point of view, is the difference between the subjects' reported use of the hint. Those who solved the problem as a whole failed to report that the hint was of any use to them, while the group that progressed through stages reported (with but one exception) that the hint was an aid. Our question is whether the "whole" subjects actually used the hint without being aware of it. If this is so, then we would expect that protocols taken during problem solving might miss many of the steps involved in arriving at a solution.

First, it is clear that the subjects who failed to report the use of the hint in fact solved the problem much quicker than the group for which no hints were given. On the average, the majority of subjects found the solution within less than a minute after the hint was given. When no hints were given, only 20% of the subjects found the solution, even though they were allowed to work on the problem for half an hour. Did the "whole" subjects notice the hint but were perhaps simply unwilling to admit that they used it? This seems unlikely. Subjects who solved the problem in steps seemed to have no hesitancy in referring to the hint as they described their solution. Why should the "whole" subjects hold back? The conclusion seems to be that the hint played an important part in bringing about the solution, even though the subjects were not consciously aware of its role. If the subject does not realize such an obvious step in his or her protocol behavior, then our protocol records are going to be incomplete.

We must assume, then, that as people work on a problem, they proceed through a series of strategies and operations, which are reflected in their verbal description of their own mental operations. The steps going on internally, however, are not all faithfully represented in the verbal output. What we can observe will only be a partial description of the actual internal processes.

The conclusion, then, is that only a portion of a person's cognitive activities is going to be available for external examination. The record will be most complete if people are encouraged to verbalize their detailed thought processes, and if protocols are taken during the actual performance of the activity. Even Maier's "whole" subjects might have been aware of their use of the hint if they had been told beforehand to monitor their thought processes and to talk aloud as they groped for a solution. Despite its shortcomings, the protocol analysis is a powerful tool in attempting to reconstruct the events that go on during problem solving and to explore the kinds of cognitive strategies that operate in these complex tasks.

We have observed many people attempting to solve the DONALD + GERALD problem, and the typical result is very much like the fumbling, tortuous path of the subject in our example. Why do people not do better? For example, here is a very efficient solution to the DONALD + GERALD problem. Note how simple it seems:

HOW GOOD IS HUMAN PROBLEM SOLVING?

$$
\begin{array}{l}
(\text{Column} \quad 6\ 5\ 4\ 3\ 2\ 1) \\
\qquad \text{D O N A L D} \qquad D = 5. \\
+\ \text{G E R A L D} \\
\hline
\qquad \text{R O B E R T}
\end{array}
$$

1. $D = 5$, so T must be $\emptyset$ (with a carry to column 2).
2. Look at column 5: $O + E = O$. This can happen only if $\emptyset$ or $1\emptyset$ is being added to O. Therefore, E must be 9 (plus a carry) or $\emptyset$. But T is already $\emptyset$, so E must be 9 (with a carry from column 4).
3. If E is 9, then in column 3 A must be 4 or 9 (with a carry in either case). E is already 9, so A must be 4.

4. In column 2, L + L plus a carry = R plus a carry to column 3. R must be odd. The only odd numbers left are 1, 3, and 7. But from column 6, 5 + G = R, so R must be greater than 5. So R must be 7, which makes L = 8 and G = 1.

5. In column 4, N + 7 = B + carry. Therefore, N is greater than or equal to 3. The only numbers left are 2, 3, and 6, so N is 3 or 6. But if N were 3, B would be $\emptyset$, so N must be 6. That makes B = 3.

6. That only leaves the letter O and the number 2: O = 2.

$$\begin{array}{r} 5\ 2\ 6\ 4\ 8\ 5 \\ +\ 1\ 9\ 7\ 4\ 8\ 5 \\ \hline 7\ 2\ 3\ 9\ 7\ \emptyset \end{array}$$

In all our experiences with this problem we have never seen a solution this direct and efficient.[3] Nonetheless, this solution to the problem shows what is possible, even if it is seldom achieved. The question is: Why don't people solve the problem this way?

Limits imposed by short-term memory

Human problem solving is actually quite limited by the constraints of short-term memory. Think about it: your ability to make mental predictions is very poor. It is only when you have experience with some topic that you are able to think ahead. We all hear stories of the extraordinary ability of the chess master to look ahead a vast number of moves, of skilled players of games and sports to foresee every possible move by their opponent, or of skilled mathematicians who can see ahead to the proof of some exotic theorems. Rubbish.

Consider the game of tic–tac–toe. We contend that tic–tac–toe is at the very limit of human cognitive ability, yet it is about as simple a game as possible. Here are the rules (for the benefit of readers whose game might differ). The board, illustrated at the very top of Figure 14-9, has only 9 squares. The players move alternately, putting symbols in the squares (the symbols are usually **X** and **O**). The first person to get three of his or her symbols in a straight row (horizontally, diagonally, or vertically) wins the game. Once a symbol is put down it cannot be changed.

---

[3] A solution very close to this one is presented by Sir Frederic Bartlett in his book *Thinking* (1958, p. 53). However, we are slightly suspicious of the report provided by Bartlett, because some of his other protocols give evidence that they were written down by the subject some time *after* the problem had been attempted. This is a very poor way to collect data: a person's recollections of what has been done tend to be better than what was actually done (see Bartlett's protocol VI, p. 55).

Almost everyone can play this game perfectly, never losing. Thus, two skilled players always draw and so the game is considered quite uninteresting. How can we contend that tic–tac–toe is at the very limit of human cognitive ability? For anyone who knows the game, this seems like an outrageous statement: let us explain.

Consider the game shown in Figure 14-9, starting at the top. Player **O** has moved first, into the center square. Pretend you are player **X** and that you have never played before. As a result, you must think through all the possible implications. There are 8 squares left into which you can move, but a little bit of thought lets you realize that the symmetry of the board and **O**'s centralized move essentially reduce the moves you must consider to 2. All the other possible moves are really the same as one of the two shown in the second row of Figure 14-9.

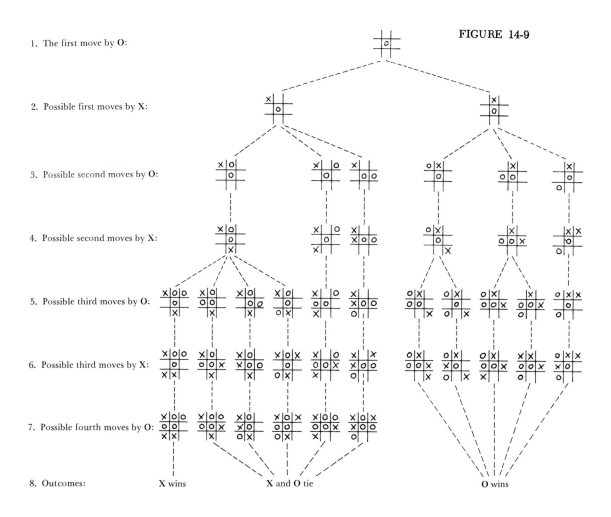

FIGURE 14-9

1. The first move by O:

2. Possible first moves by X:

3. Possible second moves by O:

4. Possible second moves by X:

5. Possible third moves by O:

6. Possible third moves by X:

7. Possible fourth moves by O:

8. Outcomes: X wins   X and O tie   O wins

Suppose you move to one of these two squares, then what? Player **O** will respond in a way that presumably makes it possible for him or her to get three pieces in a row. So excluding all moves by **O** that do not result in 2 **O**'s in a row (with an empty square in the third location), each of your two possible first moves has three possible return moves by **O**: these six possible moves are shown in the third row of Figure 14-9.

Each of these moves puts 2 **O**'s in a row, forcing your next move (shown in the fourth row of the figure). But now, depending upon what your second move was, **O** can move any one of four different ways (considering only situations that lead to as many ways of getting three **O**'s in a row as possible). By the time you have planned ahead to your third move, there are 11 different possible configurations. If you can follow those 11 ways out a few more steps, you will find that only one leads to a winning position for you; the rest lead to ties or to a win by **O**. But remember that we are discussing your first actual game in which you would have to work all this out in your mind, trying to determine which moves to make.

There is simply no way that a person can keep in mind the set of possibilities illustrated in Figure 14-9: the limits on short-term memory capacity prevent it. If tic–tac–toe were played by sheer reasoning, the game would not be possible. But we all know that the game is trivial. Why?

Planning ahead in tic–tac–toe—and planning ahead in all problem-solving situations—is done with the aid of previously learned structures. Nobody plays tic–tac–toe in the manner illustrated in Figure 14-9. More important, nobody has to. Several things happen. First of all, the results of some patterns of moves are learned directly: they only have to be figured out once, and then they just have to be remembered. Thus, most players know that if they start by placing a piece in the center square, they are guaranteed either a win or, at worst, a tie. Similarly, most players know that if the other player started with a move to the center square the proper response must be a move to one of the corner squares: any other move guarantees a loss.

Second, the goal of the game is redefined in a fashion that makes the planning easier. Thus, experienced players have discovered that there is an easier goal than the official one of "to get 3 marks in a row." The experienced player realizes that the configuration known as an *open two*, 2 marks in a row with an empty (open) square in the third position, is necessary for a win; a *double open two*, 2 open two's constructed from 3 pieces, guarantees a win. Thus, the game becomes an attempt to form a double open two, using only 3 pieces. (Every one of the 5 board configurations on the right half of row 5 that leads to a win by **O** contains a double open two.)

Redefining the game shortens the amount of planning that has to be done. Remembering the winning and losing configurations of past games also reduces the amount of planning that has to be done. Practicing different configurations of the game leads to perfection in playing through both processes. And so it is with all mental skills: practice and experience with a particular type of problem not only adds familiar patterns and responses to memory, but also enables one to redefine the situation into forms that are easier to deal with.

Is the ability of humans to think and plan ahead really as limited as the analysis of tic–tac–toe might imply? The answer is both yes and no. Yes, the limitations of short-term memory are indeed very restrictive. It simply is not possible to plan very far ahead in doing problems. But no, the human is not such a limited thinker. Two major things overcome the limitations of short-term memory: *Overcoming the limits*

> External aids to thought
> The capacity and flexibility of long-term memory.

External aids. We overcome the limits of short-term memory by using external aids—mostly pens and pencils. Do not underestimate the power of writing things down. External aids are very powerful in allowing us to plan ahead. Moreover, in order to write something down, some thought must be given to the nature of the writing, and this may itself considerably aid the thinking process. In order to write down helpful numbers or words, symbols or maps, pictures or sketches, some abstraction of the actual problem must occur to transform it into a writable form. This means that a symbolic notation must be devised. We have already seen how the problem **If the puzzle you solved before you solved this one . . .** was made trivial by the substitution of the symbolic names **puzzle A** and **puzzle B**. Symbolic notation is a very powerful tool in thinking, for it lets one symbol stand for complex concepts, and allows complex interrelationships among concepts to be summarized and manipulated directly. External aids to thought thus have several different virtues.

Long-term memory aids. The expert at any task has had years of practice. To give an accurate number for the amount of training required is difficult, but we estimate at least 1000 to 5000 hours are required to reach the top amateur or professional levels of performance. This is true for all tasks that we have analyzed, whether it be learning how to read, to race an automobile, play the piano, sing, play soccer, juggle, or become a professional psychologist. Of course, each of these tasks differs considerably from the others and the type of training that is required is different. But the need for thousands of hours holds true for all. What happens with all those hours of practice? One thing that is certainly involved is the acquisition of large amounts of structured knowledge—memory schemas—into long-term memory.

Consider our favorite example: the expert chess player (say an International Grand Master). The expert chess player is often thought to have some unique mental ability. This is simply not true. Well learned, meaningful configurations of things are much easier to retain and to work with than are configurations that make no sense.

To understand this point, consider how well you can remember a sequence of letters. For most people, about 10 letters is the limit. Try it, read the following sequence of letters once and then try to repeat it aloud (without looking at the page):

   X P C W P T L M S Q

Ten unrelated items are about the limit of what can be recalled (unless you use one of the special techniques of Chapter 9). Each letter is a single psychological unit and must be represented separately in memory.

Now consider what happens if the letters are organized into some meaningful configuration. Read the following sequence of ten letters once and then try to repeat the letters aloud (without looking at the page):

   PROCESSING

Not only are these ten letters easy to remember, but you probably do not even think of them as ten letters. They form a single psychological unit, a word. They need only be represented in memory as a single item. Indeed, it is easy to remember much longer sequences of letters in this way.

Try to recall this sentence after reading it once:

> The book *Human information processing* introduces students to the scientific study of the mind.

Here, despite the fact that there are 80 letters, the task is quite easy. Of course, you do not think of it as a sequence of letters. Indeed, you may not even have thought of the parts of the sentence as being composed of words. Thus, the title of this book, *Human information processing*, can simply be remembered as a single unit, not as three words, and it certainly need not be regarded as 26 different letters.

The configurations of pieces in chess games are treated by the chess masters in the same way as you treat the configurations of letters in sentences. In fact, many configurations have been given names, and are quite familiar to expert players. Games follow logical sequences of moves, and when two experts compete there are systematic patterns to the configurations. By taking advantage of these regularities, skilled chess players appear to have superior mental abilities in looking ahead and in planning possible moves. But this skill is actually due to their great familiarity with the game, which allows them to view configurations of pieces as single psychological units. This familiarity is not easy to develop. It takes years of study, many hours each day, to reach this level of performance. But when skilled chess players are asked to remember meaningless board configurations, or even patterns of pieces taken from the games of unskilled players, their apparent superb memory and analytical skills deteriorate, much as your ability to remember letters drops considerably when they no longer form meaningful words.

So far, we have examined problem-solving. Another major category of mental activity is labeled *decision making*. Here, a specific choice of alternatives is offered someone who must then select one course of action. Decision making is a part of problem solving, of course, just as problem solving plays a role in decision making. But there are enough new problems introduced in the formal study of decision processes that it makes sense to examine them separately.

DECISION MAKING

Decisions pervade our lives. We are continually faced with alternative courses of action, each of which must be evaluated for its relative merits. Sometimes, the decision depends upon the reactions of others; sometimes chance factors are involved; often, decision making is accompanied by a perplexing mixture of success and failure.

It is a very difficult psychological task to compare several courses of action and finally select one. First, if each course of action has any complexity to it, it strains the limited capacity of short-term memory simply to picture a single alternative and its implications, let alone carry several in mind simultaneously in order that they might be compared with one another. Second, if the alternatives are complex ones, then there is no clear way to do the comparison, even if the several choices could all be laid out one in front of the other. And finally, there are always a number of unknown factors that intrude upon the situation: Some of the results of the action are only problematical—who knows what will really happen? Some of the results of the decision depend upon how someone else will react to it, and often that reaction is not even known by the other person yet. It is no wonder that the sheer complexity of reaching a decision often causes one to give up in despair, postponing the event for as long as possible, sometimes making the actual final choice only when forced, and then often without any attempt to consider all the implications of that choice. Afterward, when all is done and it is to late to change the act, there is time to fret and worry over the decision, wondering whether some other course of action would have been best after all.

Human cognitive limitations interact with human actions. Thus, in our study of human decision making, we have to be especially concerned with realizing the distinction between the rules people ought to follow, and those they actually do follow. The distinction can be difficult to make, since people often describe their behavior as deliberate and logical, even when it is not. When people make a decision that appears to be illogical from the viewpoint of an outsider, usually it turns out that the decision was sensible from the position of the decision makers, at least in terms of the information they were thinking about at the time. When the apparent error is pointed out to them ("Why did you move the pawn there? Now I can take your queen!"), they are likely to respond that they simply "forgot" some important information ("Oh damn, I saw that earlier, but then I forgot about it!"). This poses difficulties in our efforts to study the decision processes. Which behavior do we study—the actual, erratic acts, or the systematic, purposeful ones? The answer, of course, is both.

DETERMINING
VALUES

The function of rational, decision theory is to identify the information that is relevant to a decision and to specify how the information should be put together to arrive at a conclusion. The major principle of rational decision making is that of *optimization:* All other things being equal, pick the alternative with the greatest value.

This simple maxim of acting in order to maximize the gains and minimize the losses seems to be a perfectly plausible assumption on the surface. But in this simple form, it is of relatively little value for a theory of human decision making. The problem is that different people evaluate gains and costs differently.

A basic issue raised by the notion of optimization is to determine how people assess values and costs in a decision-making situation. The psychological worth a person associates with a course of action or an object is said to be the *utility* for that object. The task of decision theory is to determine how people assign utilities to objects and then, how these utilities are used during the course of decision making.

The psychological value of money

A natural place to begin a study of utilities is with the psychological worth of money. Clearly, the utility of money is not simply its face value: among other things, it must depend critically on a person's wealth. One dollar must surely represent a far greater utility to beggars than to the people they beg from.

Consider this simple experiment. Suppose you were just given a present of $20. The arrival of the money was unexpected and there are absolutely no strings attached to it. Think about how happy this gift makes you. Now, seriously consider the amount of happiness generated by the gift of $20. How much money would the gift have to be to make you exactly twice as happy? What about four times as happy, or eight times as happy? (Notice that this is the magnitude estimation scaling technique discussed in Appendix A as it applies to money.[4] Try the experiment before reading the next paragraph.)

People differ in their responses to this thought experiment—as well they should. Someone who is a relative pauper cherishes the gift of $20; someone who receives a monthly allowance of $1000 would not be much affected by the gift: Hence, their evaluations of the situation differ. Nonetheless, almost everyone would agree that the money would have to be more than doubled in order to double the happiness that it brings. In fact, the usual answer is that the monetary amount must be **quadrupled** in order to double the happiness (utility). That is, the utility of money appears to increase as the square root of the monetary value.

Do not take this exact relationship too seriously. The important lesson of the example is that the psychological value of an item, even so well known an item as money, does not increase in direct proportion to the numerical value. In general, it increases more slowly.

What happens when we are not dealing with simple quantities like money? How do we assign values to complex objects and situations? The abstract nature of the problem is perhaps best illustrated by examining a situation not too closely related to reality; in this way we can avoid past experiences interfering with the consideration of the issues. So forget reality for a moment and view this scenario with us.

The value of complex alternatives

How to choose a mate. In a faraway land, where women are the rulers and sultanas are still in style, the Maga of Kantabara wished to purchase a mate to add to her collection. So she called before her the two best qualified brokers in all the land and requested them to go forth and seek for her a new mate. Now, by long, scientifically established tradition, the Maga had determined the most important attributes in a mate. Thus, she required that each of the prospective candidates undergo a test on several critical dimensions. Each would then be assigned a numerical value ranging from −5 to +5, depending upon his skills and attributes: Zero points if he were average, +5 if superb, −5 if perfectly awful.

The two brokers returned, each with one candidate: Shar and Malik. Their price was the same: Their individual evaluations are shown in Table 14-1.

[4] The experiment was first performed by Galanter (1962).

Table 14-1   Evaluation of Prospective
Mate

Dimension	Candidate	
	Shar	*Malik*
Military skill	2	1
Sexual skill	5	−1
Conversational skill	−2	4
Intelligence	−4	3
Personality	4	3
Physical attractiveness	2	2
Prestige of family name	3	1

Broker's verbal description of candidates:

SHAR: A man from a family of high prestige. Will add to the reputation of the court. A pleasure to be with, attractive, with fine military skills. Is top rated in his knowledge and employment of the amatory arts.

MALIK: A remarkably intelligent, personable choice. An attractive mate, with a high level of conversational ability to entertain you and your guests. Comes from a good family and has a good knowledge of military skills.

Decision strategies.   An examination of the Maga's choice situation indicates that the basic issue is how to compare all the various dimensions. How should she combine the virtues of sexual skill with those of intelligence: These are two different things.

The first step toward a solution is to make sure that all the values are on a common scale. It is important that the +3 given to Shar's prestige has just as much psychological worth to the Maga as the +3 assigned to Malik's intelligence. But let us assume that this first problem is solved, that each of the ratings assigned along the dimensions have been carefully worked out so that they can be compared directly.[5]

---

[5] One way of doing this is to transform each rating value onto a single scale, such as monetary value. Suppose there were two candidates, A and B, who were identical on all dimensions but one. On that dimension, A rated higher than B. How much monetary difference in purchase price would be necessary to offset the difference in ratings? The prospective buyer can be offered a choice of candidate A at a given price or candidate B at a reduced price. If a reduction in the price

FIGURE 14-10

The problem of combining the dimensions still remains. Try making the decision: Which one should the Maga choose? How do you deal with the various ratings on the various dimensions?

Let us attack the problem by considering two quite different strategies for combining the values of the multidimensional mates in order to reach a decision: We call these two strategies *overall impression* and *dimensional comparison*.

Overall impression. In this strategy, each candidate is examined separately and a single figure of merit determined that represents the overall value of the candidate. The same procedure is performed on each

---

of B of, say, $1000 were sufficient to offset the lower rating of B on the dimension, then the one rating-difference has the same psychological worth as $1000. By offering a number of such choices for different ratings and different dimensions, it is possible to express the rating on each dimension on a common monetary scale.

candidate, and the one with the highest overall utility is selected. Thus, the values associated with Shar add up to a total of 10. For candidate Malik, the same procedure produces an overall rating of 13. According to this decision strategy, the Maga should purchase Malik for her mate.

Dimensional comparison. In this strategy, the alternatives are compared directly, one dimension at a time. First, the difference between the alternatives is assessed for each dimension. Then the final judgment is based on analysis of these dimensional differences. In this case, Shar wins on military and sexual skills, personality, and family prestige. The results of the dimensional analysis put Shar as the winner on four dimensions, Malik on 2, with a tie on one dimension. A simple decision rule is to choose the candidate preferred on the most dimensions: This makes Shar the winner, 4 to 2.

Assessment of the strategies. Here, then, are two strategies, each giving a different answer. What should the Maga do? That is her problem. But what about most people, which strategy do they follow? The answer is both: now one, now the other. Both strategies seem to be a part of the procedures followed by people in actual situations. Each has virtue and deficiency. In the method of overall impressions, each alternative is assessed by itself and then summarized by a single value. This procedure is probably the most accurate, but it is also the hardest to do: The assessment of a given alternative is relatively difficult. In the method of dimensional comparison, the comparison between alternatives along a single dimension is relatively easy to do, even if the result is less efficient. There is a trade-off between the complexity of the decision rule, its accuracy, and the ability of a person to perform the necessary evaluation.

Actually, we have presented the problem of making this choice in a rather cold-blooded fashion. In usual situations, it is not possible to come up with such a complete numerical assessment. In fact, even when some efficient businessman or government administrator manages to convince the decision makers to prepare such an assessment of the alternatives, usually the actual person who must make the decision is not satisfied. Thus, given this scientifically proven rating scale for prospective mates, the Maga is most likely to respond, "Well, that's all very well for making the initial selections of candidates, but maybe you had better just let me be alone with each one for an evening—find out what he is really like, you know."

The Maga is clearly correct in her dissatisfaction with such a precise listing of the values of the candidates: Certainly, there is more to the alternatives than can be captured in the numbers. The main virtue of the numerical assessment is that it allows for rational, complete decision making. But there is no question that many important subtleties are ignored. However, unfortunately, personal interviews are even worse. The difficulties of comparing two complex alternatives are now compounded by the limitations of personal encounters. In a personal interview, even the most trivial of events often carries high weight. Suppose one of the candidates stumbles on the rug while leaving, or wears a distasteful color, or does something else both accidental and annoying: "That Malik, he is much too clumsy to be a Maga's mate. Certainly Shar seemed quite graceful."

What is being optimized?

Even after values have been assigned, does the decision maker always choose the highest valued alternative? Suppose that a student, Bob, has carefully saved his money in order to purchase a single-lens reflex camera. He is working his way through school, so in fact it has been difficult to raise the money needed. He has $190, and whatever is left over from buying the camera he intends to put aside toward his textbooks for next semester.

One weekend, Bob gets a ride with a friend to Los Angeles (some 100 miles away), where he knows he can get a good buy on the camera of his choice. He trudges around the city all day, from camera store to camera store. In the morning he finds store A, where the price is $185. At noon, he finds B, where the price is $165, and at 4 P.M. he is at store C, where the price is $170. Clearly, Bob should go back to store B. But he is hungry and tired. He has not eaten all day. He has to meet his friend soon for his ride back, so the actual choice is between going back to store B (saving $5) and not having time to eat anything or staying at store C, paying the extra $5, but being able to stop off for a sandwich and some rest before heading back. Bob is very likely to choose the latter alternative today, when he compares his hunger and tiredness with the savings of $5. At the moment, this is a logical decision. Tomorrow, Bob may very well regret the decision, for then, when yesterday's tiredness and hunger no longer seem very important, he realizes that he will have to work for two more hours in the cafeteria to make up the $5.

The problem one faces in trying to analyze our ability to understand the actual decisions made by someone else is hampered because we do not and cannot ever know all the variables that entered into the situation. ("Yes, I know I made a mistake in leaving too soon, but I had to go to the bathroom.") The principle of maximization is assumed to underlie every decision. When the time comes for the actual choice to be made, however, it may be that new variables have entered into the situation and some of the old ones are not considered. Thus, even when a decision is made to pursue an apparently foolish choice, we assume that it is done logically and sensibly, considering the information involved in the analysis. An apparently illogical choice of decisions can be made simply because when it came to the final moment, the psychological utility for getting some rest or of minimizing the intellectual effort was greater than the utility thought to be gained by a more prolonged, thorough analysis of the alternatives. The properties of short-term memory which cause a low limit on the number of comparisons that can be made at any one time will often turn out to be one of the most important determiners of the actual choice. Our basic assumption is that each decision does optimize psychological utility, even though the bystander (and perhaps the decision maker also) may later wonder why that choice was made.

THE LOGIC OF CHOICE

Almost without exception, people agree that their own decision processes ought to be logical. Moreover, formal theories of decision making assume logical consistency: Preferences among objects ought to be consistent with one another. If A is preferred to B and B to C, then logically A should be preferred to C. Transitivity of this sort is a basic property that just ought to hold anytime different objects are compared to one another. Let the symbol $>$ stand for a preference of one object over another, and the symbol $=$ stand for a complete indifference between two objects; the basic rules for logical choices can be summarized as

1. If $A > B$ and $B > C$, then $A > C$.
2. If $A = B$ and $B = C$, then $A = C$.
3. If $A = B$ and $C > 0$, then $A + C > B$.

These three rules constitute a sensible set of postulates about decision behavior. Indeed, if the rules are described properly, so that the mathematical framework is removed, they simply sound like obvious common sense. Those who study decision making, however, have discovered that there is a difference between the rules that people believe they follow and the rules that they actually do follow. Thus, although these three assumptions form the core of most decision theories, it is also realized that they do not always apply. There are some clear examples of instances in which each rule is violated.

There are several ways in which the decision theorist can deal with these difficulties. One is to ignore them, assuming that the violations of the rules occur only in special circumstances, and not in the situation described by the theory under study. Alternatively, the decision maker can try to incorporate the violations into a theory, showing how they result from certain performance limitations of humans. Here are some anecdotal illustrations that demonstrate examples of violations for each of the three basic rules.

$$\text{If } A > B \text{ and } B > C, \text{ then } A > C$$

Consider the decision problem of Steve, a student trying to choose a course to fulfill his social science requirement. Three courses are available—psychology, sociology, and anthropology. Assume that his preferences among these courses are based mainly on three characteristics: the quality of teaching in the course, the grade he expects to get (which includes the difficulty of the work and the toughness of marking), and his personal interest in the material. In order to make a rational decision he rates the courses on these three dimensions:

Course	Quality of Teaching	Expected Grade	Interest in Material
Psychology	High	Low	Medium
Sociology	Low	Medium	High
Anthropology	Medium	High	Low

Sociology versus psychology. When Steve goes to register, he finds the usual long lines of students waiting to sign up for the courses. He has to decide on a course fairly quickly or it will be closed before he has a chance to enroll. Suppose he starts in the psychology line. As he stands there, he begins thinking about his choice between psychology and sociology. Psychology has a higher quality of teaching, but he expects a lower grade, and the material is not as interesting as sociology. Thus, sociology rates higher than psychology on two out of the three dimensions. So he really prefers sociology to psychology, since a sensible decision rule is to choose the course that rates highest on the largest number of dimensions. Therefore he should switch into the sociology line. Suppose he does.

Anthropology versus sociology. Now Steve is in the sociology line. He begins thinking about his other option, anthropology. Anthropology rates higher than sociology on both the quality of teaching and on the expected grade, although it is somewhat less interesting. Using the same decision rule as before, he now discovers that anthropology is clearly preferable to sociology and the sensible thing to do is to switch to the anthropology line. Suppose he does.

Psychology versus anthropology. After arriving in the anthropology line, however, Steve cannot stop thinking about psychology. After all, it rates higher than anthropology on both teaching quality and interest. Perhaps he should reenter the psychology line.

This circularity in behavior represents intransitivity in his choices among the courses. If A stands for anthropology, B for sociology, and C for psychology, then apparently he prefers A to B and B to C, but also C to A:

$$A > B > C > A > B \cdot \cdot \cdot .$$

Moreover, these vacillations in his choice behavior appear even though he is following a simple and consistent rule for making his choices.

When considering the choices among complex objects, this situation is not atypical. Frequently, the decision problem involves dealing with large numbers of dimensions, weighing the values of each dimension and, finally, devising some strategy for combining the evaluations. When the objects are complex, the opportunity for inconsistency is large.

$$\text{If } A = B \text{ and } B = C, \text{ then } A = C.$$

The importance of small differences: rule 2

This time, the scenario is the purchase of a new car. Gertrude, the customer, has decided on a sports car with a base price of $4500. Now the salesperson begins to offer some extras in the hope of building up the overall price of the car.

Gertrude has chosen the red hatchback model. Certainly, the machined aluminum hubs would spectacularly improve the overall appearance. The seller argues skillfully that the hubs are only $59 extra: Since the car costs $4500, the extra cost of the hubs is negligible. This is probably true. Gertrude claims to be indifferent between paying $4500 and $4559 for a car. Thus, if A is the cost of the car and B is the cost of the car and hubs, then in the mind of the customer, A = B.

Now we make the argument over again: The black leather dash only costs $37.95. This is a must if the top will be down most of the time. Moreover, there is really no difference between paying $4559.00 and $4596.95. Thus, if B is the cost of the car and hubs and C = B + cost of dash, then in the mind of the customer, B = C.

Now, what about a white tonneau cover? Gertrude may move the price over the $5000 mark before she realizes that the sum of her small indifferences has led to a large difference. Certainly she is not indifferent between a cost of $4500 and $5000.

FIGURE 14-11

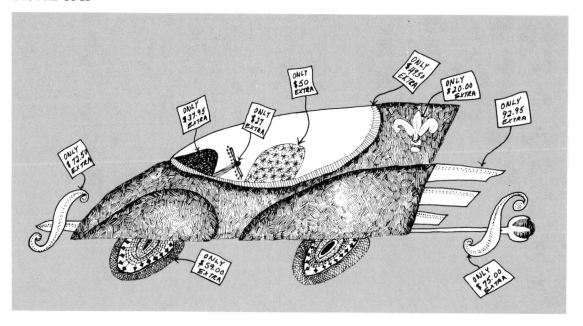

But having gone through the experience, indifference now operates in reverse to make it difficult to undo the sequence. Gertrude may feel that she could really forego the simulated alligator-hide panels in the doors but that would only save her $29.95, a paltry amount, given that she is spending $5000 on the car. Maybe she should just pay the extra money rather than bother to determine the exact combination of extras that she can do without that will significantly reduce the price of the car. The skillful salesperson always avoids mentioning the base price or cumulative cost of the extras. Emphasis is placed on the trivial amounts of each increment relative to the total cost. The shrewd seller stops just before the customer begins to consider the possibility that although A = B and B = C, A does not necessarily equal C.

$$\text{If } A = B \text{ and } C > 0, \text{ then } A + C > B.$$

The Tokyo–Paris problem: rule 3

There is a very popular counterexample to this rule, well known among economists and decision theorists. It goes like this. Suppose your name was just picked as the prize winner of a raffle. You are given a choice of prizes. Which do you prefer: an all-expense-paid week's trip to Tokyo, or an all-expense-paid week's trip to Paris? Let us assume that you are really indifferent

FIGURE 14-12

between these two choices and would be willing to let the flip of a coin decide. Call the psychological value of the trip to Paris P and that for the trip to Tokyo T. Since you are indifferent, we have established that P = T.

Now, would you rather have someone give you a bottle[6] of wine or not? We assume your choice is to receive the gift. Therefore, the psychological value of the receipt of a bottle of wine is W, W > 0. Now, suppose you get the bottle of wine only if you choose the trip to Paris. You should now have a clear preference for the Paris trip: P = T, and W > 0, therefore P + W > T. You don't agree? Right, the logic does not apply. Somehow the offer of wine is really quite inconsequential in this decision.

The problem is not that wine has no value. In isolation, most people would prefer having the free wine to not having it. The issue here is the way the values depend upon the context in which they appear. In this situation, wine is clearly irrelevant to the choice problem. In other situations, the same bottle might be the deciding factor.

RISKY DECISION MAKING

Decisions in real life frequently must be made in uncertain situations. Choices often require both assessing the utilities of the various possible outcomes and taking a gamble on what is actually going to happen. The value of the decision to carry an umbrella depends upon the chance of rain. The question of whether or not one should buy life insurance is intimately connected with the chances of living for some specified amount of time. A choice of political strategies depends on the chance that the opponents will adopt certain countermeasures. This addition of chance factors to the situation does not change the basic principle of optimization, but in considering people's decision behavior, both utilities and chance factors must be included.

Utility in risky choices

Consider the following set of choices. Would you prefer:

1. $0.10 with certainty or one chance in ten of obtaining $1.00.
2. $1 with certainty or one chance in ten of obtaining $10.
3. $10 with certainty or one chance in ten of obtaining $100.
4. $100 with certainty or one chance in ten of obtaining $1000.
5. $1000 with certainty or one chance in ten of obtaining $10,000.

---

[6] The traditional example among decision theorists involves martinis rather than wine. You, in turn, may wish to substitute your own preference for a bottle of wine. But if you do, make it just a very small amount of the item of your preference.

6. One million dollars with certainty or one chance in ten of obtaining ten million dollars. [After Markowitz (1952, p. 150).]

We make two predictions about your pattern of preferences in this situation. The first is that you will not be indifferent between these choices. That is, for choice 1, for example, you will tend to prefer the gamble to the certain winnings: You would rather gamble on winning $1 than take 10¢ for sure. Similarly, you probably prefer to gamble on $10 than take $1 for sure, and perhaps you may prefer to gamble on a 10% chance of winning $100 rather than receive $10 with certainty. But at some stage you will reverse your pattern of preferences and begin choosing certain winnings to the chance situation. Unless you place an extremely high utility on the excitement of risk, it is unlikely that you would choose the opportunity of trying for $10,000,000 with a 10% chance over the outright gift of $1,000,000.

The second prediction is that the point at which you switch over from gambling to taking the sure thing will depend on your present wealth. The richer you are, the more willing you will be to gamble for higher stakes. In extremely reduced circumstances, you might even prefer the certain gift of a dime to the chance of winning $1. This is a good experiment to try on your friends, since you can collect the data quickly and easily. Select several acquaintances including some from high-income and some from low-income backgrounds. Starting with the first choice and going down the list, ask them which they prefer, the certain sum of money or the gamble. Note the points at which their preferences change from a sure thing to a gamble. The richer they are, the higher the number of the choice at which they cross over.

The switch-over in preference from the gamble to the certainty is at the point at which utility for money begins growing less rapidly than its dollar value. When $100 with certainty is chosen over a 10% chance of winning $1000, then utility for $1000 is **less than** ten times $100. Here, then, we have the basic situation for decision-making under risk. When outcomes are uncertain, both chance and utility must be considered. To deal with these, two new concepts must be added to our discussion: *probability* and *expected value.*

Probability

The *probability* of an event is simply the long-run expectation of the relative frequency with which the event will occur. Probability values range numerically from zero through one. When an event has a probability of zero, we can say with a great deal of certainty that we never expect the event to occur. The probability that the result of a single coin flip will be both heads and tails is zero. For events with probability of one, we say with extreme confidence that it will always occur: Because everyone dies, the probability of death is one. It is conceivable that in the future this probability will be changed. Similarly, it is possible that something with a probability of zero occurrence will actually happen: It simply is never expected to.

When an intermediate value of probability is assigned to an event, this means that over the long run it is expected to happen a certain percentage of the time. An event with a probability of .28 would be expected to occur about 28% of the time in a long series of observations. Heads are expected to turn up about 50% of the time in a long series of coin flips. This does not mean that it is known exactly how many times a given event will occur. It simply means that, statistically speaking, the event is expected to happen with a particular frequency.

Probability theory is the mathematical machinery for determining the likelihood that various events or combinations of events are going to occur. Often, the assignment of probabilities can be made by an analysis of the physical characteristics of the device that is producing the events: The fact that a die is six sided and is evenly balanced produces an expected probability that any number on the die will show up on the average of $\frac{1}{6}$ of the time. Sometimes the nature of the physical mechanisms underlying the occurrence of the event are not well understood, so the probability is determined by observations of its relative frequency in the past. If someone claims that the probability of rain on any given day in California is about .01, this figure is an estimate, based on the past history of rain in the state.

These are objective probabilities based on the physical properties of a given situation. As we shall see in a moment, they do not necessarily coincide with an individual's personal assessment of how likely it is that a given thing will happen.

Expected value   When the outcomes are probabilistic, decision theory prescribes that the rational decision maker attempts to maximize the long-run expected gains. Both the probabilities of events and their values must be considered in selecting an optimal course of action. A simple gambling situation illustrates the basic principle for combining these two aspects of a decision situation.

Suppose you are given an opportunity to play the following game. A coin is flipped. If it lands on heads, you get $10; if it lands on tails, you pay $5. Should you play the game?

The *expected value* for this gamble is simply the expected winnings or losses in the long run. The calculations are straightforward. The two possible events that can occur in the situation are equally probable:

There is an equal chance of winning or losing. The probability of heads is .5 [p(head) = .5], and when the coin does turn up heads, the value of that event is $10 [$V$(head) = $10]. When the coin turns up tails, you lose $5, so V(tail) = −$5. These probabilities and values are simply combined to give the overall expected value (*EV*) for the game.

$$EV = [V(\text{head}) \times p(\text{head})] + [V(\text{tail}) \times p(\text{tail})] \, .$$

$$EV = \$10 \times .5 + (-\$5) \times .5 \, .$$

$$EV = \$2.50 \, .$$

Over the long-run, then, you should win an average $2.50 for each flip of the coin. After playing the game 1000 times, you should come out about $2500 ahead.

In any situation in which probability values can be assigned for each outcome, the overall expected value can be computed. To make an optimal decision, the strategy or course of action that yields the highest expected value in the long run should be selected. This, of course, does not necessarily mean that you will win on every try. It only means that repeated choices of the strategy yielding the highest expected value will produce the largest long-run gains in a decision situation.

The expected-value computation gives the optimal decision choice, but obviously, few people understand the procedure or, even if they do, bother to make these computations before making a decision. (You can be sure, however, that gambling casinos, insurance companies, and similar businesses do make them with skill and devotion.) Now let us work our way toward what a person actually tends to do.

Subjective probability

If you were given a pair of dice, how likely do you think it is that you could roll a 7? Devices such as a pair of dice have no memory. Each roll of dice is completely independent of each other roll (we are assuming fair dice and a fair game). It does not matter whether a 7 has come up on every roll for the last 100 trials in a row, or whether a 7 has never come up: The dice themselves have no way of knowing what has happened. Yet a gambler will often bet that a 7 will come up next because, "It hasn't come up in the last 100 tries and now, by the law of averages, it has to." Such a bet results from subjective notions about probability. Coins, dice, and wheels cannot remember what has gone on in the past, so that the probability of various events is always the same on every try, regardless of what has happened previously.

This judgment of the actual objective probabilities by humans in their subjective perception of the likelihood of an event is called *subjective probability*.

Representativeness
and availability

It often appears that a person's subjective probability of an event comes about by an assessment of how characteristic the particular event is of the process thought to underlie its generation.[7]

Suppose we have just made a survey of all the families in California that have exactly six children. We find that about $\frac{1}{3}$ of the families have three boys and three girls. Now, suppose we consider the birth order of the children of these families. Which ordering do you think is more likely,

a: G B B G B G

b: B B B G G G

When people think of random order, they usually think of things "mixed together." Clearly, the first sample (*a*) is more representative of the random process that determines the order of arrival of boys and girls. Accordingly, most people believe it to be a more likely event—that is, the subjective probability of sequence *a* is judged to be appreciably greater than the subjective probability for sequence *b*. In fact, both sequences are equally likely. Given that a family has three boys and three girls, there are exactly 20 possible birth orders that could take place: All 20 are equally likely. Yet sequence *a* appears to be representative of a random sequence, whereas sequence *b*, in the minds of most people, is not. After all, there is a simple pattern: how could that be the result of a random process?

The problem here is actually very simple. People clearly lump together such different sequences as

a: G B B G B G

c: G B G B B G

d: B G B G G B

e: B G G B G B

as being similar. Hence, they can imagine many different ways of getting a sequence "like" *a*, *c*, *d*, or *e* (18 ways, to be exact), but only two ways of getting a sequence "like" *b* (B B B G G G, and G G G B B B). Of course, that was not the question: The comparison was between the **exact** sequences *a* and *b*, not similar sequences. Nonetheless, the lesson is instructive: People expect the world to behave in a representative fashion.

[7] The ideas for this description of representativeness and of decision making based upon the construction of mental scenarios of the possible outcomes is from the work of Daniel Kahneman and Amos Tversky.

A second, related way of determining subjective probabilities of an event is to consider all the past instances you can remember: The more "accessible" the event in your memory, the more probable it is judged to be. Consider, for example, which is more likely:

    a: that an English word starts with the letter **k**;

    b: that an English word has a **k** in the third position.

If you think of all the words you can that satisfy either *a* or *b*, it is quite clear that it is easier to find the former than the latter. Hence, most people will judge possibility *a* to be much more likely than possibility *b*. In fact, there are about three times as many words with a **k** in the third position as there are words that start with **k**. The problem is that human memory is not organized in a way that makes it easy to retrieve words by their middle letters, whereas it is organized to make it easy to retrieve them by their initial letters (or initial sounds).

This judgment by "availability" taints subjective probability estimates. If you are asked to judge whether mathematics professors are any good or not, you will base your answer on a consideration of the ones you can remember, even though you can know only a tiny fraction of the thousands of professors who teach mathematics in schools across the nation.

These explanations of the assessment of subjective probabilities through judgment of the **representativeness** of the sample and the **availability** of the events in memory often lead to three generalities about subjective probabilities:

1. People tend to overestimate the occurrence of events with low probability and underestimate the occurrence of events with high probability.
2. People tend to exhibit the *gambler's fallacy*, predicting that an event that has not occurred for a while is more likely to occur in the near future.
3. People tend to overestimate the true probability of events that are favorable to them and underestimate those that are unfavorable.

CONCLUSION

In this chapter, we have described some of the rules a decision maker follows in comparing alternatives, gathering information, and then reconsidering the choice. The choices of a rational decision maker are determined primarily by the expected values associated with the possible decisions, the probabilities of the events, and the payoffs and penalties of various outcomes. One should select the course of action that maximizes the gain. Although people appear to operate according to the principle of optimization, they do not necessarily do so in a manner that is readily predictable. Internal variables, such as boredom and fatigue, are often added into the decision equation. Moreover, the limitations of short-term memory often force people into strategies that minimize cognitive strain, thereby forcing them either to neglect considering all the important variables or to use a decision strategy that, while logical, is less than optimal and perhaps even inconsistent.

To make contact between the prescription for rational decision making and the actual behavior of people, objectively defined quantities must be translated into their subjective equivalents. In general, the subjective expected utility model is a reasonable description of much of human choice behavior. But a person's estimates of probabilities and assignment of utilities do not always remain stable. In most cases, this is as it should be. The utilities for events should vary as a person gains or loses, since utility is, after all, a function of the total wealth of the owner. Different people should and do have different judgments of the value of the same event. Subjective probability also varies. A unique event may stand out in one person's memory and not in another's, leading the former to judge it as a much more probable occurrence than it actually is.

The theories of decision making stand as a **prescription** for optimal behavior. Faced with decision situations, you will find it useful to analyze the situation according to the outlines presented here and to assess the values and costs associated with each possible decision strategy. But if you do so, do not trust your memory: Write things down.

A major portion of the situations and phenomena described in this chapter are intimately related to the use of memory. Short-term memory limitations play an important role in determining the strategies used in both decision making and in the solving of problems. Similarly, long-term memory plays an important role in the assessment of information, again critical to many of the issues discussed in all the sections of this chapter. It is important to remember that memory is best thought of as comprised of organized structures: memory schemas. A schema combines information relevant to some aspect of experience, and whenever any particular schema is retrieved, all the information within it is made available at once. This turns out to be important in the formation of subjective probabilities, as our discussion on that topic showed: there is a tendency to determine if a given situation is representative of "typical" situations, but typicality is assessed through what one can retrieve from memory.

REVIEW OF TERMS
AND CONCEPTS

In this chapter, the following terms and concepts that we consider to be important have been used. Please look them over. If you are not able to give a short explanation of any of them, you should go back and review the appropriate sections of the chapter.

The difference between well-defined and ill-defined problems
Protocol
Problem-behavior graph
  states of knowledge
  operations
  backing up
Problem-solving strategies
  forward search
  backward search
  goals and subgoals
  heuristics and algorithms: the differences between them
Limitations of protocols
The role of short-term memory in problem solving
  how limitations can be overcome
  symbolic notation
Optimization
Utility
Decision strategies
  overall impression
  dimensional comparison
Transitivity
  what causes transitivity to fail
Risky decision making
  probability
  subjective probability
  expected value
Representativeness and availability
The gambler's fallacy

Terms and concepts you should know

Note that the topics of problem solving and thinking are closely related, so the Suggested Readings for Chapter 15 should also be consulted.

SUGGESTED READINGS

Two books on methods for problem solving that might prove useful in actual situations are Wickelgren's (1974) *How to solve problems* and Adams' (1974) *Conceptual blockbusting*. Wickelgren's book concentrates primarily upon well-structured problems, especially problems from mathematics, science, and engineering. The book by Adams is focused more on creativity and the development of novel ideas with which to attack ill-structured issues. Both books have many exercises and strategies; together, they cover a large portion of real situations and involve problem solving.

Problem solving

Allan Newell and Herbert Simon at Carnegie–Mellon University have made the most important contributions to the study of problem solving in recent years. Their book (Newell & Simon, 1972) is an important study that should be pursued by anyone seriously interested in this topic. Unfortunately, the book is very advanced and difficult reading. Moreover, it only covers a small set of possible topics of problem solving. An interesting study and computer simulation of problem solving and game playing is performed by Eisenstadt and Kareev (1975). The use of the problem behavior graph to study the *missionary and cannibals* problem is discussed by Greeno (1974) and Thomas (1974). The paper by Simon and Reed (1976) on strategy changes is interesting.

In many ways, the best treatment of problem solving is still that presented in one of our favorite texts on psychology: Woodworth's *Experimental psychology*, published in 1938. The revision of that book by Woodworth and Schlosberg is also good (so try to find Woodworth, 1938, or Woodworth & Schlosberg, 1954: ignore the 1971 revision of the book—you will not find problem solving in it.)

Many of the very best experiments in problem solving are summarized in the book of readings compiled by Wason and Johnson-Laird, *Thinking and reasoning* (1968: paperback). DeGroot's work on chess (1965, 1966) is both important and interesting.

Perhaps the most comprehensive modern treatment at a relatively introductory level is that provided by Barry Anderson in Chapter 6 of his comprehensive textbook *Cognitive psychology* (B. Anderson, 1975: pages 195–290). The book by Davis (1973) is entitled *The psychology of problem solving*, but it has surprisingly little overlap with the approach we take.

One of the major concepts in problem solving not covered in this chapter is that of *set*, sometimes called *fixation*. An excellent introduction to this topic can be found in the *Scientific American* article "Problem-Solving" by Scheerer (1963).

Some classic studies on problem solving are the book *Productive thinking* by Wertheimer (1945), the semihandbook *How to solve it* by Polya (1945), and the study *The mentality of apes* by Köhler (1925). Some symposia on problem solving have been printed as books: Green (1966), Kleinmuntz (1966–1968), and Voss (1969).

A review of the effects that groups have upon problem solving can be found in Hoffman's article "Group Problem Solving" in the book edited by Berkowitz (1965).

Decision making   Much of the literature on decision making is mathematical, requiring some knowledge of probability theory (although a little bit will go a surprisingly long way, if you simply refuse to be intimidated by the apparent complexity of the equations). An excellent introduction to mathematical decision theory is provided in the book, *Mathematical psychology: an introduction*, by Coombs, Dawes, and Tversky (1970). For anyone who is seriously interested in the material discussed here, it is a valuable introduction. For those less mathematically inclined, there are a number of *Scientific American* articles relevant. Most of the good ones are included in the book edited by Messick, *Mathematical thinking in behavioral sciences: Readings from Scientific American* (1968). The analysis of the perceptual and mental abilities of chess players comes from DeGroot (1965, 1966).

The analyses of various decision rules, and especially the discussion on subjective probability and the role of representativeness and accessibility, come from the works of Kahneman and Tversky. (See Kahneman & Tversky, 1972, 1973; and Tversky & Kahneman, 1973). Some of the discussion on the logic of choice was suggested by the experiment of Tversky (1969).

A good number of the important papers on decision theory have been collected together in the Penguin paperback book by Edwards and Tversky (1967). Chapters 1 and 2 of that book are especially important, since they provide reviews of the literature up to 1960. Several of the examples used in this chapter come from Chapter 7 by Tversky (examples on transitivity relations).

A complete review of the recent theories is provided by Luce and Suppes in an article in the *Handbook of mathematical psychology,* Volume III (1965), "Preference, Utility, and Subjective Probability." This article is extremely advanced, however, and should be read only after you have read many of the articles in the Edwards and Tversky collection and then only if you have a reasonable mastery of probability theory and linear algebra.

If you wish to know how to use decision theory in your everyday life, there are three delightful books you can turn to: Epstein's *The theory of gambling and statistical logic* (1967), Raiffa's *Decision analysis: Introductory lectures on choices under uncertainty* (1968), and Williams' *The complete strategist* (1954).
Theory of Gambling and Statistical Logic (1967), Raiffa's *Decision Analysis: Introductory Lectures on Choices under Uncertainty* (1968), and Williams' *The Complete Strategist* (1954).

Epstein's book does what its title suggests: It analyzes in marvelous detail many gambling games and chance situations, through the standard (and some nonstandard) games of the gambling casino, to the stock market, duels and truels, horse racing, and what have you. The book uses a straightforward expected value analysis of these games, and you can enjoy it (and learn some useful strategies), even if you are unable to follow the mathematics, which do get a bit messy at times.

Raiffa tells how an individual ought to go about choosing a course of action, even when the set of possibilities looks discouragingly complicated and the real values and probabilities are difficult to estimate. Raiffa is a Professor of Managerial Economics, and he has used the techniques described in the book in many different business situations. The book is easy to follow and may even prove to be useful.

As in problem solving, the treatment of decision making by Barry Anderson in Chapter 8 of his text *Cognitive psychology* (1975) is interesting, treating a variety of topics related to those of this chapter, although with different emphasis.

15 The mechanisms of thought

PREVIEW

Human thought capabilities are powerful, yet limited in interesting ways. Consider the limitation in attention: concentration on one task generally causes a deterioration in the performance of other tasks. Now consider some positive aspects: meaningful sights and sounds can be perceived properly even when there are numerous irrelevant visual and auditory materials present. The perceptual processing is very efficient, primarily by relying heavily on conceptualizations and expectations. There are other interesting and important properties of human thought. Tasks that have been practiced for sufficiently long periods appear to become "automated": they can be performed with little or no conscious attention. Novel tasks or unexpected aspects of familiar tasks demand conscious attention. Whenever demands are placed on conscious processing resources, there tends to be severe interference with whatever other cognitive tasks are going on at the same time.

Thinking, attention, and memory are all intimately intertwined. When thinking intently we can sometimes fail to notice the events around us. When there are many sights and sounds in the environment, we can be distracted from our thoughts. In the terms of our earlier chapters, thinking is a conceptually directed process, but outside events can still cause data-driven processing to take place, distracting the thought processes. Memory plays a critical role in thought, both guiding the operations of the thought processes and limiting their power.

In this chapter we analyze the mechanisms of information processing systems that might be responsible for human thought processes. What are the mechanisms of memory, thought, and the analysis of information? Here, we explore some of the phenomena of thought. We talk of conscious and subconscious problem solving, different states of awareness, and the different trade-offs in efficiency that result from different ways of doing the same task.

Our examination of the possible mechanisms of thought is highly dependent upon our existing understanding of computers. But beware: when you read these sections, remember that the mind is not a computer. Be wary of hasty, simple comparisons between the computers built by people and the brain structures of people. Nevertheless, the principles of information processing are highly relevant to all systems that make use of information, including the human mind. The general principles of information processing must apply to all systems that manipulate, transform, compare, and remember information. Thus, this chapter is a combination of speculative explorations of the phenomena and mechanisms of human thought. No answers are given, although many are suggested. The discussions of this chapter center around the most exciting and important mysteries remaining in the study of human information processing.

THINKING

The mind proceeds along its path, leaving provocative traces of its progress. Each of us is a psychologist—we have been since we were born. We observe ourselves, watching the experiences, watching our reactions, taking part in the decision making. But often the acts that we do surprise even us, and the ways by which we reach conclusions or form judgments can be unsolved mysteries. Sometimes we will mentally decide upon one course of action, but find ourselves performing another. Sometimes we can only tell what we ourselves believe by the emotions and tensions that accompany our experiences and actions.

Although each of us is privy to the thoughts and images of our own mind, we are also outsiders to ourselves, unable to observe or participate in all phases of the thinking process. Indeed, sometimes another person can tell more about us than we can, for another person is able to watch our actions and expressions, to see how long we take to respond, and to evaluate our behavior with a detachment seldom possible by we who are involved. Moreover, another person can probe into our actions delicately or brutely, watching how we respond to the probes and thereby inferring the operations of our mental processes.

The psychologists have a problem: how can they come to understand the workings of another mind? All that is accessible for study is the behavior of the person, the actions, movements, responses, and words. True, we can ask a person to describe the thoughts and images that pass through the head, but whether that person is ourselves or another, the descriptions are fragmentary and incomplete. Worse, they may be inaccurate, for the observation of one's own thought is subject to the same difficulties and misperceptions as is the observation of some external set of events. And the act of observing one's own inner thoughts can change the course of those thoughts.

Self-awareness and consciousness may be of fundamental importance in complex decision making and in learning. It may be that we learn by conscious reflection upon the outcomes of our actions and upon consideration of the causal link among the acts and outcomes. Simple decisions can perhaps be made by the mind without conscious processing. But complex decision making, decisions that fundamentally change the course of one's mental or physical actions, these may require conscious planning and self-awareness. The study of conscious thought is a good place to begin.

Conscious and subconscious modes of thought   Humans are conscious of their own actions and thoughts. This consciousness or self-awareness is a fundamental aspect of human mental behavior, but it is one that is little understood. We know little of the function of consciousness, little of the nature of the operations that are not conscious

—the processes of subconscious thought. We suspect that conscious processes are fundamental to intelligent choices, to learning, to the guidance of the organism. We suspect that there exist numerous subconscious processes that operate without this conscious guidance for a while, but that must seek supervision and direction periodically. All that we know of the nature of conscious and subconscious thought is very speculative. Nonetheless, the study of thought is too important to be ignored. It is an area of great importance to psychology and to all of us. Perhaps it is *the* most important topic of psychology. So let us begin.

Considerable time may pass between the initial phases of active, conscious work on a problem and the arrival of a solution. The solution sometimes arrives far after the initial phase of work, sometimes quite unexpectedly, accompanied by such statements as "it just popped into my head—I hadn't thought about that problem for months." The time lapse between the initial activity and the solution, during which no active work on the problem seems to be taking place, is called the period of "incubation." Incubation periods seem only to be successful in leading to solutions when preceded by a considerable amount of hard work on the problem.

Subconscious problem solving

   A survey of creative thinkers indicates that subconscious problem solving takes place so often that it has become a standard part of many people's techniques for solving problems. But this subconscious thought comes at a price. First, it does not take place unless there has been considerable preparation for it. That is, the problem solver must have thought long and hard about the problem, often for months, with lots of research and study, and repeated attempts to get to the solution. All the information necessary for the solution must already exist within the memory structures of the person, and they must have been brought to the same level of activation. Then, but only then, the person can stop active work on the problem and go about the other business of life, confident that the problem is actually still being worked on. Evidently, once sufficiently activated, the thought mechanisms can keep going by themselves.

   Activation.   When the neural circuits responsible for thought processes operate, we say that they "become active." We do not yet know the neural mechanisms of thought and memory, but evidently, once sufficient activity has been started, it is difficult to terminate it. It is something like the old joke about elephants—you know what a herd of elephants would do if it suddenly rushed down the streets, trampling cars, knocking over fire hydrants and telephone poles? Well, don't think about it. Starting right now, have no more thoughts about that herd of elephants. Whatever the mechanism, whenever the thought and memory processes have become sufficiently active, they tend to keep going by themselves. Once a memory structure has been used, it remains more accessible for future use. The attempt to retrieve one detail from memory invariably brings back a host of other details, whether or not these others are wanted.

Try the following demonstration. Try to remember where you lived 5 years ago. Go on, take a few minutes. Now retrieve the names of some of the people you knew then. It may take you awhile, but eventually you will recall some names. Now note two things. First, you do not simply retrieve the names, you also get the people's appearances, the events in which they took part, and lots of other recollections. Second, if you spent a reasonable amount of time and effort at this task, once you manage to get the search for the names started, you will not be able to stop it. Later today and tomorrow, thoughts about that time period will recur, and you are apt to find yourself occasionally lost in your memories. You have activated the appropriate memory structures, and that activation will now serve to control the cognitive system, whether you wish it to or not.

Activation comes at a price. You cannot simply set off the subconscious mechanisms to do things without paying for it. The first cost is the amount of prior effort it takes to get things going. The second cost is the amount of your normal processing resources that will be tied up by these subconscious activities. You may not be aware of the fact that they are taking place, but when you are, you are apt to be less effective at other activities you might be doing. The third price you pay is that the subconscious mechanisms are not as clever or powerful as the conscious ones. Thus, the subconscious mechanisms may work away, following paths among memory structures, activating nodes here and there, setting off new pathways, but they do not seem capable of any intelligent assessment of what they have done, nor of intelligent decision making whenever a difficult choice point is reached. You will pay the price later of having to evaluate the results and of guiding the decisions.

Whenever the subconscious processes get going actively, they will use up some of the limited mental resources available for normal daily activities. Thus, the ability to carry out even simple activities, especially planning and decision making, is curtailed. While driving a bicycle or automobile, you are likely to find yourself taking a frequent route rather than the one you had planned to take. You are quite likely to start out for the book store and end up at home instead, having been so distracted by background processing that the guidance for your trip was carried on by automatic, well-learned structures—data-driven processing—that took you on the well-learned path home, rather than the special route to the book store. It is not uncommon to find oneself in the position of doing the same task over again, as in the case of the chemist in this quotation:

> I remember one morning I took my bath, shaved, took another bath, and in reaching out for a dry towel suddenly became aware that this was my second bath and that my mind had been deeply concentrated on a problem for half-an-hour. [Platt & Baker, 1931, quoted in Woodworth & Schlosberg, 1954, p. 839]

Sometimes you can be an observer of your own thoughts, not controlling them but simply noting the directions they follow. The famous French mathematician Poincaré speaks of nights of excitement during which thought and problem solving get done in spite of oneself. To Poincaré, the preliminary period of work that seems to be necessary to start the subconscious processing sets the "atoms" of the mind going in frantic activity:

> What is the role of the preliminary conscious work? It is evidently to mobilize certain of these atoms, to unhook them from the wall and put them in swing . . . They flash in every direction through the space (I was about to say the room) where they are enclosed, as would, for example, a swarm of gnats or, if you prefer a more learned comparison, like the molecules of gas in the kinematic theory of gases. Then their mutual impacts may produce new combinations. [H. Poincaré, "Mathematical Creation." In J. R. Newman (Ed.), *The world of mathematics*. Vol. 4. New York: Simon and Schuster, 1956, p. 2049]

Poincaré believes that the subconscious operations fit together old knowledge into new combinations, but when that has been accomplished, then conscious activity is necessary both to evaluate what has been formed and also to do any necessary calculations. Poincaré observed that even the most simple arithmetic or algebraic calculations cannot be done subconsciously. The conscious deliberate manipulations required to do arithmetic or algebra can only be done by conscious mechanisms. The subconscious is good for undisciplined, creative manipulations of ideas: it is this disorder, suggests Poincaré, that can lead to creative new discoveries.

The development of digital computers has produced powerful tools for use in the study of mental processes. Computers are information-processing systems. They can manipulate information and make decisions. Knowledge of information processing is essential if you are to understand the tools of the study of thought mechanisms. Now, before we begin, please

SOME PRINCIPLES
OF PROCESSING

note carefully that the mind is not a digital computer. But, although the machinery is different, when it comes to the abstract, scientific principles of information processing, there are general rules that will apply, regardless of what device is being spoken of. So the science of information processing is relevant to us, even if the engineering may not always be. This science, by the way, is now being called *Cognitive Science.*

What is an information-processing system? For our purposes, it has three essential ingredients: a *memory,* a *processing unit* that can perform a specific set of operations, and ways of getting information into and out of the system, the *input–output* (or IO) mechanisms (See Figure 15-1).

FIGURE 15-1

A simple information-processing system.

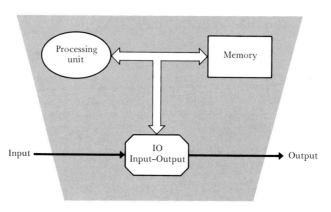

The processor   The processor is the part of the system that actually carries out the system's operations. The processor can look at information within the memory. It can perform operations such as comparing two memory units to see if and how they differ, or deciding which of several operations to perform next, or setting into motion searches of memory or chains of reasoning. In general, the processor controls and performs the actions of the system. The processor does its tasks by following instructions that are stored within the memory systems. A sequence of instructions that accomplishes some specific action is called a *program.* Whenever the processor is in operation, it is following some particular program of instructions. In following a program, the processor may then require some additional information, which is available either by appropriate searches of the memory system or by seeking the information in the environment (by means of IO operations).

Memory   The operations of a memory system have already been discussed in considerable detail in Chapters 8 through 16. For the moment, however, we can simply regard memory as the place where information is kept. Note, however, that there are two different aspects of the information. First, the information within memory can be used as *data,* as the facts that are used by the processor as it performs its operations. Second, the information can be used as *programs*, as sequences of instructions that are to be followed. These instructions guide the actions of the processor. Note that there is no fundamental difference between data and programs. An extremely important and powerful property of information-processing systems is that programs stored within the memory can be treated as data: programs can be examined, evaluated, and modified. Alternatively, programs can be *executed*, followed as instructions in guiding the operations of the system.

An important characteristic of information-processing devices is that the information in memory has meaning only because of the way it is interpreted by the processing units. The same information may have different interpretations at different times. The processor can examine the information in memory and interpret the information as instructions that are to be followed. These instructions, in turn, define how other information in memory is to be interpreted.

What is the product of 24 times 7? To do this problem you probably have to do some small amount of processing. (Please do the work—figure out what the answer is.) Suppose we now asked you the same question: what is the product of 24 times 7? The second answering of the question requires almost no effort; you should be able to state the answer immediately, without recomputing it. This trivial example illustrates the difference between getting an answer through computation (as you probably did the first time) and through memory (as you probably did the second time).

The trade-off between memory and processing

There is never a fixed rule about what information must be stored within memory and what actions are performed by the processor. In general, there is a trade-off one can make between doing a lot of processing (and requiring little information to be stored within the memory) or doing little processing but requiring a lot of information to be stored within the memory. The trade-off is important. It determines a good deal of the strategies that we follow as we learn material. Let us use day-arithmetic to illustrate the nature of the trade-off with a more complex example than simply multiplying two numbers together.

Let the days of the week represent the numbers 1 through 7, with Monday being 1. Then, solve these problems:

Day-arithmetic

Wednesday + Tuesday = ?   *(the correct answer is Friday)*

Tuesday + Friday = ?

Thursday + Saturday = ?

When you solve problems such as those posed by day-arithmetic, there are a number of possible strategies that you could use. We examine three. There are other possible strategies, and you may prefer the method you used to any of our three. Still, the comparison is valuable. All strategies have virtues, all have deficits. Which is best depends upon why (and how often) the day-arithmetic game is played.

In doing day-arithmetic, basically it is necessary to devise some sequence of operations that will be performed on the days. This sequence is a program. The strategy determines what the program looks like. A program consists of a sequence of individual steps, or instructions, with each step stating some operations that must be performed. In doing a task as simple as day-arithmetic, no new operations have to be learned: everything you need to know to do the task you already know. The only thing that must be learned is how to put together the instructions into a program. So, let us now look at the programs that result from following the three different types of strategies. We are interested in the instructions and operations followed by the program and in the role of memory.

The day-digit transformation strategy. The first strategy that we consider is perhaps the most obvious and the easiest to devise. It also requires the most effort to perform. Basically, the strategy goes like this. The first step is finding the correspondence between the days of the week and the numbers. One way is to learn this table:

Monday	1
Tuesday	2
Wednesday	3
Thursday	4
Friday	5
Saturday	6
Sunday	7

If you do not wish to memorize this table, you could derive it whenever it was needed by counting up from Monday. Whichever way, the first step is to learn the relationship between the days and the numbers. Then, to add two days together, you simply transform each day to the appropriate number, add the two numbers together, and then transform the answer back to a day. Thus, **Tuesday + Friday** becomes transformed into $2 + 5$. The answer is 7, which is **Sunday.**

There is a problem when the sum of the days yields a number greater than 7. In this case, you must subtract 7 from the answer before converting it to a day. Thus, Thursday + Saturday becomes transformed into $4 + 6$. The sum is 10. Subtracting 7 gives 3, which can be transformed back into the answer **Wednesday.**

This is the day-digit transformation strategy. Now let us put together the sequence of instructions that should be followed to use it. The resulting program is composed of a sequence of operations and use of memory. We use all capital letters to mark the operations in a program (that is, terms such as TRANSFORM, REMEMBER, etc.). Here is the program for doing day-arithmetic by means of the day-digit transformation strategy:

Given the problem, **what is day-1 + day-2?**

1. TRANSFORM day-1 to a number: CALL that number *n1*.
2. REMEMBER *n1* in short-term memory.
3. TRANSFORM day-2 to a number: CALL that number 2.
4. ADD n1 + n2. CALL the total *T*.
5. IF *T* is GREATER-THAN 7, THEN SUBTRACT 7 and CALL the new number *T*.
6. TRANSFORM the number *T* to the appropriate day.
7. STATE that day as the answer.

With this program, a number of operations are necessary, identified by being printed in all capitals: TRANSFORM, REMEMBER, ADD, IF-THEN, CALL, GREATER-THAN, SUBTRACT, STATE. With the exception of TRANSFORM, all of these operations are assumed to be known prior to the start of the problem.

Note that the TRANSFORM operation can be done in two ways. First, it can be accomplished by a *table lookup.* Second, it could be done by a counting strategy. In the first technique, table lookup, one simply memorizes the table showing the combination of days and digits we presented earlier: there are seven combinations to learn. In the second technique, counting, one simply remembers that *Monday = 1,* and then counts from there. What is Thursday? Starting with Monday, go through the days of the week until you reach Thursday, simultaneously adding one to a mental counter (or moving the fingers). Table lookup is faster and requires less effort to use. Counting is slower, but is much easier to learn. Which technique is better is determined by how often the total task needs to be done. The table lookup strategy for TRANSFORM suggests the second strategy for the entire task.

The table lookup strategy. If you can learn to change the seven days of the week into numbers by simply learning the seven combinations, why not just learn all the day–day combinations in much the same way? Here is what the resulting table looks like:

	Monday	*Tuesday*	*Wednesday*	*Thursday*	*Friday*	*Saturday*	*Sunday*
Monday	Tuesday	Wednesday	Thursday	Friday	Saturday	Sunday	Monday
Tuesday		Thursday	Friday	Saturday	Sunday	Monday	Tuesday
Wednesday			Saturday	Sunday	Monday	Tuesday	Wednesday
Thursday				Monday	Tuesday	Wednesday	Thursday
Friday					Wednesday	Thursday	Friday
Saturday						Friday	Saturday
Sunday							Sunday

There are 28 combinations that need to be learned. The strategy is simple (once the table is learned): look up the two days in the table and report the answer. The corresponding program is also simple.

What is day-1 + day-2?

1. FIND the memory structure corresponding to the pair **day-1 and day-2**.
2. STATE the value of that memory structure as the answer.

The rule strategy. The *table lookup* strategy requires memorization of a large table. But examination of the table reveals some interesting consistencies. Thus, adding *Sunday* to a day is like adding zero to a number: there is no change. Similarly, whenever *Saturday* is added to a day, one simply needs to go backwards one step from that day. It turns out that it is possible to make a simple set of rules for doing the task. Here is the program that results from the use of a rule strategy:

What is day-1 + day-2?

1. IF one of the days is:
   A. *Sunday,* THEN STATE the other day as the result.
   B. *Monday,* THEN INCREMENT the other day once and STATE the result.
   C. *Tuesday,* THEN INCREMENT the other day twice and STATE the result.
   D. *Friday,* THEN DECREMENT the other day twice and STATE the result.
   E. *Saturday,* THEN DECREMENT the other day once and STATE the result.
2. Otherwise, apply a table lookup strategy with the following table:

	Wednesday	*Thursday*
Wednesday	Saturday	Sunday
Thursday		Monday

Comparing the strategies. Now, let us examine the differences among the three strategies. Notice the tradeoffs.

The *transformation strategy* uses the tools of arithmetic. It does not require much practice or training, but it does require quite a bit of mental processing. Thus, the transformation strategy requires a good deal of processing, a medium amount of short-term memory use, and little or no learning.

The *table lookup strategy* requires the most amount of material to be learned: 28 day–day–digit relationships. But once those get learned, it is the easiest to apply, requiring very little processing and very little short-term memory use.

The *rule strategy* is a general overall compromise. It requires a medium amount of processing, and a medium short-term memory load. In turn, 8 different items must be learned: the rules for 5 of the days and a table with 3 entries. In summary:

	Processing load	Short-term memory load	Amount to be learned
Transformation strategy	high	medium	low
Table lookup strategy	low	low	very high
Rule strategy	medium	medium	medium

This particular set of trade-offs among processing load, short-term memory, and amount to be learned is typical of all mental tasks. There are almost always several methods for doing a task. Each method has virtues and difficulties. Which method should be used depends upon for what purpose the task is needed and how many times it is going to be performed. Thus, in this particular example, if the day-arithmetic task is only going to be done once or twice, you should certainly not spend much effort learning strategies: use the transformation strategy. If it is to be done many, many times for several months, then the table lookup strategy is best. If the task is only going to be done a medium amount of time, then the rule strategy is best, for the rules can be learned with a few minutes study, and the processing load is medium.

There is an important basic principle:

> *There is a trade-off between memory and computation. Complex tasks often can trade ease of performance for amount of information that must be learned.*

The more material learned, the more information stored in long-term memory, the less computation needs to be performed, and so the easier the task becomes. If you work hard to learn a task, it becomes easy to do. If you exert little effort at learning, the task remains difficult.

Division of a processing system into a processor, a memory, and input–output functions allows us to examine such basic principles as the role of data and programs and the trade-off between processing and memory. But the system is too simple to get at some other issues relevant to the

Time sharing and multiple processors

study of human thought processes. Most important, the system is only capable of doing a single task at a time: this is a severe limitation.

People can do several tasks at the same time. Granted, there are limits to the things that can be done together (as we showed in Chapter 7), but certainly we can walk while we talk, think while we bathe, draw while we sing. Unfortunately, not all possible tasks can be done at the same time. We cannot take part in two different conversations by listening to the voice of one person while at the same time speaking on some unrelated topic to another. Even though the mouth and the ear are separate organs, they cannot be divided up that way. We cannot think very satisfactorily about solving a complex problem when talking about some other topic. Even tasks that can be done simultaneously deteriorate when conditions change: when attending to difficult traffic conditions, the driver of an automobile will tend to slow up or stop speaking to the other occupants.

There are two major ways by which two different actions can be carried on at the same time: *time sharing* and *multiple processing*.

Time sharing.   Time sharing is a scheme for taking advantage of lulls in demands upon a processor. Suppose you are holding a telephone conversation with someone, trying to arrange a date for a picnic. You suggest possible dates and there is a long silence on the telephone as the other person checks the calendar, discusses the date with other people, and finally comes back with a counterproposal. As far as you are concerned, this situation is *input–output limited (IO limited)*. That is, the rate at which you can proceed with the conversation is determined by how long it takes to get a response to your last question (your last output). What do you do while waiting? Whenever a processing system encounters an IO limited task, the processor is idle, doing nothing except waiting for an input to arrive. During this idle time, why not do some other task? Time sharing is a scheme for using time made idle while waiting for more information. The telephone conversation is simply one illustration of a task that allows for time sharing. A task that has any idle time at all is potentially a candidate for time sharing.

Suppose you are in a lecture, listening to a slow-moving speaker: no reason why you should not time share, thinking about other things while the speaker laboriously repeats the same point three times. All that is necessary is that you check on the progress of the lecture periodically, just to make sure that a new topic has not been introduced. Of course, if you are in a conversation with a fast-speaking, fast-thinking person, you cannot time share: the conversation moves so rapidly that if you start thinking about something else, you are likely to miss some important point. The only difference between the slow-moving speaker and the fast-moving conversation is the amount of time you have to do other tasks. The limit with time sharing is how fast you can change from one topic to another.

In order to do time sharing, you must be able to stop doing one task and start another, remembering all the important aspects of where you left off on the first task. If you are in the middle of doing a mental multiplication when someone interrupts you with a question, then unless you can save the current contents of your short-term memory and some marker about which operation you were doing at the time of interruption, you will not be able to resume the problem from exactly the point where you left off.

FIGURE 15-2

To do time sharing, there must either be some way of saving the information relevant to the state of the problem when the task was switched, or the switching can only take place at natural breaks, at places where there is no need to save temporary results. Humans do time share. In some sense we must, for during the course of the day we start and stop many different tasks, sometimes resuming a task we started hours previously. We often time share whenever there are small gaps in the demands upon us, gaps that are specified in seconds. The limitations on our abilities to time share are the limitations on our short-term memory structures that allow us to reconstruct exactly where we must have been working when we left off.

Note that most computers today do time sharing by this scheme, but the computers are usually especially designed to make the task easy. In computers, there are special instructions and operations that save and restore all of the temporary memory structures used by a program. When the program is interrupted, it stores away all its temporary results. When the program resumes, it restores all its temporary memory, letting it find its place exactly and precisely, without any confusion. Even so, a computer system has to be very careful about how it switches back and forth among tasks, for any error or failure to save information can lead to problems. For this reason, there are often "protected" operations that will not allow themselves to be interrupted, and the supervisory program that controls the time-sharing operation often makes numerous checks of the status of all its shared programs before switching from one task to another. All these checks take time. Quite often a considerable percentage of the processing power of a computer is involved with the "overhead" of checking and scheduling the different programs that are to be time shared.

Multiple processors.   Time sharing is not the only way to do several tasks at the same time. The easiest way is to simply have two separate processors: each can work at its own task at the same time without any need for interfering with the other. For example, if you have two different problems to solve, do one yourself and ask a friend to do another: now you have two processors working, in parallel, and there is no interference between the two tasks (unless your friend needs help and continually interrupts you with questions).

One reason we can tap our fingers while thinking is that the control systems for tapping are quite separate from those for thinking, and there is simply no interference. We have different processors for these tasks. We cannot speak and listen at the same time, however, because the same processors are used for both these tasks, and the performance of one prevents the system from doing the other.

There is no reason why a system cannot have several different processors, each working at the same time. This adds considerable power, but with a possible danger. Suppose the two processors conflict. Suppose one of them wanted to do a particular operation when the other wanted to do the opposite? That cannot be allowed: something must intervene. Several possibilities exist. It could be that the two separate processors had separate responsibilities that never overlapped. In this way, there would never be conflicts. In Figure 15-3 we show how two processors can

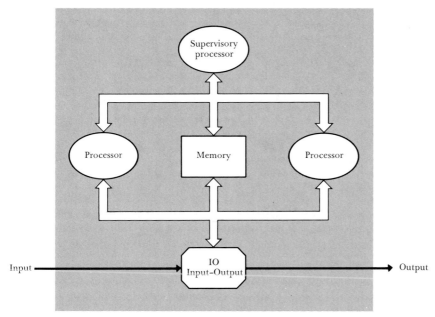

An information-processing system with two processors and a supervisory processor.   FIGURE 15-3

be watched over by a third, supervisory processor, whose sole job is to resolve any conflicts.

Consider the system shown in Figure 15-3 as a special supervisory processor to resolve conflicts. The supervisor must have some interesting capabilities. It must know what the tasks are that are being performed by the processors that it controls. It probably does not need to know the details, just the nature of the tasks. The supervisor's job is to evaluate what each processor does, compare the performance of the various ones, and resolve any conflicts that are involved. The supervisor must therefore be aware of the general functions and operations of the units it supervises.

A major job of the supervisor is to control just what operations the information-processing system will be performing. Any powerful system will always have a rich set of options available to it. Its memory structures may contain numerous programs that can be followed, the environment may present a rich set of data to the input–output sensors, providing many possible things to be analyzed. The actual choice of operations can be directed by several different control mechanisms.

The supervisory processor usually has some particular goal (or set of goals) that it is attempting to accomplish. The supervisor can evaluate the performance of the system according to how well it moves toward these goals. This is high-level, *conceptually-guided control.* Presumably the supervisor does not watch over the individual instructions or operations being done, but rather only over the choice of particular strategies and programs. Then it oversees the general progress. The programs themselves exert control by explicitly specifying specific operations that the system should perform. Thus, we say that the actual sequence of operations is under *program control.*

No intelligent system can afford to be completely controlled by its prior plans and goals without keeping alert to new developments and occurrences in the environment. (It is all very well to have all your processing directed toward understanding this chapter, but it might be wise to monitor your environment in case the room catches on fire—you must be both conceptually driven and data driven.) Thus, in addition to conceptually guided control and program control, the system must also allow itself to be guided by external events. The events can interrupt the flow of processing, allowing whatever operations are necessary to deal with the arriving data to take place, at least far enough to determine whether these new events are important or not. This is *data-driven control.*

Let us look more closely at these three different modes of control: *conceptually guided control, program control,* and *data-driven control.*

Conceptually guided control. Whenever the supervisor attempts to satisfy its goals, it exerts conceptual guidance on the flow of processing. It directs other processors to perform their operations, probably by specifying the programs that are to be followed. As the results of the operations performed become available, the supervisor evaluates them: it may decide to change the course of processing. Moreover, the supervisor continually evaluates all the information being made available, so that the interactions among processors may lead to new directions of processing, or perhaps the interpretation of newly arrived environmental events might suggest other courses of action. Thus, both the results of operations of the processors and the interpretations of newly arriving data are evaluated by the supervisor to determine the course of future operations. Whatever the source, new information may suggest to the central guiding controller that it should change the course of activity, perhaps terminating some actions or initiating some new actions, perhaps maintaining some ongoing ones. The ability to control the operations of one level of processing by some higher, more central level is conceptual guidance.

Program control. Program control is the simplest control structure: the instructions that comprise the program are followed in sequence, and the next operation that is to be performed is predetermined by the program.

Data-driven control. What happens when new input information arrives at the system? In most systems, including the human, there are usually specialized processing mechanisms—specialized processors—for doing the initial analysis of the arriving information. These specialized units can do simple manipulations of the data: they can start the process of pattern recognition and interpretation of the data. But usually a full analysis of the data requires consideration by the supervisory processor of the programs and other processors under its control. Therefore, there is usually some system designed to interrupt the activity of the supervisory processor and to bring the newly arriving data to its attention. Then, it is up to the supervisory processor to decide what actions to take.

Exactly as in the discussion of time sharing, several things must be noted about this interruption of ongoing activity. First, interruptions would severely disrupt a system unless there were some way of automatically ensuring that the interruption did not cause any information to be lost. Any temporary results that have just been determined must be saved safely until the interrupted task resumes. Similarly, the place must be kept: the operation that was being performed at the time of the interruption must be remembered so that activity can resume again.

Second, when activity is interrupted, it slows down the rate at which operations get performed in that activity. Thus, one would expect the performance of the supervisor to deteriorate if it were subject to frequent interruption.

Finally, the arrival of data can cause a temporary interruption of the ongoing activity to allow the data to be identified. Then the flow of processing resumes from where it was at the time of interruption. Alternatively, the interruption could introduce sufficient new considerations into the course of processing that the control changes in a direction dictated by the data. The processing is data-driven only in the latter situation.

The problem for the psychologist is to understand the mechanisms of thought. This chapter has presented some of the possible machinery for putting together the knowledge that we have of memory, perception, and problem solving. In this book, we have made considerable progress in analyzing the basic components of thought: the analyses of sensory processes, perception, attention and pattern recognition, memory, language, and the developing structure of the child's capabilities all spoke to the basic underlying mechanisms. The previous chapter on problem solving touched upon issues of direct concern to the discussions of this chapter. Unfortunately, as we have stressed repeatedly throughout this chapter, we are not yet ready to make definite statements about the overall system that comprises the mind. But still, let us go on to examine a few

HUMAN THOUGHT MECHANISMS

interesting phenomena, remembering as we do so our discussions of a processing system that has several different processors capable of working independently, but being monitored by some supervisory process. Let us see what insights into the operation of the human mind are provided by our analyses.

Dual processing units in the human   The human brain is roughly symmetrical, with the left and right halves having approximately the same structures. We have already discussed the division of brain structures and some of the specialization of functions that occur between the hemispheres (Chapter 11). One hemisphere of the cerebral cortex seems specialized to handle language functions. Just how the functions of the other should be characterized is unclear, but it is usually thought of as specialized to handle functions related to time and space.

Consideration of the dual nature of the human brain structures has obvious implications for the structure of human mental functions. Unfortunately, the implications are far more potent than the actual evidence, and there has been an understandable tendency for some commentators to let their imaginations run wild in discussing the division of responsibility between the two hemispheres. Let us proceed cautiously, seeing just what firm conclusions can be drawn.

First, there seems no doubt that for most people, one brain hemisphere is highly specialized for language functioning. Second, it seems clear that one can find tasks specific to either hemisphere. Most people can hear speech slightly better with the right ear (which feeds most of the sound to the left hemisphere) than with the left ear, and these same people can perform slightly better at nonspeech auditory tasks with their left ear. Similarly, comparisons between visual pictures are done slightly better by most people when the pictures are presented just to the left of the point at which they are looking (and therefore get sent to the right hemisphere). Comparisons among visually presented words are done slightly better by these same people when the words are presented just to the right of the point at which they are looking (and so get sent to the left hemisphere). There is a long list of tasks that appear to get done better by one hemisphere than the other. There are two characteristics of the list:

1. The differences between the hemispheres are never very large.
2. It seems necessary that *both* hemispheres be active in order for the superiority of one to show up.

Why might these results occur? If the two hemispheres were indeed very highly specialized processors, should not a large difference be apparent? Why does it matter whether or not both hemispheres are busy at the same time? The answers to these questions seem to lie in the nature of the interconnections between the two hemispheres. Both cerebral cortexes of the brain are interconnected by a massive layer of fibers: the *corpus callosum.*

The brain may contain two independent processors, but they communicate with one another over a highly effective, rich set of interconnections. Thus, unless something is done to prevent intercommunication, one never can be sure just where a particular piece of processing gets done. Presenting information to one half of the visual field does indeed send all the information initially to one half of the brain, but in a few milliseconds that information is also available at the other half. (Most sensory systems send their information directly to the two hemispheres anyway, so that even without the corpus callosum, both hemispheres of the brain get very similar information, regardless of how it arrived at the organism.)

One of the functions of the interconnections between the hemispheres is to transfer information between the two halves. But another function appears to be involved in the synchronization of functions, preventing duplication and competition of efforts. Evidently, activity at one location in one hemisphere of the brain *suppresses* activity at the corresponding location in the other hemisphere. The suppression seems to take place by inhibiting the activity of corresponding neural circuits in the other hemisphere (in the same fashion as the inhibition of neural circuits described in Chapter 6).

The two brain hemispheres appear to handle the problems associated with conflicts among independent processing units by massive interconnections among the structures and by special neural circuits designed to prevent both hemispheres from working at the same task at the same time. If the communication medium—the corpus callosum—is severed, then of course the two hemispheres must function independently, and then it is possible for both to conflict, leading to the strange circumstances described in Chapter 11.

Suppose the mind were organized so that there were many separate   *Meditation*
processing units, each capable of performing predefined operations upon the structures in memory, and with one overseeing, supervisory processor that monitored, evaluated, and generally made decisions for the overall processing of the mind. This model is probably as good as we can get today for our picture of the organization of the mind. To simplify our discussion, let that central *Supervisor,* the overseeing, controlling, self-

evaluating operation, be called **S**. Suppose we could turn **S** off: what then?

When voluntary, conscious control of mental functioning is turned off, the mind enters some novel states of awareness. The inner voice that most of us continually experience, that voice that comments upon what we do, approving, disapproving, sometimes just repeating the words we hear, read, speak, and write, that voice finally goes away. But when the inner voice stops, then what? And how does one silence the inner voice?

Methods for controlling states of the mind are very old and very well known among some societies. Until recently, these techniques were not widely known within western civilization, but now they have become widely publicized and practiced. The techniques of religious and personal meditation are designed to change one's mental state. Drug states and hypnotic states may have related functions.

The most common and the most effective way to control one's mental states is by the use of a *mantra*. Basically, if you want to turn off **S**, that central inner voice of consciousness, you face a problem. **S** is a meddlesome device, tending to be data driven by any events that occur, whether they be external or internal. The easiest way to take care of **S** is to give it something distracting to do. Let **S** spend all of its resources doing something irrelevant, and then the mind can function free of **S**'s influence. The mantra is just such a technique.

A mantra is defined by the dictionary as "a mystical formula of innovation or incantation in Hinduism and Mahayana Buddhism" [*Webster's new collegiate dictionary*]. Most frequently today, the mantra is simply a word that a person continually repeats, over and over again. We view the mantra as an attentional device. It is much like the shadowing technique described in Chapter 7, it keeps the attentional capacity of the mind occupied, it gives **S** something to do, and it effectively skips the supervisory, directive nature of the inner conscious mechanisms.

There is more to meditation than simply saying a mantra. Some forms of meditation are intimately related to religious or philosophical concerns, and meditation by saying the mantra is only one of a number of different activities. But let us only be concerned here with the act of meditation through the use of a mantra. Meditation is practiced by many people, twice a day, for 15 to 20 minutes a session. Those who meditate claim it is relaxing and soothing, and numerous claims about the overall effect on the body's activities and mental structures are made by proponents of meditation. Again, without worrying about the claims, consider the meditation itself.

First, how does one do it? A simple set of rules was formulated by Benson (1975), a researcher who has studied the physiological properties of meditation. Four components are necessary:

1. A quiet environment.
2. A mental device.
3. A passive attitude.
4. A comfortable position.

The *quiet environment* would seem to be necessary to prevent outside events from intruding upon the meditative state. In our terms, the quiet environment avoids data-driven processing resulting from events in the environment. A *mental device* is necessary to keep **S** under control by giving it something specific to do. The specific task can be concentration upon sounds such as breathing, repetition of a mantra, prayer, or even deep visual concentration on an object. Whatever the activity, it must be simple to do, but it must occupy the mind (more accurately, it must occupy **S**).

The *passive attitude* is necessary for dealing with thoughts that do intrude. Let them intrude, but neither pursue them nor suppress them. Trying to suppress an unwanted thought can activate the whole processing system, leading to mental activity. Following a train of thought also leads to unwanted activity. Both following a thought and suppressing it require the aid of **S,** and that is exactly what is not wanted in meditation. So to meditate, just let happen what does happen; do not attempt to exert any control.

A *comfortable position* seems necessary, for discomfort will cause data-driven inputs to the system, requiring attention to deal with the discomfort. Note that the position cannot be too comfortable, however, or else there is a tendency to fall asleep. Benson believes that the various positions of kneeling, swaying, or sitting in a cross-legged position have evolved to prevent falling asleep.

Benson provides specific instructions on how to meditate. A good, decent, nonsecret mantra is the word "one." Actually, almost any simple, short word will do. But Benson suggests "one" as simple, convenient, and effective. In addition, he recommends concentration upon one's own breathing. Here is how to meditate:

> Sit quietly in a comfortable position and close your eyes. Relax. (A good way to do this is by progressive relaxation—mentally relax your toes, your heels, your ankles, and so on, up to your eyebrows, forehead, and even your scalp. Do this one muscle group at a time.) When you are relaxed, stay that way. Become aware of your breathing. Benson suggests that each time you breathe out, you should say the word "one" silently to yourself.
>
> That's all there is to it. Remember to keep relaxed and to breathe naturally. Concentrate on your breathing. Do this for 10 to 20 minutes. You can check your watch. (Don't jump up right away

after meditating, since your metabolic rate may be lower than it usually is.)

The meddlesome nature of S Pity poor **S**, our central supervising consciousness, turned off in meditation by distracting it to do meaningless activities and bypassed in problem solving by feeding the subconscious all the relevant information and then waiting for the report. But there is more to come: **S** gets in the way of performing skilled activities.

Picture a tennis player. The opponent has just hit the ball and our hapless player is critically concerned about this particular shot, so **S** provides useful advice:

> I have to hit that ball. Keep that racket straight—watch the wrist, keep it stiff. Flex those knees. Maybe I should shift the racket grip. Don't forget to follow through. Watch out for a slice—step into it, don't wait. Now.

S is being meddlesome, again. By the time our player has followed up on all of **S**'s suggestions the ball has long since whizzed past. Conscious control mechanisms are slow. They cannot keep pace with fast moving events. To do a skill well, one must do it automatically, subconsciously, without **S**'s obtrusive comments.

Professional athletes know that they cannot think about what they are doing. They must practice so thoroughly that every movement they might wish to make can be done subconsciously. Their actions must be smooth and rapid. But more, they must also eliminate **S** from interfering. Even if their actions could be carried out accurately with the guidance of **S**, once **S** gets going, evaluating and supervising, it also takes control, and so the actions are likely to be interfered with.

Most professional athletes have developed techniques for ignoring or turning off their inner voices. They do so by techniques not unlike those just described for meditation. The difference is that the athlete must not turn off sensory information: it is very important that the system process all relevant information. Indeed, in playing sports, one wants a system that is primarily data driven with conceptual guidance only to provide high-level strategy. Our supervisor, **S**, is welcome—even essential —for *high-level planning*. But once a strategy has been determined, the actual activities cannot afford to wait for conscious supervision.

Athletes have developed many different techniques. Some tennis players look for the seams of the tennis ball as it comes at them: they cannot see the seams, but the concentration keeps **S** occupied and also, nicely, gives the sensory system information about the ball's location. Some base-ball pitchers concentrate upon the center of the catcher's glove. Again, this gives **S** some meaningless activity to do, but simultaneously provides relevant sensory information.

There are similar tactics used in other activities. Musicians must learn their pieces so well that they can play them in public even if **S** insists on worrying about the audience. Piano soloists—who must play without music—learn their pieces so well that they know the proper notes will be played even if their mind panics at the thought of the critical audience. The piece must be known so well that one can enter the "mindless state," playing without conscious awareness of the activity.

Remember the trade-off between processing and memory that we discussed earlier in this chapter? Although a tremendous amount of information must be acquired into memory in order for every component of a skilled task to be prelearned, prestored, once that task has been accomplished, think of the tremendous burden that has been released from the processing mechanisms—and from the supervisory responsibilities of **S.** By learning large amounts of information specific to a task, a person is capable of performing the task even when mental activities are otherwise occupied or when the computations would take longer than the time allowed.

The virtues of S

Let us not get carried away in our critique of the role of the central supervisory function played by **S**: on the whole, **S** is necessary for the proper functioning of the cognitive system.

We have already discussed how a central, supervising, monitoring function is absolutely necessary for any system that is doing complex processing. Decision making, the following of logical, ordered steps in thought, and the evaluation of the path of these thoughts must be performed by **S**. It is quite likely that **S** is an essential component of the learning process. Whenever thought is required, **S** is essential.

But many activities must be performed faster than the sequential decision-making processes can operate—faster than thought, if you will. For these activities, **S** is not needed: **S** is too slow and gets in the way. But **S** can only be discarded for well-learned activities. For activities that have not been well learned, or for activities that are novel and require considerable decision making, **S** is essential.

States of awareness

One result of the complex nature of the human processing mechanisms is that it can enter a number of different *states of awareness*. Thus, a person "captured" by a book or theatrical performance can be transported mentally into the situation being depicted, entering a trancelike state in which the normal awareness of the real environment is suppressed. Deep thought or day-dreaming can produce similar results. Meditation produces a special state of awareness.

There are a number of normal states of awareness. The most common one experienced by everyone is that of sleep: the special mental state that everyone enters with reasonable regularity. Other special states require special conditions: meditative states, religious trances, states induced by hypnosis, fatigue and emotions, and drug-induced states.

The different states of self-awareness present some curious situations for the individual. Here we are, normal human beings, reading this book. But we are also aware of ourselves reading the book. Who is the "we" that is aware? Who is the "we" that is doing the reading? We can go further. We can imagine the way an outside observer would view the scene. We can imagine looking down from a high vantage point upon the space in which we are working. And now, we are aware of our awareness of all these different levels.

Abnormal states.   The different levels of self-awareness are normal. They allow us to view situations at many different levels of description and they increase our power to deal with different situations. But sometimes these levels get confused. Sometimes we fail to distinguish among the various "we's" of the situation.

Consider the common *déjà vue* experience. Most of us have experienced the state of "previously experiencing" some current event. That is, some event in which we are partaking feels as if it is a reenactment of some past experience. But the feeling is strange, for it is not possible to predict what will happen next. But when the next happening occurs, it feels as if it were fully expected. There are various explanations for the phenomenon of *déjà vue.* The explanation most consistent with our understanding of processing structures revolves around the close interaction between perception of an event and memory: the memory system both stores the ongoing experiences and also provides information necessary to interpret them. It would not take much of an error on the part of the supervisor to confuse which information was coming from memory and which was going into it.

Auditory, tactile, kinesthetic, and visual hallucinations occur with surprising frequency. They seldom occur for the individual who is in a normal state. But when fatigued or aroused, under stress, deprived of sleep or food, under the influence of drugs, or suffering from a mental disorder, then hallucinations become more frequent. Considering the wide variety of human experiences, considering the powerful mental apparatus that we all have for generating fantasies and imagined occurrences, the strange phenomenon is that we are not more often misled by delusions and anomalous experiences.

We suspect that mental states such as *déjà vue* and hallucinations are caused by confusions in the conscious, supervisory mechanisms about the source of information being processed. As we saw in the earlier chapters of this book, the process of properly perceiving the elements in the environment requires a combination of data-driven and conceptually driven processing, combining information from past experiences with information arriving at the sensory systems. Suppose the supervisor that is involved in interpreting the ongoing processing confuses newly arriving information with information provided by the memory system about past experiences. This can lead to three forms of abnormal states:

déjà vue (previously encountered)
> When perceptions that are really based upon information from sensory inputs are thought to have come from memory: the present experience appears to have been experienced previously.

jamais vue (never encountered)
> When it is not realized that the current experience is the same as something in memory, either because the information from memory is mistakenly thought to be the result of perception or because the memory system fails to make an appropriate match: the present experience seems to be a novel one, even if it really is a familiar event, one that has been encountered many times before.

hallucination
> When perceptions that are really based upon information from memory are thought to have come from information provided by the sensory systems: the present experience is hallucinatory.

Sleep.   Sleep seems best characterized by a depression of the normal processing of a person, most especially a reduction in the processing of sensory inputs. In addition, there is a general relaxation of the motor control system and (except for "sleep walking") no complex motor movements are usually performed while asleep.

A depression of perceptual processing does not mean a cessation, however. Some sensory events are processed. There is a good likelihood that a sleeper can be awakened if called by name. Sensory events are often incorporated into ongoing dreams. But there is no evidence whatsoever that learning takes place during sleeping: the deeper levels of processing of sensory inputs do not appear to take place.

What is dreaming? Dreams are not a result of sleep. Dreams can occur during waking hours, and then it is called *daydreaming*. Daydreams rarely are as elaborate as night dreams, but perhaps they rarely are given the same opportunity to develop in a sensorily deprived, quiet environment. During sleep, dreams seem to be characteristic of the lighter stages of sleep, not the deep states. What function do dreams play? What are the sources of dreams? Are dreams necessary? These, and related questions, remain unanswered—and with our present knowledge and techniques, they are unanswerable.

The overall electrical response of a large proportion of the cortical area of mammalian brains changes distinctly as an animal goes from being fully awake, through a state of relaxation, and finally to a sleeping state. When alert, the electrical response of its brain, as measured from the external surface of the skull, shows a rapid, irregular pattern. The irregularity of the pattern is presumably due to the fact that different cortical cells in different areas of the brain are operating independently of each other. But as the organism relaxes, regular oscillations at a rate of 8 to 12 Hz appear in the electrical brain recording. This pattern suggests that a large percentage of the brain cells are operating together in a synchronized way. These repetitive firing patterns are labeled *alpha waves,* and the term *alpha blocking* describes the change from the regular cyclic activity of the relaxed state to the irregular desynchronized brain response of an alert, active organism. As the organism falls asleep its brain responses go through a number of distinctive stages associated with various levels of sleep, from drowsy sleep (very light) to deep sleep (see Figure 15-4).

The early theories about sleep tended to view it as a response to lack of stimulation. That is, there was an arousal system that kept an animal alert and awake. In the absence of arousal, there was sleep. Thus, alertness was the result of the arousal activity: Sleepiness was a result of low arousal. This theory is wrong. It turns out that sleep is under the control of specific "sleep centers" in the brain. Animals tend to maintain a 24-hour sleep–awake cycle even when deprived of all sensory information.

Early workers in the field of sleep research found it useful to distinguish the four different stages of sleep shown in Figure 15-4. Dement and Miller (1974) now distinguish between *stages* and *states* of sleep: the first state corresponds to stage 2 of Figure 15-4 and the other state contains stages 3, 4, and 5. The first state is characterized by *rapid eye movements,* so it is called the REM state. The other state is not, so it is called NREM (no REMs). It is believed that when someone is in state REM, then dreams are occurring. In state NREM, no one is quite sure what mental activities go on. About 20% of the time that someone is wakened from an NREM state they do report dreams. If they do not report dreams, they nonetheless can usually report "thinking" about something.

WAVES

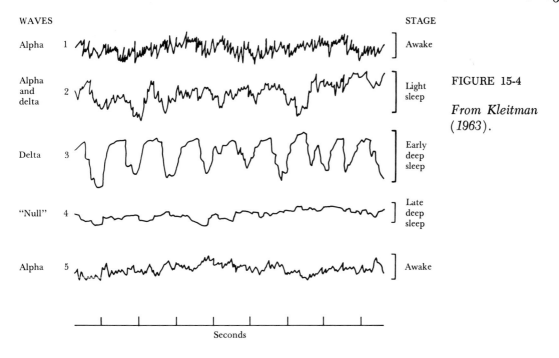

		STAGE
Alpha	1	Awake
Alpha and delta	2	Light sleep
Delta	3	Early deep sleep
"Null"	4	Late deep sleep
Alpha	5	Awake

Seconds

FIGURE 15-4

From Kleitman (1963).

Most dreams occur in the REM state, which corresponds to the lightest stage of sleep. The three most important characteristics of REM sleep are:

1. A lack of motor control. That is, the muscles are completely relaxed: voluntary movement is not possible. Even normal tendon reflexes do not operate.
2. The brain appears to be alert, aroused, and in many respects mental activity cannot be distinguished from the awake state.
3. There are spurts of activity, bursts of short-lasting events. Of these, the most well known is the rapid eye movement. In addition, there are muscle twitches, sudden changes in pupil size, sharp fluctuations in penile tumescence, brief twitches of the muscles of the middle ear (quite analogous to the rapid eye movements), brief irregularities in heart rate, and a reasonable amount of electrical activity (see Dement & Miller, 1974, page 285).

The REM state is therefore characterized by mental activity, but no motor activity, and with a decrease in processing of sensory information.

The picture of processing just described is still incomplete. We have produced a rough sketch, not a finished work. In considering the discussions of this chapter, certain cautions should be observed.

In this chapter we have mentioned a number of the phenomena of

THE ANALYSIS OF HUMAN THOUGHT

human mental behavior: conscious and subconscious thought, memory activation, the trade-offs between memory and processing, the differences between the left and right hemispheres of the brain, meditation, altered states of awareness, and sleep. We have also considered the analysis of information-processing systems that contain memories, processing structures, and supervisory control structures. Presumably, the principles of processing structures can explain the phenomena of human thought. But we have not made that step: all we have done is to place the ideas side by side. As psychologists, we are not yet ready to piece together the mechanisms of the mind.

Although the processing structures described in the chapter are over-simplified in a number of respects, they provide many concepts highly relevant to our understanding of mental processes. It is useful to consider the roles of the mechanisms of the human mind, of instructions and programs, of processors and memory systems. It is useful to realize that there are several possible organizations of the system. Finally, it is valuable to consider the possible role of a supervisory processing structure to help in evaluating, scheduling, and guiding the other processes. Note that the reasons that caused us to consider these aspects of processing do not depend upon the details of *how* the human cognitive system is really put together. Thus, we know that the brain is constructed of neural circuits (as in Chapters 6 and 11) that send signals to one another, spreading their activation along neural pathways. These neural circuits are the structures that interact with each other and that send new information to memory. The processors, memories, and input–output structures of the mind are constructed of neurons, and this fact does not change or detract from the usefulness of our analysis.

Here are the important points. First, the concepts introduced by the idea of a *program* are quite powerful. A program is a sequence of operations that guide the performance of information-processing mechanisms. Programs are flexible: they can be changed. Circuits that are wired together do not have this flexibility. The neural interconnections that we discussed in Chapter 6 can do powerful operations, but always in the same fixed, standardized fashion. The specialized receptors of the sensory system are not flexible enough for all the demands placed upon the human. In addition to the fixed circuits, we need modifiable programs. A program can be:

> modified
> examined
> performed.

These properties are important: it is the flexibility of programs as controlling devices that gives information-processing systems their power and that distinguishes them from fixed, nonmodifiable circuits.

Processing systems can take many forms. In this chapter, we showed how several different processors could work simultaneously, independently of each other. But too much independence can lead to conflicts, so some sort of supervisory system is necessary. It is tempting to speculate upon the nature of the supervisory systems, especially in their implications on the role of human consciousness and self-awareness, and we did not completely resist that temptation. But the speculation should be recognized as provocative suggestion rather than scientific fact.

In this chapter, the following terms and concepts that we consider to be important have been used. Please look them over. If you are not able to give a short explanation of any of them, you should go back and review the appropriate sections of the chapter.

REVIEW OF TERMS AND CONCEPTS

Why it is difficult to get scientific evidence about human thought
Conscious and subconscious modes of thought
   activation
Information-processing systems
   memory
   processing unit
   input–output (IO)
   program
   trade-off between memory and processing
Time sharing
   IO limited processes
   remembering the place in the program
Multiple processors
   sharing the load
   possible conflicts
   supervisory process
   conceptually guided control
   program control
   data-driven control
Hemispheric specialization
   language specialization
   corpus callosum
Supervisor
   meditation
     the role of the supervisor
     mantra

Terms and concepts you should know

difficulties of supervision
  skilled performance
    the trade-off between memory and processing
  the power of supervision
States of awareness
  anomalous states
  normal states
    sleep

SUGGESTED
READINGS

Much of the psychological literature on thought is actually about problem solving, which was discussed in the previous chapter, so start with the references listed there. The books by Miller, Galanter, and Pribram (1960) and by Bruner, Goodnow, and Austin (1956) are perhaps the classics in this field, and they provide useful starts. Unfortunately, the stimulating ideas of those have not been much improved upon in the years since their publication. The 1975 *Annual Review of Psychology* article (Neimark & Santa, 1975) should probably be examined, if you wish to be thorough, but do not expect any exciting information. The book by Falmagne (1975) on reasoning is perhaps the most valuable spot to start for the recent experimental literature.

In distinction to studies of the normal thought processes, studies of altered states of awareness do exist in relative profusion: for some reason, the unusual is more studied than the usual. Graham Reed's (1972) book, *The psychology of anomalous experience* is an excellent introduction to the entire area, complete with plausible explanations of many of the phenomena. We recommend this book highly. Siegel and West (1975) present a colorful book on hallucination (colorful in the literal sense that it contains numerous drawings made by artists in drug-induced states of awareness). The entire book provides a good starting point for the scientific literature on this topic, but although much of the book makes for fascinating reading, do not expect any answers or explanations. Adam Smith's (1975) best seller *Powers of mind* presents a healthy introduction to the whole business of meditation and other levels-of-awareness.

Ornstein's (1972) book and collected readings (Ornstein, 1973) on the nature of consciousness, with emphasis on altered states of behavior, are excellent scientific introductions. For the start of scientific theories about the nature of consciousness, see Mandler (1975a; but also see his book, 1975b).

Hypnosis is reviewed by Hilgard and Bower (1975). Studies of sleep are reported in the book by Petre-Quadens and Schlag (1974). In the book on sleep, we recommend starting with Chapter 12 (by Dement &

Miller), then moving to Chapter 15 (by Dement & Villablanca), then to Chapters 1 and 2. Studies of the two hemispheres of the human and implications for thought processes are reviewed in the Suggested Readings for Chapter 11. However, the papers by Gazzaniga and Hillyard (1973) and by Kinsbourne (1973) are relevant to the discussions of control structures in this chapter: they present interesting evidence of the division of tasks between the hemispheres.

Books on information-processing systems that will be helpful for this chapter are surprisingly difficult to find. Both Raphael (1976) and Hunt (1975) give useful reviews of the literature on artificial intelligence relevant to problem solving, but with little discussion of the mechanisms of computers. Arbib's (1972) book on artificial intelligence and brain theory is an interesting approach to the analysis of the brain.

The processing structures described in this chapter (especially in Figures 15-1 and 15-3) are actually very simple by modern standards. Although they do contain the basic fundamental components, more sophisticated structures are possible. In particular, there has been considerable work on other types of processing mechanisms that have relevance to the understanding of human thought processes. For instance, we believe that studies of *production systems* will lead to important new insights in our knowledge of thought mechanisms (see Newell, 1973). In addition, systems organized around active memory units seem to be a promising new set of developments: see the papers on memory schemas by Norman and Bobrow (1975, 1976), Bobrow and Norman (1975), and the ACTOR system of Hewitt, Bishop, and Steiger (1973: unfortunately, this paper is not easy to find). An important new language for computers that is relevant to the study of processing systems is reported by Bobrow and Winograd (1977).

16 Social interactions

PREVIEW

Although the same principles of information processing govern interactions among people as govern interactions with the physical world, the interpretation of the social world is somewhat more complex than interpretation of the physical world. Thus, despite the similarity of principles, social interactions provide interesting new problems. Interpersonal interactions are rich and complex. Much of the behavior of one person is based upon the real and imagined behavior of another.

In this chapter we analyze a number of the phenomena of interpersonal behavior. Not surprisingly, our analysis is based upon the role of internal models of the world. Each of us attempts to understand the actions of people (both ourselves and others) by constructing models of people and situations and then assessing the possible causes of behavior. A particularly important issue is the way by which we assign the causes of events to the situation and to the personalities of the people involved. People make up reasons for the causes of other people's behavior—sometimes quite inappropriately. In addition, people justify and rationalize their own actions. The study of how people perceive the causes of the behavior of themselves and others is called *attribution theory*. This theory plays an important role in the topics covered in this chapter.

One way of classifying social interactions is in how well they follow well defined patterns. We talk of behavioral patterns—of schemas, prototypes, stereotypes, scripts, and games. We examine the role of such generalized patterns on behavior.

We finish the chapter with a discussion of a social bargaining situation in which the agreement requires the cooperation of both participants. However, the roles that the participants decide to play can determine the outcome. In general, the higher the aspiration of the participant, the greater will be his or her result.

In reading this chapter, it is important to attempt to understand how the principles of the preceding chapters apply. The central theme of the chapter is the manner by which individuals form models of the world, and then use those models to predict and to understand events. This process is exactly the same as the process discussed in the chapters on pattern recognition and perception. Memory schemas play an important role in guiding interpretations. To realize that the other people in a situation also have their models of the world and of the events that concern them adds new complexity, but also helps explain the richness of interpersonal relations. Note that we really do not specify fully and exactly the form of the internal models used in social interactions. Although the phenomena that we discuss are highly suggestive of these models, we are still not yet ready to construct them in detail. This is another task that is left for the future.

PROTOTYPES AND SCHEMAS

> Woodward knew that Bernstein occasionally wrote about rock music for the *Post*. That figured. When he learned that Bernstein sometimes reviewed classical music, he choked that down with difficulty. Bernstein looked like one of those counter-culture journalists that Woodward despised. [Bernstein & Woodward, 1975, p. 15]

One of the most powerful aspects of human intellect is the ability and tendency to construct models of the world, to predict occurrences and to establish expectations of one's experiences. This capability is of great importance in perception, where expectations and context play an important role (as discussed in Chapters 1 and 7). Conceptually guided processing —processing based upon high-level knowledge of the world—plays a fundamental role in the use of our perceptual and memory systems.

The same capabilities that serve so well in perception and memory also apply in the perception and interactions with people. Memory schemas characterize the people with whom we interact and the social situations in which we take part. These schemas provide us with social *stereotypes*, knowledge about the typical people and situations that we expect to encounter. Actually, people and events are not easily stereotyped. The notion that persons fall into a simple category that immediately classifies their behavior in all sorts of situations is simply not true. Consider the common stereotype of a miser: thin miserly people, wheezing and snorting their way through life, holding on to every penny, denying themselves and others even the slightest pleasure, continually counting their possessions (and perhaps always carrying an umbrella and clutching tightly a pocketbook). The image we have just painted is extreme, yet probably many of you are able to imagine some particular person who fits reasonably closely the major attributes described.

Years of study of the characteristics of people fail to find the consistencies required by simple prototypes. Warm, friendly, loving people are not always as friendly as their stereotype might suggest. Misers can sometimes be generous. Cool, calm people lose their tempers. But despite the fact that actual people do not fit well into simple stereotyped classifications, these stereotypes appear to be a common property of a person's belief about the actions of other people. Thus, our models of the world and of other people appear to govern our expectations and our perceptions, even if the categorizations oversimplify, even if in many instances they are wrong.

Stereotypes and prototypes provide both powerful and dangerous tools. Their virtues lie in the efficiency and power of processing, deductions, and memory storage they provide. For example, prototypes can be used to short-circuit the learning process. A prototype for medical surgeons can tell us a good deal about the probable characteristics of an individual instance. Thus, when we hear about a particular new person who is a surgeon, we can assume a person with highly trained skills, who probably can control knives, scissors, needle, and thread with considerable skill, and who probably is an expert at carving a turkey or slicing roast beef. Of course, we will discover a new instance for which all of the features do not apply, such as when we learn of a surgeon who cannot stand the sight of blood, or who is very emotional and outgoing. Sometimes we have to adapt the range of possible values for the characteristics of our prototype. Still, the internal memory schema provides the basic organizing structure for integrating the new information into our general memory prototype.

Another advantage of prototypes for processing is that they let us respond quickly and efficiently to external events. If we had to examine all the detailed features of an object each time we viewed the world or to rediscover its expected behavior, we might never have any time or processing resources left to do anything else. Prototypes provide a useful summary of the information one normally expects to find in interactions with the world.

When it comes to considering prototypes for event sequences (later on we call these prototypes *scripts*), a number of special advantages become apparent. A prototypical sequence of events for some common activity, such as going to a movie, can be useful in helping to plan the activity beforehand, as well as in guiding behavior and anticipating problems. The prototype gives a basic structure for encoding and remembering the activity: All that has to be remembered are those features that deviate significantly from the expectations embedded in the prototype.

Prototypes of people and groups have some of the same virtues as prototypes of objects and situations. Prototypes of different types of people can be useful in helping deal with various social interactions. The stereotype of professors might include the kinds of clothes they wear, their usual interests, their probable views on various issues, plus the appropriate ways to address and respond to them. This can be a great help in dealing with professors in a social context. However, some special issues related to the use of prototypes in interpersonal situations can pose problems. First, the stereotype can lead to false deductions about the characteristics of a person, much as the quotation from the book by Bernstein and Woodward at the beginning of this chapter illustrated. These false deductions, in turn, can shape the whole nature of the interactions with people, including refusal to have anything to do with particular people.

Social stereotypes

Making attributions about people is usually a very uncertain business. Any given piece of behavior in isolation can usually be interpreted in a wide variety of ways, and the desire for consistency tends to lead to attempts to assimilate potentially discrepant evidence into a preexisting stereotype. If one encounters a hairless, three-legged creature and the community agrees that it is a dog, then there is compelling evidence for making some adjustments in any preexisting stereotype of dogs. This kind of evidence is not usually available for adjusting stereotypes of people or groups.

A large number of social stereotypes for groups and, in particular, for nationalities or racial groups are based on little or no firsthand personal knowledge. They are derived from the media or the social milieu, with little opportunity for testing and modifying through direct personal contact. For example, consider how you would react if you discovered that one of your friends was living with Iggy: Iggy is a famous rock singer. You have never met Iggy, so your first temptation is to characterize Iggy according to the common ethnic prototype: long hair, bizarre clothes, lots of jewelry, and an overbearing personality. Moreover, you are apt to draw conclusions about your friend based upon the relationship with Iggy.

One problem with stereotypes about people is that, once they are applied, they are difficult to check or to correct. Iggy may really wear a wig and be a quiet and considerate person. It is relatively easy to discover that some dogs have only three legs instead of the expected four: it is obvious just by looking at such a discrepant case. It is not so easy to determine whether a particular set of personality traits is appropriate. Because expectations so readily guide perception and interpretations, and because motivations for behavior are generally ambiguous, preexisting stereotypes about individuals may automatically lead you to perceive those traits, even if they are not actually there.

If the individual or group is positively valued, these types of problems may not be so serious. Problems do arise, however, if the prototype being dealt with is negatively valued, as in the case of prejudice or racism.

Being sane in insane places   The tendency to judge people's behavior according to prototypes can severely bias one's interpretations of a situation. A fascinating example of misconceptions of a person's behavior was demonstrated through an experiment by Rosenhan (1973). In this study, the experimenters had themselves committed to various mental hospitals. Once they entered the hospital, they acted in their usual manner. Rosenhan's question was how long would it take the hospital staff to realize that there was nothing abnormal about these patients and, therefore, to release them. (The hospital staff was unaware that there was an experiment taking place or that the patients had made up a story about their alleged symptoms in order to get admitted.)

The problem is that people who are patients in a mental institution are assumed to have mental abnormalities. But people who have mental problems quite often act normally. It is necessary to view the whole pattern of their behavior in order to classify them appropriately. Moreover, these experimenter–patients were classified in terms of very general, rather vague diagnoses (schizophrenia—a term that applies to a wide variety of ailments). As a result, these patients found that they had severe difficulty in convincing the hospital staff that they really were normal. Some of the patients failed completely and had great difficulty in getting higher authorities to check their stories and verify that they were really involved in an experiment (and thus, to get released).

The task is really a difficult one for the staff of the hospital. Imagine that you are in charge of a large group of mental patients, some of whom usually show no abnormal signs. One person walks around talking to herself, another repeats the same unessential operation over and over again, evidently unaware that he has done that operation before. Other patients play games or read or watch television. Some patients keep telling you that they are really normal (although they are very accurate at diagnosing the problems of others). And one patient walks around claiming to be in a psychological experiment, stating that he is really normal, and writing down everything that happens in a notebook. Who is to say which patients are normal? After all, if they were really normal, how did they get admitted in the first place?

In this experiment, the stereotypes of the hospital situation and of patients' behavior overcame the efforts of the fake patients to get out. Interestingly, although it was sometimes difficult to convince the hospital staff that they were really normal, the fake patients found it easy to convince the other patients. Even when they were finally released (after an average stay of almost three weeks), the experimenters had to settle for a diagnosis of "schizophrenia with symptoms in remission." That is, the medical staff did not classify them as normal, but rather as mentally disturbed people whose symptoms had temporarily subsided.

When they were admitted, the patients described their problem as that of "hearing voices." This auditory imagery is a typical sign of some classes of schizophrenia. The experimenters were truthful about all other aspects of their history. Once admitted, they no longer claimed to hear voices, but instead acted normally. However, the staff still persisted in attributing their behavior to the standard stereotypes of clinical abnormal behavior. Thus, note-taking by the experimenters was permitted, but was sometimes taken to be a clear sign of the persistence of the abnormalities.

Although Rosenhan's study has been taken by some people to be an indictment of mental institutions and of the ability to make accurate diagnoses, we see it as an illustration of the pervasive powers of prototypes. People must use a variety of sources of evidence in dealing with the world. If a person deliberately seeks out a clinical psychologist or psychiatrist and claims to have heard voices, this seems to be valid evidence for some abnormality. Not only is it unlikely to think that a patient would lie about all the symptoms, but even if a patient did lie, the lie itself is illustrative of another difficulty. Certainly, a clinician should not ask about each patient "Is this person really just a subject in a psychological experiment?" Similarly, once a patient has been admitted, it is only natural for the institutional staff to overlook the normal behavior and to focus upon minor quirks that appear abnormal. Most real patients exhibit a good deal of normal behavior: their difficulties usually only cover restricted areas of behavior. We find it no surprise at all that the staff found it easy to accept the classification of the fake patients, and that it was very difficult to convince anyone besides the other patients that they really were normal.

ATTRIBUTION THEORY

Imagine you are observing Professor Salton teaching a class. One student, Sue, arrives late. When Professor Salton notices Sue coming in, he interrupts what he was saying and begins to berate her for her lateness. As he gets into it, his voice rises, his face turns red, until finally he goes back to the lecture.

To what do you attribute Professor Salton's behavior? Specifically, is his anger attributable to his personality or his attitude or is it determined by the situation? Maybe this is an important class, one that was planned. Maybe Sue was supposed to get some material ready for Professor Salton. But perhaps the professor is a tyrant, and Sue just an innocent victim. How does someone determine the cause of another's behavior? This is the main issue of *attribution theory*: the study of how people perceive the causes of behavior.

Attributing the cause of another's behavior

Probably the first tendency upon reading the story about Professor Salton and Sue is to make a dispositional attribution. That is, a natural response is to infer that the Professor's behavior reflects his basic personality characteristics (his dispositions). Professor Salton would seem to be a rather hot-tempered individual. After all, being late for a class should not be sufficient cause to make such a fuss.

It is typical to assume initially that another person's behavior is caused primarily by personal factors such as enduring traits or values rather than by specific aspects of the situation itself. When we form models of other people and of situations, we have some choices in assigning the causes of people's actions. The way a person behaves is a function of both the situation and of the particular characteristics of the person. When we simply see one action on the part of an individual, there is no real evidence by which to determine the cause of their behavior. There are essentially two causes for a person's behavior: the situation or the person. Causes due to the situation are called *situational, conditional, external,* or *extrinsic* causes. Causes due to the person are called *personality traits, dispositional, internal,* or *intrinsic* causes.

To make the causal attribution properly, we really need more information. If Professor Salton's behavior results from his temper, we should be able to see the same behavior in other situations: when someone interrupts him in his office, or when a colleague argues against his ideas. If the dispositional attribution is correct, we would expect to find a similar angry response in these situations.

Suppose the dispositional interpretation is wrong. There could really be other factors in the classroom situation. Is it only late arrivals that trigger the Professor's ire, or is it any disturbance in the class? If Professor Salton's response is specific to latecomers, does it apply to all late students on all occasions or maybe only to Sue herself? Perhaps it is specific to this particular occasion.

People almost automatically make attributions about the causes of behavior. As we saw in Chapter 13, the tendency to determine the cause of an event is an important component of learning to deal with those events. Determining causal factors is a common and essential component of behavior. But attributing causes to a single event is risky. It leads to errors. To make more accurate assessments, we need to act more like scientists, observing people in a variety of contexts. We can only make inferences after observing different people in the same situation and the same people in different situations.

To make attributions properly, we need to be amateur scientists, making a series of observations and forming our opinions on the consistencies that are observed. In the example that opened this section we have no way of knowing whether Sue is always late for class, or whether Professor Salton acts that way to everyone, or whether there was something special about the situation that led to the behavior.

When we see people putting money into the coin box of a bus, we attribute the cause of their behavior to the situation: you are supposed to put money into the box in order to pay the bus fare. When we hear a person in the audience talking loudly throughout a play, we attribute the behavior to the personality traits of that person: you are not supposed to talk during a play. In both these cases, attribution of the causes of behavior is made easy by our general experience with these situations. We could be wrong, of course. The person talking in the audience could really be a part of the play, and in that case the behavior is determined by the situation itself.

In most circumstances, we make inferences by watching people's behavior in a variety of situations. We can summarize the observations that we make with a set of diagrams. Part (*a*) of Figure 16-1 shows what happens when we examine four different people (**P1–P4**) in four different situations (**S1–S4**): 16 different combinations in all. If a particular type of behavior is noticed only for one person, but for all situations, then we get the pattern of results shown in the shaded boxes in the figure. This behavior seems to be specific to person **P2**, and to hold across all situations. We conclude that something is special about the person: the behavior is *person specific.*

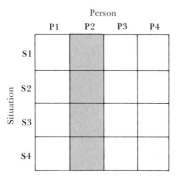

(*a*) Person-specific behavior

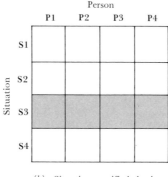

(*b*) Situation-specific behavior

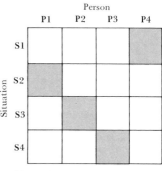

(*c*) An interaction between person and situation determines behavior

FIGURE 16-1

If a particular type of behavior is noticed for all people, but only for one type of situation, the pattern of results is shown in the shaded boxes of Part (*b*) of the figure. We conclude that there is something special about the situation: The behavior is *situation specific.*

Finally, we might find that the particular behavior is noted only for certain people in certain situations as shown in Part (*c*) of the figure: Person **P1** only shows it in Situation **S2**, Person **P2** in Situation **S3**, **P3** in **S4**, and **P4** in **S1**. We might also find that some people or some situations never seem to give rise to the behavior. In these cases, we would say that there was a specific interaction between people and situations that leads to the particular behavior.

Attributing the causes of our own behavior An interesting situation arises when we judge our own actions. Note that just as we form impressions of others, we also form impressions of ourselves, sometimes with even less accurate information being applied to our own behavior. How do we come to understand ourselves? In many ways, we are as much observers of our own behavior as we are of others. We do have some other sources of information that can guide our analyses of ourselves: we have participated in all of our own activities, so we have a wide variety of experiences to use as guides. We also participate in our mental decision processes: something only we have access to. But, as we have seen in the chapter on thinking, the mental events of which we are aware may only tell part of the story of what is occurring. Moreover, that part of the theory may be erroneous.

Interestingly enough, people tend to attribute their good behavior to their own virtuous personalities, and their bad behavior to the situation. But they tend to attribute other people's bad behavior to those people. In part, we see that a person's self-observations suffer from a lack of thoroughness and detachment from the situation. After all, when we ourselves lose our temper and get angry at some event, we perceive the event as being directly responsible. But when we observe another person getting angry at similar events—or more importantly, when another person gets annoyed with us—we can note whether that person regularly gets angered or not, and we can often attribute the other person's behavior more to the person than to the situation. Of course, the situation triggers the behavior, but triggering is not the same as causing. If the other person is angered at us, even if we concede that we were partially responsible, we tend to put the blame on the other person.

There are interesting speculations about the role that people's observations about themselves play in determining their own behavior. For example, fat people are often pictured as being jolly, pleasant people. There are at least three different interpretations of this statement:

1. Fat people really are jolly—the same factors that cause them to be fat contribute to their personality and cause them to be jolly.
2. Fat people would not normally be any more or any less jolly than the rest of us. But they become jolly because social factors direct them toward jolliness. We expect fat people to be jolly, and so we act as if they were. In turn, fat people also believe that fat people are jolly. Moreover, fat people also see others reacting to them as if they were indeed jolly. Therefore, they believe that they themselves must be jolly, and this belief eventually does lead to jolliness. This causes others to continue to react to their jolliness, continuing the behavior.
3. Fat people are not any more or any less jolly than the rest of us. But we expect fat people to be jolly, and so we act as if they were.

Here we have three different reasons for our perceptions that fat people are jollier than the rest of us. Reason 1 is that there is some fundamental cause of jolliness that fat people have. Thus, Reason 1 states that it is really true that fat people are jolly, and so our perceptions are correct. Reason 2, however, says that environmental causes are responsible for the jolliness of fat people: our belief that they should be jolly makes it happen. Reason 3 states that it is all in the eyes of the beholder: fat people are not any jollier than anyone else, but if we believe they are, then that is how we perceive them to be.

Of grasshoppers and things.[1]   Do you like fried grasshoppers? Suppose a polite, popular professor of one of your classes brought some in to class and asked if any of the students were willing to try them. How much do you think those students who took up the offer and actually ate some grasshoppers would actually change their opinion of the taste for the better?

Suppose the same sort of thing happened in another class, this one taught by a bossy, aggressive, and unpopular professor. Here, too, the students are brought fried grasshoppers, but they are offered quite differently. The professor places a grasshopper in front of each of 15 students and says, "Eat." Obviously, the students do not have to obey if they do not wish to, but of those that do, how many do you think would actually change their opinion of the taste for the better?

Most people would favor the mild, pleasant approach and, in fact, this approach is usually much more successful in actually getting people to eat grasshoppers than the efforts of the bossy, obnoxious professor. But what about the opinions of those who eat the grasshoppers? Why did they eat them?

The students in the pleasant professor's classes like their teacher. If they were asked to do something somewhat distasteful, well, the professor really is nice so why shouldn't they do it; after all, it will please the professor. But they still dislike the whole idea.

The students of the obnoxious professor feel rather differently. Why should they do something special? Who cares about the professor's feelings; after all, does the professor care about theirs? But then why should they eat the grasshoppers? Well, maybe because they don't really taste so bad after all.

If one performs a distasteful action with no apparent rationale, why, then, maybe the action is not so bad after all. Hence, the nonintuitive prediction that doing an action "voluntarily" for an obnoxious person may influence your opinion in a positive direction more than doing the same action voluntarily for a pleasant person who also wishes you to change your opinion in the same way.

[1] For a discussion of the experiments from which this example was drawn, see Zimbardo and Ebbesen, 1969.

In general, people attribute the causes of their own actions either to the situations themselves or to their own characteristics. This means that people will use the exact circumstances as a way of assessing the cause of their actions.

Suppose you wish to convince someone to campaign for a political cause—say the *Protect the Sea Urchin* cause. Most people do not know much about sea urchins, nor do they care to. If you want zealous converts preaching your side of the issue, how best can you recruit them? Suppose money is no object (the Japanese sea urchin industry is financing the campaign, say). One way to get people to preach your message is to pay them. The problem is that if you pay your workers too much, they will have no reason to believe in what they are doing. The money is sufficient cause to explain their behavior. Surprising as it may seem, you should pay them as little as possible, and then work them hard. The more disagreeable the task, the more likely they are to believe in the truth and righteousness of what they are doing. After all, if the task is so miserable, why else would they be doing it, except that it is a just cause?

From eating grasshoppers, to political campaigning, to praising a child for good behavior, the lesson is the same. People will attribute their own behavior to their own good qualities—if you give them the chance to do so. But if you overpay, or overpraise, or make their behavior a personal favor, then the result is that people will believe that they performed their actions because of the situation they were in.

People will sometimes manipulate the situation so as to provide a reason for their behavior. If you wish people to think highly of you, only do tasks that you know you can do well. Of course, you will never accomplish new things this way, but you will be judged well. If you think you are going to do badly at something, then make the task as difficult as possible, so the failure in performance will be blamed on the task rather than on you.

It was reported that some students at the Berkeley campus of the University of California stated that they feared flunking out of the university, and so selected the most difficult courses of study. As one student put it, "It's better to flunk out of physics than sociology." Similarly, students who doubt their ability to write good term papers may delay working on their paper until the very last moment, thereby guaranteeing a low grade. But now there is an external reason for the grade: after all, "It was written at the last minute." As the student counselor pointed out, "It is easier to accept a C this way than to have actually tried hard and risked getting the same grade." This type of behavior is self-destructive: it guarantees failure at a task. Of course, it provides the individuals with situational excuses for failure, thereby preserving their own image of themselves.

FORMING
IMPRESSIONS

We have discussed the rather global tendency of people to attribute the causes of an individual's behavior to personality characteristics. Let us now examine how different sources of information about personality are combined to form some overall impression of an individual. How does one derive an overall judgment from the mix of positive and negative information that one usually encounters? Is it simply a matter of totaling up the pros and subtracting the cons, or are there other ways of combining the information? Here we examine a specific arithmetic rule that describes the combination of information.

*Information
integration*

To make the issues more concrete, consider the following rather simple task. You are told that *Peggy is a sincere person.* The term *sincere* is one that has been judged as a highly likable trait. (In a study done by N. Anderson, 1968, the word "sincere" was judged to be the one that was most favorable or desirable out of a list of 555 personality traits.) The experiment in which you are participating asks you to assign a number to how well you like Peggy after only this one-word description: you should be willing to think pretty highly of her, say 5 points worth.

Now suppose you are told something else good about Peggy, but not quite as good as being sincere: she is also orderly ("orderly" is only 185 on the list of 555 words); suppose this phrase alone is worth 2 points. If positive evaluations are simply *added,* then because the terms sincere and orderly are both judged to be good, a person having both these qualities should be judged to be better than a person having only one of them: the total positive evaluation should be 5 plus 2, or 7. If, on the other hand, the individual values are *averaged* in arriving at an overall judgment, then a person who is described as being both sincere and orderly should be judged somewhat less favorably than someone who is described only as sincere. In fact, in controlled experiments, it is this latter situation that happens. A person who is described as both sincere and orderly is judged less well than one described as sincere alone: People tend to average information when forming overall impressions.

Figure 16-2 shows the results of one experiment investigating this question. Various combinations of judgments by subjects were examined. Basically, the subjects were given one or two paragraphs describing the activities of various American presidents. The paragraphs had been chosen on the basis of initial ratings as to the extent to which they portrayed a favorable picture of the president. Different paragraphs were rated individually as portraying the president in a low, neutral, or highly positive light. The question was how various combinations of these paragraphs would affect the subjects' overall judgments of the statesmanship of the presidents.

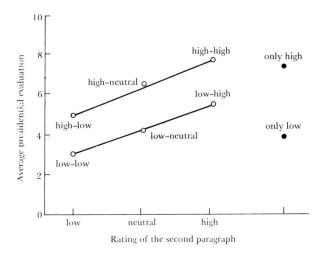

Judgments of U.S. presidents after reading descriptive paragraphs about   FIGURE 16-2
them. The six judgments shown by open circles were made after reading
two paragraphs about each president: the two judgments shown by filled
circles were made after reading only a single paragraph. The adjectives
low, neutral, *and* high *state how each of the paragraphs describes the*
statesmanship of the president being described. (From N. Anderson,
in Contemporary developments in mathematical psychology. Volume II:
Measurements, psychophysics, and neural information processing, *edited*
by David H. Krantz, Richard C. Atkinson, R. Duncan Luce, and Patrick
Suppes. W. H. Freeman and Company. Copyright © 1974.

The vertical axis of Figure 16-2 indicates the subjects' overall judgments of the statesmanship of the presidents after reading the paragraphs indicated on the curves. The important result, in terms of the averaging hypothesis, is shown by the two solid dots on the right side of the graph. The ratings of presidents after people had only read *one* paragraph about them, a single *high*-value paragraph, is essentially equal to the impression resulting from reading *two* high-value paragraphs. In addition, a high paragraph alone yields a higher rating than the combination of a high paragraph and a neutral one, or a high combined with a low one. Both these results are precisely what one would expect if the overall rating is a result of averaging the individual paragraph values. A similar pattern of results occurs when the single paragraph is low in value, although the low–low rating is below that of a single low paragraph. (See N. Anderson, 1973a, for more details.)

By now, there is a great deal of evidence to indicate that we tend to combine information by some process akin to averaging. This is not only true of interpersonal judgments and impressions of people, but also describes how we formulate judgments about almost anything, whether it be an automobile, or the choice between Shar and Malik (see Chapter 14). We tend to look at the overall information structures and produce something like an average value of that information. By this means, individual sources of information get integrated into one overall picture.

Order effects   In addition to the type and amount of information received, the order in which information is received is extremely important in determining the resulting impression. Two different factors are working here. First, there is the *primacy* effect: information received first seems to be weighted most highly. Second, there is the *recency* effect: information received last tends to be best remembered. The two different effects might seem contradictory, but they are not. For one thing, both operate to the detriment of the information presented in the middle of an argument. For another, the primacy effect tends to be longer lasting. Unless the material at the end of a presentation is integrated thoroughly, the recency effect will only be temporary.

The powerful effect of order was first pointed out by Solomon Asch (1952), who showed that the same words can be used to describe someone and make entirely different impressions depending upon the ordering of the words. Consider some person, **P**. Suppose that according to different people you have asked, **P** has been described as

*smart, artistic, sentimental,
cool, awkward, faultfinding.*

Form an overall judgment of **P** using the rating scale below:

+4	+3	+2	+1	−1	−2	−3	−4
highly		moderately		slightly		considerately	
	considerably		slightly		moderately		highly

Now consider another person, **D**. Again, suppose that six different people have provided adjectives describing **D** as:

*faultfinding, ackward, cool,
sentimental, artistic, smart.*

Form your overall opinion of **D** using the same scale as you used for **P**.

When Anderson and Barrios (1961) did this experiment, their subjects rated **P** with an average value of 1.4, roughly midway between *moderately favorable* and *slightly favorable*. They rated **D**, on the other hand, at a value of −0.7, *slightly unfavorable*. Exactly the same words are used in describing both individuals. The only difference is the order in which the adjectives are presented.

These order effects have several possible explanations. One is that the initial impressions formed by the first pieces of information to be received about a topic provide a substantive core of knowledge or *memory schema* into which all other information is integrated. This is an *assimilation* model in which new information is assimilated into the memory structures formed by the older information and is thereby colored by the prior knowledge. Another possible explanation is based on attention: More attention is paid to the first information received and later information tends to be ignored, or at least not processed so deeply. Of course, this strategy of allocating attention might be a result of the same phenomenon that produces the assimilation effects: Once a core impression is formed, little attention is paid to other pieces of information.

It is not easy to decide which of these explanations is the most appropriate one since both predict similar experimental results. The key is to realize that, in terms of its contribution to an overall impression, there are two separate aspects associated with any piece of information.

PATTERNS OF SOCIAL INTERACTION

Stereotyped patterns of interaction

Just as there are stereotypes for people and for common activity patterns, a good deal of our social interactions also seem to follow set patterns. In many cases, it is as if the individuals are in a play, each acting out a prescribed part according to a mutually agreed-upon script. The outcome is known in advance and the rules are followed implicitly. These social *scripts* seem to be automatically invoked whenever the context is appropriate.

The simplest and most tightly constrained of the stereotyped interaction patterns are rituals. Consider two friends, Mike and Ben, who pass one another on the street, each rushing on the way to some location. They are obliged to engage in a brief greeting ritual, perhaps just nodding or waving, or perhaps exchanging a few phrases as they meet and pass on. On the surface, this ritual would appear to be a sort of automatic response with almost no meaning. This must not be correct, however, since if either of the individuals does not play the part appropriately, it can have important effects. Suppose Mike looks straight at Ben, but reacts only with a clench of the jaw, then quickly looks away. This behavior is likely to be interpreted by Ben as a deliberate attempt to avoid contact. It is likely to cause Ben to search for the reasons for Mike's behavior. Alternatively, Mike could violate the brief greeting ritual by attempting to prolong it unduly. For example, Mike may insist on stopping Ben and talking about some event that happened the previous day. If the interaction persisted despite Ben's protest of an important appointment, then Ben would probably wonder about the real motives behind Mike's behavior. Is something the matter with Mike? Is this prolongation of what should be a brief greeting a request for help of some sort? The point is that even these brief rituals have some very definite rules and expectations on the part of both participants. Any violation of those rules interrupts the smooth execution of the script and alerts the individual to some possible problem.

In order to be competent in social interactions, people must know how to play out these rituals. There are many subtle variations of the rituals that depend on such factors as exactly where the individuals are located, how long it is since they have seen each other, and the nature of the relationship between them.

One interesting study of the stereotyped interactions among people is that of transactional analysis (or TA). Here, the rituals people follow are used as the basis of an analysis of all human transactions. The result is an interesting approach to the treatment of interpersonal difficulties. We cover this topic in the next section.

I'm information processing, you're information processing

When Freud first started the scientific study of people's motives and behavior, he postulated a set of internal states and processes. Freud thought there were three controlling states: the *id*, the *ego*, and the *superego*. Since the time of Freud, many people have attempted to analyze the structures of interactions among people. Many of the approaches are quite compatible with the picture that we have described of human information processing and of the construction of internal models.

An interesting case to pursue is that of transactional analysis, or TA as it is usually called. This analysis was originally formulated by the psychiatrist Eric Berne (1961, 1964) and has been popularized by many other people and institutes since then. TA combines an engaging mixture of Freudian analysis with information-processing views (although this opinion might perhaps be more in our minds than in actuality). We find it an insightful exercise to let the books about TA trigger our own interpretations of interpersonal behavior.

According to the TA approach, human personality, and thus human behavior, is governed by three ego states (three states of self), commonly called the *Parent,* the *Adult,* and the *Child.* Each of these states represents a distinct type of knowledge as well as a distinct mode or style of interacting with the world. The *Parent* ego state represents the values and precepts we have acquired from significant others in our life and, in particular, our parents. It is an internalization of parental beliefs and standards and is analogous to Freud's superego. When our Parent ego is in control, our behavior tends to be judgmental or critical. The Parent ego, however, is also the source of our nurturance and protective behavior.

The *Child* state is the playful noncritical child in us all. It is the primary source of emotional behavior, both of laughter and of anger. Our Child can be impulsive and petulant; it can also be creative and joyful. The internal Child is most closely akin to Freud's id.

Finally, our *Adult* state is our information-processing state. The Adult is the ego state that gathers data, weighs evidence, anticipates consequences, and makes predictions about outcomes. Unlike the Parent, the Adult is objective and nonjudgmental. Unlike the Child, the Adult is disciplined and reality oriented.

These three states then coexist in all personalities. For the mature, healthy individual, the states function harmoniously together, each making its appropriate contribution to the overall behavior. If functioning properly, the Adult should play the role of an executive supervisor who mediates between the demands of the inner-Child and the proscriptions of the inner-Parent. It is the Adult information processor that knows when it is appropriate to play, when it is appropriate to be judgmental or nurturing, or when the individual should be task oriented and settle down to get some job done.

According to TA theory, various disturbances in these three stages can interfere with the proper coordination in an individual's behavior and personality. One possible problem is that one state tends to dominate the behavior to the exclusions of others. This can produce the constant Parent who is invariably critical or forever helpful, the constant Child who never grows up and will never be serious, or the constant Adult who is unemotional and calculating, never letting feelings or value judgments interfere with rational behavior. Alternatively, there may be no stable state, with the result being unpredictability and vacillation, a general inability to develop consistent systematic approaches to problem solving and in dealing with the environment.

Within the TA model, interactions between people are referred to as *transactions* and the characteristics of those transactions depend on which states of the participants are involved. A *complementary transaction* is when one individual attempts to communicate with a specific state of another and the recipient responds appropriately. Thus, a person who has suffered the death of a friend or relative may grieve, thereby being under control of the inner-Child. The transaction will be complementary if the person's partner responds with the appropriate consoling, caring, parental type of behavior. A crossed transaction results if the recipient produces an unexpected response to a communication attempt. For example, if the partner responds with a rational analysis of death (the inner-Adult) or a plea for equal consolation (the inner-Child), then the communication would be disrupted or crossed. Finally, some transactions have underlying motives or intentions quite different from what the surface message would imply: "Why don't you come up to see my etchings" would appear to be a straightforward Adult-to-Adult invitation, but of course, it has an entirely different meaning.

As a theory of information processing, transactional analysis is intuitively appealing and quite compatible with the general philosophy presented in this book. The different ego states can be translated into different sources of information in the data base and different types of supervisory processes for operating on that information. After all, the use of models and expectations in negotiating with the world and with others has been a main theme of this book. The fact that TA represents a relatively comprehensive theory of human information processing means it provides a model of the world that individuals can use to analyze their own behavior and patterns of social interaction.

We believe that analyses of interpersonal situations are important. The models in Chapter 15, with monitor, interpreter, and a supervisory processor, all represent attempts at such an analysis from the framework of human information processing studies of psychology. The TA approach represents another type of analysis. Both approaches need a lot of development. The information-processing models have not yet been developed sufficiently to apply to the complex interpersonal behavior of the world outside the laboratory. The TA models are not well justified on scientific grounds: their assumptions and characteristics are vague, and the data that have led to their development are not of scientific quality. We are encouraged, however, that progress is being made.

Scripts   In the preceding chapters we examined problem solving and thinking. There we saw that cognitive activity is controlled by analyses of the situation and an attempt to get toward some goal. In addition, we saw that different control structures watched over the performance of activities, monitoring and supervising the things that took place. Thus, there were strategies to be followed, and differing states of awareness that had high-level control of the situation. Finally, behavior was controlled in several ways, particularly through data-driven processes—controlled and

directed by the events in the environment, and conceptually driven processes—controlled and directed by inner plans and strategies. Many of
our interactions in life, with other people, institutions, and ourselves,
seem to follow set patterns. Thus, we have standard ways of behaving
in restaurants, libraries, stores, and at parties. In the library script, for
example, the following events might take place.

Title: *Script for searching for a particular book in library.*
Purpose: (1) *to find a sought-for book;* (2) *to search in the area of
the sought-for book for other books of interest.*
Constraints: *Minimal interactions with others; to be quiet and in-
conspicuous to avoid bothering others.*

The Sequence of Events
> Enter library, go to card catalog.
> Look up name of book in catalog. (Use problem-solving routines
> if the book name is not known, or if the name that is known
> cannot be found.)
> Find out where in library the sought-for book is located. (Do not
> trust memory, write it down.) Go to appropriate section of the
> library.
> Search library shelves for book. Search all shelves nearby for re-
> lated books of interest. (If the sought-for book is not found,
> maybe a search of nearby shelves will find it or produce an
> adequate substitute.)
> Take books found to table and see if they will be usable. Look
> in them for references to other books that might be useful.
> Wander about section of library: something interesting might
> come into view.
> Take books to checkout counter.
> Leave library.

This is a script that could be followed in going to libraries to obtain a
book. It is flexible enough to account for a variety of actual situations,
although it certainly cannot account for all our visits to libraries. When
we go with other people, then social interactions will change the order
of events. When we go with different purposes in mind, then different
scripts must be invoked. Thus, the general category of scripts for **Visit
the Library** might have many subcategories, such as:

Visit library *(in order to):*
> *get a particular book* (the script we have just seen)
> *look up a particular fact*

> *check the recent scientific journals*
> *find a quiet place to do some work*
> *show someone else a book*
> *put some books on the reserve list for a class.*

Notice that these scripts will all be primarily data driven, controlled by the situation with little room for individual variation. Scripts of this form could be called *situation-driven scripts*.

A second kind of script is much more controlled by the individual. Thus, the way that a parent interacts with a child, or a professor with a student or with another professor is affected much more by individual variables. These situations are also controlled by the environment and by societal factors. Our culture has established certain expectations for the scripts for parents, for professors, for personal interactions, and these *culturally driven* aspects of behavior can be just as important as situation-driven and person-driven influences.

The real importance of individual scripts comes into play when dealing with situations much more under the control of the individuals who are involved: *person-driven situations*. These situations usually take place when people are somewhat removed from official roles imposed by society. Here we find the difficulties and pleasures of interpersonal interactions playing major parts. Here it is that the nature of the transactions between individuals becomes important, when "crossed transactions" can occur, when misunderstandings can easily arise.

The study and analysis of scripts is just beginning. A whole set of issues has yet to be resolved. All scripts have a common structure for encoding information (such as the *Title, Purpose, Constraints* and *Event Sequence* structure in the example). What are the basic categories of information needed to specify scripts of this type? How are scripts organized and catalogued in our memory system? The ways in which script information is organized will determine the most effective cues for retrieving a script. Are scripts encoded into some hierarchical structure? Can we retrieve scripts on the basis of place information (like being at the library), or do the purposes and objectives have to be integrated into the retrieval cues? What are the possible combinations and variety of features that can serve as good cues for retrieving and activating scripts?

THE PROCESSES OF SOCIAL INFLUENCE

- A used-car salesman accidentally finds his customer's bank book. He refuses to look at it, fearing that if he knows too much, he will not drive as good a sale for himself.
- The president of a large corporation is about to undertake some delicate negotiations with the union. Business is bad, and she wants to

make sure that the bargaining will be favorable for the company. She decides she has the best chance of success if she sends a low-ranking company official to negotiate for her.

- An 18-year-old switchboard operator, working alone in her office in New York, is raped and beaten. Escaping momentarily, she runs naked and bleeding into the street, screaming for help. A crowd of 40 passersby gathers and watches as, in broad daylight, the rapist tries to drag her back upstairs; no one intereferes. (From Latané & Darley, 1970.)

These are decisions made within a social context. The final outcome will depend on the actions not only of a single individual, but also of the other people involved in the situation. Sometimes the participants are strangers who provide an audience with subtle social pressures on the behavior of everyone involved. Sometimes the participants are partially cooperative, so everyone can gain if they can come to an agreement on a mutually beneficial decision. Sometimes the participants are protagonists, seeking to optimize their own gain at anyone else's expense. The introduction of social factors into the study of human decision making takes us beyond the point where rational strategy can be specified, with the decisions made in isolation, independent of the pressures of others. To understand decision behavior in a social context, we must study the issues of negotiations, threats, conflict, compliance, social models, and attitudes.

When people operate within a social context, the opinions and actions of others become a part of the analysis of costs and gains. Whether or not a family decides to purchase a new car or color television set may depend much more upon their perception of the reactions of colleagues and friends than of the actual finances or need for the item.

Part of the difficulty in real life decision making lies with the uncertainty faced by each individual decision maker. Most real decisions are difficult, so there is conflict and dissonance over the actual choice. Should you call the fire department when smoke pours into the room? Of course, unless the smoke has a simple, natural explanation, or unless several other people have already called. Individuals must decide for themselves how to act when the unexpected occurs. But they know that life is complicated and filled with peculiar situations in which action can lead to embarrassment or even danger for the person who acts. To the simple assessment of the decision situation, there must be added a consideration of the aftereffects of each action.

Let us start the analysis of social influence processes by considering what happens in some reasonably lifelike experimental situations: We consider the actions of people left in smoke-filled rooms, or confronted with bizarre frisbee players, or involved as witnesses to crimes.

Bystander
behavior

The plight of Kitty Genovese, beaten to death in full view of her neighbors over a 30-min period, none of whom called the police; the murder of Andrew Mormile, stabbed and left to bleed to death in a subway train in the presence of eleven passengers, none of whom tried to help; the rape of the switchboard operator described in the introduction of this chapter—these are the types of events that motivated Latané and Darley (1970) to investigate why bystanders fail to act.

Here we are dealing with a situation with certain specific ingredients: There is uncertainty as to the appropriate behavior involved; other people are facing the same situation; the opportunities for communication are limited or not exercised. Somehow, each individual must decide whether there is an emergency and then decide on the appropriate course of action. Latané and Darley have carried out a series of ingenious studies of decision behavior in these situations. Both their techniques and their results are instructive.

Throwing frisbees. The setting was Grand Central Station in New York City. The experimenters, two women, sat opposite each other on benches in the waiting room, throwing a newly acquired frisbee back and forth. After a few minutes of play, the frisbee was accidentally thrown to a bystander (who, in fact, was a confederate of the experimenters). The confederate's function was to establish a model or focal point for the reactions appropriate to a stranger in these circumstances. The confederate either enthusiastically joined in the frisbee game, or she belligerently kicked at the frisbee, expressing her opinion that the game was both childish and dangerous. In some of the experimental conditions, the confederate left the situation after voicing her opinions; in others, she remained while the women tested the reactions of the real bystanders. The experimental test consisted of throwing the frisbee to each of the bystanders on the benches: A bystander was counted as cooperative if he or she returned the frisbee to the women at least twice.

Generally, the bystanders interpreted and acted in the situation according to the model provided by the confederate. If the confederate was uncooperative they too were uncooperative, often moving away, muttering comments similar to those of the confederate. When the confederate was cooperative, however, there was almost 90% cooperation among the bystanders; indeed, the problem became one of trying to terminate the game rather than trying to stimulate participation. The **vocal behavior** of the confederate and her **continued presence** made all the difference. If the confederate merely let the frisbee lie where it landed and said nothing, her lack of interest did not inhibit participation by others. If she voiced disdain and then left, the bystanders joined in the game after she left: Grand Central Station became a playground.

The smoke-filled room. Subjects were sitting in a room, filling out a "marketing questionnaire," when suddenly smoke began to trickle in through a ventilator. As they worked on the questionnaire, the smoke continued coming in until, "by the end of four minutes, enough smoke had filtered into the room to obscure vision, produce a mildly acrid odor, and interfere with breathing [Latané & Darley, 1970]."

The way people respond to the situation depends upon whether they are working alone or with others. When the subjects were working alone, 75% of them responded rationally to the possibility of fire. They investigated the smoking ventilator and went out into the hall to report the incident. But when two other people were in the same room, by far the majority of subjects failed to report the smoke. They attempted to wave the smoke away and persevered with the questionnaire, until the experimenters compassionately terminated the experiment.

The lady in distress. Again, subjects were sitting in a room filling out a "marketing questionnaire." As they worked, they could hear the "marketing representative" as she moved around in an adjoining office. Four minutes after they began work on the questionnaire, a loud crashing sound came from the office, accompanied by a woman's scream and the (tape recorded) moans: "Oh, my God, my foot . . . I . . . can't move . . . it. Oh, my ankle . . . I . . . can't . . . can't . . . get . . . this thing off . . . me." When the subjects were working alone, 70% of them responded to the situation by offering assistance. But when they were working in the presence of two others (actually, confederates of the experimenter who were instructed to make no responses to the cries), only 7% responded to the woman's distress.

No time to help. Sometimes social factors can influence behavior in strange ways, even when the person involved is all alone, and even when the action goes against the stated beliefs of the person. Darley and Batson (1973) asked students from the Princeton Theological Seminary to participate in a study related to religious education and vocations. The students were given instructions in one building where they were told that they were to go to a neighboring building and give a brief talk. Some of them would talk about job possibilities, while others would talk on the Biblical parable of the Good Samaritan. (Recall that in the Good Samaritan parable, the religiously affiliated priest passed by a person who had been waylaid by robbers, while a lowly Samaritan, a religious outcast, stopped and gave help.) The students were asked to think about the talk as they walked to the other building. Prior to leaving for the other building, students were told they had different amounts of time before they had to present their talk. A relatively leisurely group of students were told "It will be a few minutes before they are ready for you." The relatively pressed group of students were told, "Oh, you're late! They were expecting you a few minutes ago—you'd better hurry."

The experiment was actually conducted in the alley between the buildings. As the students passed through the alley, they encountered a person (a confederate of the experimenters) who was slumped over in a doorway coughing and groaning, apparently in need of help. The experimental question was twofold: Would the students' perception of how much time they had affect their willingness to stop and help? Would thinking of the parable of the Good Samaritan when encountering the person in distress increase the chance of helping?

The answer to the first question is *yes* and to the second *no*. Two-thirds of the students who thought they had some time did stop and help. For those who thought they were in a hurry, however, only one out of ten stopped to offer assistance. The attempt to make helping behavior salient apparently did not work. The group of people who were going to give the Good Samaritan speech were no more willing to help than any of the others.

Bystander apathy   These studies demonstrate some of the factors that influence our willingness to intervene in uncertain social situations. Generally, people tend to follow the course of least resistance, and where possible, conform to the actions of their neighbors. But these acts are not necessarily unsocial, nor do they necessarily demonstrate a lack of consideration for the plight of others. Rather, they tend to show how complex the actual decision process must be.

Consider the plight of the New York telephone operator described in the opening paragraphs of this section. Would you have gone to her rescue? Probably not, since the problem for the decision maker witnessing the actual event is not nearly so simple as the short description here conveys. The crowd or the noise would attract your attention. Going over to watch, you would see a naked woman screaming for help while a man tried to carry her to a building. "What is going on?" you ask the person next to you, who replies "I don't know." How serious could it be? Nobody else seems to be doing anything. Maybe someone is making a movie, maybe it is a domestic quarrel, maybe the man is trying to help her. So you shrug your shoulders and walk off, mumbling that New York City certainly is a strange place.

The situation would have been quite different had you been all alone when you saw the woman and her pursuer. In this case, some of the other explanations do not seem so plausible, and it is very likely that you would be concerned and would take some action. Crowds of people seem to provide for a *diffusion of responsibility* which reduces the perceived obligations of individuals to act. This does not mean that crowds of people always lead to apathy or inaction, as the actions of lynch mobs prove.

Moreover, they can often lead to good behavior, as when a group of people band together to help out in the aftermath of a natural disaster. The point is that individual decision making is a difficult and unsettling task, and social conformity usually acts to simplify the decision problem for the individual. Individuals are constantly faced with doubt about the correctness of a choice. The reactions of other people provide a valuable source of information that can reduce the uncertainty about the possible interpretations of a situation: "I must be doing the right thing. Look how many other people agree with me." The fact that most of the crowd agrees simply because others appear to agree with them is irrelevant because this fact is not known. The reactions of others also indicate some of the contingencies associated with possible actions. In the presence of a passive crowd, individual action may not be supported, and consequently a person may be exposed to considerable risk.

But what about the theological students from Princeton who did not stop to help the person in the alley? In this situation, there was no audience, but the students faced a conflict. Should they help the people who were waiting for them in the next building, or should they stop and help the lone stranger in distress? When in a rush, 90% of the students decided to bypass the stranger, in some cases stepping over the body on their way to the next building.

People may actually help out more in emergencies than would be predicted on the basis of the experiments we just discussed. With a series of somewhat more likely events where the simulated emergency was the collapse of a passenger on a crowded New York subway train, passengers were much more willing to help. One experiment was carried out on a subway train where the next train stop was 7 minutes away. In these studies, bystanders helped the victim. In some of the experimental conditions virtually 100% assistance was recorded. In fact, the psychologists doing the study were really not able to test their ideas because passengers would go to the victim's aid before the experimental situation was fully established. These results are consistent with the earlier ones. The subway provides a captive audience with little else to do. Under these circumstances, the chance that a bystander will help is ten times greater than for a Princeton student who is in a hurry. (These studies were done by Piliavan, Rodin, & Piliavan, 1969; and Piliavan & Piliavan, 1972.)

In the situations we just discussed, there was some uncertainty about the appropriate interpretation of and response to the situation. Now we look at a situation in which there is no ambiguity at all about the correct interpretation or the correct response. But the social pressures toward conformity go directly against the evidence: What happens then?

Conformity

Consider this scenario. A person (call him Chris) is brought into the laboratory to participate in a simple perceptual study involving people's ability to discriminate the length of lines. When Chris arrives, five other subjects are already waiting, so he takes the sixth seat near the end of the table. The experimenter enters the room, wearing a white lab coat, carrying a clip board and related materials. She explains that she has asked the six subjects there to help her in a study of visual judgments. In particular, she is interested in how well people can discriminate among lines of different lengths. Since she is testing a large number of people, she is working with groups of six at a time in order to be more efficient.

The task is really quite simple. One each trial, the subjects will be shown a test line (labeled x) and three comparison lines (labeled a, b, and c). The subjects are to indicate which comparison line is most similar in length to the test line (see Figure 16-3). Each subject will answer in turn —thus Chris will answer sixth because of his seating position. As the subjects respond, the experimenter records each of their judgments in turn and then goes on to the next trial.

FIGURE 16-3

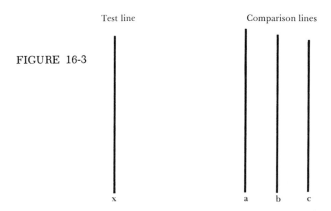

As the experiment proceeds, Chris finds that the discriminations are relatively easy and his answers usually agree reasonably well with the answers of the others. But then things change. A rather simple choice is given, one in which everyone would normally agree to the answer. Chris has determined that line b is the proper answer. But while waiting for his turn to respond, he discovers that all the other subjects have chosen c as the answer. What should Chris do?

Note the conflict. While it is true that the comparison lines are close to each other in size, there is no doubt at all in Chris' mind that b is the correct answer. He had made this decision as soon as the lines were shown. To his amazement, each of the preceding five subjects chooses line **c**. How can this be? Everyone was watching the same display. Moreover, in previous trials, Chris had agreed with the other subjects, except on very difficult choices when there were divergent opinions anyway. Now they all disagree with him. What has happened?

The answer, of course, is that the experiment is rigged. The other five subjects are really confederates of the experimenter, and they have been told just how to respond. The experimenter is not interested in perception at all, but rather in the extent to which subjects will conform to a majority opinion even when they have to go against the evidence of their own senses. Interestingly enough, in the initial studies the experimenter was trying to demonstrate that people would *not* conform to a discrepant opinion or attitude when they had firm evidence to the contrary. The results were just the opposite.

About ¾ of the people who are placed in Chris' position will conform and choose the incorrect response on at least some of the trials. About ⅓ will conform all of the time. The tendency to conform increases with the number of confederate subjects. It can be counteracted if one confederate disagrees with the majority opinion and states the answer that is actually correct.

Conformity of belief occurs, but at considerable emotional cost. When subjects respond against their own perceptual judgments, they sometimes suffer a good deal of psychological conflict. They report feeling anxious, or feeling "distant" from the other subjects. They often show the physiological signs of heightened emotion: sweating, trembling, an increase in pulse rate and blood pressure.

Any major discrepancy between one's own thoughts and the actions of others presents a very difficult situation. Different individuals will devise different explanations of the discrepancies, but the result usually relies heavily on the actions or inactions of others. Perhaps the most important observation, however, is not that people tend to conform, but rather that it can be a traumatic and difficult thing to do. Conformity to strong social pressures can have a great psychological cost. We see these reactions more vividly in the next series of studies.

Compliance

Closely allied to the mechanisms of conformity is the use of authority as a means of inducing another person to do as you wish. Sometimes authority carries with it an implied threat for failure to comply; sometimes authority is perceived as benevolent, so the demands add positive value that may offset whatever costs might be involved; sometimes authority implicitly or explicitly takes over the decision process: The task gets done because the participants do not need to make any judgment whatsoever, they simply do as they are told.

The following studies provide a good introduction to some of the factors operating in compliance with authority. We present the scenario in some detail in order to give you a chance to play the role of a subject. Try to imagine the situation and predict how you would behave.[2]

Imagine that you have answered an advertisement to serve as a subject in a psychological study of learning at Yale University. You enter the impressive buildings of the interaction laboratory at Yale and go to the designated room, where you are met by a scientist in a white coat. Another subject has already arrived. The scientist explains that he is studying the relationship between punishment and learning. In particular, he is interested in how much punishment is best for learning and in whether the relative ages and sexes of the teacher and students affect the rate of learning.

After drawing lots to decide who is to be the "teacher" and who the "learner" (it turns out that you draw the slip marked **teacher**), both of you are taken to an adjacent room. The learner is strapped into the apparatus ("in order to prevent excessive movement"), and an electrode is fixed to his wrist with special jelly ("in order to avoid blisters and burns"). While you are present, the experimenter reassures the learner that, although the shocks he will receive may be extremely painful, they will not cause any permanent tissue damage. He then takes you back to the experimental room and explains your part in the study.

Your task is to teach the learner a list of words. You are to read the complete list of word pairs, then go back to the beginning and start reading the words one at a time. You read the first word of a pair, then four test words. The learner is to press a button indicating which of the four test words was part of the original pair. You give him an electric shock each time he makes an error. For each successive error, the shock level is increased by one step. The apparatus for delivering the shocks has a series of switches for setting different shock levels. The intensities range from 15 volts up to 450 volts in 15-volt steps. The lowest intensities are marked **Slight Shock** and the highest intensities marked **Danger: Severe Shock**, then **XXX**.

After some practice with the procedures, the trials begin. As you proceed through the word list, the learner gets about one correct response in every four. For each error you increase the shock levels according to the experimental design. After several repetitions of the list, the shock intensity is at 300 volts. At this point, the subject starts to pound

---

[2] The description of this study and the quotations were taken from Milgram (1963).

on the wall of his booth. The experimenter tells you to allow 5 to 10 sec for a response, than treat the failure to respond as an error and carry on with the procedure. After the next test word, there again is pounding on the wall, but because there is no response, you administer the 315-volt shock. When you turn to the experimenter for advice, he appears completely passive and simply requests that you "Please continue." If you show continued reluctance, he may inform you that "The experiment requires that you continue," or "You have no other choice; you must go on." How far would you be willing to go?

We have explained the situation in considerable detail to allow you to imagine how you would expect to behave in this set of circumstances. When Yale psychology majors were given the same kind of description and asked to predict, there was general agreement that people in this situation would refuse to continue with the experiment. On the average, they expected that most people would not administer shocks much beyond the 240-volt range, regardless of the inducements of the experimenter. They predicted that only an insignificant minority of the subjects (1–3%) would be willing to continue on to the most intense shock levels (450 volts). Informal polling among psychiatrists and colleagues of the experimenter produced similar predictions.

In the actual experiment, all of the subjects administered shock levels of 300 volts or higher. Twenty-six of the 40 subjects, 65%, were willing to administer the maximum shock levels of 450 volts. These results were completely unexpected. They have stirred up considerable controversy, both on their social implications and on the ethics of psychological experimentation.

The experiment was actually a hoax. No electric shock was being presented: The man pretending to be the learner was actually one of the experimenters, playing the role of learner and acting out his responses to the fake shocks according to a well-rehearsed script. The real subject in this experiment was the person playing the part of the teacher. The real question being studied was how far the relatively minor inducements of the psychologist would cause the subject to go in presenting shocks.

The results are the more surprising in light of the fact that each subject's decision to go on with the deliverance of shock was obviously difficult and painful. The subjects were "observed to sweat, tremble, stutter, bite their lips, groan, and dig their fingernails into their flesh. These were characteristic, rather than exceptional responses to the experiment." For subjects who refused to continue, a typical explanation indicates the depths of their conflict:

He is banging in there. I'm gonna chicken out. I'd like to continue, but I can't do that to a man. . . . I'm sorry, I can't do that to a man. I'll hurt his heart. You take your check. . . . No, really, I couldn't do it.

The subjects appeared to be in a severe emotional conflict with themselves as they struggled with the anxiety involved in compliance to authority. One observer who watched the experiment through a one-way mirror commented:

I observed a mature and initially poised businessman enter the laboratory, smiling and confident. Within twenty minutes he was reduced to a twitching, stuttering wreck who was rapidly approaching a point of nervous collapse. He constantly pulled at his earlobe and twisted his hands. At one point, he pushed his fist into his forehead and muttered, "Oh God, let's stop it." And yet he continued to respond to every word of the experimenter and obey to the end. [Milgram (1963)]

These emotional effects are not restricted to situations as dramatic as the shock experiment. Even in the seemingly innocuous line-judging experiment mentioned previously, subjects underwent considerable trauma when they were faced with the problem that the judgments of others did not conform to their own perceptions.

What exactly does the experiment demonstrate? This work and the studies that followed it have been widely cited as evidence for a general human tendency to defer to authority. One must be extremely cautious, however, in drawing such a sweeping conclusion. Clearly, people try to evaluate the entire pattern of events when engaged in making decisions about the most appropriate course of action. In this particular experiment, the unimpeachable reputation of science was behind the quiet, smooth voice of the experimenter. The subjects must balance their own mental anguish (and the apparent anguish of the learner) against the possible utility of the experimental results. They should refuse to proceed with the experiment only when their own personal anguish exceeds their perceived value of the study.[3]

---

[3] In this experiment, as in all such experiments where there is some deception of subjects, the experimental session is followed by a *debriefing* stage. Here the subjects are told the exact nature of the experiment, informed of the exact conditions that were studied, and introduced to the "victim" who was, in actuality, one of the experimenters. Moreover, in this particular experiment, the subjects received

Actually, it is possible to argue that the subjects were absolutely correct in their assessment of the situation when they continued to deliver the shock, even at the highest levels. After all, the experimenter asked them to continue, thereby implying that there would be no permanent damage. And, in fact, they (and he) were correct: It turned out to be an experiment in which no one was getting shocked after all.

These results may not have anything to do with any natural or enduring trait of obedience, but they do represent a rather depressing picture of the way people evaluate and respond to a particular set of circumstances. What is most surprising, is not that people will comply, but their assessment of the relative values in the situation—the apparent high degree of positive value and prestige assigned to the institutions of science relative to the personal costs of inflicting pain on someone. Critics of the experiment have pointed out that the experimenters themselves were exhibiting a behavior pattern quite similar to their subjects. The fact that they were willing to conduct such an experiment and impose upon their subjects such tension and discomfort represents a similar weighting of the value of science relative to the discomfort of the subjects.

Although there has been vocal opposition to this type of experiment, the subjects who undergo these do not seem to share this point of view. After such studies every subject is carefully debriefed, and the intent and implications of the study are fully explained. In most cases, the subjects have felt the experiment was useful and that their personal experience in it was instructive. They seemed to believe that they had learned a valuable lesson about the necessity of acting according to their own principles, and not to follow authority so readily (see Milgram, 1964). Nevertheless, these experiments still pose important issues for all of us, both as individuals and as members of society. Milgram has summarized the issues in this way:

---

a full description of the experiment at a later date and were visited to determine the long-term effects (see Milgram, 1964, for a full report).

It is unfortunate that subjects must sometimes be hoaxed in the initial stages of experiments of this kind, but so far, no one has discovered any other way of collecting the scientific information required to assess theories of human behavior. But the standard ethics of the profession require that all subjects always be debriefed after such experiments. Often, the subjects feel that the experiment was a worthwhile experience for them; that they have learned something useful about themselves.

In most psychological experiments, there is no deception. In the majority of cases, the experimenter really is studying what he or she claims. Many an experimenter trying to study something so innocuous as hearing comes to grief because the subject keeps waiting for the trick, when in fact there is none. Many readers of this book will be asked to serve as subjects in psychological experiments. If you do so, after the experiment is over you have the right to request a complete explanation of the experiment and a copy of the final report (although this might take a year or so to be produced). Most experiments are valuable experiences: you can learn a lot about yourself.

With numbing regularity good people were seen to knuckle under the demands of authority and perform actions that were callous and severe. Men who are in everyday life responsible and decent were seduced by the trappings of authority, by the control of their perceptions, and by the uncritical acceptance of the experimenter's definition of the situation, into performing harsh acts.

What is the limit of such obedience? At many points we attempted to establish a boundary. Cries from the victim were inserted; not good enough. The victim claimed heart trouble; subjects still shocked him on command. The victim pleaded that he be let free, and his answers no longer registered on the signal box; subjects continued to shock him. At the outset we had not conceived that such drastic procedures would be needed to generate disobedience, and each step was added only as the ineffectiveness of the earlier techniques became clear. . . .

The results, as seen and felt in the laboratory, are to this author disturbing. They raise the possibility that human nature, or—more specifically—the kind of character produced in American democratic society, cannot be counted on to insulate its citizens from brutality and inhumane treatment at the direction of malevolent authority. A substantial proportion of people do what they are told to do, irrespective of the content of the act and without limitations of conscience, so long as they perceive that the command comes from a legitimate authority. If in this study an anonymous experimenter could successfully command adults to subdue a fifty-year-old man, and force on him painful electric shocks against his protests, one can only wonder what government, with its vastly greater authority and prestige, can command of its subjects. [Milgram, 1965]

INTERACTIVE DECISIONS

The previous situations all involved pressures put on an individual. But the decision was still relatively simple, one that had to be made alone by the individual. A second basic type of social context is where several participants interact with each other, to bargain or to debate, so that the eventual course of action is determined by the mutual decisions reached by all the participants. Several different factors enter into this process. For one, the interests of the different parties may differ, so that an optimal decision for one is not optimal for the other. In this situation, some sort of compromise must be reached. For another, there may be a lack of communication among the participants, so that it is not always possible to discuss the possible decisions and their implications. For example, in business negotiations, each side does not usually know the details of the problems of the other. In negotiations between nations, there is often mutual distrust, so communication is strained.

Some of the factors operating in interactive decision making can be illustrated by a prototypical situation: bargaining. The bargaining situation is both competitive and cooperative. It is competitive because two opponents—a buyer and seller—seek to maximize their own gains through negotiation: Usually, the optimal outcome for one is not the optimal outcome for the other. But bargaining can also be cooperative: The participants must agree upon a price if either is to gain and the transaction is to be completed. Communication is allowed, but restricted. In the simplest case, bargaining is conducted impersonally with no social pressures allowed. All communications are limited to the negotiations about price and quantity. Bargaining is usually a decision-making situation in which each participant has incomplete knowledge: Neither one knows the payoff matrix of the other.

We start our analysis of bargaining with an example from the marketplace. We want to pit a **buyer** against a **seller** in a social decision-making situation to see the kinds of interactions that take place. You should try the task: It is informative as well as fun. The example works best if you try it with a friend. (The necessary decision matrices have been inserted in the book in a way to make it possible for two people to play the game.) Ideally, you should play one of the parts and have a friend play the other. (If you cannot find a partner in this enterprise, it is surprisingly satisfactory for you to take both roles, alternating between being buyer and seller.) It helps to play-act, putting yourself in the role of the part you are going to play.

Now decide which part each participant wishes to play, the **buyer** or the **seller.** Then, locate the figure in the text that contains the description of the parts, and have each participant read the appropriate description (either Figure 16-4 or 16-5 depending on which part you have chosen). Do not read both descriptions; that would hamper the ability to play the role demanded of you satisfactorily.

Each participant knows the rate structure of his or her business: the dependence of the profit or loss on the price and quantity that is bought or sold. The relation among price, quantity, and profit is a complex one, however, with a number of different factors interacting to make the structure somewhat different than intuition might suggest. Thus, both the buyer and the seller have prepared a profit table for their use that gives the

Both buyer and seller should read this section.

FIGURE 16-4

THE BUYER

You are trying to buy corn. You are the owner of a small grocery store, chosen to negotiate for a cooperative of independent grocery store owners. The small neighborhood grocery store is in severe economic difficulties because of competition from the large supermarket chains. Last year, times were hard, and a number of small stores were forced to declare bankruptcy or to sell out at very poor prices to representatives of the supermarkets. This year, many of the independent store owners are in debt from previous years. At least one family has had large medical bills, unpaid at this time. This year, the stores have agreed to group together in purchasing farm commodities, hoping that their mass purchasing power will enable them to buy large enough quantities of foods that their purchases prices will not be too high compared with that of the supermarkets. Furthermore, you are ready to purchase corn early, hoping to gain a time advantage over the markets which are not yet ready to begin negotiations. (The produce sections of the large markets are suffering from a strike of their personnel.) You are presently the only buyer in large commercial quantities. Thus, you represent the only outlet for corn. You wish to get the largest possible profits for your grocers. (Now read the section entitled *The bargaining procedure,* p. 653.)

FIGURE 16-5

THE SELLER

Imagine that you are trying to sell corn. You are the owner of a farm, chosen to negotiate for a farm cooperative. Last year there were severe problems in the farms, with drought and disease combining to create severe difficulties on the various individual small farms which are represented by the cooperative. This year things were much better, but many of the farm families are heavily in debt from the preceding year. At least one family has had large medical bills, unpaid to this time. It is important for you to negotiate a good price for this year's corn crop. This year you have harvested the crop early, so that at the present time you are the only source of corn in commercial quantities. Thus, you represent the only source of supply. You wish to get the largest possible profit, since your farmers need it. (Now read the section entitled *The bargaining procedure,* p. 653.)

figures necessary for the bargaining situation. Obviously, these tables must be kept highly confidential. Neither the seller nor the buyer should know the payoff matrix for the opponent. A sample of these tables is shown in Figure 16-6 (both buyer and seller may examine these illustrations). Across the top of each table are listed the quantities of the commodity involved. Down the left side are listed the prices for each unit amount of quantity. The numbers in the table show the profits if the bargain is settled at the specified price and quantity.

In the simplified segments of the profit tables shown here, there is conflict; the buyer is best off by the purchase of a large quantity at a low price; the seller is best off with a small quantity at a high price. (The actual tables to be used in the negotiations are more complex than this, as a study of both complete tables will indicate, but please do not study them both until after the negotiations are complete.)

FIGURE 16-6

Buyer's Guide (Example)

Price	Quantity		
	5	6	7
	Profits		
100	6	7	8
90	6	8	9
80	7	8	10

Seller's Guide (Example)

Price	Quantity		
	5	6	7
	Profits		
100	3	2	2
90	2	2	1
80	2	1	0

(Note that these are simplified tables, used only to illustrate the situation. Do not use these figures in the actual negotiations.)

FIGURE 16-7

Buyer's Guide[a]

Price	1	2	3	4	5	6	7	8	9	10	11	12	13	14	15	16	17	18
																		Quantity / Buyer's Profit in Cents
240																		
230	7	6	0															
220	17	26	30	28	15	0												
210	27	46	60	68	65	60	50	24	0									
200	37	66	90	108	115	120	120	104	90	70	33	0						
190	47	86	120	148	165	180	190	184	180	170	143	120	91	42	0			
180	57	106	150	188	215	240	260	264	270	270	253	240	221	182	150	112	51	0
170	67	126	180	228	265	300	330	344	360	370	363	360	351	322	300	272	221	180
160	77	146	210	268	315	360	400	424	450	470	473	480	481	462	450	432	391	360
150	87	166	240	308	365	420	470	504	540	570	583	600	611	602	600	592	561	540
140	97	186	270	348	415	480	540	584	630	670	693	720	741	742	750	752	731	720
130	107	206	300	388	465	540	610	664	720	770	803	840	871	882	900	912	901	900
120	117	226	330	428	515	600	680	744	810	870	913	960	1001	1022	1050	1072	1071	1080
110	127	246	360	468	565	660	750	824	900	970	1023	1080	1131	1162	1200	1232	1241	1260
100	137	266	390	508	615	720	820	904	990	1070	1133	1200	1261	1302	1350	1392	1411	1440
90	147	286	420	548	665	780	890	984	1080	1170	1243	1320	1391	1442	1500	1552	1581	1620
80	157	306	450	588	715	840	960	1064	1170	1270	1353	1440	1521	1582	1650	1712	1751	1800
70	167	326	480	628	765	900	1030	1144	1260	1370	1463	1560	1651	1722	1800	1872	1921	1980
60	177	346	510	668	815	960	1100	1224	1350	1470	1573	1680	1781	1862	1950	2032	2091	2160
50	187	366	540	708	865	1020	1170	1304	1440	1570	1683	1800	1911	2002	2100	2192	2261	2340
40	197	386	570	748	915	1080	1240	1384	1530	1670	1793	1920	2041	2142	2250	2352	2431	2520
30	207	406	600	788	965	1140	1310	1464	1620	1770	1903	2040	2171	2282	2400	2512	2601	2700
20	217	426	630	828	1015	1200	1380	1544	1710	1870	2013	2160	2301	2422	2550	2672	2771	2880
10	227	446	660	868	1065	1260	1450	1624	1800	1970	2123	2280	2431	2562	2700	2832	2941	3060

[a] From Siegel and Fouraker (1960, pp. 114–115).

In the actual negotiations each participant will have a complete table. Each should start bargaining at a favorable position, but both will eventually have to make concessions. The following rules of fair play should be followed:

- You either accept an offer or make a counter-offer.
- Bargaining is in good faith. That is, any offer is always valid. Even if an offer is rejected at first, either party may later decide to accept it. At that time, whoever made the original offer must agree to abide by it.
- No agreements which involve losses for either party are acceptable.
- All offers are to be made in writing, each offer stating both a price and a quantity.
- No talking.

Now, try it. We have provided both a buyer's and a seller's profit table. If two of you are negotiating (and using only one book) sit at a desk with the buyer on the left. We have located the tables in the book so that each of you will be able to see only the appropriate table. The two tables are on pages 656 and 659 for the buyer and seller, respectively. The **buyer's guide** is on the **left** side of the book, the **seller's** is on the **right,** and there is a page of text between them. Hold the page separating the two tables vertically to act as a shield.[5]

When the negotiating game is over, it is time to examine the processes by which an agreement was reached. Note how each person's behavior influenced that of the other. In determining a bargaining stance, each participant had to consider the constraints imposed upon the other, even though it was not known exactly what they might be.

The process of negotiation

Level of aspiration. One factor that plays an important role in the bargaining behavior is the level of aspiration of the bargainers. Think back on your own performance. Initially, you probably started off by examining the range of profits possible from the various price–quantity combinations of the table, selecting a target range for the amount of gain you hoped to make. Then, you made your bids in such a way that you would end up somewhere near your goal. Probably you were rudely awakened to reality by the initial bids of your opponent, since

---

[5] If you are playing both parts, do it honestly. Get yourself in the mood of the buyer and make an offer in writing on a piece of paper. Then, turn to the seller's table, get yourself in the mood of the seller, and examine the offer. Using the profit and the history of the previous offers, either accept or make a counteroffer. Then go back to the role of the seller. The tables are complex enough so that you will have difficulty in gaining any unfair advantage, if you play the game honestly. But remember that neither buyer nor seller is supposed to know anything about the other's profit table.

the initial bids most likely left you with little or no gain. From this point on, the bargaining usually proceeds somewhat like a fencing match, with each participant trying to keep profits at an acceptable level, while at the same time attempting to discover what range of prices and quantities seem to be acceptable to the opponent. The final goal that you were trying to attain is called the *level of aspiration* (*LA*).

Level of aspiration plays an important role in much human behavior, since it tends to dominate the way that people will act in a wide variety of situations. A person who traditionally sets a high value of LA acts quite differently than one who sets a low level. Often, the pattern of success is determined by the setting of the LA, with the person who sets a high value producing more achievement than the person who is more modest in ambition. The achievement could result from one of two reasons, of course. A person who sets high values of LA may be more competent and skilled than a person who sets a low value of LA. Alternatively, someone who sets the high value may thereby force a good performance, both by refusing to settle for results too far removed from the target and by the extreme self-confidence that often accompanies the setting of high goals.

In the bargaining situation illustrated here, for example, the end result is determined by the joint agreement reached by the two bargainers: The LA value set by each bargainer has a strong influence on that end point. The participant who sets and keeps a high value of LA may very well end up with more profit than the one who sets a low value. This is not because the winner has a unique ability or any inherent advantage at the bargaining table. The high LA person simply refuses to give concessions that would fall below his or her LA.

In addition to these general effects of LA, several other aspects of the bargaining situation have been discovered in the series of experiments performed by Siegal and Fouraker. [The bargaining game, including the tables, comes from the book in which Siegal and Fouraker reported their experiments (1960).] One central point concerns the different types of strategies adopted by the bargainers.

There are a number of different variations of the bargaining procedure possible, and the strategies of the bargainers vary with the situation. In the situation illustrated here with the tables, neither bargainer knew the profit tables of the other. This experimental situation is called *incomplete–incomplete:* Each person has incomplete knowledge of the opponent's profit table. What happens, however, when one person knows both profit tables but the other only knows his or her own—the situation called *complete–incomplete?* The result depends upon the negotiation strategy selected by whoever has the complete knowledge. Two possible strategies are especially interesting: One can be called *fair;* the other can be called *ruthless.*

Seller's Guide[a]

Seller's Profit in Cents

Price	1	2	3	4	5	6	7	8	9	10	11	12	13	14	15	16	17	18
240	230	440	630	800	950	1080	1190	1280	1350	1400	1430	1440	1430	1400	1350	1280	1190	1080
230	220	420	600	760	900	1020	1120	1200	1260	1300	1320	1320	1300	1260	1200	1120	1020	900
220	210	400	570	720	850	960	1050	1120	1170	1200	1210	1200	1170	1120	1050	960	850	720
210	200	380	540	680	800	900	980	1040	1080	1100	1100	1080	1040	980	900	800	680	540
200	190	360	510	640	750	840	910	960	990	1000	990	960	910	840	750	640	510	360
190	180	340	480	600	700	780	840	880	900	900	880	840	780	700	600	480	340	180
180	170	320	450	560	650	720	770	800	810	800	770	720	650	560	450	320	170	0
170	160	300	420	520	600	660	700	720	720	700	660	600	520	420	300	160	0	
160	150	280	390	480	550	600	630	640	630	600	550	480	390	280	150	0		
150	140	260	360	440	500	540	560	560	540	500	440	360	260	140	0			
140	130	240	330	400	450	480	490	480	450	400	330	240	130	0				
130	120	220	300	360	400	420	420	400	360	300	220	120	0					
120	110	200	270	320	350	360	350	320	270	200	110	0						
110	100	180	240	280	300	300	280	240	180	100	0							
100	90	160	210	240	250	240	210	160	90	0								
90	80	140	180	200	200	180	140	80	0									
80	70	120	150	160	150	120	70	0										
70	60	100	120	120	100	60	0											
60	50	80	90	80	50	0												
50	40	60	60	40	0													
40	30	40	30	0														
30	20	20	0															
20	10	0																
10	0																	

Quantity

FIGURE 16-8

[a] From Siegal and Fouraker (1960, pp. 114–115).

The fair strategy.   If the two opponents are fair, reasonable people, then it may actually be detrimental for one to have too much information about the other. What happens is this. When one of the bargainers knows both profit tables, that person can see just what the reasonable values of profits might be for both participants. Most of the price–quantity values which yield large profits for one person are unreasonable for the other person, hence they are avoided. The fair bargainer aims for a target price and quantity that will tend to equalize profits for both participants—a "fair" solution. This person sets a low LA value.

The opponent, however, does not know both profit tables, and typically sets a high initial LA value. Moreover, the rapidity at which the opponent starts offering reasonable profits is reinforcing. The offers of reasonable profits from the informed participant support the estimates of how much can be gained. The uninformed one often wins out, for the bargainer with complete information encounters a long string of failures by attempting to stick to reasonable demands. The bargaining situation produces strong pressures to try to salvage some profits and give in to the opponents (if no agreement is reached, no profits can be obtained). It is clear that the person who is fair can be handicapped by too much information.

The ruthless strategy.   If the bargainer who has complete information is also ruthless in a determination to maximize profits, the information can be used to manipulate systematically the opponent's level of aspiration. Basically, the ruthless person only needs to know the general principles of learning theory, namely that a history of reinforcements for positive behavior and lack of reinforcements for negative behavior can have a powerful influence on performance. The reinforcements for negative behavior can be very small, so long as they are applied and withheld consistently. Thus, one ruthless, completely informed bargainer in this situation started out by offering the opponent no chance at all for profit. Then, small increments in profit were offered only for large concessions. Whenever the opponent proved reluctant to make concessions, the informed bargainer changed bids to give zero profit to the opponent. The end result was that the completely informed bargainer realized a substantial profit, whereas the incompletely informed person was very pleased with the small amount that was salvaged. The advantage of learning theory, when used properly, is that not only can it lead to beneficial results for the ruthless player, but that the history of small reinforcements is so pleasing, the uninformed bargainer is not only satisfied but is willing to play (and lose) again.

In all these examples of social decision-making, no personality factors were operating. Everything was carried out (or should have been) in a cold, impersonal manner. What if personalities had been allowed to intrude, what then? According to the basic principles of decision theory one should maximize profits, and thus personality factors should really make no difference. This, of course, is false. Consider what might have happened could you perceive the plight of your opponent. Would not the whole bargaining structure be changed if it were known that one participant was evil, profit-minded, and ruthless: totally aware of the opponent's problems but completely unmoved by them, caring only for personal profit no matter what the cost to others?.

SUMMARY

In many ways this chapter has focused on the individual's assessment of the world through observations and attributions of causality. Bystanders of events consider both the actual occurrences and also the actions of other bystanders in determining what action to take. The individual participant does not usually realize that each of the other bystanders might also be observing the others and attempting to determine what he or she should do. So each person may see that the others are not responding to the events, and draw the obvious conclusion that nothing is happening that requires any action.

In situations of negotiation and bargaining, similar evaluations take place. Each individual attempts to understand the behavior of the others, and the skilled negotiator carefully manipulates their behavior and the ensuing interpretations of what is happening. Experienced negotiators are well aware of their own temptation to interpret their opponents' actions, and are careful to avoid learning too much about them in order to reduce any tendencies to sympathize with their opponents.

The analysis of bargaining tactics presented here makes the interaction look cold-blooded and ruthless, but that was not the intent of the examples. The point was to illustrate the way in which the interpretation of the behavior of others can affect interpersonal interactions. Friendly, cooperative interactions follow these same principles, except that mutual trust and understanding become the guiding principles.

Not all actions of people are selected after conscious, careful deliberation. Many patterns of action tend to be ritualized, selected automatically by the memory system according to an analysis of the situation, and then followed by the participants without any particular awareness of their actions. These ritualized interactions are characterized by *scripts*. Unless people are aware of the rules they are following, they may find themselves trapped within a script, following a behavior pattern that is unproductive, misleading, or sometimes highly emotional. Some forms of clinical analysis of interpersonal behavior have focused upon this aspect of interactions, and we examined one such system in this chapter: transactional analysis.

If people are made aware of the situations in which they take part and of the stylized interactions that often result, they can learn to improve their own interpersonal relations. The analyses of transactional analysis provide some insight to human behavior, first by focusing upon styles of supervisory control of a person's behavior (the three ego states labeled Adult, Child, and Parent) and also by making participants aware of the games in which they engage. The insights can be quite effective, even if they are not correct. This is probably because the simple realization that other people have some of the same problems and desires as oneself immediately leads to some improvement in understanding others, and the awareness of the ritualized behavior patterns into which we all fall helps one to break out of an undesirable pattern. Stepping back from an interpersonal situation—especially one wrought with emotional feelings—and asking oneself "What is happening? What roles are the participants playing? How is everyone interpreting the actions of the others?" can be invaluable steps towards the understanding and improvement of the interactions—again, even if the particular analyses offered by a particular therapeutic system are not scientifically reliable or accurate.

REVIEW OF TERMS AND CONCEPTS

In this chapter, the following terms and concepts that we consider to be important have been used. Please look them over. If you are not able to give a short explanation of any of them, you should go back and review the appropriate sections of the chapter.

Terms and concepts you should know

Prototypes
Schemas (also see Chapter 10)
   stereotypes
Attribution theory
   situational causes
     (external, extrinsic, conditional)
   dispositional causes
     (personality traits, internal, intrinsic)
   making attributions
     person-specific
     situation-specific
     interactions
Forming impressions
   the difference between averaging and adding
   order effects
     primacy
     recency
     attention

Patterns of interaction
   rituals
   scripts
   transactions

We have found the book *Social psychology: A cognitive approach* by Stotland and Canon (1972) to be a good review of many of the topics discussed in this chapter.

Attribution theory has been widely explored by a number of people. The best introduction is probably the series of papers on attribution by Jones, Kanouse, Kelley, Nisbett, Valins, and Weiner (1972). The article by Kelley in that series is especially important. The article by Jones (1976) summarizes some recent work. The origins can be traced to the influential book by Heider (1958). We find Heider's book to be an important statement about many aspects of people's knowledge: the book was premature, in that the field is only now ready for many of the ideas that it discusses. Crosby (1976) presents an interesting study of self-assessment of deprivation: the conditions under which people feel deprived relative to their perception of what they should be receiving.

Norman Anderson has put together an extensive series of studies on the means by which people combine different sources of information. The best survey of this work is in his book (1977). Some applications are reported in N. Anderson (1976 and 1973b). The work on serial position effects is presented in Anderson and Barrios (1961), as well as in the other sources. N. Anderson (1974) provides a good review of Anderson's theory of integrating information.

An early theory about the way people attributed the causes of behavior was the theory of cognitive dissonance. People act to reduce their internal conflicts, went the theory, and the resulting flurry of experiments that were produced provided interesting and speculative reading. Unfortunately, the theory floundered for lack of specificity. It simply was not possible to agree on the meaning of dissonance, or on the interpretation of experimental results. Actually, it was often easy to interpret the results of experiments after the results were known, but not so easy to decide exactly what dissonance theory would predict prior to the actual running of the experiment. Scientific theories must be able to predict, however, for otherwise their utility is severely limited. We suspect that many of the notions of dissonance theory were correct, but at the time the theory was proposed, there simply was not enough known to make the theory sufficiently precise.

Those of you interested in reading up on dissonance theory might wish to examine several of Leon Festinger's books on this topic; perhaps starting with his *A theory of cognitive dissonance* (1957) and including the very delightful study by Festinger, Riecken, and Schachter, *When prophecy fails* (1956).

The experiment on grasshoppers was actually performed by E. E. Smith in an unpublished Armed Forces report (1961). This experiment is discussed in some detail (along with a replication and expansion of it) in the book on attitude change by Zimbardo and Ebbesen (1969). The grasshopper experiment is discussed starting on page 40 and then again on page 72. Bem's book on beliefs (1970) also covers this material.

The scientific literature on transactional analysis is scanty, but the popular literature is voluminous. Perhaps the best starting point is two of Berne's early works: Berne (1961) is the technical presentation of his ideas; Berne (1964) is the popular presentation titled *Games people play*. We have found James and Jongeward (1971) a useful popular source of information.

The material on conformity, in which subjects are led to respond according to the responses of their fellow subjects rather than their own beliefs derives primarily from the work of Solomon Asch. This work is reviewed in Asch's text *Social psychology* (1952). An excellent review is Crutchfield's article, "Conformity and Character" (1955). Asch's work can also be found in his 1955 *Scientific American* article. A review of the literature on conformity is provided by Allen's discussion, "Situational Factors in Conformity" (1965).

The material on bystander apathy comes from the book by Latané and Darley, *The unresponsive bystander* (1970). A very excellent short summary of the work can be found in the *American Scientist* article by Latané and Darley (1969).

The work on compliance with authority, the unexpected willingness of subjects to forego their own personal judgment and obey the requests of the experimenter, comes from the work of Stanley Milgram (1963, 1965). We also recommend that you read Milgram's reply to critics, in which he explained in some detail exactly how he conducted the aftermath of the experiment, the debriefing and thorough discussions of the experiments with his subjects (Milgram, 1964). See Milgram's book on obedience (1974).

The example on bargaining comes from the book by Siegal and Fouraker, *Bargaining and group decision making: Experiments in bilateral monopoly* (1960).

T. C. Schelling discusses the tactics of strategic negotiations in his book *The strategy of conflict* (1963). This is a fascinating book, one that may be considered immoral by some circles. Anyone who reads Schelling's book should also read the one by Anatol Rapoport, *Fights, games, and debates* (1960). Both these books make excellent introductions to discussion on game theory. In addition, three excellent articles have appeared in *Scientific American*. [All are included in the book of reprints edited by Messick, *Mathematical thinking in behavioral sciences: Readings from Scientific American* (1968).] The three articles are: Morgenstern, "The Theory of Games" (1949); Hurwicz, "Game Theory and Decisions" (1955); Rapoport, "The Use and Misuse of Game Theory" (1962).

An important set of material, not discussed in this chapter but very much related, is the way by which people form beliefs and attitudes. Two excellent small books are available on this topic: one by Bem on beliefs (Bem, 1970); one by Zimbardo and Ebbesen, *Influencing attitudes and changing behavior* (1969). A technical handbook on how to go about changing attitudes is provided by Karlins and Abelson (1970). Jacobo Varela, an applied psychologist from Montevideo, has applied many of these psychological principles to the social and interpersonal problems of daily life. His book (Varela, 1971) summarizes his philosophies and is highly relevant to the material covered within this chapter.

While on the topic of attitude change, Eugene Burdick's popular novel, *The 480* (1965) discusses how a thorough computer analysis of voting patterns was used to alter a hypothetical election. The analysis is not completely hypothetical; similar analyses are actually done by various companies that simulate the beliefs of the American voting populace in manners not unrelated to the discussion that occurred in this chapter.

A not-so-amusing discussion of an attempt to alter attitudes comes from McGinniss' discussion of *The selling of the president, 1968* (1969). The most reassuring thing about this book is that, despite all its sophistication, many of the techniques simply did not work.

17 Stress and emotion

PREVIEW

Many different sources of information interact to control what a human does—thoughts, hormonal level, nutritional needs, the perceptual system, the memory system. So far in this book, we have concentrated on the pure information-processing systems, systems that pick up information from the environment or from memory. In the study of emotions, we are dealing for the first time with systems that directly involve biochemical factors in their operation, systems for which the chemical state of the body is one of the more important inputs.

In our studies, one dominant theme has repeatedly emerged. The mind actively engages the environment. It models the world, predicting and interpreting current events within the context of past experience. We have studied these activities in perception, memory, problem solving, and decision making. Now we will discover many of the same principles interacting with emotion. This is to be expected. In the complex behavior and thought of people, the environment is important only because of the interpretation given to it.

Uncertainty, a failure to observe an expected event, a disruption in the pattern of otherwise smoothly flowing response sequences, an anticipation of the inability to cope with a pending event—these seem to lead to many human emotions and stresses. A real or anticipated mismatch between what occurs and what is expected has important consequences. Our internal model of the world guides our actions. Unexpected events and inadequacies of the predictive mechanisms cause the biochemical responses that we then interpret as emotions and stress.

In this chapter we briefly review some of the concepts of stress and emotion. By no means do we cover all the possible effects of emotions; we do not even cover all emotions. Rather, the emphasis is on how cognitive factors can influence the initiation of emotional states and then, in turn, influence the person's responses to those states.

The important point is that environmental situations do not cause stress or emotion: it is a person's interpretation of the situation that leads to emotional responses. People perform mental simulations of the occurrences of the world, predicting the events that will occur and predicting their ability to control those events. When the predictions are undesirable, or when it appears that there is little that can be done to control that state of affairs, then emotional responses are likely to develop. Similarly, if the real occurrences are not at all what was expected, emotions will be triggered. The human system contains an intimate interaction of predictions and interpretations of the world with biochemical and neural mechanisms that activate the body. This chapter introduces the study of these interactions.

STRESS

Words like *expectations, uncertainty, disruption, discrepancy, dissonance,* and *conflict* are key words in the experimental analysis of human emotion and motivation. In many types of motivational situations, the organism acts as if something were monitoring the ongoing cognitive processes, watching for potential trouble spots in dealing with the environment, and signaling when difficulties arise. The comparison mechanism is primarily concerned with the results of cognitive processing. So long as things are within sensible limits, it remains quiet. But when something is encountered that is new or discrepant from what is expected or potentially threatening, it acts like an interrupt mechanism, alerting the organism to the potential problem and mobilizing resources to deal with it. The result is a change in the general level of arousal or activation. It can range from high levels under stress and fear to low levels when the environment makes no demands at all on the organism.

How to produce stress

In a stress-provoking situation, the important factors are not the objective facts of the situation, but the individual's appraisal of them. This close dependency on cognitive factors has made stress a particularly difficult topic to study in the laboratory.

For example, in one experiment, psychologists attempted to study the stress reaction in soldiers undergoing combat training, using live ammunition (Berkun, Bialek, Kearn, & Yagi, 1962). They were surprised at the apparently low levels of stress associated with the combat training. The trainees simply refused to believe that the Army would place them in a position where they could get hurt. They assumed (falsely) that being perched precariously on a tree with bullets whizzing all around ("sniper training") must be safer than it seems, or the Army would not permit it.

Similar difficulties are found in other experimental studies of stress. Most subjects assume that any ignoble treatment in an experiment must be part of the test manipulations. Their reluctance to give up their image of a benevolent experimenter, one who would not subject them to any real risk or harm without good reason, tends to counteract the effects the experimenter is trying to achieve.

Although these problems make it difficult to study stress under controlled conditions, they do underscore the importance of cognitive factors in determining emotional responses. If things are staged correctly, stress can be induced. A roller coaster ride can be made far more stressful (without changing the ride itself) by adding a few signs about the reliability of the track:

Warning. Loose track. This section under repair. Do not use while red flag is up (a big red flag is perched on the sign).

Amusement park operators do not dare such tricks, even in jest, for the very success of the ride depends upon the conflict between the knowledge that things must be safe and the external appearances of danger.

The various, well-publicized tests of "space stations" in which a number of volunteers are placed aboard a space simulator and locked up for some few months, also fail in their attempts to mimic stressful conditions. The knowledge that one is really on the ground, being observed all the time by television and various physiological measuring devices, takes away most of the reality of the experiment. Yes, the simulation does help in answering questions about the reliability of the toilets and other equipment, but human responses will be severely affected by the knowledge that this is only a test.

In general, the success of simulated environments in making people react normally depends a good deal on how successfully the simulation mimics reality. This difference between the psychological response to simulated and real experiences has been the basis of at least one science fiction solution to the problem of making astronauts perform coolly and competently during a real space mission, even in the face of massive equipment failure. The trick in the science fiction story was simple: The astronauts thought they were being run through one of the more realistic space simulators.

Conflict is perhaps the most frequent source of everyday stress and anxiety. It can arise whenever something interferes with attempts to achieve a particular goal. There could be an obstacle that prevents a desired action from being performed, there might be difficulty in choosing among outcomes, or perhaps there might be undesirable side effects associated with the activity. Whatever its source, conflict is unpleasant and stressful: It has been proposed as a major motivator for aggressive behavior.

In a classic study of conflict, frustration was introduced into children of kindergarten age (Barker, Dembo, & Lewin, 1941). In the first part of the experiment, children were presented with a playroom containing a curious mixture of toys. The toys were without all their components: ironing boards without irons; water toys without water. The various deficiencies in the toys did not seem to bother the children in the least. They made imaginative use of the toys and seemed to enjoy constructing elaborate and imaginative games out of what was available.

Their behavior changed, however, when they were provided with a glimpse of a better world. They were allowed to look at toys for which no parts were missing and which were much more elaborate and intriguing to play with than the ones they had been given. The next day when they were again allowed to play with the original toys, the effects of this experience became apparent. The children were no longer satisfied with the motley collection that was available. They squabbled among themselves, they were belligerent to the experimenter, and they were destructive to the toys.

In the chapter on learning (Chapter 13), we noted the pheomenon known as *learned helplessness*. Here, animals (including humans) are placed in situations where their responses appear to be irrelevant to controlling the situation. The situation can be one in which no response seems appropriate, or where only inappropriate responses have been learned. If the situation continues long enough (or is repeated in different environments), the result is often a generalized feeling of helplessness, a feeling of general inability to cope with the world. One major determiner of stress and emotion is people's knowledge of their own ability to control a situation.

When people are placed in an environment that they feel unable to change or for which they have no satisfactory repertoire of responses, general anxiety seems to prevail. If the person does try to react to the situation, the attempted responses are often inappropriate. This increases the feeling of anxiety. Someone who is well trained and experienced in the same situation does not feel anxious or emotional under the same environmental circumstances. The major difference between these people is the ease with which they are able to produce responses appropriate to the situation (and their confidence in their ability to produce the appropriate responses).

Closely related to these issues are the emotional responses generated when some ongoing activity is interrupted. Interruption seems to be a primary source of difficulty, leading to feelings of frustration and of a general inability to respond after the interruption. The planned activities are no longer relevant, and no new sequence of actions has yet been considered. Thus, immediately following the interruption of some ongoing activity, there will be a lack of adequate responses, a general knowledge that the planned and activated response possibilities are irrelevant, and therefore a buildup of emotional states. Once emotional responses build up in the human, then the perceived situation changes, for the person starts responding to the perception of those emotional changes as well as to the general situation.

Chapter 16 discussed two different situations that led to emotional responses. Both situations required people to conform to a course of action that was contrary to their beliefs. In one situation, people's perceptions of the relative lengths of lines seemed contrary to those of others. In the other situation, people were asked to deliver painful electric shocks to others under the gentle request of a scientist who explained that it was necessary for the good of science. Neither of these situations would appear to be inherently stressful on the surface. Stating an opinion about the length of a line would not seem difficult. Deciding to obey or disobey a calmly made request would not seem inherently difficult. In neither case were the people themselves threatened or in a dangerous situation. But the discrepancy between perceptions or beliefs and the required behavior produced highly emotional, stressful reactions for the people involved.

A major source of stress seems to be an inability to control the environment. People who experience situations where there is no harmony between their planned responses and the situation seem to undergo stress. A belief that one has the coping skills required to master the contingencies of the world seems necessary. When such a belief is broken, the results can be feelings of helplessness and hopelessness, which can lead to withdrawal, neurotic depression, and even to death.

All the situations discussed to this point seem to have some common principles. All hinge upon the structure of people's internal beliefs about the situation facing them. Basically, there are two classes of conditions that seem to produce stress. First, there are situations in which people's internal models are inadequate. Second, there are situations in which the internal models lead to an undesirable result that people feel powerless to prevent.

Cognitive causes of stress

Inadequate models occur either when there is some novel situation for which past experience offers no guidelines, or when there is a discrepancy between actual events and expected events. In either case, the difficulty is that no adequate internal model for the situation exists. This situation characterizes stress by novelty, by unexpected events, by inadequate knowledge of the situation, or by interruption of an ongoing activity.

Feelings of helplessness occur either whenever people feel themselves incapable of coping with the task before them or when the situation is such that there can be no adequate response. Thus, if an engine fails on a commercial airline flight, the people on board feel stress. The passengers have absolutely no control over the situation. Many people feel much safer driving in automobiles rather than flying in airplanes, despite the fact that automobiles are much less safe and they are aware of the statistics. The difference is that one has some control of the situation in an automobile, but no control at all in the airliner.

A third cause of stress is stress itself. Once emotional responses begin to build up, people will start responding in terms of their perception of these emotional changes as well as to the general situation. The buildup of emotion brings further pressure to act, but the responses that are attempted are often inappropriate, thereby leading to even greater anxiety and stress (which again increases still further the pressure to respond).

Performance under stress   In general, it is useful to consider two levels of our responses to stress. One is the internal physiological level, which is largely responsible for mobilizing the body's biochemical resources to counteract the stress. The other level is the cognitive interpretive level, which is involved in the deployment of cognitive resources to try to cope with a stress-provoking situation. We will consider both of these levels, starting with the cognitive level.

Cognitive responses to stress.   In times of stress and, in particular, of imminent danger, the behavior of people changes but not always in ways that are well suited to deal with the problem at hand. Consider the following situation:

> A crowd of people are in a theater, watching a movie. Suddenly there is smoke and flames. Excitement builds up. Some people rush to the exits and try to open the doors by pushing on them. The doors remain closed. The people push harder, throwing themselves at the doors. They bang, push, shove, but all to no avail. The doors seem to be locked—they withstand all the assaults.
>
> Later on a fire fighter tries the doors. They open easily. The doors were unlocked, but they must be pulled inward to open. During the fire, the panic-stricken people were trying to force the doors open by pushing them outward.

This type of situation has happened. Other similar tragedies occur. People have been killed by persisting in attempts to open doors the wrong way. People have been trapped in the rear seat of two-door vehicles because they were unable to push the front seat forward even though they were trying to push the seat latch, because in some cars the seat latch will not release if there is any pressure pushing against the seat. This arrangement works against the natural responses of a panicked person who only tries to push harder when resistance is encountered.

SCUBA divers have drowned for similar reasons. There are numerous reports of poorly trained divers panicking when they encounter relatively minor mishaps. Often these divers were cold and tired and, in a sudden need to reach the surface, neglected to release the heavy bag of game weighing them down or the lead weights (designed with special easy to release levers). The necessary response was not attempted during the diver's frantic struggle to swim up when weighted down.

All of these situations illustrate a narrowing of perception and a tendency for stereotyped behavior under conditions of high threat and stress. The person in danger seems to concentrate all attentional resources upon one aspect of the situation. When attention is focused upon a single narrow aspect of the problem, it becomes impossible to examine the total situation and generate alternative responses. Without alternatives, the only action possible is to try harder what you just tried before: if a door or seat will not move, push harder; if you are struggling to surface for air, struggle harder.

Easterbrook (1959) has suggested that a state of emotional arousal tends to reduce the number of different cues that a person might utilize in a given situation. This can function as an adaptive response if the excluded cues do not contain vital information. Mandler (1975b) has suggested that an overall reduction in processing efficiency under conditions of high stress and anxiety may result from competition for the limited cognitive resources among both the situational cues being focused upon and also the additional cues that result from the aroused emotional state. Since the arousal cues are nonfunctional, they only add an extra burden to the processing load. Finally, there seems to be a change in the way failures are dealt with. Under ordinary circumstances (without unusual stress), if a response continues to fail to achieve a desired outcome, we will eventually try to reassess the situation in order to generate some alternatives. Under conditions of high stress, it becomes very difficult to do this. We appear to get locked into a maladaptive cycle that can be described as "If at first you don't succeed, try again—but harder."

The management of stress-provoking situations. How can the debilitating effects of stress be avoided? Obviously, either the environment or the person's responses must be changed. Thus, one approach is to attempt to arrange the environment so that the predicted natural responses of people will be the ones that are successful. Sometimes it is impossible to do this. The alternative then is to train people how to deal with stressful situations.

The first solution is so well recognized that it is incorporated into many laws. Thus, most public meeting halls are required to have fire exits plainly marked with automatic, battery-operated lights. Most important, the doors are required to open *outward*, never inward. Some communities do not even allow doorknobs: A long bar is placed on the door so that pressure against it opens the door. The natural flow of a panicked crowd of people would automatically open the door. A similar situation can be observed for many stairways in public buildings. In states of emergency, people run to the stairs and run down as they try to escape from the building. Once they start moving down, there is a tendency to keep going, past the ground floor and on into the basement or garage area. This can lead to people being trapped beneath the building. A solution is to make it difficult to pass the ground floor. You may have noticed that in many public buildings the stairway from the upper floors terminates at the ground floor. Stairs leading to the lower levels are located elsewhere, or are separated from the stairwell above ground by a separate door or gate that closes them off. In fact, this door typically has to be pulled inward to open, making it hard for a fleeing crowd to accidentally pass through. The extra effort required to go below the ground floor can be a lifesaver in times of emergency, even though it is regarded as a nuisance to people using the stairway under normal situations.

If the environment cannot be altered, then people must be trained to cope more rationally with dangerous situations. The SCUBA diver must be trained to respond appropriately even when there has been no air for 30 sec. Automobile and motorcycle drivers and pilots must learn to apply appropriate responses in the face of danger. Highly trained responses to anticipated stressful conditions can go a long way toward reducing panic when the actual situations occur. The more closely the practice drill resembles the potential dangerous situation, the better the chance that the practiced responses will be performed in an actual emergency. It is important that simulated emergencies be practiced over and over again (to the point called "overlearned") so that the person responds automatically and efficiently to the particular situational cues. Indeed, a person who is well practiced for emergencies may not experience the same emotional state as the untrained person. The knowledge that the situation has been successfully coped with before is often sufficient to reduce stress reactions considerably. If emotional reactions are related directly to deviations from one's expectations, then one of the byproducts of a high degree of practice is to provide the individual with the range of models needed to anticipate possible mishaps, together with the full knowledge that the models work: the situation has been met and handled successfully before.

The same principles behind the need to practice responding in dangerous situations also apply to anyone who must perform skilled acts under stressful conditions. Actors and musicians who perform in front of large audiences often become stressed prior to a performance. As a result, their performance is liable to deteriorate. The solution is to have practiced their parts over and over again so that the actions can be done automatically and without any need for thought or decision making. Only when the performance is so well learned that it requires little or no conscious attention can the performer feel confident of an immunity to the disrupting effects of stress.

Physiological responses to stress. A neural subsystem that is involved in the deployment of cognitive and attentional resources would seem to require certain characteristics:

- The system must interact closely with the cognitive processes carried on in the higher cortical centers.
- The system should both monitor and control the efficiency of cortical processing.
- The system should be sensitive to the incoming sensory information so that it can alert the organism when certain incoming signals require priority in the attention and processing given to them.

There exists a neural system with most of these properties. Running through the part of the brain called the midbrain is a loosely packed set of neurons that are interconnected to much of the rest of the brain. The normal activation of the brain depends on the integrity of this area: It is called the *reticular activating system (RAS)*; see Figure 17-1.

The reticular activating system. The sophistication of the reticular function is suggested by the abundance and the complexity of its interconnections with the rest of the central nervous system. Sensory messages pass by the RAS on their way to the cortex. In addition to its sensory-communication network, the reticular system connects directly with brain centers located immediately above it, and also sends out enormous numbers of fibers that connect diffusely throughout the cortex. Communications travel in both directions. The cortex receives large numbers of fibers from the reticular system, and in turn can send messages directly back. Simply from an anatomical point of view, the reticular system is in an ideal position to play a central role in the coordination and integration of the neural traffic in the central nervous system. Studies of the reticular system are just beginning to reveal how central this role is.

Generally, the RAS appears to modulate the overall activity levels of the cortex, affecting the efficiency with which incoming sensory data are processed. Suppose a flash of light or a click is presented to an animal. The flurry of neural impulses generated in the sensory system travels to the sensory receiving area of the cortex where it sets off responses in a large number of cortical brain cells. The synchronized activity of these cortical units can be measured with a gross electrode: It is called an *evoked potential*. In an anesthetized animal, this cortical response to incoming signals seems to die down quickly and is restricted mainly to the region of the cortex that first receives the sensory signals. In an alert animal, the neural response travels widely throughout the cortex and can easily be detected at many different recording locations.

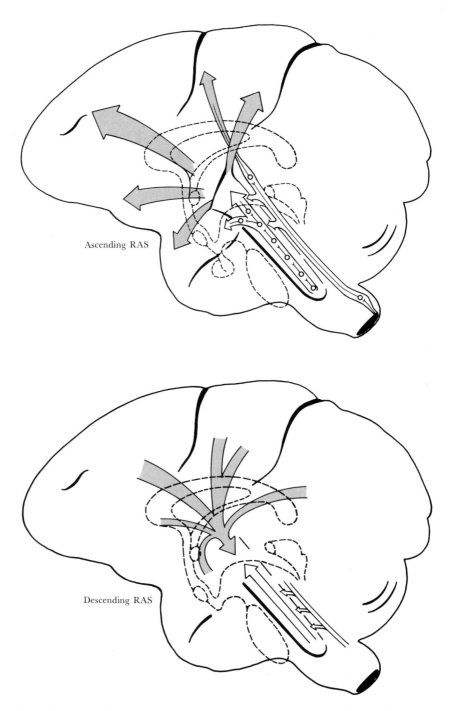

Ascending RAS

Descending RAS

FIGURE 17-1   *Top: The ascending reticular activating system. Bottom: Mutual interaction of messages from the cortex downward and from the reticular activating system upward. From Lindsley (1957).*

The anesthetized animal's insensitivity to signals may thus be due to the failure of the cortex to process the sensory messages beyond the sensory reception areas. Since anesthetics have their primary influence by desensitizing the reticular system, this result suggests that efficient cortical processing depends on a properly functioning reticular system.

There is considerable evidence for this general thesis. If the RAS is activated by an electrode at the same time as an external signal is presented, both the magnitude of the neural response in the sensory cortex and the extent of the spread of activity throughout cortical areas are increased. Similar influences can be found for single cells in the sensory pathways. Neurons in the visual pathways, for example, which are not responding to an incoming signal may suddenly become very active when an electrode embedded in the reticular system is turned on. Reticular activation, however, does not invariably produce an increased sensitivity in the sensory transmission pathways. Activating some areas of the reticular system seems to have the opposite effect—it reduces rather than increases neural activity levels to sensory events.

Changes in the reticular activation level, then, seem to be capable of producing widespread alterations in the conductivity of both cortical and sensory pathways. In turn, the reticular system is influenced by the activity in these networks. Some cells in the RAS seem to be sensitive to activity in any of the sensory systems and may respond with equal vigor to the occurrence of a visual, auditory, tactile, and even an olfactory stimulus. This type of cell appears to be primarily sensitive to the overall level of sensory traffic, rather than to specific characteristics of the sensory message. They are most frequently found in the lower half of the RAS. Other reticular cells are more selective in their responses. Some seem to be primarily monitoring information in a particular modality and are sensitive only to changes in the characteristics of the appropriate signal. These distinctive response patterns have been the basis for dividing the RAS into two separate areas. The lower half, primarily concerned with the gross levels of sensory activity, appears to be sluggish and relatively unselective in its response. Its primary function may be to maintain a lower limit or a background level of arousal or activity. The upper part of the reticular system (often called the *diffuse thalamic projection system*) is more sensitive to transient changes in the level of stimulation and may play a basic role in alerting the organism to changing environmental conditions and modulating the flow of sensory traffic in response to changing environmental demands.

Here is a neural structure capable of monitoring the volume of traffic in the sensory system, of detecting transient changes in environmental stimulation, of altering the characteristics and efficiency of cortical processing, of amplifying or attenuating messages on their way to the cortex, and of receiving messages from higher brain centers which control its own activity. It has important influences on the activity of the organism, ranging all the way from control over sleeping and waking cycles to specific alterations in attention and the efficiency of cortical processing. To an engineer, it has all the earmarks of a communications controller, a system responsible for coordinating the information flow in the nervous system and for controlling the allocation of computations and analytic facilities of the higher nervous centers. We are not quite ready to state this conclusion, however, no matter how intuitively plausible it sounds. Although the data collected so far give us a good start on understanding the RAS, we are still far from understanding the complete story.

Biochemical responses to stress.   Prolonged exposure to stress-provoking situations can gradually overwhelm a person's biochemical defense mechanisms. The result is a weakened individual with lowered resistance who is highly vulnerable to diseases of almost any type.

Selye (1974) has suggested that there is a specific pattern of biochemical reactions that constitutes the body's standardized response to stress. According to Selye, it does not matter whether the stress arises from physical or psychological causes, nor whether the stress is associated with pleasant or unpleasant experiences: the biochemical response patterns are the same. These responses are characterized as the "*nonspecific* response of the body to *any demand* made upon it" (Selye, 1974).

The biochemical responses to stress are controlled primarily by the interaction of several neural and biochemical centers of the brain: the hypothalamus, and the pituitary and the adrenal systems. Once started, the stress response appears to go through three distinct stages known as the *General Adaptation Syndrome* (*GAS*). The first stage of response occurs with the initial exposure to stressful conditions: the *alarm reaction.* This reaction is associated with an increased adrenaline discharge, increased heart rate, reduced body temperature and muscle tone, anemia, and temporary increases in blood sugar levels and stomach acidity. When severe enough, these reactions can lead to the state of clinical shock.

If the source of stress persists, the alarm stage gives way to the second stage: the *stage of resistance.* At this point, the symptoms of the alarm stage disappear as the body mobilizes numerous defense systems to counteract the stressor agent. The major role in this defensive reaction is played by the hypothalamic, pituitary, and adrenal systems. These systems promote an increased development of antibodies and a heightened level of metabolic activity. In addition, there is an increase in the rate of release of chemicals into the blood stream—in particular, an increased release of

Normal   Stressed

Adrenals

Thymus

Lymph nodes

Inner surface
of stomach

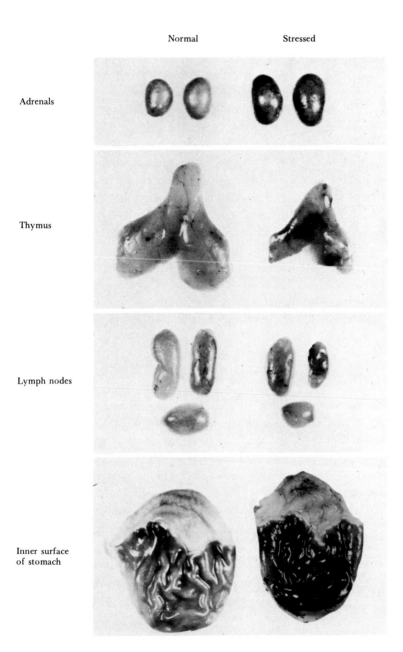

Characteristic symptoms of stress syndrome: enlarged and discol-   FIGURE 17-2
ored adrenals, involuted thymus and lymph nodes, and ulcerated stom-
ach wall. From Selye (1952).

the blood sugar stored in the liver. These factors can be responsible for the development of a number of pathological conditions: one result of prolonged stress is the occurrence of ulcers in the stomach and gastro-intestinal tract. Another is the condition known as hypoglycemia, in which the body's sugar reserves become depleted to such dangerously low levels that any sudden energy demands can exhaust the remaining supply. Hyperactivity in the hypothalamic, pituitary, and adrenal systems during the stage of resistance can also have very profound effects on the physical characteristics of the associated structures (Figure 17-2).

Eventually, the biochemical systems will no longer be able to maintain these high levels of resistance and will give way to the final stage of the GAS, the *stage of exhaustion*. At this point, the adaptation reserves of the organism have been totally depleted. This final condition is irreversible and the individual will inevitably die. The biochemical responses to stress are *nonspecific* in their sensitivity to initiating factors. The same biochemical response patterns occur regardless of the nature of the stressor agent. The general adaptation syndrome can be activated by temperature changes, infections, intoxicants, injury, surgical trauma, as well as psychological conflict, threat, or a persisting inability to cope with the environment.

INTERPRETING EMOTIONAL AROUSAL

A mismatch between expectations and reality can cause a general activation of physiological and cognitive processes. A central issue for the theorist is whether there is a single arousal mechanism that simply alerts the organism and allows any possible response to occur, or if the activation pattern is different for different causes? The proposal that emotional arousal is nonspecific and based on a single underlying mechanism has been called the Juke Box Theory of Emotion (Mandler, 1962).

Emotions: one or many?

As the name implies, according to the Juke Box Theory, the arousal of emotion is somewhat analogous to placing a coin in a juke box: The machine is lit up, ready to go, equally ready to play anything in its collection. The actual behavior is determined only when a particular button is pushed. Emotional activation begins when the coins enter the machine. Environmental factors then select the resulting behavior, just as the pushing of a button selects a particular record.

As with all analogies, the parallels are not meant to be taken literally. One important factor in emotional responses not covered by the analogy is that with emotions, the very events that lead to the response are those that then control the behavior, once the system is activated. This puts a strong bias on what behavior will result from an emotional state.

An alternative theoretical possibility is that activation mechanisms are different for different emotions. After all, are you not aware of the differences in the way your body is aroused by hunger or by cold, fear, or sex? The answer is yes, but no. On the one hand, it is clearly possible to divide the types of neural activation into two general classes: those that excite and those that calm. One set of emotions seems to result from activation of the *sympathetic nervous system* and leads to general tenseness, especially of muscles that help support the body (the so-called antigravity muscles). The typical human pattern is tenseness of the knees, an erect body, clenched hands and jaws. The heart-rate rises, the blood vessels constrict, and there is a rise in blood pressure. In terms of emotions, these are often the symptoms of rage, hate, or anger. Another set of emotions appears to have symptoms that are almost the complete opposite. It results from activation of the *parasympathetic nervous system*. There is a slowing of heart rate, dilation of blood vessels, and a reduction of blood pressure. The limbs tend to bend. In terms of emotions, these are often the symptoms of pleasurable states, of satiation from overeating, for example.

There should be little doubt that body states of tenseness can be distinguished from states of relaxation, at least in the extreme cases. But can finer distinctions be made within those two classes? On this point, the evidence is not so clear. At least one theorist, for example, has argued that these two basic emotions are simply outgrowths of the body's normal defenses against cold and heat (Stanley-Jones, 1970). Contraction of blood vessels and all the related results are part of the defense against cold. Dilation of blood vessels and the resulting relations are part of the defense against heat. According to this theory, a whole set of emotional states have become attached to these two basic physiological reactions. The distinctions we feel among the states—the reason that we do not often confuse being warm with being sexually excited, or being cold with being angry—is that cognitive factors have taken control. Thus, the same cognitive factor that causes relaxation of blood vessels will also cause us to interpret the resulting body states as those of love, not simply overheating.

The problem in resolving the issue comes from the limitations of conscious awareness. In principle, all the psychologist wishes to know is whether such things as tenseness caused by fear can be distinguished from tenseness caused by anger, or even cold. In practice, it is not easy to find out.

Physiological measures. We have mentioned that during emotional arousal many physiological indices change. The obvious question is whether there is a distinctive pattern in the physiological responses associated with the various emotions. How does the physiological state of an organism differ in different emotional states?

In one experiment (Ax, 1953), the subjects were connected up to a variety of physiological monitors and then angered or frightened by the activities of the laboratory assistant (who was actually a confederate of the experimenter). Fear was induced by the assistant's inept handling of the equipment; anger was induced by some well-chosen remarks.

There were some differences in the overall pattern of physiological responses to these two emotions. But the exact activity pattern depends not only on the strength of the emotional arousal, but also on the total context. Moreover, it is difficult to tell whether the physiological differences reflect true underlying physiological causes, or simply reflect the results of the emotional response. Ax found that angry subjects had decreases in heart rate and increases in muscle tension and diastolic blood pressure, whereas fearful subjects breathed faster. But these could have resulted from the subjects' attempts to cope with their perception of fear and anger. Physiological responses are affected by whether or not the individual expresses anger openly. Moreover, even if the internal arousal patterns differ somewhat for different emotions, there is still the question of whether these arousal patterns are distinctive enough to provide the individual with reliable cues about the emotion being experienced.

Biofeedback. Why not take a person's word for it and simply ask people to express what they are "feeling." Even if the question can be answered, there is no way of knowing how much the answer is determined by cognitive factors that created the body states and how much from an actual assessment of those states. Moreover, it is possible to have perfectly controllable body states that a person is unable to describe.

Wiggle the second finger of your hand. Now wiggle the third finger of the same hand. Describe what you did differently these two times. It is simply not possible. Yet the fact that you have such precise control over your finger movements proves that your brain can consciously exert the proper motor commands to move those fingers. Suppose you had to teach someone how to wiggle their fingers—or their ears? How would you start? There is no way to do it by description; you need to use more sophisticated techniques. So it might be with emotional body states. "But," you may complain, "I always know when I am hungry because my stomach rumbles and growls." Wrong. People who have had their stomachs removed still feel the same "stomach pangs." Why do you sometimes feel those pangs only after you have looked at your watch? The feeling is real. But the cause is not accurately known.

One method of trying to assess people's knowledge of body states is to monitor the system and see if people can respond accurately when something happens. Most of the early experiments were failures. In one heroic attempt, a subject was asked to predict which of two lights was going to flash on. The actual light that was turned on was determined by the subject's heart rate: One light went on whenever the rate increased; the other when it decreased. After 5000 trials, there still was no sign of any ability to predict the correct light.

Today, however, it is common practice to have subjects control all sorts of internal body states of which they have no apparent awareness, but they need some external help to do it. If we ask you to meditate, to change the pattern of your brain's electrical activity, for example, you probably wouldn't even know how to begin. But that does not matter; you can be trained, even though you are completely unable to describe what it is that you are doing (just as you cannot describe how you move your finger).

The trick is to use an electronic apparatus that can monitor the electrical signal from the brain (or other body processes) that is to be controlled. For controlling brain waves, this is rather easy to do. Electrical leads are connected to the scalp and the resulting electrical potential is amplified and monitored. This potential is, in turn, used to control the pitch of a tone produced by an audio oscillator. The subject hears this tone over earphones. Normally, the brain activity of people contains a very slow (about 10 Hz) component of reasonably large amplitude whenever they are not thinking about or looking at something; this is the alpha rhythm mentioned previously.

The subjects' task is to produce this alpha activity while they are in an alert, wide-awake state. The way we do this procedure in our own laboratory is as follows: When there is no alpha component in their brain records, the subjects hear a steady, unchanging tone over earphones. But the more alpha rhythm they produce, the lower the pitch of the tone: They are told to make the tone go as low as possible. After some training, many people can turn their alpha rhythms on or off at will.

The control over internal processes such as heart rate and brain waves is possible, though not necessarily easy. It requires some way of making these internal states easily observable to the subject. Thus, the recent evidence tends to refute the view that people are relatively powerless to do anything about what goes on in their own bodies. But most of the recent evidence concerns the ability of people to control their own body functions, and **to control** is not necessarily **to be aware of.**

Interpreting emotions through context   Probably the most elegant experimental demonstration of the interaction between cognitive factors and physiological states in determining emotional experiences is the classic experiment by Schachter and Singer (1962). They felt that to support a cognitive model of emotions it was necessary to demonstrate two basic propositions. First, whether or not people interpret internally aroused states as emotions depends on the context in which the internal arousals occur. If there are alternative explanations for the states, the feelings will not be seen as emotional. To demonstrate this, an experiment should show that if two groups of people are in identical states of physiological arousal, different interpretations about the source of the arousal will lead one group to believe they are undergoing an emotional experience while the other group does not believe this.

The second proposition is that, for people who perceive themselves to be in an emotional state, the exact emotion will depend on the context in which they find themselves. In other words, felt emotions can be changed simply by altering the external circumstances. To demonstrate this proposition requires that two groups of people with identical physiological arousal interpret their emotions entirely differently because of differences in the contexts that they are experiencing.

The experiment. In a very imaginative experiment, Schachter and Singer found support for both of the propositions in the same study. Their experiment proceeded as follows. They started by gathering a group of subjects who had volunteered to participate in an experiment that was supposed to be studying the effects of a new vitamin compound called "Suproxin" on visual acuity. When the subjects arrived for the experiment, they were asked if they minded being injected with the vitamin. If they agreed, they were injected by the attending physician. The actual drug injected was *adrenalin* (or more properly, *epinephrine*), one of the hormones that is normally released into the bloodstream in a wide variety of emotional situations. The point of the adrenaline injections was to create a state of physiological arousal that was "almost a perfect mimicry of a discharge of the sympathetic arousal in the subject's nervous system."

Next, Schachter and Singer manipulated the likelihood that different groups of subjects would attribute the physiological effects they would experience to an emotional arousal. They did this by varying what subjects were told to expect as side effects of the drug. One group, the *informed* condition, was told accurately what to expect from the injection: "Your hands will start to shake, your heart will start to pound, and your face may get warm and flushed." Another group, the *misinformed* condition, was misled about the symptoms: "Your feet will feel numb, you will have itching sensations over parts of your body, and you might get a slight headache." A third group, the *uninformed* condition, was told only that the injection was mild and harmless and would have no side effects.

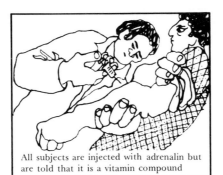

FIGURE 17-3

All subjects are injected with adrenalin but are told that it is a vitamin compound

INFORMED GROUP
Subjects are told they may have side effects of flushed face, trembling hands, and increased heartbeat

UNINFORMED GROUP
Subjects are told that shot will give them no side effects

INFORMED–EUPHORIC
Subject enters room in which another person is laughing, dancing about, and playing games

INFORMED–ANGER
Subject is given insulting questions to answer, another person filling out questionnaire exhibits loud anger

UNINFORMED–EUPHORIC
Subject enters room in which another person is laughing, dancing about, and playing games

UNINFORMED–ANGER
Subject is given insulting questions to answer, another person filling out questionnaire exhibits loud anger

Subject interprets physical sensations as drug side effects and does not follow example of other person

Subject interprets physical sensations as drug side effects and does not follow example of other person

Subject interprets physical sensations as emotional arousal and joins in euphoric behavior with other person

Subject interprets physical sensations as emotional arousal and joins in angry behavior with other person

The environmental conditions.   After being injected, the subjects were put into waiting rooms "to give the injection time to take effect." When a subject entered a waiting room, someone else was already there. Two of the several experimental conditions used for controlling the environment the subject experienced are of interest to us: one called *euphoric*, the other called *anger*. There are now four experimental groups: *informed-euphoric, uninformed-euphoric, informed-anger,* and *uninformed-anger*. In addition to these experimental groups, several *control* groups experienced the environmental conditions, but without receiving injections of adrenaline.

Euphoria.   In the euphoric condition, when the subject entered the waiting room, a rather playful fellow subject was already there. This other person was having a gay time, flying paper airplanes, playing with things in the room, and practicing basketball with a crumbled paper and wastebasket. The subject was continually invited to join the fun.

Anger.   In this condition, the subject was led to the waiting room and asked to fill out a long, rather infuriating questionnaire. A typical question on the form was

With how many men (other than your father) has your mother had extramarital relations?

>   **4 and under _____**
>   **5 through 9 _____**
>   **10 and over _____.**

This question had no function but to annoy the respondent. The other person who was in the waiting room at the same time showed increasing agitation and finally ripped the questionnaire up in rage, slammed it to the floor, denounced it, and stomped from the room.

The results.   Now consider what these various conditions have done. Here are subjects whose biological systems are in a state of arousal and who are left alone in a room with a strangely behaving person. If an emotion simply resulted from a reaction to the combination of internal arousal state and the environment, there should be no difference between the performance of the subjects **informed** about the feelings generated by the drug and those **uninformed.** If the arousal state is specific to a particular type of emotion and independent of the environment, then both the subjects in the **euphoric** group and in the **anger** group should respond similarly. If the environmental factors have strong influence, then they should each act by responding to the behavior of the partner in the waiting room.

What was discovered was very simple. The **informed** subjects calmly went about their tasks, either quietly waiting or filling out the questionnaire, and ignored the antics of their partner. The **uninformed** subjects, however, tended to follow the behavior of their partner, becoming euphoric or angered according to their partner's mood.

Here, then, are two groups of subjects, the informed and the uninformed, with identical internal arousal states and identical environmental experiences. Yet they do different things. Why? One expects the internal feelings being aroused, attributes them (correctly) to the drug injection, and is able to go about their jobs, ignoring the antics of the other person in the room. The others, however, feel their hearts pounding and their faces getting flushed. They have no explanation for these feelings, but they do make sense if they are euphoric or angered. Hence, with no explanation, the subjects are easily manipulated into one of these states.[1]

A MODEL OF EMOTIONAL AROUSAL

There is a large list of experiments that have now been performed which generally support these main points: emotional states are manipulable by the combination of three different factors—*cognitive processes* (expectations), *physiological states*, and *environmental influences*. To say that cognitive factors play an important role in the manipulation of emotional behavior does not mean that we are necessarily consciously aware of our cognitions. When we become angered or threatened by someone's remarks or actions, our logic may tell us there is nothing to be concerned about, while our internal responses may tell us differently. In this case, we can have a large discrepancy between our rationalizations of our behavior and the actual behavior.

To translate the active interpretive theory of emotion into a working system means that we must have several interesting interactions among the processes controlling behavior. First, we need an ongoing system that creates an internal model of the world to provide the expectations that are so important for emotions. That is, a central feature of the system must be cognition: the active development of a picture of the world, including the past, present, and expectations about the future. In addition, we need an assessment of how well things are coming along. How well are our expectations being met? What predictions can we make for the future if things continue along in the same way?

---

[1] In the debriefing, following the experiment, the subjects were told the exact nature of the experiment, informed of the exact drug with which they were injected and the proper side effects, and told that the partner in the waiting room was, in actuality, one of the experimenters.

As we explained previously in footnote 3 of Chapter 16 (page 650), some deception is sometimes necessary in conducting psychological experiments, but whenever this is done the experiment is always followed by a debriefing session in which the exact nature and purpose of the experiment is explained.

Next, we need some way of correcting aberrant behavior. Suppose there is a mismatch between expectations and events. Suppose we must get a term paper in by Friday, or we may fail the course. But examination of how far we have gotten indicates that we are not going to make it. Panic. Tension.

How does the system cause panic? Obviously, it can do the cognitive operations that lead to the prediction that the deadline will not be met. But how does knowledge of that fact change the heart rate, muscle tension, sweat, blood pressure, and even the hunger system?

The basic model is shown in Figure 17-4. This model emphasizes the comparison between a person's expectations and the actual events of the world. The expectations are generated by a person's *cognitive processes,* with the aid of past experiences (from the memory system). This is conceptually driven analysis: it provides a general set of expectations of behavior.

The analysis of the actual environmental situation is a data-driven process. Basically, it consists of *perceptual analysis* of the incoming information. (Perceptual analysis itself must involve both data-driven and conceptually driven processing, and most certainly uses the information stored within memory. But for the purposes here, the perceptual analysis is the source of information about the environment, and so plays the role of a data-driven process.)

The mechanism that compares the expectations with reality is called the *cognitive comparator* in the figure. It matches the real-world events against the internally generated expectations. When there is a sufficient mismatch of expectations with actual events (or when expectations are for a highly undesirable state for which there seems to be no way of

FIGURE 17-4

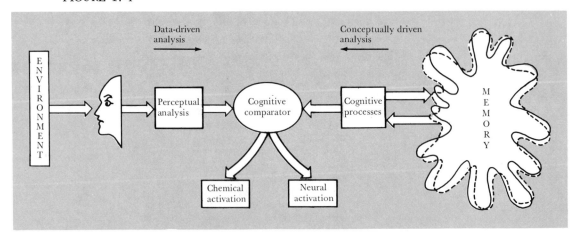

coping), then the cognitive comparator triggers the release of appropriate chemicals (mostly hormones) into the biochemical structure of the
body. This changes the neural activation of brain structures. These biochemical changes will, in turn, be picked up by the normal monitoring
systems of the body and will become part of the information used by the
cognitive processor.

The whole picture might look like Figure 17-5. Note what we have
shown. The cognitive system can control biological emotional processes.
Similarly, the biochemical system can control actions. The whole picture
is a circular, feedback control system. If actions are not going well, the
cognitive system is likely to send out error messages by means of chemical
stimulation—it might shoot adrenaline into the system. But this stimulation might be exactly the opposite of what is needed. Today we seldom
need to kill tigers. Instead, we need to solve intellectual problems. The
rise in tension and body states is likely to be disastrous for the solving of
problems. Furthermore, it is not unlikely that the poor human whose

FIGURE 17-5

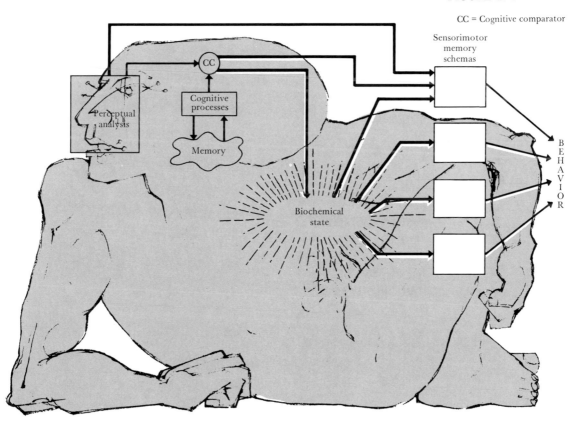

CC = Cognitive comparator

Sensorimotor
memory
schemas

CC

Perceptual
analysis

Cognitive
processes

Memory

Biochemical
state

BEHAVIOR

system has just activated itself might notice all the physiological changes occurring—increased heart rate, deep breathing, tension, sweating—and conclude that he or she is frightened. Then things really can get out of hand, for if someone is frightened, the natural response is to run. *(All this for a term paper.)*

The system we have outlined works simultaneously in all directions. The cognitive aspect of fear can cause biochemical (hormonal) stimulation of the body. But, in turn, the inflow of hormones into the body can lead to fear. How are we ever to tell which causes which? Why do we care? The important thing about this system is the way the various pieces interact with one another. Cognition and emotion are intimately intermingled with each other.

REVIEW OF TERMS AND CONCEPTS   In this chapter, the following terms and concepts that we consider to be important have been used. Please look them over. If you are not able to give a short explanation of any of them, you should go back and review the appropriate sections of the chapter.

Terms and concepts you should know

Stress
   the role of cognitive interpretation
   learned helplessness
   inability to cope
   interruption
   frustration
Performance under stress
   attentional factors
   attending to the stress itself
   the role of training
   how to change the environment
Physiological responses to stress
   hormonal changes
   the general adaptation syndrome
      alarm reaction
      stage of resistance
      stage of exhaustion
Interpreting emotion
   the juke box theory
   biofeedback: sensitivity to internal states
   the Schachter–Singer experiment
      the basic experimental design
      the conclusions

A model of emotional arousal
    data-driven and conceptually driven comparisons
    the role of perceptual analysis
    cognitive processes
    cognitive comparator

Without any doubt, the most thorough book on motivation and emotion is the massive review by Cofer and Appley, *Motivation: Theory and research* (1964). This 958-page volume discusses most of the concepts discussed in this chapter and obviously much more. Some of the book is rather advanced, and some of the work is a bit dated by now, but still the book remains one of the best sources of information. Selye has probably written more on the topic of stress than any other person: see his book *Stress without distress* (1974), for example. The book by Cofer and Appley also covers the earlier research on stress. Lazarus (1966) has provided some of the information used in this chapter. The effect of stress on performance is reviewed in Chapter 4 of Norman (1976). The basic model of performance under stress comes from the work of Easterbrook (1959). Seligman's (1975) work on helplessness provided the background material for our discussion of the state of depression, especially that caused by a general feeling of helplessness in coping with the world.

    The studies on interpreting emotional arousal are reported in Schachter (1967), Schachter and Singer (1962), and Schachter and Wheeler (1962). These earlier papers are reviewed in the article "Emotion" by Mandler (1962). A much more recent review and synthesis of the studies is provided by Mandler's (1975b) book, *Mind and emotion*. In general, this book is the best source that we have found for theoretical views on emotion. See also the small collection of papers edited by Weiner (1974).

    Schachter's (1971) book *Emotion, obesity, and crime* ties together work from several different areas, starting with the Schachter and Singer study reported in this chapter. Schachter and Rodin (1974) present an interesting set of studies portraying the performance of obese people as essentially data-driven individuals, reacting to events in the environment and therefore easily distractible.

SUGGESTED
READINGS

APPENDIX A
Measuring psychological variables

SCALING

Listen to some music. How loud is it? The obvious immediate response is to say something like **not very,** or **extremely.** This will hardly do. We need some precise way of specifying what is heard; some way that will allow us to generalize across many people and make predictions of impressions about new sounds. Moreover, to understand how the nervous system operates, we must be able to match subjective impressions of loudness with the known properties of the physical sound and of the sensory system. Basically, we need precise quantitative numbers, not words like "but it is very loud." For the problems discussed in this book, we need some way of scaling or measuring our perceptions of loudness, pitch, brightness, and hue.

Let us put some numbers to the psychological dimensions. The task is to determine the exact numerical relationships that hold between the physical and the psychological experiences. To do this requires a method of measuring psychological impressions: a scaling technique. It is not enough to assign numbers to psychological experiences; we need to be concerned about the mathematical meaning that we can attach to the numbers so assigned.

Scale types

Nominal scale. For example, if numbers are assigned arbitrarily to different objects—something like the way the uniforms of baseball and football players are numbered—we have performed a valuable service by allowing the different objects to be identified. This assignment of numbers fulfills a naming requirement, but quite clearly, the particular values of numbers that have been assigned are irrelevant. Hence, this type of assignment of numbers to objects is the weakest possible use of numbers to scale something. The numerical scale so formed is called a *nominal scale* (nominal for naming).

Ordinal scale. The next level of sophistication in scaling comes about when the numbers assigned to the objects bear some correspondence to the mathematical properties of numbers. The most common next step in scaling is to order the objects to be scaled so that the assignment of numbers reflects the ordering. This type of scale is called an *ordinal scale* (ordinal for order). Scales for hardness of rocks or quality of lumber, such that the larger the number, the harder the rock or the higher quality the lumber, are ordinal scales. Similarly, if the people in a room are numbered by lining them up in alphabetical order, giving the first person in line the number 1 and proceeding down the line, we have established an ordinal scale. Someone with a number of eight is not twice someone with the number four; that name simply starts later in the alphabet.

Interval scale.   Better than an ordinal scale is one in which the differences between the numbers represent the differences in psychological value. Scales in which the intervals between numbers represent a meaningful concept are called *interval scales*. The normal temperature scales used in the home are interval scales (Farenheit and Celsius). The temperature chosen to be labeled 0° is completely arbitrary, but the difference in temperature between an object that is 80° and one that is 70° is exactly the same as the difference between an object that is 40° and one that is 30°. Ratios are meaningless. An object with a temperature of 80° does not have twice as much heat as an object with a temperature of 40°. In an interval scale, only the differences among the scale values are meaningful. The value that is assigned to be zero is quite arbitrary and could be changed without affecting the validity of the scale.

Ratio scale.   Finally, among the most desirable of the methods of scaling is the technique that leads to meaningful intervals and ratios among the numbers assigned: the *ratio scale*. Thus, when someone's height is specified in inches, if we get a value of 80, it means that person is twice the height of someone whose height is 40. Both the intervals and the zero point are meaningful in a ratio scale. The specification of temperature on the Kelvin scale or as absolute temperature leads to a ratio scale. Length, height, weight, and monetary value are all examples of ratio scales. Ratio scales are not the highest form of scale type, for the particular number assigned to an object is still somewhat arbitrary. After all, we can say that someone's height is 80 inches, 6.67 feet, 203 centimeters, or 2.22 yards. Multiplying all the scale values by a constant does not destroy any of the interval or ratio properties of the scale.

Absolute scale.   Occasionally, we can find examples of absolute assignment of numbers to objects, so strictly determined that we cannot change the numbers at all, not even by multiplication, without affecting the relationships that hold among the items. Such a scale is called an *absolute scale*. The number of things in a pile is counted on an absolute scale.

Scaling techniques   There are many ways by which psychologists go about the business of assigning numbers to psychological attributes. Two basic procedures are now used most widely. The first method is called *confusion scaling*, the second *direct scaling*.

Confusion scaling.   With this procedure, the psychological distance of two objects is determined by the number of times that they are confused with one another. Suppose that we wish to determine the relative spacing of the psychological **sweetness** of different amounts of sugar (sucrose) concentration. Suppose we take an accurately measured cup of distilled water and put in it exactly 1 teaspoon of sugar. This would produce a solution with some amount of sweetness to it. Call this amount the *standard sweetness*. Now, make up ten other sugar solutions, five with concentrations progressively less, five with concentrations progressively more than the standard, giving eleven different concentrations of sugar water, each differing from the next in very tiny steps, perhaps like this:

*Amount of Sugar Dissolved in 1 Cup of
Distilled Water*

.5 teaspoon		1.1 teaspoons
.6 teaspoon		1.2 teaspoons
.7 teaspoon	*1.0 teaspoons*	1.3 teaspoons
.8 teaspoon	*(the standard)*	1.4 teaspoons
.9 teaspoon		1.5 teaspoons

By asking subjects to taste a pair of concentrations, always comparing the **standard** with one of the other solutions (called the **comparison**), indicating which they believe to be sweeter, we determine relative sensitivity to taste.[1]

When concentrations were relatively similar (such as the comparison between 1.0 and 1.1 teaspoons), there would often be confusion. When concentrations were very different (as with the comparison between ably typical set of results is shown in Figure A-1.

This set of results shows just how accurately a person can discriminate between two different levels of sweetness, a standard value of 1.0 and a comparison value given by the points along the horizontal axis. This function is called a *psychometric function*. It plays an important role. We see that when comparing, say, the standard with a concentration of 1.4, the solution of 1.4 is judged to be sweeter than the standard about 88% of the time. Thus, the judgment is in error 12% of the time. If we look at Figure A-1, we see that the judgment of sweetness is also in error about 12% of the time when the concentration slightly less than .7 is compared with the standard of 1.0.

---

[1] In an actual experiment, of course, we would probably specify sweetness in terms of molar concentration of sucrose, not simply as teaspoons per cup of distilled water. In making the comparisons, we would use people with a good deal of experience at this task. They would be asked to compare solutions in identical containers by sipping a measured amount of the fluid and then spitting out each sample so that nothing was swallowed. After each taste, the mouth would be rinsed with some neutral fluid, probably distilled water. The order of the comparison substance and the standard would vary randomly, with the subjects never knowing which solution was the standard: They would simply be asked to say which fluid was sweeter, the first or the second sampled.

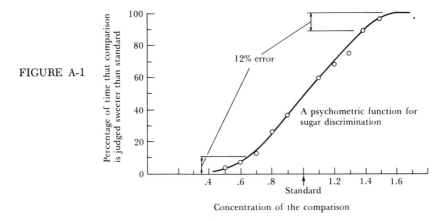

FIGURE A-1

A psychometric function for sugar discrimination

12% error

Percentage of time that comparison is judged sweeter than standard

Concentration of the comparison

If concentrations of 1.4 and .7 are equally often confused with the standard, does that mean that they are equally distant from the standard in terms of their psychological scale values? The method of confusion scaling is based on this assumption:

- **Two physical differences that are equally often confused are psychologically equal.**

This is the basis of confusion scaling. It allows us to equate differences between psychological scale values: Hence, it specifies the objects measured on an *interval scale*.

Confusion scaling has played an extremely important role in the history of psychology. It is the basis of the most widely used and most important result of psychological scaling procedures: the *intelligence scale (IQ)*. Further discussion of the assumptions and implications of this method of scaling is presented in Appendix B.

Direct scaling. An alternative method of assigning numerical scale values to psychological phenomena is quite a bit simpler than the method of confusion scaling: We simply ask people to assign numbers to physical attributes in ways that are proportional to their subjective impressions. This direction procedure originated with the work of Professor S. S. Stevens at Harvard University, and the rest of this section is devoted to a description of the method and the several techniques for using it.

Magnitude estimation   The basic technique is simple. One simply presents a signal to the subjects and asks them to judge it relative to a standard. Stevens (1956) describes the genesis of the technique in these words:

It all started from a friendly argument with a colleague, who said, "You seem to maintain that each loudness has a number and that if someone sounded a tone I would be able to tell him the number." I replied, "That's an interesting idea. Let's try it." We agreed that, as in any problem of measurement, we would need first to decide on a modulus—a size for our unit—so I sounded a loud tone and we agreed to call its loudness 100. I then presented a series of other intensities in random order and, with a readiness that surprised both of us, he assigned numbers to them in a thoroughly consistent manner.

That was my first use of the method. Only after working with this procedure for a couple of months did I discover—or rediscover—that it is basically similar to the method used by Richardson and Ross (1930), which I had described in 1938 (Stevens and Davis, 1938). How easily one forgets!

Anyhow, the evidence accumulated over the past two years suggests that, if properly used, the method of magnitude-estimation can provide a simple, direct means of determining a scale of subjective magnitude. The method has wide potential utility, but like all psychophysical methods it has its pitfalls and its sources of potential bias. In any given situation, most of the distorting factors can probably be discovered and either avoided or balanced out of the experimental design [p. 21].

After years of experience with magnitude estimation as a tool for measuring subjective experience, it would appear to be a reliable, robust method. It is simple and effective. It gives reliable answers, so reliable that it can be used in a class as a demonstration of scaling without any fear that the answers will come out wrong. In fact, the main difficulties with the method come when the experimenter tries to help it along by suggesting that the subject might limit the numbers used; or by presenting the standard over and over again, lest the subject forget what it was like; or perhaps by collecting many trials of responses to get a good statistical reliability. All of these improvements make things worse. As Stevens says, the experimenter "should keep hands off and let the observers make their own judgements." In fact, it is not even necessary to present the standard. Let the subjects assign whatever numbers they feel appropriate to each stimulus as it is presented. This is much more natural for the subjects than arbitrarily telling them what number they should use for that first one. Actually, today most experimenters do not use numbers. They use instead a procedure called *cross-modality matching* (described a couple of sections hence).

The power law   For many sensory functions, the psychological impression of the physical intensity follows a simple mathematical function: the *power function*. For example, loudness and brightness increase in subjective magnitude proportionally to the $\frac{1}{3}$ power (the cube root) of the physical intensity of the sound or light. Heaviness increases with the 1.5 power of the actual weight of an object; psychological judgment of the duration of a sound increases almost linearly (to the power 1) with the actual time span as measured in seconds. In general, for many sensory phenomena,

$$J = kI^p,$$

where J is the Judgment of psychological magnitude, I is the physical Intensity, p is the *p*ower, the size of the exponent that governs the relationship between physical and psychological magnitude, k is an arbitrary constant, simply serving to get the psychological magnitude into the actual numbers used by subjects. If loudness grows with the cube root of sound intensity, then $p = \frac{1}{3}$ or .3. If a sound intensity of 1 were assigned a response of 100 by the subject, then $k = 100$. Thus, we would predict that a sound intensity of 8 would receive a response of 200 by the subject. The relationship is called a power law, because we raise physical intensity to a power (I^p) to get psychological magnitude. (Note that this is not an exponential function—the expression p^I would be exponential. In a power function, the variable of interest, I, is raised to a power. In an exponential function, the variable of interest is in the exponent.) The relationship is also called Stevens' Law, after the psychologist who has developed the technique, promulgated the
Table A-1   procedure, and verified its applicability to a large variety of areas.

"How much" versus   We can distinguish between two kinds of sensations, one that deals with
"what kind"   the question **how much,** the other with the question of **what kind** or **where.** It would appear that Stevens' law of the power function applies to all relationships between physical and psychological variables that deal with the question of **how much.** The distinction between these kinds of sensations is simple, but important.

The psychological continuum that deals with **how much** of something is present is *additive;* it changes from one level to another by adding on to or subtracting from whatever is already present. Weight is an additive dimension, since we increase and decrease weight by adding on or taking away mass. Moreover, we assume that the psychological correlate of heaviness comes about through the number and rate at which the neurons respond: More weight means more responses. Loud-

Table A-1

Judgment	Power
Loudness (one ear)	.3
Brightness, dark-adapted eye, target of 5°	.3
Smell of coffee odor	.55
Taste of saccharine	.8
Taste of salt	1.3
Taste of sucrose	1.3
Cold (on arm)	1.0
Warmth (on arm)	1.6
Thickness of wood blocks as felt by fingers	1.3
Heaviness of lifted weights	1.5
Force of a handgrip	1.7
Loudness of one's own voice	1.1
Electric shock applied to fingers (60 Hz)	3.5
Length of a line	1.0

ness, intensity of a smell or taste, force of a handgrip, and felt intensity of an electric shock all appear to be additive dimensions. They all yield power functions. They all intuitively fit the notion of something increasing. Such an additive continuum is named a *prothetic continuum*.

The psychological continuum that deals with **what kind** or **where** is *substitutive;* it changes from one value to another by substituting the new for the old. If pressure is applied to the skin, pressure changes are additive. They are performed by increasing or decreasing the amount already being applied. Pressure is a prothetic dimension. But, if we vary the location of the pressure on the skin, that is a substitutive action. We take away the old pressure and replace it with one at a different location. The psychological correlate of a substitutive dimension comes about by one group of neurons ceasing their responses and a different group starting. Pitch, apparent inclination of the body, felt location of an object, and location of a sound all appear to be substitutive. These dimensions do not necessarily yield power functions. They all fit the intuitive notion that something has been replaced. Such a substitutive continuum is named a *metathetic continuum*.

Interpretation of the power function

The power function is simply stated as $J = kI^p$. By taking logarithms of both sides of this equation, we find that

$$\log J = p \log I + \log k.$$

This is a simple result. It means that plotting the logarithm of psychological intensity on the vertical axis of a graph and the logarithm of physical intensity on the horizontal axis gives a straight line which has a slope of p and an intercept of log k. Alternatively, the points can be plotted on the special graph paper which has both axes stretched out logarithmically—the graph paper which is called log–log paper. This simple relationship makes it easy to test the power function: When the results are plotted on log–log paper they ought to lie in a straight line.

FIGURE A-2

From Stevens (1961a).

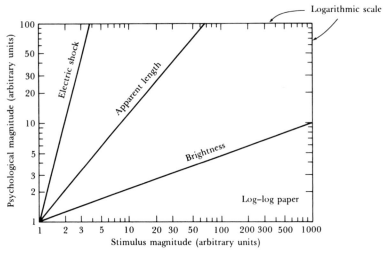

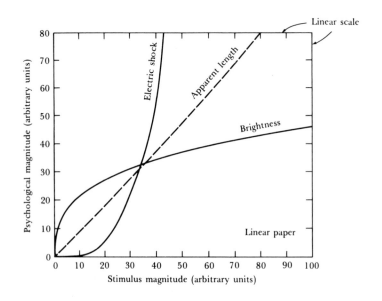

As you can see from Figure A-2, the log–log portrayal is extremely simple and easy to work with. Note, by the way, that judgments of apparent length vary almost exactly with actual length. The exponent of the power function is 1.0, which means that $J = kI$. Because $p = 1$, the power law reduces in this case to simple proportionality.

It is possible to use magnitude estimation procedures to judge almost any psychological dimension that is additive (or prothetic). Sellin and Wolfgang (1964) used this technique as a tool for measuring the way that society viewed the seriousness of crimes and of punishments. For example, subjects (juvenile court judges, police officers, college students) rated the seriousness of crimes. They judged that stealing and abandoning a car is .1 times the seriousness as robbing a man of $5 and wounding him. The robbery increases in the seriousness of the crime by a factor of 2.5 if the robbery victim is killed. Ratings on the seriousness of a robbery as a function of the amount of money stolen produced a power function with an exponent of .17. Thus, in order for one crime to be considered twice as serious as another, about 70 times the amount of money must be stolen [$70^{.17} = 2$].

Range of applicability

Figures A-3 & A-4

One difficulty with magnitude estimation is its reliance on numbers. How does one assign a number to a sensation? Look at the brightness of this book page. What number do you assign to it? 10? 1000? 45.239? Serious objections to the magnitude-estimation procedure have often been raised, usually because one feels that the rules we have learned

Cross-modality matching

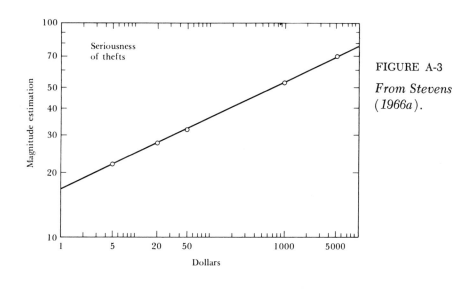

FIGURE A-3

From Stevens (1966a).

FIGURE A-4

From Stevens (1961a).

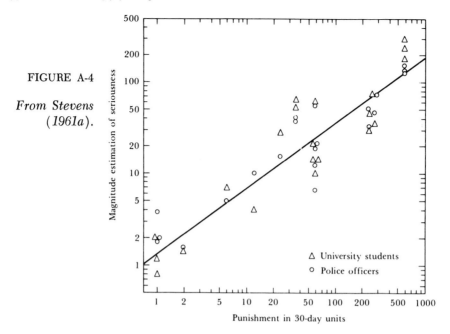

about the mathematics of numbers somehow must force the results to be power functions, even though the underlying psychological sensations are not. One answer to this criticism is to ask why there is such consistency in the results when we give many different people the same task. Surely, people's experiences must differ, so one would expect that difference to be reflected in the estimations. But if there were some artifact in the procedure which always produced power functions, why should pitch and position be exempt?

FIGURE A-5

From Stevens (1966a).

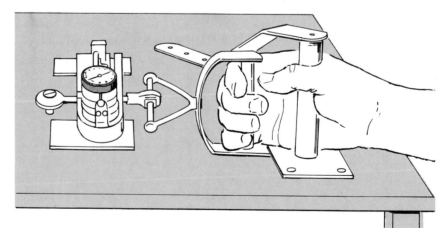

A simple way to avoid the criticism, however, is simply to avoid the use of numbers. The easy way is to have people judge the subjective magnitude of one event by producing an outcome that they feel is equal in subjective value.

One simple method is to have subjects listen to different sound intensities, say, and tell us their loudness by squeezing their hand as hard as they feel the sound to be loud. We measure the squeeze pressure with a dynamometer. Alternatively, we could have someone adjust the intensity of a tone until it sounded as loud as a light was bright, or draw a line as long as sandpaper was rough, or adjust an electric shock to have the same psychological magnitude as the strength of the odor of coffee. Does this seem a strange method to you? Try it (see the experiment described later in this section). The description is strange, but in practice it is quite simple and direct.

We can predict what the results of these cross-modality matches should be. Let us compare two continua, A and B. We do standard magnitude-estimation experiments for each, finding that for intensity values of I_A and I_B, the judgments of psychological magnitudes J_A and J_B are represented this way:

For estimates of A:

$$J_A = k_A I_A{}^a.$$

For estimates of B:

$$J_B = k_B I_B{}^b.$$

Now, if we ask our subjects to observe a signal from A that has intensity I_A and produce a value of intensity on B, I_B, so that the two psychological impressions are equal, we know that

$$J_A = J_B,$$

and so

$$k_A I_A{}^a = k_B I_B{}^b.$$

Thus, if we solve for the value of I_B necessary for the judgment of B to match that of A

$$I_B{}^b = \frac{k_A I_A{}^a}{k_B}$$

and, taking the bth root of both sides,

$$I_B = k I_A{}^{a/b}, \qquad \text{where} \quad k = \frac{k_A}{k_B}.$$

Thus, we still get a power function when we plot the intensity of B that the subjects claim matches the subjective impression of the intensity of A. The exponent of the power function obtained by cross-modality matching is given by the ratios of the exponents which we get in a magnitude estimation experiment.

Table A-2   The Exponents (Slopes) of Equal-Sensation Functions, as Predicted from Ratio Scales of Subjective Magnitude, and as Obtained by Matching with Force of Handgrip[a]

| | *Ratio Scale* | | *Scaling by Means of Handgrip* | |
Continuum	*Exponent of Power Function*	*Stimulus Range*	*Predicted Exponent*	*Obtained Exponent*
Electric shock (60-cycle current)	3.5	0.29–0.72 milliampere	2.06	2.13
Temperature (warm)	1.6	2.0–14.5°C above neutral temperature	.94	.96
Heaviness of lifted weights	1.45	28–480 gm	.85	.79
Pressure on palm	1.1	0.5–5.0 lb	.65	.67
Temperature (cold)	1.0	3.3–30.6°C below neutral temperature	.59	.60
60-Hz vibration	.95	17–47 dB re approximate threshold	.56	.56
Loudness of white noise[b]	.6	59–95 dB re .0002 dyne/cm²	.35	.41
Loudness of 1000-Hz tone[b]	.6	47–87 dB re .0002 dyne/cm²	.35	.35
Brightness of white light	.33	59–96 dB re 10^{-10} lambert	.20	.21

[a] From Stevens (1961a).

[b] There is a technical issue here that often causes confusion. We specified that the exponent for loudness judgments as a function of sound intensity had a value of .3. Yet the table shown here lists the exponent as .6. Why the discrepancy? The answer is simply that sound is measured both in units of energy and amplitude. Sound *intensity* refers to energy measurements; *sound pressure level (SPL)* refers to amplitude measurements. Sound energy is proportional to sound amplitude squared ($I \approx A^2$). Hence, if we write the power function, we find that

$$J \approx I^{.3} \approx (A^2)^{.3} \approx A^{.6}.$$

Both exponents are correct: .6 applies when sound pressures are measured; .3 when sound intensities are used.

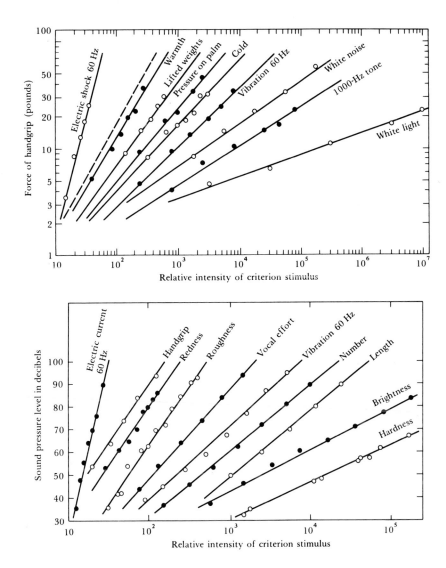

Top: Equal-sensation functions obtained by matching force of handgrip to various criterion stimuli. The relative position of a function along the horizontal axis is arbitrary. The dashed line shows a slope of 1.0 in these coordinates. Bottom: Equal-sensation functions obtained by matches between loudness and various criterion stimuli. The relative positions of the functions are arbitrary, but the slopes are those determined by the data. From Stevens (1966d).

FIGURE A-6

How to scale   *Method.* Take a piece of lined paper and letter the lines from A to H (8 lines). You will write your responses on these lines. You will be presented with a series of stimuli in irregular order. Your task is to tell the immediate psychological impression they make on you by assigning numbers to them. Don't try to make any computations; simply write down what comes to mind.

The first item shown to you is the standard. Assign a value of 1 to it. Then as you look at the other stimulus items, assign numbers such that they reflect your subjective impression. For example, if a stimulus seems 20 times as intense, assign the number 20 to it. If it seems $\frac{1}{5}$ as intense, assign the numbers .2 (or $\frac{1}{5}$) to it, and so on. Use fractions, very large numbers or very small numbers. Just make each assignment
Figures A-7 & A-8 proportional to your subjective impressions.

Write down your answers in order down the answer sheet. Do **not** look at previous responses. It would be best to cover each response

FIGURE A-7

AREAS

Take a blank piece of lined paper and label the lines from A to H. Now, judge the *area* of each circle relative to the *area* of the standard. No computations, simply write down your subjective impression. The standard circle is assigned a value of 1. Cover all the other circles and then

expose them to view one at a time. If you think a circle is five times the area of the standard, write down 5 for its value. If you think it is 1/10, write down 1/10. Do *not* look back over either your answers, the other circles, or the standard.

This is the **standard** circle: Call its area 1.   /Standard

Now, cover the circles below. Cover the standard. Expose only one of the circles below at a time.

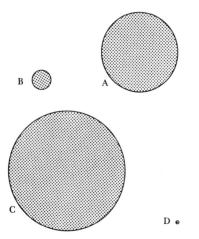

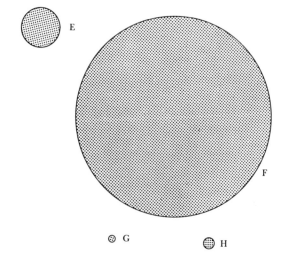

FIGURE A-8

NUMBER OF DOTS
Take a blank piece of paper and label the
lines from A to H. Now, judge how many dots
each square contains relative to the number
in the standard. No counting, simply write
down your subjective impression. The number
of dots in the standard square is assigned
a value of 1.

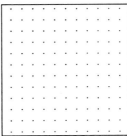

Standard

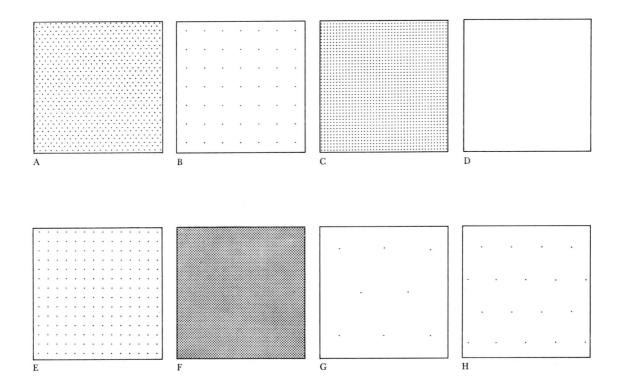

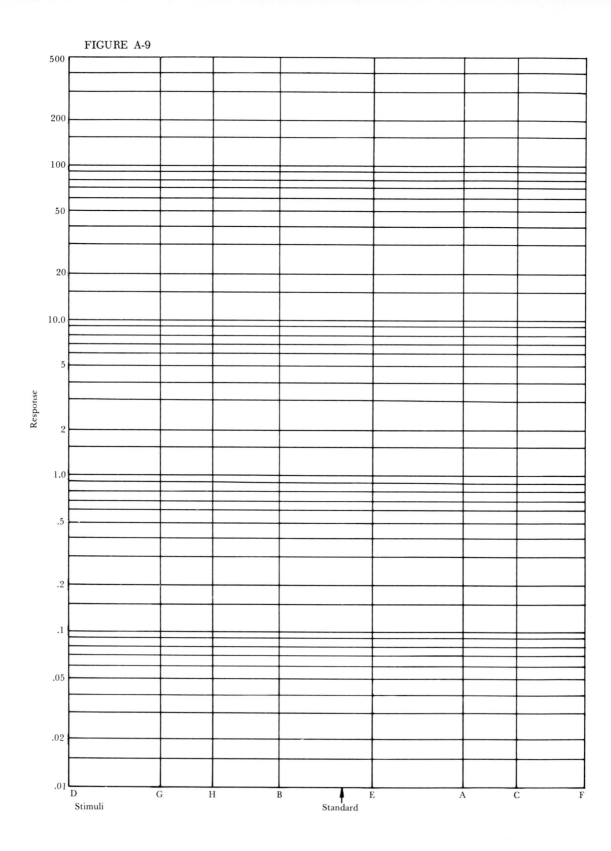

FIGURE A-9

as you make it. Don't be concerned if you think you forgot what the original standard looked like. Everything will work out fine.

Remember, make assignments according to your immediate impressions. The standard is 1. If something looks 5 times as much as the standard, give it a number 5. Now do both the experiments in judging areas and numerosity.

Analysis of results. Plot the number you assigned to each stimulus item for both area judgments and numerosity on Figure A-9 (use different symbols, and use pencil so you can erase). (You might find the fraction-to-decimal conversion factors listed in Table A-3 to be useful.) Note that we have already put the stimulus items at their proper location along the horizontal axis of each graph. The scales for both horizontal and vertical axes on the graph are spaced logarithmically. That is, we have used log–log paper for the graph. This type of paper should make your data points fall along straight lines. Actually, there will be a lot of statistical variability ("noise") in the points, so they will not actually fit a straight line. But if you draw the two best possible straight lines through the points, one for areas and the other for numerosity, the deviations should not be too bad.

Table A-3   Conversions of Fractions to Decimals

$\frac{1}{32}$	.03	$\frac{9}{32}$	.28	$\frac{17}{32}$	.53	$\frac{25}{32}$	.78
$\frac{1}{16}$	.06	$\frac{5}{16}$	.31	$\frac{9}{16}$	.56	$\frac{13}{16}$	.81
$\frac{3}{32}$	.09	$\frac{11}{32}$	.34	$\frac{19}{32}$	.59	$\frac{27}{32}$	.84
$\frac{1}{8}$	.13	$\frac{3}{8}$	.38	$\frac{5}{8}$	.63	$\frac{7}{8}$	.88
$\frac{5}{32}$	.16	$\frac{13}{32}$	.41	$\frac{21}{32}$	.66	$\frac{29}{32}$	.91
$\frac{3}{16}$	.19	$\frac{7}{16}$	.44	$\frac{11}{16}$	.69	$\frac{15}{16}$	.94
$\frac{7}{32}$	.22	$\frac{15}{32}$	.47	$\frac{23}{32}$	.72	$\frac{31}{32}$	.97
$\frac{1}{4}$	.25	$\frac{1}{2}$	.50	$\frac{3}{4}$	.75		

$\frac{1}{2}$	.50	$\frac{1}{9}$	.11	$\frac{1}{16}$	.063	$\frac{1}{40}$	.025
$\frac{1}{3}$	.33	$\frac{1}{10}$	.100	$\frac{1}{17}$	.059	$\frac{1}{50}$	.020
$\frac{1}{4}$	.25	$\frac{1}{11}$	.091	$\frac{1}{18}$	.056	$\frac{1}{60}$	.017
$\frac{1}{5}$	.20	$\frac{1}{12}$	.083	$\frac{1}{19}$	.053	$\frac{1}{70}$	.014
$\frac{1}{6}$	.17	$\frac{1}{13}$	.077	$\frac{1}{20}$	.050	$\frac{1}{80}$	.013
$\frac{1}{7}$	.14	$\frac{1}{14}$	.071	$\frac{1}{25}$	.040	$\frac{1}{90}$	.011
$\frac{1}{8}$	.13	$\frac{1}{15}$	.067	$\frac{1}{30}$	.033	$\frac{1}{100}$	.010

Cross-modality matching. Remember that one objection to magnitude estimation procedures is that they require subjects to produce numbers

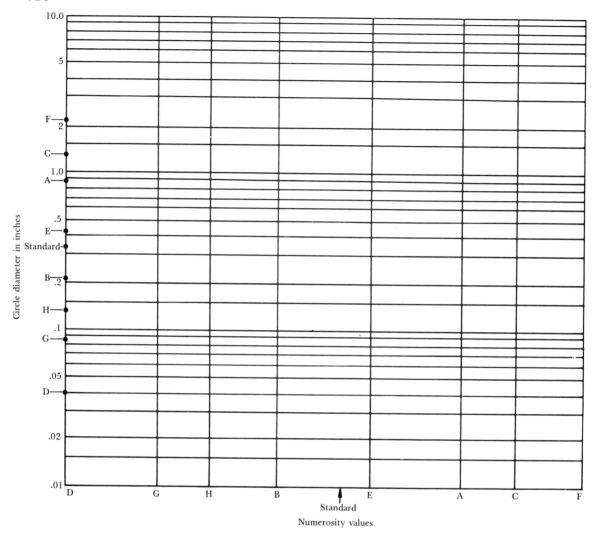

FIGURE A-10

as responses, a rather arbitrary scheme. But we need not use numbers. Go back through the assessment of numerosity again. But this time, respond by drawing a circle instead of giving a number. Draw a circle whose area is as large as the dots are numerous. That is not as difficult as it seems. If the dots look to be five times more numerous than the dots on the standard, simply draw a circle whose area is five times that of the standard circle. In fact, you should not think of numbers at all: Just look, and draw whatever feels right.

Analysis. Plot circle size against numerosity. To make this easy for you, we provide a graph, Figure A-10, with the numerosity stimuli already placed along the horizontal axis. You can plot circle size on the vertical axis. Circle size should be specified on the graph as the size of the circle diameter, measured in inches (use pencil again). (The table of conversions between fractional inches and decimals, Table A-3, will be of use to you.)

See whether you can predict your results. Look back at the magnitude estimation functions for these two stimuli. Find the numerical response you gave to numerosity value C. Now look up on the magnitude estimation function for the area size that would have given the same response. (You will have to draw the best straight line through your points and interpolate the answer, since it is unlikely that one of the sizes of circles we gave you will match exactly the number you are looking up.) Now you know how the numbers predict that circle area matches with numerosity. In fact, by checking several values of numerosity and circle area, you can draw the complete predicted function: How well do they match?

Perhaps the best spot to start is with the papers by Stevens. He has clearly elucidated the issues and problems faced in measuring psychological attributes. The basic article on scaling, which describes the various types of scales, is Chapter 1 of the *Handbook of experimental psychology*, edited by Stevens (1951). This chapter does not discuss magnitude estimation techniques nor the power function: That was developed after 1951. Another excellent introduction to measurement theory comes from the article by Galanter in the book *New directions in psychology I* by Brown, Galanter, Hess, and Mandler (1962).

A good review of many of the results is provided by Stevens' article (1961a) in the book *Sensory communication,* edited by Rosenblith (1961). The application of the scaling techniques to social issues and opinions (such as illustrated in this section by the rating of seriousness of crime) can be found in Stevens (1966a,b, 1968). The study on rating the seriousness of crime and punishment was done by Sellin and Wolfgang (1964). An interesting expansion of power functions to account for changes that result from masking and glare can be found in Stevens (1966c).

A mathematical description of scaling (with emphasis on various variations of confusion scaling) can be found in Chapters 2, 3, and 4 of Coombs, Dawes, and Tversky, *Mathematical psychology: An introduc-*

SUGGESTED READINGS

tion (1970). An even more advanced treatment, for those of you with the necessary mathematical background, can be found in Chapter 1 of Volume 1 of the *Handbook of mathematical psychology* (Luce, Bush, & Galanter, 1962–1965) in the article, "Basic Measurement Theory" by Suppes and Zinnes (1963). In addition, the two-volume work on measurement theory by Krantz, Luce, Suppes, and Tversky, (1971) will treat this topic in perhaps more detail than you will wish to get, at this point.

Note that the methods of magnitude estimation are not universally accepted by everyone. In particular, the procedure called *functional measurement* developed by Norman Anderson has been especially useful in a wide variety of applications (we discussed some of this work in Chapter 16). For a treatment of this work, see N. Anderson (1976, 1977). (Also see the papers and books recommended in the Suggested Readings of Chapter 16.)

APPENDIX B
Operating characteristics

THE DECISION PROBLEM

In most real decisions that we must make, there is no answer that is guaranteed to be correct. For most situations, it is necessary to choose among virtues and evils, hoping to minimize the chance of misfortune and maximize the chance of good.

In this section, we analyze one common, simple form of decision making. The situation can be described by the following description. First, there is some information that the decision maker uses to help reach his decision. This information comes from the observations of the decision maker. We represent the results of the observations by the letter **O**. Second, the only choice open to the decision maker is to decide which of two acts, **A** or **B**, he will choose to do. Finally, the choice of decision can be correct or incorrect. Thus, we have the simple chain of events with four possible outcomes shown in Figure B-1. The prototypical example is that of the following, a dice game.

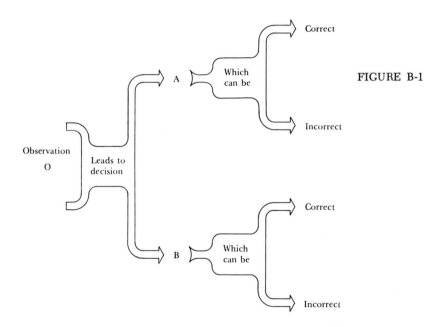

FIGURE B-1

You are gambling while playing a guessing game. Your partner throws three dice. Two of the dice are normal, one die is very special in that three of its sides are marked with the number "3" and the other three sides with the number "0." Your job is to guess which side the special die came up on; you are told only the total scores from all three dice. (Obviously, if the total is 2, 3, or 4 the special die must be "0"; if

THE DICE GAME

the total is 13, 14, or 15, the special die must be "3.") You are told that the score is 8. What should you respond?

Your observation **0** *is* 8.

Alternative **A:**   Decide that it was a 3.
Possible results: 1. It was a 3. You win the bet.
                             2. It was a 0. You lose your money.

Alternative **B:**   Decide that the 3 did not turn up.
Possible results: 1. It was a 3. You lose your money.
                             2. It was a 0. You win.

The important thing to notice about this situation is that, on the average, you cannot help but make mistakes. There is no possible way of guaranteeing perfect performance.

To analyze the dice game, consider all the possible ways that it can come out. First, how many possible results are there? Well, the lowest number that is possible comes if the two regular dice both turn up "1" and the special die comes up "0": that gives a total of 2. The highest number comes if the two regular dice both come up 6 and the special die comes up 3: that gives a total of 15. Thus, there are 14 possible outcomes, ranging from 2 through 15.

Now consider the chance that we can get any one of those 14 scores, given that the special die was a 3 or a 0. To do this, we have to figure out how many ways the dice can turn up to give any particular score. Here is how we do that.

Suppose the total were 8: this can happen in different ways, depending upon whether the special die is 3 or 0.

If the special die is a 3:

> The two regular dice must total 5: There are four ways for that to happen. The two regular dice can come up 1 and 4, 2 and 3, 3 and 2, or 4 and 1.

If the special die is 0:

> The two regular dice must total 8: There are five ways for that to happen. Two regular dice can come up 2 and 6, 3 and 5, 4 and 4, 5 and 3, or 6 and 2.

In fact, for all the possible scores of the dice, we get the number of possibilities shown in Table B-1.

Now, suppose that we observed a score of 10. How many ways can that happen? Looking at Table B-1, we see that this can happen in 3 ways if the special die is 0 and 6 ways if the special die is 3: There is a total of 9 ways that the 3 dice can combine to give a 10. Thus, because we know that we got a score of 10, we also know that, on the average, $\frac{6}{9}$ of the time this will be a result of the special die coming up a 3 and $\frac{3}{9}$ of the time from the special die coming up 0. So, if we guess that a score of 10 means that the special die is a 3, we will be correct 6 out of every 9 trials and incorrect 3 out of every 9 trials, on the average. If you are a gambler, you would say that a score of 10 means that the odds of the special die being a 3 are 2 to 1 (six to three).

It would seem to be sensible to say the special die is 3 whenever the total is 10, because the odds favor it. In fact, look at this: *The criterion rule*

Total	Proportion of Times Special Die Is 3
7	$\frac{3}{9} = \ \ 33\%$
8	$\frac{4}{9} = \ \ 44\%$
9	$\frac{5}{9} = \ \ 56\%$
10	$\frac{6}{9} = \ \ 67\%$
11	$\frac{5}{7} = \ \ 71\%$
12	$\frac{4}{5} = \ \ 80\%$
13	$\frac{3}{3} = 100\%$

On the average, the percentage of times that calling the special die 3 will be correct rises steadily as the total score rises, with the chance being more favorable than not as soon as the total is 9 or greater. A good decision rule, thus, would appear to be "Say that the special die is 3 whenever the total score is 9 or greater." Let us see what this would cause to happen.

Hits and misses. Suppose we tossed the dice 100 times, and on each toss had to decide whether the special die was a 3. We use the decision rule of responding "Yes" every time a total of 9 or more occurs. Now go ahead to Table B-1. We will answer **yes** (the die is a 3) for a score of 9, 10, 11, 12, 13, 14, and 15. Otherwise we will say **no**. But there are 36 possible combinations of the regular two dice, and if the special die is a 3, only 26 of them give totals of 9 or greater. (We can get scores less than 9—scores of 8, 7, 6, and 5—in 10 ways.) Thus, we will be correct by saying **yes** 26 out of every 36 trials on which the special die really is a 3. We **miss** 10 out of every 36 trials that the special die really was 3.

The proportion of times that we get a **hit** by correctly deciding **yes**, the 3 has turned up, is represented as $p(\text{yes}|3)$. The vertical bar ($|$)

Table B-1

*Number of Ways This Can Happen
if the Special Die Is a*

Total	0	3
0	0	0
1	0	0
2	1	0
3	2	0
4	3	0
5	4	1
6	5	2
7	6	3
8	5	4
9	4	5
10	3	6
11	2	5
12	1	4
13	0	3
14	0	2
15	0	1
16	0	0
Total Combinations:	36	36

means "conditional" or "given." Thus the terms read "the proportion of
hits is equal to $p(\text{yes}|3)$, which is the proportion of yes, given that a 3
actually was rolled on the special die." In this example the hit rate or
$p(\text{yes}|3) = \frac{26}{36} = 72\%$. Similarly, the **miss** rate $p(\text{no}|3)$, is $\frac{10}{36}$ or 28%.

False alarms. What about when the special die really was a 0? We
respond **yes** anytime the total score is 9, 10, 11, or 12. Thus, out of the
36 combinations of the two regular dice when the special die is a 0,
exactly 10 of them lead to a total score of 9 or more, the other 26 combinations lead to a total score of 8 or less. Saying **yes** for the wrong
event is called a **false alarm**. In this example, the false-alarm rate is $\frac{10}{36}$:
$p(\text{yes}|0) = \frac{10}{36} = 28\%$.

Moving the criterion. We can adjust how often we correctly guess
that the special die turned up "3" by adjusting the critical score at
which we change from an answer of "yes" to "no." But, as the critical
score varies, so do the hits and the false alarms. The hit and false-alarm
rates are related; increasing one always increases the other. In fact,

the exact relationship between the hit and false-alarm rate is very important in decision theory. Call the critical score on which we base our decisions the *criterion*. Whenever the dice total equals or exceeds the criterion, we say that the special die is most likely to be a "3"; otherwise we say that it is probably a "0."

Criterion	False-Alarm-Rate		Hit Rate	
	Fraction	Percentage	Fraction	Percentage
1	$\frac{36}{36}$	100	$\frac{36}{36}$	100
2	$\frac{36}{36}$	100	$\frac{36}{36}$	100
3	$\frac{35}{36}$	97	$\frac{36}{36}$	100
4	$\frac{33}{36}$	92	$\frac{36}{36}$	100
5	$\frac{30}{36}$	83	$\frac{36}{36}$	100
6	$\frac{26}{36}$	72	$\frac{35}{36}$	97
7	$\frac{21}{36}$	58	$\frac{33}{36}$	92
8	$\frac{15}{36}$	42	$\frac{30}{36}$	83
9	$\frac{10}{36}$	28	$\frac{26}{36}$	72
10	$\frac{6}{36}$	17	$\frac{21}{36}$	58
11	$\frac{3}{36}$	8	$\frac{15}{36}$	42
12	$\frac{1}{36}$	3	$\frac{10}{36}$	28
13	$\frac{0}{36}$	0	$\frac{6}{36}$	17
14	$\frac{0}{36}$	0	$\frac{3}{36}$	8
15	$\frac{0}{36}$	0	$\frac{1}{36}$	0

The operating characteristic. It is easier to see the relationship between false alarms and hits if we plot them together, as shown in Figure B-2. This relationship is called an *operating characteristic.*[1] This curve shows explicitly how changing the criterion (the numbers beside the points) changes both the percentage of hits and the percentage of false alarms.

Another way of seeing how the decision rule must always be related to the trade off between hits and false alarms is to look again at the distribution of total scores shown in Table B-1. This time, draw a diagram of the distributions (Figure B-3). This is the same information originally presented in the table, but now it is clear why there must always be errors. The distribution of dice scores when the special die

[1] Originally, this relationship came from the study of radar receivers attempting to determine whether the signal seen was a real one or simply noise. Hence, the curve was called a *Receiver Operating Characteristic* or *ROC* curve. The term *ROC curve* is still widely used in the psychological literature.

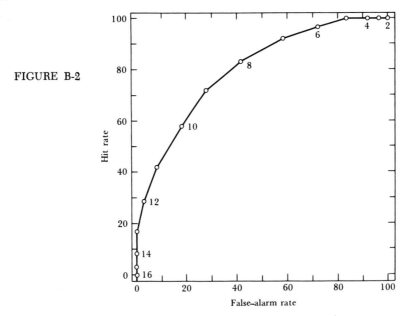

FIGURE B-2

THE OPERATING CHARACTERISTIC

FIGURE B-3

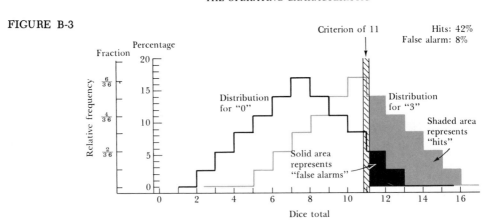

is a 0 (the distribution on the left) overlaps considerably with the distribution of scores when the special die is a 3 (the distribution on the right). There is nothing that can be done about that overlap: If the dice total is 8, it could be a result of either outcome of the special dice. In the figure, a criterion of 11 is drawn in. For this criterion value, we decide to say that the special die is a 3 if we get a dice total of 11 or more, so the chance that we are correct is the chance that we get an observation of 11 or more from the distribution shown on the right. The chance of a false alarm is the chance of an observation of 11 or more from the distribution shown on the left. Thus, simply by examining how much of each distribution lies to the right of the criterion, we can see the way the relative hit- and false-alarm rates vary as we move the criterion back and forth. This, of course, is exactly what we did in drawing the operating characteristic.

The operating characteristic shows how performance varies as we vary the decision rule. Now, what happens if we make the task easier? Suppose we change the dice game so that the special die has a 6 on three sides and 0 on the other three sides. What then? We leave this as a problem for the reader. Draw the new distribution of observations of the dice scores for the special die coming up a 6. (You already have the distribution for the case when the special die is 0.) Now draw the operating characteristic. It should include the point that has a hit rate of 83% and a false-alarm rate of 8%. If it does not, you had better review this section on operating characteristics.

The diagram of the distributions points out something else about the decision rule: If we simply adopt a strategy of saying "3" whenever the dice total exceeds the criterion, we are wasting information. There are times when we have absolutely no doubt about the accuracy of our response, and there are times when we know that we are simply guessing: How does the decision rule describe this? The answer is simple. Whenever we get a low total on the dice, say between 2 and 4, we are certain that the special die was a 0; whenever we get a high score, say between 13 and 15, we are certain that the special die was a 3. With a value of 8 or 9 for the total score, we are guessing. Thus, we can say more than simply **yes** or **no** whether the special die is likely to be a 0 or a 3: We can also assign a statement of how confident we are in that response. We can easily qualify our answers by adding a statement like "I am very certain," or "I am pretty certain," or "I am really just guessing" to our statement of **yes** or **no**. When this is done, we see that there are really six responses:

Confidence ratings

Yes, the special die is a 3 and I am
   very certain
   certain
   not certain

No, the special die is a 0 and I am
   not certain
   certain
   very certain

These six responses can be ordered according to the dice score, with a response of "very certain that it is a 3" always coming from the highest total and "very certain that it is a 0" coming from the lowest.

If we draw the way responses come from the distributions of dice totals, we might get something like that shown in Figure B-4.

FIGURE B-4

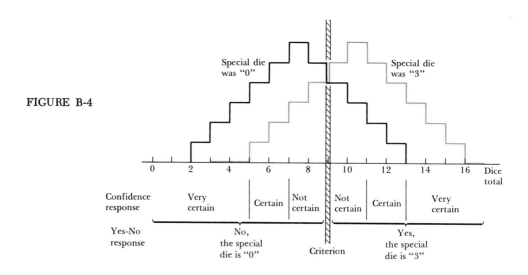

These confidence ratings are extremely useful. Note that we can treat the six different responses somewhat as if we had six different criteria for responding. Thus, the operating characteristic can be drawn to reflect confidence ratings, rather than the criteria illustrated previously. To do this, simply note that the chance of responding **yes** with a confidence of **certain** or greater is given by the chance that the dice total is **11** or greater. Thus, in the illustration shown in Figure B-4, the translation between criteria and confidence ratings looks like this:

To Simulate a Criterion of	*Combine These Responses*
13	**Yes—very certain**
11	**Yes—very certain** and **certain**
9	Any response of **yes**
7	**No—Not certain** and any response of **yes**
5	**No—Not certain, certain,** and any response of **yes**
2	Any response whatsoever

Note that in order to plot the operating characteristic we do not really need to know what the criteria are. All we need to know is what the hit and false-alarm rates are for the various responses.

Suppose we did the dice game for 200 times. Furthermore, suppose that on 100 trials the special die came up 0 and on 100 trials it came up 3. After the experiment, we sort out the responses according to whether they resulted from a 3 or 0 on the special die. Suppose that this is what we found.

Responses	*Number of Occurrences When Special Die Was*	
	0	*3*
A. Yes—very certain	0	17
B. Yes—certain	17	41
C. Yes—not certain	11	14
D. No—not certain	30	20
E. No—certain	25	8
F. No—very certain	17	0
TOTAL:	100	100

Now, without bothering to figure out what criterion each response represents, we simply realize that we can treat these responses as if each came from a criterion, if we lump together all responses of a certain confidence or **greater:**

Response	*(Special Die Was 0)* *False-Alarm Rate*	*(Special Die Was 3)* *Hit Rate*
A	0	17
B or A	17	58
C, B, or A	28	72
D, C, B, or A	58	92
E, D, C, B, or A	83	100
F, E, D, C, B, or A	100	100

If we plot the hit and false-alarm rates, we get the operating characteristic (Figure B-5)—the same curve shown in Figure B-2.

This is exactly how we analyze real data, the only exception being that in a real experiment the numbers would not come out quite so cleanly. People are inconsistent in where they place their criteria. These inconsistencies are relatively small, however.

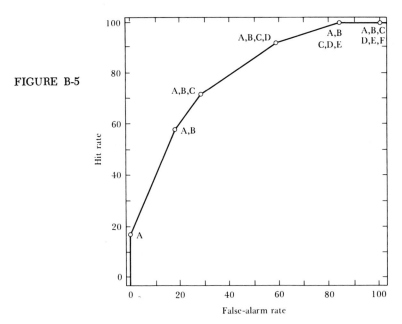

FIGURE B-5

The normal We ask human subjects to listen to a very weak signal that is presented
distribution periodically over a pair of earphones. We want to find out whether or not
they can hear the signal. The question is actually much more complex,
however, because the subjects are always hearing something: They must
decide whether what they heard resulted from the signal presented, or
whether it was simply a result of the normal fluctuations in hearing that
occur. These fluctuations come about for many reasons. In fact, in many
experiments, we add noise to the earphones in order to see how well the
subjects can pick out the signal from the noise.

   The situation for the subjects is very much like the situation described
for the dice game. They listen during the interval when the signal could
be presented and end up with some observation, much like our rolling
the dice and ending up with some total score. The question is, "Did that
observation come from the signal or just from noise"? The analogous question for the dice game, of course, is, "Did that total result from the special
die being a 0 or a 3?" We assume the subjects who try to detect the signal
choose some criterion: If their observation exceeds that criterion they
say "signal." Otherwise they say, "no signal." From the hit and false-alarm
rates, we try to determine the separation of the distributions that they
must be using to make their decisions. Then, from our determination of

the distributions, we try to decide how the auditory system must be converting the signals.

Let us now work through some examples. Before we do, however, we need to introduce a special type of distribution of observations, the *normal distribution*.

When we played the dice game, we developed the distribution of outcomes of the dice (Figure B-3). In general, however, a different type of distribution is frequently encountered. This distribution is called the *normal distribution*, and is an extremely useful one to know about. It is widely used in many fields of study, including psychology, and it usually turns out that even if the actual distributions under study are not normal, the normal is an excellent approximation to the true one. A drawing of the normal distribution is shown in Figure B-6. Notice

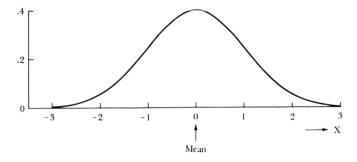

FIGURE B-6

that it looks very much like the distribution for the dice game, except it is drawn smoothly, rather than with steps. This is because the total score from a dice game can only take on an integral value—it must be a number like 6 or 7, it cannot lie between. The normal distribution, however, can take on any real number, positive or negative. The normal distribution shown here is characterized by one number—the mean or average value. As it is drawn, it has an average value of zero. If it were to have an average value of, say, 1.5, the distribution would simply be shifted to the right, so that its peak was at 1.5: This is shown in Figure B-7.

The values of the normal are shown in Table B-2. Here we see the height of the curve for different values along the horizontal axis. In addition, we also show the percentage of the curve that lies to the right of any criterion. It is this latter figure that we use for computing the operating characteristics.

What we usually care about is how far apart the mean values of two distributions are from one another. Suppose we do the experiment

Table B-2   The Normal Distribution Height and Percentage of the Curve (Area) to the Right of Any Criterion

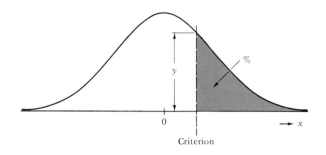

Criterion	Y	Percentage		Criterion	Y	Percentage		Criterion	Y	Percentage
−3.0	.004	99.9		−1.0	.242	84.1		1.0	.242	15.9
−2.9	.006	99.8		−.9	.266	81.6		1.1	.218	13.6
−2.8	.008	99.7		−.8	.290	78.8		1.2	.194	11.5
−2.7	.010	99.7		−.7	.312	75.8		1.3	.171	9.7
−2.6	.014	99.5		−.6	.333	72.6		1.4	.150	8.1
−2.5	.018	99.4		−.5	.352	69.2		1.5	.130	6.7
−2.4	.022	99.2		−.4	.368	65.5		1.6	.111	5.5
−2.3	.028	98.9		−.3	.381	61.8		1.7	.094	4.5
−2.2	.035	98.6		−.2	.391	57.9		1.8	.079	3.6
−2.1	.044	98.2		−.1	.397	54.0		1.9	.066	2.9
−2.0	.054	97.7		0	.399	50.0		2.0	.054	2.3
−1.9	.066	97.1		.1	.397	46.0		2.1	.044	1.8
−1.8	.079	96.4		.2	.391	42.1		2.2	.035	1.4
−1.7	.094	95.5		.3	.381	38.2		2.3	.028	1.1
−1.6	.111	94.5		.4	.368	34.5		2.4	.022	.8
−1.5	.130	93.3		.5	.352	30.1		2.5	.018	.6
−1.4	.150	91.9		.6	.333	27.4		2.6	.014	.5
−1.3	.171	90.3		.7	.312	24.2		2.7	.010	.4
−1.2	.194	88.5		.8	.290	21.2		2.8	.008	.3
−1.1	.218	86.4		.9	.266	18.4		2.9	.006	.2

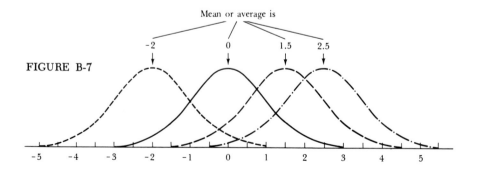

FIGURE B-7

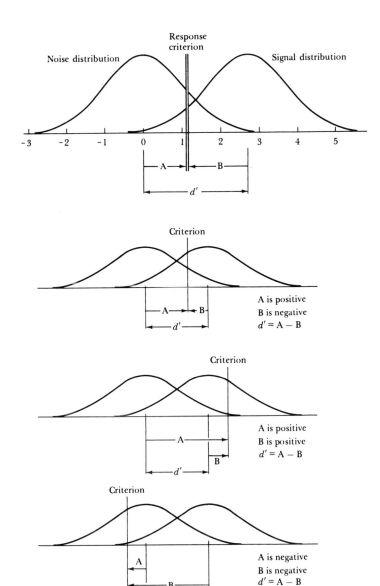

we mentioned in which we ask the subjects to try and detect a signal that we present. We want to find out how far the distribution of observations that results from noise is from the distribution which results from the signal. We think that the situation is characterized by Figure B-8.

We want to discover both exactly where the signal distribution is located relative to the noise distribution and also where the criterion is. To start, call the mean value of the noise distribution 0. There is good reason for doing this, in the absence of signal the average observation ought to be around zero. Moreover, since we only care about the *relative* separation of the two distributions, it doesn't really matter what number we call the mean value of the noise (our measurement will be on an *interval scale;* see Appendix A). We call the distance from the mean of the noise distribution to the criterion A, the distance from the mean of the signal distribution to the criterion B, and the distance from the mean of the noise distribution to the mean of the signal distribution d'. The symbol d' is used for historical reasons: That is what it has been called in the psychological literature. Both A and B are distances from the mean value of distribution. If the criterion is to the right of the mean, A and B are postive. If the criterion is exactly at the mean, then the distance value is 0. If the criterion is to the left of the mean, the distance is negative. Thus $d' = A - B$.

Suppose one subject gives us a false-alarm rate of 14% and a hit rate of 95%. We can immediately determine A: If we look up 14% in Table B-2, we see that the criterion must be located a distance of 1.1 units to the right of the noise distribution. Thus, $A = 1.1$. Similarly, we see that a hit rate of 95% requires that the criterion be 1.6 units to the left of the mean of the signal distribution (the criterion value is at -1.6). Thus, $B = -1.6$. Now we know that $d' = 2.7$. And that is all there is to it.

PROBLEMS

The fire-sprinkler problem

At this point, we can probably learn most about the use of operating characteristics and about the normal distributon by working a few problems.

We are installing a sprinkler system as part of a fire-alarm system for a building. Now we wish to install the temperature control that will turn on all the sprinklers whenever a fire occurs. The control is located near the ceiling of a large store room. The roof is made of tin, and there are no windows in the room. Questions: To what temperature should we set the control? If the temperature is set too low, (say 130°), then on very hot days, when the outside temperature goes as high as 110°, it is quite likely that the hot air will rise to the ceiling of the storeroom and be heated even more by the sun warming up the tin roof. Thus, it would not take long for the air temperature to reach 130° and set off the system: a *false alarm.*

If, however, the temperature is set higher, say 180°, it is quite likely that a fire could develop and destroy a good deal of the items in the storeroom before the flames got high enough to heat the air at the ceiling to a temperature of 180°. Thus, we would fail to report many fires, at least while they were still small enough that the sprinkler system could put them out. This would be a *miss*. Where do we set the temperature?

To solve this problem, we need information about hits and false alarms. We need to know the probabilities with which these occur. Ideally, we would set up a test situation and watch what happens over, say, a 3-month period, carefully counting the occurrences of hits (correct triggering of the system to a fire), misses (failure to respond within, say, 5 min of a fire), false alarms (triggering of the system in the absence of a fire), and correct rejections (no response from the system in normal conditions). Then we could plot an operating characteristic.

The way we plot the operating characteristics is to vary the temperature setting of the control, collecting information about the hit and false-alarm rate at each temperature setting. Thus, if we set the control at 140°, we might observe that the actual room temperature reaches that value on one day out of every five—giving a false-alarm figure of 20%—and we might also note that 88% of the fires that we set caused the room temperature to reach that value within the 5 min we require—a hit rate of 88%. This, then, is the first point on our curve: $p(\text{alarm}|\text{fire}) = 88\%$; $p(\text{alarm}|\text{no fire}) = 20\%$.

This one point is actually sufficient, if we believe that everything is normally distributed. We can now compute the value of d' and then compute what the rest of the curve should look like.

If we go back to the table of the normal distribution, Table B-2, we see that if we have a false alarm rate of 20%, the criterion must be to the right of the highest point on the distribution, at about .8: That is, the value of A is 0.8. A hit rate of 88% means that the criterion must be located to the left of the highest point on the distribution, at a point around −1.2. Thus, $B = -1.2$. Now d' is simply the distance that the two distributions are apart, and that is given by $0.8 + 1.2 = 2.0$. Our fire-alarm system has a d' of 2.0. The entire curve, therefore, looks like that shown in Figure B-9.

Now, to complete our information about the setting of the temperature limit we can simplify our procedure: All we do is find out what the false-alarm rate would be at different temperatures. To get this information, we can install an automatic temperature recorder in the building for a few months. Then, we look at the distribution of temperatures reached throughout that period. We might find that at a temperature of 150°, there was a false alarm only 10% of the time, at a temperature

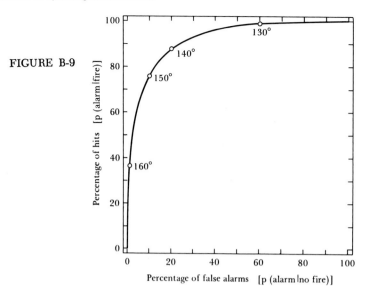

FIGURE B-9

of 160° only 1% of the time, and at a temperature of 130°, 60% of the time. These values then determine points on the operating characteristic, as shown.

At this point, it is obvious that we can never survive with a d' as low as 2.0. If we set the false-alarm value at a level acceptable to the fire department, say 1%—a temperature setting of 160°—then our insurance company will complain that we will only detect a fire with a chance of $\frac{37}{100}$. If we try to detect the fire with a chance as high as $\frac{9.5}{10}$, we will have a false alarm rate of close to 40%—clearly unacceptable to the fire department. It is quite clear that we can never solve the problem by trying to adjust the temperature setting of the sprinklers and alarms. We have to raise the d' value.

Suppose that both the fire department and the insurance company agree that an acceptable hit and false alarm rate would be 99% and 1% respectively. What value of d' would we have to have?

Memory   From experiments in memory, we know that if a list of 30 names is presented to you once (for about 2 sec per name), an hour later the retention of that list will be very low. In fact, for any individual name, $d' = 0.8$.

Suppose that both the fire department and the insurance company agree that an acceptable hit and false-alarm rate would be 99% and 1% respectively. What value of d' would we have to have?

your false-alarm rate to be 8%, what percentage of the names do you remember?

Consider a version of the three-dice game in which the special die has *The dice game* **O** on three sides and **S** on the other three sides. Using the normal dis- *revisited* tribution as a good approximation of the dice distribution, what is the relationship between d' and the value of S?

Assume that there is a fixed criterion at 11. This means there will be a false-alarm rate of 8%. Thus, if S is 3, we see from our dice-game table that the hit rate is $\frac{15}{36}$ or 42%. Going to the normal distribution tables, $A = 1.4$, $B = 0.2$, so $d' = A - B = 1.2$. The relationship between d', hit rate, and false-alarm rate (assuming a fixed criterion of 11) is shown in Table B-3. The relationship between d' and S is plotted in Figure B-10. Now, you should try to complete both the table and the figure.

Table B-3

Value of S	False-Alarm Rate	Hit Rate	A	B	A − B = d'
0	8%	8%	1.4	1.4	0
1	8%	—	1.4	—	—
2	8%	—	1.4	—	—
3	8%	42%	1.4	0.2	1.2
4	8%	—	1.4	—	—
5	8%	—	1.4	—	—
6	8%	83%	1.4	−1.0	2.4
7	8%	—	1.4	—	—
8	8%	—	1.4	—	—

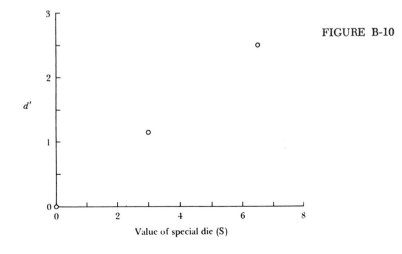

FIGURE B-10

d'

Value of special die (S)

The decision theory discussed here grew out of the engineering literature and it has mostly been applied to the study of sensory processes: to psychophysics. Because it was first applied to the analysis of detecting signals in noise, it usually goes under the name of *Signal Detection Theory*, or sometimes simply *SDT*. Thus, to find this topic in book indices, one must usually look for "signal detection theory" or sometimes for "d'"

The best overall introduction to the many uses of the decision theory discussed here is the book by David Green and John Swets: *Signal detection theory and psychophysics* (1966). This book does get very technical, but much of the material in the early chapters can be followed without too much difficulty even by those whose mathematics is weak. Some of the latter chapters review the various uses of the decision theory to other areas of psychology.

The chapter by Egan and Clarke (1966) in Sidowski's book on experimental methods offers another very good introduction to the technique. The book of collected readings edited by Swets (1964) gives a collection of uses, but this is very technical material. Signal detection theory has now become a standard tool used in the analysis of many experiments. It has proven to be particularly important in the study of memory. Uses of the technique are numerous, and can be found in many of the areas of psychology.

Bibliography

USING BASIC REFERENCE MATERIAL

The reader who is interested in learning more about the issues discussed in this book can look in a number of different places for more material. The most important sources are the *Annual Reviews*, the *Psychological Abstracts*, the *Citation Index*, and the various journals in the field.

The *Annual Reviews* are a series of volumes published every year that survey the research findings in the field. They are published by Annual Reviews, Inc., Palo Alto, California. Although these books are published yearly, some of the specific areas are covered less frequently—perhaps once every third or fourth year. Use of the *Annual Reviews* is perhaps the fastest way to get up to date in any research area. They are difficult to use, however, because they are written for advanced readers, and some of the reviews tend to be incomprehensible even to them. Nonetheless, you can carefully examine the chapter in the *Annual Review* that covers the area of your interest, ferret out the references to the more important recent papers, and then find the papers themselves in the library. Often the papers on a topic are easier to understand than the reviews of those papers.

Annual reviews

Although *Annual Reviews* are published on a number of topics, the two that will contain almost all the material relevant to the topics of this book are *Annual Reviews of Psychology* and *Annual Reviews of Physiology*.

Psychological Abstracts is a journal published by the American Psychological Association that contains abstracts of all technical papers published in a very large list of journals. By looking up a topic in the index of the abstracts, it is possible to trace the papers that might be of interest. The abstracts themselves give a general summary of what that paper is about, thus letting one know whether the actual article ought to be examined.

Psychological abstracts

The main difficulty with the abstracts is that they tell you too much: You will be led to more papers than you can possibly examine. This usually is a result of the fact that you cannot find the exact area you wish to read about in the index: Thus, if you use an index term like "memory," you are likely to be referred to something like 500 papers. The one paper you really ought to read is probably somewhere in that list of 500, but you will never find it. Your job is to use the index and abstracts so cleverly that you can reduce that large initial number of papers to a more manageable size. It can be done with some thought: Basically, look up more specific terms. This difficulty has virtue, however, for often the abstracts lead you to a paper or research area that is even more interesting than the one you were originally seeking. Many a person has discovered his true interest by accidentally finding a paper in his wanderings through the abstracts.

The abstracts are bound in yearly editions: You have to examine each year's editions for the topic in which you are interested. It is always best to start with the most recent year and work backward.

Often you find a particularly good paper, but one that is rather old. The problem is to discover what new material has been published on this same topic. The way to do this is through the *Science Citation Index* (published

The science citation index

quarterly by the Institute for Scientific Information, Inc.). Here you look up the paper in which you are interested: The citation index tells you what recent papers have been published that refer to it. This is an excellent way to search forward from a paper to the recent work. This method fails sometimes, both because you get led astray with papers that cite the one you have but are, in fact, on a completely different topic, and also because not all the good papers you ought to read will get around to referencing the paper you happen to have.

The *Citation Index* is also bound in yearly editions, so you have to look up your favorite old paper in each year to see what new ones might have referred to it.

The journals   When all these methods fail, you can go directly to the journals. The journal presentation is often very technical, but sometimes surprisingly simple to read. The best thing to do is to find out the names of a few journals that cover the field that interests you (you can find the names of the journals in the references in this book), and then simply browse through the stacks in the library, including the stack of unbound, recent issues of the journal. Then you will probably both stumble across interesting articles and also discover references to earlier articles. Sometimes, when you find a journal that appears to cover the area in which you are interested, it makes sense to turn every page of the journal and examine all the articles, starting with the most recent years and going back as many years as your interest holds out. This technique of "brute force" search is not really so laborious as it sounds, and almost every serious scientist has done this task several times. (Do not shun the older issues. Because of the peculiar history of psychology, many of the most fascinating papers and books seem to have been published in the years around 1890 through 1910).

The journals you will find to be of most interest are:

American Journal of Psychology   (General experimental psychology)
British Journal of Psychology   (General experimental psychology)
Canadian Journal of Psychology   (General experimental psychology)
Cognition   (Theoretical and philosophical papers, as well as experimental ones)
Cognitive Psychology   (Both theoretical and some experimental articles dealing with memory, perception, cognition)
Journal of the Acoustical Society of America (*JASA*)   (Theoretical and experimental papers on hearing and speech recognition)
Journal of Cognitive Science   (Theoretical papers from psychology, artificial intelligence, linguistics)
Journal of Experimental Psychology   (Experimental papers on almost any topic in psychology. This journal is now published under four separate subtitles: *Animal Behavior Processes; General; Human Learning and Memory;* and *Human Perception and Performance*)
Journal of the Optical Society of America (*JOSA*)   (Theoretical and experimental papers on vision)

Journal of Verbal Learning and Verbal Behavior (Experimental papers mainly concerned with human memory studies)

Nature (Short reports on a variety of fields (the British version of *Science*))

Perception and Psychophysics (Experimental papers, primarily)

Psychological Bulletin (Contains review articles on specialized topics. Good for summarizing the research and opinions on a topic)

Psychological Review (Contains theoretical articles in current areas of interest)

Quarterly Journal of Experimental Psychology (General experimental papers)

Science (Occasional long survey articles, frequent short, technical papers)

Scientific American (Good introductory articles)

Vision Research (As the name implies)

GENERAL READINGS

Throughout the text, we reference particular books and articles that ought to be read for the individual chapters. In addition to these, there are several excellent general sources, books that you will probably want to scan to get a more thorough knowledge of psychology in general. Here is a small number of those books we feel are best suited for the reader who has finished this book and wishes to go on. It is not a complete list.

R. S. Woodworth & H. Schlosberg. *Experimental psychology.* New York: Holt, 1938, 1954, 1971. An excellent treatment of all of experimental psychology. Long used as the standard text for graduate students. There are three versions of this text in existence: the original text by Woodworth (1938), the one by Woodworth and Schlosberg (1958), and a new, revised one (Kling and Riggs, 1971). The 1938 version of the book is a remarkable document. It contains discussions on many important issues, issues that were not covered in the 1958 version. In many ways, the 1938 edition of the book is more valuable than the 1958 one, but you will have to decide this for yourself by browsing through both of them. The newest edition promised to bring the virtues of the earlier editions more up to date, but in our opinion it did not. It is a disappointing book.

G. A. Miller, E. Galanter, & K. H. Pribram. *Plans and the structure of behavior.* New York: Holt, 1960. A brief treatment of many of the issues presented in this book, with a framework that may sound familiar. This was one of the very first books to introduce information processing into psychology—a well-written book, easy to understand.

D. E. Wooldridge. *The machinery of the brain.* New York: McGraw-Hill, 1963: paperback. An excellent introduction to the operation of the brain and its implications for behavior. We have often assigned this book as supplementary reading for our course. Wooldridge also has several other books that should interest you, although they are not directly concerned with psychological issues.

C. H. Coombs, R. M. Dawes, & A. Tversky. *Mathematical psychology:*

An introduction. Englewood Cliffs, New Jersey: Prentice-Hall, 1970. Much modern psychological theorizing uses mathematical models. This book provides an excellent introduction to all of this work.

G. A. Miller & R. Buckhout. *Psychology: The science of mental life.* New York: Harper and Row, 1973. An excellent summary of psychology, including an historical survey.

REFERENCES

Adams, J. L. *Conceptual blockbusting: A guide to better ideas.* San Francisco: Freeman, 1974.

Albers, J. *Interaction of color.* New Haven: Yale Univ. Press, 1963. (*Also see* Bucher (1961).)

Allen, V. L. Situational factors in conformity. In L. Berkowitz (Ed.), *Advances in experimental social psychology.* Vol. 2. New York: Academic Press, 1965.

Anderson, B. F. *Cognitive psychology: The study of knowing, learning, & thinking.* New York: Academic Press, 1975.

Anderson, J. R. *Language, memory and thought.* Hillsdale, N.J.: Lawrence Erlbaum Associates, 1976.

Anderson, J. R., & Bower, G. H. *Human associative memory.* Washington, D.C.: Winston, 1973. (Distributed by Halsted Press, Wiley, New York.)

Anderson, N. H. Likeableness ratings of 555 personality-trait words. *Journal of Personality and Social Psychology,* 1968, *9,* 272–279.

Anderson, N. H. Integration theory applied to attitudes about U.S. presidents. *Journal of Educational Psychology,* 1973, *64,* 1–8. (a)

Anderson, N. H. Cognitive algebra: integration theory applied to social attribution. In L. Berkowitz (Ed.), *Advances in experimental social psychology.* Vol. 7. New York: Academic Press, 1973. (b)

Anderson, N. H. Information integration theory: A brief survey. In D. H. Krantz, R. C. Atkinson, R. D. Luce, & P. Suppes (Eds.), *Contemporary developments in mathematical psychology. Vol. II: Measurement, psychophysics, and neural information processing.* San Francisco: Freeman, 1974.

Anderson, N. H. How functional measurement can yield validated interval scales of mental quantities. *Journal of Applied Psychology,* 1976, in press.

Anderson, N. H. *Information integration theory: A case history in experimental science.* New York: Academic Press, 1977.

Anderson, N. H., & Barrios, A. A. Primary effects in personality impression formation. *Journal of Abnormal and Social Psychology,* 1961, *63,* 346–350.

Anstis, S. M. What does visual perception tell us about visual coding? In M. S. Gazzaniga & C. Blakemore (Eds.), *Handbook of psychobiology.* New York: Academic Press, 1975.

Arbib, M. A. *The metaphorical brain: An introduction to cybernetics as artificial intelligence and brain theory.* New York: Wiley (Interscience), 1972.

Arnheim, R. *Art and visual perception.* Berkeley: Univ. of California Press, 1969. (a)

Arnheim, R. *Visual thinking*. Berkeley: Univ. of California Press, 1969. (b)

Arnold, M. B. (Ed.). *Feelings and emotions: The Loyola symposium*. New York: Academic Press, 1970.

Asch, S. E. *Social psychology*. Englewood Cliffs, N.J.: Prentice-Hall, 1952.

Asch, S. E. Opinions and social pressure. *Scientific American,* 1955, *193,* 31–35.

Atkinson, R. C. Mnemotechnics in second-language learning. *American Psychologist,* 1975, *30,* 821–828.

Atkinson, R. C., & Shiffrin, R. M. The control of short-term memory. *Scientific American,* 1971, *225* (2), 82–90.

Averbach, E., & Coriell, A. S. Short-term memory in vision. *Bell System Technical Journal,* 1961, *40,* 309–328.

Ax, A. F. The physiological differentiation between fear and anger in humans. *Psychosomatic Medicine,* 1953, *15,* 433–442.

Backus, J. A plea for conformity. *Journal of the Acoustical Society of America,* 1968, *44,* 285.

Baddeley, A. D., & Warrington, E. K. Amnesia and the distinction between long- and short-term memory. *Journal of Verbal Behavior,* 1970, *9,* 176–189.

Baddeley, A. D., & Warrington, E. K. Memory coding and amnesia. *Neuropsychologia,* 1973, *11,* 159–165.

Bahrick, H. P., Bahrick, P. O., & Wittlinger, R. P. Fifty years of memory for names and faces: A cross-sectional approach. *Journal of Experimental Psychology: General,* 1975, *104,* 54–75.

Bandler, R., & Grinder, J. *The structure of magic: A book about language & therapy*. Palo Alto, Calif.: Science and Behavior Books, 1975.

Barbizet, J. *Human memory and its pathology*. San Francisco: Freeman, 1970.

Barker, R. G., Dembo, T., & Lewin, K. Frustration and regression: An experiment with young children, *University of Iowa Studies in Child Welfare,* 1941, *18,* No. 286.

Barlow, H. B. Single units and sensation: A neuron doctrine for perceptual psychology? *Perception,* 1972, *1,* 371–394.

Barlow, H. B., Hill, R. M., & Levick, W. R. Retinal ganglion cells responding selectively to direction and speed of image motion in the rabbit. *Journal of Physiology,* 1964, *173,* 377–407.

Bartlett, F. C. *Thinking: An experimental and social study*. New York: Basic Books, 1958.

Beach, F. A., Hebb, D. O., Morgan, C. T., & Nissen, H. W. (Eds.). *The neuropsychology of Lashley*. New York: McGraw-Hill, 1960.

Békésy, G. von. On the resonance curve and decay period at various points on the cochlear partition. *Journal of the Acoustical Society of America,* 1949, *21,* 245–254.

Békésy, G. von. *Experiments in hearing*. New York: McGraw-Hill, 1960.

Békésy, G. von. *Sensory inhibition*. Princeton, N.J.: Princeton Univ. Press, 1967.

Bem, D. J. *Beliefs, attitudes, and human affairs*. Belmont, Calif.: Wadsworth, 1970.

Benson, H. *The relaxation response.* New York: Morrow, 1975.

Berko, J. The child's learning of english morphology. *Word,* 1958, *14,* 150–177.

Berkowitz, L. (Ed.). *Advances in experimental social psychology.* Vol. 2. New York: Academic Press, 1965.

Berkun, M. M., Bialek, H. M., Kearn, R. P., & Yagi, K. Experimental studies of psychological stress in man. *Psychological Monographs,* 1962, *76* (15, whole no. 534).

Berlyne, D. E. Children's reasoning and thinking. In P. Mussen (Ed.), *Handbook of child psychology.* New York: Wiley, 1970.

Berne, E. *Transactional analysis in psychotherapy.* New York: Grove Press, 1961.

Berne, E. *Games people play.* New York: Grove Press, 1964.

Bernstein, C., & Woodward, B. *All the president's men.* New York: Warner Paperback Library, 1975.

Bever, T. G. The cognitive basis for linguistic structures. In J. R. Hayes (Ed.), *Cognition and the development of language.* New York: Wiley, 1970.

Blakemore, C. Central visual processing. In M. S. Gazzaniga & C. Blakemore (Eds.), *Handbook of psychobiology.* New York, Academic Press, 1975.

Blakemore, C. Nachmias, J., & Sutton, P. The perceived spatial frequency shift: Evidence for frequency-selective neurons in the human brain. *Journal of Physiology,* 1970, *210,* 727–750.

Bobrow, D. G., & Collins, A. M. (Eds.). *Representation and understanding: Studies in cognitive science.* New York: Academic Press, 1975.

Bobrow, D. G., & Norman, D. A. Some principles of memory schemata. In D. G. Bobrow & A. M. Collins (Eds.), *Representation and understanding: Studies in cognitive science.* New York: Academic Press, 1975.

Bobrow, D. G., & Winograd, T. An overview of KRL, a knowledge representation language. *Journal of Cognitive Science,* 1977, *1,* 3-46.

Bower, G. H. Analysis of a mnemonic device. *American Scientist,* 1970, *58,* 496–510.

Bower, T. G. R. *Development in infancy.* San Francisco: Freeman, 1974.

Boynton, R. M. Color, hue, and wavelength. In E. C. Carterette & M. P. Friedman (Eds.), *Handbook of perception.* Vol. V. New York: Academic Press, 1975.

Bransford, J. D., & Johnson, M. K. Considerations of some problems of comprehension. In W. G. Chase (Ed.), *Visual information processing.* New York: Academic Press, 1973.

Bredberg, G., Lindeman, H. H., Ades, H. W., West, R., & Engstrom, H. Scanning electron microscopy of the organ of Corti. *Science,* 1970, *170,* 861–863.

Brewer, W. F. There is no convincing evidence for operant or classical conditioning in adult humans. In W. B. Weimer & D. S. Palermo (Eds.), *Cognition and the symbolic processes.* Hillsdale, N.J.: Lawrence Erlbaum Associates, 1974.

Broadbent, D. E. *Decision and stress.* New York: Academic Press, 1971.

Brooks, L. R. Spatial and verbal components of the act of recall. *Canadian Journal of Psychology,* 1968, *22,* 349–368.

Brooks, L. R. Visual and verbal processes in internal representation. Talk presented at the Salk Institute, La Jolla, California, 1970.

Brown, R. *Social psychology.* New York: Free Press, 1965.

Brown, R. The first sentences of child and chimpanzee. In R. Brown, *Psycholinguistics: Selected papers of Roger Brown.* New York: Free Press, 1970.

Brown, R. Development of the first language in the human species. *American Psychologist,* 1973, *289,* 97–106. (a)

Brown, R. *A first language: The early stages.* Cambridge: Harvard Univ. Press, 1973. (b)

Brown, R., & Bellugi, U. Three processes in the child's acquisition of syntax. In E. Lennenberg (Ed.), *New directions in the study of language.* Cambridge, Mass.: M.I.T. Press, 1964.

Brown, R., Galanter, E., Hess, E. H., & Mandler, G. *New directions in psychology I.* New York: Holt, 1962.

Brown, R., & Hanlon, C. Derivational complexity and order of acquisition in child speech. In J. R. Hayes (Ed.), *Cognition and the development of language.* New York: Wiley, 1970.

Bruce, B. Case systems for natural language. *Artificial Intelligence,* 1975, *6,* 327–360.

Bruner, J. S. The course of cognitive growth. *American Psychologist,* 1964, *19,* 1–15.

Bruner, J. S., Goodnow, J. J., & Austin, G. A. *A study of thinking.* New York: Wiley, 1956.

Bucher, F. *Joseph Albers. Despite straight lines.* New Haven: Yale Univ. Press, 1961.

Burdick, E. *The 480.* New York: Dell, 1965. (Originally published by McGraw-Hill, New York, 1954.)

Campbell, F. W., & Maffei, L. Contrast and spatial frequency. *Scientific American,* 1974, *231,* 106–114 (November).

Carraher, R. G., & Thurston, J. B. *Optical illusions and the visual arts.* Princeton, N.J.: Van Nostrand-Reinhold, 1968.

Carterette, E. D., & Friedman, M. P. *Handbook of perception.* New York: Academic Press.

Volume 1: Historical and philosophical roots of perception. (1974).

Volume 2: Psychophysical judgment and measurement. (1974).

Volume 3: Biology of perceptual systems. (1973).

Volume 4: Hearing (1976).

Volume 5: Seeing (1975).

Volume 6: Feeling, tasting, smelling, and hurting (in preparation).

Volume 7: Language and speech. (1976).

(*Volumes 8* through *10* will cover a much broader range of topics, including cognitive performance, and ecological perception. These volumes were still in the planning stage and details were not available at the time this book was written.)

Chapanis, A. The dark adaptation of the color anomalous measured with lights of different hues. *Journal of General Physiology*, 1947, *30*, 423–437.

Chomsky, N. The formal nature of language. In E. H. Lenneberg (Ed.), *Biological foundations of language*. New York: Wiley, 1967.

Chomsky, N., & Halle, M. *The sound pattern of English*. New York: Harper, 1968.

Clark, E. V. What's in a word? On the child's acquisition of semantics in his first language. In T. E. Moore (Ed.), *Cognitive development and the acquisition of language*. New York: Academic Press, 1973.

Cofer, C. N. (Ed.). *The structure of human memory*. San Francisco: Freeman, 1976.

Cofer, C. N., & Appley, M. H. *Motivation: Theory and research*. New York: Wiley, 1964.

Cohen, G., & Martin, M. Hemisphere differences in an auditory stroop test. *Perception & Psychophysics*, 1975, *17*, 79–83.

Collins, A. M., & Loftus, E. F. A spreading–activation theory of semantic processing. *Psychological Review*, 1975, *82*, 407–428.

Conel, J. L. *The postnatal development of the human cerebral cortex*. Vols. I–VI. Cambridge: Harvard Univ. Press, 1939–1963.

Conrad, R. Errors of immediate memory. *British Journal of Psychology*, 1959, *50*, 349–359.

Coombs, C. H., Dawes, R. M., & Tversky, A. *Mathematical psychology: An introduction*. Englewood Cliffs, N.J.: Prentice Hall, 1970.

Corballis, M. C., & Beale, J. L. Bilateral symmetry and behavior. *Psychological Review*, 1970, *77*, 451–464.

Coren, S. Brightness contract as a function of figure–ground relations. *Journal of Experimental Psychology*, 1969, *80*, 517–524.

Cornsweet, T. N. Information Processing in Human Visual Systems. *Stanford Research Institute Journdl*, 1969, feature issue No. 5.

Cornsweet, T. N. *Visual perception*. New York: Academic Press, 1970.

Cotton, J. W. Models of learning. *Annual Review of Psychology*, 1976, *27*, 155–188.

Craik, F. I. M., & Lockhart, R. S. Levels of processing: A framework for memory research. *Journal of Verbal Learning and Verbal Behavior*, 1972, *11*, 671–684.

Crosby, F. A model of egoistical relative deprivation. *Psychological Review*, 1976, *83*, 85–113.

Crutchfield, R. S. Conformity and character. *American Psychologist*, 1955, *10*, 191–198.

Dale, P. S. *Language development: Structure and function*. New York: Holt, Rinehart, and Winston, 1976.

Dallos, P. *The auditory periphery: Biophysics and physiology*. New York: Academic Press, 1973.

Darley, J. M., & Batson, C. D. From Jerusalem to Jericho: A study of situational variables in helping behavior. *Journal of Personality and Social Psychology*; 1973, *27*, 100–108.

Davis, G. A. *Psychology of problem solving: Theory and practice.* New York: Basic Books, 1973.

DeGroot, A. D. *Thought and choice in chess.* The Hague: Mouton, 1965.

DeGroot, A. D. Perception and memory versus thought: Some old ideas and recent findings. In B. Kleinmuntz (Ed.), *Problem solving: Research, method, and theory.* New York: Wiley, 1966.

Dement, W. C., & Miller, M. M. An introduction to sleep. In O. Petre-Quadens & J. D. Schlag (Eds.), *Basic sleep mechanisms.* New York: Academic Press, 1974.

Dement, W. C., & Villablanca, J. Clinical disorders in man and animal model experiments. In O. Petre-Quadens & J. D. Schlag (Eds.), *Basic sleep mechanisms.* New York: Academic Press, 1974.

Denes, P. B., & Pinson, E. N. *The speech chain.* Murray Hill, N.J.: Bell Telephone Laboratories, Inc., 1963. (Available from the business office of the local Bell System Telephone Company.)

de Sausmarez, M. *Bridget Riley.* Greenwich, Conn.: New York Graphic Society Ltd., 1970.

Deutsch, D., & Deutsch, J. A. (Eds.). *Short-term memory.* New York: Academic Press, 1975.

Deutsch, J. A. The physiological basis of memory. *Annual Review of Psychology,* 1969, *20*, 85–104.

Deutsch, J. A. (Ed.). *Physiological basis of memory.* New York: Academic Press, 1973.

Deutsch, S. *Models of the nervous system.* New York: Wiley, 1967.

DeValois, R. L., & DeValois, K. K. Neural coding of color. In E. C. Carterette & M. P. Friedman (Eds.), *Handbook of perception. Volume V: Seeing.* New York: Academic Press, 1975.

DeValois, R. L., Abromov, I., & Jacobs, G. H. Analysis of response patterns of LGN cells. *Journal of the Optical Society of America,* 1966, *56*, 966–977.

Dick, A. O. Iconic memory and its relation to perceptual processing and other memory mechanisms. *Perception & Psychophysics,* 1974, *16*, 575–596.

Dodwell, P. C. *Visual pattern recognition.* New York: Holt, 1970.

Easterbrook, J. A. The effect of emotion on the utilization and the organization of behavior. *Phychological Review,* 1959, *66*, 183–201.

Eccles, J. C. *The neurophysiological basis of mind.* London and New York: Oxford Univ. Press, 1953.

Eccles, J. C. Possible ways in which synaptic mechanisms participate in learning, remembering and forgetting. In D. P. Kimble (Ed.), *The anatomy of memory.* Vol. I. Palo Alto, Calif.: Science and Behavior Books, 1965.

Edwards, W., & Tversky, A. (Eds.). *Decision making.* Harmondsworth, Middlesex, England: Penguin Books, 1967.

Egan, J. P., & Clarke, F. R. Psychophysics and signal detection. In J. B. Sidowski (Ed.), *Experimetnal methods and instrumentation in psychology.* New York: McGraw-Hill, 1966.

Eisenstadt, M., & Kareev, Y. Aspects of human problem solving: The use of internal representations. In D. A. Norman, D. E. Rumelhart, & the LNR Research Group. *Explorations in cognition.* San Francisco: Freeman, 1975.

Enright, J. T. Stereopsis, visual latency and three-dimensional moving pictures. *American Scientist,* 1970, *58,* 536–545.

Epstein, R. A. *The theory of gambling and statistical logic.* New York: Academic Press, 1967.

Escher, M. C. *The graphic work of M. C. Escher.* New York: Meredith Press, 1967. (1st ed. 1961.)

Estes, W. K. Memory, perception, and decision in letter identification. In R. L. Solso (Ed.), *Information processing and cognition: The Loyola symposium.* Hillsdale, N.J.: Lawrence Erlbaum Associates, 1975.

Evans, R. I. *Jean Piaget: The man and his ideas.* New York: Dutton, 1973.

Falmagne, R. J. (Ed.). *Reasoning: Representation and process in children and adults.* Hillsdale, N.J.: Lawrence Erlbaum Associates, 1975.

Farb, P. *Word play: What happens when people talk.* New York: Knopf, 1974. (Paperback published by Bantam, 1975.)

Farnham-Diggory, S. (Ed.). *Information processing in children.* New York: Academic Press, 1972.

Fay, R. R. Auditory frequency stimulation in the goldfish (*Carassius auratus*). *Journal of Comparative & Physiological Psychology,* 1970, *73,* 175–180.

Fay, R. R., & MacKinnon, J. R. A simplified technique for conditioning respiratory mouth movements in fish. *Behavioral Research Methods and Instrumentation,* 1969, *1,* 3.

Festinger, L. *A theory of cognitive dissonance.* New York: Harper, 1957.

Festinger, L., Coren, S., & Rivers, G. The effect of attention on brightness contrast and assimilation. *American Journal of Psychology,* 1970, *83,* 189–207.

Festinger, L., Riecken, H. W., & Schachter, S. *When prophecy fails.* Minneapolis: Univ. of Minnesota Press, 1956.

Fillmore, C. J. The case for case. In E. Bach & R. G. Harms (Eds.), *Universals in linguistic theory.* New York: Holt, 1968.

Fillmore, C. J. Toward a modern theory of case. In D. A. Reibel & S. A. Schane (Eds.), *Modern studies in English.* Englewood Cliffs, N.J.: Prentice-Hall, 1969.

Fink, M., Kety, S., McGaugh, J., & Williams, T. A. (Eds.). *Psychobiology of convulsive therapy.* New York: Halsted Press, 1974.

Flavell, J. H. *The developmental psychology of Jean Piaget.* Princeton, N.J.: Van Nostrand-Reinhold, 1963.

Flavell, J. H. Role-taking and communication skills in children. *Young Children,* 1966, *21.*

Flavell, J. H., Botkin, P. T., Fry, C. L., Wright, J. W., & Jarvis, P. E. *The development of role-taking and communication skills in children.* New York: Wiley, 1968.

Flavell, J. H., & Wellman, H. M. Metamemory. In R. V. Kail & J. W. Hagen (Eds.), *Memory in cognitive development.* Hillsdale, N.J.: Lawrence Erlbaum Associates, in press.

Fleming, J. D. The state of the apes. *Psychology Today*, 1974, *8*, 31–46.

Flock, H. R., & Freedberg, E. Perceived angle of incidence and achromatic surface color. *Perception & Psychophysics*, 1970, *8*, 251–256.

Fodor, J., Bever, T., & Garrett, M. *The psychology of language*. New York: McGraw-Hill, 1974.

Fromkin, V. A. Slips of the tongue. *Scientific American*, 1973 (December), 110–117.

Fromkin, V. A., & Rodman, R. *An introduction to language*. New York: Holt, Rinehart, and Winston, 1974.

Galanter, J. The direct measurement of utility and subjective probability. *American Journal of Psychology*, 1962, *75*, 208–220.

Garcia, J., Hankins, W. G., & Rusiniak, K. W. Behavioral regulation of the milieu interne in man and rat. *Science*, 1974, *185*, 824–831.

Garcia, J., & Koelling, R. Relation of cue to consequence in avoidance learning. *Psychonomic Science*, 1966, *4*, 123–124.

Gazzaniga, M. S. *The bisected brain*. New York: Appleton, 1970.

Gazzaniga, M. S., & Blakemore, C. *Handbook of psychobiology*. New York: Academic Press, 1975.

Gazzaniga, M. S., & Hillyard, S. A. Attention mechanisms following brain bisection. In S. Kornblum (Ed.), *Attention and performance IV*. New York: Academic Press, 1973.

Geldard, F. (Ed.). *Cutaneous communication systems and devices*. Austin, Texas: The Psychonomic Society, 1973.

Gentner, D. Evidence for the psychological reality of semantic components: The verbs of possession. In D. A. Norman, D. E. Rumelhart, & the LNR Research Group, *Explorations in cognition*. San Francisco: Freeman, 1975.

Geschwind, N. The organization of language and the brain. *Science*, 1970, *170*, 940–944.

Geschwind, N. The apraxias: Neural mechanisms of disorders of learned movement. *American Scientist*, 1975, *63*, 188–195.

Gibson, A. R., & Harris, C. S. The McCollough effect: Color adaptation of edge-detectors or negative afterimages? Paper presented at the annual meeting of the Eastern Psychological Association, Washington, D.C., April, 1968.

Gibson, J. J. *The perception of the visual world*. Boston: Houghton, 1950.

Gibson, J. J. *The senses considered as perceptual systems*. Boston: Houghton, 1966.

Ginsburg, H., & Opper, S. *Piaget's theory of intellectual development: An introduction*. Englewood Cliffs, N.J.: Prentice-Hall, 1969.

Gold, P. E., & King, R. A. Retrograde amnesia: Storage failure versus retrieval failure. *Psychological Review*, 1974, *81*, 465–469.

Gombrich, E. H. *Art and illusion*. New York: Pantheon, 1960.

Gombrich, E. H., Hochberg, J., & Black, M. *Art, perception, and reality*. Baltimore, Md.: John Hopkins Univ. Press, 1972.

Gordon, B. The superior colliculus of the brain. *Scientific American*, 1972, *227*, (6), 72–82.

Graham, C. H. (Ed.). *Vision and visual perception*. New York: Wiley, 1965.

Gray, C. R., & Gummerman, K. The enigmatic eidetic image: A critical examination of methods, data, and theories. *Psychological Bulletin*, 1975, *82*, 383–407.

Greeff, Z. *Graefe-Saemisch Hb. ges. augenheilk, II*, Kap. 5, 1900, 1.

Green, B. F., Jr. Current trends in problem solving. In B. Kleinmuntz (Ed.), *Problem solving*. New York: Wiley, 1966.

Green, D. M., & Swets, J. A. *Signal detection theory and psychophysics*. New York: Wiley, 1966.

Greeno, J. G. Hobbits and Orcs: Acquisition of a sequential concept. *Cognitive Psychology*, 1974, *6*, 270–292.

Gregory, R. L. *Eye and brain: The psychology of seeing*. New York: McGraw-Hill, 1966.

Gregory, R. L. *The intelligent eye*. New York: McGraw-Hill, 1970.

Gross, C. G. Inferotemporal cortex and vision. *Progress in Physiological Psychology*, 1973, *5*, 77–123. (New York: Academic Press.)

Gross, C. G., Cowey, A., & Manning, F. J. Further analysis of visual discrimination deficits following foveal prestriate and inferotemporal lesions in rhesus monkeys. *Journal of Comparative and Physiological Psychology*, 1971, *76*, 1–7.

Gross, C. G., Rocha-Miranda, C. E., & Bender, D. B. Visual properties of neurons in inferotemporal cortex of the macaque. *Journal of Neurophysiology*, 1972, *35*, 96–111.

Guzmán, A. Decomposition of a visual scene into three-dimensional bodies. In A. Grasselli (Ed.), *Automatic interpretation and classification of images*. New York: Academic Press, 1969.

Haber, R. N. (Ed.). *Contemporary theory and research in visual perception*. New York: Holt, 1968.

Haber, R. N. Eidetic images. *Scientific American*, 1969, *220*, 36–44.

Hagen, J. W. Strategies for remembering. In S. Farnham-Diggory (Ed.), *Information processing in children*. New York: Academic Press, 1972.

Harris, C. S. Perceptual adaptation to inverted, reversed, and displaced vision. *Psychological Review*, 1965, *72*, 419–444.

Hecht, S., & Hsia, Y. Dark adaptation following light adaptation to red and white lights. *Journal of the Optical Society of America*, 1945, *35*, 261–267.

Heider, F. *The psychology of interpersonal relations*. New York: Wiley, 1958.

Held, R. Dissociation of visual functions by deprivation and rearrangement. *Psychologische Forchung*, 1968, *31*, 338–348.

Held, R., & Richards, W. *Perception: Mechanisms and models. Readings from Scientific American*. San Francisco: Freeman, 1972.

Held, R., & Richards, W. *Recent progress in perception. Readings from Scientific American*. San Francisco: Freeman, 1976.

Hewitt, C., Bishop, P., & Steiger, R. A universal modular ACTOR formalism for artificial intelligence. Stanford, California: Proceedings of the Third International Conference on Artificial Intelligence, 1973.

Hilgard, E. R., & Bower, G. H. *Theories of learning* (4th ed.). New York: Appleton, 1975.

Hillyard, S. A., & Picton, T. W. Event-related brain potentials and selective information processing in man. In J. Desmedt (Ed.), *Cerebral evoked potentials in man: The Brussels symposium.* London: Oxford Univ. Press, 1977.

Hirsch, H. V. B., & Jacobson, M. The perfectible brain: Principles of neuronal development. In M. S. Gazzaniga & C. Blakemore (Eds.), *Handbook of psychobiology.* New York: Academic Press, 1975.

Hochberg, J. *Perception.* Englewood Cliffs, N.J.: Prentice-Hall, 1964.

Hochberg, J. In the mind's eye. In R. N. Haber (Ed.), *Contemporary theory and research in visual perception.* New York: Holt, 1968.

Hochberg, J. The representation of things and people. In E. H. Gombrich, J. Hochberg, & M. Black, *Art, perception, and reality.* Baltimore: Johns Hopkins Univ. Press, 1972.

Hochberg, J., & Beck, J. Apparent spatial arrangement and perceived brightness. *Journal of Experimental Psychology,* 1954, *47,* 263–266.

Hoffman, L. R. Group problem solving. In L. Berkowitz (Ed.), *Advances in experimental social psychology.* Vol. 2. New York: Academic Press, 1965.

Horemis, S. *Optical and geometrical patterns and designs.* New York: Dover Publications, 1970.

Horton, D. L., & Turnage, T. W. *Human learning.* Englewood Cliffs, N.J.: Prentice-Hall, 1976.

Hubel, H. D., & Wiesel, T. N. Receptive fields, binocular interaction and functional architecture in the cat's visual cortex. *Journal of Physiology (London),* 1962, *160,* 106–154.

Hubel, D. G., & Wiesel, T. N. Shape and arrangement of columns in cat's striate cortex. *Journal of Physiology (London),* 1963, *165,* 559–568.

Hubel, D. H., & Wiesel, T. N. Receptive fields and functional architecture in two nonstriate visual areas (18 and 19) of the cat. *Journal of Neurophysiology,* 1965, *28,* 229–289.

Hubel, D. H., & Wiesel, T. N. Receptive fields and functional architecture of monkey striate cortex. *Journal of Physiology (London),* 1968, *195,* 215–243.

Hulse, S. H., Deese, J., & Egeth, H. *The psychology of learning.* New York: McGraw-Hill, 1975.

Hunt, E. B. *Artificial intelligence.* New York: Academic Press, 1975.

Hunt, E. B., & Love, T. How good can memory be? In A. W. Melton & E. Martin (Eds.), *Coding processes in human memory.* Washington, D.C.: Winston, 1972.

Hunter, I. M. L. Mental calculation. In P. C. Wason & P. N. Johnson-Laird (Eds.), *Thinking and reasoning.* Harmondsworth, Middlesex, England (also Baltimore): Penguin Books, 1968.

Hurvich, L. M., & Jameson, D. *The perception of brightness and darkness.* Rockleigh, N.J.: Allyn & Bacon, 1966.

Hurvich, L. M., & Jameson, D. Opponent processes as a model of neural organization. *American Psychologist,* 1974, *29,* 88–102.

Hurwicz, L. Game theory and decisions. *Scientifc American,* 1955, *192,* (2), 78–83.

Huttenlocher, J., & Burke, D. Why does memory span increase with age? *Cognitive Psychology*, 1976, *8*, 1–31.

Ingle, D. Two visual mechanisms underlying the behavior of fish. *Psychologische Forschung*, 1967, *31*, 44–51.

James, M., & Jongeward, D. *Born to win: Transactional analysis with Gestalt experiments*. Reading, Mass.: Addison-Wesley, 1971.

Jarrard, L. E. (Ed.). *Cognitive processes of nonhuman primates*. New York: Academic Press, 1971.

Johnson-Laird, P. N. Experimental psycholinguistics. *Annual Review of Psychology*, 1974, *25*, 135–160.

Jones, E. E. How do people perceive the causes of behavior? *American Scientist*, 1976, *64*, 300–305.

Jones, E. E., Kanouse, D. E., Kelley, H. H., Nisbett, R. E., Valins, S., & Weiner, B. *Attribution: Perceiving the causes of behavior*. Morristown, N.J.: General Learning, 1972.

Judd, D. B. Basic correlates of the visual stimulus. In S. S. Stevens (Ed.), *Handbook of experimental psychology*. New York: Wiley, 1951.

Julesz, B. Binocular depth perception of computer-generated patterns. *Bell System Technical Journal*, 1960, *39*, 1125–1162.

Julesz, B. Binocular depth perception without familiary cues. *Science*, 1964, *145*, 356–362.

Julesz, B. *Foundations of cyclopean perception*. Chicago: Univ. of Chicago Press, 1971.

Jung, R. Allgemeine neurophysiologie. In *Handbuch der inneren medizen*. Ed. V/1. Berlin and New York: Springer-Verlag, 1953.

Kahneman, D. *Attention and effort*. Englewood Cliffs, N.J.: Prentice-Hall, 1973.

Kahneman, D., & Tversky, A. Subjective probability: A judgment of representativeness. *Cognitive Psychology*, 1972, *2*, 430–454.

Kahneman, D., & Tversky, A. On the psychology of prediction. *Psychological Review*, 1973, *80*, 236–251.

Kandel, E. An invertebrate system for the cellular analysis of simple behaviors and their modifications. In F. O. Schmitt (Ed.), *The neurosciences, third study program*. Chapter 31, pp. 347–370. Cambridge: M.I.T. Press, 1974:

Karlins, M., & Abelson, H. J. *Persuasion: How opinions and attitudes are changed*. Second edition. Berlin and New York: Springer-Verlag, 1970.

Kaufman, L. *Sight and mind: An introduction to visual perception*. New York and London: Oxford Univ. Press, 1974.

Kavanagh, J. F., & Mattingly, I. G. (Eds.). *Language by ear and by eye. The relationship between speech and reading*. Cambridge: M.I.T. Press, 1972.

Kepes, G. (Ed.). *Vision and value series: 1. Education of vision; 2. Structure in art and in science; 3. The nature and art of motion; 4. Module, proportion, symmetry, rhythm; 5. The man-made object; 6. Sign, image, symbol*. New York: Braziller, 1965, 1966.

Kimura, D. Cerebral dominance and the perception of verbal stimuli. *Canadian Journal of Psychology*, 1961, *15*, 166–171.

Kimura, D. Left–right difference in the perception of melodies. *Quarterly Journal of Experimental Psychology*, 1964, *16*, 355–358.

Kinney, G. C., Marsetta, M., & Showman, D. J. *Studies in display symbol legibility, part XII. The legibility of alphanumeric symbols for digitalized television*. Bedford, Mass.: The Mitre Corporation, November, 1966, ESD-TR-66-117.

Kinsbourne, M. The control of attention by interaction between the cerebral hemispheres. In S. Kornblum (Ed.), *Attention and performance IV*. New York: Academic Press, 1973.

Kinsbourne, M., & Wood, F. Short-term memory processes and the amnesic syndrome. In D. Deutsch & J. A. Deutsch (Eds.), *Short-term memory*. New York: Academic Press, 1975.

Kintsch, W. *Learning, memory, and conceptual processes*. New York: Wiley, 1970.

Kintsch, W. *The representation of meaning in memory*. Hillsdale, N.J.: Lawrence Erlbaum Associates, 1974.

Klahr, D. (Ed.). *Cognition & instruction*. Hillsdale, N.J.: Lawrence Erlbaum Associates, 1974.

Klatsky, R. L. *Human memory: Structures and processes*. San Francisco: Freeman, 1975.

Kleinmuntz, B. (Ed.). *Problem solving*. New York: Wiley, 1966.

Kleinmuntz, B. (Ed.). *Concepts and the structure of memory*. New York: Wiley, 1967.

Kleinmuntz, B. (Ed.). *Formal representation of human judgment*. New York: Wiley, 1968.

Kleitman, N. *Sleep and wakefulness*. Revised edition. Chicago: Univ. of Chicago Press, 1963.

Kling, J. W., & Riggs, L. A. (Eds.). *Woodworth/Schlosberg's experimental psychology*. Third edition. New York: Holt, 1971.

Köhler, W. *The mentality of apes*. London: Routledge and Kegan Paul, 1925. (2nd ed., 1927.) Available in paperback from Vintage Books, New York, 1959.

Kosslyn, S. M. Information representation in visual images. *Cognitive Psychology*, 1975, *7*, 341–370.

Kosslyn, S. M., & Pomerantz, J. R. Imagery, propositions, and the form of internal representations. *Cognitive Psychology*, 1977, *9*, 52–76.

Krantz, D. H., Luce, R. D., Suppes, P., & Tversky, A. *Foundations of measurement*. Vol. 1. *Additive and polynomial representations*. New York: Academic Press, 1971.

Kreutzer, M. A., Leonard, C., & Flavell, J. H. An interview study of children's knowledge about memory. *Monographs of the Society for Research in Child Development*, 1975, *40*, (1, Serial No. 159).

Kryter, K. D. *The effect of noise on man*. New York: Academic Press, 1970.

Kuffler, S. W. Discharge patterns and functional organization of mammalian retina. *Journal of Neurophysiology*, 1953, *16*, 37–68.

Lashley, K. S. Mass action in cerebral function. *Science*, 1931, *73*, 245–254.

Lashley, K. S. In search of the engram. *Symposium of the Society of Experimental Biology*, 1950, *4*, 454–482.

Lashley, K. S. The problem of serial order in behavior. In L. A. Jeffress

(Ed.), *Cerebral mechanisms in behavior: The Hixon symposium.* New York: Wiley, 1951.

Latané, B., & Darley, J. M. Bystander apathy. *American Scientist,* 1969, *57,* 244–268.

Latané, B., & Darley, J. M. *The unresponsive bystander.* New York: Appleton, 1970.

Lazarus, R. C. *Psychological stress and the coping process.* New York: McGraw-Hill, 1966.

Leask, J., Haber, R. N., & Haber, R. B. Eidetic imagery in children: II. Longitudinal and experimental results. *Psychonomic Monographic Supplements,* 1969, *3* (3, Whole No. 35).

LeGrand, Y. *Light, colour, and vision.* London: Chapman & Hall, 1957.

Lenneberg, E. H. *Biological foundations of language.* New York: Wiley, 1967.

Lettvin, J. Y., Maturana, H. R., McCulloch, W. S., & Pitts, W. H. What the frog's eye tells the frog's brain. *Proceedings of the IRE,* 1959, *47* (11), 1940–1951.

Lettvin, J. Y., Maturana, H. R. Pitts, W. H., & McCulloch, W. S. Two remarks on the visual system of the frog. In W. A. Rosenblith (Ed.), *Sensory communication.* Cambridge: M.I.T. Press, 1961.

Levy, J. Possible basis for the evolution of lateral specialization of the human brain. *Nature,* 1969, *224,* 614–615.

Levy, J. Psychobiological implications of bilateral asymmetry. In S. J. Dimond & J. G. Beaumont (Eds.), *Hemisphere function in the human brain.* New York: Halsted Press, 1974.

Levy, J., Trevarthen, C., & Sperry, R. W. Perception of bilateral chimeric figures following hemispheric deconnexion. *Brain,* 1972, *95,* 61–78.

Lindsley, D. B. Psychophysiology and motivation. In M. F. Jones (Ed.), *Nebraska symposium on motivation.* Lincoln: Univ. of Nebraska Press, 1957.

Lindsley, J. R. Producing simple utterances: How far ahead do we plan? *Cognitive Psychology,* 1975, *7,* 1–19.

Linton, M. Memory for real-world events. In D. A. Norman, D. E. Rumelhart, & the LNR Research Group, *Explorations in cognition.* San Francisco: Freeman, 1975.

Loftus, G. R., & Loftus, E. F. *Human memory: The processing of information.* New York: Halsted Press, 1975.

Lorayne, H., & Lucas, J. *The memory book.* New York: Stein and Day, 1974. (Also published in paperback by Ballantine Books, 1975.)

Luce, R. D., Bush, R. R., & Galanter, E. (Eds.). *Handbook of mathematical psychology.* 3 volumes. New York: Wiley, 1962–1965.

Luce, R. D., & Suppes, P. Preference, utility, and subjective probability. In R. D. Luce, R. R. Bush, & E. Galanter (Eds.), *Handbook of mathematical psychology.* Vol. III. New York: Wiley, 1965.

Luckiesh, M. *Visual illusions.* Princeton, N.J.: Van Nostrand-Reinhold, 1922. (Also available in paperback from Dover Publications, 1965.)

Luria, A. R. *The mind of a mnemonist.* Translated by L. Solotaroff. New York: Basic Books, 1968.

Luria, A. R. *The man with a shattered world: The history of a brain wound.* Translated by L. Solotaroff. New York: Basic Books, 1972.

Luria, A. R. *The working brain: An introduction to neuropsychology.* Translated by B. Haigh. New York: Basic Books, 1973.

Madigan, S. A., & McCable, L. Perfect recall and total forgetting: A problem for models of short-term memory. *Journal of Verbal Learning & Verbal Behavior,* 1971, *10,* 101–106.

Magritte. See Sylvester (1969).

Maier, N. R. F. Reasoning in humans. II. The solution of a problem and its appearance in consciousness. *Journal of Comparative Psychology,* 1931, *12,* 181–194.

Maier, S. F., & Seligman, M. E. P. Learned helplessness: Theory and evidence. *Journal of Experimental Psychology: General,* 1976, *105,* 3–46.

Mandler, G. Emotion. In R. Brown *et al.* (Eds.), *New directions in psychology.* New York: Holt, 1962.

Mandler, G. Consciousness: Respectable, useful, and probably necessary. In R. L. Solso (Ed.), *Information processing and cognition: The Loyola symposium.* Hillsdale, N.J.: Lawrence Erlbaum Associates, 1975. (a)

Mandler, G. *Mind and emotion.* New York: Wiley, 1975. (b)

Mark, R. *Memory and nerve cell connections.* London and New York: Oxford Univ. Press, 1974.

Markowitz, H. The utility of wealth. *Journal of Political Economics,* 1952, *60,* 152–158.

Massaro, D. W. *Experimental psychology and information processing.* Chicago: Rand McNally, 1975. (a)

Massaro, D. W. (Ed.). *Understanding language: An information-processing analysis of speech perception, reading, and psycholinguistics.* New York: Academic Press, 1975. (b)

Mayzner, M. S. Studies of visual information processing in man. In R. L. Solso (Ed.), *Information processing and cognition: The Loyola symposium.* Hillsdale, N.J.: Lawrence Erlbaum Associates, 1975.

McCollough, C. Color adaptation of edge detectors in the human visual system. *Science,* 1965, *149,* 1115–1116.

McGhie, A. *Pathology of attention.* Baltimore: Penguin Books, 1969.

McGinniss, J. *The selling of the president, 1968.* New York: Trident Press, 1969.

Mershon, D. H., & Gogel, W. C. Effect of stereoscopic cues on perceived whiteness. *American Journal of Psychology,* 1970, *83,* 55–67.

Messick, D. M. (Ed.). *Mathematical thinking in behavioral sciences. Readings from Scientific American.* San Francisco: Freeman, 1968.

Milgram, S. Behavorial study of obedience. *Journal of Abnormal Psychology,* 1963, *67,* 371–378.

Milgram, S. Issues in the study of authority: A reply to Baumrind. *American Psychologist,* 1964, *19,* 848–852.

Milgram, S. Some conditions of obedience and disobedience to authority. *Human Relations,* 1965, *18,* 574–575.

Milgram, S. *Obedience to authority.* New York: Harper & Row, 1974.

Miller, G. A. Decision units in the perception of speech. *IRE Transactions on*

Information Theory, 1962, *8*, 81–83.

Miller, G. A., Galanter, E., & Pribram, K. H. *Plans and the structure of behavior.* New York: Holt, 1960.

Miller, G. A., & Johnson-Laird, P. N. *Language and perception.* Cambridge, Mass.: Belknap Press, (Harvard Univ. Press), 1976.

Miller, R. R., & Springer, A. D. Implications of recovery from experimental amnesia. *Psychological review*, 1974, *81*, 470–473.

Milner, B., Corkin, S., & Teuber, H. L. Further analysis of the hippocampal amnesia syndrome: 14-year followup study of H. M. *Neuropsychologia*, 1968, *6*, 215–234.

Moore, T. E. (Ed.). *Cognitive development and the acquisition of language.* New York: Academic Press, 1973.

Moray, N. *Attention: Selective processes in vision and hearing.* New York: Academic Press, 1970.

Morgenstern, O. The theory of games. *Scientific American*, 1949, *180* (5), 22–25.

Mountcastle, V. B. (Ed.). *Interhemispheric relations and cerebral dominance.* Baltimore, Md.: Johns Hopkins Press, 1962.

Mueller, C. G., Rudolph, M., & the Editors of the Time-Life Books. *Light and vision.* New York: Time, Inc., 1969.

Murdock, B. B., Jr. The retention of individual items. *Journal of Experimental Psychology*, 1961, *62*, 618–625.

Murdock, B. B., Jr. The serial effect of free recall. *Journal of Experimental Psychology*, 1962, *64*, 482–488.

Mussen, P. (Ed.). *Handbook of child psychology.* 2 volumes (revised). New York: Wiley, 1970.

Myers, R. E. Transmission of visual information within and between the hemispheres: A behavioral study. In V. B. Mountcastle (Ed.), *Interhemispheric relations and cerebral dominance.* Baltimore, Md.: Johns Hopkins Press, 1962.

Neimark, E. D., & Santa, J. L. Thinking and concept attainment. *Annual Review of Psychology*, 1975, *26*, 173–205.

Neisser, U. Visual search. *Scientific American*, 1964, *210* (6), 94–102.

Neisser, U. *Cognitive psychology.* New York: Appleton, 1967.

Nelson, K. Concept, word and sentence: Interrelations in acquisition and development. *Psychological Review*, 1974, *81*, 267–285.

Nelson, K. The nominal shift in semantic-syntactic development. *Cognitive Psychology*, 1975, *7*, 461–479.

Newell, A. Production systems: Models of control structures. In W. G. Chase (Ed.), *Visual information processing.* New York: Academic Press, 1973.

Newell, A., & Simon, H. A. *Human problem solving.* Englewood Cliffs, N.J.: Prentice-Hall, 1972.

Newman, J. R. (Ed.). *The world of mathematics.* Vol. IV. New York: Simon and Schuster, 1956.

Newport, E. L., Gleitman, H., & Gleitman, L. R. Mother, I'd rather do it myself: Some effects and noneffects of maternal speech style. In C. A.

Ferguson & E. C. Snow (Eds.), *Talking to children*. Cambridge: Cambridge Univ. Press, in press.

Norman, D. A. (Ed.). *Models of human memory*. New York: Academic Press, 1970.

Norman, D. A. *Memory and attention: An introduction to human information processing* (2nd ed.). New York: Wiley, 1976.

Norman, D. A., & Bobrow, D. G. On data-limited and resource-limited processes. *Cognitive Psychology*, 1975, 7, 44–64.

Norman, D. A., & Bobrow, D. G. On the role of active memory processes in perception and cognition. In C. N. Cofer (Ed.), *The structure of human memory*. San Francisco: Freeman, 1976.

Norman, D. A., Gentner, D. R., & Stevens, A. L. Comments on learning: Schemata and memory representation. In D. Klahr (Ed.), *Cognition & instruction*. Hillsdale, N.J.: Lawrence Erlbaum Associates, 1976.

Norman, D. A., Rumelhart, D. E., & the LNR Research Group. *Explorations in cognition*. San Francisco: Freeman, 1975.

Olson, G. M. Developmental changes in memory and the acquisition of language. In T. E. Moore (Ed.), *Cognitive development and the asquisition of language*. New York: Academic Press, 1973.

Ornstein, R. E. *The psychology of consciousness*. San Francisco: Freeman, 1972. (Also published by Viking, 1972.)

Ornstein, R. E. *The nature of human consciousness*. San Francisco: Freeman, 1973. (Also published by Viking, 1973.)

Paivio, A. *Imagery and verbal processes*. New York: Holt, 1971.

Paivio, A. Perceptual comparisons through the mind's eye. *Memory and Cognition*, 1975, 3, 635–647.

Palmer, S. E. Visual perception and world knowledge. In D. A. Norman, D. E. Rumelhart, & the LNR Research Group, *Explorations in cognition*. San Francisco: Freeman, 1975.

Paris, S. G. Integration and influence in children's comprehension and memory. In F. Restle, R. M. Shiffrin, N. J. Castellan, H. R. Lindman, & D. B. Pisoni (Eds.), *Cognitive theory*, Vol. 1. Hillsdale, N.J.: Lawrence Erlbaum Associates, 1975.

Patterson, R. D. Noise masking of a change in residue pitch. *Journal of the Acoustical Society of America*, 1969, 45, 1520–1524.

Patton, R. M., Tanner, T. A., Jr., Markowitz, J., & Swets, J. A. (Eds.). *Applications of research on human decision making*. NASA-SP-209. Washington, D.C.: National Aeronautics and Space Administration, Office of Technology Utilization, 1970.

Penrose, L. S., & Penrose, R. Impossible objects: A special type of illusion. *British Journal of Psychology*, 1958, 49, 31.

Peterson, L. R. Short-term memory. *Scientific American*, 1966, 215 (7), 90–95.

Peterson, L. R., & Peterson, M. Short-term retention of individual items. *Journal of Experimental Psychology*, 1959, 58, 193–198.

Petre-Quadens, O., & Schlag, J. D. (Eds.). *Basic sleep mechanisms*. New York: Academic Press, 1974.

Pettigrew, J. D. The Neurophysiology of binocular vision. *Scientific American*,

1972, *227*, 84–95 (August).

Piaget, J. *The origins of intelligence in children*. New York: International Univ. Press, 1952. (1st ed., 1936.)

Piaget, J. *Six psychological studies*. Edited by D. Elkind, translated by A. Tenzer. New York: Random House, 1967. (Published in paperback by Vintage Books, 1968.)

Piliavin, I. M., Rodin, J., & Piliavan, J. A. Good samaritanism: An underground phenomenon? *Journal of Personality and Social Psychology*, 1969, *13*, 289–300.

Piliavin, J. A., & Piliavan, I. M. Effect of blood on reactions to a victim. *Journal of Personality and Social Psychology*, 1972, *23*, 353–361.

Pirenne, M. H. *Vision and the eye* (2nd ed.). London: Associated Book Publishers, 1967.

Pirenne, M. H. *Optics, painting, and photography*. London and New York: Cambridge Univ. Press, 1970.

Platt, W., & Baker, B. A. The relation of the scientific "hunch" to research. *Journal of Chemical Education*, 1931, *8*, 1969–2002.

Plomp, R., *Experiments on tone perception*. Soesterberg, The Netherlands: Institute for Perception RVO-TNO, 1966.

Poincaré, H. Mathematical creation. In J. R. Newman (Ed.), *The world of mathematics*. Volume IV. New York: Simon & Schuster, 1956.

Polya, G. *How to solve it*. Princeton, N.J.: Princeton Univ. Press, 1945.

Polyak, S. *The vertebrate visual system*. Chicago: Univ. of Chicago Press, 1957.

Pomeranz, B., & Chung, S. H. Dendritic-tree anatomy codes form-vision physiology in tadpole retina. *Science*, 1970, *170*, 983–894.

Posner, M. I. Psychobiology of attention. In M. Gazzaniga & C. Blakemore (Eds.), *Handbook of psychobiology*. New York: Academic Press, 1975.

Posner, M. I., Nissen, M. J., & Klein, R. M. Visual dominance: An information processing account of its origins and significance. *Psychological Review*, 1976, *83*, 157–171.

Posner, M. L., & Snyder, C. R. Attention and cognitive control. In R. L. Solso (Ed.), *Information processing and cognition: The Loyola symposium*. Hillsdale, N.J.: Lawrence Erlbaum Associates, 1975.

Postman, L., & Phillips, L. W. Short-term temporal changes in free recall. *Quarterly Journal of Experimental Psychology*, 1965, *17*, 132–138.

Pritchard, R. M. Stabilized images on the retina. *Scientific American*, 1961, *204*, 72–78.

Pylyshyn, Z. W. What the mind's eye tells the mind's brain: A critique of mental imagery. *Psychological Bulletin*, 1973, *80*, 1–24.

Rachlin, H. *Introduction to modern behaviorism*. San Francisco: Freeman, 1970.

Raiffa, E. *Decision analysis: Introductory lectures on choices under uncertainty*. Reading, Mass.: Addison-Wesley, 1968.

Raphael, B. *The thinking computer*. San Francisco: Freeman, 1976.

Rapoport, A. *Fights, games, and debates*. Ann Arbor: Univ. of Michigan Press, 1960.

Rapoport, A. The use and misuse of game theory. *Scientific American,* 1962, *207* (6), 108–118.

Rasmussen, G. L., & Windle, W. F. (Eds.). *Neural mechanisms of the auditory and vestibular systems.* Springfield, Ill.: Thomas, 1960.

Ratliff, F. *Mach bands: Quantitative studies on neural networks in the retina.* San Francisco: Holden-Day, 1965.

Ratliff, F. Contour and contrast. *Scientific American,* 1972, *226,* 90–101 (June).

Ratliff, F., & Hartline, H. K. The response of *limulus* optic nerve fibers to patterns of illumination on the receptor mosaic. *Journal of General Physiology,* 1959, *42,* 1241–1255.

Reddy, R. (Ed.). *Speech recognition: Invited papers presented at the IEEE symposium.* New York: Academic Press, 1975.

Reed, G. *The psychology of anomalous experience: A cognitive approach.* London: Hutchinson Univ. Library, 1972.

Reed, S. K. *Psychological processes in pattern recognition.* New York: Academic Press, 1973.

Reitman, J. S. Mechanisms of forgetting in short-term memory. *Cognitive Psychology,* 1971, *2,* 185–195.

Restle, F., Shiffrin, R. M., Castellan, N. J., Lindeman, H. R., & Pisoni, D. B. (Eds.). *Cognitive theory.* Vol. 1. Hillsdale, N.J.: Lawrence Erlbaum Associates, 1975.

Revusky, S., & Garcia, J. Learned associations over long delays. In G. H. Bower (Ed.), *The psychology of learning and motivation: Advances in research and theory.* Volume 4. New York: Academic Press, 1970.

Reynolds, R. *Mind models: New forms of musical experience.* New York: Praeger, 1975.

Richardson, L. F., & Ross, J. S. Loudness and telephone current. *Journal of General Psychology,* 1930, *3,* 288–306.

Riggs, L. A., Ratliff, F., Cornsweet, J. C., & Cornsweet, T. N. The disappearance of steadily-fixated objects. *Journal of the Optical Society of America,* 1953, *43,* 495–501.

Riley, B. See de Sausmarez (1970).

Rips, L. J., Shoben, E. J., & Smith, E. E. Semantic distance and the verification of semantic relations. *Journal of Verbal Learning and Verbal Behavior,* 1973, *12,* 1–20.

Robinson, D. W., & Dadson, R. S. A redetermination of the equal-loudness relations for pure tones. *British Journal of Applied Physics,* 1956, *7,* 166–181.

Robinson, J. O. *The psychology of visual illusion.* London: Hutchinson, 1972.

Robson, J. G. Receptive fields: Neural representation of the spatial and intensive attributes of the visual image. In E. C. Carterette & M. P. Friedman (Eds.), *Handbook of perception. Vol. 5: Seeing.* New York: Academic Press, 1975.

Rock, I. *An introduction to perception.* New York: Macmillan, 1975.

Rodieck, R. W. *The vertebrate retina: Principles of structure and function.* San Francisco: Freeman, 1973.

Roederer, J. G. *Introduction to the physics and psychophysics of music.* New York: Springer-Verlag, 1975.

Rosch, E. H. On the internal structure of perceptual and semantic categories. In T. Moore (Ed.), *Cognitive development and the acquisition of language.* New York: Academic Press, 1973. (a)

Rosch, E. H. Natural categories. *Cognitive Psychology,* 1973, *4,* 328–350. (b)

Rosch, E. H. Cognitive representations of semantic categories. *Journal of Experimental Psychology: General,* 1975, *104,* 193–233.

Rosch, E. H., Mervis, C. B., Gray, W. D., Johnson, D. M., & Boyes-Braem, P. Basic objects in natural categories. *Cognitive Psychology,* 1976, *8,* 382–439.

Rosenblith, W. A. (Ed.). *Sensory communication.* Cambridge: M.I.T. Press, 1961.

Rosner, B. S. Brain functions. *Annual Review of Psychology,* 1970, *21,* 555–594.

Rosenhan, D. L. On being sane in insane places. *Science,* 1973, *179,* 250–258.

Rozin, P., & Kalat, J. W. Specific hungers and poison avoidance as adaptive specializations in learning. *Psychological Review,* 1971, *78,* 459–486.

Rumelhart, D. E. *An introduction to human information processing.* New York: Wiley, 1977.

Rumelhart, D. E., & Norman, D. A. Accretion, tuning and restructuring: Three modes of learning. In R. Klatsky & J. W. Cotton (Eds.), *Sematic factors in cognition.* Lawrence Erlbaum Associates, in press.

Rumelhart, D. E., & Ortony, A. The representation of information in memory. In R. C. Anderson, R. J. Spiro, & W. E. Montague (Eds.), *Schooling and the acquisition of knowledge.* Hillsdale, N.J.: Lawrence Erlbaum Associates, 1976.

Russell, W. R., & Nathan, P. W. Traumatic amnesia. *Brain,* 1946, *69,* 280–300. (A slightly condensed version has been reprinted in C. Gross & H. Zeigler (Eds.), *Readings in physiological psychology.* New York: Harper and Row, 1960.)

Saltz, E. *The cognitive bases of human learning.* Homewood, Ill.: Dorsey Press, 1971.

Schachter, S. Cognitive effects on bodily functioning. In D. C. Glass (Ed.), *Studies of obesity and eating in neurophysiology and emotion.* New York: Rockefeller Univ. Press, 1967.

Schachter, S. *Emotion, obesity, and crime.* New York: Academic Press, 1971.

Schachter, S., & Rodin, J. *Obese humans and rats.* Potomac, Md.: Lawrence Erlbaum Associates, 1974.

Schachter, S., & Singer, J. E. Cognitive, social and physiological determinants of emotional state. *Psychological Review,* 1962, *69,* 379–399.

Schachter, S., & Wheeler, L. Epinephrine, chlorpromazine and amusement. *Journal of Abnormal Psychology,* 1962, *65,* 121–128.

Schade, J. P., & van Groenigen, W. B. Structural organization of the human cerebral cortex: Maturation of the middle frontal gyrus. *Acta Anatomica,* 1961, *47,* 74–111.

Schank, R. C. Conceptual dependency: A theory of natural language understanding. *Cognitive Psychology,* 1972, *3,* 552–631.

Schank, R. C. *Conceptual information processing.* Amsterdam: North-Holland; New York: American Elsevier, 1975.

Scharf, B. Critical bands. In J. V. Tobias (Ed.), *Foundations of modern auditory theory.* Vol. I. New York: Academic Press, 1970.

Scheerer, M. Problem solving. *Scientific American,* 1963, *204* (4), 118–128.

Schelling, T. C. *The strategy of conflict.* Cambridge: Harvard Univ. Press, 1963.

Schmitt, F. O. (Ed.). *The neurosciences: Second study program.* New York: Rockefeller Univ., 1972.

Schmitt, F. O., & Worden, F. G. (Eds.). *The neurosciences: Third study program.* Cambridge: M.I.T. Press, 1974.

Schneider, G. E. Contrasting visuomotor functions of tectum and cortex in the golden hamster. *Psychologische Forschung,* 1967, 1968, *31,* 52–65.

Schneider, G. E. Two visual systems. *Science,* 1969, *163,* 895–902.

Seitz, W. C. *The responsive eye.* New York: Museum of Modern Art, 1965.

Sekuler, R., & Levinson, E. Mechanisms of motion perception. *Psychologia— An International Journal of Psychology in the Orient,* 1974, *17,* 38–49.

Selfridge, O. Pandemonium: A paradigm for learning. In *Symposium on the mechanization of thought processes.* London: HM Stationery Office, 1959.

Seligman, M. E. P. *Helplessness: On depression, development, and death.* San Francisco: Freeman, 1975.

Seligman, M. E. P., Maier, S. F., & Solomon, R. L. Unpredictable and uncontrollable events. In F. R. Brush (Ed.), *Aversive conditioning and learning.* New York: Academic Press, 1971.

Sellin, T., & Wolfgang, M. E. *The measurement of delinquency.* New York: Wiley, 1964.

Selye, H. *The story of the adaptation syndrome.* Montreal: Act, 1952.

Selye, H. *Stress without distress.* New York: Lippincott, 1974.

Shepherd, G. M. *The synaptic organization of the brain.* London, New York: Oxford Univ. Press, 1974, pp. 15–34, 46–57.

Shiffrin, R. M. Capacity limitations in information processing, attention and memory. In W. K. Estes (Ed.), *Handbook of learning and cognitive processes. Volume 4: Memory processes.* Hillsdale, N.J.: Lawrence Erlbaum Associates, in press, 1976.

Shiffrin, R. M., & Geisler, W. S. Visual recognition in a theory of information processing. In R. L. Solso (Ed.), *Contemporary issues in cognitive psychology: The Loyola symposium.* Washington, D.C.: Winston, 1973. [Distributed by Halsted Press, Wiley, New York.]

Siegal, S., & Fouraker, L. E. *Bargaining and group decision making: Experiments in bilateral monopoly.* New York: McGraw-Hill, 1960.

Siegel, R. K., & West, L. J. (Eds.). *Hallucinations: Behavior, experience, and theory.* New York: Wiley, 1975.

Simon, H. A., & Reed, S. K. Modeling strategy shifts in a problem-solving task. *Cognitive Psychology,* 1976, *8,* 86–97.

Simon, H. A., & Simon, P. A. Trial and error search involving difficult problems: Evidence from the game of chess. *Behavioral Science,* 1962, *7,* 425–429.

Sinclair-deZwart, H. Language acquisition and cognitive development. In

T. E. Moore (Ed.), *Cognitive development and the acquisition of language*. New York: Academic Press, 1973.

    I. Introduction. *Scandinavian Journal of Psychology*, 1961, *2*, 11–20. (a)

    II. External reinforcement of conservation of weight and of the operations of addition and subtraction. *Scandinavian Journal of Psychology*, 1961, *2*, 71–84. (b)

    III. Extinction of conversation of weight acquired "normally" and by means of empirical controls on a balance scale. *Scandinavian Journal of Psychology*, 1961, *2*, 85–87. (c)

    IV. An attempt at extinction of the usual components of the weight concept. *Scandinavian Journal of Psychology*, 1961, *2*, 153–155. (d)

    V. Practice in conflict situations without external reinforcement. *Scandinavian Journal of Psychology*, 1961, *2*, 156–160. (e)

    VI. Practice on continuous versus discontinuous material in conflict situations without external reinforcement. *Scandinavian Journal of Psychology*, 1961, *2*, 203, 210. (f)

Smedslund, J. The acquisition of substance and weight in children.

    I. Introduction. *Scandinavian Journal of Psychology*, 1961, *2*, 11–20. (a)

    II. External reinforcement of conservation of weight and of the operations of addition and subtraction. *Scandinavian Journal of Psychology*, 1961, *2*, 71–84. (b)

    III. Extinction of conservation of weight acquired "normally" and by means of empirical controls on a balance scale. *Scandinavian Journal of Psychology*, 1961, *2*, 85–87. (c)

    IV. An attempt at extinction of the usual components of the weight concept. *Scandinavian Journal of Psychology*, 1961, *2*, 153–155. (d)

    V. Practice in conflict situations without external reinforcement. *Scandinavian Journal of Psychology*, 1961, *2*, 156–160. (e)

    VI. Practice on continuous versus discontinuous material in conflict situations without external reinforcement. *Scandinavian Journal of Psychology*, 1961, *2*, 203–210. (f)

Smith, A. *Powers of mind.* New York: Random House, 1975. (Adam Smith is a pen-name. The book might be filed in some libraries under the author's real name: G. J. W. Goodman.)

Smith, E. E., Shoben, E. J., & Rips, L. J. Structure and processes in semantic memory: A featural model for semantic decisions. *Psychological Review*, 1974, *81*, 214–241.

Soby, J. T. *René Magritte.* New York: Museum of Modern Art, 1965.

Solso, R. L. (Ed.). *Contemporary issues in cognitive psychology: The Loyola symposium.* Washington, D.C.: Winston, 1973. (Distributed by Wiley.)

Solso, R. L. (Ed.). *Information processing and cognition: The Loyola symposium.* Hillsdale, N.J.: Lawrence Erlbaum Associates, 1975. (Distributed by Wiley.)

Sperling, G. Information in a brief visual presentation. Unpublished doctoral dissertation, Harvard Univ. 1959.

Sperling, G. The information available in brief visual presentations. *Psychological Monographs*, 1960, *74* (Whole No. 11).

Sperling, G., & Speelman, R. G. Acoustic similarity and auditory short-term memory experiments and a model. In D. A. Norman (Ed.), *Models of human memory.* New York: Academic Press, 1970.

Sperry, R. W. Cerebral organization and behavior. *Science,* 1961, *133,* 1749.

Sperry, R. W. Hemisphere disconnection and unity in conscious awareness. *American Psychologist,* 1968, *23,* 723–733.

Sperry, R. W. Lateral specialization in the surgically separate hemispheres. In F. O. Schmitt (Ed.), *The neurosciences, Third Study Program.* Cambridge: M.I.T. Press, 1974.

Squire, L. R. Amnesia for remote events following electroconvulsive therapy. *Behavioral Biology,* 1974, *12,* 119–125.

Squire, L. R. Short-term memory as a biological entity. In D. Deutsch & J. A. Deutsch (Eds.), *Short-term memory.* New York, Academic Press, 1975.

Squire, L. R., & Chace, P. M. Memory functions six to nine months after electroconvulsive therapy. *Archives of General Psychiatry,* 1975, *32,* 1557–1568.

Squire, L. R. Slater, P. C., & Chace, P. M. Retrograde amnesia: Temporal gradient in very long term memory following electroconvulsive therapy. *Science,* 1975, *187,* 77–79.

Stanley-Jones, D. The biological origin of love and hate. In M. Arnold (Ed.), *Feelings and emotions.* New York: Academic Press, 1970.

Stein, B. E., Magalhães-Castro, K. B., & Kruger, L. Superior colliculus: Visuo-topic–somatotopic overlap. *Science,* 1975, *189,* 224–226.

Stevens, K. N., & House, A. S. Speech perception. In J. V. Tobias (Ed.), *Foundations of modern auditory theory.* Vol. Two. New York: Academic Press, 1972.

Stevens, S. S. (Ed.). *Handbook of experimental psychology.* New York: Wiley, 1951.

Stevens, S. S. The direct estimation of sensory magnitude—loudness. *American Journal of Psychology,* 1956, *69,* 1–25.

Stevens, S. S. The psychophysics of sensory function. In W. A. Rosenbith (Ed.), *Sensory communication.* Cambridge: M.I.T. Press, 1961. (a)

Stevens, S. S. To honor Fechner and repeal his law. *Science,* 1961, *133,* 80–86. (b)

Stevens, S. S. A metric for the social consensus. *Science,* 1966, *151,* 530–541. (a)

Stevens, S. S. On the operation known as judgment. *American Scientist,* 1966, *54,* 385–401. (b)

Stevens, S. S. Power-group transformations under glare, masking, and recruitment. *Journal of the Acoustical Society of America,* 1966, *39,* 725–735. (c)

Stevens, S. S. Matching functions between loudness and ten other continua. *Perception & Psychophysics,* 1966, *1* (1), 5–8. (d)

Stevens, S. S. Ratio scales of opinion. In D. K. Whitala (Ed.), *Handbook of measurement and assessment in behavioral sciences.* Reading, Mass.: Addison-Wesley, 1968.

Stevens, S. S., & Davis, H. *Hearing: Its psychology and physiology.* New York: Wiley, 1938.

Stotland, E., & Canon, L. K. *Social psychology: A cognitive approach.* Philadelphia: Saunders, 1972.

Stromeyer, C. F. Further studies of the McCollough effect. *Perception & Psychophysics,* 1969, *6,* 105–110.

Stromeyer, C. F., III. Eidetikers. *Psychology Today,* November 1970, 76–80.

Stromeyer, C. F., & Mansfield, R. J. Colored aftereffects produced with moving images. *Perception & Psychopsysics,* 1970, *7,* 108–114.

Stromeyer, C. F., III, & Psotka, J. The detailed texture of eidetic images. *Nature,* 1970, *225,* 346–349.

Stroop, J. R. Studies of interference in serial verbal reactions. *Journal of Experimental Psychology,* 1935, *18,* 643–662.

Suppes, P., & Zinnes, J. L. Basic measurement theory. In R. D. Luce, R. R. Bush, & E. Galanter (Eds.), *Handbook of mathematical psychology.* Vol. I. New York: Wiley, 1963.

Swets, J. A. (Ed.). *Signal detection and recognition by human observers.* New York: Wiley, 1964.

Sylvester, D. *Magritte.* Catalogue of an exhibition of paintings by René Magritte, 1898–1967. London: The Arts Council of Great Britain, 1969.

Talland, G. A. *Deranged memory.* New York: Academic Press, 1965.

Talland, G. A. *Disorders of memory and learning.* Harmondsworth, Middlesex, England: Penguin Books, 1968.

Talland, G. A., & Waugh, N. (Eds.). *The pathology of memory.* New York: Academic Press, 1969.

Teuber, H. L. Perception. In J. Field, H. W. Magoun, & V. E. Hall (Eds.), *Handbook of physiology, Section 1: Neural physiology.* Vol. 3. Baltimore: Williams & Wilkins, 1960.

Thomas, J. C., Jr. An analysis of behavior in the Hobbits–Orcs problem. *Cognitive Psychology,* 1974, *6,* 257–269.

Thompson, R. F. *Physiological psychology. Readings from Scientific American.* San Francisco: Freeman, 1972.

Thompson, R. F. *Progress in psychobiology. Readings from Scientific American.* San Francisco: Freeman, 1976. (a)

Thompson, R. F. The search for the engram. *American Psychologist,* 1976, *31,* 209–227. (b)

Thornton, J. W., & Jacobs, P. D. Learned helplessness in human subjects. *Journal of Experimental Psychology,* 1971, *87,* 367–372.

Tobias, J. V. (Ed.). *Foundations of modern auditory theory.* Vols. I and II. New York: Academic Press, 1970, 1972.

Trevarthen, C. B. Two mechanisms of vision in primates. *Psychologische Forschung,* 1968, *31,* 299–337.

Tulving, E., & Donaldson, W. (Eds.). *Organization of memory.* New York: Academic Press, 1972.

Turner, J. *Cognitive development.* London: Methuen, 1975.

Tversky, A. Intransitivity of preferences. *Psychological Review,* 1969, *76,* 31–48.

Tversky, A., & Kahneman, D. Availability: A heuristic for judging frequency and probability. *Cognitive Psychology,* 1973, *5,* 207–232.

Tversky, A., & Kahneman, D. The belief in the law of small numbers. *Psychological Bulletin,* in press.

van Bergeijk, W. A. Variation on a theme of Békésy: A model of binaural interaction. *Journal of the Acoustical Society of America,* 1962, *34,* 1431–1437.

Varela, J. A. *Psychological solutions to social problems.* New York: Academic Press, 1971.

Vasarely, V. *Vasarely I* (Trans. H. Chevalier). Neuchatel, Switzerland: Editions du Griffon Neuchatel, 1965.

Vasarely, V. *Vasarely II* (Trans. H. Chevalier). Neuchatel, Switzerland: Editions du Griffon Neuchatel, 1971.

Verheijen, F. J. A simple after image method demonstrating the involuntary multi-directional eye movements during fixation. *Optica Acta,* 1961, *8,* 309–311.

Vernon, M. D. (Ed.). *Experiments in visual perception.* Harmondsworth, Middlesex, England: Penguin Books, 1966.

Voss, J. F. (Ed.). *Approaches to thought.* Columbus, Ohio: Charles F. Merrill, 1969.

Wagner, H. G., MacNichol, E. F., Jr., & Wolbarsht, M. L. The response properties of single ganglion cells in the goldfish retina. *Journal of General Physiology,* 1960, *43,* 45–62.

Wald, G. The receptors for human color vision. *Science,* 1964, *145,* 1007–1017.

Waltz, D. Understanding line drawings of scenes with shadows. In P. H. Winston (Ed.), *The psychology of computer vision.* New York: McGraw-Hill, 1975.

Warrington, E. K., & Weiskrantz, L. An analysis of short-term and long-term memory defects in man. In J. A. Deutsch (Ed.), *Physiological basis of memory.* New York: Academic Press, 1973.

Wason, P. C., & Johnson-Laird, P. N. (Eds.). *Thinking and reasoning.* Harmondsworth, Middlesex, England: Penguin Books, 1968.

Webb, W. B. *Sleep: An experimental approach.* New York: Macmillan, 1968.

Weber, R. J., & Castleman, J. The time it takes to imagine. *Perception & Psychophysics,* 1970, *8,* 165–168.

Weiner, B. (Ed.). *Cognitive views of human motivation.* New York: Academic Press, 1974.

Weintraub, D. J. Perception. *Annual Review of Psychology,* 1975, *26,* 263–289.

Weisstein, N. Beyond the yellow-Volkswagen detector and the grandmother cell: A general strategy for the exploration of operations in human pattern recognition. In R. L. Solso (Ed.), *Contemporary issues in cognitive psychology: The Loyola symposium.* Washington, D.C.: Winston, 1973. (Distributed by Wiley.)

Werblin, F. S. The control of sensitivity in the retina. *Scientific American,* 1973, *228,* 70–79 (January).

Wertheimer, M. *Productive thinking.* New York: Harper, 1945.

Wever, E. G. *Theory of hearing.* New York: Dover, 1970.

Whitfield, I. C. *The auditory pathway.* London: Arnold, 1967.

Whitfield, I. C., & Evans, E. F. Responses of auditory cortical neurons to stimuli of changing frequency. *Journal of Neurophysiology,* 1965, *28,* 655–672.

Whitty, C. W. M., & Zangwill, O. L. (Eds.). *Amnesia.* London: Butterworth, 1966.

Wickelgren, W. A. *How to solve problems: Elements of a theory of problems and problem solving.* San Francisco: Freeman, 1974.

Wightman, F. L., & Green, D. M. The perception of pitch. *American Scientist,* 1974, *62,* 206–215.

Williams, J. *The complete strategist.* New York: McGraw-Hill, 1954.

Williams, M. D. Retrieval from very long-term memory. Unpublished doctoral dissertation. Univ. of California, San Diego, 1976.

Winograd, T. A program for understanding natural language. *Cognitive Psychology,* 1972, *3,* 1–191.

Winograd, T. *Language as a cognitive process* (in preparation).

Winston, P. H. Learning to identify toy block structures. In R. L. Solso (Ed.), *Contemporary issues in cognitive psychology: The Loyola symposium.* Washington, D.C.: Winston, 1973. [Distributed by Halsted Press, Wiley, New York.]

Winston, P. H. (Ed.). *The psychology of computer vision.* New York: McGraw-Hill, 1975.

Woodworth, R. S. *Experimental psychology.* New York: Holt, 1938.

Woodworth, R. S., & Schlosberg, H. *Experimental psychology.* New York: Holt, 1954.

Young, M. N., & Gibson, W. B. *How to develop an exceptional memory.* Radnor, Pa.: Chilton, 1962.

Zimbardo, P., & Ebbesen, E. *Influencing attitudes and changing behavior.* Reading, Mass.: Addison-Wesley, 1969.

Zwicker, E., & Scharf, B. Model of loudness summation. *Psychological Review,* 1965, *72,* 3–26.

Zwislocki, J. Analysis of some auditory characteristics. In R. D. Luce, R. R. Bush, & E. Galanter (Eds.), *Handbook of mathematical psychology.* Vol. III. New York: Wiley, 1965.

Author index

Numbers in italics refer to the pages on which the complete references are listed. Names of painters, photographers, and composers mentioned in the text are also listed in the Author Index.

Subject index